JAMES
KAY-SHUTTLEWORTH

Frontispiece Sir James Kay-Shuttleworth

JAMES KAY-SHUTTLEWORTH

Journey of an Outsider

R.J.W. SELLECK

THE WOBURN PRESS

First published in 1994 in Great Britain by
THE WOBURN PRESS
Newbury House, 890–900 Eastern Avenue,
Newbury Park, Ilford, Essex IG2 7HH

and in the United States of America by
THE WOBURN PRESS
c/o International Specialized Book Services, Inc.
5804 N.E. Hassalo Street, Portland, Oregon 97213-3644

British Library Cataloguing in Publication Data

Selleck, R.J.W.
  James Kay-Shuttleworth: Journey of an Outsider
  I. Title
  941.08092

  ISBN 0-7130-0187-9 (cloth)
  SIBN 0-7130-0198-4 (paper)

Library of Congress Cataloging in Publication Data

Selleck, R.J.W. (Richard Joseph Wheeler), 1934–
  James Kay-Shuttleworth: Journey of an outsider/R.J.W. Selleck.
  p. cm.
  Includes bibliographical references and index.
  ISBN 0-7130-0187-9 (cloth) ISBN 0-7130-0198-4 (paper)
  1. Kay-Shuttleworth, James, Sir, 1804–1877–Biography.
  2. Educators–England–Biography. I. Title.
  LA2375.E542E397 1994
  370'.92–dc20
  [B]
                                                    93-10868
                                                       CIP

Typeset by Vitaset, Paddock Wood
Printed in Great Britain by Bookcraft (Bath) Ltd

Contents

Acknowledgements

This book could not have been completed without assistance from the Australian Research Grants Scheme, Monash University, and, most importantly, the Spencer Foundation.

I wish to acknowledge the assistance of librarians, archivists and other staff at the Baillieu Library, University of Melbourne; Bamford Chapel, Norden Road, Rochdale; the Bodleian Library, Oxford (New Library); the British Library (including the Newspaper Reading Room at Colindale); Bury Central Library; Chetham's Library, Manchester; Department of Education and Science Library, London; (Lord Shuttleworth's) Estate Office, Cowan Bridge; Gawthorpe Hall; Giggleswick School; the Institute of Education Library, University of London; John Rylands Library (Deansgate), Manchester; Lambeth Palace Library; the Lancashire Record Office; Leeds District Archives; Local History Archives, Central Library, Manchester; Local Studies Library, Castle Gates Library, Shrewsbury; Macfarland Library, Ormond College, University of Melbourne; Main Library, Monash University; Medical Library, John Rylands Library, University of Manchester; National Library of Wales; New College, Edinburgh; National Register of Archives, London; Penzance Library; Public Record Office, London – both Kew and Chancery Lane; Record Office, House of Lords; Royal Manchester Infirmary; Royal College of Physicians, Edinburgh; Royal Medical Society, Edinburgh; Staffordshire Record Office; University College, London; University of Edinburgh Library, particularly Special Collections; University of Leeds Library; the University of London Library, and University of Sheffield Library.

Many individuals have helped in the collection of material, commenting on parts or all of the manuscript, directing me to new sources, helping to prepare the manuscript, and in various other ways. I am grateful to Dr Richard Aldrich, Dr Marion Amies,

Professor Harold Attwood, Mr B.C. Bloomfield, Professor Joan Burstyn, Professor W.F. Connell, Professor Graeme Davison, Dr E. Cunningham Dax, Dr Gwyneth Dow, Ms Vivienne Kelly, Ms Sheonagh Martin, Professor Sheldon Rothblatt, Mrs Heather Sharps, Mr J.G. Sharps, Mr Claude Sironi, Mrs Pamela North, Dr John Penman, Dr John Pickstone, Mrs Anne Selleck, Dr Andrew Spaull, Dr Martin Sullivan, Dr Marjorie Theobald, Dr David Warwick, Dr Katherine Webb, Ms Rosamund Winter, Miss Anne Young and Mrs Janet Young.

I owe special debts to the inter-library loan staff of the Main Library, Monash University, and to Ms Lorraine Elliott, Mr Peter Gill, Professor Peter Gordon, Professor Humphrey Kay, Ms Joan Mottram, Miss Imelda Palmer, Dr Margaret Pawsey, Professor Brian Simon, Ms Anne Waldron, and Dr Ailsa Zainu'ddin.

My principal debt is to Lord Shuttleworth. No biographer could have asked for more generous treatment. He and Lady Shuttleworth provided thoughtful hospitality, and he made available the papers at the John Rylands Library, his Estate Office in Cowan Bridge, and Leck Hall in the most open possible way. He arranged access to other sources and to family members, and commented on, and sometimes corrected, the manuscript. But the responsibility for the conclusions reached in this book is mine, not his.

List of Illustrations

Acknowledgements of Illustrations

The portraits of Charlotte Brontë and Elizabeth Gaskell are reproduced by kind permission of the National Portrait Gallery, London. The photographs of Gawthorpe Hall on pages 198 and 266 are reproduced by kind permission of the National Trust.

Grateful acknowledgement is made to Lord Shuttleworth for permission to reproduce the portrait of Janet Shuttleworth on page 181, and to Mrs Janet Young for the portrait of Sir James Kay-Shuttleworth on page 328.

Abbreviations

Add. mss	Additional manuscripts, British Library
BPD	*British Parliamentary Debates*
BPP	*British Parliamentary Papers*
CB	Charlotte Brontë
DNB	*Dictionary of National Biography*
EG	Elizabeth Gaskell
EN	Ellen Nussey
EO,CB	Estate Office (Lord Shuttleworth's), Cowan Bridge
FND	Frederick North diaries
FPPE	*Four Periods of Public Education*
FR,MSS	*First Report of the Statistical Society, Manchester*
Janet K-S	Janet Kay-Shuttleworth
JPK	James Phillips Kay
JPK-S	James Phillips Kay-Shuttleworth
JS	Janet Shuttleworth
JSJ	Janet Shuttleworth's journal
K-SP	Kay-Shuttleworth papers (John Rylands Library, Deansgate)
LBD	Lovelace Byron Deposit
MCCE	Minutes of the Committee of Council on Education
MG	*Manchester Guardian*
MPC	*The Moral and Physical Condition of the Working Classes*
MPC2	Second edition of above
MPCCE	Minutes of the Proceedings of the Committee of the [Privy] Council on Education
NEMSA	North of England Medical and Surgical Society
NEMSJ	*North of England Medical and Surgical Journal*
PBHM	Proceedings of the Board of Health, Manchester
PLCP	Poor Law Commission Papers
PLC	Poor Law Commission
PMSS	Papers of the Manchester Statistical Society
PRO	Public Record Office, London

RPLC 1/2, etc.   First/Second, etc. Annual Report of the Poor Law
                 Commissioners
RTPC   Report on the training of pauper children
SP   Shuttleworth papers (Estate Office, Cowan Bridge)
SR,MSS   *Second Report of the Statistical Society, Manchester*
TCHS   *Transactions of the Congregational Historical Society*
UK-S   Ughtred Kay-Shuttleworth

A note on first names

James Kay-Shuttleworth had a grandfather, an uncle and at least one cousin
called James. They did not play large parts in his life, and are not the source
of much confusion. His father, a brother and a son were called Robert. They
played much larger parts in his life, but at different times, and can, therefore,
be reasonably easily distinguished. His mother and sister were named
Hannah Kay, and his wife and daughter, Janet Kay-Shuttleworth. They
played large parts in his life, and can easily be confused. I have tried in the
text to make clear which of them is being referred to. In the notes, 'Hannah
Kay' and 'Janet K-S' always refer to the older woman, that is, to his mother
and to his wife. When letters to his sister or daughter are referred to, their
relationship to him (or to the person who wrote the letter) is indicated in
brackets. Thus, if he wrote to his sister, the entry would read 'JPK-S to
Hannah Kay (sister)'; if he wrote to his daughter, it would read 'JPK-S to
Janet K-S (daughter); and if his son, Ughtred, wrote to his daughter, Janet, it
would read 'UK-S to Janet K-S (sister).

A note on surnames

James Phillips Kay-Shuttleworth was born James Phillips Kay. He added his
wife's surname to his on their marriage. He almost always spelled his name
without a hyphen, but it has become customary for the family to use the
hyphen, and that practice has been followed in this book.

Preface

G.M. Young, Whiggish, witty and wise, wrote of James Phillips Kay-Shuttleworth that 'if history judged men less by the noise than by the difference they make, it is hard to think of any name in the Victorian age which deserves to stand above or even beside Kay-Shuttleworth's'. Matthew Arnold, poet and school inspector, who knew him and laboured in the schools he had helped to create, had a similar view. He recalled that politicians such as Lord Lansdowne and Lord John Russell appreciated his skills, 'followed his suggestions, and founded upon them the public education of the people of this country'.

No one fostered this view of his achievements more assiduously than Kay-Shuttleworth himself, and Frank Smith's valuable biography, published in 1923, and written with Kay-Shuttleworth's eldest son looking over his shoulder, perpetuated this estimate by devoting more than two-thirds of its pages to his educational work. This is to distort his life. Kay-Shuttleworth's educational endeavours were of great importance and are the main reason for his frequent appearances in the historical literature, but he had a range of interests which make him a fascinating figure in English social history. Cotton (in plenteous times and in famine), Congregationalism, cholera epidemics and Chartism were important in his life. He mixed (often uneasily) with handloom weavers, East Anglian paupers, dissolute women in the London parish of St George in the East, Tractarian bishops, the Whig aristocracy at Bowood, Unitarians, tenant farmers, cottagers and coal miners in north-west Lancashire, ambitious medical practitioners, Somerset House civil servants, Manchester manufacturers, the Brontës at Haworth, prelates and powerful politicians, illegitimate children and the children of idiots and felons in Poor Law workhouses, and the gentry of northern England. To read his life is to be introduced not only to educational battles, but to exciting episodes in the history of religion, medicine, social science, the family, public health, literature, industrialization, politics and public administration. It is to study the class struggles of nineteenth-century Britain, and the often agonized relations of men and women.

This biography tries to capture some of the complexity and richness of Kay-Shuttleworth's life. He was an intense man, ambiguous, authoritarian, and riddled with idealism, ambition, uncertainty and contradiction. A Dissenter who conformed, he adopted the lifestyle of the landed gentry against whom he had once fought; an advocate of Victorian family values, he made a controversial and anguished marriage; at one stage of his life he prayed much, though later he came to place a lot of trust in statistics; he recited the *Masque of Anarchy* to turbulent crowds in the early 1830s and condemned Chartist agitators at the end of the decade; as a young doctor he sought the support of Manchester's cotton masters (and one of their daughters for a wife) while denouncing their selfishness. He was a civil servant eager to instruct his political masters, a novelist who was better known, and better, as a pamphleteer, an enthusiast destroyed by his enthusiasm, and an advocate of civil order who spent a short time in a German gaol.

Kay-Shuttleworth's public life was buffeted by the winds of social, economic and religious dispute. Having left his family's cotton business, he sought acceptance from the urban, professional middle class among whom he worked and the landed gentry into whom he married. He could not, of course, expect it from the aristocracy and he did not require it from the labouring classes whom he wished to educate. In the end his acceptance was only partial and he became a victim of the social structure he had so sternly defended. Disappointed in his public life, his private life in disarray, Kay-Shuttleworth in his declining years was a tragic figure who sought and obtained some vicarious satisfaction through his son's political career. But he was altogether more interesting than he himself, his supporters and his detractors have suggested. His was a life crowded with achievement, contradiction and distress, a fascinating mirror of the cruel age of which it was a product.

R.J.W. Selleck
Melbourne, 1992

1 · James Phillips Kay and family

When James Phillips Kay was born, on 20 July 1804 in Rochdale, he entered a family familiar with Mammon and haunted by God. He spent his life in the service of both masters and some of his contemporaries thought that in the process he served himself well. Few understood the price which he had paid for success or how evanescent that success was to appear, even in his own lifetime, and even to him. Consumed by a tormented search for recognition and self-respect, he was unable to recognize how easily he could turn hard-won success into tragedy, defeat or black farce. Nevertheless, in the course of this search he grew to love some people as best he knew how and in return some of them loved him; he knew triumph and defeat, exultation and humiliation, but rarely equanimity, and never serenity. His Rochdale family initiated him into a struggle from which he could not escape and which he did not win.

Kay's struggle derived in part from the ambiguous political and social circumstances of his family which, like others in late eighteenth- and early nineteenth-century Lancashire, changed its economic base from farming to textile manufacture and thus made its contribution to that drama of dislocation, excitement and suffering which was the Industrial Revolution. The Kays emphasized, and sought to inflate, their contribution by claiming to be related to John Kay (1704–64), the inventor of the flying-shuttle.[1] Whether or not they were correct, they came from Bury, the same area as John Kay. It is difficult to separate them from the complex network of Kays who had lived in Bury and nearby towns such as Rochdale for more than two centuries and who made the records more intricate by frequent use of the same first names and by marrying other Kays.

James Kay's grandfather assisted the confusion: his name was also James Kay and on 15 May 1761 he married Mary Kay from Birtle.[2] Originally farmers, James and Mary Kay, who lived at Bass Lane in

Walmersley near Bury, started woollen manufacturing and by 1794 (James was then in his sixties) were conducting a fustian manufacturing business in Bury and owned or rented a warehouse in Blue Boar Court, Manchester. They had blazed a new trail and their six sons, Richard, Robert, James, William, John and Thomas, followed the trail into the family manufacturing business, though they retained their skill in agricultural pursuits such as haytenting and mowing which the family's transitional economy required. Ann, the Kays' only daughter, made another transition: whereas her mother, Mary, could not sign her name on her marriage certificate, Ann was literate. When James Kay died in 1802 he had not made a greater fortune than was 'ordinarily possessed by any yeoman engaged partly in manufacturing and partly in farming as was then the custom', but he had laid the foundations on which his eager sons could build. They were busy building when Mary Kay died seven years later.[3]

Of James and Mary Kay's sons, James in particular pursued an adventurous career. He learned the cotton trade as an apprentice at Cockey Moor, and at Brooksbottom established one of the first large cotton mills in the neighbourhood of Bury. One of his apprentices, Nicholas Hoyle, remembered James as 'a first rate man of business' who had a fine memory and 'great powers of calculation'. He may have lost composure when 'an alarm of rioters' threatened his premises at the time of Peterloo, but during the Napoleonic wars, according to John Parks, a surgeon who knew the Kays well, James's foresight, resolution and decisiveness had been of great value to the family. Gradually the sons (except Thomas, the youngest, who seemed to be overawed by his brothers' aggression and remained with his father at Bass Lane) set up on their own. Richard and John entered the woollen trade at Limefield – John eventually left to work alone at Lark Hill – William after a period in Manchester went to Liverpool, and even before his father's death Robert had established himself as a fustian manufacturer in Rochdale, though he still used the same Manchester warehouse in Red Lion Street, Back Square, as did the Kays at Bass Lane.[4]

Robert, the fustian manufacturer, was James Phillips Kay's father. He married Hannah Phillips of Birmingham on 22 September 1803 and for the first two decades of their marriage Robert, though considered less interested in business success than some of his brothers, involved Hannah and their children (there were eventually six) in a determined, restless and fruitful search for financial

FAMILY TREE : JAMES PHILLIPS KAY

KAY

PHILLIPS

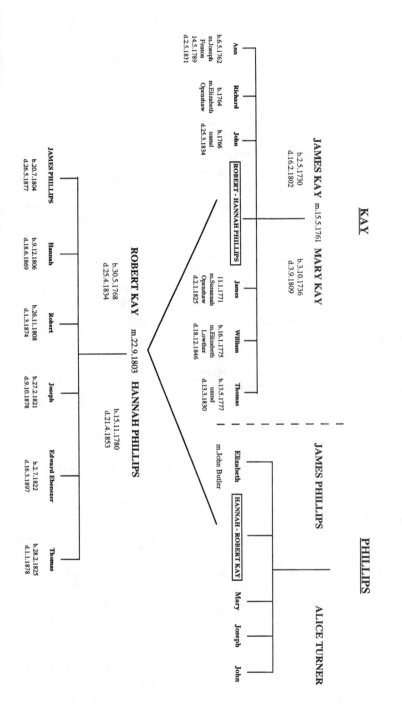

JAMES KAY m.15.5.1761 MARY KAY

JAMES PHILLIPS   ALICE TURNER

b.2.5.1730
d.16.2.1802

b.3.10.1736
d.3.9.1809

Ann
b.6.5.1762
m.Joseph
Fenton
d.2.5.1831

Richard
b.1764
m.Elizabeth
Openshaw

John
b.1766
unmd
d.25.3.1834

James
11.1.1771
m.Susannah
Openshaw
d.2.1.1825

William
b.16.1.1775
m.Elizabeth
Lowther
d.18.12.1846

Thomas
b.13.5.1777
unmd
d.13.3.1830

Elizabeth
b.15.11.1780
d.21.4.1853
m.John Butler

ROBERT · HANNAH PHILLIPS

HANNAH · ROBERT KAY

ROBERT KAY m.22.9.1803 HANNAH PHILLIPS

b.30.5.1768
d.25.4.1834

b.15.11.1780
d.21.4.1853

Mary   **Joseph**   **John**

JAMES PHILLIPS
b.20.7.1804
d.26.5.1877

Hannah
b.9.12.1806
d.18.6.1869

Robert
b.26.11.1808
d.1.3.1874

Joseph
b.27.2.1821
d.9.10.1878

Edward Ebenezer
b.27.1.1822
d.16.3.1897

Thomas
b.28.2.1825
d.1.1.1878

independence. From 1800 for about eight years he operated the fustian manufacturing business in Rochdale and maintained a Manchester warehouse. At least twice a week, usually on Tuesdays and Saturdays, he stayed in Manchester in the Griffin Inn at Dangerous Corner, having advertised his presence so that those who wished to trade with him would know his whereabouts. By 1808 his interests had expanded and he moved his business to Heywood while keeping a Manchester warehouse in Blue Boar Court. By 1817 he had taken another warehouse, probably a larger one, in Hodson's Court, and the following year he added cotton spinning to his manufacturing interests at Heywood. He was still running the dual Heywood business in 1821 and had diversified further by beginning woollen manufacturing from Brookshaw in Bury. By 1825 he was describing himself as a woollen manufacturer and merchant, was employing a London agent, and had business interests in America. Shortly afterwards Robert Kay could afford to retire from business or at least to reduce his activities greatly, while continuing to provide an adequate supply of servants for his family who lived in the comfortable Meadowcroft House in the countryside on the outskirts of Rochdale.[5]

Robert achieved his success despite some difficult economic times, and his progression through fustian and woollen manufacturing and cotton spinning to the often anxious, if profitable, life of a merchant suggests that he had the entrepreneur's resourcefulness, adaptability and willingness to take risks. He and his family had joined the new industrialists who watched as the seasonal rituals of agricultural life moved to the periphery of their existence. Residential stability certainly went: between 1803 and 1825 the Kays lived at Rochdale, at Manchester in Ardwick, at Salford in Regent Road, Ordsall Lane, and Leaf Square, Pendleton – and at Meadowcroft near Rochdale.[6] These shifts were confined to a relatively small district but Robert Kay knew a larger world, for London, which he visited in the course of his business, and even America entered into his plans.

His decision to turn his back on this world was partly caused by ill-health; he had high blood pressure – 'fullness of blood in the head' was how his contemporaries described his condition. But religious motives helped to make him content with a 'moderate fortune' rather than continuing the pursuit of financial gain which preoccupied some of his brothers.[7] In the thrusting entrepreneurial environment in which he lived this was an eccentric choice, but Robert Kay had decided that, having satisfied Mammon, he would ensure his own salvation and that of his family and other people within reach.

Religion was not a recent Kay discovery. Robert's father, James, was originally Presbyterian but by the end of his life he had made a common contemporary transition and had become a Congregation-alist. He was one of the founders of the Park Chapel whose first trust deed lists his six sons as trustees. He and his wife were buried under the singing pew and three of their sons were also buried in the chapel. However, even so respectable a resting-place was no guarantee of a life well lived, and Robert had serious fears about his brother James. James may have been the family's most adroit businessman, have lived in a style commensurate with his wealth, and left his children considerable property, but as he lay dying he began to experience 'great alarm as to futurity'. He called upon Robert's assistance, which was given with such single-minded fervour that Robert rarely left his brother's sickbed for the two weeks before he died.[8] The sight of James's perturbation may have influenced Robert's decision to retreat from business, for he took it not long after his brother's death in December 1824.

James's choice of Robert in his moment of dire necessity indicates Robert's reputation for religious fervour. John Hall, a cotton manufacturer who had known the Kay brothers for most of his life, remembered him as a young man taking his mother on horseback to church every Sunday – she rode behind him on a pillion. Robert Porter, a provision dealer from Heywood who also knew Robert well, reported that he had never known a man 'of a more pure Christian disposition, or who in all respects strove to live a more pious life'.[9] Consumed with the importance of individual salvation and fearful that the snares of this transient world might enslave his fellow men and women, as for a time they had James, Robert Kay lived with a passionate puritanical ardour which makes 'pensive' seem a pallid description.

The tradition of Dissent was embedded in the Kay family. Robert was a follower of Henry Pendlebury, who helped establish Non-conformity in the Bury area and at Bass Lane itself, and was one of the 2,000 clergymen ejected from their livings when they did not comply with the requirement of the Act of Uniformity (1662). Nonconformists did not need the memory of such a man to remind themselves of religious conflict, for in the mid-1820s they still had serious grievances. They were required to pay a church rate which might be used to repair the parish church, a perpetual reminder of the religion against which they were dissenting. At the important milestones of human existence, birth, death and marriage, there were further reminders: the only births registered by the state were those in the baptismal registers of the parish church; the parish churchyard was everyone's burial ground, but Nonconformists could be buried there only according to the rites of the Established Church or in silence; and they could be married legally only according to the same rites. In addition public office, whether civil or military, was still denied them and, though the practice of occasional conformity and Indemnity Acts had eased this disability, there was a price to be paid, if only the constant reminder that Nonconformists were second-class citizens. And, of course, the universities were closed to them.[10]

Robert's wife, Hannah, also came from a strong Dissenting background. Her father, James Phillips, resolutely supported the Unitarian Joseph Priestley when Church and King mobs burned Priestley's home in the Birmingham riots of 1791. Her mother, Alice Turner, was the daughter of James Turner, the first Baptist minister of the Cannon Street Chapel, Birmingham, and a man of influence and 'elevated character'. The marriage of Robert Kay and Hannah Phillips, which thus mingled Baptist, Unitarian, Presbyterian and Congregational strands, symbolized the complex web of early nineteenth-century Dissent. Congregationalism came to dominate the marriage, but that was because Hannah was more flexible than Robert and not because her religious feelings were shallow. The son of a Congregational minister, who baptised some of the Kays' children and was closely associated with the family, described her as a woman of 'very superior mind', dignified, gentle, and neat and orderly in her domestic habits. He thought that her excellencies of character 'were substantially grounded upon the principles of the religion of Jesus Christ', and that she was 'in person, manner, and actions, a fine specimen of a *Christian* Lady'.[11]

Hannah Kay endorsed the part which Robert played in Congregational affairs. He continued to give financial backing to the Park Chapel of which his father had been a founder, and became a member and financial supporter of William Roby's famous and markedly Calvinistic Congregational Chapel in Cannon Street, Manchester, where one of his children was baptised. When in 1806 under Roby's leadership the Lancashire Congregationalists formed a Union (while still professing a belief in the fierce democracy of the local congregation which was reflected in their older name of Independents), Kay became its treasurer and held the position until he resigned in 1817. He had earlier (in 1798) organized Congregational preaching in Heywood, and in about 1800 had tried to unite the congregations of Heywood, about three miles from Bury, and nearby Ashworth in a building which he provided at Bamford. Some Methodists who were sharing the facilities left, objecting to the Calvinist tone of the preaching, but by 1801 a small Congregational chapel had been built at Bamford in a spot 'sweetly shaded by pines and poplars'. To emphasize the continuity of Robert Kay's interests William Roby preached at its opening.[12]

Robert, his brother William, and his sister Ann contributed liberally to the establishment of the chapel, watched over its building, and frequently discussed church affairs with the minister or deacon, especially while the Kays lived at Rochdale or Bury, but also while they were living in Manchester, where Robert enlisted the support of some wealthy Congregationalists for the Bamford Chapel. After he reduced his business concerns Robert Kay spent two days a week in an itinerant ministry accompanying Thomas Jackson, the minister at Bamford. They moved among the villages visiting the poor and the sick and distributing the tracts which Dissenters considered 'happily calculated, under the divine blessing, to diffuse sacred knowledge, and to promote the best interests of mankind'. In accordance with his request he was buried in the Bamford Chapel under the pew 'where he used to sit and listen to the Gospel'.[13]

Jackson preached an uncompromising gospel. He refused to come to Bamford unless given complete liberty to preach 'according to the best of my light and knowledge', unless the teaching of writing, which he regarded as a means of furthering worldly gain, was forbidden in the Sunday school, and unless Sunday school anniversaries were celebrated with plain hymns and not 'those pieces which render a place of worship more like a play house than a house of God'. Despite the best efforts of 'prudent and decisive' deacons, Jackson precipitated bitter divisions in the small community. Some of his congregation thought him too legalistic and too Arminian: while affirming that salvation was a gift of God, he had moved from strict Calvinistic predestination to a belief that God's grace could be rejected by humans who, therefore, had to prepare themselves to welcome that grace when it was offered. The records of the Bamford Chapel reported that 'the contentious and uneasy' separated for a time from the rest of the community and, with a well-placed confidence in the congregation's Biblical knowledge, they included a cryptic reference to 'Numbers 16', the account of Core's rebellion against Moses and Aaron. Though the earth did not open and swallow Jackson's enemies, 'a better spirit seemed slowly but gradually to pervade the congregation' and the dispute ended. It did not affect Robert Kay's relationship with Jackson as they continued to work closely together. His Arminianism, his preoccupation with conversion and his itinerant ministry marked Robert Kay as a fervent child of the Evangelical revival.[14]

The Kays and the Phillipses had earthier sides to their character. Hannah's two brothers lived tragic lives. The elder, Joseph Phillips, a spirited and attractive man whose popularity led him into 'convivial excesses', died in his thirties from the effects of a blow in the side. John, the other brother, became addicted to alcohol early in life and his 'sottish habits' turned him into a tragic figure unsuccessfully battling delirium tremens, poverty and imprisonment. Neither man satisfied the hopes of his pious parents.[15] If Hannah or Robert looked to their immediate family for cautionary tales there was plenty of material.

Most of the Kay brothers were given to the free living which worried James as he faced eternity. Contemporaries described them as strong, forceful, impatient men who combined business acumen with a willingness to work as hard as any labourer they employed. They indulged in trials of strength – Robert once carried eighteen score of wool on his back up the steps of a warehouse, putting his foot only once on each step. These competitions, which in Robert's case may have damaged his spine and heart, and the barely restrained intensity of all they did, made the Kays seem driven men who, according to some of their acquaintances, 'wore out their strength before their time'.[16]

Even friends anxious to speak well of the Kays described them as men of 'strong appetites' and 'great animal vigour' who honoured the customs of the time and place by living too freely. Richard became excessively corpulent and died before he was 60 afflicted with liver problems; James helped himself too generously from his own hospitable table and suffered a similar fate; John's incessant business activity forced him into an early retirement to which he could not adjust; and Thomas, overshadowed in other ways by his brothers, matched them by becoming overweight, contracting diseases of the heart and liver, and dying of dropsy. William and particularly Robert lived more staid lives, though Robert, who suffered from shortness of breath and was to die of a heart attack, had to be cupped on the back of the neck from time to time to reduce his blood pressure. He was sufficiently a Kay, and sufficiently unconcerned by warnings against alcohol, to make specific provision in his will that the ale, wine and spirits he left behind should be Hannah's.[17]

The Kays were not simply men who lived and worked too hard. Their lives had an anxious vehemence which made them seem barely in control of their forceful personalities. Insistent on having their own way, passionate and hot-tempered, they chafed under opposition – 'they could not brook it', said Samuel Wilkinson, a weaver who was well acquainted with them. Illness made these qualities conspicuous in John Kay when in his retirement he became partially crippled, a sad fate for an exceedingly active man who had been keen on bowling and hunting. He became solitary and morose and, according to Dr Parks, gave vent to his frustration by 'passionate impatience of contradiction to his strong will'.[18]

The Kays' sister, Ann, displayed the same edgy and disturbing energy as her brothers. She married Joseph Fenton, a member of a family travelling the same upward path as the Kays: they farmed, and had gone into woollen manufacturing and banking. Like Robert, Ann was deeply religious and watched over the Bamford Chapel, which she helped to found, with intense anxiety. Quick-tempered and compulsively active, she could not tolerate any want of energy or industry in others. To her household duties, which included the care of two children, she added the supervision of a dairy, and brewing for all the servants on the large farm which she helped to run. In the afternoons, 'dressed with great neatness as a lady', she often called on neighbouring farms and cottages, distributing gifts, visiting the sick, collecting money for religious purposes and assisting the deserving poor. She rose at six, if necessary at five, in order to find more time for her activities, and sometimes prepared breakfast for her servants before they came downstairs to begin the day's work, in order to re-prove them for what she judged to be their indolence. Not surprisingly her activities were a subject of wonder in the neighbourhood, and the inhabitants of many a cottage must have quaked as they saw her bearing down upon them full of good works and imperious energy.[19]

Though Robert Kay was often described as quiet and sedate, the force of his religious convictions suggests that hidden fires were burning. The son (also called Thomas) of the minister, Thomas Jackson, believed that he shared the characteristics of his brothers and sister but that he restrained them by a firmer temperament.[20] In any case, James Phillips Kay and the other children of Robert and

Hannah were members of an extended family which pursued wealth, pleasure and God (or a combination of the three) with wholehearted and febrile intensity.

Robert and Hannah Kay may be said to have had two families. The first consisted of James Phillips (born on 20 July 1804, ten months after his parents' marriage), Hannah (9 December 1806) and Robert (26 November 1808). After a gap of almost thirteen years the 'second' family began: Joseph (27 February 1821), Edward Ebenezer, usually called Ebenezer (2 July 1822), and Thomas (28 February 1825). Whatever the reasons for the gap, its existence meant that James was in his seventeenth year, at work and living away from home, when Joseph, the first child of the 'second' family, was born. He experienced family life as the eldest male child and as the focus of parental expectations in a small family which exposed him to the perilous emotions of his parents. The names the Kays chose for their first three children were gestures to familial piety: through a fortunate economy, 'James' honoured both his grandfathers, while 'Phillips' recalled his maternal grandfather's surname. Hannah was named after her mother; Robert after his father. The Kays turned in on themselves, and by their children's names tied themselves tightly into their immediate family.

In their day-to-day living the Kays were part of a small, close-knit community. They associated with many members of the Kay and Fenton families and, though disputes erupted, their very sharpness reinforced young James's consciousness that uncles, aunts and cousins were a prominent part of his environment. The Phillips family, centred on Birmingham, was further away, but close links were kept. The chapel, whether in Manchester or Salford, Bury or Bamford, helped to constrain the Kay children within a known and limited world. Its stern theology did not tempt to intellectual adventure, and its congregation became a centre of interest, a locus for celebration or anxiety, a force for social unity and a source of friends. The business links which Robert Kay forged with other cotton families, who were often Congregationalist, meant that people who might visit the Kays during the week would meet them again at the chapel on the Sabbath. Shared religion, friendships and business pulled the small, intense family in which James Kay grew up into the vital but confined world of northern English Dissent.

The powerful and vulnerable personality of Robert ('dear Papa', as Hannah called him when addressing the children) pervaded the family's emotional transactions. He was twelve years older than Hannah and the sole source of the family's income – Hannah might have been less dependent a generation earlier, when her spinning or weaving could have had some financial importance. Certainly James was later to be left in no doubt about his financial dependence when letters from his mother were delayed until his father placed under their cover the money he needed. Hannah accepted this relationship, but she was neither resentful nor dully dutiful. She was an intelligent and, within the middle-class mores of the time, an independent woman who had worked away from home before her marriage. It was her task to communicate with any absent children (she once remarked that Robert had 'commissioned' her to write) and her fluent and frequent letters reveal that she was more at ease with the pen than was Robert. Some of the Kays even thought that Hannah influenced Robert's business decisions in undesirable ways.[21]

It was Robert, however, whom his children saw as the source of power. He made the arrangements for his boys' careers, and sometimes left Hannah to acquaint them with his decision. Once Robert's opinion was known a problem could be solved; if he offered reassurance it would soothe; his opinions were close to law, his wishes decisive; protecting him when he was ill or under stress from business was a paramount duty; gratitude for his goodness was natural, as were obedience and respect – there was relief in the family on one occasion when James's views were found to coincide with his father's.[22] Around Robert's concerns, whether in business, good works, family disputes, or the guiding of his brother into eternity, the family was organized. Except that the Queen had not yet ascended the throne, Robert might be described as a Victorian father.

For all the authority accorded and unquestioningly accepted by him, Robert Kay was an uncertain man. The God who consumed his waking hours could not protect him against insidious depression – he was 'low' or 'nervous' or, in words James was accustomed to use, 'afflicted by the *blue devils*'. Faced with a bad debt in London, he would retreat into himself, become enveloped in a cloud of solitariness, unable or unwilling to discuss the cause of his worry, while Hannah warned the children not to mention the problem. Stronger than Robert but made subservient by her strength, Hannah often had to act as a go-between, interpreting him to the children and to that extent experiencing reality through him. She explained his business concerns as well as she could with the limited information she was given; she replied to James's requests for his father's opinion on a career decision; she told the children how much their father missed them, just as she did the congratulating when a success had been obtained. Writing to his children later in life James captured this aspect of his mother's relationship to his father:

> Grandma lived a simple, pure, religious life. She taught us all to think of the gentle pious example of our father – to remember his continual charity – his love of God which was above the fear or favour of man – his preference of a good conscience to wealth – his singular meek, patient, and forgiving disposition.[23]

Emotionally, James Kay's father was forbidding, inaccessible, saintly and self-absorbed. His mother was more accessible, but equally threatening to peace of mind. In all the letters she wrote to him one note is missing entirely: uncomplicated or unconditional love. Hannah Kay was deeply concerned about her son's health and spiritual welfare, but her affection was hedged with conditions or obligations. James had been greatly helped by his father, he must make due recompense; his behaviour had been good, but he should not become careless, and should remember that much would be expected from him because he had been given much. When he pleased his father, he had to beware of self-confidence; he must work hard, but if he gained recognition, her warnings against worldliness or pride pushed rejoicing away.[24]

The careers of Robert's and Hannah's sons were retrospective evidence of their aspirations: four of their five boys pursued worldly recognition with success. (Their daughter had to be satisfied with triumphs of a more domestic kind.) James was the best known, but Robert was an important calico printer, Joseph a Queen's Counsel and a judge of the Salford Hundred Court of Record, and Ebenezer, who was knighted, a Queen's Counsel and a Lord Justice. Three of the boys have *Dictionary of National Biography* entries, a remarkable score for a family struggling into the middle class and a score not likely to have been attained had their parents not encouraged ambition. Yet, in a manoeuvre which was emotionally draining to James, Hannah expected success from him, warned him against enjoying its fruits, and diminished any sense of achievement he felt by attributing his success to Providence, to whom he was enjoined to show gratitude.[25]

Robert's and Hannah's preoccupation with the dangers of worldly success was fuelled by fear – they themselves had felt the perilous attraction of wealth and respectability and had fought hard to gain them. With an ambivalent fervour characteristic of nineteenth-century Nonconformity, they sought their salvation in the next world while cherishing their dangerous prosperity in this. Indeed, Robert Kay could afford to scale down his business activities only because of the fulfilment of his prolonged and determined search for success. As if to remind him of his past, some of his brothers urged him to end his retirement and manage a business venture they were planning. He decided to refuse when he discovered that the salary was £150 per annum instead of the £500 or £600 he had expected. He expressed his and Hannah's anger by accompanying his refusal with an offer to give his services for nothing at times when they were busy.[26] Old habits died hard and, though worldly wealth might constitute a snare and a delusion, he still considered himself a labourer worthy of his hire.

Out of their own confusion Robert and Hannah created a harsh emotional environment for their children, for they accompanied their simultaneous exalting and diminishing of success with the habit of exaggerating their children's faults. Much later in life, pondering the upbringing of his own children, James reflected how habitual, slight punishments produce 'the injurious impression on a child's mind that he is gravely and fatally in error'. His mind went back to his own childhood: 'I remember the bad effects of such a feeling on myself. It is fatal to the degree of self respect without which no good and true things can be done.'[27] He was to do some good and true things, but the emotional rewards from them, or from the success and recognition he obtained, could never permanently give him a sense of being valued, worthy and loved. Ease and self-confidence were not part of his personality, and rejection, which he often experienced, found him utterly vulnerable.

In June 1822 the Rev. John Clunie, owner and headmaster of the Leaf Square Grammar School in Pendleton, Salford, consoled himself for the failure of his hopes to climb 'a few of the pinnacles of Parnassus' with the thought that, if 'my works' (his students) turned out to be valuable, 'no wise man would say I had lived in vain', particularly as he sent out '10 or 12 volumes every year'. Among these volumes was James Kay, whom Clunie judged to have more promise than had his young brother Robert. Before they went to Leaf Square, James and Robert may have been educated at home by a tutor, but James attended the school from 1815 to 1819, when he was between the ages of 11 and 15, and he may have started there earlier and finished a little later.[28]

In August 1814, shortly before he took control of the school, Clunie stated the principles on which it was to be based. 'The pious and reflecting parents among Protestant Dissenters', he said, had long regretted that their sons had few opportunities to obtain a classical education, while 'the sons of the Establishment' had numerous grammar schools and 'those seats of learning which have been honourably designated the Two Eyes of Britain'. These parents also feared that in these institutions education might be provided at the expense of their sons' moral and religious principles, 'a sacrifice far too great for the highest possible attainments in learning and science'. Just such sentiments had in the eighteenth century led to the establishment of Dissenting academies (designed to train clergy and later, laymen) and schools, both of which became renowned for adding to the classical curriculum the new studies of science, modern languages, history and geography.[29]

Leaf Square Grammar was in this tradition. The Lancashire Congregational Union had resolved in 1809, when Robert Kay was its treasurer, to establish an academy to educate young men for the ministry, and a grammar school 'embracing the most liberal plan of education . . . for the Youth of Protestant Dissenters'. Any profits from the school were to support the academy, which was established in June 1811 and immediately began to struggle. Though its life was extended by some substantial donations, including 50 guineas each from Robert Kay and his brother, William, it was dissolved in December 1813. The grammar school, which had started in January 1811, was taken over by Clunie in 1815 and he ran it as a private venture for about 40 years.[30]

Learned, intellectually ambitious and very devout, Clunie made a deep impression on James Kay, who continued to correspond with him in later life. Clunie, a classical scholar, was able to offer his pupils these studies, while the Dissenting tradition from which the school originated ensured the usual emphasis on mathematics and science – it employed no less a person than John Dalton as a mathematics tutor, but as he departed in 1813 he did not teach James Kay. At Leaf Square Grammar a secular education was not acquired at the expense of a pupil's religious development. As Clunie wrote to Kay after he had left school,

> If you tread with delight the walks of science, and feel inspired by the air of all genuine eloquence and poetry, why should you not equally – infinitely more – be enraptured with the sacred scenes, where David tuned his harp, Isaiah soared higher than 'ad sidera', Jeremiah wept in strains so plaintive that none other ever surpassed them, or where He that 'taught with authority' uttered his sublime parables and heavenly discourses.

Robert and Hannah Kay had put the education of their sons in safe hands.[31]

Kay left two memorials of his schooldays. They are like different bells, one of which was to sound often in the future and to send its echoes thudding through his life, while the other rang a few times, then gradually ceased to sound. The first was a prize gained in 1815 for 'diligence in composing his themes' and foretelling the dedicated conscientiousness which marked his life. The second memorial, his earliest surviving piece of writing, was some verse produced in June 1819, when he was almost 15 years old and influenced by Samuel Butler's brilliant satire, *Hudibras*. If his parents recognized their son's debt to this mocker of the early Dissenters, they could console themselves that it had been written more than 150 years earlier, and that James's untitled poem contained no trace of Butler's mockery.[32]

It was addressed to his sister, Hannah, and began:

> You are again my best resort
> And as you took my last in sport
> Altho' a *teazing plaguing* letter
> I've sent you this perhaps a better

Its 37 lines end with him contemplating a future parliamentary career:

> Pleading strongly all my Country's laws
> *Ranting* loudly for a little cause
> And p'rhaps upon th'Examination
> You'll see me represent a Nation
> Then stand up an old grey-headed *Member*
> Boast my *age* and all my deeds remember
> Howe'er I'm yours in Hudibrastic
> Or rather Man in Periphrastic
> Thro' ev'ry passing day
> *Your Mother's* Son *Jim Kay*

Kay was not going to be a serious challenge to Butler, though he entertained visions of fame and public recognition – he even imagined himself sitting among the 'titled great' with Robert Walpole, England's first prime minister. Yet for all its awkwardness and laboured posturing, the poem attempts a high-spirited humour which did not appear again in the 58 years of writing that were left to James Kay.

After he left Leaf Square Grammar Kay worked for about three years in his birthplace, Rochdale, at Fenton and Roby's Bank, of which his uncle, Joseph Fenton, who had married the aggressively pious Ann Kay in 1789, was a partner. The Fentons lived first at Crimble but moved to Bamford Hall, about three-quarters of a mile away, after Joseph bought the Bamford estate in 1816. While Kay worked at the bank he lived with his uncle, aunt and two cousins, James and John. He faced the prospect of life in that highly organized home with trepidation.[33]

The gathering at Bamford Hall provides a vignette of the middle class which had ridden to prominence on the vehicle of the Industrial Revolution. In their hands the Hall became a symbol of money made in textiles which was now seeking security and respectability in land. Its owner, Joseph Fenton, was one of the country bankers who had come into existence since the mid-eighteenth century and who, while investing in land, continued to develop their textile interests. The Kay–Fenton marriage was a common alliance among cotton families, who thus protected and consolidated their financial position.[34] Ann Fenton's passionate Nonconformity expressed a common religious position. And James Kay represented the younger generation, which was moving away from the textile trade and agriculture towards a professional occupation.

Country banking did not retain its attraction for long. Kay spent sufficient time at Fenton and Roby's to learn something of the business, but soon made clear his wish to study medicine. For reasons which are unknown, his father opposed his wish, and a protracted struggle developed, drawing from John Clunie a sympathetic comment about 'all the scenes and privations' through which his ex-pupil had passed. Eventually Robert Kay conceded that banking did not satisfy his son and arranged for him to work in the cotton trade, an occupation which proved equally unattractive. By mid-1824 he had worn down his father's resistance and it was agreed that he would go to Edinburgh to study medicine. A satisfied Clunie wrote: 'I always conceived that you had little business to be at the bank . . . and none to be at the looms.'[35]

Kay's time in Rochdale was not wholly wasted. His uncle's partner, the Roby of Fenton and Roby, had a local reputation in literary matters and stimulated Kay's interest in English poetry. He was sufficiently adventurous to read the modern poets, Byron, Shelley and Wordsworth, and was also fond of Milton, particularly *Comus*. He wrote to Clunie of his determination to pursue a literary as well as a medical career, and while working in the bank he had passed that gloomy milestone in a writer's career, the first rejection slip. He received it for his short poem, 'To the echo in a sea shell', which he had sent to the *Bolton Express* with the suggestion that he might be paid for it. The editor pointed out that the poem needed to be 'very considerably altered', and that it was usual to contribute small pieces of poetry gratuitously. The rejection did so little to abate Kay's fervour that Clunie advised him not to allow his literary or medical ambitions to undermine his religious commitment.[36]

An unknown friend had a similar fear, for having expressed regret at being without Kay's company, he warned against 'bad companions' who threatened religion and morality. There was little chance of going astray in Ann Fenton's household, and in fact Kay was expressing his religious commitment in a way much valued among Congregationalists. He became superintendent of the boys' Sunday school at Bamford Chapel and applied knowledge he had acquired of the Sunday school system in Manchester with such enthusiasm that the Bamford school improved rapidly and had to be enlarged in 1822. As he was assisted by Thomas Jackson, the son of the uncompromising minister his father had assisted, the missionary efforts of the fathers were being emulated by the sons.[37]

Not all of Kay's endeavours were successful: once when he tried to impress his scholars with a chemical experiment, 'an irritating and noxious gas' drove them from the room. Jackson was more successful. A shoemaker with what Kay later described as 'a very humble elementary education', he taught oratorios and anthems which the choir practised for months (sometimes nearly every night of the week) before singing them in the chapel, led by Jackson on his violin. What Jackson senior with his preference for plain hymns thought is not known, but Kay taught the Sunday school during the dispute between Jackson and his congregation and, as Sunday school superintendent, would have been directly involved in the debate over the teaching of writing. In the end it was decided that no writing would be taught on Sunday, but it was offered to the boys on Saturdays and to the girls on Monday evening. Thus early in his life Kay saw how religious opinion could impinge on educational policies. There was no personal clash between Kay and Jackson senior, who allowed him to establish a laboratory for chemical experiments in a room in his own house.[38]

Kay and the young Thomas Jackson sometimes took the senior scholars and the most active teachers on long walks. Kay remembered climbing the Knowl Hill and descending Balderstone and Brooks-bottom; he also recollected clambering up a steep scar in Bamford Wood expecting to have thrown off the party, only to find Jackson close behind him, though his body was withered by illness and he was crippled in both foot and leg. These wanderings gave Kay some knowledge of the handloom weavers who lived in the villages and hamlets or in the lonely stone cottages. The industrialization, which his family had assisted, swept away the cottages and transformed the countryside, but in novels written decades later Kay left his memorial of that countryside and its people.[39]

Kay often listened to Jackson's sermons and he left a portrait of his friend's carefully prepared discourses, which were characterized 'by much of the quaintness of the old divines, and deeply tinctured by a severe form of Calvinistic theology'. The geniality of Jackson's disposition, Kay said, gave 'a winning sweetness' to what was otherwise a harsh manner, 'so that the sternest doctrines of his creed were not repulsive from his lips'. In recording these memories Kay forgot his own youthful enthusiasm. A fragment of a speech or a letter to his boys' Sunday school shows him spinning an intricate web of rhetoric, just as Jackson and other preachers had done in the large bare Congregational chapels Kay knew so well. 'My dear lads', he began, having taken a text from *Ecclesiastes*:

> You have perhaps ere this heard of the death of some notorious sinner[,] one who had despised the warnings of conscience and the rebuke of the righteous and the fearful ravages of disease – whose daring impiety was a proverb – whose midnight intemperance was the terror of society – in whose character there was nothing to love and the assembly of everything that could disgust[,] who had it might be in his earlier and more happy years married the woman of his love and had gathered around his fireside the innocent prattling objects of his affection . . . but who in what manner it matters little to say had gradually or at once become the terror I have told . . . it would scarcely be possible to imagine a more affecting picture than to watch at

midnight by the light of some few stray sticks which her little ones had gathered the wife whom he had linked to his miserable carreer [*sic*] in the bare and shelterless desolation of his garret exposed to the pitiless beatings of the storm nestling in her bosom upon the broken boards the slumbers of her children which hunger and cold united to disturb and listening with terror for the staggering heavy footfall that announced his return from some midnight scene of riot in all the violence of drunken madness and raving impiety [–] you have stood perhaps at the grave of such a man . . .[40]

John Ashworth, whose evangelizing activities and religious tracts became well known, met Kay some 40 years later, identified himself as one of his Sunday-school scholars, and vividly described being presented with the school's first prize. Before the presentations were made Kay 'mounted the platform and made a speech', and when the time came to receive his prize Ashworth, whose family was too poor to afford 'the clogs' he longed to wear on his feet, threaded his way through the audience 'as softly as though I were a cat' and walked 'blushingly' on to the platform. He returned to his place and cried; some of the boys, he thought, had sneered at his poverty. For Kay, if not for all his pupils, Ashworth had much respect.[41]

The fervent young Kay accompanied the deacons on Sunday visits to remote districts in the hills of Blackstone Edge and Todmorden or along the range from Knowl Hill to Rowley Moor. More than 40 years later, though he scarcely remembered what attracted him to 'this simple, earnest, grave man', he wrote of one of the deacons, John Crabtree:

> his pious conversation on the way – our arrival at a weaver's cottage in some far distant 'fold' on the edge of a wild moor – the simple breakfast of oatcake, or oatmeal porridge and milk – the gathering of the neighbours, and the primitive scriptural greetings sometimes uttered – the simple services, and the quaint, rather dogmatic discourse of my friend John.

The midday meal of eggs, bacon and oatcake was followed by the walk back to Bamford, the arrival in the twilight or at night, and Crabtree's wholehearted efforts to persuade him to become a missionary. He failed, but Kay founded a missionary society at the Sunday school to raise money for those who had answered the call to evangelize. As for himself, he had glimpsed other worlds and 'longed to go to the university to study science, history, and metaphysics'.[42]

John Clunie thought that Kay was 'powerfully stimulated and

passionately devoted to study', and when his longing to go to university had triumphed over his father's opposition, Kay flung himself into his medical studies, as if seeking an immediate outlet for his pent-up frustration. Soon these studies, his literary efforts, and new and pressing social concerns consumed his attention, but the values of the Bamford chapel and its Sunday school were too deeply ingrained to be easily displaced. Later he claimed that his Sunday school experiences were what first made him think about popular education, though by the time he expressed this view his educational activities had established his reputation and had given shape and purpose to his life, so that he may have read more into his Bamford days than they actually contained. Nevertheless, gatherings of Edinburgh's sophisticated medical world, impressed by the sharpness of Kay's intellect, the power of his personality and his brilliance as a speaker, might have been surprised to discover how little changed he was from the intense young man who had conducted the Sunday school under Bamford's pines and poplars.[43]

2 · The medical student, 1824–27

In Hugo Arnot's famous description, Edinburgh's Old Town was compared to a turtle. Edinburgh Castle was the turtle's head, the High Street the ridge of its back, the wynds and closes which fall away from the High Street its 'shelving sides', and the Palace of Holyroodhouse its tail. The Castle looming through the mist which rolled in from the North Sea was a familiar sight to Kay during his three winters in Edinburgh, as his studies at the medical faculty, and at the hospital where he did his clinical work, brought him daily through the streets of the Old Town. By the time Kay came, the aristocracy and the middle classes had left the Old Town's tall, narrow, stone buildings, the aristocracy preferring country living and perhaps a town house in London, while the middle class had moved into the elegant, spacious but less dramatic streets of the New Town. Built in the late eighteenth and early nineteenth centuries, and separated from the Old Town by the stagnant North Loch, the New Town was a striking product of that 'late and sudden flowering of Scottish culture', the Scottish Enlightenment. Though he worked in the Old, Kay boarded in the New Town, amid a middle class whose rich intellectual, literary and legal life had not been greatly affected by the loss of the aristocracy.[1]

In the early nineteenth century Edinburgh's population grew rapidly: from 67,000 in 1801 to 136,000 in 1831. Driven from the rural areas by the enclosures, the demolition of cottar houses and the Highland clearances, and attracted by the hope of work or higher wages, people crowded into the city, especially into the wynds and closes which their betters had left. Not primarily an industrial city, Edinburgh's economy was supported by agriculture and sheep farming for which it provided financial and commercial services, by a ring of industries around the city, and by small industries within it. Edinburgh was essentially residential, the legal, ecclesiastical and banking centre of Scotland, a city of lawyers, bankers, professors, merchants, writers and country gentlemen who put their profits into buildings in the New Town. And it still provided a home for the craftsmen whom it had harboured for centuries. As Youngson remarked, 'it was . . . a city of infinite variety; a city of professional service, of craft service, of menial service; a city of handsome homes, fine public buildings, wealth and enjoyment' – if one could forget the poverty and misery of the Old Town.[2]

By the mid-1820s, the major figures of the Scottish Enlightenment (Adam Smith and David Hume, Henry Raeburn, the artist, or the architect, Robert Adam) had left the scene, though the philosopher, Dugald Stewart, remained to personify the Enlightenment's belief that the advances made by Newton and Bacon in science might be repeated in social and political matters if their methods were thoroughly applied. But the 1820s were years of religious renewal which witnessed a striking growth of Evangelical influence. In any case, an Edinburgh whose intellectual life was influenced by Francis Jeffrey and the *Edinburgh Review* which he edited, or Henry Cockburn, who later became Lord Advocate and whose *Memorials of His Time* left so lively an account of the period, or Walter Scott, remained a vital city. In law, literature, science, economics, philosophy and music it offered Kay a stimulating cultural environment to which he responded with a student's enthusiasm.[3]

Above all, for Kay, there was medicine. The medical faculty had been established in 1726 by George Drummond, Edinburgh's most influential eighteenth-century civic leader, and his friend John Munro, a surgeon who had studied medicine at Leyden. Greatly impressed with Leyden, Munro modelled Edinburgh's medical faculty on it – so thoroughly that the first five professors to be appointed had been trained there. As well as helping to create a faculty Munro established a family monopoly. His son, grandson and great-grandson, each called Alexander and distinguished by the dynastic addition of *primus*, *secundus* or *tertius*, held the chair of anatomy in unbroken succession from the first days of the faculty until the resignation of Munro *tertius* in 1846, a reign of 120 years. The Town Council, which controlled the university, handled its responsibilities so effectively that Edinburgh became one of Europe's best medical faculties and Scottish students were joined by many from Ireland, England, North America and parts of Europe. The Council had developed an institution which, even its enemies conceded, had a significance far beyond the municipal.[4]

Students were attracted to the medical faculty by Edinburgh itself, which was one of Europe's largest cities. The teaching was in English, tuition was relatively cheap, being non-residential the university imposed fewer restrictions on students, it had no religious tests (obviously important for a Dissenter such as Kay), and as its professors were paid little or no salary and relied on the fees paid by their students, a premium was placed on effective teaching. Moreover, the course for the MD did not have rigid subject requirements so that students might vote with their feet when a professor displeased them. Finally, the Royal Infirmary of Edinburgh, part of the founders' plan and one of their heaviest debts to Leyden, provided the opportunity, available nowhere else in England or Scotland, for practical clinical teaching.[5]

When Kay came to Edinburgh in 1824 the medical faculty's reputation was beginning to decline. The class fee system had earlier begun to ossify as professors were reluctant to support the establishment of new chairs, or even to appoint assistants, for fear that their incomes would be reduced. These incomes were going to men who were inferior to the giants of the earlier age, as nepotism of the Munro kind had eventually taken its toll: of the ten medical professors appointed between 1786 and 1807, eight were the sons of Edinburgh medical professors. The story that Munro *tertius* read his grandfather's lectures on anatomy with such lazy faith that students of Kay's era heard him remark 'When I was in Leyden in 1719' seems, unfortunately, to be apocryphal. But he did little to enthuse his students. Sir Robert Christison, a student in 1815 and later a medical professor at Edinburgh, thought that Munro's lectures were clear and precise, but remembered his classes as being 'the frequent scene of disturbance and uproar', caused, no doubt, because Munro taught with 'an unimpassioned indifference, as if it were all one to him whether his teaching was acceptable and accepted or not'. Charles Darwin, who was in Edinburgh failing to get a medical degree for two of the three years in which Kay was there, thought that Munro's lectures were 'as dull as he was himself, and the subject disgusted me'. In anatomy and in other subjects, extramural teachers, some of them aggressive and brilliant lecturers, set up in competition, and when the university tried to prevent their courses being accepted for the MD, the Town Council insisted that they be recognized. Such difficulties, however, had not yet made a serious dent in the medical faculty's prestige.[6]

There was little in Kay's family or social background to prepare him for medicine, but he did the best he could. He took advice from Dr James Lomax Bardsley, who had just brought his newly acquired Edinburgh MD to Manchester. He secured letters of introduction to Edinburgh friends from Dr William Johns who, before coming to Rochdale, had been a Congregational missionary in India – he was expelled when the East India Company decided that the Christian missions were alienating a populace it wished to exploit in peace. Dr James Williamson, another co-religionist who was working in Leeds, gave Kay information on the courses he should study, the books he required, and places to find accommodation. His mother acted on Williamson's advice, but despite her efforts Kay boarded in four places in his first six months.[7]

Early in Kay's time at Edinburgh the wooden spire of the Tron Church caught fire – Henry Cockburn left a memorable description of 'a calm and triumphant gilded cock' on the top of the spire looking down disdainfully on the crackling flames before plunging into them. Sights more typical of Kay's routine were described by 'Scotus', the acerbic correspondent of *The Lancet*, when he reported on a lecture given by Dr Andrew Duncan, senior, then much past his peak. Evoking 'the dreary sensations' which accompanied the opening of an Edinburgh winter's campaign of lectures, Scotus recalled 'the College or the hospital, enveloped in wreaths of snow or the thick folds of a fog just freshly wafted from the waves of the Forth on a December morning'. He climbed three or four flights of dimly lit, stone steps on his way to the lecture theatre, a room in which the black walls were dripping with moisture and which was lit by one 'half-starved gas lamp'. The stove burning in a corner did little to warm the students, and when Duncan arrived, preceded by a servant carrying a taper, he had to call for more light before he could read his lecture. As the lecture gradually 'dwindled down to an almost inaudible susurration', neither Scotus nor the freezing students learned much.[8]

Though Kay became accustomed to such scenes in his first Edinburgh session, which began in early November and lasted until May, his enthusiasm was not diminished. He studied anatomy, chemistry and materia medica (pharmacology), and over 50 years later a fellow student and friend, William Charles (usually called Charles) Henry, could remember Kay's impact. Henry thought him unprepared for his scientific studies, though he may have been misled by the fact that Kay had come to Edinburgh with the works of great poets and his own compositions buzzing in his head. Moreover,

Henry's idea of a suitable preparation was rather exalted as he belonged to one of Manchester's most influential medical and scientific families and had been privately tutored in chemistry by John Dalton. Henry was struck by Kay's obsessive determination to succeed and the manner in which he flung 'his whole mental power and inexhaustible energies' into his studies, so that he had outstripped most of his contemporaries by the end of his first winter. 'He became a marked personage in the classrooms, where his earnest never-swerving attention to lectures, his massive forehead, and the high intellectual cast of his features impressed all, professors as well as students, with a prevision of his certain subsequent distinction'.[9]

On Williamson's advice Kay joined the Royal Medical Society, an influential body of students, who formed its basis, and some medical professors and extra-mural staff. Kay was soon regarded as the Society's best debater, apart from Dr William Cullen, a member of another Edinburgh dynasty who was considerably older and already a lecturer in anatomy. 'Over his fellow-students', Henry remembered, 'he achieved an easy triumph, overbearing all opposition in a torrent of vigorous expression, imagery and argument'. Charles Darwin, who thought that 'much rubbish was talked' at the Royal Medical Society, nevertheless agreed that there were some good speakers 'of whom the best was the present Sir J. Kay-Shuttleworth'. Kay's reputation increased when he read a paper on muscular contractibility. Henry considered the paper ingenious but unsound, yet it was adjudged a remarkable performance and gave rise to a long and animated discussion – a very successful outcome for so early an appearance before the Society. Reports of Kay's triumph were welcomed at Bamford Hall and at home. His sister gave him the important news that 'Dear Papa' was very pleased, warning, as her parents might have done, that those at home had 'as much reason to pray to be kept from pride as you have from vanity'.[10]

In the reminiscences of Charles Henry, the young Kay is full of drive and strength, a man who swamps his opposition by the force of his personality and the passion of his arguments, rather than one who relies on precise and elegant persuasion. Henry admitted that Kay was not as exact in thought or close in reasoning as he was later to become, and remarked that 'the rhetorical faculty was unquestionably far more developed than the logical'.[11] Certainly Kay's behaviour showed traces of the unwillingness to brook opposition for which his uncles were noted, and it sometimes seemed that he dared not listen to what others had to say lest his own uncertainties be exposed.

Sometimes, however, the aggressive debater disappeared and a more uncertain young man emerged. In his first session at Edinburgh he had an experience which he did not recount until 33 years later. He told the story in unusually simple and direct prose, as if, even after that length of time, he did not want to drop his guard.

> I remember the first time I entered a dissecting-room, the porter showed me in early in the morning. I was fresh from a pure home. There was a corpse on the table covered by a sheet. I had an awe of death, and of the cold and livid ruin which it had made. I sat down in silence. I waited perhaps an hour. What thoughts passed through my mind! Then suddenly entered a group of initiated students. They stripped the sheet from the subject. It was a female form. The conversation jarred on my ears – wrung my heart. It was jesting, ribald, even profane. Even the Professor who entered, and who is a man of pre-eminent skill and knowledge [presumably Munro *tertius*], said nothing to rebuke this tone. My blood was almost curdled in my veins. At that moment I could not conceive it possible that I should spend every livelong day of many months in rooms crowded by such bodies, over which would swarm the votaries of a great but thus degraded science.[12]

An early nineteenth-century dissecting room did not need happenings of this kind to be a chamber of horrors, but Kay eventually overcame his repugnance to the study of anatomy. Yet more than three decades later, he had not shaken himself free of his tendency to idealize women, of the emotional hesitancy betrayed in the words 'female form', and of the expectation that authority would behave honourably. This James Kay, so very different from the marked personage of the classrooms, would swiftly have been recognized by Robert and Hannah.

Hannah Kay recognized another emotional symptom after her son had been in Edinburgh less than two months, when, 'knowing your studious mind will leave nothing unaccomplished however much you may undertake', she reminded him that it was not necessary to accomplish everything in one year. She attributed his 'dejection of spirits' to his 'constitutional disposition to it and too intense study'. If she had not come to this conclusion, she informed him, 'I should feel a little more uncomfortable about you'. She gave the usual fruitless (and dispiriting) advice : 'endeavour to relax a little if you can afford time', but be grateful for being busy because the effects of 'inapplication' were lamentably injurious.[13] In the future, moods of depression often enveloped Kay, and already there were signs that the intense single-mindedness, which impressed his teacher and fellow-students, could bring him to the brink of emotional exhaustion.

It was early in 1825, while Kay was at Edinburgh, that his uncle James called Robert Kay to his death-bed, and provided the subject for the only surviving letter from Robert to his son. In this stark, urgent letter Robert gives his feelings stiff but powerful expression:

> My Dear Jas.
> Will easily conceive that while I have been attending some Friends to their long Homes and others while they have been walking thro' the Valey of the shadow of Death and beheld their anxiety and at times their distraction of mind as they approach'd the gates of the Grave and the borders of Eternity, that the words of the wise man would sometimes occur to my mind, vanity of vanities all is vanity. . .

Addressing his son in the third person, Robert warns him about the success James had been pursuing:

> could he have seen his Uncle Jas. and heard him state his anxiety of mind and at times his dispare at the recollections of his past spent Life, am persuaded that the enchanting prospects which the enemy of mankind often presents to the sanguine Minds of unexperienced youth, wou'd in great measure have lost their force, and tho' we find it recorded that while we are seeking happiness in anything short of God, we are seeking it in broken Cisterns that can hold no Water and will of course disappoint our expectations, yet we still persue and still prove the assertions of the wise man, who had far greater opportunities of trying all things, than we can possibly enjoy; instead of listening to the word of God which says seek ye first the kingdom of God and his righteousness and all things else shall be added to you, we too often are seeking in the first place the Honor the riches and the pleasures of this perishing World forgetting that the Wisdom that cometh from above is what *alone* can ennoble the mind and render us truly great and happy here and hereafter oh Jas. cou'd I persuade him in the first place to make his peace with God thro' the merits of a D^n Saviour, am persuaded he wou'd find Wisdom flow into his mind in far superior way to anything he can possibly imagine and then his persuits (*sic*) of other wisdom wou'd be properly directed and to proper ends, and persuaded he his (*sic*) convinced that life is very uncertain and that we any of us may die any day and is it not best to be prepared. . .

Still addressing his son in the third person (perhaps his urgent emotions could comprehend no more than another object for salvation), Robert Kay told him about a cousin also named James, the son of the James whose salvation was in peril. He had abandoned trade, was seeking a private tutor, and intended to go up to Oxford, forbidden to respectable Dissenters, 'to fit himself for a gentleman as he says but what will become of him God only knows he his (*sic*) now a pitiable object'. Robert ended the letter:

> I am extremely busy with my own little Business and my Brother's affairs am afraid the[y] will never be settled peaceably; he will be glad to hear that he has another Brother and that his Mother is doing well, I don't know that we have much news here at present have recd a letter from Thos. Jackson shall send it first opportunity; enclosed he will receive ten pounds his Mamma Sister and little Brothers join in love to him believe me to be
> Your affectionate father
> Robt Kay[14]

His brother's entry into eternity and the temptations facing his eldest son had almost obliterated from Robert Kay's mind the danger and eventual happiness which attended the birth of his youngest son.

Writing to her brother a week later, Hannah Kay provided a different view of the world. She was surprised and grieved that their father had given no details about the birth of the baby, but she reported that the letter from James, which had revealed this failure, supplied them with some 'merriment'. Robert Kay had not been the least amused but, having had the grace to be 'rather ashamed', had stalked out of the room. The arrival of 'the little stranger', Hannah wrote, had brought them 'inexpressible joy', particularly as it had been 'a long dread event' and the object of fearful anticipation. Hannah Kay, the mother, was 44 when the child, named Thomas, was born, and her daughter wrote frankly: 'We can never be sufficiently thankful that whilst so many are being carried off on every side by the hands (?) of death our beloved Mamma is once again spared to us.'[15] The women's world at Meadowcroft was closed to Robert Kay whose eyes were fixed on his own 'little Business' and the greater business of the world to come.

The ordinary life at Meadowcroft and among the family's relatives and friends was also reported to James by both Hannahs. They told him when his brother Robert was apprenticed to an apothecary in Portsea – the less promising Robert once ruefully told his brother that it would never be allowed for the apothecary to prescribe for the physician. In lively, affectionate and somewhat sentimental letters, Hannah (his sister) informed James how she had followed him in spirit on his journey to Edinburgh, how she mourned and grieved over his lonely situation, and thought of him at night in his dull little room; his mother spoke frankly of the 'noisy and boisterous' older boys and of her wish 'for a school for them during the day to be out of my way'. She also told him how much his father missed him – 'I never knew your Papa feel so acutely on any occasion, Oh make him every compensation in your power by sturdy attention to your studies, and that consistency of conduct which you have hitherto maintained'. James was exhorted to be economical – a £10 Bank of England note which he had been sent 'will not I am sure be improperly appropriated – because you know the extent of our means . . . your good father . . . seems so well satisfied with the path chosen and adopted – but . . . my dear lad a word of caution do be as economical in your expenditures as possible'. Robert Kay's dominion over his family was also recorded – 'he is so very kind towards all of us more so I think than ever' – as was his trust in Providence – 'In a conversation last night he mentioned that he placed no confidence in men and wished to depend upon a gracious Providence who had hitherto so wonderfully dealt with his family'.[16]

His mother's letters also took in the Fentons' decision to build a large factory at Hooley Bridge despite the difficult financial times; the intention of one of James's cousins, William Kay, to study medicine in Edinburgh, her uncertainty about the wisdom of their lodging together and her opinion that William was inadequately prepared; his father's failure to dissuade another cousin from 'running off' to contract an ill-advised marriage; family disputes at Bass Lane and Limefield which drained Robert Kay's patience and energies; James Kay's property settlement – he left about £30,000 which Hannah feared the family would not use well; a series of deaths of relatives and friends which drove Hannah to the conclusion that 'We live in a dying world and it is a dying time'. His sister also brooded over mortality, deciding that the sudden death of a distant relative was 'a solemn warning to act and to work while it is day for the night cometh when no man can work'. She was unselfconsciously and cruelly confident that the dead man would not be present when they met their friends in glory – 'he was summoned to appear after a life of neglected privileges before the Holy Tribunal almost without warning'.[17] Other reports came from friends. Thomas Jackson submitted to his 'General' a report of the juvenile regiment which he commanded at Bamford and remarked on the dreadful chasm left by

James and his brother Robert, who had also worked in the Sunday school. He warned against allowing science and philosophy to 'usurp the place of Piety and religion', and asked Kay to send him an address which he could read to the Sunday school. And Dr William Johns revealed that he had some kinship with Robert Kay: 'Dr. Jarrold visited yesterday – my wife is unwell from miscarriage – my paper on worms was published in the Lancet'.[18]

It was this vital, parochial, intolerant, paternalistic, God- and Mammon-obsessed world that Kay re-entered when he returned to Rochdale after his first session in Edinburgh.

Kay's sister told him that the family were agog with expectation as they awaited his return from Edinburgh. She watched figures moving through the trees near Meadowcroft until that of her 'dear Jemmy' (as she called him) appeared. The reunion was short for Kay moved to Manchester where he spent the six months before the next university session working at the Manchester Infirmary. He had considered a stint at a bank in Edinburgh during the summer recess, but his parents had not liked the idea and Robert Kay arranged for him to work at the Infirmary where he would gain valuable experience and make important contacts.[19]

Kay returned to Edinburgh for his second session in late October 1825 with his confidence lifted by the good opinion he had earned at the Infirmary and by his attendance at a course of clinical lectures given by Bardsley. During this session his main study was the practice of physic with Dr James Home. On 25 March 1826, towards the end of the session, he began a three-month spell at the New Town Dispensary where he gained practical experience as he had numerous patients under his immediate care. Partly because of this work Kay did not return to Rochdale during the recess, but completed a summer course of lectures in chemistry, in which he assisted in the performance of experiments under the guidance of the outstanding Edward Turner. He attended lectures in anatomy, which had become a major interest, and he obtained the eagerly sought honour of serving as a clinical clerk (a medical assistant) for most of the summer clinical courses conducted by Dr William Alison. He also spent some time in Dublin furthering his anatomical studies.[20]

During his third and final session, which began in November 1826, Kay attended further lectures in chemistry, the institutes of medicine (physiology) and midwifery. He took the extra-mural lectures on surgery given by another of Edinburgh's famous medical figures, James Syme, and continued his practical studies: he spent three months as a clerk in the Fever Hospital with Drs Robert Graham and Alison, and from 1 February until December 1827 he worked as a clerk and then as resident clerk in the medical wards at the Royal Infirmary, where Alison was again one of his colleagues.[21] Meanwhile Kay prepared the thesis which he had to defend as part of his final examination due in April 1827.

Of equal importance with his studies was his election by a large majority as Senior President of the Royal Medical Society for the 1825–26 session, an honour which was obtained, according to Christison, only by 'the choicest of our students'. One of his first tasks was to present to the Society a portrait of Dr Andrew Duncan who, however scathingly Scotus wrote of him, had been the Society's president six times and was largely responsible for obtaining its Royal charter. Kay's brilliant speeches on occupying the chair of the Society and at its annual dinner strengthened the students' conviction that they had chosen their president wisely.[22]

Hannah Kay's reaction to her son's triumph was not enthusiastic. She admitted that the Bible did not require him to relinquish honours which had been legitimately earned, but – 'I do not wish you to be frequently the President of dinner table or one of a dinner party, and if it expose you to such temptations I care not how soon your Presidency closes.' She was sure that 'no one can rise from such entertainments in any degree better for it', and she objected to the midnight rambles on which he was going, though she enjoyed his descriptions of them. Worried by his excitement, she had 'sat down in the quiet of this evening because you are much upon my mind and I am anxious to bring you down from your elevation now and then to the concerns and cares that are familiar to us, as a means of doing you much good'. She hoped that he was not in danger of forgetting his family, but 'I more fear your forgetfulness of Him in whom we all live and have our being.' He was to read his Bible and to pray daily, for Daniel 'in his elevated station in a court sought his God in fervent prayer, three times a day, and I am sure you are in equal danger in your elevation and surrounded probably with as many tempters'. 'All this', Hannah said with relentless truthfulness, 'is because I love you so much and have so continually [your] best interests at heart.'[23] When his mother equated an anxiously sought and jubilantly reported triumph with a temptation to evil, and attributed her action to love, Kay's uncertain sense of his own worth was made more precarious. His response then, and throughout his life, was to pursue recognition even more feverishly, in the vain hope that further achievements would appease the demons of self-doubt which had not been satisfied by earlier successes. He was set on a course of emotional destruction.

There was a danger as old as fame to which his mother may have suspected he was exposed. If he encountered it, the company included a cousin, James Openshaw Kay, who came to Edinburgh in November 1825 to study medicine. Hannah Kay was aware that the quarrelsome Kays carried their rivalry into the activities of their children, and she warned her son to set an example to his cousins in Edinburgh, 'who will watch you very closely and be ready to report anything to your disadvantage'. In the same letter she indulged in some of this rivalry herself, reporting caustically that James Openshaw Kay had sent back a box of game soon after his arrival in Edinburgh. She passed on her daughter's wish to know 'what Proffessor (*sic*) he attended for the game'. By February 1826 James Openshaw Kay had abandoned Edinburgh and his medical studies, but he wrote to his cousin requesting a minor favour and reporting an event which had happened shortly before he left Edinburgh.

> I went for the fun of the thing to see the poor romantic girl I introduced to you. There she was at the old station and came running to meet me, and gave me her address written under the light of *a Lamp* in Leith Walk. When we parted she shed tears, and the beautiful impression in her fine black eyes I shall not forget.

'I am much better of the –', he immediately continued, 'though when I drink any wine I have much pain after in making –. Should I continue taking the drops?'[24] If 'station' is taken to imply the meeting place for a prostitute, and 'pox' is placed in the first of the deliberately left blanks, one of James Openshaw Kay's activities (and perhaps his cousin's) becomes clear. The interpretation and the interpolation do not require an unreasonable reading of the letter, but in the absence of any further evidence, the conjecture cannot be guaranteed.

Kay did not answer this or two later letters from his cousin, who charitably attributed his silence to 'your old complaint, study', and whatever the sexual experiences (if there were any) the association had brought Kay, he was not cured of this old complaint. In the course of his study he developed professional relationships of great importance, especially through the clerical clerkship with Alison. A member of a distinguished Edinburgh family, William Pulteney Alison (1790–1859) completed an MD at Edinburgh at the age of 21. In 1815 he became physician at the newly founded New Town Dispensary and, seven years later, professor of the institutes of medicine and, by virtue of that professorship, a physician in the clinical wards of the Edinburgh Infirmary. He wrote widely and his views on physiology were influential, but his kindliness, conscientiousness and compassion made him one of the best-liked members of the Scottish medical profession. As Alison's clerk, Kay had to keep admission records, write case histories, and record the physician's comments on treatment. According to Henry, Kay's reports went beyond simple recording and 'were coloured and adorned with his imaginative power, and perhaps influenced by preconceived views, yet bore the impress of his mind'. A calm and cautious physician, who placed great stress on exact observation, Alison listened 'with a benignant smile to Mr. Kay's rapid, fervent, brilliant, but not always correct diagnoses; and in a few well-weighed words pointed out the error, when such there was, and defined the true character of the disease'. Alison was impressed with his clerk's 'extraordinary mental power and stern unwearied industry', and Kay preserved a lifelong admiration for Alison.[25]

Alison gave considerable support to the scientific investigations Kay had begun. In 1826 he drew on his thesis to present the Royal Medical Society with another paper which he called 'Physiological experiments and observations on the cessation of the contractibility of the heart and muscles in the asphyxia of warm-blooded animals'. In an unusual achievement for a student, a version of this paper was later published in the *Edinburgh Medical and Surgical Journal*. During a paper which Alison gave to the Medico-Chirurgical Society of Edinburgh, he referred in some detail and favourably to the work of 'my friend Dr J.P. Kay'. The *Edinburgh Medical and Surgical Journal*, when reviewing Alison's contribution, said that its most novel part was its description of Kay's experiments, showing how effectively Alison had used his name and influence to bring Kay under notice.[26]

He rendered Kay a still more important service. While working with Alison at the New Town Dispensary, Kay began to see the world of poverty and suffering outside the polite chambers of the Royal Medical Society. Established in 1815, the New Town Dispensary was supported by subscribers who, in return for their donations, elected the office-bearers and had the right to recommend

'such poor patients as they wish to receive aid'. Unlike the Old Town
Dispensary, which had bitterly opposed its establishment, the New
Town Dispensary provided medicines and medical (including obstet-
ric) assistance on its premises and in the homes of the poor. Such
practices, Henry Cockburn remarked, were thought 'Impractical,
and dangerously popular!', especially by the Old Town Dispensary
which 'demonstrated the beauty of the sick poor being obliged to
swallow their doses at a public office'. The newcomer survived the
controversy which erupted at its foundation, and through it Kay
gained an insight into the conditions of Edinburgh's poor.[27]

    This insight was sharpened during his time at the Infirmary and
the Fever Hospital because there was an outbreak of typhoid fever.
Kay remembered leaving the Royal Medical Society late at night and
climbing the staircases of the Old Town to visit patients. He came to
know the tall buildings in the 'steep narrow avenues' which speared
down from the ridge of the High Street, and he worked in the wynds
of the Canongate and in the Cowgate where the buildings which
once housed the wealthy had been converted into 'barracks' for the
poor. Five or six storeys above the street, in rooms with decorated
ceilings and fireplaces, Kay discovered families racked with poverty
and illness. He once found that an 'Irishman's pig', brought in as a
suckling, had grown so large that it was almost impossible to remove.
The filth on the stairs disgusted him and he became convinced that
'the lees of the population' who had settled in the barracks would
perish from illnesses which defied medical knowledge.[28]

    The Fever Hospital, Queensberry House in the Canongate near
Holyroodhouse and once the home of the Dukes of Queensberry,
made a lasting impression. Kay thought it large, gloomy and
architecturally depressing, and in his *Autobiography* he wrote that 'if
the scenes of the Canongate and Cowgate could ever have been
blotted from my mind, the suffering and mortality of Queensberry
House would be indelible'. In 1827 he gave a now unknown
acquaintance the only contemporary account of his feelings:

> In hospitals we see the worst features of the character of Man – they
> are in these Golgothas distorted by vice the victims of misery and
> disease and its consequences writhing under the agony of present
> torture with neither philosophy nor religion to point to consolation or
> hope. These wards hold the vilest and most abject the abandoned of all
> happiness and virtue in their worst often their hopeless extremity.[29]

Alison's attitude to the abject and abandoned made as deep an impression on Kay as did their plight. Fifty years later he remembered that 'the old crones of the neighbourhood' or, as he also described them, 'dirty garrulous old women' would gather around the entrance to a stair and when Alison descended beg for money or press him to visit another patient. They made the symbolically revealing journey from the Old Town to Alison's New Town residence, and in the early morning he would find 'these wretched tottering women' gathered around his door to continue their importunities. Kay's description lacks some of Alison's compassion, but their association sharpened questions stirring in Kay's mind. Drawing on his own observations, Alison argued that disease could in part be attributed to poverty. The fever grew worse in winter, not simply because the poor were intemperate or lazy – common contemporary explanations – but because they were poor. Many of his patients, he reported, belonged to families whose working members had been unemployed for considerable periods, and 'the most malignant cases of contagious fever commonly originate in the crowded hovels' where the unfortunate poor 'herd' together. Alison forced Kay to realize that the poverty, disease and misery which so troubled him were not just personal problems – they were social disasters and required explanations which went beyond the failings of individuals. He helped Kay frame questions which were to preoccupy him all his life.[30]

As Kay said in his *Autobiography*: 'I came to know how almost use-less were the resources of my art to contend with the consequences of formidable social evils'. Daily experience had 'burned into me' the realization that neither medical skill nor charity could cure 'this social disease'. He confronted harsh questions:

> Were this degradation and suffering inevitable? Could they only be mitigated? Were we always to be working with palliatives? Was there no remedy? Might not this calamity be traced to its source and all the resources of a Christian nation devoted, through whatever time, to the moral and physical regeneration of this wretched population?

As Kay struggled with these questions, news from Rochdale warned him of the precariousness of business success and of the turbulent forces challenging the social order. The difficult economic years of 1825–26 directly affected his family: there were runs on Fenton and Roby's bank; Robert Kay watched a mob destroy the power looms at Bass Lane and then survived the collapse of his London agent's business; a cousin, Richard Kay, faced a bad debt of £2,000, and an acquaintance attempted suicide. Hannah Kay informed her son of the unparalleled distress of the poor and of his good fortune to be in the comparative safety of the medical world, where he would have been unaware of 'the extensive agitation and distress felt in the Commercial Hemisphere'. Far from being unaware, Kay had widened his enquiries:

> I gradually began to make myself acquainted with the best works on political and social science, and obtained more and more insight into the grave questions affecting the relations of capital and labour and the distribution of wealth, as well as the inseparable connection between the mental and moral condition of the people and their physical well-being.[31]

It was impossible in Edinburgh at this time to struggle with such questions without confronting the formidable intellectual presence of Adam Smith – indeed, the very words in which Kay expresses his enquiries suggest Smith's influence. Kay does not say when he read *The Wealth of Nations*, though he was later to quote directly from it, but, like so many thinkers of his time, he was deeply attracted by the intellectual power of Smith's writings, a power which has not been tamed, despite the efforts of ideologues in his own time and later to tap it for their own purposes. If Kay ever attempted a detailed analysis of Smith's economic and social theories, it has not survived, and Kay never gave them a systematic or exclusive adherence. But Smith's influence is evident in Kay's writings from the early 1830s onwards. Kay shared Smith's belief in progress, in the historical evolution of society, which is driven by the desire of human beings for self-betterment, and which culminates in laissez-faire capitalism. Smith's advocacy of the competitive market as a powerful and useful social mechanism, which advances civilization and personal liberty, found a ready adherent in Kay, who in commercial matters was an advocate of free trade and a minimum of government intervention. The division of labour, so crucial in Smith's thinking, appears in Kay's social analysis, and following Smith, he acknowledged both its contribution to the increase of wealth and to the diminishing of human initiative and intelligence, the making of people, under certain conditions, 'as stupid and ignorant as it is possible for a human creature to become'. And Smith's views on government's responsibility to ensure the education of 'the inferior ranks of people' were crucial for Kay's thinking. 'The more they (the inferior ranks) are instructed', Smith wrote, the less liable they are to the delusions of enthusiasm and superstition, which, among ignorant nations, frequently occasion the most dreadful disorders. An instructed and intelligent people, besides, are always more decent and orderly than an ignorant and stupid one.

Smith provided in these two sentences a text which Kay was to restate and to elaborate throughout his life.[32]

Adam Smith had died in 1790, though Dugald Stewart, his friend, biographer and interpreter, was still active in Edinburgh when Kay was there. However, another Scot who helped to form Kay's thinking was much more accessible. Thomas Chalmers was Professor of Moral Philosophy at St Andrews, a position he had taken in 1823 after eight years as a parish minister in Glasgow. After a lacklustre start as a clergyman, Chalmers had undergone a conversion and became a fervid Evangelical, renowned for his preaching. Kay probably met Chalmers when he visited Edinburgh, as after Kay had left the city, he wrote to Chalmers in a tone which assumes some personal familiarity.[33]

Some of Chalmers's social and educational ideas attracted Kay. While in Glasgow Chalmers had been shocked by the condition of the poor, particularly the dispossessed from the countryside and the desperately impoverished Irish immigrants in the crowded slums. Deeply influenced by Malthus, Chalmers considered that compulsory poor relief would increase social misery and convert poverty into pauperism by destroying responsibility among the poor and making them dependent on paid officials. He regarded poverty as a natural condition which provided an opportunity for the rich to display their charity, and at St John's parish in Glasgow, Chalmers organized an elaborate system of charitable assistance which he believed could eventually replace the relief of poverty through the poor rate. Education was of great importance to Chalmers. He started a Sunday school in each of the 25 districts into which he had divided his parish and began to build day schools, fortified by his belief that, as well as making the Bible accessible, education would advance social order and moral respectability. He looked forward to the time when 'many a lettered sage as well as many an enlightened Christian will be met with even in the very lowest walks of society, when the elements of science and philanthropy and high scholarship will so ripen throughout the general mind of the country as to exalt it prodigiously above the level of its present character and accomplishments'. Chalmers did not imagine that these lettered sages from the lower orders would rise above their position in society – they were not being given the means of 'abandoning their status' but of 'morally and intellectually exalting it'.[34]

Chalmers reported what he regarded as the successful realization of his plans at St John's in a three-volume study, *The Christian and Civic Economy of Large Towns*, which was published between 1819 and 1826. The actual success of his plans and the clarity and humanity of his social vision have been vigorously disputed. William Alison issued a strong challenge and, though their dispute did not reach a climax while Kay was studying in Edinburgh, he could hardly have been unaware of the different approaches adopted by the two men. Confronted by the slums of Edinburgh's Old Town and convinced that poverty and disease were linked, Alison regarded social reform as a precondition for the reform of the individual. Chalmers, driven by Evangelical enthusiasm, believed that the individual had to be saved before society could be reformed. Both Alison and Chalmers taught Kay that the poverty and suffering in large cities posed unique social problems, both set him in search of a remedy, and Chalmers stressed the part education might play. They also confronted him with a conflict for which, after he had left Edinburgh, he sought his own solution. When Adam Smith's influence is added, Scotland contributed markedly to the thinking of the young James Phillips Kay.[35]

Kay did not take part in the lively student journalism of his day. His medical studies may have prevented him, but there was also a clash of temperament, for journals such as the *New Lapsus Linguae* had a lightness of tone, wit and irreverence which were foreign to his nature. It is hard to imagine Kay contributing to a publication which remarked that another journal was almost its equal 'at least in point of assurance and scurrility'. Yet, amidst his medical and social preoccupations poetry remained an obsession. At an annual dinner of the Medical Society Kay mocked those who 'limp in the stilts of Grecian verse' but never write a rhyme in English. To Charles Henry, Kay poured out his love of Milton and the Romantic poets, recited his favourite passages, or read his own compositions. With a fellow student, John Addington Symonds, who came from a medical family in Oxford, Kay shared an idealistic friendship, based in part on their belief that as poets they shared a kinship denied to the votaries of science.[36]

Some of the poems Kay wrote at this time were privately published in 1842 under the title *Cynedrida, a masque; the river of the under-*

world; and other poems. They reveal a dark and melancholy young man. *Cynedrida*, the longest and most ambitious poem, was inspired by Milton's *Comus* and took its title from Sharon Turner's *The History of the Anglo-Saxons.* Turner, according to Kay, described Cynedrida as a noblewoman, who was left at sea in an open boat off the shore of France as a punishment for sorcery and who drifted to Wales and became a heroine in British history. *Cynedrida* and other poems are set in strange and gloomy places and crammed with weird and doomed knights, phantoms, malevolent spirits, crazed maidens, giants and Titans, skulls, vast baronial halls resounding with riot, wild oceans, skeletons and spectres, goblins, lividly lit caverns prepared for demonic festivals, and lovers whose only union is in death. Kay painted these haunted lands with such humourless enthusiasm that the poems often toppled into farce. A setting he provided in *Cynedrida* was

> *A gibbet in a solitary place, beneath the wall of a castle. A Spirit seated in the noose, swinging on the rope; another on the top of the gibbet.*

> FIRST SPIRIT
> Forsooth, a pleasant swing. Where have you been?

> SECOND SPIRIT
> A palsied sacristan had made a grave,
> Death pushed him in. I shovelled in the earth,
> And tolled his knell.

Henry let Kay off lightly when he remarked that the poems manifested originality and creative power but were 'by no means . . . models of artistic and finished execution'. Symonds placed his friendship at risk by telling Kay that there was 'a ruggedness in the versification' which did not produce 'a striking effect', and that he was too fond of rhyming certain words. The examples he provided gave a telling commentary on the mood of Kay's poetry: 'storms and forms', 'womb and gloom', and 'gloom and tomb'.[37]

The preoccupation of the poems with death reflected the concerns of contemporary poets, yet Kay was doing more than obey a poetic convention. D.G. Paz has remarked on their 'intense sense of alone-ness – even of alienation'. The loneliness is remarkable, for though Kay produces images of an eagle 'sublime, alone,/Wheeling on his silent flight' and an Arab riding freely in the desert, the loneliness in the poems is rarely confident or defiant. They are peopled with men and women who are placed in settings of violence and destruction, and who are themselves destroyed or who destroy others. Cynedrida is choked by her lover as she tries to prevent him from going to certain death in battle; a minstrel, after a lonely and perilous journey through the underworld, is drowned, crazed and alone, in a storm; a captive troubadour grows old believing that freedom comes only with death; an Alpine hunter exults as the wild deer he has shot crashes down a mountain; a baron announces his own death when he hears that his crusader son has been killed; a novice takes a vow and renounces his lover. Kay may be left to sum up his concerns:

> In the lazar-house we dwell
> Where the dying dream of hell;
> Where the madman shakes his chain,
> And the harlot's tears are rain.[38]

In Kay's relentlessly anxious poetry, people and landscapes are blurred. Of a minstrel, he wrote:

> In the dread roar of waters lost,
> Tortured in writhing eddies, tost
> I' th' Phlegethon of desperate agony,
> The minstrel swept, as wanderers in the war
> Of thunders, strife of winds, or staggering jar
> Of earthquake wrath, caught by the whirlwind's blast,
> Or smitten by the bolt, whose sense hath passed.

With such passages in mind Symonds warned Kay against the use of contractions such as I' and th' and complained that his poetry had a 'multitude of images' which

> do not stand out sufficiently – you do not take pains enough to set them off to the best advantage – you think too rapidly – you give us the momentary vision of a beautiful figure but it is immediately displaced by another ... After reading your piece one's mind is conscious of having seen a great number of splendid objects but is confused and cannot form a distinct remembrance of particular ones.[39]

Despite this advice, Kay continued to write poetry in which image and meaning were submerged by the wild words which flooded across his pages. He seemed to fear that if readers were allowed time to study a landscape or to savour a mood, they would see faults and begin to doubt. In his clinical diagnoses Kay attempted to drive his colleagues to support his conclusions by the force of his personality, and his poetry also conducted an assault on his readers' doubts. Moreover, whoever speaks in the poems, whether it is Cynedrida, a spirit in a seashell, a roistering baron or a doomed warrior, will, if the speech goes on for long enough, begin to sound like James Kay. His rhetoric worked at the Royal Medical Society because the intensity of his feelings could be communicated by demeanour as much as by words. But left to do its work on the printed page, Kay's poetry revealed the loneliness and uncertainty at the centre of his personality. He could not leave his readers to their own devices in case they turned away from him. They had to be harried until they went where he wanted them to go, or were so dazzled by what he had to say that they did not know where he had taken them.

> The left side of the Chest of a Rabbit was opened. The pericardium cut and a ligature having been passed round the Aorta and a pulmonary artery at their origin. An interval was allowed to elapse during which the Animal breathed well though rapidly with the right lung. The ligature was then tied close to the root of the arteries. Respiration proceeded well with the right lung and continued about a minute and a half when struggles and violent convulsive gasping ensued and the animal died exactly as in Asphyxia. The struggles had ceased in three minutes and a half . . .

So, James Kay, confronting death in his medical research as well as in his poetry, and writing the thesis on which he worked during his second and third sessions at Edinburgh. His topic was asphyxia in warm-blooded animals and he challenged the French anatomist and physiologist, Marie-François-Xavier Bichat (1771–1802), who claimed that death occurred when respiration was suspended because the venous blood, having been denied exposure to the air, was unable to make the left ventricle of the heart contract. Bichat claimed that only arterial blood could stimulate the left cavities of the heart and that venous blood was actually poisonous. Through a series of ingenious and unsqueamish experiments on rabbits Kay refuted this argument and offered his own explanation. His thesis was an ambitious and, considering his youth and the prestige of Bichat, a brave study. It challenged Alison's belief that the great majority of theses 'cannot be expected to contain any thing worthy of being published'.[40]

The language of the thesis is simple, even laconic. On one occasion Kay decided not to repeat an experiment because even 'the most eager adventurer in Physiology' found 'much that is deeply repugnant to the feelings in its pursuits',[41] but the tone of the thesis is usually detached. He had separated himself from the profoundly disturbing experiences encountered in the New Town Dispensary, the Infirmary and the Fever Hospital; and the hectic world of his poetry was far distant. The socializing power of his medical training and his desire to succeed helped him to accept the empowering belief that he possessed an exact and objective knowledge, and could write with the confident detachment of a scientist. Admittedly his chances of obtaining an MD depended on his satisfying his teachers that he had acquired their values as well as their knowledge. But his thesis was not a conventional technical exercise. Kay was fascinated by the problems he studied, his experiments were cleverly designed and satisfying, except to the rabbits, and his sharp scientific curiosity and determination shine through the calm reporting.

The process of examination was prolonged. Three months before the graduation day, 2 August 1827, Kay and the other candidates applied for the Preliminary Examination in Arts, a private examination held in the home of a professor and designed to test not only medical knowledge but also literary attainments, especially knowledge of Latin. This examination completed, Kay submitted his thesis to a professor who approved it and signed it, with a comment in Latin to match the Latin in which the thesis was written; Kay's thesis was actually signed by two professors, Alison and Robert Graham. His mastery of Latin may not have been as firm as this procedure suggests, for he could have been assisted by a 'grinder', one of a depressed race of scholars who polished up the student's uncertain Latin and who, according to the cynics, sometimes wrote the thesis. The next ordeal was an examination by two professors in the presence of the Faculty of Medicine on different branches of medicine. Though the examination was conducted in Latin, the linguistic demands were not high: when James Williamson was advising Kay about what faced him in Edinburgh, he remarked that he should have 'no difficulty in acquiring a facility in speaking such Latin as is used at examinations'. Nevertheless, for Kay, anxious and desperately determined to succeed, the examination was a demanding trial. He was next required to prepare written comments (again he could have the assistance of a grinder), on two aphorisms of Hippocrates and two specially chosen medical cases. Then he had to have his thesis printed according to a set format and give a copy to each member of the Faculty of Medicine whose bookshelves must have groaned under the load of knowledge they had gratuitously received. On graduation day Kay was required to defend his thesis, though not very strenuously – one critic claimed that the graduates' degrees were being engrossed and signed as the 'sham battles' were in progress in the classrooms. Kay shared his graduation with Charles Henry and, perhaps to Hannah Kay's surprise, his cousin, William Kay.[42]

Before Kay celebrated his graduation day, there was a shock. Early in May 1827 in the midst of the examinations he collapsed, physically and mentally exhausted. Robert Kay rushed to Edinburgh and his son recovered quickly – by 10 May Robert informed Hannah that they had gone on a long walk against his wish, and that James had

> felt the effect of it for two days after, but is gradually getting better, I take him a short walk every day, sometimes two; to divert him from his studies and brace his nerves, Dr Allisons [*sic*] advises it; think he will in a few days be as well as he was before his attack . . .

He told Hannah how he, James and William Kay, who had come to the assistance of his cousin, went one morning to hear Dr Graham lecture on botany 'at the Bottanick Gardens about 1½ miles in the country, the finest Gardens I ever saw, he was numerously attended, but it was too much for Jas. he was badly tir'd, wednesday better and this morning quite well'. Robert's eccentricities of spelling and expression were accompanied by his equally familiar religious preoccupations – the second half of his letter discussed some sermons and gave his views on certain religious practices. His letter ended: 'Jas. joins me in Love to you all, kisses to the little fellows not forgetting H pray for us we are after all in a world of temptation and sin with deprev'd natures, must conclude, believe me to be yours sincerely R. Kay'.[43] James Kay passed his examinations, but his collapse and earlier mood of depression revealed the emotional cost at which his success was being purchased.

Kay remained in Edinburgh until the end of the year, continuing as resident clerk at the Infirmary. Despite the last-minute difficulty, he had been strikingly successful. His intellectual horizons had been dramatically widened as he struggled to comprehend the social and economic problems which Edinburgh thrust before him. He had his poetic quiver full of arrows he hoped to fire into the world. He had made friendships with Henry and Symonds which, with some difficult interludes, were to last a lifetime. Professionally, he had made a fine start: he had completed the course in the minimum time of three years; his experimental work had been well received; he had acquired a reputation as a speaker; he had gained Alison's support and his clerkship; he had triumphed at the Royal Medical Society. The reports of his teachers were full of praise: 'the greatest zeal and assiduity . . .

highest opinion of him as a student and gentleman . . . student of the first class . . . indefatigable in attention to patients . . . uncommon proficiency . . . intelligence, activity, humanity . . . uniformly gentlemanly conduct . . . constant fidelity, and zealous attention'. Kay had every reason to accept James Syme's opinion that he could look forward to attaining the 'first ranks' in the medical world.[44]

The first step into those ranks was difficult. Kay faced the problem that troubled most medical graduates: in what way, and where, should he take this first step? At a time when home remedies, the herbalist and the unlicensed midwife commanded strong loyalty, and medical science had not acquired a powerful mystique, the beginning medical practitioner faced considerable difficulties. He needed capital: suitable premises and the drugs to dispense were expensive. So were appearances – an air of affluence in clothing, and a carriage. Robert Kay, especially with his reduced business activities, could not afford to set his son up in practice. Nor was James Kay in the fortunate position of Charles Henry who remarked candidly, as he canvassed his own options, that it would be unwise for him to set up practice in London when his prospects in Manchester were promising 'from family connections and from my father and grandfather having both exercised the profession here'. With the advantage of being a third-generation medical practitioner, the 23-year-old Henry confidently advised Kay on how to build a medical practice by applying for a job in Edinburgh which he knew his friend did not want and would not get. 'Do not be deterred by the fear of obtaining a situation which you do not desire', he said:

> By offering yourself as candidate now, you will render your success on
> the next vacancy more certain by familiarizing the Governors with
> your name and inducing them to make enquiry as to your character
> and acquirements, a scrutiny which cannot but rebound to your honor
> and interest.[45]

Kay chose to go into practice in Manchester. The city was large and growing rapidly, he had some knowledge of it and, though his connections did not remotely match Henry's, he could expect good will from the cotton and Nonconformist circles in which the Kays were known. He may have been encouraged by Charles Henry's opinion that Manchester would furnish them both with sufficient employment, and hoped that Henry's influence might help him. Perhaps he thought along the same lines as George Eliot's Mr Lydgate, who at about this time decided:

A born provincial man who has a grain of public spirit as well as a few ideas, should do what he can to resist the rush of everything that is a little better than common towards London. Any valid professional aims may often find a freer, if not a richer field, in the provinces.[46]

Kay did not contemplate a London position, but he valued freedom and riches. At the beginning of 1828 at the age of 23, Dr James Kay set out to make his name in Manchester.

3 · A Manchester doctor, 1828–35

In July 1835 Alexis de Tocqueville, a subtle and observant traveller, stood outside Manchester looking at where the Irwell on its slow way to the Irish Sea was joined by three canals and the winding streams of the Medlock and the Irk. A pall of black smoke had converted the sun into a rayless disc; the soil was uncultivated; the rutted roads were full of puddles; and heaps of dung, rubble and 'putrid, stagnant pools' lay between houses or in public places. On the hilltops 30 or 40 factories, 'palaces of industry' he called them, towered above the homes of the poor, blocking light and air and perpetually imprisoning them in fog. In Manchester's labyrinthine streets de Tocqueville found evidence of wealth: splendid stone buildings with Corinthian columns set amidst the 'sombre stretch of brick work' which dominated the town. Elsewhere, in marshy land below river level, narrow twisting roads were lined with dilapidated buildings, and beneath them a sunken corridor led to cellars, 'damp, repulsive holes' into which 15 people might be crowded. The noise of the city assaulted him - 'the footsteps of a *busy* crowd, the crunching wheels of machinery, the shriek of steam from boilers, the regular beat of the looms, the heavy rumble of carts'.[1]

Thomas Carlyle, visiting Manchester three years later, was struck by the noise which broke the silence at half-past five in the morning when 'all went off like an enormous mill-race or ocean-tide. The Boom-m-m, far and wide. It was the mills that were all starting then, and creishy [greasy] drudges by the million taking post there'. A few years later another sound preoccupied him as he pondered the 'huge, inarticulate question' which had been put at Peterloo by the 'poor Manchester operatives, with all the darkness that was in them and round them' – 'What do you mean to do with us?'[2]

De Tocqueville, acutely aware of contradiction and ambiguity, struggled with that question when he wrote of Manchester:

From this foul drain the greatest stream of human industry flows out to fertilise the whole world. From this filthy sewer pure gold flows. Here humanity attains its most complete development and its most brutish; here civilisation works its miracles, and civilised man is turned back almost into a savage.[3]

Without De Tocqueville's eloquence, but intensely, James Kay was to portray Manchester's contradictions in his life and work. The town's miracles, its brutishness, its population turning away from civilization as he knew it, came to obsess him. Kay gave his answer to Carlyle's question and told the Manchester operatives what he meant to do with them, only to find himself confronted with another question: what was he to do with himself?

'Cotton made modern Manchester', Asa Briggs has said. It brought the mills and the warehouses, the industries which serviced them and the merchants, manufacturers and bankers who owned them. Like a great magnet, the city sucked from the surrounding countryside and from across the Irish Sea the 'operatives' whose condition was to trouble Kay. In 1801 Manchester had a population of 70,000; by 1831 it had grown to 142,000; in 1841 the population was 217,000. Cotton goods accounted for half the value of British exports in 1830 and the home trade was of almost equal importance. The industry's manufacturers and merchants exercised a profound influence on commercial and political life, and though the mill workers were not the first with some class-consciousness, and the factories not the earliest examples of industrial capitalism, the use of power-driven machines in large spinning mills introduced the factory system and the changes which fascinated observers such as de Tocqueville.[4]

These changes ensured that Manchester was racked by social disturbances. Peter Gaskell, a doctor with whom Kay became acquainted, wrote in 1833 that the condition of the labourers was 'the slumbering volcano, which may at any time shatter the whole fabric to atoms, and involve in one common ruin, themselves, the master, and the manufacture'. It was already an old story. In 1808, Manchester's weavers had struck successfully for a wage increase; in 1810 there was a spinners' strike; in 1812 the town and the surrounding districts were disturbed by riots, torchlight demonstrations and machine-breaking; in 1817 a group of men, mostly weavers, attempted to march to London demanding parliamentary reform and a remedy for other grievances. Two years later there was Peterloo. The 1820s, especially the financial crisis of 1826, saw much anxiety among the middle class, while radicals, unionists and the leaders of the Ten Hours movement struggled to advance their causes. The radical Archibald Prentice, reflecting on the riots of 1829, which Kay saw, spoke of the gap between the manufacturers and the working men. The two classes 'were arrayed against each other in a hostility which daily became more bitter', for the working people thought the masters 'grievous oppressors' while the masters considered the workers 'unreasoning and brutal incendiaries'.[5]

There were other tensions in Mancunian society, the agitation for parliamentary reform being most conspicuous. Through the 1832 Reform Act Manchester received its first parliamentary representation and the liberal elements of its middle class achieved a significant victory in their struggle to wrest power from the Church and landed aristocracy. Especially between 1820 and 1840 lords of the manor, including the Mosleys who presided over Manchester, felt 'the chill blast of middle- and working-class hostility', and though the demise of the aristocracy was by no means swift, those of its members who sought political office were forced to concede that the Act had brought power to a new electorate and to pay at least a token obedience to sober middle-class values.[6]

Efforts to reform local government further increased the volatility of the political situation. In 1828, when Kay set up in practice, Manchester retained the semi-feudal structure which had existed since the sixteenth century. However, unusual in this as in so much else, Manchester's local affairs were already in middle-class hands so that the campaign for municipal incorporation, which elsewhere was directed at breaking the power of the manorial lords, was in Manchester largely an internecine warfare within the middle class. Since late in the eighteenth century the city's court leet, magistracy, vestry and police commission had been controlled by an oligarchy of Churchmen and Tories who were challenged in the 1820s by a liberal, Nonconformist group in which the Unitarians were most active. Wealthy, well educated and entrepreneurial, Unitarian families such as the Gregs, Kennedys, Percivals, Murrays, Heywoods, M'Connels, Potters and Henrys (a number of whom played significant parts in Kay's life) were spread through Manchester's banking, professional and business world and found a convenient home in the

Literary and Philosophical Society. Though not without internal differences, the Unitarians gained coherence from resentment at the discrimination which they, more than most Dissenters, faced, from an aggressive desire for the authority to which they believed their wealth entitled them, and from a tight web of kinship and inter-marriage. In the struggle for incorporation liberal groups such as the Unitarians were forced to seek support outside their class from shop-keepers and artisans, thus increasing the complexity of Manchester's class alliances.[7]

The conflict surrounding the Reform Bill and incorporation, the attempts to make Manchester's operatives orderly, and their efforts to remedy their grievances had flung the city into a maelstrom of class warfare. For Kay this warfare was not a background against which he could pace through the routines of his daily business. He plunged into the midst of the battle and fought with the enthusiasm which his father's generation had brought to business or simply living. Though he had some victories, he was badly wounded, and for the rest of his life bore the scars of his time in Manchester.

In February 1828, Kay announced his arrival in rented premises at 40 King Street by writing *The Lancet* a long and uncompromising letter, which expressed his astonishment at another doctor's opposition to the recently invented stethoscope. He refuted the claim that the instrument had been abandoned in the clinical wards of the Edinburgh Infirmary and insisted that it would soon be 'suicidal to professional reputation to object to the stethoscope'. John Symonds congratulated his friend, but warned that 'the dry juiceless minds' of the medical profession might associate the letter with 'predominance of Fancy, impetuosity of conclusion, fervour of youthful judgement and a parcel of other stupid notions'. Symonds regretted its publication in *The Lancet*, which was linked with a party for whom 'I cannot help saying I feel the most intolerable disgust' – the journal was 'steeped with all the malignancy of the ruffianly John Bull [and] all the blackguardism of Cobbett'. Symonds's was not an uncommon reaction to *The Lancet* whose editor, Dr Thomas Wakley, had launched a violent attack on the medical establishment. As far as Symonds was concerned, Kay had aligned himself with radical forces in the medical world.[8]

However radical, Kay had high ambitions. He was determined to join the privileged ranks of the physicians who, secure in the possession of a university degree (which in some cases had been bought), treated internal diseases, and prescribed but did not dispense medicines. In the turbulent medical world in which Kay had to make his way, general practitioners were beginning to evolve from the ranks of the surgeon-apothecaries – surgeons who added the making and dispensing of medicines to their surgical skills, or apothecaries who, going in the reverse direction, took on patients and practised some surgery as well as maintaining their original function, the making of medicines. The term 'general practitioner', which came into use at this time, marked the growth in confidence of a group who were condescended to and feared by the colleges of physicians and surgeons which ruthlessly protected their own wealth and status. The emergence of the general practitioner blurred the traditional divisions and, at a time when neither physicians nor surgeons waited for patients to be referred to them, made competition fierce and explicit.[9]

To make matters more difficult, the medical profession was overcrowded. Its status was rising among the middle class, even if it lacked the prestige of a commission in a fashionable regiment, and ambitious young men such as Kay rushed to join it. In 1841, there were five times as many medical practitioners in Manchester and Salford as there had been in 1801, a period in which the population had trebled. The growth was specially intense from the early 1820s to the mid-1830s, the very time at which Kay was striving to establish himself. As well as competition from medical colleagues, there were the 'outsiders' – midwives, druggists and other denizens of the medical world whom the profession considered 'quacks'. While many individual medical practitioners earned high praise from their patients for their skill and humanity, the ability of medical science to produce cures for even trivial complaints was still unimpressive, so that the gap between the quack and the professional was often uncomfortably narrow and the competition threatening.[10]

Although Kay was a newcomer with neither adequate capital nor family connections, he swiftly made clear his intentions. On 5 April 1828, only a few months after his arrival in Manchester, he applied for the position of honorary physician at the Manchester Infirmary, a coveted appointment which marked the pinnacle of professional recognition. Physicians were elected by the subscribers who supported the Infirmary. The elections, often occasions for the display of party and personal prejudice, could be bitter and, because of the canvassing, expensive – in the mid-1830s one doctor spent £690, mostly for the hire of vehicles to bring voters from neighbouring towns.[11]

As a young and inexperienced physician, Kay might be thought naively over-ambitious to have applied, except that Charles Henry was one of his opponents. The candidates were eventually reduced to Kay, Henry and George Freckleton, a widely travelled and experienced doctor. At the election meeting on 17 April, when the subscribers were addressed on behalf of the candidates, Henry was supported by the liberal Unitarian merchant, George William Wood, and the Conservative Hugh Hornby Birley, who had led the Manchester Yeomanry in their charge at Peterloo. Kay also endeavoured to embrace Whig and Tory, being represented by the Anglican Benjamin Braidley, later a boroughreeve, and the Congregationalist merchant, Samuel Fletcher. Wood mentioned that Henry's father, William, now in 'delicate health', had once held the position in the Infirmary to which his son aspired, and Birley also stressed Henry's 'personal merit and hereditary claims'. Kay had to rely on his Edinburgh referees and his university record. He was not helped by Fletcher, who remarked that his 'intense application to his studies' had seriously affected his health – 'for his only relaxation consisted in a change of study'. Fletcher also pointed out that though Kay 'could not derive credit from the lustre of a name, which would endure, when, perhaps, even the locality of Manchester might be unknown', he came from a family long connected with the town and 'extensively and honourably engaged in its commercial pursuits'. Henry won convincingly, getting 380 votes to Freckleton's 184 and Kay's 124. Reflecting on the event 40 years later, Henry remarked: 'It was not, of course, a contest of comparative professional merit, but of local interest, and my father, who had himself formerly filled the same office, carried the election by a large majority in my favour.' Before the election Hannah Kay had told her son: 'If it be for your good you will be successful, if not it will be well ordered by *Him* who sees the end from the beginning.' She added: 'Leave it there but use all lawful means.' Unfortunately for Kay the Providence on which Hannah relied proved less effective than a William Henry in delicate health.[12]

After the election Kay placed the customary newspaper advertisement, thanking 'my rivals and their friends, for the very gentlemanly way in which the opposition has been conducted, and for many assurances of cordial feeling'. He reaffirmed his desire to become an Infirmary physician – it could not 'be abated by any other

professional advantage, and is not prompted by such hopes alone' –
and assured everyone that nothing would prevent him becoming a
candidate when next there was a vacancy. His defeat revealed how
important it was to win acceptance among the powerbrokers of
Manchester's middle class. Kay was still an outsider seeking to enter a
world in which medical, economic and religious forces were
intricately interwoven.[13]

He took a step towards joining that world when in 1829 he became
a member of the Manchester Literary and Philosophical Society. At
its foundation in 1781 14 of the society's 24 members were medical
men and, though the percentage of doctors had dropped, the
profession continued to wield influence. In its early days the society
provided a means of cultural self-expression for Manchester's
middle-class elite, particularly for radical Dissenters such as the
Unitarians, who were excluded from political power and social
recognition. It retained some of this function in the 1820s but by
then membership had become a mark of social acceptance, at least
among the middle class. As a contemporary commentator remarked,
'To rank as a member of the "Literary and Philosophical Society of
Manchester", would add consequence to the character of any man.'
Kay tried to add to the consequence of his own character in
November 1830 when, while speaking to the society about his
experimental work, he exhibited the diseased lung of a rabbit. When
not giving papers Kay could speak to John Dalton, the society's
presiding genius, and other influential members.[14]

When Kay joined the society his medical career had entered a new
phase: he was one of the two foundation physicians at the Ardwick
and Ancoats Dispensary. Like the Infirmary, dispensaries depended
upon charity (chiefly subscribers), were governed by a committee
chosen from the subscribers, and elected their medical staff. They
took no in-patients and were therefore cheaper than hospitals and, as
well as dispensing drugs, provided home visiting and an out-patient
service which the hospitals had been slow to develop. Usually staffed
by honorary physicians and surgeons, a full-time apothecary, and
a collector whose task was to raise money, they attended to the
'deserving poor' who were supposed to be recommended by subscribers. In practice the mobility of urban life meant that the personal
link between the philanthropists and the objects of their charity was
often broken, and the dispensaries received recommendations from
people who had not checked to see how 'deserving' were the poor
they sent. The dispensaries were frequently so crowded that, as Kay

pointed out, the physicians could provide only hasty attention, yet despite their limitations and condescension, they were an attempt to respond to health problems among the urban poor which had been neglected by the hospitals.[15]

The Ardwick and Ancoats Dispensary originated when the Manchester Infirmary Board, pressed to establish a dispensary to assist the inhabitants of that district, concluded that they were too far from Piccadilly, where the Infirmary was situated, and involved the Board in 'a positive pecuniary loss' because the district lacked 'opulent inhabitants' (that is, potential subscribers) and had 'very numerous poor'. In June 1828, a group of four doctors (which included Kay and two others just beginning private practice) asked the board's support for an independent dispensary which they were proposing to establish. Relieved not to have the responsibility for the dispensary, the Board gave its support, and the dispensary was opened on 11 August 1828 in a rented house at 181 Great Ancoats Street. For the next seven years Kay was required to attend twice a week at 9 o'clock in the morning to treat the poor and to ponder the dispensary's unambiguous rule that only those who could not afford to pay for medicines were proper objects of charity. He knew that from such a population he was unlikely to treat many patients who would later attend him privately, and he had to contend with the fact that dispensary doctors were accorded an uncertain status. A *Lancet* editorial, reflecting a fear that the growth of dispensaries might affect private practice, derided them as 'open frauds and impositions' and dismissed their doctors as 'the most ignorant of impostors' who had obtained their places by 'shuffling and knavery'.[16]

However, there were some advantages. A dispensary post was increasingly seen as a step along the path to an Infirmary appointment. The fact that Kay, who had his Edinburgh experience to draw on, sought to establish the dispensary only four months after his rejection by the Infirmary suggests that he considered that the medical charity might have what Webb calls 'succession value'. In addition, the relative ease with which patients could get access to dispensaries meant that their medical staff, unlike hospital physicians who usually did not see a patient until the disease was well advanced, could observe the progress of a disease from beginning to end – they had 'the unrivalled opportunity for the study of disease as natural history'. The dispensary also provided sufficient facilities to enable Kay to continue some experimental work, and as it had a few students, mostly apothecaries, he could contribute in a small way to provincial

medical education. Finally, the dispensary flung Manchester's con-
trasts into Kay's face: home visiting ensured that he had a first-hand
acquaintance with the living conditions of the poor; and he was also
brought into contact with powerful, self-made cotton men, such
as the Scots George Murray, James and John Kennedy and James
M'Connel who were among the dispensary's subscribers and committee men. Around them hung the scent of wealth and, for a young
physician seeking to build a private practice, the possibility of
contacts with wealthy clients.[17]

Building that practice, Kay's main aim, was not proving easy. Both
a student friend, who noted that Kay had made 'a good connection'
and asked whether this meant that he had forged a link with other
practitioners or with families who had a predisposition to illness, and
a distressed Symonds, who attributed Kay's delay in answering
letters to the 'gloriously urgent' demands of his practice, were too
optimistic. On 29 December 1828, with his practice about a year old,
Kay was forced to ask his father for money to pay for his lodgings.
When sending the money Hannah Kay characteristically reminded
him that his intermingling with the world was dangerous to his best
interests, that he had 'unspeakable cause of gratitude if you review
the past to think how wonderfully your way has been made', that
'every *indulgence* had been afforded you independent of your absolute
wants', and that all that was required of him was 'a more entire
consecration of yourself to God and the more useful duties of your
profession'. Symonds was afraid that Kay would not 'condescend to
the patient drudgeries that private practice demands' or put up with
'the prejudices of the ignorant and vulgar' long enough for them to
get to know his worth. Ambitious, intense, absorbed in the study of
medicine, insistent on his views yet riddled with doubt and anxiety,
Kay was not likely to develop a relaxed bedside manner. John Crosse, a
successful contemporary, reflected: 'People wish not only to be cured
but to be amused and some must be duped into the bargain.' Kay
would not have duped his patients, but he was more inclined to lecture
than to listen and more interested in arguing than in amusing.[18]

However, he did not allow the problems of his practice to dampen
his enthusiasm and early in 1830 he began planning a medical
journal. His co-editor was Dr James Williamson, who had advised
him when he was preparing for his studies in Edinburgh and who was
continuing to play a leading part in the medical and civic affairs of
Leeds. Kay needed this powerful ally because the *North of England
Medical and Surgical Journal*, as the journal was eventually called (the

first title proposed was the 'Manchester and Leeds Medical and Surgical Journal'), faced competition from the *Midland Medical and Surgical Reporter*, which had been founded in 1828 by Charles Hastings, another Edinburgh graduate who had distinguished himself at the Royal Medical Society and was now in Worcester. Symonds informed Kay that the *Reporter* had considerable support, and at one time Kay and Williamson seemed interested in forming a coalition, but Hastings's editorial colleagues would not agree. Williamson believed that the *Reporter* was not of high quality and would not last, and he and Kay worked enthusiastically to piece their journal together. Kay was the more active figure but, despite an illness, Williamson gave dedicated assistance.[19]

The first issue, which appeared in August 1830, was aggressively provincial. Kay and Williamson insisted that the numerous medical practitioners in the northern counties were not well served by the existing medical journals, which were biased towards the cities, especially London. They believed that even in 'the most secluded districts of the empire' diligent observers were studying diseases, so that a journal primarily concerned with the 'local results of original investigations' would attract more attention than one published in a 'distant city'. Insisting that they were free of party prejudice and influenced only by 'a sincere desire of assisting the dissemination of knowledge', they proposed to cover a range of studies including medical statistics, in which Kay was becoming interested.[20] Through the model of science they adopted – the systematic accumulation of knowledge based on experiment and observation, through their conscious provincialism and their determination to improve the professionalism of medical practitioners, Kay and Williamson gave expression to the views of their progressive colleagues.

They published a series of solidly researched and often original contributions. Edmund Lyon, a physician at the Manchester Infirmary, wrote two articles on the medical topography and statistics of Manchester which were of unusual interest, and other important local practitioners such as Edward Carbutt and John Roberton, who combined social reform with his medical activities, as well as friends such as Symonds, and Kay and Williamson themselves, provided articles. Reports of provincial medical happenings added topicality and, true to their Scottish training, the editors stated that, though favoured with many theoretical discussions, they 'respectfully, but urgently' asked their contributors 'to favour us with the results of their *clinical experience*'.[21]

Not reluctant to favour his readers with his own work, Kay contributed four, perhaps five, articles. Two drawn directly from his dispensary experience announced themes which often recurred in his later work. Entitled 'Physical condition of the poor', the first article discussed the gastralgia and enteralgia suffered by many of his dispensary patients. Kay attributed their illness to poor diet caused by poverty, and blamed the poverty on Irish immigration and the low wages resulting from the introduction of the power loom. He took his readers inside the working-class homes and, though his sympathy was somewhat condescending, he showed that differences in physical comfort between the various grades of society, 'from affluence, ease, and luxury, down to indigence, labour and want', influenced their differing patterns of health. Poverty bred disease. In the second essay Kay brought the same honesty, and the same sense that he was observing a foreign species, into the cotton mills. He had become aware of damage done to the lungs of cotton workers by the 'great quantities of short filaments and foreign particles' with which they came in contact, and he claimed that the chronic bronchitis, which often resulted, could lead to phthisis. Later writers have credited him with being among the first to describe byssinosis, the lung disease caused by the inhalation of cotton dust.[22] Whatever the medical value of his observations, Kay had seen, inside the mills and the homes of the poor, that manufacturing arrangements could destroy health. Earlier than most of his contemporaries, he began to grapple with issues of public health and occupational safety.

Despite both editors' enterprise the journal collapsed. The fourth and last issue appeared in May 1831; it gave the impression that business was continuing as usual and contained no epitaph. In fact the journal faded away without overt fuss or recrimination, another victim of the economics of publishing. There had been moments of hope: *The Lancet* produced a lengthy summary of articles in the first issue, and Williamson and Symonds passed on some favourable comments to Kay. But the support had not come. The journal's failure was made more galling when Symonds reported the 'shabby' manner in which Hastings, at a meeting of the Provincial Medical Association, had ignored the contribution of the *North of England Medical and Surgical Journal* and 'bedaubed with praise' his own *Midland Reporter*.[23]

In the pages of his journal Kay appears in working-class homes and in factories as a dispensary doctor from the middle class who remained an outside observer, even when he was sympathetic. Confidently middle-class in those surroundings, he knew, when he was at the Literary and Philosophical Society, that he was on the periphery of power, that he was an outsider again, though of a different kind. As a provincial medical practitioner, and as such a member of a profession seeking its own acceptance, Kay adopted a tactic common among aggressive outsiders: he took on the responsibilities of leadership and helped to found a journal which gave a voice to the new forces in provincial medicine. The journal's failure was another reminder that he was a long way from acceptance.

> Nothing talked of, thought of, dreamt of, but Reform. Every creature one meets asks, What is said now? How will it go? What is the last news? What do *you* think? and so it is from morning till night, in the streets, in the clubs, and in private houses.

On 8 May 1831, two months after Greville had confided his thoughts to his diary, John Symonds asked Kay if he was 'violent in the politics of the day or like me do you preserve a philosophic indifference to the subjects that convulse the people about you'. In Manchester, the most important of the towns which the Reform Bill proposed to enfranchise for the first time, the struggle for parliamentary reform was hard fought and, as E.P. Thompson has remarked, there were times when revolution seemed possible in England. In December 1831, as the Lords continued to reject Lord John Russell's increasingly cautious Bills, Kay wrote to William Rathbone Greg, a member of the cotton family with whom he had become friendly, expressing 'gloomy forebodings' and predictions of a revolution. He did more than write letters to friends. Earlier in 1831 he produced a pamphlet whose title announced his position: *A Letter to the People of Lancashire, concerning the future of the commercial interest by the return of members for its new boroughs to the reformed Parliament.* It was his first and remained his most exuberant polemic.[24]

In the anonymous pamphlet Kay disguises himself as an old and wealthy Nonconformist who lives in a charmingly grotesque house on a peaceful estate set on a range of hills overlooking Manchester. He attacks John Wilson Patten, the previous Tory Member for the county, and praises the decision to replace him with 'one of the most wealthy and influential members of the commercial community', Benjamin Heywood, a leading banker and a liberal Unitarian. A

powerful commercial district such as Manchester, Kay argued, should
be represented by men of commercial experience, 'long accustomed
to the most extended view of the relations of trade, and to the most
enlarged ideas concerning its economy'. The passionately fluent
pamphlet reveals Kay as an admirer of Lord John Russell, an advocate
of free trade and the abolition of slavery, an opponent of the corn
laws, an ardent reformer, and a believer in commerce which 'increases
the comforts and luxuries of life, and rapidly assists the progress of
civilization', the dissemination of wealth, knowledge and arts, and
the reduction of jealousies between nations. The influence of Edinburgh and Adam Smith could hardly have been more obvious.[25]

In Manchester, 'that great city of industry', Kay saw 'the fearful
strength of that multitude of the labouring population, which, for the
present, lies like a slumbering giant at their feet'. But, important
though such fears were to become in later life, they were overwhelmed in the *Letter* by his violent opposition to the Tory establishment. He sneered at 'the chartered venality' of the electoral system,
and at the party 'self-styled "*conservative*," but which is always the
advocate of *rottenness and corruption*'. Oxford and Cambridge were
'gloomy seat(s) of monkish prejudice', the patronage of the Church
had been abused, and the aristocracy were the idle rich: they wasted
hours 'in *ennui*, in frivolous dissipation, in exhausting excitement, in
plotting factions in clubs'. He insisted that 'We do not love lords,
because they give us races in their parks, and lectures on the dignity
of the aristocracy at our dinners.' He was not going to be deluded by
'the eternal smiles of an aristocrat, whose grin ever keeps his lips
apart, like a cast iron mantrap waiting for its prey'. Kay's commitment
was so intense that his emotions threatened to consume him, but the
Letter remains just under control.[26]

When he had completed his pamphlet, the old Nonconformist
declared, he would return to the seclusion of his estate. His creator
abandoned whatever safety his anonymous pamphlet had given him
and worked publicly for reform. Many years later John Bright, by
then an institution in British politics, remembered hearing the 27-
year-old Dr Kay speak at a Reform Bill meeting in Rochdale, their
common birthplace. Kay quoted from the *Masque of Anarchy*:

> Rise like lions after slumber
> In unvanquishable number!
> Shake your chains to earth, like dew
> Which in sleep had fall'n on you:
> Ye are many, – they are few.

Shelley had written the poem in 1819 when the news of Peterloo reached him in Italy, and when Kay quoted it, he, Shelley and Bright were for a moment part of a radical tradition of protest.[27] Kay and Bright left it in later life, but in their youth they were swept along by the swelling tide of reform.

Kay was delighted when, in the election in December 1832 which followed the passage of the Reform Bill, Manchester returned the Whigs, Mark Philips from the prominent Unitarian manufacturing family and Charles Poulett Thomson, Vice-President of the Board of Trade. Kay also had the satisfaction of speaking at a dinner to celebrate the election to the seat of Rochdale of his cousin, John Fenton, with whom he had remained in close contact since his days in the bank. Another cousin, Mary Kay, the daughter of the James Kay whose death had so disturbed Robert, shared a further Whig triumph when her husband, John Fort, was elected to the seat of Clitheroe. Despite these family interests, Kay concentrated on one of the two county electorates, the southern division of Lancashire. It also returned two Whigs, G. W. Wood, who had supported Henry in the election for the Infirmary, and the aristocrat, Charles William Moly-neux, from Croxteth in Liverpool. Kay's assiduity in Molyneux's cause was noticed by Charles Pascoe Grenfell, Molyneux's brother-in-law. In January 1833 he wrote to Kay, expressing the hope that an illness Kay had contracted would not prevent his visiting Croxteth to meet Lord Sefton. He thought that Kay should get to know the father as well as the son whom he had 'so zealously supported during the recent contest'.[28]

Molyneux trusted Kay and relied on him to keep him in touch with his constituency, though with an aristocratic disregard for the niceties he sometimes referred to him as 'Dr Kaye'. For his part Kay kept Molyneux supplied with material on the political questions of the day, particularly as they affected the cotton interest. He also undertook the chores of electioneering, and at least on one occasion prepared some 'hints towards an address' which Molyneux did not use. Grenfell favoured Kay with his views on political issues and their association ripened into friendship. Kay sent some of his political writings which Grenfell praised, considering that only a Tory or a bigoted Churchman could oppose them, and he made a practice of answering Kay's letters promptly, even if they reached him as he was about to go hunting.[29]

One of the first issues faced by the Reformed Parliament in which Molyneux sat was Lord Ashley's Factory Bill. Because of the manner in which child and adult labour were interlocked in the mills, the Bill, which limited the hours of work for children between the ages of nine and 18 to ten hours a day, would simultaneously have secured a ten-hour day for adults. It was a crucial test of the response of the Parliament to working-class demands for reform. Opposition from the manufacturers caused the Bill to be delayed to enable another royal commission to investigate the issue, a decision carried by one vote on a motion of John Wilson Patten who, unscathed by Kay's denunciation, had been returned unopposed in the new seat of North Lancashire. Only a few weeks earlier Molyneux had thanked Kay for keeping him informed on the factory question which he was studying closely. He did not want the House 'misled by erroneous remarks and false views of claptrap humanity', especially as he believed that the interests of 'the trade of the county and that of the capitalists are in my mind so wrapt up with and dependent on the welfare of the operatives that we cannot consult one without the other'. He had some sense of the difficulties in his position because he remarked that it was 'very difficult to persuade the ignorant that [in supporting the manufacturers] I was not advocating cruelty and oppression'.[30]

As soon as Wilson Patten's motion was passed, Molyneux put Kay's name forward for appointment as a commissioner, understanding from some remarks which Kay had made that he was 'quite ready to undertake the task'.[31] Public affairs and wider ambitions than Manchester could satisfy had begun to beckon to the dispensary doctor. The commission was headed by Edwin Chadwick, and Kay was not among the commissioners whom Chadwick sent storming around the country. Lord Grey's government produced a Bill which embodied Chadwick's findings and weakened the proposals in Ashley's Bill, though it tightened the means of enforcing them. On 18 July 1833 the government's Bill defeated Ashley's, a result which Kay favoured, and the Ten Hours movement was given a clear idea of the intentions of the new Parliament.

Kay's preoccupation with national politics continued after the passage of the Factory Act. On 8 July 1834 Lord Grey resigned as Prime Minister and William IV endeavoured to persuade Lord Melbourne, the most conservative of the Whigs, to form a coalition with the support of political opponents such as Wellington and Peel. An anxious Kay pressed Molyneux for news but Molyneux, writing from Brooks's, informed Kay that he was in 'as complete a state of suspense and anxiety' over the state of the negotiations 'as you can be in the remote and dismal regions from which you write'. He gave Kay a sniff of the political excitement when he described the scene at the club: 'everybody's mouth is open in this room and all you hear is one man asking another if he has heard anything'. As it happened, the government limped along until November when Melbourne manoeuvred the King into dismissing him, Peel formed an administration and Parliament dissolved in December for a general election. Lacking knowledge of Melbourne's stratagems, Molyneux expressed the common reaction of astonishment at 'so sudden, so wild and capricious an assault upon the peace of the country by our Patriotic monarch'.[32]

For Molyneux and Kay the election had particular significance. Kay had decided for personal and professional reasons to play a less public role. Meanwhile, and before the dissolution, Molyneux expressed doubts about his political future, and when his father, the Earl of Sefton, announced his intention 'not to spend a farthing' on any election, Molyneux decided to end his political career. Candidly exposing his personal and class values, he confessed to Kay: 'The fact is that I am as little suited as possible except by my rank and situation in the county to fill the place of Member.' He had 'neither talent nor power of attention for the business', he could not break 'the weight of my old habits and pursuits', he hated being confined in London, the situation of being a MP was 'most irksome', and 'I shall think that day one of the happiest of my life in which I know that I no longer fill it'. He professed himself aware of the gratitude he owed friends – 'more particularly a few such as yourself, who have exerted themselves to place me where I am' – and admitted that he should have given earlier notice of his feelings.[33]

Grenfell was 'mortified beyond expression' by Molyneux's decision: 'I frequently said – I will write to Dr Kay today – but when it came to the point I could say so little that I wished to *utter*, that I determined upon silence.' Grenfell, Molyneux and Kay were overtaken by events. When Molyneux first informed Kay of his intentions he believed that there might not be a dissolution. When the dissolution occurred, Molyneux realized that he had left his announcement too late and began an unenthusiastic campaign. Ruefully, but without a sense of shame, he praised Kay's 'activity and zeal' which were 'truly wonderful and must be crowned with success', and expressed regret that Kay, who in the crisis had put aside his desire to reduce his political activity, was not working 'for one as zealous as yourself'. Not surprisingly, the campaign was underfinanced and badly organized, and at the election in January 1835 Molyneux was defeated.[34]

Despite this disappointment Kay's involvement in politics had brought him satisfaction, in addition to that of trying to influence major social debates such as those on the Reform and Factory Acts. He had become a trusted confidant and a respected organizer in the Molyneux camp, in wider Whiggish circles he was known to be interested in public appointments, and he had gained some understanding of politics and politicians at the local level. If at some stage he decided to stand for Parliament himself, Molyneux's loss would do him no harm and his own reputation for industry and dedication to the cause might considerably assist him.

> The Cholera's coming, oh dear! oh dear!
> The Cholera's coming, oh dear! oh dear!
> Take care of yourselves, or you'll feel very queer,
> For the Cholera's coming, oh dear! oh dear!
>
> The doctors combined have found out a way
> To diddle their patients out of their pay;
> For if in your bowels you ever feel queer,
> They'll tell you the Cholera Morbus is there . . .
>
> With the doctors' consent, I will give them advice,
> For though it is simple, it yet may suffice;
> For the very best way this infection to cure,
> Is to feed all the *hungry*, and clothe all the *poor*.

With angry bravado the *Poor Man's Advocate* of 31 March 1832 gave its views on the cholera epidemic which was sweeping England. Throughout 1832, as the Reform Bill agitation simmered or exploded, this frightening enemy moved unpredictably around the country, missing some towns, striking others, and in the end killing some 32,000 people. On 18 June 1831 the Privy Council, which had responsibility for matters of health and had been watching the epidemic advance across Europe, set up an advisory Board of Health. The Board produced a plan by which local boards of health were established across the country. Manchester's was operating by 10 November 1831, and a week later James Kay made his first appearance as a member.[35]

The cholera bacillus, *vibrio cholerae*, is carried in the victim's faeces, urine or vomitus and transmitted in contaminated food or water. Lacking a germ theory, the medical establishment was racked by disputes over the cause of cholera. Contagionists, who included most of the College of Physicians, believed that it was passed on by person to person contact. From this view followed the policies of quarantine and of isolating the victims in cholera hospitals, as well as a fear of paupers or vagrants, who might carry the disease into unaffected areas. Anti-contagionists attributed cholera not to personal contact but to a vapour or miasma generated by decaying organic matter or other refuse. They were therefore committed to cleaning up the overcrowded, dirty and unsewered districts which places like Manchester had in abundance. There were bitter debates between contagionists and anti-contagionists, but the majority of medical practitioners, particularly by the end of the epidemic, had become contingent contagionists: while accepting that cholera was contagious they allowed a place for 'predisposing' causes which included overcrowding, poverty, filth, bad food and water, and intemperance. Kay was a contingent contagionist; he worked in a cholera hospital but led efforts to clean up the working-class areas of Manchester, to pave the streets and to improve waste disposal, arguing, as he had before the cholera broke out, that the environment in which the poor lived increased their susceptibility to disease.[36]

Bereft of a theory which convincingly accounted for the origins of cholera, medical practitioners were more than usually open to influence from political pressure groups. Some manufacturers and merchants were attracted to anti-contagionist views as a counter to quarantine measures, which had a deleterious effect on business and trade. However, too simple a link between economic interests and medical theory cannot be made, as contagionists were as prominent as anti-contagionists among conservative groups. Moreover, the stress of the anti-contagionists or the contingent contagionists on diet, intemperance, contaminated water, decomposing vegetable matter, filthy houses and unpaved roads did not gain acceptance simply through an absence of an agreed scientific explanation, but reflected an increasing desire to control the working classes by shaping the environment in which they lived.[37]

Whatever the political or humanitarian considerations, there were practical reasons for Kay to work on a local Board of Health. To be seen energetically confronting a national crisis helped improve the social standing of medical practitioners and increased their ability to differentiate themselves from the quacks they despised. Prominence on the board increased Kay's chances of rising within his intensely competitive profession, particularly as it brought him into direct contact with the Infirmary physicians, all of whom were members, and with the powerful manufacturers and businessmen, who were well represented on the board. Kay flung himself into its work with unstinting energy, even though his political activities continued throughout the epidemic. Too anxious ever to be uncomplicatedly happy, Kay came closest to contentment when a cause consumed him and, by enabling him to feel part of a greater good, flooded him with a sense of personal worth. His excitement is preserved in his *Autobiography* written 45 years later, and contemporaries noted that he had been 'indefatigable in his attention to the working classes during the time of the cholera'. His very commitment and a belief in the significance of his contribution may explain Kay's later claim that he had been the board's secretary. He had not, but he did not disgrace the example which William Alison had given him.[38]

The first reported case of cholera in Manchester did not occur until June 1832 so the board had about eight months to prepare. It announced that 'there is reason to think that personal communication with the sick' was what most contributed to the spread of cholera but, displaying its uncertainty, also concluded that those most liable to be victims of the disease included the occupiers of crowded, dirty and ill-ventilated buildings, the badly clothed, the ill-fed and the intemperate. It set scavenging parties to work, tried to persuade landlords to clean up their properties, organized the whitewashing of houses and factories, and made arrangements for the burial of cholera victims and for the inspection of boats on canals. Kay helped to establish cholera hospitals and took part in discussions with the vestry and the churchwardens who, as guardians of the poor rate from which the Board of Health was financed, were determined to ensure that expenses were kept under tight control. The jealousies became evident when the board had to rescind its appointment of a treasurer because the churchwardens had decided to keep the accounts themselves.[39]

The local board, in response to a decision of the Central Board, used Manchester's police districts to set up 14 district boards each of which was allocated three or four medical practitioners and a druggist – Kay shared the tenth district with Charles Henry and another local board member and strong anti-contagionist, Henry Gaulter. Kay suggested that the district boards should be used to undertake a detailed study of the state of the houses and streets. He wanted the districts to be subdivided into small sections and two or more inspectors placed in each section. The inspectors were to be chosen from 'the most respectable inhabitants of the vicinity' in order that the state of the streets and houses might convince these influential men that the public health 'was depressed by moral and physical evils'. In November or December 1832 the inspectors were given a set of questions devised by Kay. They were to ask if the houses were in good repair, clean, whitewashed, well-ventilated, and dry or damp; they were to enquire about the proprietor of the houses, the number of families or lodgers they held, the existence of private privies, the willingness of tenants to clean streets and houses, the health of the tenants, their 'habits of life', occupations, and the state of their clothing, food and fuel. Attention was also directed to the streets, courts and alleys: were they narrow, ill-ventilated, paved, did they contain 'heaps of refuse, pools of stagnant fluid, or deep ruts', what was the condition of the public and private privies, and how close were they to canals, rivers, or marshy land?[40]

Drawing on the findings of these inspectors, Kay published in April 1832 the first edition of his pamphlet, *The Moral and Physical Condition of the Working Classes Employed in the Cotton Manufacture in Manchester* – 'one of the cardinal documents of Victorian history', G.M. Young has called it. Part of Kay's inspiration for this early piece of social research is indicated by his use of a quotation from Thomas Chalmers on his title page: 'Many schemes of amelioration are at all times afloat. We hold, that without the growth of popular intelligence and virtue, they will, every one of them, be ineffectual'. It is a very personal document, much more deeply felt than his poetry, in which Kay exposed his ideas with a raw and sometimes unconscious honesty.[41]

The pamphlet is awkward to approach. Many commentators have found no difficulty in mining it for statements which suit their arguments, for contradiction is a fundamental feature of the pamphlet and cannot be resolved by slotting Kay unequivocally into one or another camp. Developments in Kay's thinking have been obscured because the pamphlet's second edition, published only seven months after the first, is what is usually consulted. There are important differences between the two editions which illuminate changes in Kay's thought at a crucial period of his life. Interpretations of the pamphlet have also suffered from the belief that it was written in response to the sights Kay had seen as he treated cholera victims, a belief made more tenable because Kay expressed it himself. However, the substance of the pamphlet was presented in a paper to the Literary and Philosophical Society on 23 March and published in the first week of April 1832, two months before cholera came to Manchester. The fear of cholera created an atmosphere which permitted Kay to collect the material he needed; but his pamphlet was the work of the dispensary, not the cholera doctor.[42]

The opening pages of the first edition of *The Moral and Physical Condition of the Working Classes* sound a note rarely heard before in English intellectual history. Pain, said Dr Kay, warned the human body of illness, but the social system had no similar warning of moral or physical ills and might take no action to remedy them until threatened with social convulsion. Unlike the English, the governments of some continental countries had sought knowledge of their society through statistical investigations. Ordinary means of study, Kay proclaimed, might yield approximations to truth, but their results 'are never so minutely accurate as those obtained from statistical investigations' nor, because they relied on 'partial evidence', would they convince the public. His own evidence was not founded on 'general opinion' or dependent 'merely on matters of perception'; instead, it was based on material which 'admitted of a statistical classification'. Kay was expressing a new faith, the belief in scientific objectivity and certainty in social matters.[43]

In the first of the pamphlet's two sections Kay produced tables, constructed from the returns of the inspectors, from which he painted a picture of the poorer parts of Manchester. He described streets containing 'heaps of refuse, deep ruts, stagnant pools, ordure'; houses built on mounds of clay and divided by narrow streets which had become gullies, 'down which filthy streams percolate'. Other narrow and unpaved streets were 'the common receptacles of offal and ordure', because the houses were built back to back and had 'no yard, no privy, and no receptacle of refuse'. Near the centre of Manchester, in 'a mass of buildings inhabited by prostitutes and thieves', the one privy, which served 380 inhabitants, was in a narrow passage 'whence its effluvia infest the adjacent houses, and must prove a most fertile source of disease'. With fascinated disgust Kay acquainted middle-class Manchester with the conditions under which the poor lived.[44]

The evils were so remarkable in some districts, he said, that 'more minute' description was required. He chose Little Ireland, a low-lying swampy area between a high bank carrying the Oxford Road and a bend in the Medlock. Two hundred three-storeyed houses, whose chimneys hardly protruded above the road, were crowded into 'an extremely narrow space' and were inhabited by 'the lowest Irish'. In many cellars the floor was barely above the river level, so they were constantly damp and often flooded. Sewers were unable to carry away the surface water or the slops thrown down from houses, privies were inaccessible through filth, and cellars consisting of two rooms each nine or ten feet square, were crowded. The houses were surrounded by some of Manchester's largest factories whose chimneys 'vomit forth dense clouds of smoke, which hang heavily over this insalubrious region'.[45]

From the streets Kay went into the houses, especially those in which the Irish lived. He found them without furniture apart from a few chairs, a table, some cooking materials and one or two beds 'loathsome with filth'. Often a single bed accommodated a whole family and to Kay it seemed that 'a heap of filthy straw and a covering of old sacking' hid the family 'in one undistinguished heap'. Kay drew on one of his articles in the *North of England Medical and Surgical Journal* to give a fastidious description of the daily life of mill workers. He told of their rising at five o'clock, their long working hours, their poor food and their eating habits: 'The family sits round the table, and each rapidly appropriates his portion on a plate, or, they all plunge their spoons into the dish, and with an animal eagerness satisfy the cravings of their appetite.' About half the children born in Manchester, Kay calculated using Roberton's figures, were the offspring of parents 'so destitute or so degraded, as to require the assistance of public charity, in bringing their offspring into the world'. These children were often 'abandoned to the care of a hireling or neighbour' while the mother returned to the mill; and, Kay claimed, more than half of the children of the poor died before the age of six.[46]

Believing, as he did, that the moral and physical degradation of the poor were intimately linked, Kay asked whether pauperism, by which he meant living on the poor rates, was associated with moral and physical degradation. Like many a middle-class liberal, he believed that 'the artificial structure of society', that is, the Poor Law, provided a false security which bred apathy, led the poor to rely on charity and encouraged them to neglect to provide for 'the contingencies of the future'. Using statistics provided by the churchwardens he satisfied himself that pauperism had increased alarmingly, especially where there was 'moral and physical depression'. With pauperism went beer- and gin-shops, crime, an absence of religious observance,

an excessive dependence on the medical charities of the town, poor
health and 'a licentiousness capable of corrupting the whole body of
society', a 'moral leprosy of vice', which defied statistical capture
and which Kay could not bring himself to name, except to call it
'sensuality' and to relate it, in a footnote, to the number of illegitimate births.[47]

The second section of Kay's pamphlet began with a hymn to
Manchester: the buildings of its merchants which were 'monuments
of fertile genius and successful design', the 'masses of capital' which
they had accumulated, and their creation of a system of commerce
which 'stretches its arms to the most distant seas, [and] attests the
power and the dignity of man'. Yet discordant noises disrupted the
hymn. Riots, machine-breaking, incendiarism, even rebellion
threatened, and 'political desperadoes' were ever ready to tempt the
population to 'the hazards of the swindling game of revolution'. Yet
he had also heard the cries of need and he knew that want did 'prey
upon the heart of the people'. How could commerce, that powerful
promoter of civilization, produce the evils which afflicted the
working classes? To answer that question Kay was forced to examine
the basis of his political beliefs.[48]

The beliefs, which owe a patent debt to Adam Smith, survive the
examination. The evils arise *'from foreign and accidental causes'*, Kay
insists, and later claims that *'so far from being the necessary results of the
commercial system, [they] furnish evidence of a disease which impairs its
energies, if it does not threaten its vitality'*. How then do the evils arise?
Kay suggested that the 'eager antagonization of commercial
enterprize' had through the pressure of business and time, but not
through a want of humanity, caused too rapid and uncontrolled an
expansion. Then he offered a more ominous explanation: 'the
colonization of the Irish', he claimed, was 'one chief source of the
demoralization, and consequent physical depression of the people'.
Using a medical metaphor, Kay argued that 'the contagious example
of the ignorance and barbarous disregard of forethought and
economy, exhibited by the Irish, spread'. Though a source of cheap
labour, the Irish soon became 'burdens on the community whose
morals and physical power they have depressed; and dissipate wealth
which they did not accumulate'. He painted a grotesque picture of a
population corrupted by the Irish: children born to impoverished
parents would eke out an existence, growing steadily more hungry,
dissipated, destitute and debauched. 'Even war and pestilence', he
decided, 'when regarded as affecting a population thus demoralized,

and politically and physically debased, seem like storms which sweep from the atmosphere the noxious vapours whose stagnation threatens man with death.'[49]

Kay next explained that the restrictions placed on commerce were a major cause of the moral, physical and economic suffering of the labouring population. He rehearsed arguments for free trade, insisting that unrestricted commerce would make 'redundant labour' merely 'an evil of brief duration, rarely experienced'. He then advanced the first of his suggestions for improvement, the spread of education. A reduction in the hours of labour, such as that required by the Ten Hours movement, which was not preceded by 'the relief of commercial burdens' and 'the introduction of a *general system of education*', was a delusion. Kay's comments were brief and general, and announced themes which are not developed until his later works: education is a social activity directed to improving the poor; it should go beyond the rudiments of learning and offer the child instruction 'in the nature of his domestic and social relations, of his political position in society, and of the moral and religious duties appropriate to it'; it should also provide some general knowledge as a source of rational amusement and as an introduction to the exact sciences likely to be connected to the child's future vocation. These were conventional liberal views and did not as yet bear Kay's personal imprint; in fact he often quoted the words of other writers, including Chalmers.[50]

Kay next stressed the need for capitalists to take an enlightened attitude to their employees, and drew attention to a provident society in Liverpool in which 'influential inhabitants' helped to instruct the poor in domestic economy and the virtues of 'sobriety, cleanliness, forethought, and method'. Finally, he returned to public health measures. Non-resident proprietors in search of high rents had, he believed, let their land to 'avaricious speculators' who, 'unrestrained by any general enactment, or special police regulation', had built the unplanned, wretched houses in the narrow, unpaved streets which he had described. 'Private rights', he argued, 'ought not to be exercised so as to produce a public injury'; the law should protect the rights of communities against 'the assaults of partial interests'. Streets should be built according to a plan determined by a body of commissioners; landlords should be compelled to provide drainage and to pave their parts of the street; houses should be whitewashed once a year and have receptacles for refuse; and inspectors should examine the houses which, if declared to be unhealthy, should be repaired at the expense of the landlords. As Chadwick himself later acknowledged, these remarkable recommendations, whose precision contrasted with the generalities he had written about education, foreshadowed the public health movement with its governmental intervention at the bidding of expert inspectors. In 1832 public health was more important to Kay than education, and led him, only a few pages after he had extolled the virtues of unfettered commerce, to propose restrictions which affected the profits and entrepreneurial activities of the middle class.[51]

In his concluding paragraphs Kay wrote of relations between capitalists and workers, and his view of the 'cordial sympathy' which ought to unite them. 'Capital', he insisted, 'is but accumulated labour: their strife is unnatural. Greed does not become the opulent; nor does turbulence the poor.' He saw value in 'general combinations of workmen' and remarked that a capitalist who thought only of the results of labour was treating his employees as 'a mere animal power necessary to the mechanical processes of manufacture', and this he described as 'a heartless, if not a degrading association'. The 'operative population' was one of the most important elements in society and because of its numbers potentially of great power. If the higher classes, whom Kay regarded as the fountain from which the 'cordial sympathy' might flow, neglected the operative population, others would take advantage of its ignorance and excite its distrust. He ended where he had begun, stressing the significance of knowledge in preserving the fabric of society.[52]

In that search for knowledge Kay was a child of the Enlightenment, especially as mediated by his Scottish teachers, and his pamphlet was a testament to his belief in the power of reason: study and understand the lives of the poor, make their living conditions known to the middle class and reform will follow. Knowledge given statistical expression was more persuasive because it borrowed the authority of objective science. And persuasiveness was the more urgent because the middle class was separated from the working class not only geographically – Kay pointed out they had left Ancoats and similar districts to build comfortable homes in the countryside – but also imaginatively. The poor, as Pickstone has said, had become 'a separate mass', an 'other' which had to be classified and quantified if it were to be understood. Though Kay had not gained access to its inner sanctum, he understood the middle class; the poor were different and could not be understood without carefully acquired learning.[53]

Kay's trust in reason was so profound that it had begun to erode his belief in the all-wise Providence which ruled the world according to hidden and often seemingly arbitrary laws. Kay paid tribute to Providence but his pamphlet assumed, as did the Unitarians with whom he mixed freely, that the world was ultimately rational and therefore accessible to human knowledge. Despite Kay's concern at the state of religion in Manchester, his pamphlet contained little sense of a deity, either unitarian or trinitarian, little feeling of spirituality, no intimations of the numinous. His Congregationalist deity was being remade in Kay's own image, secularized and converted into a controlling intelligence whose laws might be discovered. Kay had not discarded his earlier beliefs but they were gradually being transformed.

Yet Kay's changing theological beliefs could not conquer profound emotional forces which warred against the optimistic view that humans were perfectible through reason. Evil stalks through the filthy streets, the towering mills and cruelly crowded houses of Kay's Manchester – drunkenness, improvidence, sensuality, idleness, apathy, greed, neglect and exploitation of children, ignorance and irreligion. This diseased society is, in Messinger's words, suffused by 'a subconscious sense of Manichean struggle between the forces of light and the forces of darkness'.[54] Manchester is seen through the lens of his Congregational childhood. It is a depraved form of 'the world' which his father left in order to secure salvation, about which John Crabtree spoke on their twilight walks through the Lancashire hills, and against which his mother was ceaselessly warning him. A Nonconformist morality, formed in childhood's cruel and powerful mould, shaped Kay's shocked vision. Yet the true Kay was neither the rational, enlightened thinker nor the pessimistic Congregationalist, but both and both at once. The pamphlet was a record of the moral and physical conditions of Manchester's working classes, but also of the contradictions which tormented the man who observed them.

The contradictions are reflected in Kay's attitude to the working class. He frequently attributed their demoralization to their own failings, and towards the Irish in particular he displayed the destructive prejudices of his race, religion and class: they had demoralized the English operatives, their habits were filthy, they multiplied without 'moral check', they were barbarians and savages. The working class, but the Irish especially, were scapegoats who bore away Kay's guilt for the horrors of urbanization and industrialization, leaving unscathed his respect for the teachings of the political economists. In his blackest passages the pauper boarding-houses became 'fertile sources of disease and demoralization' because the tenants of 'these disgusting abodes' were prone to contagion. From the working class and the pauper steals the poison which threatens the physical and moral health of society.[55]

Yet Kay sometimes wrote with an unusual understanding of the cotton workers. He insisted that their 'prolonged and exhausting labour' prevented the development of their moral and mental faculties. He sensed the deadening effects of work 'in which the same mechanical process is incessantly repeated', and he saw that factory labour, by causing the intellect to slumber in 'supine inertness', was destroying the mill workers. 'To condemn man to such severity of toil is, in some measure, to cultivate in him the habits of an animal.' He was one of the earliest observers to grasp that the process of industrialization was changing not merely the working habits but the very character of the people. Mill workers

> are drudges who watch the movements, and assist the operations, of a mighty material force, which toils with an energy ever unconscious of fatigue. The persevering labour of the operative must rival the mathematical precision, the incessant motion, and the exhaustless power of the machine.

For Kay, in this remarkable mood, the cotton mills diminished moral and intellectual power as they had reduced light and air, and destroyed 'all the distinguishing aims' of the human species. The cotton workers had been brought to a state in which they had 'neither moral dignity nor intellectual nor organic strength to resist the seductions of appetite'. Kay could not sustain this insight, but at times he could see beyond the glories of commerce and industry to the human misery on which they were based.[56]

A little before Kay, writers such as C.T. Thackrah, W.R. Greg and John Roberton had discussed the state of the working population, but their writings did not have the same impact.[57] Though Kay began his pamphlet with a call for dispassionate statistical analysis, he was soon overwhelmed by his feelings and he exposed the conditions of working class life with a searing and unreflecting honesty. Had he been more cautious and self-conscious, he might have noticed his contradictions and produced a more consistent analysis. But then his pamphlet could have lost its compelling immediacy. Kay was trapped within his own analysis, so that we see not only the condition of the working class, but also the response of a liberal member of the middle class with all his ambiguities and contradictions, his condescension and sympathy, his anger and fear, his leaps of understanding and his failures of imagination. Kay's pamphlet is a 'cardinal document' of English social history as much for what it reveals about the middle class as for what it has to say about its subject, the working classes.

The pamphlet was also very brave. It was not wise or prudent, to choose words to which Kay became addicted, for a doctor who was endeavouring to build his practice and be elected to the Infirmary, to risk alienating the cotton masters by so graphic a description of the condition of their labour force. The *Manchester Guardian* immediately recognized that Kay had exposed social and moral ills which had surprised most people, even the 'comparatively well-informed', and the *Poor Man's Guardian* was also supportive. Even the *Union Pilot*, which denounced Kay for his desire 'to preserve the whole system', described as 'truly creditable' his 'unreserved exposition of the astounding evils which, in his enquiries, he found besetting the working classes'. Dr Henry Gaulter, a fellow member of the board of health, testified to Kay's impact by criticizing him, claiming in 1833 that the pamphlet seemed to many of 'the more easy inhabitants as little less than a malicious libel on the town'. Twelve years later a most important student of Manchester drew on the pamphlet. Kay's 'recorded impressions', Friedrich Engels said, 'tallied exactly with my own', and he commented that Kay's was 'an excellent book although the author confuses the workers with the working class in general'.[58]

Kay reported the anger of the more easy inhabitants to Thomas Chalmers when, in June 1832, he implied that he had been subjected to 'the most bitter animosity and fractious opposition'. By November he expressed his relief that 'the inconsiderate hostility which was at first raised by a few of those capitalists, who considered themselves *attacked* (!)' was now 'almost entirely assuaged'. In its place was springing up a readiness to remedy evils 'whose existence cannot be denied'. However, not even Kay's new optimism could hide the fact that his pamphlet had further strained his relations with Manchester's powerful middle class.[59]

In June 1832, two months after his pamphlet was published, the first case of cholera was diagnosed in Manchester, and Kay soon realized that he and his medical colleagues faced opposition. The reports of cholera in other towns, the whitewashing of houses, the scavenging parties, the watchers placed on the canals, the placards' dire warnings – these and other measures added to the fear created by the appearance of the cholera itself. When the deaths began, the board's pressure for swift burials affronted the poor's religious beliefs and their attachment to their burial rituals, particularly the wake. Resentment of the medical profession's support for the burial policy fed on the long-nurtured anger against the bodysnatching gangs, some of whom had made great profits by robbing graves or stealing bodies from undertakers. Then the 1832 Anatomy Act provided that, if they were not claimed within a certain time, the bodies of those who had in life been maintained at public expense or who had died in workhouses or charitable institutions, could be used to satisfy the insatiable demand of the anatomist. These provisions again affronted the religious beliefs of the poor, denied them dignity, linked them with convicted murderers (whose bodies were available for dissection), and used their bodies to benefit the wealthy who had easy access to doctors. Finally the cholera hospitals, symbols of the interference of authority, loomed as deathly prisons which incarcerated the poor and brought contagion into the districts in which they were located. Despite the hopes of Kay and other medical practitioners, a cholera doctor worked in an atmosphere of suspicion and hostility which increased his social marginalization.[60]

The hostility did not diminish Kay's vigour. Throughout the epidemic he remained on the Board of Health, a faithful attender of meetings, a preparer of placards and resolutions, a participant in debates on the burial difficulties or the problems of medical officers and, on some occasions, a spokesman who put the board's case for financial support to public meetings of the vestry. He also acted as physician to the Knott Mill cholera hospital, an old cotton factory which had been filled with iron bedsteads, and he visited the houses of the first 250 people to die of cholera in pursuit of an understanding of the disease. That pursuit led him into an argument with one of his medical colleagues who complained, with some but not sufficient justification, that Kay had entered the Swan Street hospital, where he had no authority, and interfered with a patient's treatment.[61]

Kay's handling of one of the first cases of cholera, a family from Little Ireland, gives some insight into his approach. After the death of the father, Richard Bullock, Kay had the mother, Ellen, and her three children spirited away in the cholera van (according to him, willingly) to the Knott Mill hospital, before the 'excitable Irish population' realized what had happened. Despite Kay's ministrations the mother and children died. Henry Gaulter, whose account of these incidents was written in 1833 and was therefore less susceptible to memory's self-justifying lapses than Kay's account in his *Autobiography*, claimed that Ellen Bullock feared going into hospital and had to be locked up at night to prevent her throwing herself into the Medlock. He also claimed that it was a long while before the reputation of the hospital recovered from the Bullocks' deaths: they had entered the hospital 'well and sorely against the wishes of the woman and her friends, having yielded to the earnest solicitations of the medical men, and they had not been heard of again until they were borne away to be laid in the same grave'. Not surprisingly 'the mob' which assembled at the gates of the hospital 'accused the doctors of poison, and even of darker crimes'. A fervent anti-contagionist and opposed to cholera hospitals, Gaulter was out of sympathy with most of his fellow board members, but there is no reason to disbelieve his account. Significantly, on 18 June, four days after the death of the last of the Bullocks, the board decided to prepare a placard warning against 'violent conduct' towards doctors. Large crowds had gathered at the gates of the Knott Mill hospital and there was 'evidently increasing hostility' to the medical staff. The placard said that 'medical gentlemen', who were 'greatly risking themselves, and giving, gratuitously, services of the most laborious and painful kind', had been 'grossly and insultingly attacked'. When in August 1832 Kay helped to produce another placard aimed at removing the 'prejudice' against going to hospitals, he was helping to defend his own practices.[62]

Even if motivated by ideological differences, Gaulter left a memorable comment on the resentment created by the board's activities:

> The perpetual appearance of fresh placards headed by this frightful word [cholera] – the daily parade of reports – the procession of the sling exciting and wounding the curiosity of the passengers – the rattling of the cholera van through the streets – the dead-cart followed by a mourner or two at an awful distance, moving slowly towards a remote burying-ground branded with the double stigma of poverty and infection – all this ostentation of pestilence was most pernicious. Nor was the hospital system, though organized with the most benevolent intentions, productive of less mischief.

Kay did not hesitate to impose hospitalization on the poor, but given the state of medical knowledge and the seriousness of the emergency, he had little alternative. Had cholera sufferers been left in their homes, Kay and his medical colleagues would probably have been accused of callous neglect and irresponsibility. Moreover, as the epidemic developed, it became clear that cholera doctors ran serious professional and personal risks. Some found their private practice at risk as patients left them from fear of contagion, and as they moved about the filthy streets and the unsewered houses they were exposing themselves to conditions in which, according to their own theories, they ran the risk of contracting cholera. Mortality among doctors was not high, but it was higher than in any other middle-class profession, and their vulnerability was emphasized by the deaths of eight nurses at the Swan Street hospital.[63]

A bitter confrontation over cholera hospitals occurred in September 1832 after an elderly Irishman, having been refused admittance to the Swan Street hospital to see his four-year-old grandson whose parents had died of cholera, returned the next day to discover that the boy was dead and buried. He exhumed the body and found that it was headless and that a brick had been put in the coffin to replace the head, which presumably had been used for dissection. In the riot that followed, an angry crowd destroyed a cholera van, broke into the hospital, took patients home, and was not dispersed until troops arrived and the Riot Act was read. This spontaneous demonstration of working-class hostility against cholera hospitals and body-snatchers was defended by the *Poor Man's Advocate*, which pointed out that it was 'no proof of "brutal ignorance" in the people, insisting on having the bodies of their friends and relatives buried whole and entire'. The blame was attributed to a recently appointed dispenser of medicines who had disappeared. In a massive understatement, the Board of Health spoke of 'the possible prejudice likely to arise in the minds of the public against cholera hospitals'. Meanwhile Kay worked on a committee entrusted with drawing up a placard to explain the 'unfortunate circumstances' and to express the board's regret. He was also signatory to a smug letter from the Knott Mill hospital which deplored the dispenser's 'gross violation of the orders of the Board', supported the medical officers at Swan Street, and noted that 'not even the slightest incision has been made in any subject' in the Knott Mill hospital, without the consent of the friends of the deceased. The letter also insisted that 'no feeling of courtesy to the Medical Profession' should prevent the board from prosecuting the offender if they so wished.[64]

By the end of October 1832, about six weeks after this incident, the board began to scale down its activities as the number of cholera cases dropped. The winter saw the end of the epidemic in Manchester, though the board did not congratulate itself and dissolve until October 1833. By then Kay had published a second edition of his pamphlet, which was 'greatly assisted by the marginal notes of approbation and dissent' made by Thomas Chalmers to whom he had sent a copy of the first edition. The new edition appeared in November 1832 and contained an introductory letter to Chalmers which extolled his work for the poor, implied his support for Kay's views, and enabled Kay to hit back at his critics. He attributed the lack of knowledge of the condition of the people to a remote aristocracy living in an 'Arcadian stillness', to merchants who were absorbed with business, and to manufacturers burdened by taxation, restrictions on trade and confrontation with a gloomy and rebellious working class. He admitted that a few manufacturers still wished to hide the condition of the working classes, but he insisted that he was not willing 'to screen those from just contempt, who are so blind to the true interests of their own order, or so fearful of the propositions of every quack, that, deaf to the appeals of humanity, they represent the people to be happy and contented'. In a menacing image he wrote of 'the dense masses of the habitations of the poor, which stretch out their arms, as though to grasp and enclose the dwellings of the noble and wealthy, in the metropolis, and in our large provincial cities'. The supposedly incurable social evils in these 'mighty wildernesses of buildings' could, however, be cured. In an almost providential way cholera would lead to the Boards of Health becoming 'permanent organized centres of medical police, where municipal powers will be directed by scientific men, to the removal of those agencies which most powerfully depress the physical condition of the inhabitants'.[65]

Additions to the text of the pamphlet developed the thinking expressed in the introductory letter. A typically agitated description of the polluted Irk and the Gibraltar and Allen's Court districts buttressed an argument for street-widening which involved the destruction of houses and a factory; the keeping of pigs which reduced the common area at the back of some houses into a 'dung-heap and a receptacle of . . . putrescent garbage' enabled Kay to call on the commissioners of the police to obtain power to erect a common slaughterhouse; and he wanted the authorities to interfere in the conduct of gaols and gin-shops. His attitude towards workers' assemblies, union co-operatives and strikes hardened, and his increasing fear of social unrest led to a more detailed discussion of education as a means of protection:

> Alarming disturbances of social order generally commence with *a people only partially instructed*. The preservation of *internal peace*, not less than the improvement of our national institutions, depends on the education of the working classes.

He summarized his position starkly: 'That good government may be stable, the people must be so instructed, that they may love that *which they know to be right*.'[66]

Perhaps under Chalmers's influence, Kay stressed religious instruction through the newly established Christian Instruction Societies. A society operating from the Mosley Street Independent Chapel, which Kay attended, sent visitors into the homes of the poor 'for the purpose of conversing with the inmates on the great truths of the gospel', to lend them tracts and books, and to attract them to worship. Kay asked for more infant schools, for domestic economy to be taught to girls, and for 'a general system of education', which was to be 'so extensive and liberal as to supply the wants of the whole labouring population'. Though determined, as Adam Smith had been, that the ignorant were 'properly, the care of the state', he did not yet discuss how a general system of education would be provided or who would control it.[67]

Kay reiterated his concern that the poor would become demoralized and dependent if incentives to prudence and virtue were removed, and he welcomed the appointment of a commission of inquiry into the Poor Laws (he could not know that it would have a profound effect on his life). He argued that the distribution of poor relief should approximate as closely as possible to 'that by which a well regulated private bounty is administered'. Invoking the condescension of the old order, Kay declared himself in favour of

> that sympathy with the distresses of the poor, and that gratitude for relief afforded – that acknowledged right to administer good counsel, and that willingness to receive advice – that privilege of inquiring into the arrangements of domestic economy, instructing the ignorant, and checking the perverse – all which attend the beneficent path of private charity.[68]

Yet his approach to public health and education was undermining this disintegrating and paternalistic world. In the second edition of his pamphlet, Kay's support for medical police and the Christian

Instruction Societies, his growing fear of working-class instability, and his distrust of their associations, showed an increased separation from the poor he studied and a growing determination to restructure their environment. The social imaginativeness of the first edition was still present, but the rioters outside the cholera hospitals had affected him more than he realized.

When writing his *Autobiography* Kay remembered how during the epidemic his thoughts and sympathies had become 'entirely fixed' on the miseries of Manchester's poor. He recalled the days and nights he had spent in their homes, in the streets and in cholera hospitals, the suffering and death he had observed, and his realization that he had little power 'to alleviate excruciating pain or to prolong life'. He also remembered 'outbursts of popular suspicion and fury' and the 'frantic insurrection' of the mob which had 'gutted a cholera hospital'. He decided to draw a curtain on these scenes.[69]

Drawing the curtain was easier in old age than in youth, and in the years immediately following the cholera epidemic Kay was preoccupied with the moral and physical condition of the working classes. He explained to Thomas Chalmers in November 1832 that ill health and professional duties had eaten up the time which he hoped to spend 'in directly aiding, by my own personal exertions, some practical schemes of benevolence'. By the beginning of 1833 the circumstances had changed and Kay launched himself on a hectic round of activity in support of what he described to Chalmers as 'this best cause'. He made a painless contribution to the cause in March by expressing to a parliamentary enquiry into public walks his concern that 'the operative population of Manchester' had nowhere to exercise in the open air. He provided a map, marking in red the parts of the town where the poor lived, and in green the places where he thought parks might be built.[70]

He had more time-consuming activities. Throughout the early 1830s he was active in the Manchester Mechanics' Institute, which had been started in 1824 under the leadership of Benjamin Heywood, the banker whom Kay had praised in his *Letter*. The Institute, like similar institutions established in Glasgow, Edinburgh and London a few years earlier, aimed to teach mechanics and artisans the scientific principles on which their trades were based. Heywood meticulously explained to Lord Brougham, perhaps the most prominent and

powerful supporter of mechanics' institutes, that Manchester's Institute had not been started by mechanics but by the employers, who
intended 'to watch over its infancy ourselves, to put it in the way of
gaining strength and good experience, and then I apprehend but not
till then – to leave its chief management to the mechanics'. In the
light of this approach it is not surprising that in Manchester (and later
in many other places) the mechanics' institute was not strongly
patronized by the artisans and mechanics it was supposed to serve.
But its aims and hopes persisted, and for a time in the 1830s Kay was
one of its directors, and often sat in a prominent position in the
company of the 'gentlemen of science and station' who attended its
annual meetings or the lecture programmes it conducted. Through
these activities Kay may have come into contact with Roland
Detrosier, an autodidact of impressive ability, who in the 1820s and
1830s worked vigorously in Manchester for educational and social
reform, and who in 1829 established the 'New Mechanics' Institution', designed to give workers control over their own education.
Detrosier does not appear in Kay's correspondence and no precise
contact between them can be documented, but 30 years later Kay
showed that Detrosier had left a mark on his mind.[71]

The Manchester and Salford District Provident Society was
another of Kay's social interests. It was established on 20 March 1833
with Heywood as treasurer and Kay and his lifelong friend, William
Langton, who worked in Heywood's bank, as two of its secretaries.
Among early subscribers were the Kennedys and the M'Connels and
one of the committee members was Robert McAll, the minister at the
Mosley Street Independent Chapel, who now had the chance to
watch Kay at work among the Unitarians. The society aimed at 'the
encouragement of frugality and forethought, the suppression of
mendicity and imposture, and the occasional relief of sickness and
unavoidable misfortune among the poor'. Visitors appointed by the
society (often clergymen and especially Unitarians) were to call
weekly at the houses of the poor to advise on financial management,
to encourage them to make deposits with the society, and to acquaint
them 'with the sympathy of the wealthier classes, and the advantages
of their advice'. A rumour that the society was to distribute general
financial relief to the poor sent the society scurrying to its rules,
which Kay and Langton had drawn up. They instructed subscribers
to give a ticket but no money to beggars. When beggars brought
their tickets to the society, the visitor of the district in which a beggar

lived would make certain that the case was one of 'extreme and temporary distress'. A successful beggar was then given a form to take to the weekly meeting of the society's board which, after investigation, might 'exercise their discretion' and provide an order for food, or in exceptional circumstances, bedding, clothing or fuel. Obviously impetuous charity was not going to be encouraged. Yet, despite its bureaucratic paternalism, the society received support; it had 964 depositors at the end of its first year and 3,851 at the end of its third.[72]

In 1834 Kay published a pamphlet in the form of a letter to George Murray, the President of the Ardwick and Ancoats Dispensary, which grew out of his experiences as a dispensary doctor and as an official of the Provident Society. In *Defects in the Constitution of Dispensaries* Kay argued that the use of medical charity had increased more rapidly than the population, and he revealed that he had begun to ask himself 'to what extent I am a minister of good, and how much evil accrues from my visitations'. The dispensary doctor was flooded with patients who were recommended by people who hardly knew them, who regarded their treatment '*more as a right* than *as a boon*', and who showed the doctor little respect or gratitude. Kay linked the Provident Society and the Ardwick and Ancoats Dispensary by suggesting that the dispensary should join the relatively new ranks of self-supporting dispensaries whose subscribers were guaranteed medical attention and might even choose their doctor from a panel elected by the dispensary board. He suggested that the society's visitors should encourage the poor to become subscribers and he provided figures which, he claimed, proved that the workmen's wages were sufficient to enable them to pay their subscriptions. As a result of such schemes, he concluded, 'we should no longer be instrumental in diminishing that noble self-reliance, which has been the boast of the English peasantry, and in substituting for the generous pride of independence, a sickly craving for sympathy.' The Manchester and Salford District Provident Society was a manifestation of Kay's increasing impatience with philanthropy that had not done its sums in his way.[73]

During the course of their work for the society Langton and Kay became involved in establishing a statistical society. Kay's interest in statistics had been evident since his days as editor of the *North of England Medical and Surgical Journal* but, as Langton remembered things 42 years later, the establishment of the society was his suggestion. It is more likely that the initiative was Kay's – certainly Chalmers thought so, for he informed Kay that it did him 'great credit to have originated such an institution in Manchester'. In any case Langton and Kay worked harmoniously. On a tour through the Peak District with his friends, the cotton manufacturers Samuel and William Rathbone Greg, Kay had further discussions, and on 2 September 1833 at Claremont, the home of Benjamin Heywood, a group of like-minded men took up a collection to establish the Manchester Statistical Society. The new society was to discuss 'subjects of political and social economy' and to promote statistical enquiries with a 'total exclusion of party politics'. To high-mindedness they added social exclusiveness and self-satisfaction, declaring themselves to be 'gentlemen accustomed for the most part to meet in private society, and whose habits and opinions are not uncongenial'. The importance they placed on 'agreeable social inter-course' became obvious when they were confronted with financial difficulties and decided to raise money in ways other than expanding their membership, in case the society's 'social character' was dis-rupted by the influx of new members. They tackled their task with earnestness, being motivated by a 'strong desire . . . to assist in pro-moting the progress of social improvement in the manufacturing population by which they are surrounded'.[74]

'By which they are surrounded. . . .' There is the hint of a threat to the congenial company in the comfortable room. Because the early members of the society included John and James Kennedy, another cotton man, Samuel Robinson, James and Henry M'Connel, Thomas Potter, Mark Philips, the Member for Manchester, as well as Hey-wood, Samuel and William Greg, Langton and Kay, the congeniality could be expected. They shared, most of them, Unitarianism, the occupations of the cotton trade and banking, and membership of so many committees that on occasions they might have wondered which one it was that they were attending. Also they were, or were later to become, bound by family links – for example, two of Heywood's sons married two of Langton's daughters, Samuel Robinson was Heywood's brother-in-law and John Kennedy's son-in-law, and Kay was to make a determined effort to become James Kennedy's son-in-law. In addition they shared a particular view of statistics. For William Greg, statistics, far from being 'a dry collection of figures and tables, possessing no interest, and leading to no result', were of surpassing importance. 'Without accurate data on which to ground our enquiries', he insisted, 'we can never attain to any adequate knowledge of the various influences which modify the Social State.' Any political philosophy not based on a statistical foundation was 'speculative and uncertain, and can never attain the dignity and the value of a *Science*'. The London Statistical Society, founded a few months later than its Manchester counterpart, expressed the faith which underlay both institutions. Its 'first most essential rule' was 'to exclude carefully all *opinions* from its transactions and publications, – to confine its attention rigorously to facts, – and, as far as it may be found possible, to facts which can be stated numerically and arranged in tables'.[75]

Kay and the Manchester Statistical Society had decided that a social science was possible, that the techniques of observation and experiment which had been so fruitful in the physical and chemical sciences, and with which Kay's medical training had made him familiar, would have similar success if applied to moral and social problems. In the belief that he would find secure and tightly defined truth, Kay worked with the fervour and intolerance of the neophyte. It was necessary, he told the Statistical Society, 'that all the information collected should be presented in a statistical form and that vague generalizations and personal impressions should, as much as possible, be avoided'. His remark in his pamphlet of 1832 that the approximations to truth which traditional methods produced could never be 'so minutely accurate as those obtained from statistical investigations' had received an institutional expression.[76] Kay hoped that the evils and suffering with which Manchester confronted him might be reduced or removed if these social truths could be discovered and understood. Through the Manchester Statistical Society he was developing the position which he had announced in *The Moral and Physical Condition of the Working Classes*.

Kay was not alone in such hopes for the society was itself an expression of an interest in statistical work which led a historian of the movement to describe the 1830s and 1840s as 'the era of enthusiasm'. In France and in Germany there was considerable activity and the writings of the Belgian statistician, Adolphe Quetelet, were most important. In 1835, just as the Manchester society was getting into its stride, he published *Sur l'homme* in which he wrote of 'the average man' around whom he grouped measurements of human traits in accord with the normal probability curve. England had conducted censuses each decade from 1801; actuarial statistics had advanced reasonably rapidly; medical statistics were improving; national criminal statistics, driven in part by a controversy over

capital punishment, began to be published by the Home Office in
1810; and some statistics were being collected on education and the
health of factory children. In 1833, the year the Manchester society
began, the Board of Trade, then a small department with mainly
advisory responsibilities, established a statistical department, and the
British Association for the Advancement of Science added a statistics
section. The Manchester Statistical Society was part of a new and
exciting intellectual movement.[77]

One of the society's first projects was a study of the working
population of Manchester. Benjamin Heywood commissioned an
agent, an 'intelligent Irishman', to conduct a house-to-house survey
in a predominantly working-class area. The agent was given questions
on the country of origin of the people in the district, their religion,
the condition of their accommodation, the ages of their children,
their educational history, standards of literacy and occupations. The
results of the survey were expressed in tabular form (which should
have pleased the London Statistical Society), and Heywood reported
them to the Statistical Section of the British Association for the
Advancement of Science in Edinburgh in 1834.[78]

Today's sophisticated research workers might permit themselves
the flicker of a smile at the study's crude methodology and at the
simple-mindedness with which the results were reported. They
would be unwise, for, with the survey which Kay had organized for
the Board of Health, it was one of the earliest examples of social
survey research. Moreover, in this pioneering investigation the
Manchester Statistical Society hit upon a durable research strategy:
they chose a topical issue which involved working with people of low
socio-economic status, designed a questionnaire, hired a research
assistant to do the field work, appropriated the results with the
minimum of acknowledgement, turned them into statistical tables,
and delivered the findings as a paper to a learned society. The
Manchester Statistical Society got all this right, first time, in 1834,
with the help of an intelligent Irishman. Even the manner of
reporting has a familiar ring. The agent, 'research assistant', had
trouble getting answers – some people refused him admission to their
homes and others were absent when he called. But though 'the return
was not as complete as we would wish' there was 'no reason to dispute
its correctness'. It was a 'fair and impartial' account of 4,102 families
from 'the poorest class of the labouring population of Manchester'.
Again Heywood got it right: the measured tone, the qualification
made, then put aside, the reassuring objectivity, the solid conclusion.

To monitor and to devise research of this kind as well as to conduct its ordinary business, the society usually met monthly in the home of one of its members, including Kay's on at least one occasion. He was treasurer in the first year of the society's life and was on the executive committee in its second. He helped to formulate its rules, took an active part in discussions about its future, presented plans and estimates for public swimming baths for the 'operative population', played a part in Heywood's survey, assisted in a larger study which followed, floated an unsuccessful proposal for an investigation into the problems faced by handloom weavers, and presented papers on miners in Derbyshire, on religious instruction of the working classes (this was read in the presence of Poulett Thomson and led to another enquiry), and on the defects in dispensaries – his pamphlet made its first appearance as a paper given to the society in November 1833. When speakers were required to lecture at the Mechanics Institute on political economy, Kay spoke on wages. He was also involved in the most important of the society's early projects, a study which illuminated the inadequacies of education in Manchester and provided a model for later investigations.[79]

Kay's approach can be seen in a proposal he developed to study 'the habitations of the poor'. Taking a district containing houses of a particular rental, Kay sought to discover the number, age, sex, employment and wages of each family member, the number in the family who were employed or on poor relief, the condition of the dwelling, the literacy of the adults, the nature of their amusements, and whether or not they were members of a benefit society or subscribed to a mechanics' institute. He then proposed to use this information to make comparisons with districts of higher or lower rental, and to classify the houses according to the occupations of those who lived in them. He developed his plan in elaborate detail but this small section is sufficient to show its modernity. However tentative and undeveloped, it is recognizably survey research, and Kay is trying to create objective numerical data from which he could derive a picture of the lives of the poor.[80]

That belief in objectivity masked a typical ambiguity in Kay's thinking. His characteristic assumptions, carried forward from his *Letter* and his 1832 pamphlet, were that the social system which had advanced commerce and enriched and diffused civilization could not be 'inconsistent with the happiness of the *great mass of the people*',[81] yet that, simultaneously, many in the working classes were morally and physically degraded. By concentrating all his attention and research

on the working classes, Kay, at least by implication, identified them
as the source of society's problems. It was they who had to be understood, their behaviour which had to be changed, while the aristocracy
and the middle classes, with whom political power actually lay, were
left without scrutiny.

By their problems you shall know them. The invocation of
objectivity served a political purpose for it invested the questions Kay
asked with a cloak of scientific detachment which disguised the
political assumptions he had made. Despite the information these
early social scientists collected, despite the tables they filled with
statistics (or probably, because of the tables they filled with statistics)
they had made a fundamental but never closely examined judgement
that the poor were the source of Manchester's problems. The interests
of the merchants and manufacturers, determined to preserve their
recently obtained power, slipped out of sight. For the working classes
there were to be public health, provident societies and education. For
the powerful, statistics, the collection of quantified information,
knowledge that helps to define and control. Social science was born
into a power struggle.[82]

The membership of the society demonstrated its political nature:
bankers, merchants, manufacturers, physicians, but no statisticians.
When in his *Letter* Kay was inveighing against aristocratic control of
Parliament, he had insisted that 'our representatives shall be upright,
independent, sagacious merchants, too rich to accept a bribe, and too
astute to be deceived', he might have been talking about the
Manchester Statistical Society. A debate about its name exposed its
political orientation – 'the name was a sort of compromise', the
cautious Heywoood reported to Brougham; 'the Political Economy
Club might have been more appropriate'. The topics the society
chose to investigate revealed its preoccupations; no papers on
statistical theory or methodology but on down-to-earth problems –
the condition of the working classes, their education and health and,
early in the society's proceedings, an analysis by Samuel and William
Greg of evidence given to Chadwick's 1833 commission in which the
Gregs came to the conclusion that the factory system was vindicated.
Yet perhaps most indicative of its political intent was the swift link
which the society established with government.[83]

The link was established through Charles Poulett Thomson, who
as well as representing Manchester was Vice-President of the Board
of Trade, and was interested in its recently established statistics

department. In March 1833, six months before the Manchester Statistical Society was formed, Poulett Thomson had asked Kay for some statistical information to use in the Factory Act debate. In November Poulett Thomson congratulated Kay on the establishment of the society, pointing out that the deficiency in the system for the collection of statistics could only be made up from 'private undertakings, such as that which you have instituted at Manchester'. When he met with the society in the same month, he argued somewhat ominously that the government could not obtain statistical information throughout the country because of the expense, and because 'the organization requisite for such a system would be more difficult in a free than a despotic state'. Enquiries from government might be considered 'inquisitorial', but would be regarded with less suspicion if conducted by voluntary associations. Poulett Thomson hoped that the society's work might draw attention to 'the great economical interests of this part of the country, and to a question of paramount importance, the best means of ameliorating the social condition of the labouring classes'. Thus, in these early days of social and educational research in England, researchers were enjoined to meet the wishes of government, even if these could not be made public. Scientific detachment, it seems, was not compromised by working on problems chosen by the powerful.[84]

By late 1834 Kay had been in Manchester for six years and his activities at the Statistical Society and elsewhere had made him well known in liberal middle-class circles. *The Moral and Physical Condition of the Working Classes* had received an important analysis in the *Westminster Review* and a notice in *Tait's Edinburgh Magazine*. Writers such as Peter Gaskell, the Factory Act campaigner George Condy, and Benjamin Heywood used the pamphlet as an authoritative source as, later, did Leon Faucher, editor of the Parisian journal, *Le Courier Français*, and Engels. Kay's political activities had brought him to the attention of people such as Grenfell, Molyneux, John Bright and Poulett Thomson, while through the Statistical Society he met the powerful Whig politicians, Viscount Morpeth, sixth Earl of Carlisle, and Lord Kerry, who wrote to Kay a number of times on statistical matters, and offered to put Kay's name forward for membership of the London Statistical Society. At about this time, no doubt through such contacts, he was introduced to the circle of the London

Benthamites, including James and John Stuart Mill and Nassau Senior, who were soon to be of importance in his intellectual and political development. He also met Alexis de Tocqueville, who attended a meeting of the Manchester Statistical Society, spoke with Kay, and gave a description of Little Ireland which draws on Kay's or perhaps results from his having been taken there by Kay. The young Cavour was another to seek out Kay when visiting Manchester.[85]

Kay was sufficiently well-known to be the butt of public and private jokes. On one occasion Dr Edward Carbutt, renowned for his eccentricities and sarcasm, was heard to remark when Kay was summoned from the dinner table to attend a patient: 'Confound it, I quite forgot to tell my servant to send for me.' The *Squib*, a journal which described itself as 'a satire on passing events in Lancashire', also attacked the serious-minded Kay. It included an item on a book he was supposed to publish: 'A TREATISE on the PROPAGATION OF SEA COCKLES, with a full account of their Habits and Amours. By Dr. J.P.K.' On 31 October 1832, as the second edition of his pamphlet was in preparation, the *Squib* announced that there was shortly to be published

> The DIARY of a PHYSICIAN, (after Blackwood's). Being an Essay on the *Manners*, *Customs*, and *Habits*, of *Fashionable Life*, with *Cuts*; to which will be added a *K.* to the *Art of Introduction*, to the Higher Class; same size, and intended for binding with, 'The Moral and Political Condition of the Working Classes.' – By *M. D. K.* 8vo, bound in *Brass*.

The author had not been given free admission to all the Public Rooms, the *Squib* continued, and so had not had 'that early opportunity of introducing himself to the *elite* of Fashionable Society he anticipated'. He was said to be ready to trade six copies of the announced work, and a '*gratuitous prescription*', for admission tickets to the Exchange and Portico News Rooms.[86]

Other prominent Mancunians were mocked by the *Squib*, but Kay had neither the same sense of humour nor the self-confidence to be amused, especially as, about this time, he was more than usually intent on becoming acceptable in fashionable society. He was courting Helen Kennedy, whose mother, June, was the widow of James Kennedy, a member of the powerful Unitarian cotton family whose acquaintance Kay had many opportunities to make through the dispensary and his other activities. This courtship is the first known example of Kay's relationships with women other than his mother and sister. He was about 27 when it began, and the extent of his sexual experience (whatever may have happened with the girl in Edinburgh to whom his cousin James had introduced him) can only be guessed at. Certainly the stern physician mocked by the *Squib* would not seem immediately attractive to women (or for that matter, men) and, as his courtship of Helen Kennedy showed, he was not a quick learner.

The affair surfaced in idyllic circumstances: at Elleray on Lake Windermere where June Kennedy was holidaying with her six children in the autumn of 1833. In reply to 'the very agreeable things' in a letter which Kay had written her, she welcomed his coming to Elleray. They had plenty of room, the weather was beautiful and they were so entranced with the Lake District scenery that they were reluctant to return to Manchester. However, suffering lurked beneath the placid surface of June Kennedy's warm and unaffected letter. As the family doctor, Kay had helped the Kennedys through the distress caused by the death of a child, and had simultaneously come to see June as a sympathetic figure to whom he could pour out 'my pursuits, my prospects, my hopes – and lastly my heart'. While pouring out his emotions to the mother, he lost his heart to her daughter and, some 18 months before the visit to Elleray, had confided his feelings to his mother and June Kennedy. For all her sympathy, once she was involved in the politics of marriage, which newly rich cotton families treated cautiously, June Kennedy refused to allow her eldest daughter to marry a physician with uncertain financial prospects. She insisted that any engagement wait on an improvement in his financial affairs and that in the meantime he should not declare his feelings to Helen. She had given Kay's struggle for professional success a double urgency.[87]

At Elleray the 18 months' truce collapsed, and Kay spoke to Helen, who was the same age as he, while they were out walking. He obtained what he described as an 'implied compact' – he might hope for an engagement if he waited a little longer and was discreet in the attentions he paid her. He did neither: on 4 January 1834, about three months after the visit to Elleray, Kay arrived at Ancoats Hall, the Kennedys' home, carrying a written proposal. He did not deliver his letter but he and Helen and June Kennedy had a distressing meeting which left each of them shaken. To lack of money, and probably suspect political views, Kay had added a blatant disregard for etiquette. A looming rejection had stoked his fear of being found unworthy and eroded his judgement of reality as well as his appreciation of etiquette.[88]

Helen Kennedy asked him not to come to Ancoats for some time as his presence brought 'nothing but unhappiness to all, but more particularly to yourself and to me' and, understanding his temperament, she begged him not to let 'this painful subject dwell too deeply on your mind'. The desperate Kay took no notice and on 4 February June Kennedy had to remind him of the promises he had 'never thought necessary to attend to'. Yet while threatening to prohibit visits to Ancoats until such time as he could 'pay them with propriety', she insisted that she was 'as warmly your friend as ever I was in my life'. He had, however, to remember that 'there is such a thing as prudence'.[89] Kay's increasingly erratic and importunate behaviour showed he cared neither for propriety nor prudence.

On 10 February, only six days after June Kennedy's reminder of his failed promises, Kay showed how importunate he had become, and how out of touch with reality. He sent Helen a shortened version of the undelivered letter of 4 January. 'Dear Miss Kennedy,' his astonishing letter began, 'To lose your friendship, would be the source of so much suffering to me, that I am sure you would not willingly punish me so severely.' He continued:

> When I risk the possession of what I prize so highly, by declaring that I have long felt for you an affection, to describe which friendship is much too feeble a word, I feel, the presumption implied in the avowal of such a sentiment may expose me to a diminution of the kind confidence with which you have regarded me. Nevertheless, I can neither extinguish the sentiment, nor would its extinction contribute to my happiness.

Accordingly he asked her to accept 'the undivided affection which I offer you'. They had known each other long and closely, and she realized that he was 'of a peculiar temperament – having capacities for enjoyment and suffering so attuned, that the disappointment of my affections, when once placed on a legitimate object, would not be with me, a momentary feeling'. This was 'the only plea which I will prefer'.

His pain would be reduced if he believed that her happiness would be promoted by her refusing him. But he did not want to risk the 'bitter regret' he would suffer if he failed to ask her to marry and thus forfeited the pleasure of 'ministering to your happiness'. He was not rich and had not been fortunate, but he had enjoyed as much success as a man of his age could hope for, and she could estimate his prospects, position in society, connections and ability. If she

Extract from a letter from James Phillips Kay to Helen Kennedy, 10 February 1834 consented 'to share the results of my exertions', all his powers would be concentrated on securing for her 'the station which you ought to fill'. Mrs Kennedy knew of his sentiments, had no objection to him personally, and in fact held him in esteem and high regard. He had endeavoured to promote her happiness with much sacrifice to himself, and was willing to undergo any suffering for the same end. He would always regard the sentiment he avowed as fortunate, whether it brought him happiness or disappointment, because it had inspired him 'with nobler purposes and firmer and more virtuous resolutions, than any feeling which I have ever cherished'. He signed himself 'Affectionately and unalterably yours, J.P. Kay', and appended a serenade in eight verses.[90]

The letter is neither sensitive nor subtle, for, although it is a proposal, the feelings of the writer rather than the recipient are its central concern: the risks James Kay is running, his sacrifices and suffering, his desire for Helen's happiness, the disappointment he is contemplating, the bitter regret he does not wish to contemplate, his despondency, his own peculiar temperament. Occasionally in the serenade, though he is still self-preoccupied, some genuine feeling peeps through his literary and emotional contrivances:

> But in my soul the secret still
> Hath grown, until its power
> Usurps the mastery of my will;
> And, at this midnight hour,
> Beneath thy lattice, am I come to tell,
> How long this heart hath loved thee, and how well!

But almost always his love for Helen Kennedy is hidden by his determination to win her consent, and his desperate fear that he will not, so that his proposal's tense, self-regarding (but not self-aware) sentences constantly unbalance into pomposity. It is hard to know which is the more frightening, Kay's lack of appreciation of the likely impact of his letter or his failure to understand his own feelings. A close personal relationship in which he became involved had a good chance of ending in tragedy or black farce.

Helen Kennedy replied gently that she did not want to cause him pain, but 'principle' and a regard for 'your happiness and my own' prevented her from entering into an engagement. 'I do not say that you are an indifferent person to me', she wrote, 'and I hope you will believe that I am grateful for your preference.' June Kennedy was more forthright. On 15 February, insisting that she had Helen's support, she pointed out that he had broken his promises and paid little attention to her wishes, so: 'I have no confidence in your discretion, and must tell you determinedly that I *cannot* and *will* not permit your visits here at present.' He was to rally his mind, give himself up to duty, prove that he could be as resolute as he was superior in talent, take care of his health for he could not misuse it without sin, and be assured that she felt for him 'the most sincere and warm friendship'.[91]

On the same day Kay wrote an aggressive letter to June Kennedy. 'With so full a view of my character and so long a trial of my affections what have you seen wrong in me? With such a claim upon your sympathies will you destroy me?' he asked. 'Before we part at this crisis,' he insisted, 'let us have a few last words, lest we deceive ourselves.' Then Kay showed that for him, as well as for June Kennedy, marriage had prudential considerations. The patronage of the Kennedys, especially if displayed by marriage to their daughter, could ensure his professional success, while withdrawal of that patronage would do much harm. A physician from Port Glasgow was soon to settle in Manchester, hoping for 'the patronage of the circle which my connection with your family would ensure to me'. That connection, he asserted, was of value only because it ensured her friendship and because of his affection for Helen. But as the Kennedys had raised prudential objections, he had produced some of his own. Frustrated and despairing, he attributed June Kennedy's rejection to the anxieties which afflicted her, insisted that there was no bitterness in his remarks, and expressed his thwarted affection, battered pride and damaged professional prospects in a cry of grotesque self-pity: 'I hope there is little pain in the world like mine.'[92]

June Kennedy wrote a compassionate answer whose importance she signalled by saying that she had stayed home from church to write it. She assured Kay that she felt for him 'an affection little short of maternal', but wondered why he was not content with the high estimation in which he was held – 'why ask *that*, which in present circumstances it would be contrary to my duty to grant, both on your account and her own?' She promised to write to a brother in Port Glasgow so that Kay's potential rival would learn that he faced opposition rather than support; she stressed that Kay would continue to be her personal physician; and she vowed that she would ostentatiously display her support for him. 'Do you not suppose, my dear young friend', she wrote with an affection Kay had put severely to the test, that I can ever forget the claims you have upon me, do you think I can cease to remember your watchful care, your kind and tender attentions to my poor dying child, your affectionate consolations to myself, your unwearied solicitude by night and by day, believe me it is impossible, I must ever feel the greatest interest in, and the most lively gratitude to one to whom I owe so much.[93]

Still Kay could not let things be, and he replied with a disturbed letter in which his affection, as was often the case, issued in a duty – the need 'to show you what you are about to do before it is done'. He spoke of his long forbearance and eventual decision to declare his love to Helen ('I do not know how to trifle with the feelings of an amiable woman'), the possible damage to his professional prospects ('If I no longer occasionally appear with your family after having been in some sort inseparable from them, one conclusion only can be found viz. that I am banished'), and his fears for the future. His angry and anguished self-righteousness inoculated him against the warmth and concern of June Kennedy's letter, but made it harder for her to retain that warmth. In her reply she admitted that her affection for him may have 'occasioned admissions which I ought not to have allowed' but which seemed to have conveyed more 'than I ever contemplated'. She pointed out: 'I never for a moment accused you of mercenary motives, if you suppose so, you did both me and your-self injustice.' Then, in commenting on his financial position, she permitted herself a sentence whose ambiguity was surely deliberate: 'That was, and is, the only objection I shall advance.'[94]

In an amazingly insensitive tribute to her tolerance, Kay chose this moment to ask her opinion of a letter he had written to the Duke of Northumberland which formed the preface of a book he was about to publish on asphyxia. 'It must be excellent,' she managed to say, 'because I who am an ignorant person feel as if I understand it perfectly. . . . I hope to see it published soon, and that the enlightened author may reap all the advantage which in my poor opinion he is so well entitled to.' The affair did not end on this bizarre note. Within a month Kay had returned to the charge, forcing June Kennedy to say, 'You may overpower me by entreaty, and perplex me by false promises, but half an hour's calm reflection will always bring me back to the same, and only rational conclusion': he should visit her house only if invited. And she passed on Helen's 'decisive wish' that he should realize that 'everything between you and her is now at an end'.[95]

A few days later Kay told James Williamson that he was considering abandoning medicine. Williamson thought that his success had been 'distinguished in relation to those of your own standing', and attributed his limited prosperity to the overcrowding of the profession and to his having given 'direct offence by the plain, and powerful, enunciation of truth, on many of the topics of political economy, and general politics'. It was dangerous for a medical man to become involved in politics because a 'mere drudge and plodding routinist is thought a safer and more judicious practitioner, than the man who writes and speaks especially out of his profession'. Williamson also suggested that Kay had dissociated himself from 'that class of the religious world in Manchester, where you had most legitimate hold' – Kay's frequent mixing with the Unitarians may have alienated his co-religionists. Williamson decided that if Kay could make £300 a year he should stay in Manchester, though that income would not justify 'a matrimonial connection'. With exclusive dedication to his profession he might hope to obtain £500 or £600 a year, but not for three or four years. This was not advice which Kay wished to hear, particularly as it was realistic. His situation was not unusual: a medical practitioner without powerful connections could easily spend ten years before achieving a reasonable income. Of course Kay was still young, but as Webb has remarked, his feelings of despair were no less real because of that.[96]

While Kay struggled to come to terms with his position in Manchester his father's health was failing. He was frequently called to give medical attention but, despite his ministrations, Robert Kay died of heart failure on 25 April 1834. Kay immediately assumed leadership of the family, as his mother expected him to do. His brother Robert, now married and living in Birmingham but plagued by anxiety and depression as he struggled to expand his apothecary's business by selling medical tests and equipment, had always consulted him as if he were a superior being. Hannah, his sister, willingly trapped by custom and her own generosity, looked to his advice while she devoted her life to her mother and the upbringing of her three youngest brothers. A letter from Robert McAll, the minister of the Mosley Street Independent Chapel, praised Kay's attention to his father and his father's holiness, but there is no other reference to Robert Kay's death in the surviving correspondence. However, dutiful son that he was, Kay knew that his advancement had not been as rapid as his father had hoped. Yet, as he stood for his father's burial in Bamford Chapel amidst the scenes of his boyhood, newer scenes – Edinburgh and Manchester, the Royal Medical

Society and the Manchester Statistical Society, cholera hospitals and Reform Bill meetings, Little Ireland and Ancoats Hall – intruded between him and the harsh but simpler world of his childhood.[97]

An outsider at Bamford, Kay had the Kennedys to remind him, on his return to Manchester, that he was still an outsider there. Early in May 1834, as if to signify the end of the relationship, Kay sent 'Mrs James Kennedy' a bill for four years' medical attention to herself, her family and servants. But in August, again in the Lake District, Kay moved briefly back into the Kennedy circle. Helen's 25-year old sister, Jane, begged him to attend Amelia, another sister, at Rydal where they were holidaying. She admitted that recent events had made her request a painful one, but she made it 'without any doubt of your sympathy and assistance or of your misunderstanding it'. 'My mother is in Scotland', she said. 'We are quite inexperienced. You are the physician upon whose skill and friendship we can depend.' Kay paid a brief visit to Rydal and, although Helen returned to Manchester immediately he arrived, his relations with the Kennedys were cordial. By mid-September Amelia had recovered sufficiently to be propped up with pillows and to be driven about in the phaeton. Then, as the swallows began to leave Rydal, the Kennedys and other holiday makers moved in slow procession back to Manchester.[98]

The autumnal calm was broken in October or early November when, again in the absence of her mother, Jane Kennedy gave Kay a shattering piece of information: Helen had fallen in love with another member of the Kennedy circle, Thomas Hamilton, a solicitor. Jane Kennedy thought that Kay received the news with 'generosity and forbearance', and explained that no one except another sister, Eliza, had known of the relationship until immediately before his visit to Rydal. Distressed by Amelia's illness, they had rejected their first thought which was to tell him the news, and he had assumed, as they guessed he would, that Helen's leaving Rydal was due to the events earlier in the year. Jane Kennedy explained that she had tried to speak to him on a number of occasions but had not been able to bring herself to do so. She realized that Kay's mother 'will blame much, but that unhappily is only just', and admitted that 'it will be a relief to my mother to know that you have been told all', adding that her mother had suffered from extreme anxiety because of the fear that Kay might misunderstand her conduct towards him.[99]

Kay asked what he should do and an embarrassed Jane Kennedy told him that he should 'consult *your own feelings* in all respects. Ask anything you wish, you are well entitled'. She did, however, request him to keep the matter confidential as only the near relatives knew of the surprising turn of events, and she remarked that his behaviour had 'if possible increased both our regard for you and our regret for what has happened'. Kay tested this regard the next day by sending her a note which he said was never to be shown to her sister. 'A prudent man', he admitted, 'would not reply to your note in the state of agitation which I suffer', but he had 'lost all claim to such a character'. He had re-read the correspondence which had passed between him and the Kennedys since March and had decided that he was justified in believing that Helen Kennedy had 'preferred me to any other person'. With more dignity than he had been able to muster earlier in the year, he expressed his regard for the family and for Helen, and gave an assurance that he would give 'the most solicitous attention' to the family, stressing that his attitude was one of 'an instinct not of a calculation' and that if they ceased to wish for his professional advice 'it will be a burden to me to give it'. Only at the end of his letter did his bitterness get the upper hand. He recalled two adages 'so ominous that I remember them with fear': 'Let not the ashes of our love be hatred' and 'Canst it be possible that those who suffer only remember their former affliction?' He also wrote to Helen Kennedy. Having erased one outburst of self-pity ('I am altogether absorbed by the contemplation of my overwhelming misfortune'), he told her more directly and simply than he had previously managed that he could 'never hope to fill the void you would have me make in my heart'. He said this not to make her grieve 'but that you may not unjustly think that I loved you briefly or that I can cease to do so'. Neither of them had been sullied by contact with the world, he remarked somewhat enigmatically, and ended his letter by deciding to say no more, lest he create 'one fresh grief' by what he wrote.[100]

Kay vented his anger in a flurry of aggressive exchanges with two friends and members of the Statistical Society, William Langton and John Douglas. The nature of their supposed offence is not clear, though Kay's imperious bitterness is very obvious. Their generosity and a dawning sense of reality in Kay ensured that the friendships survived the exchange. 'I do not understand all that has passed', Kay admitted to Douglas. To Jane Kennedy he had written, 'We have I fear played out a sad drama of follies.' The more extraordinary follies were his, and the greatest sadness. The drama had revealed that behind the cholera doctor issuing instructions to his patients and the pamphleteer who confidently prescribed for the nation, there lurked a 30-year-old so lacking in self-confidence and self-awareness that rejection could drive him beyond all bounds of prudence, propriety or even dignity.[101]

During his disastrous courtship of Helen Kennedy Kay continued to work on medical matters other than the building up of his practice. In 1834 he produced *The Physiology, Pathology, and Treatment of Asphyxia* in which he republished but also extended some of his earlier research challenging Bichat's work. Kay also demonstrated the implications of his research for the treatment of 'suspended animation', particularly the resuscitation through artificial respiration of those rescued from drowning. The introductory letter to the Duke of Northumberland was aimed at changing some instructions issued by the Royal Humane Society, of which the Duke was President, and persuading the society to accept Kay's views. The letter gave a clear, popular account of the problems discussed in more technical terms in the book.

Kay had every reason to be gratified by the reception of *Asphyxia* which established him as a medical researcher of some skill. Nearly 90 years after publication it was the subject of favourable comment by Sir James Mackenzie. In his *Diseases of the Heart*, he praised Kay's ingenious experimental work and sharp observations, some of which, he concluded, were in advance of what was being done in the 1920s. The gloss may have been dulled when Dr David Williams of Liverpool claimed in the *Lancet* that Kay had failed to give him credit for an 1823 article in the *Edinburgh Medical and Surgical Journal* in which he had anticipated one of Kay's conclusions. Kay replied that when he had written his article in the same journal in 1828 neither he, nor Alison, nor those who had heard him deliver papers on his findings were aware of Williams's article. He pointed out that when he learned of it in 1831 he had added a note of acknowledgement to his article on asphyxia in the *North of England Medical and Surgical Journal* and had retained that note when the article was reproduced in *The Physiology, Pathology, and Treatment of Asphyxia*, as he had 'conceived it to be most natural and just to print everything as it first appeared'. Williams was understandably aggrieved that in a book devoted to asphyxia his work had been confined to a note, even if Kay could claim, probably legitimately, that his research was more advanced and more comprehensive than Williams's. Nor would Kay have been satisfied when a colleague from Liverpool, W.H. Duncan, reported that Alison, while confirming his and Kay's ignorance of Williams's earlier work and acknowledging that Kay's work was based on more numerous and varied experiments, had the previous winter mentioned Dr Williams's paper as 'prior to Dr. Kay, and tending to establish the same point', and had added Williams's name to 'Dr. Kay's as authorities on which I rely'. Alison had reiterated the high esteem in which he held Kay but wanted to do justice to all. Kay decided that 'a precedency in the merit of having made these discoveries' was a question 'only very remotely connected with the advancement of science', and he declined any further discussion. The controversy seems to have lapsed but neither Kay nor Williams could have been completely satisfied.[102]

Kay also became involved in efforts to establish new medical societies. A meeting of the West Riding Charitable Society at Pontefract in July 1833 floated the idea of a North of England Medical and Surgical Association (NEMSA). A committee, chaired by James Williamson, met at Wakefield on 4 October and approved the establishment of an association to promote medical science, publish papers on important topics, collect statistics, and record hospital and clinical experiences – aims remarkably close to those Kay had held for his journal. It was decided to form four district associations, one of which was to cover Lancashire, and on 29 January 1834 at the York Hotel in Manchester, a committee, of which Kay was a member, decided to organize a district association. Nine months later the committee was planning to meet a similar group from Yorkshire to frame rules for a general association, but progress left much to be desired. Just as Kay's journal had met competition from a journal launched by Charles Hastings, so this association competed with Hastings's Provincial Medical and Surgical Association. Most Manchester doctors supported the NEMSA, but the rival association was strong in Liverpool. As the NEMSA struggled, Kay's emotional condition worsened. He was in the midst of the Helen Kennedy affair and he took out his many frustrations on Williamson. 'Reiterated admonitions, and taunts on my alleged habits of procrastination, and on my criminal indifference, and apathy on the subject of the association are almost the only topics of your letters', Williamson complained. He did not wish to lose Kay's friendship, but 'the tone of some of your late letters, has been very trying to my sentiments of regard for you'.[103]

As Kay quarrelled with Williamson and the NEMSA faded, another medical society took shape. The York Hotel meeting in January 1834 had decided to establish a medical library, reading room and society, but matters languished until August when two enthusiastic doctors started a canvass of their colleagues to persuade them to pledge £2.2.0 each to start the society. Kay was one of the first to pledge support – among those who declined were Charles Henry and a doctor who said that he read nothing except newspapers. On 4 September the Manchester Medical Society was begun. It swiftly evolved an elaborate set of rules and organized the library and reading room. Kay was a member of its council and regularly attended its meetings, ordering numerous books for the library and presenting it with a copy of the *North of England Medical and Surgical Journal*. Its relatively speedy success may have been some consolation for the slow progress of the NEMSA.[104]

On 4 May 1835 Charles Henry resigned from the Manchester Royal Infirmary to further his chemical studies in Germany, thus reopening the door which he had previously closed on Kay. On 9 May, with five other physicians, Kay announced his candidature, claiming that he was mindful of 'warm support' given seven years earlier and that he had endeavoured to make himself 'not unworthy of the kind promises of future favour then extensively made to me'. He launched himself into the public round of electioneering with vigour, and as the Infirmary Board examined the medical qualifications of the candidates and made arrangements for the poll, including the provision of a room in which women trustees could vote, Kay strove to gain every advantage. He advertised widely, had an active supporting committee and pressed his family into service. The weekly meeting of the Infirmary Board on 25 May, three days before the election, announced a substantial benefaction of 30 guineas from his cousin James Openshaw Kay. On the same day the *Manchester Guardian* carried a report of a meeting of the Mechanics' Institute attended by Lord Brougham, who sat on the platform with 'several gentlemen of high standing and respectability', including Benjamin Heywood, John Dalton, and Dr J.P. Kay. Two days earlier Kay had advertised his book on asphyxia in the *Guardian* and included extracts from a number of favourable reviews.[105]

By the time the election took place at the Infirmary in Piccadilly on 28 May, the only candidates remaining were Kay and Dr Charles Phillips, a physician at the Chorlton-upon-Medlock Dispensary. Phillips won easily, 503 votes to 324. The next day Kay prepared the requisite advertisement thanking his supporters and assuring them that he would try to justify their preference by 'continued attention to the duties of my station, hoping that at some future period the honourable responsibilities of physician to this most important charity, may be committed to my care'. In 1832, reflecting on Kay's involvement in politics, John Symonds had remarked: 'Perhaps it is not a matter of importance to you whether you get patients or not'. Looking back at the election late in his life, Charles Henry well understood why Kay had been rejected: he had involved himself in politics 'more eagerly than was prudent or consistent with medical success', allowing Phillips to obtain the support of the conservatives who were the most influential group among the trustees. For Kay, who might have expected this reaction, the defeat came as a shattering blow. He had waited and worked for seven years to obtain a position vital for his professional success and his personal self-esteem. It had been denied him. Despite his work at the dispensary, at the Board of Health, with the journal, the various medical associations, and the statistical and provident societies, he was still an outsider. Undoubtedly his personality contributed to his failure, but he was also a victim of the conflicts within middle-class Manchester. First Helen Kennedy, who had married on 29 April, a few days before Henry's resignation, and then the Infirmary trustees had preferred a safer man.[106]

He collapsed emotionally and physically, just as he had at the end of his studies in Edinburgh. He recorded in his *Autobiography* that he was told to seek a complete change of scene and occupation, 'live much in the open air, and divert my thoughts from subjects which had become a source of exhausting feeling and thought'. His political activities and his efforts to expose 'sanitary and social evils' had worked against him, and he feared that his second failure meant that a career as a physician in Manchester was 'likely to be closed by the denial to me of the chief means of scientific study'. While in this state of depression and uncertainty he was offered, for two years and through the influence of Nassau Senior, the position of Assistant Poor Law Commissioner in Norfolk and Suffolk. He accepted and was sworn in at Chancery Lane on 11 July 1835.[107]

There is a dubious air of calculated rationality in the account Kay gave of his last weeks in Manchester. By the time he wrote his *Autobiography*, memory had formed a protective cocoon around his suffering, hiding from his ageing mind the despair of 1835. A collapse of health and his Infirmary disappointment may explain why he left

Manchester but they do not explain why, after a decade's intense commitment to medicine, he fled from the profession and never resumed it. Why did he not, for example, get the benefit of the open air of Suffolk and Norfolk by trying to build a medical practice there? He had earlier considered playing a wider part in public life than that of a provincial physician, as was shown by his efforts to be appointed to Chadwick's commission, and an unsuccessful attempt he made for a similar position in 1833. But when he did leave Manchester his behaviour, far from being a decisive career change, was marked by uncertainty, secrecy and haste. Without tidying up his affairs he cut himself adrift from his private practice, the dispensary, the medical associations, and the statistical and provident societies which had consumed so much of his attention. He left his mother and sister to fend off questions from friends who had only a partial understanding of his new appointment, instructing them to give no information about the date of his return to Manchester or even about whether he planned to return. He left letters unanswered and bills unpaid – including that of the printer of his election material. Patients delayed treatment expecting that he might come back, landlords kept rooms for him, and the handling of his father's estate was delayed. His writings had shown an interest in the administration of the Poor Law, but his appointment as an assistant commissioner was not a thoughtful change of career direction but a hasty and embarrassed flight from the scene of major personal and professional setbacks.[108]

The James Kay who left Manchester in July 1835 was a tragic figure. He had come seven years earlier knowing that he faced a struggle to establish himself but buoyed by his Edinburgh triumphs. He had done what was required for success. He had joined the Literary and Philosophical Society, made connections with important families, and been active at the dispensary and the Board of Health. He had founded and edited a medical journal and, through that journal and the medical associations, had played his part in the profession's efforts to establish its own identity. He had continued his scientific investigations and had published a well-received book. Yet he had failed: economically, because his private practice was not substantial enough for him to contemplate marriage; professionally, because he had not gained acceptance at the Infirmary; and, in his family's eyes, because he was abandoning his medical career.

He was also an outsider politically. He had rejected the aristocracy. He had unusual insight into, and some sympathy with, the problems of the working class, but he was deeply ambivalent towards their culture and, as the Knott Mill hospital taught him, they were suspicious of him. To the conservative middle class he was a liberal Dissenter whose pamphlet had painted an unjust picture of Manchester and who wanted local government to be strengthened so that it could interfere in some of their activities. His opinions on sanitation and occupational health, the use of statistics, the power of education and the possibility of a social science might not have condemned him to the intellectual loneliness of the pioneer, but in many quarters they were advanced and suspect. In his religious beliefs he was in a similar position, having moved away from the simple fervour of his Bamford days towards a more rationalistic religion, though he had not adopted the theology of the Unitarians. Finally, as his courtship of Helen Kennedy and his quarrel with Williamson proved, he could not count on personal charm to smooth his way: at the best of times he was anxious and intense and, when faced with rejection, was driven by his own insecurity into irrational and unconventional behaviour. At most levels of his life – his personal popularity, his self-esteem, his relationship with his family, his position in Manchester's class battles, his professional status, economic standing, political opinions and religious beliefs – he was more isolated, more markedly an outsider, more at the mercy of the swirling tides of his time than he had been on his arrival from Edinburgh. Manchester, to which he had given so intensely, had refused him everything. Sick, depressed, ashamed of his failures, and remembering Ancoats Hall and Piccadilly as the sites of especially demoralizing defeats, he fled to the East Anglian countryside.

The scenes there were very different from those which greeted de Tocqueville when he looked at Manchester's factories and reflected:

> Here is the slave, there the master; there the wealth of some, here the poverty of most; there the organised efforts of thousands produce, to the profit of one man, what society has not yet learned to give. Here the weakness of the individual seems more feeble and helpless even than in the middle of a wilderness. . . .[109]

The day before he wrote these words de Tocqueville spoke to Kay at the Statistical Society, not knowing that Kay was preparing to leave Manchester because he had learned only too well of the individual's weakness in the face of larger forces.

4 · Assistant Poor Law Commissioner, 1835–39

Early in Kay's new career Thomas Frankland Lewis, one of the three Poor Law Commissioners, suggested that he should consult another assistant commissioner, Major Francis Bond Head. 'I suppose', Head asked Kay, 'you are fond of hunting?' Kay replied that he was inexperienced because, in the parts of Lancashire which he knew best, high stone walls divided the fields. 'Then', Head remarked,

> you have just the most profitable experience. Think what you do when you are riding your horse at a high stone wall. You settle well in the saddle. You let him know by the pressure of your knees that you have a firm resolve. Perhaps you let him feel the spur, and you put him at his work with a will which convinces him that you will take no denial, but over he must go.

From someone called 'Galloping' Head this was predictable advice; predictably the uncertain James Kay took it.[1]

The power of being an assistant Poor Law commissioner did not corrupt Kay. It had a more disastrous effect: he became a zealot who stormed through Suffolk, and later Norfolk, determined to banish the curse of pauperism. Manchester had rejected him, but in East Anglian paupers he found a clientele which needed his ministrations desperately. A protest that they did not, or a reluctance to listen to him, merely reinforced Kay's belief in the paupers' need, and he worked the harder to overcome their hesitancy.

Before the passage of the 1834 Poor Law Amendment Act, the legislative basis of nineteenth-century poor relief was the Elizabethan Act for the Relief of the Poor (1601). It made each parish responsible for the poor within its boundaries and required the levying of a compulsory rate, which was collected and controlled by unpaid officials, the overseers of the poor. Poor relief, though seen as a personal service given in familiar surroundings by people known to the recipients, reaffirmed the social and economic hierarchy. The poor were at the mercy of overseers, drawn principally from the ranks of shopkeepers and farmers, who were in turn supervised by the gentry in their capacity as magistrates. As, over the centuries, parishes interpreted the law for themselves, a uniform national policy did not develop. Nevertheless, poor relief came to be regarded as a right. To attempt reform was to threaten the equilibrium of English social life, for the Poor Law trapped the poor and their betters in an intricate and ancient web of vested interest, dependence and class conflict.[2]

The chief protagonist of the Poor Law Amendment Act, Edwin Chadwick (Manchester-born and married to Rachel Kennedy, a cousin of Helen Kennedy), insisted that the Old Poor Law had corrupted English society. At high cost to the ratepayer it had rewarded the indolent and the deceitful, mocked the efforts of the independent labourer, and robbed paupers of initiative and self-respect. Chadwick attacked officials who winked at fraud, benefited from it or were cowed into accepting it; farmers who relied on poor relief to cover the inadequate wages they paid; excessively lenient magistrates; and laxly administered workhouses which sheltered violent, degraded or apathetic paupers. They were particularly disturbed by the allowance system, which permitted the giving of relief outside the workhouse by the payment of an allowance. Throughout the 1820s it was widely believed that the cost of poor relief, and especially of the allowance system, had grown inordinately. Assessments of the Old Poor Law and the cost of outdoor relief are still subjects of controversy, but contemporary opponents pointed to growth in the annual bill. From £1,500,000 in 1775 it had risen to £8,000,000 in 1818 and, though the price of bread had dropped by one third, poor relief still cost £7,000,000 in 1832. Calls for its abolition, which owed much to Malthus even if they distorted what he had said, became frequent.[3]

The economic difficulties of the 1820s, culminating in bad harvests from 1828 to 1830, and the eruption of rural violence in the Swing Riots of 1830, emphasized that the Poor Law had not provided the stability which might have reconciled property owners to its cost. However, it was one thing to be aghast at its expensive ineffectiveness; it was another to find a remedy. The Whig government, lacking policies to guide it through the Poor Law's minefield and pre-occupied with Parliamentary Reform, procrastinated until 1832 when it appointed a Royal Commission. Four of the commission's seven members had Benthamite links, which were strengthened in

1833 when Chadwick, who had been Bentham's private secretary, joined it. Chadwick and his friend (and Kay's patron) Nassau Senior, previously Professor of Political Economy at Oxford, produced the *Poor Law Report*, which provided the basis for the Poor Law Amendment Act passed in August 1834.[4]

The Act bore clear marks of Bentham as interpreted by Chadwick. It established the Poor Law Commission with power to decide how relief would be given. Assistant commissioners were to enforce the commission's policies, and parishes were to be joined into larger Unions administered by elected boards of guardians who appointed the Union's officials. Poor relief was to be given only in the workhouse, so that an end could be made to outdoor relief – 'the great source of abuse', the *Poor Law Report* called it. Thus the workhouse came to symbolize the New Poor Law, though it had been in existence for centuries, and parishes had long had the power of denying relief to those who refused to enter it. Through the workhouse, the New Poor Law separated the labour of the pauper from that of the able-bodied. Simultaneously, its administrators enforced Bentham's principle of 'less eligibility' – the condition of the recipient of relief was to be less eligible (or more unpleasant) than that of the independent worker. So, in the pitiless logic of the New Poor Law, pauperism would eventually be ended, dignity restored to the labourers of England, and the burden of the poor rates lifted.[5]

With the Act passed, the government appointed the three Commissioners whose work was to be supervised by Lord John Russell, the Home Secretary. Chadwick had a formidable grasp of Poor Law affairs and had been the driving force in formulating the Act, but he was passed over for Thomas Frankland Lewis, a Tory (which helped to defuse claims of Whig jobbery), George Nicholls, who had experience and some reputation in Poor Law reform and J.G. Shaw-Lefevre, a young Whig whose appointment has been described as 'an out-and-out job'. An embittered Chadwick was made secretary, given some hope of eventually becoming a Commis-sioner, and informed that his lack of rank and station had prevented his appointment. There was truth in the claim, but fear of Chadwick's doctrinaire and insensitive integrity also made the government reluctant to appoint him. He held unrelentingly to the belief that 'the process of dis-pauperizing the able-bodied is in its ultimate effects a process which elevates the condition of the great mass of society'.[6] Also possessed by this belief, James Kay descended upon the paupers like an Old Testament prophet come to call them to judgement.

Kay arrived in Suffolk early in August 1835, and from February 1836, after the illness of the assistant commissioner, Sir Edward Parry, Norfolk was added to his responsibilities. He administered both counties until he was transferred to London in July 1838.

However, he made his first mistake before he left Manchester. In 1834 Edmund Ashworth from the Bolton cotton family suggested to Edwin Chadwick that the shortage of labour in the northern textile districts might be relieved by migration from the pauperized south. Pressure from others, including the Gregs, followed, and eventually the Commissioners instructed Kay to investigate. On 22 July 1835, only eleven days after his appointment as an assistant commissioner, he sent a report from his home in St Peter's Square. He argued that, though migration from the northern counties explained much of the increase in Lancashire's population, 'one source of a vast supply' was Ireland. As he had done in his 1832 pamphlet, Kay expressed 'the deepest and most sincere commiseration of the sufferings of that gallant but degraded race', and then blamed the Irish for the decline in 'the manners, habits and domestic comfort' among the people of the cotton districts.[7]

Kay set about obtaining 'exact statistical data'. He calculated that the steam power in operation or likely to be introduced in the next two years required an additional 90,000 people, and claimed that, unless other arrangements were made, the Irish 'would come over in crowds'. Migration from the south would provide an alternative, while relieving the distress in those districts. He suggested that an agent in Manchester might mediate between the millowners and the assistant commissioners from the south to ensure a proper selection of workmen. He believed that the most suitable were widows, or craftsmen such as shoemakers and blacksmiths, with large families – he clearly had child labour in mind. The migrants were to go to country districts where they would have an easier transition from agricultural life and avoid the evils of the city. Kay visited families who had migrated from the south, inspected various cotton establishments, and decided that the migrants might earn three times as much as a southern labourer. He concluded: 'A more gratifying tour I never performed, as nothing could be more cheering than the gratitude which the immigrants universally expressed for the change which the Commissioners had accomplished in their condition'.[8]

In case the Commissioners overlooked this best of all possible worlds, Kay wrote them a long letter from London about a week later emphasizing that the supply of labour should be related to a demand 'so legitimate as to be in every respect unquestionable, and, with such caution, that the supply never can overstep the actual wants of the manufacturers'. Kay saw the agent as 'the Protector of the interests of the labourers' against manufacturers and he detailed a tabular register he wanted the agent to construct. Indefatigable and obsessional, he listed questions which Boards of Guardians in the south might ask potential migrants, and he proposed a 'manual of directions'; with a hint of encouragement he would have written it himself. He also told the Commissioners that the southern labourers should not wear 'that distinguishing southern dress, the *smock frock*, nor the half boot, by both of which they would be distinguished from the population of the district'. With enlightened masters, they would become 'more and more accustomed to the long labour of the factories' while the 'independent, intrepid, and active workmen of the north' might learn softer ways from their 'gentle southern countrymen' and 'smooth the ruggedness of their exteriors, and the uncouthness of their address'.[9]

Kay's use of internal migration to combat overpopulation and social disruption was a variant of the more drastic remedy of emigration and appealed to the manufacturers, though many of them considered the appointment of an agent as unnecessary centralization. The scheme, which operated from October 1835 until May 1837 when it collapsed amidst a deepening depression, probably did not add significantly to the migration which was taking place independently, and did not fulfil Kay's expectations. But its failure owed nothing to lack of endeavour. Of the 4,323 migrants from 17 counties who came north, 2,711 were from Norfolk and Suffolk, the next most prolific contributor being Buckinghamshire with 389.[10]

Kay was an easy target for opponents of the New Poor Law. In 1836 a letter in *The Times* attacked the conflict between his migration policies and his pamphlet, which a defensive Kay described as 'this slight work'. In the same year John Fielden, the Radical cotton manufacturer who had known Kay in Manchester, identified him as an authority on the 'pernicious effects' of factory labour and condemned his efforts to persuade the gentry and farmers to send the 'redundant supply' of rustic infants down into the manufacturing districts, and the parents to comply in this species of what is called '*home colonization*'! A proposition at which I shudder, when I recal (*sic*) to mind the fate of the '*Factory Apprentice*', and one that I should have thought Dr. KAY himself would not have been the man to promulgate . . .

He flung Kay's own words back at him when explaining that weavers would not enter the factories because of the long hours, and he referred to their mental and physical anguish, which drove them to cheat their sufferings 'by the false excitement procured by ardent spirits'.[11]

In 1841, three years after migration had finished, the Ultra Tory, G.W. Ferrand, suggested that the plan, like the New Poor Law itself, had 'originated in a deep-laid design between the rich cotton spinners of Lancashire and the Poor-law commissioners and assistant commissioners'. The Tory Radical, Richard Oastler, was more explicit. He mentioned *The Moral and Physical Condition of the Working Classes*, then angrily insisted that Kay had told the labourers of Suffolk and Norfolk that the factories were 'very fine, comfortable places'. Because of 'the lying delusions of that plausible demon of the Government, the poor children were transported by their own consent, thus obtained by threat and delusion, from their native fields, into the horrors of the pestilential factory'. This same Dr Kay, Oastler thundered, 'could never make a hundred pounds a-year by his wits in medicine; by his skill in deluding the poor, he makes just £1500 a-year!!' Oastler had more than doubled the salary which Kay received, but he had scored a palpable hit and, ironically, used the pamphlet which had made Manchester's cotton families suspicious of Kay to undermine his new work.[12]

The effectiveness of the attack was increased by ignoring safeguards (such as the appointment of agents) which Kay recommended but, after all allowances have been made, he was following the age-old policy of shifting the poor from their homes while preserving the system which produced their poverty.

Kay began his work in East Anglia with typical enthusiasm. He arrived in Ipswich on Monday 3 August 1835 at 3.15 a.m. and by 8 o'clock had called at the Golden Lion Inn to meet Charles Mott, the assistant commissioner whom he was replacing. They spent the day visiting workhouses, and in the evening Kay prepared to summon the churchwardens and overseers to a meeting. The next day he made an assessment of the average poor rates of Ipswich's twelve parishes for the past three years. In the evening he wrote to the Commissioners at Somerset House about what he had accomplished, the difficulties he faced, and the insolence of the paupers. 'I am much pleased', he said, 'with my new occupation. I think its functions will soon be familiar to me.'[13]

Those functions were demanding. Kay had to report upon the parishes in his district, a process which necessitated many nights in rough inns and much travelling, often by horse and gig. Before forming the parishes into Unions he was required to establish the average Poor Law rates, confer with landowners, and persuade Boards of Guardians to give him the necessary two-thirds majority. He often confronted hostile farmers, politicians, clergy, magistrates and overseers, and usually met their hostility head-on by giving a speech (of some hours in length) in which he exposed 'the confusion, waste, fraud and approaching ruin' wrought by the previous administration. When a Union was established he supervised the election of a Board of Guardians, watched the appointment of officials to prevent jobbery, ensured that a suitable workhouse was built, superintended the sale of disused parish workhouses, and enforced the regulations. Inspection of the new Unions increased his travelling and ensured that the one guinea *per diem*, added to his annual salary of £700, was soon exhausted. Though they had a clerk to assist them, assistant commissioners were under great pressure.[14]

East Anglia's geographic and cultural isolation and its predominantly rural character contrasted strongly with industrialized Manchester. In the flat, water-dominated landscape of the fens, Kay, a stranger and a northerner, had to contend with a parochial and intimate world in which petty jealousies, political feuding and economic difficulties nourished suspicion and resentment. The squire and parson retained more influence than they had in Manchester, but East Anglia had provided fertile conditions for the Swing Riots of 1830. Nevertheless, Suffolk and Norfolk had advantages for an assistant commissioner, who could count on the support of the propertied classes. Cheaper poor relief was doubly attractive because agricultural profits had been reduced after 1815, and the increased population strained an economy hit by the decay of its weaving industry. Of almost equal importance to the promise of financial savings was the hope that the Poor Law would tame a rebellious and destructive agricultural labouring force. The Norfolk gentry, having taken a close interest as the boundaries of the Unions were negotiated and the workhouses built, could leave the Boards of Guardians in the control of farmers with the comfortable knowledge that their interests were similar.[15]

Moreover, in the eighteenth century Suffolk and Norfolk had begun to group parishes into incorporations, hoping to produce a more liberal and economic system of poor relief by establishing larger houses of industry than an individual parish could provide. Kay commented that Suffolk's houses of industry 'afford such excellent means of applying the proper test at once, that, perhaps, the most extensive and earliest proofs of the correctness of the principles on which the new law is founded will be derived from this county'. By 1837 this claim looked prescient. Opposition had been bitter and the cities, especially Norwich, still presented problems, but most rural incorporations had given way to Unions – 15 in Suffolk and 18 in Norfolk – and the five rural incorporations, which had not agreed to dissolve themselves, were functioning very much as if they were Unions.[16]

Kay could afford to congratulate himself, and he did. When he left a newly formed Union in late September 1835, he remarked that the guardians were 'in good humour with their duties, and grateful to me'. He was even more delighted when leaving Blofield, a wealthy suburb of Norwich, where he had at first faced opposition; now, the Union was 'in the condition of a frog which burst while trying to swell itself to the size of an ox'. He described interchanges at meetings in which he crushed an opponent's objections, only to apologize to the Commission for writing about 'so insignificant a person. He has neither connections nor influence, and is altogether unworthy of further notice'. At other times he basked in praise from Boards of Guardians, such as that at Aylsham, which was grateful for 'the aid they have received from their Assistant Commissioner, Dr Kay, who has most kindly explained all doubtful points of the Law, and given most valuable advice on whatever subject was under discussion'.[17] They could be relied on to support Kay's crusade against the iniquities of the Old Poor Law.

'Crusade' is not too strong a word. Kay saw the pauper population as sunk in lethargy and self-destructive dependence. According to his trusted statistics, pauper children died younger than the children of independent labourers, and a pauper population had more idiots, 'more victims of scrophula, more defective and helpless beings'. A pauper's wife, Kay announced, was more likely to be a slattern, his cottage less clean, his children worse fed, he himself more profligate. Because the allowance system permitted wages to be obtained without labour 'the natural and useful relation of the labourer to his employer was destroyed; the terms of the contract for labour were dissolved; the docility and respectful demeanour of the servant gradually diminished'. The fabric of society was threatened with dissolution:

> The more intimate and close the connection between the employer and the labourer, the greater will be the strength and compactness of the social body. Whatever tends to interfere with this relation, to impair the integrity of this union, weakens the social structure. When this connection is dissolved the social compact seems virtually at an end among the mass, and external force alone can sustain what was hitherto cemented by internal cohesion.

Kay was more frighteningly certain than he had been in Manchester. Perhaps because he understood the city and had experienced its horrors, he could sometimes see the working classes as victims of a system over which they had no control. In the agricultural south, to which he was a stranger, his vision was harsh, sharp, bright, unfiltered by experience. He placed the blame unambiguously on the pauper: 'Instead of putting their shoulders to the wheel they [the paupers] fall down in the mud', calling for the parish to assist them.[18]

To stamp out such practices Kay attended the first interview of paupers by the new Boards of Guardians in order to demonstrate 'the manner of *addressing paupers*'. He had them brought back after the interview to hear the board's decision as to whether they would receive poor relief, hoping to impress them with the guardians' authority. Where paupers were judged insolent Kay called additional meetings 'with a view of subduing this refractory spirit'. After following this policy in a rebellious Union, he noticed that, when the guardians rode home through the parish in the evening, they were 'respectfully saluted – caps and hats were doffed, and curtsies made'. In fact, he reported, '*The Paupers universally now doff their hats to the Relieving Officers when they meet them, and when receiving relief at the Pay Table, bow or curtsey respectfully before they retire, and during their attendance maintain silence and decorum in the presence of the Officer*'.[19]

Kay believed in 'less eligibility' and applied the workhouse test with enthusiasm, though he became more cautious with experience. He instructed the workhouse masters to put paupers immediately to work, to enforce silence, order and decorum during meals, to demand cleanliness and neatness in the wards and yards, and to observe scrupulously 'the hours of rising and rest, of meals, labour and religious exercises' – all of which were to be marked by the ringing of a bell. In some ways Kay's workhouses were more like monasteries than the 'bastilles' his opponents denounced. When he noticed that some supposedly destitute paupers had personal possessions, 'boxes, china, articles of clothing, &c.', he directed that they should be collected, marked with the paupers' names and placed in a storeroom. In one workhouse where this was done, the master found 'considerable quantities of bread secreted . . . (showing how abundant the dietary is), and likewise soap and other articles, purloined from the workhouse stores'. 'As a result of this procedure', Kay noted, 'twelve able-bodied female paupers left the house, saying they preferred labour out of doors'. The bitterly contested practice of making able-bodied married paupers sleep in separate rooms at first caused Kay no concern, though (as with the workhouse test) he came to modify his views. He enforced the Commission's dietary rules strictly. If Oliver Twist, whose story was being published while Kay was in East Anglia, had asked for more, Kay would have consulted the regulations before answering him.[20]

The pauper had become an opponent. In the workhouse and the cottage Kay found imposture, fraud and violence, the more easily because he was looking for it. His indignation blinded him to the desperate buoyancy which helped paupers survive: he complained that two beer shops had been built to cater for the paupers at Heckingham in Norfolk, when they were allowed out of the house on Sundays; but he was too offended by the flagrancy of the offence to wonder at the resilience of the women paupers, who dressed themselves in clothes they had stored in nearby cottages and 'flaunted about the neighbourhood in company with the young men'. The village of Snape in Suffolk was more violent. It was inhabited by a 'lawless population of paupers, disbanded smugglers and poachers, who extorted the scale allowance from the reluctant overseers by threats of violence'. These paupers entered a meeting in December 1835 in 'a most insulting manner', two of them so abjectly intoxicated that they could not walk unless supported by colleagues. Two others, notorious poachers in Kay's opinion, assaulted a butcher at the door of the inn where the meeting was being held. They were summoned before a magistrate and fined 30/- each in default of gaol. To Kay's scandalized amazement 'they instantly paid the money', having been recipients of the full allowance for large families, and later 'ferociously threatened' the guardians who were on their way home from the meeting.[21]

There were more subtle practices which Kay believed he was well equipped to detect. He could not rely on a commanding physical presence to overawe paupers as he was slim and, though above medium height, not tall. But his large forehead made larger by premature baldness, his aquiline nose and his pale blue eyes, blazing with intensity, made him a formidable inquisitor. He assured the Commissioners that his skills had been honed in hospitals where he had witnessed 'the worthless among the poor' trying to obtain free medical treatment. He told of a 'delicate female' who had been bled each alternate day, blistered twice in the week, occasionally leeched, kept on a low diet, pierced at the one time with six or seven four-inch-long acupuncture needles, and forced to drink a pint of a particular type of oil daily. Though she accepted this treatment without murmur, her malingering was somehow discovered. On another occasion a sturdy, tall and well-dressed man who looked like 'an inferior farmer' came to plead on behalf of a sick widow. Kay questioned him.

> You are a neighbour?
> Yes.
> Does she live in your house?
> No.
> Do you live in hers?
> Why – yes.
> Now sir, answer, as though you were on your oath. Do you, or do you not, sleep with that woman?

After some confusion the man answered in the affirmative, to be met with Kay's aggressive question: 'Do you come here to ask this board of guardians to give you further support for the maintenance of your mistress?'

Cases of sexual misconduct (which Kay mostly described through the actions of women) particularly concerned him. He commonly reported, as he did of Plomesgate, that the workhouses were 'literally brothels' frequented by sailors and poachers and inhabited by 'single women each with one, two, three, four or even five bastards!' He wrote of a woman who had had two children by her husband before he was transported. She had two more by another man before he abandoned her to the care of the parish whose officials were hesitant to press the case against him. They were unsure whether he was the legitimate father or had been guilty of bigamy – and only difficult-to-obtain information from the Antipodes could solve their dilemma. Kay discovered that the woman had two more children by a third man, and he informed her, when refusing outdoor relief, that he had previously found children dependent on the parish because they were the offspring of marriage with a convict husband, or from a bigamous union, or through adultery, but never before had he encountered an example 'in which all three crimes were centred in the one individual'.[22]

Kay reported with horror in December 1835 that a woman in Sudbury had received an allowance for 'four bastards', the results of 'illicit intercourse' with three different men. To make her disgusting profligacy worse, 'this abandoned harlot' kept a shop which probably earned enough to support her family. Kay produced a variation on the less eligibility principle: if allowances for 'the mother of a bastard' were as large as those for a widow with a child, the motive for marriage would be 'exceedingly diminished'. He was still more shocked by a woman living in the Stowmarket workhouse who, after her husband had been transported, had two illegitimate children by Jude Fletcher, a cripple. When Kay asked to see 'this wretch, who had thus wantonly desecrated the asylum of his infirmity', he was shown into '*the SCHOOL ROOM*, and found that Jude Fletcher the crippled pauper and adulterer, was the schoolmaster of the workhouse' and had been teaching the children morality '*since* the birth of his first illegitimate child'. Furthermore, the governor of the workhouse did not know whether Fletcher and the woman were still sleeping with each other and could not, in any case, prevent it. As Kay recounts these cases, his is the outraged voice of the middle-class Dissenting male, shocked by the sexual mores of the paupers but blind to their suffering. And, one senses, with the shock came an unacknowledged fascination – a fascination which his uncles and great-uncles, those passionate men of strong appetites and animal vigour, might have acknowledged more openly.[23]

Investigations before the Board of Guardians did not satisfy Kay. Though paupers sometimes locked their doors against Poor Law officers and insulted or even assaulted them, Kay wanted them to be followed into their cottages. He followed them in himself, preferring to be alone and 'without confessing who I was and what my object was'. He described an old couple in Bury St Edmunds who had been on poor relief for four years, and whose goods were seized and sold, despite 'considerable excitement among some humane persons', for the substantial sum of £234.6.9. Kay recorded that two of their ten Bibles, three Prayer Books and one New Testament had been gifts from the Society for Promoting Christian Knowledge and had never been opened.[24] Admiring his own inquisitorial skills, impressed by the salutary dread with which his presence struck recalcitrant paupers, rendered myopic and impregnable by a fanatic's certainty,

Assistant Commissioner James Phillips Kay criss-crossed Suffolk and Norfolk, as close to personal fulfilment as he was ever to come. In June 1836, as the first year of his appointment ended, he told Samuel Robinson, the cotton manufacturer and founder member of the Manchester Statistical Society, that he usually travelled 200 or 250 miles a week in an open carriage, lived mostly on bread and water, and was extremely healthy. His district was already depauperized, he claimed, and rate savings in Suffolk alone would amount to £150,000 for the year. 'The effect of the Law is almost magical, and I may confess to you privately that I have lived a new life of high moral and intellectual enjoyment in effecting and witnessing this mighty change.'

Yet, in these moments when he derived 'an almost unqualified and unalloyed satisfaction from my pursuits', he was haunted by ambition, by the desire to 'get on' and so still the doubts which drained him of self-belief. He feared that when the demands were reduced 'I may feel the want of that incessant stimulus, and constant reward which they have hitherto afforded'. If so, he should be constrained to demand from the Commissioners 'as the reward of my past exertions some other and more active duties'. He did not tell Robinson that he had asked Chadwick in January 1836, when he had been in Suffolk for less than five months, for a hint as to his likely destination 'after my mission is completed in this County'.[25] In the midst of his new life of high moral and intellectual enjoyment, Kay was wondering how long the cause would continue to consume him.

Kay's mother and sister joined him in mid-1836 at Cromer, a coastal resort 25 miles north of Norwich, having remained in Manchester for ten or eleven months, trying to come to terms with his appointment and his unfinished business. His mother decided that, though they missed him, they were thankful for his new office, 'and think we can discern the goodness of God in it towards yourself in an especial manner'. His sister was less certain and, as early as November 1835, asked whether someone less talented could supervise the running of the Unions he had formed. She thought it 'very ignoble work'.[26] Her life had become inextricably linked with her mother's after her father's death and James's appointment as an assistant commissioner. As her brother Robert had married and left home, she and her mother were left with her three youngest brothers – Joseph, 14 years old, Ebenezer, 13, and Thomas, ten. Faced with the demanding task of their upbringing, the 54-year-old Hannah Kay looked to her unmarried 28-year-old daughter for support. Both mother and daughter accepted that James would act in a paternal role, the more easily because he was nearly 17 years older than Joseph and as keen to exercise authority in the family as he was in the Unions. Furthermore, his departure for Suffolk emphasized that he intended to follow his career where it led him, expecting his mother and sister to make the adjustments necessary for the functioning of the family.

Robert Kay had left his family well provided for: Hannah received the use of the house and all its contents (including all wines, ales and spirits) until her death or remarriage, when all went to the children. She also received a legacy of £7,000 (it fell to £4,000 if she remarried), and each child was left a legacy of £2,000, Hannah's (the daughter's) being protected from the designs of any future husband. The correspondence allows only fleeting glimpses of the investments which made up the rest of the estate for which James, Robert and their mother were executors. It is clear, however, that James Kay made the crucial decisions. His mother's and sister's letters are full of subservient comments: 'Dearest Mamma and Bobby are so very anxious to do everything correctly and as they think you would have done and approved . . . I have said or done nothing nor shall I do till I know your mind . . . as you especially directed.'[27]

Having abandoned the apothecary's trade in order to start a calico and woollen printing business in Manchester, Robert Kay also consulted his brother regularly. He did not want 'Mamma' worried about his activities, no doubt because of bad debts he had accumulated and the borrowing he was forced to undertake, and in 1837 he admitted that he had lost 'time and money but neither hope nor energy nor the determination to do right'. By the end of 1838 his prospects had improved, though James Kay remained doubtful. 'I hope he does not need me to be at his elbow to stimulate and to caution him', he wrote to his mother. 'And I wish him above all things to remain prudent in his expenses.'[28]

To conduct his war against pauperism, Kay needed his mother to assume key responsibilities. She ran their Manchester home in St Peter's Square, arranged the education of her youngest sons, and controlled the day-to-day finances. After the shift to Cromer, she organized the letting of their home and sold some of the furniture and Kay's gig. The only surviving letter from Kay to his mother dates from this period and combines explicit and cautious instructions with awkward affection. 'I also think you are a wonderfully clever person at getting rid of the furniture so very snugly and so well', he wrote, adding,

'I must say in fine that I think you are a clever sort of old woman.'[29]

Meanwhile, with the three boys at boarding-school and ample money for servants, mother and daughter had time for the niceties of middle-class life. While in Manchester they visited the Murrays, Langtons, Robinsons, and the Kennedys at Ancoats Hall. (Kay was still in touch with the Kennedys, though his mother warned him not to write too often – 'it is not good for your mind'.) They gossiped about friends such as Charles Henry, and kept him informed about the affairs of various Kays, Fentons and Forts. But beneath the civilities, the duties of a widow's unmarried daughter were carefully, if obliquely, delineated – as was evident when Kay invited his sister to Suffolk. Their mother immediately approved of the visit, in ways which stressed its cost to her: 'I would delight in making every sacrifice which would induce her to comply with your wish more especially because I think it would be delightful for you to be together'. Despite the fragile health which her mother was intently bestowing on her, Hannah expressed joy at the prospect of being able to render Kay 'any and every little attentions in my power'. Yet it was 'now more than ever my duty to devote myself entirely to her [mother]. I have more than one void to try to fill up'. Though she was sure that her mother wished them to be together, she would then be quite alone 'and I do not know of any one with whom she would be comfortable to be left'.[30]

Hannah went to Suffolk after arrangements had been made for Kay to reduce the perils of travel by meeting her in London; their mother stayed with Robert and his wife. The protectiveness of mother and son reflected, and helped to create, the feeling that Hannah was venturing into a dangerous world when she moved outside the family circle. After a most successful visit she returned, better informed on the Poor Law but hiding the pace at which Kay was working. Her mother did not hide her manipulative musings: 'I am often ready to wish I were not so selfish as to require her, and think it would be a much more useful station for her to occupy to travel with you'. Emphasizing her dependence by expressing surprise at her independence, she remarked that, though her daughter was very kind, 'I was able to do [without her] so much better than I expected'. The younger Hannah had a choice of waiting on her mother or her brother; to each of the three, that seemed natural.[31]

What both Hannahs thought strange was that they saw little of Kay at Cromer. The shift from Manchester had been a considerable sacrifice, for they exchanged a comfortable home for a cottage and left the Dissenting, cotton community in which they felt accepted. Their reward in this rural coastal town, whose ways and people were strange to them, was to see Kay once every two weeks. 'I seldom visit my sweet home more than once in a fortnight', he told Robinson, but that day was 'a sort of domestic sabbath'. Neither this cloying affection, nor the sabbath rest he took on his fortnightly visit, could have satisfied the two women.[32]

Matters worsened in July 1836 when Kay, having decided that his brothers should live at Cromer and have private tutors, added to his mother's problems by suggesting that Henry Nicholls, the son of the Poor Law Commissioner, should stay at the cottage for a time, probably as a tutor. Resisting this suggestion, his distressed mother insisted that she was not 'more nervous than usual' as he had implied, that she had never before had to share a party yard which was unpleasant 'on account of servants etc.', that the cottage was too small for a fourth boy, and that she did not want the extra responsibility as 'I have not the health and spirits I once had'. She canvassed other possibilities, but finished by saying, 'believe me when I add how much I desire you should decide as you consider will be best', though her anger flashed when she added – 'if we ever see each other again'. The letter halted Kay's plans, but did not abolish them. On 14 July 1838, two years after the first suggestion, Joseph Kay informed his brother that 'our young friend Henry Nichols (*sic*) has arrived and in five minutes we know one another as if we had been together for so many months'. What his mother thought is not known.[33]

Joseph and Ebenezer sent their brother accounts of their studies – chemistry with Nicholls; the *Hecuba* of Euripides, some Homer, some German, Isocrates, the *Iliad*, the Greek Testament, Horace, Cicero, Virgil and Euclid. Kay had ensured that the modern studies of chemistry and German accompanied their education in the classics. They were serious young men and they sent Kay considered, formal letters ('I cannot help venturing to write a few lines to thank you for the very kind advice you have sent us', Joseph began a letter), as if his authority made normal brotherly relations presumptuous. They followed his activities closely and, when Nassau Senior visited Cromer while Kay was away, they helped to secure him horses and show him the neighbourhood's most interesting places. Under the guidance of their usually absent brother, Joseph, Ebenezer and Thomas were being grounded in the social and intellectual skills necessary for a public career.[34]

In the altercation over Nicholls Hannah Kay wrote to her son: 'I wish I could express myself so as to be understood by you, but I confess I feel always unable to write properly to you.'[35] Many paupers might have echoed that sentiment, as they faced the assistant commissioner who listened without hearing. In the cottage at Cromer Kay was more benign, but he exercised authority whether he was present or absent. His mother and sister responded to his needs, giving him support which he could, and did, take for granted. To the world outside, life in the cottage might have seemed prosperous and placid. Indeed it was. Yet men and women were exploiting each other: Kay, his mother and sister; his mother, her daughter; his brothers, their sister. As it was done for the most part politely, without the conventions of class and gender having to be made explicit or seriously called into question, Kay could return once a fortnight to his domestic sabbath and his sweet home, to rest amidst its peaceful tyrannies from the high task of imposing a bleaker tyranny.

Though that task was being accomplished, it met opposition at the national and local levels which drew revealing responses from Kay. Richard Oastler saw the Poor Law's 'cold, calculating, Malthusian Philosophy' as the end of an older order of society. But for all his passion Oastler was no more vehement than some of the poor who saw themselves deprived of a right, hectored by new officials, and threatened by the workhouse – a threat given physical expression as Kay and his colleagues built new and larger *bastilles* in the new and larger Unions they were creating. As the Tories and *The Times* thundered their opposition and the beleaguered officials of Somerset House watched, the St Pancras parish fanned rebellion by establishing in January 1837 that the Commission could not direct parishes controlled by certain Acts to elect guardians in accordance with the 1834 Act. The next month an uneasy government, which faced an election, thought it expedient to establish a select committee on the Poor Law Amendment Act. Though Russell gave the committee a membership which guaranteed that it would not report unfavourably, it acted as a focus for discontent. Then, when Lefevre resigned at the end of 1838, Chadwick's guttering bitterness burst into flame as a commissionership was again denied him. To the plentiful and determined foes from without was added a secretary who saw himself serving an unjust Home Secretary and weak Commissioners.[36]

For assistant commissioners in the field the opposition was direct and personalized. Drawing the boundaries of the new Unions raised local jealousies and required the support of the larger landowners. Kay cultivated people such as Thomas Coke of Holkham, an enterprising octogenarian, who had opposed the Poor Law but, having changed his mind, gave Kay strong support, even placing his coach and four at his disposal. Kay tried to organize Unions on a basis of accessibility to the workhouse rather than in conformity with the boundaries of particular estates, and Coke allowed the Holkham estate to be divided among five Unions. Many were not so co-operative, and Kay's reports contain frequent references to obstreperous landowners or magistrates: 'one very irritable and apparently malevolent surgeon . . . one or two very restive spirits . . . miserable minority . . . unmanly and disgraceful conduct . . . on the verge of insanity . . . long notorious as crotchety people whose eccentricity borders on mental infirmity . . . a paper currency man – Fanatics of that class are always unstable people – without exception wrongheaded if not worse'.[37]

Norwich was a perpetual problem for Kay – he called it 'the Norfolk St Pancras' because a local Act gave the city substantial protection from the Commission and the Board of Guardians was heavily politicized. Both Whig and Tory, Kay said in October 1836 from the safety of King's Lynn, were 'grossly ignorant and grossly venal'. The trade second in importance to cattle and corn was 'the trade in *votes*, which are as openly sold in municipal and borough elections' as cattle and corn were at a fair. With the decline of Norwich's textile industry, there was high unemployment among weavers and the poorer classes were 'demoralized and turbulent'. Their opposition was fomented by the employment of a dozen blind men who, every market day, recited ballads about the horrors perpetrated by the Commission. Even the ardent Kay moved slowly. Although 'in that pure city of Norwich', the orders of the Commissioners had 'not yet been burned by the common hangman', he admitted that he had 'no confidence that my eloquence will prevail above the voice of faction'. It did not prevail, and eventually Kay had to warn his successor to continue his caution lest disruption from Norwich spread into Unions which were working well.[38]

While Norwich was 'an angry boil, busily generating corruption', Kay had serious troubles in Suffolk. On 16 December 1835, which was to be an important day for him, he addressed a meeting of gentry, clergy, magistrates and landowners in the Guildhall at Bury St Edmunds. The chairman may have known Kay for he remarked that he would make a 'luminous and probably voluminous statement'.

Kay expressed his faith in the New Poor Law, claiming that its 'exact and beautiful adaptation to the exigencies of the period' had produced 'a conviction not only of the justice, but of the beneficence of its provisions'. He made his standard attacks on the Old Poor Law – it reduced the labourers' wages, bred indolence and dependence, increased the profits of cottage owners by subsidizing rents, and produced 'a population of Helots to eat up the land'. He attacked over-generous diets, accepting those given to soldiers as a standard because 'paupers ought to be fed less abundantly than the men who fought the battles of our country', and he gave his audience 'some facts as to the illicit intercourse of the sexes, and their fruits'. As he drew to the end of his three-hour address he denounced the Old Poor Law overseer who had been 'accustomed to pay the paupers over his own counter, and to receive back the poor man's pittance, mulcted by his own avarice'. He condemned landlords who had made exorbitant profits from their cottages, lawyers who had benefited from unnecessary litigation, and the beadle, 'the petty persecutor of the poor', who would now descend to 'his native insignificance'. He warned that public meetings of Boards of Guardians would lead to a system of bullying, that the first enforcement of the Law would be trying and that they could expect 'the misplaced sympathies of the pseudo-benevolent'. Nevertheless, 'the country was in the state of a house on fire, with the ruin impending, and . . . it was better to encounter danger in doing well than in doing ill'. His speech was well received, and the chairman referred to the speaker's 'amusingly instructive lecture'.[39]

As Kay spoke, the law of the land was being defied in Ipswich. The Board of Guardians, apparently with his approval, decided to place the male paupers in the St Clements Street workhouse and the women paupers in another. Watched by more than 200 people, protesters destroyed the window shutters of the St Clements Street workhouse, then demolished the wall and one of the wings. The constables, fearful of violence towards themselves, did not interfere, and the disturbance ended only when the military arrived and arrested three of the ringleaders. The troops were also required the following night when a crowd gathered at the other workhouse. Kay stationed himself in Ipswich with some police and two troops of cavalry, a force he thought insufficient; then, worried about disturbances in the Plomesgate Union, he went to Wickham Market. However, on 22 December a band of paupers, spurred on by the Ipswich troubles, marched on Stradbroke. Two hundred entered the village, four abreast, to be met by the Reverend Henry Owen, four metropolitan police and a special constable (a civilian sworn in to act temporarily as a policeman). The protesters' poor organization and their residual social deference were revealed when Owen 'resolutely collared the most conspicuous leader, who was armed with a bludgeon, appended to his wrist by a sling', ordered the arrest of other leaders, quelled the conflict which followed an attempt to rescue them, and took possession of about 50 bludgeons and sticks. He then assumed his role as magistrate and condemned four of the seven arrested to four months' gaol each. As an awed eye-witness remarked, Owen was 'a host in himself'. Kay knew nothing of these events until he saw the prisoners being escorted through Wickham Market. He immediately sent a messenger to find out what had happened, and considered going into the parishes with a force of 12 or 14 policemen and special constables, and two or three magistrates, in order to protect guardians and relieving officers who were being threatened and assaulted. He took no action and returned to Ipswich, 'sure that we have not force enough to preserve the peace of the County'. He was physically exhausted, having been on the road for most of the previous three nights.[40]

The next day, 23 December, Kay reported that the paupers of Snape had guns but had been overawed by a body of constables, that a large group of paupers had attacked the workhouse at Balcamp with picks, axes and other instruments, that he needed six police at Wickham Market to protect the house of industry, and that more troops were urgently required in the district. He set out for Snape, but eventually went to Stowmarket as he was worried by a threat to its workhouse. He persuaded the magistrates to swear in 30 special constables and arranged the defence of the workhouse though, as only special constables were available, he thought that the paupers might still pull it down. He returned to Ipswich at 1.30 in the morning. The paupers 'have given us a busy week', he decided, 'but have been defeated everywhere'; however, he admitted that as he rode around the country he heard paupers 'utter most savage threats'. He had become a special constable so that he could 'take anyone into custody who threatens me with violence', but he was relieved that reinforcements had been sent, hoping that this would put 'all chance of success out of the rioters' power'.[41]

On Christmas Day Kay visited Balcamp where the guardians had given the paupers a holiday, that is, permitted them 'to get drunk out of the house with the turbulent paupers of the district'. Meanwhile at Semer, in a fight involving three magistrates (all clergymen), the weapons had included cutlasses, pistols and staves, and in Kay's opinion, the workhouse would have fallen if the police had not arrived. One magistrate's nose was cut transversely 'quite through' and, despite the attentions of a surgeon, permanently disfigured. As protests and rumours of protest rumbled around the district a fiercely exhilarated Kay found himself in a semi-military situation. He told Chadwick that he had been 'converted into a Commissioner of Police' and he deployed additional police to numerous troublespots, swore in special constables, ordered some of them to sleep in the workhouses, set up night patrols of young farmers, and made 'minute arrangements' for the defence of the workhouses. With two winter months ahead he was determined not to let the paupers triumph. Their 'premature movements', he said, retaining the military analogy, had ensured 'our victory'. The press, he thought, had been cowed; he was not.[42]

Yet in late December and early January Kay was anxious: the local authorities lacked energy, the constabulary were 'worthless' or 'worse than useless' (a few had been drunk on the evening of 26 December, and they were afraid for their farms and houses); and some magistrates were opposed to the law, some lukewarm, and others 'naturally stupid and supine'. At a dinner with magistrates, 'after the cloth was removed', Kay discussed the state of the rural police and the need for a force 'to put down burglaries – incendiarism – and to maintain a higher state of subordination in the County'. He contemplated a special Union police and took consolation that a few vigorous men scattered through the county were ready to act 'on the slightest hint from me'. He also had some doubt about the Commissioners' support. He assured them that his 'instinct' was right, that he trusted it implicitly, that '*no* measures are so bad as *half* measures'. He spoke to them, '*without reserve* as I should to my best friend; – hoping I may account them *all truly my friends since I am the ally of their great enterprise*'. If they thought him sudden or rash, they should wait till they saw the result for he had 'long been accustomed to promptitude in action'. He was trying to attain a 'mental equilibrium between energy and prudence', and he hoped that 'the errors of the last week', if their better judgement had detected any, would be atoned for by his sincerity and singleness of purpose.[43]

Kay's singleness of purpose had its reward by late January 1836 when the disturbances near Ipswich died down. However, revolt was simmering elsewhere and in April 1836 Kay had the dubious honour of being the first assistant commissioner to have a Union workhouse burned down in his district. On an earlier visit to the workhouse at Heckingham in Norfolk he found scenes of 'unparalleled disorder and iniquity', and he had been faced with clamorous opposition when he endeavoured, successfully, to win support for the formation of a new Union. He now proposed to reduce the paupers' diet and, while not separating married paupers, he wished to divide the unmarried men and women as the workhouse was little more than a 'House of ill-fame'. Aware that his proposals would cause trouble, he asked for police. Four arrived but, early in the morning of 23 April, Kay was wakened at the home of Sir William Beauchamp Proctor, whose support he had been cultivating, with the news that the workhouse had been burned down. It was a premeditated act, as the inmates had been warned, the boys being told to sleep with their clothes on and to take their shoes upstairs with them. The paupers closed ranks when Kay and the magistrates cross-questioned them, and he rapidly admitted that a large reward would be necessary 'to break the con-spiracy to conceal the circumstances'. Despite a reward of £500 the silence was not broken. Charges were laid, then allowed to lapse, and Kay had to content himself with sternness, and anger that 'indirect but unequivocal encouragement' had been given to the paupers by one or two middle-class people 'who were adverse to the dissolution of the incorporation'.[44]

In July 1836, only three months after the Heckingham fire, Bury St Edmunds expressed its anger in turbulent scenes. As Kay walked to the Guildhall for a meeting with the guardians, he became aware that 'a considerable number of the working classes of the town' had arrived there, giving 'sufficient evidence that they were ready for uproar'. Kay adhered to his principles and refused to have a public meeting of the Board of Guardians. For 15 or 20 minutes he addressed the crowd ('an assembly of considerable intelligence', the *Bury and Norwich Post* reported him as saying) in what he described as 'a conciliatory tone', though the *Post* reported Kay telling one interjector that 'if those insulting remarks were continued', he would stop talking. After his speech the crowd followed Kay and the guardians into their private meeting with cries of 'hole-and-corner work' and, when they were expelled, filled the rooms and passages of the Guildhall demanding admission. They had been particularly incensed by Kay's claim that the labourers were better fed under the New Poor Law – 'Some persons, who were evidently not ratepayers', the *Bury and Suffolk Herald* reported, 'commenced hissing and groaning, and calling out "the labourers have no meat"'.

Eventually the guardians agreed to make the changes which Kay was seeking. 'We rose as a body', Kay, who was physically fearless, reported, 'flung open the doors, and proceeded to attempt to make our way downstairs. We were jostled rather roughly. My hat was struck from my head. My coat slightly torn.' The guardians escorted Kay to his hotel 'amidst the hootings of the lowest rabble' who were led, Kay claimed, by 'a few of the more desperate radicals, and the beer shopkeepers – many of whom were recognized as leaders in the affray'. Though missiles were thrown there was no serious attempt at assault; but as Kay drove from the town 'the old women screamed loudly out of the windows, in all the streets through which I passed'.[45]

If Kay had thought more deeply about those screaming women, the burning workhouses, or the paupers whose resistance the reward could not break, he might have realized that, beneath the hostility of vested interest groups, beneath the resentment of officials who had lost power and patronage, beneath the rivalry of Whig and Tory, seethed the inarticulate anger of the poor as they watched their 'rights' being wrested from them on a promise of better things to come. But, like a true and brave zealot, he found it easier to reduce opposition to the actions of the venal, the uninformed or the stupid. He reported to the Commissioners: 'I maintained my good humour throughout the hooting – pelting – and insult. It was better to laugh at them, as I had the good fortune to be able to do, than to knock any of the most abusive down, as they most richly deserved.'[46]

By mid 1837 Kay reported that, except for 'miserable Ipswich', his two counties were tranquil. However, he was under attack from a more powerful force than the old women of Bury St Edmunds. On 27 June 1837 the Earl of Stanhope, an anti-Poor-Law campaigner, claimed in the House of Lords that 'Dr Kay had very distinctly and very candidly acknowledged that the purpose of those concerned in the management of workhouses had been to render them as like prisons, and in every respect to make them as uncomfortable, as possible.' Kay produced a letter which he asked the Commissioners to put into the Prime Minister's hands. In lumbering, convoluted prose, he informed Lord Melbourne that, 'as it has never been in my mind to think that Workhouses should be made as uncomfortable as possible, so I have the greatest confidence that I never could have uttered that sentiment in that, or in any other form of words'. Stanhope repeated the accusation, which he owed to John Lewin, a semi-professional anti-Poor-Law agitator from Wickham Market. Melbourne took no action, but Stanhope was attacked by Brougham, the Earl of Stradbroke, who had direct knowledge of Kay's work, and the Earl of Radnor, whose son-in-law was E. Carleton Tufnell, an assistant commissioner and a close associate of Kay. Stanhope's credibility was undermined by his failure to name the source of his accusations, and by the House of Lords rejection of a petition he presented because many of the signatures were in Lewin's handwriting. A select committee (to which Kay gave evidence) looked at some of his complaints, but Stanhope did not include those he had made against Kay.[47]

Seven months later Kay received an anonymous letter which contained unspecified but 'detestably libellous imputations'. Such a 'gross and assassin like slander' was designed to intimidate him, Kay believed, and in a remarkable outburst in an official letter, he told Lewis that if he discovered the identity of 'this malignant liar, I think I should brain him in a paroxysm of anger'. He had informed the Commissioners in 1836 that he was 'a thousand times more in my element if a little resistance occur, than in the trifling times of peace', and, in the same year, had sent some Norfolk papers to his mother, remarking that they praised him – 'but I have learned to be indifferent, both to praise and blame, because I get both, and often when I least deserve either'. The uncertain Kay may be recognized again in the paroxysm of anger, in the boastful crusher of resistance, and in the son who affected indifference to praise or blame yet sent his mother papers which praised him.[48]

Yet, for all his personal uncertainty, it was a mark of Kay's resilience, of his need for success and of his developing political skills that, though deeply threatened by criticism, he could adapt his policies pragmatically. He did not, for example, press Norwich too hard, revolted though he was by its behaviour, and he moderated his position on the separation of the sexes in workhouses, informing the Commissioners that he had long felt 'the impracticability of the separation of man and wife in *different* houses in the present excited state of the country'. Again after the troubles in Ipswich, in search of compromise, he briefly departed from his policy of establishing one large workhouse to explore the possibility of using a number of smaller ones. He even modified his view on outdoor relief. Faced with the distress caused by a particularly severe winter, Kay informed the Commissioners, who had asked him in February 1837 to report on 'the expediency of forbidding outdoor relief except in case of emergency or of a temporary nature', that such a prohibition was 'altogether inexpedient in my district'. There was much 'morbid feeling' and the Unions were 'totally unprepared', so while not doubting the essential correctness of the policy he suggested some convenient concessions.[49]

Kay was capable of independence from the Commissioners. Certainly he proffered effusive thanks for their support, their 'confidence in my zeal and judgement' and their 'flattering expectations of success'. He even expressed confidence that they would admonish him if he erred. But this more than ritual obsequiousness (Kay once described himself as 'but the shadow of the Commission') was sometimes overwhelmed by an independence of the sort that had led him, against his own interest, to attack Manchester's cotton manufacturers – 'I cannot too emphatically express my opinion' was the way he gave his advice on outdoor relief. He strongly but unsuccessfully advised the Commission against the premature extension of the Act into the north; he produced a circular on medical relief which Nicholls thought it would be inexpedient for the Commission to publish; he argued that assistant commissioners and not the guardians, as the Act required, should appoint auditors; and he warned the Commissioners to proceed moderately against recalcitrant Unions until they found a suitable issue on which to intervene. Kay was not a mere shadow of the Commission; he often interpreted East Anglian conditions to the Commissioners in ways which reflected the wishes of the local guardians.[50]

Moreover, Kay's administrative imagination enabled him to look towards a metamorphosis of Unions into rural municipalities which handled roads, the distribution of charities, and other matters. Administration could be consolidated, the number of clerks reduced, and 'in one convenient centre [there] would be united the executive authority of the district'. He also suggested that Boards of Guardians be given power to introduce sanitary measures in areas where the health of the poorer classes was particularly affected. Kay was angered when Boards of Guardians displayed jealousy of the central authority, but during his time in East Anglia, his was an intermediate centralism: the will of the central authority was to be done, but through local authorities which had consolidated powers previously spread haphazardly among diverse groups. His vision would have terrified Fielden or Oastler and made them think, rightly, that the old order was being undermined. They would have been wrong, however, if they thought that Kay had learned nothing from his experiences.[51]

On 10 July 1838 the Poor Law Commissioners decided that

history should repeat itself: they appointed Kay to the metropolitan district supervised by Charles Mott whom, three years earlier, he had replaced in Suffolk.[52] Though it carried no increase in salary, the move to London was a mark of favour, and gave Kay the larger stage he craved.

Kay's East Anglian experience had been crucial. He had re-established himself after Manchester's disasters, and justified himself to his friends and his family. The abandoned medical career no longer looked a defeat or an inexplicable waste, and he even permitted himself to sneer at the profession he had left. 'Medical gentlemen', he remarked of a troublesome group in King's Lynn, 'suffer under the constantly recurring disease of a morbidly increased sensibility of the nervous system. The pulses of the common air which refresh and invigorate the rest of the world, torture them.' He made many suggestions on medical relief derived from his dispensary pamphlet, a revised version of which he unsuccessfully tried to persuade the Commission to publish. But as an assistant commissioner he had wider responsibilities: he established new Unions, built workhouses, disciplined paupers, crushed opposition, exposed fraud and cut the cost of poor relief. Before giving him the London appointment, the Commissioners had frequently brought him to the city for special tasks. He had reported on the distress among weavers in Spitalfields, graphically illustrating their plight without being shaken from his belief that, even amidst great commercial distress, a well-regulated workhouse was the best means of providing poor relief. He and Dr Neil Arnot wrote an important analysis of the fever in London which took him back to issues of public health he had discussed in his Manchester pamphlet – indeed, Chadwick welcomed Kay to London because of his interest in these matters. After studying the conduct of 'dissolute women' in a London workhouse, he made a plea for the establishment of an asylum where 'this refuse of the prostitution of London may be set to work'. Always ready to offer the statistics he had collected or the results of enquiries he had conducted, Kay gave impressive testimony (in February and March 1838) to the Select Committee on education of the poorer classes in England and Wales, and also in March, to the Select Committee on the Poor Law Amendment Act. The length at which he was questioned reflected the value placed on his opinions and, to a lesser extent, his loquacity.[53]

The links which Kay had made with influential people – Lewis, Nicholls, Senior, Shaw-Lefevre, Chadwick and Tufnell – were as important as this recognition. The Earl of Kerry, whose acquaintance

he had made through the Statistical Society, wrote about his
migration scheme and may have introduced him to his brother, Lord
Lansdowne. Through Lansdowne and Lord John Russell, he had
become known in the highest Whig circles, though he had not yet
gained entry to them.[54] He had, however, become a member of a
relatively new group – the middle-class, expert administrators who
brought order, rationality and uniformity to the solution of social
problems. As Kay saw it, the variety and confusion of local practices,
their inefficiency and corruption, and their reliance on the patronage
of the squire and the parson would eventually be replaced by the
steely, scientific efficiency of a bureaucracy. In Manchester Kay had
embraced this ideal, and through his statistical research had tried to
provide it with intellectual foundations. In East Anglia he realized
that local conditions had to be taken into account, but he tried to
persuade and, if necessary, force a reluctant population to accept the
rationality of the New Poor Law. Charity and religion had to yield as,
brandishing his secular solution, his statistics and sets of government
regulations, Kay rushed to stabilize the social system. Nevertheless,
there were ironies in his position. The informed expert, who thrust
the New Poor Law's procedures on paupers, could not bring order to
his inner life. There, anxiety and uncertainty lurked, temporarily
restrained not by rational calculation but by professional success and
by working for a cause in which he passionately believed. Within his
family his authority was recognized, but he could not discard the
uncertainties which first developed in the family he now ruled.

At Christmas in 1838 some people judged that workhouse children
could be offered a dinner of meat and plum pudding. It might cause
them

> to reflect with some degree of satisfaction and contentment that altho'
> reduced to the lowest scale of civilized humanity, they are nevertheless
> kindly remembered at such a season by those, whom Providence has
> graciously placed beyond the influence of penury. . . .

The previous year, James Kay had invoked the less eligibility
principle: as many industrious and frugal labourers could not afford
beef and pudding with ale, paupers should not receive them at the
ratepayers' expense. Food for the mind was a different matter. Kay
argued that workhouse children should not be educated as unsatis-
factorily as were children of the labouring classes.[55] He had accorded

education importance in his Manchester pamphlet, but as an assistant commissioner he changed from a conventional believer to an apostle spreading a message of salvation through education.

Kay's involvement with pauper education blossomed when he came to London, but it began in Suffolk and Norfolk, especially after he had studied the apprenticeship of pauper children in 1836. He denounced the evils of apprenticeship and, believing that education provided the alternative, was closely studying the schools in his Unions by mid-1837. He began a course of educational reading and recommended that the teachers in workhouse schools follow his example. In search of better ways to prepare children for industrial employment, he visited the school at Ealing Grove run by Lady Byron, the poet's widow, and the schools of the Children's Friend Society at Hackney Wick and Chiswick.[56]

On 19 August 1837 Kay embodied his ideas on pauper education in a circular which he headed 'Poor Law Commission', in the hope that his masters would approve it for circulation throughout Suffolk, Norfolk and E.C. Tufnell's district of Kent. Tufnell, the well-connected assistant commissioner whose acquaintance Kay had made through the Statistical Society, suggested that they visit Scotland to examine the work being done by John Wood in Edinburgh and David Stow in Glasgow. Kay received an unintended preparation for the visit when the Commissioners asked him to investigate accusations of cruelty made against an institution for pauper children at Brixton. He conducted his examination on 25 August 1837, immediately before he left for Scotland, and found, among other indignities, that two boys had been chained to logs. He ordered their release, admonished the owner, and reported him to the Commissioners.[57]

The visit to Scotland may have reminded Kay of his student days but its significance was not retrospective – it put him on his road to Damascus. 'How little we knew of this subject before our visit to Glasgow', he exclaimed to Tufnell. A vision of what schools could do, all the more glittering by contrast with what he had seen at Brixton (which was high in his mind as he wrote the report of his investigation from Edinburgh), flooded Kay's mind. Now, he decided, with typically premature enthusiasm, he knew what pauper education was all about. He was convinced of 'the supreme superiority' of these Scottish schools over everything he had seen in England.[58]

Tufnell went to London, leaving a chagrined Kay to tell the Commissioners, from Cromer, that he 'rejoiced' that they had instructed Tufnell to report to them. They seem to have expected Tufnell, who had become interested in pauper education before Kay, and Charles Mott, who had written to them on the subject in late 1836, to lead the way. They interviewed Tufnell on 20 September, and nine days later he sent in his report. Bearing clear traces of the Scottish visit and recommending the employment of teachers from Glasgow, it was a safe, responsible document, more unified than the report Kay was soon to produce, but unimaginative and without a pedagogic programme. However, it was enough to frighten Mott about the 'mania of false humanity' which gave paupers a better education than the children of small ratepayers received. He could see 'nothing but dissatisfaction and mischief' resulting.[59]

On 2 October Tufnell discussed his report with the Commissioners, but may have been distracted from educational concerns because, as a staunch follower of Chadwick, he would not budge from the workhouse test and became embroiled in controversy. He was 'wearied to death with preaching theory to these dull-headed people', he said to the Commissioners on 21 October as he found himself 'environed in a perpetual ocean of difficulties and trials'. Kay, after warning the Commissioners that his 'anxiety' on the subject might 'assume the character of intrusiveness', bombarded them with urgent suggestions. Workhouse schools, especially in London, produced 'a race of young felons and vagrants' and perpetuated pauperism 'under the especial patronage of the Poor Law Commissioners'. Reform was made difficult by 'the gross inefficiency of the present schoolmasters and schoolmistresses' (usually themselves paupers), and progress could not be made without 'the creation of a normal institution' for the training of teachers. He had discussed such an institution with the Bishop of Norwich before going to Scotland; now, he was utterly convinced and he looked to an improved pauper establishment at Brixton and another at Norwood to provide models. 'I cannot refrain', he told the Commissioners, 'from urging this most important subject earnestly upon your attention'.[60]

In the months after his visit Kay accumulated educational ideas in a confused, excited rush. He read about and called upon schools in England and briefly visited Holland and Belgium with George Nicholls. His now outdated circular of 19 August gave him a beginning, and pressed for time and possessed by the neophyte's intensity, he did not closely analyse what he was collecting, but spilled out his heady amalgam of ideas in a report written in December 1837, in one day, a Monday, he claimed. Wood, Stow, Lady Byron and the industrial schools of the Children's Friend Society jostled continental reformers such as Labarre, Prinse, Pestalozzi and de Fellenberg, as Kay raided them for ideas. He took what served his purpose – sometimes more than served his purpose for he proposed two different ways of teaching reading – without worrying too much about the context from which he extracted it. The consequent *Report on the Training of Pauper Children* (published in 1838) bears unmistakable signs of the speed at which it was composed. When it was finished, however, he had wrested leadership in pauper education from Tufnell and Mott.[61] For all his speed Kay was clear about his clientele and his administrative arrangements. The workhouse children 'dependent, not as a consequence of their errors, but of their misfortunes', were often 'orphans, or deserted children, or bastards, or children of idiots, or of cripples, or felons'. They frequently had no natural guardians and the state stood *in loco parentis* for them. There were, according to Kay's finicky statistics, 44,697 of them in England, and if 'the germs of pauperism' were to be eradicated they had to be educated. Kay advocated the establishment of district schools of industry (in his August circular he called them 'common schools' and he also referred to them as 'county schools'), two in Suffolk and two in Norfolk, which would replace the numerous and unsatisfactory schools being set up in each Union. Both Tufnell and W.E. Hickson, an educational writer and later owner of the *Westminster Review*, had suggested types of district school before Kay did, but the idea became associated with him because he developed it systematically and pushed vigorously for its implementation. His district schools were to be separate from the workhouse so that the children who lived in them were free from the stigma of pauperism and the possibility of corruption by adult paupers; the schools required fewer teachers who might, therefore, be better; they would cost less. Their main task was 'the rearing of hardy and intelligent working men, whose character and habits shall afford the largest amount of security to the property and order of the community'. Kay wanted boys taught reading, writing and arithmetic, and gardening, which afforded artisans 'innocent recreation' and was a source of comfort to the family of the working man. Above all, the boys were to be introduced to work which fitted them '*for the discharge of the duties of that station which they will probably fill in after life*' – skills such as carpentering, tailoring and shoemaking, which had the additional advantage of being useful in the running of the school. Girls were to be involved in the domestic management of the school, which was to be 'subservient to the training of the girls in all the arts of household service' – scrubbing floors, lighting fires, making beds, doing the washing and laundry and helping nurses to wait on the sick.[62]

The exigencies of class and gender dominated Kay's plan, but in the context of the time his thinking was neither unimaginative nor ungenerous. Nor was it haphazard. Though Kay had not integrated them tidily into his proposals, the ideas of David Stow lurked underneath the hectic eclecticism of his pedagogy and gave his report some coherence. Stow, 44 years old in 1837, was a merchant who had been an elder in Thomas Chalmers's church and a Sunday school teacher. He did not always acknowledge his debts to continental thinkers and to the English infant-school pioneer, Samuel Wilderspin, but he was a courageous innovator, and by 1837, through the aid of the Glasgow Educational Society (which he helped to establish), he had developed the Glasgow Normal Seminary. Kay admired Stow greatly: the Glasgow Normal School, he said in 1838, was 'the most perfect school of this description with which I am acquainted'. Between Adam Smith, Chalmers and Stow, Scotland left a powerful mark on Kay's intellectual development.[63]

Part of the subtitle of Stow's major work, *The Training System*, first published in 1834, suggests why Kay found him attractive: it was a *'manual . . . which includes a system of moral training suitable to the condition of large towns'*. Stow claimed that his system had a Scriptural basis: 'Train up a child in the way he should go' was the text to which he appealed. Instruction, by which he meant teaching a child to memorize half-understood knowledge, was not training. Intellectual culture itself, he insisted, was 'too exclusively considered the all-in-all in education'. The training system, by contrast, aimed at 'the cultivation of the understanding, affections, and physical habits, not separately but combined, *at one and the same time'*. Stow stressed that children must understand what they were taught: 'If I am not told the meaning [of a word], but my intellectual powers are called upon to find it out by analysis, root, construction etc, and thus determine for myself what must be the meaning of the word – that is *training*.' At the same time it was essential for children to put what they had learned into practice. Thus, of moral training, which he considered 'the great end of all national education', he wrote: 'Training in school can only be termed *moral* training when precept is turned into practice.' A child had to develop good habits of action which might 'gradually form *a second nature'*.[64]

The sympathy of numbers – the effect, for good or ill, which a community, a crowd or a closely knit group may have on behaviour –

was important. When a new child came to his school, Stow explained, 'he instantly finds himself in a new region, and free from his old temptations – he catches the moral atmosphere of the place – and by the influence of sympathy, gradually, and imperceptibly to himself, imitates their example'. The playground, 'the *uncovered* school-room' Stow called it, was therefore crucial, for in it a child, 'amidst companions freely at play, and under the moral superintendence of the teacher', learned 'in real life' the moral values Stow wished to inculcate. Inside the classroom he favoured 'simultaneous instruction' by which all children were taught at the one time by an adult teacher – and not individually or in small groups by monitors (older children previously instructed by the teacher), as was common in schools for the poor. Stow believed that all the children would learn through trying to answer the teacher's questions, even if only half of them originally knew the answer: 'if the teacher so commands their attention as to keep their eyes upon himself, then he is quite sure that they are receiving the instruction.' He insisted, optimistically, that 'being, in some measure, at liberty to speak or not as they please, there may be a full understanding of the subject without its being brought out in words'. Simultaneous instruction took advantage of the sympathy of numbers, and used elliptical questioning and 'picturing out', a laborious blend of oral description and illustrations aimed at developing an understanding of metaphorical expressions or new ideas. Stow's emphasis on understanding, the persuasiveness of example and the sympathy of numbers turned him against prizes and rewards, and he opposed corporal punishment, claiming in 1836 that the rod had not been used in his school for two and a half years.[65]

Stow's ideas found architectural expression in the gallery, a series of steps on which the children sat, their attention focused downwards on the teacher. The sympathy of numbers and the teacher's personality had a greater opportunity to weave their powerful spells in a gallery than when 'the children are seated around a school-room, at desks, or on scattered forms; the attention of all is secured; all receive one lesson, and all learn'. An important architectural development followed when Stow began to 'classify' students, to divide them into different groups, or classes, on the basis of their ages and attainments: he built *class*rooms into which a class of children might go for a particular lesson, leaving the large *school*room typical of the monitorial system. The playground, the gallery and the class-room were the outward and visible signs of the new vision of education which Kay saw in Glasgow in 1837.[66]

Stow's methods (and, therefore, Kay's) may seem a quaint repository of educational optimism, though to be understood they need to be compared with 'mutual instruction' or the monitorial system. By the first decade of the nineteenth century Andrew Bell and Joseph Lancaster had developed versions of this system, which provided an elementary education comparatively economically: a teacher assisted by unpaid monitors, whom he or she chose and instructed, might handle more than 100 pupils. Intense personal rivalry between the founders was made worse by religious disputation: Bell's system was adopted by the Church while Lancaster's found favour among Nonconformists. But in comparison with Stow's, the similarities between the monitorial systems were more important than their differences. Stow offered access to an adult teacher, not to a child who was too little in advance of the other pupils to be able to offer a stimulating education. Moreover, his emphasis on understanding what was learned, on the moral discipline of the playground and the sympathy of numbers, implied that he expected a child to respond in a way which necessitated some individual choice. The teacher's dignity was increased by the responsibility Stow attached to the position, and both teacher and child gained dignity because of Stow's aversion to corporal punishment – he attributed the use of the rod to a desire 'to save the trouble of convincing the judgement, and impressing the conscience'.[67]

Much of Stow's system can be found in Kay's 1838 report. He wanted children ruled 'by love rather than by fear', and teachers who developed understanding instead of coercing children to remember information they did not comprehend. He wrote of simultaneous instruction, the sympathy of numbers, the gallery, and 'the uncovered classroom'; he stressed moral education and the significance of the teacher's role; he was not impressed with the use of monitors and he rejected corporal punishment. Like Stow, he valued the teaching of singing and took the advanced line of suggesting that boys and girls should be educated together. He did not discuss the model school or the normal seminary, but he mentioned a form of teacher training that was successfully used in Holland, the pupil-teacher system. Scholars with superior zeal, interest and attainments were given additional instruction, some practice in teaching and eventually some classes to teach under the supervision of the schoolmaster. They were paid and, when their 'modified form of apprenticeship' was finished, examined and, if successful, awarded a certificate of competency.[68]

Kay shared some of Stow's political assumptions. Pauper children were to be prepared for specific occupations so that they did not provide a recruiting ground for the armies of unrest and revolution. There was no hidden curriculum in Kay's suggestions – he wrote openly of social control. However, only by ignoring the independence and integrity of his pedagogy can his approach be explained simply as an effort to impose a particular set of political values on the working classes. That pedagogy was itself shaped by considerations of class, but it also offered solutions to educational problems: it was a response by Stow, and through him, Kay, to the day-to-day experience of confronting the demands and needs of students. Kay's version of 'the training system' gave child and teacher personal as well as social dignity; it fostered some individual and independent responses; it aimed to enlighten as well as to control. Like other occupations – medicine or shipbuilding or carpentry or music-making – education confronts its practitioners with immediate questions (what should be taught, how and why?) and immediate problems (keeping order, for example, or satisfying the often conflicting demands of employers and students). As they struggle to find answers, teachers produce or accept plans of action, pedagogies, which often drive them down different roads from those envisaged by those who control the schools. Schools cannot be reduced to expressions of class interest, they have a life of their own – which explains why teachers often do not recognize themselves when they read what sociologists or psychologists, or historians, write about them.

The architecture holds the clue. Galleries, playgrounds and classrooms appeared in plans prepared under Kay's instructions, and in the classrooms the desks were arranged with the children facing the teacher in order to be 'instructed and governed by him'.[69] As the century progressed the monitorial schoolroom slowly disappeared and the school became a collection of classrooms. Kay's plans brought pauper education, and eventually elementary education, to the edge of the modern era for the architecture and furniture expressed a new pedagogic vision – the meeting in a self-contained room of a teacher and a classified group of students for simultaneous instruction aimed at developing an understanding, not simply an acceptance, of what was taught. This classroom was the meeting-ground, and the battleground, where a new educational relationship was forged. When, on a productive December Monday in 1837, Kay put his pedagogic vision on paper he helped to alter the relationship between children and adults, and despite all the defects and betrayals which time has brought, the arrangements he advocated are recognizable today. They have lasted longer than the social order Kay tried to preserve, striking evidence of their independence and self-sufficiency.

Kay did more than put his ideas on paper. Immediately on his return from Scotland he and Tufnell brought teachers who had worked with Stow and Wood to some schools in their Unions. By mid March 1838 Kay had engaged six 'Scotch schoolmasters', whom he described as 'missionaries of the true faith in teaching'. Three of them moved from school to school trying to exemplify new educational possibilities and, with a similar intention, Kay sent teachers from his Unions to institutions such as the Children's Friend Society and Ealing Grove.[70]

Around one teacher, William Horne from Wood's school, a myth grew which Kay sedulously cultivated. After Horne, an exciting and energetic teacher, left the Gressenhall workhouse in Norfolk, the teacher fell ill. In his absence, William Rush, a 13-year-old pupil, took charge and, to the amazement of the guardians, ran the school successfully. Hearing of this miracle Kay visited Gressenhall and was impressed. In later life he claimed that this event had led him to suggest a similar practice in other schools. 'We began to call the most successful of these assistants pupil teachers', he remarked, implying that he had hit upon the idea and the title himself. Memory, helped by his desire to appropriate the credit, deceived Kay. The system had been in operation in Holland for more than a quarter of a century and descriptions of it were available in English. In any case, Kay mentions pupil teachers in his *Report on Pauper Education* (1838).[71]

On 13 March 1838 Kay told the select committee enquiring into the Poor Law Amendment Act that he did not expect 'to have any better teachers than are in some of the workhouses in Norfolk and Suffolk'. The Scots emphasized their usefulness by informing Kay that the children from the parochial workhouses were brutishly ignorant, vicious and disorderly, and, though they knew how to pull up twitch grass and top and tail turnips, 'beyond that they had not a single idea'. However, Kay soon realized that it was impossible to attract sufficient teachers from Scotland, and in January 1839 he again called for the Commissioners to establish a Normal industrial school near London. About a year earlier, with the co-operation of its owner, Frederick Aubin, Kay had begun to use the pauper establishment at Norwood as a prototype of a district school and as a model school for the training of teachers. Aubin contracted with certain parishes to board, clothe and educate their pauper children for a per capita payment, and while, like others who made a living in this way, he was wary of additional expense, he was genial and adaptable. The idea of using Norwood as 'a model establishment' to train teachers came in September 1837 while Kay and Tufnell were in Glasgow. Kay was attracted to Norwood because it was in the country about five miles from London, and held about 1,100 children, enough to permit their being 'classified' in ways impossible in a small workhouse. He began working with Aubin while he was in East Anglia, but found things easier at the beginning of 1838 because he was often in London preparing for, and testifying at, the select committees. After his appointment to London pauper education dominated his attention.[72]

Of course, as an assistant commissioner, Kay had other cares. His return to the metropolis saw him more supportive of the central authority. English legislation, he wrote, had consistently 'leaned towards the chartered rights of municipal bodies', which had been seen as citadels of liberty 'notwithstanding the most notorious and flagrant corruption and malversation of every kind and degree'. The public should learn that the Poor Law's 'Central Authority' was 'a mere instrument for executing the will of the Legislature responsible to, and controlled by the Houses of Parliament'. In the service of this instrument he continued to establish Unions, implement regulations, pacify Boards of Guardians, conduct investigations, and produce reports. He prepared questions about Divine Service on Sundays and circulars on medical relief and casual destitution. He became a Fellow of the London Statistical Society in 1838 and reworked some of his official reports for publication in its journal. He had to defend himself from wild accusations that he had advocated infanticide, and persuade the Commissioners to pay his personal expenses. 'I value the office I hold for reasons among which the remuneration attached to it holds no place', he said grandly, then: 'but I should not value it *at all*, if bearing in mind the nature of the duties I have to discharge, I received a remuneration inferior to that of any other of your Assistant Commissioners'. Meanwhile he pressed ahead with pauper education, leading Nicholls to claim that what had been done 'proves how much more is even now in the Commissioners' power, and opens out a new field for future operations'.[73]

Kay kept that field of operations before the Commissioners, but realizing that the unsatisfactory conditions at Norwood could not be improved without financial assistance, he asked for an interview with Lord John Russell and in October 1838 wrote him an account of what had been achieved. Norwood was fitted up according to Dutch and Prussian examples; industrial occupations had been introduced – for the boys a fully rigged mast, 70 feet high, with yards and sails had been erected. The boys made the shoes and some clothes for the institution, while the girls did its domestic duties. The simultaneous method was in use, moral training was stressed, religious instruction and divine services were available in a carefully regulated way. Kay stressed the need for a Normal school, as well-qualified teachers did not stay in workhouse schools. At Norwood, he told Russell, he had tried to create 'a Model Industrial School for the Training of Pauper children' – opening the school to the public every Friday was part of this plan. More importantly, Kay had widened his horizons and saw Norwood as an inspiration for primary education generally, not just pauper education. He was advancing towards a new field of responsibility.[74]

Russell obtained Norwood a grant of £500. In April 1839 Kay wrote a second report on pauper education, announcing that the best example of what he had been trying to achieve was 'the school of industry under the management of Mr Aubin at Norwood'. Candidates for pupil-teacherships (including the precocious William Rush) were coming from other Unions to undertake a three months' training course, and a group of pupil-teachers was being chosen from the children at Norwood itself. He stressed that the work had just begun, that more could be done with greater resources, and that the future lay not with contract establishments such as Norwood but with district schools run by the Poor Law Commission. Kay devoted much attention to pedagogic matters, particularly simultaneous instruction. To ensure its effectiveness the children had been divided into classes of 40 or 50, suitable desks had been provided, a gallery had been installed, and separate classrooms had been constructed by the use of sliding partitions. He repeated his condemnation of burdening the memory with ill-understood facts, and of corporal punishment and bribery through rewards. At Norwood, he claimed, children were being brought gently and smoothly to understanding and to sound moral values. With the help of Stow, Kay had realized what has often escaped educators since: the manner of instruction itself teaches.[75]

Kay's analysis of the effects of the programme was striking. Predictably, he mentioned that the school had produced docile children with a respect for authority, truth and property. He also remarked that, however unpromising the environment from which the children had sprung, they now at least display in their features evidence of happiness; they have confidence in the kindness of all by whom they are surrounded; their days pass in a cheerful succession of instruction, recreation, work and domestic and religious duties, in which it is not found necessary to employ coercion to ensure order. Punishment, in its ordinary sense, has been banished the school, and such slight distinctions as are necessary to mark the teacher's disapproval of what is wrong are found efficacious.

This, it should be remembered, was an education designed for bastards, orphans, deserted children, the offspring of felons, cripples and idiots, the incurable victims of scrofula, boys with 'almost universally coarse features' and girls almost all of whom were 'plain'. Kay may have been complacent but, whatever his approach to adult paupers, he was reaching out to the children with sympathy and imagination.[76]

Edward Tufnell knew Kay well and, despite their co-operation, did not particularly like him, referring to him as 'the doctor'. In 1867 he told Chadwick that Kay was 'of so jealous a nature, that he was always afraid of having his merit lessened by others, and it was only possible to work with him by keeping constantly in the back-ground'. When he wrote this Tufnell suspected Kay, probably unfairly, of having worked to prevent him obtaining an appointment he wished to secure, but there was truth in his remark. Yet the consuming uncertainty which fed Kay's need to be seen as successful could, when devoted to a cause, equip him with a fervour which carried all before him. In the case of pauper children the fervour could even mask from Kay the realization that the cause he had adopted was not an astute one for an ambitious man to take up. Perhaps in the plight of those children Kay, half unaware, saw himself, a perpetual outsider denied acceptance by the powerful, a child unable to satisfy his parents even if he could treat his mother paternalistically. Admittedly in April 1839 when Lord Lansdowne, the languidly powerful epitome of a Whig grandee, offered Kay the position of Secretary to the newly established Committee of the Privy Council on Education, success and acceptance seemed his. Yet, only seven weeks earlier, he had been asked for information about schools in Manchester. 'I have not been in Manchester for nearly three years', he replied stiffly.[77]

5 · The Committee of the Privy Council on Education, 1839-42

Human conflict, according to Henry Edward Manning, whose educational activities caused trouble for James Kay, was ultimately theological.[1] Like other profound statements this is not true, though in the educational battles of nineteenth-century Britain it almost was. Decisions on what children should be taught, and who should control the teaching, meant confronting questions about the meaning and purpose of life and led, therefore, to political, economic, social and religious conflict. Kay soon learned how turbulent the priests, in particular, could be.

The Church insisted that it should control popular education. Through the National Society for Promoting the Education of the People in the Principles of the Church of England, founded in 1811, it built schools in which all pupils, whatever their religion, read the Bible and learned the catechism and liturgy of the Church. The British and Foreign School Society, established in 1808, was supported by Nonconformists and some evangelical Anglicans, and provided Bible reading and a form of non-denominational religious instruction. The National Society had the support of the Tories, while the British Society relied on the Whigs and some radicals and socialists. The societies' differences over how popular education should be provided were made more intense because they agreed that the extension of education was becoming increasingly important.[2]

In 1833, recognizing the religious and political realities of the differences between the societies, but also trying to respond to the agreed educational needs, the Whig government granted £20,000 to supplement private subscriptions towards the building of schools for the poorer classes. It did not, however, create a department of education to administer grants, but left responsibility to the Treasury which dispersed the money through the two societies. The British Society swiftly grew dissatisfied as the National Society gained almost 80 per cent of the grant. Moreover, because the Treasury operated through the two societies, it had loose control of the grant, so that rivalry led to duplication of effort in some areas, leaving the large towns and manufacturing areas, where many thought the need for education most urgent, comparatively neglected.[3]

The battle raged indecisively until the late 1830s. Whigs and Tories, Church and Dissent, supporters of secular, denominational or non-denominational education, proponents of government grants and education rates, advocates of an education board or ministry, groups urging the establishment of Normal schools and school inspection – all produced proposals and counter-proposals, linked or overlapping or diametrically opposed. The unpopular Melbourne administration stumbled from crisis to crisis in a bitter political atmosphere, as the Tory-dominated Lords rejected its Bills with wearisome predictability and its majority in the Commons dwindled. On education as on other matters it was divided, yet for all its faltering steps, even Melbourne, who distrusted new schemes, recognized that action could not be 'escaped or deferred'. In November 1838 he asked Russell to prepare a plan for the government.[4]

Russell was a crucial figure in these difficult times. Astute and experienced, he possessed the unstudied arrogance of the aristocratic families who assumed that governing was part of their birthright. He had the advantage of belonging to the Established Church without the handicap of taking its doctrines too seriously; his attitude to Rome was reliably hostile; he thought baptism merely an outward sign and had not bothered to be confirmed, though he took Holy Communion, which he regarded as a ceremony of remembrance. He was a vice-president of the British Society from 1824 to 1861, when he succeeded his brother as president, and he personally favoured the Society's solution to the education problem. However, political pressure forced him to consider other solutions. With cautious Whiggish rationality, he had once warned Chadwick that English society might have been

> lax, careless, wasteful, injudicious in an extreme; but the country governed itself, and was blind to its own faults. We are busy in introducing system, method, science, economy, regularity, and discipline. But we must beware not to lose the co-operation of the country – they will not bear a Prussian Minister to regulate their domestic affairs. So that some faults must be indulged for the sake of carrying improvement in the mass.

He was speaking of a rural constabulary, but out of such practised but not unprincipled pragmatism his scheme for education took its uncertain shape, despite a crippled government and an Opposition baying at the scent of power.[5]

The Church also had problems. The repeal of the Test and Corporation Act in 1828 had ended its monopoly over public appointments and, as Emancipation had enabled Catholics to enter Parliament, the Church could no longer assume that those who ruled the country were its members. It was under constant attack from liberals and radicals, disestablishment was being urged, the endowments of its cathedrals were coveted, and it seemed 'politically unpopular, socially exclusive, and administratively corrupt'.[6]

In fact, in education, as in other aspects of its life, the Church was changing. In March 1838, William Ewart Gladstone, 29 years old and passionately High Church, remarked that they were experiencing 'a safe and precious interval, perhaps the last to those who are desirous of placing the education of the people under the efficient control of the clergy'. Later in his life, his views much changed, he explained that in 'the sanguine fervour of youth' he had dreamed that the Church was 'capable of recovering lost ground, and of bringing back the nation to unity in her communion'. The lost ground was not recovered; but in December 1839 Gladstone's dreams of High-Church-led unity preoccupied him. While touring the continent he went with Manning to visit Dr (the future Cardinal) Nicholas Wiseman, and at Christmas after Wiseman had taught him to use the Missal, he attended Mass, deciding that 'nothing less than a wisdom most Divine can separate & discharge the evil & the good which are so subtly combined in it'.[7]

Gladstone could afford to relax in Rome because, between February and August 1838, he and a like-minded group (the bishops called them 'the young gentlemen', and they included Manning) had captured the National Society. Gladstone was very active as the young gentlemen secured support from Lord Ashley, William Howley, the Archbishop of Canterbury, and Charles Blomfield, the Bishop of London. Their ambitious scheme included an expansion of the parochial schools and the construction of 'a regularly graduated scale of public instruction from the Universities down to the Infant Schools, the whole essentially and intricately connected with the principles and Ministers of the Church'. Each diocese was to be responsible for the starting of 'middle' schools to cover the education of lower-middle-class children, as well as for parochial schools, the raising of funds, and the establishment of a board of education with powers to inspect. The beleaguered cathedral chapters (thus supplied with new reason for their existence) were to be responsible for the local administration of the new system and were to establish diocesan training colleges. The young gentlemen also proposed a central training institution, the 'Queen's Hall', which was to be attached to King's College, London.[8]

The High Church enthusiasm stung the Whigs and, as Kay reminded Russell in 1843, his government acted in 1839 'to prevent the successful assertion on the part of the Church of the claim then put forth for a purely ecclesiastical system of education' – Kay specifically mentioned the diocesan boards and training colleges and the central training institution envisaged in the National Society's programme. In August 1838, as the Society's plans were announced, Russell was toying with a British and Foreign School Society scheme envisaging a national board, which regulated secular instruction only, and encouraged (but did not establish) Normal schools. Scripture reading was compulsory except in Jewish and Roman Catholic schools, and Dissenters were exempted from the Catechism. By October he was proposing a Bill which did not include a board but authorized Poor Law Guardians to levy a rate to assist schools which provided Scripture readings with a conscience clause for Dissenters. Thomas Spring Rice, the Chancellor, assuming that Russell would proceed by a parliamentary Bill, warned him that his plans would give the Established Church 'pride and mortified self-importance to add to party feeling'. The Church and *The Times* kept intense pressure on the government, and on 22 January 1839 Blomfield and Howley called on Russell, and in Blomfield's words 'asserted the claims of the Church to conduct the education of the people'. No politician as saturated with English political values as Russell could underestimate the power of the Church.[9]

On 12 February 1839, departing from his earlier ideas, Russell tabled in Parliament an exchange of letters between himself and Lord Lansdowne, President of the Privy Council, in which he proposed the establishment, through an Order in Council, of a committee of the Privy Council which would control the distribution of the parliamentary grant (now £30,000), run a Normal school, and appoint inspectors. As an expression of the royal prerogative, an Order in Council did not require the assent of the Lords and thus greatly reduced Spring Rice's fear of parliamentary defeat. Though there was a precedent for setting up an executive department in this way – the Board of Trade, in 1786 – Russell had instituted a strange administrative body for, as A.S. Bishop has remarked, 'a central authority was created virtually without parliamentary sanction'. The Committee of the Privy Council on Education, usually called the Committee of Council, assiduously tabled its minutes in Parliament but it was not controlled by a ministry. Yet, paradoxically, it was exposed to changes in the political wind because new governments could alter its membership at will. The original Committee had four members, all, deliberately, laymen: Lord Lansdowne, the Privy Seal (Lord Duncannon), the Chancellor of the Exchequer (Spring Rice) and the Home Secretary (Russell). When debate began to swirl around the Committee an angry Brougham, who perhaps put the first inkling of such a Committee into Russell's head, complained:

> I am ashamed . . . that after all that has been confessed . . . of the utter inadequacy of our present means of education, that all we have been able to 'screw our courage' to, has been the asking of Parliament for a paltry £30,000, and appointing a committee of noblemen to distribute it.[10]

At its first meeting in the Council Chambers at Whitehall on 11 April 1839 the Committee appointed Dr James Phillips Kay its secretary. (Strictly speaking Kay was appointed assistant secretary as Charles Greville, the Clerk of the Privy Council, was *ex officio* secretary to all its committees.) Russell later confirmed that Lansdowne appointed Kay. In his *Autobiography* Kay reports that Lansdowne asked him for the name of any gentleman who would make a competent secretary. Kay produced three names but, perhaps on 1 March 1839 before the Committee of Council had been formally established, Lansdowne offered him the job, warning that it would subject him to much opposition and might be precarious. He accepted on the understanding that he could retain his position with the Poor Law Commission as insurance against these uncertainties, and an arrangement was made by which the Commission and the Committee of Council each paid £600 a year towards his salary.[11] His appointment was not unpredictable. He had long been identified with the Whig cause; during his time as an assistant Poor Law commissioner he had become known to Russell; and he had established a reputation for being knowledgeable in educational matters. When the noblemen who ran bodies such as the Committee of Council wished to implement their social policies they turned to the ambitious middle class to supply the expertise they lacked.

Kay claimed that he influenced Russell's statement of 12 February and, specifically, that he suggested the inclusion of the Normal school. Normal schools were common in the educational baggage carried by the progressives of the time – they were also part of the rarefied milieu which surrounded the young gentlemen – and neither Russell nor Lansdowne needed Kay to remind him about them. Yet, as a matter of fact, Kay did suggest the idea to Russell in his letter of 29 October 1838 inviting him to Norwood; and he had an opportunity to remind Russell for he met him with Chadwick on 26 January 1839, presumably to discuss Poor Law matters. Only nine days later, in the letter he wrote to Lansdowne proposing the establishment of the Committee of Council, Russell spoke approvingly of the educational activities of the Poor Law Commission.[12]

Whatever Kay's influence on the statement of 12 February, he had an obvious impact on the Committee of Council's first minute, issued on 13 April, two days after its first meeting. The minute announced the Committee's approval of a scheme to establish a Normal school, a model school and a day school. In the model school general religious instruction was to be combined with 'the whole matter of instruction, and to regulate the entire system of discipline'. Special religious instruction (that is, doctrinal instruction) was to be given by the chaplain for children belonging to the Established Church and by a licensed minister in the case of Dissenters. The Scriptures were to be read daily, arrangements being made for Roman Catholics to read their own version. Similar arrangements were made for the Normal school which was to be residential. Instruction was to be given by the simultaneous method, a gallery was to be built, and moral training was at all times to be 'an object of special solicitude'. The minute also decreed that grants towards a Normal school of no more than £2,500 were to be given to each of the societies, that building grants of not more than £10,000 a year were not to be restricted to the two societies, and that inspectors were to be appointed to examine schools aided by the grants.[13]

Kay was the minute's principal author. In 1873, towards the end of his life, speaking to an audience of admirers, he claimed:

> I prepared the minute, and presented it to the Government; I attended the Cabinet Council, and it passed; and when they asked my opinion I said it would ignominiously fail. These are not the exact words, but the spirit in which I spoke.

By the time Kay made this statement it had become vital for him to have been right about everything, even failures, but he made an earlier claim in 1862. Then, because he wished to stress that the Committee of Council was consulted about the minute, he allowed it more influence. 'It was discussed by the whole committee clause by clause', he said. 'Its whole form was changed by them, and several important technical alterations were made in it'.[14] Whatever changes were made, Kay's influence is clear.

It is evident in the provisions for religious instruction, which were those he had implemented at Norwood and, too optimistically, commended to Russell in his letter of 29 October 1838 as likely to avoid sectarian difficulties. It is evident also in the stress on inspection, the importance placed on the Normal and model schools and the stipulation of simultaneous instruction and the gallery, which were not 'a few pedagogical notes thrown in by the secretary', as one historian has described them, but an attempt, in a brief official paper, to legislate for the vision which David Stow had shown him. Nor is there, as has also been claimed, a lack of clarity in Kay's mind or his minute about the nature of a Normal school. He made his ideas clear in *Recent Measures for the Promotion of Education in England*, a pamphlet he published only a few months after the minute had been issued. Moreover, he anticipated the minute in a letter to Lady Byron on 30 March 1839, two weeks before the minute was published. In the letter he defined a Normal school as 'an institution for the instruction of teachers in the *theory* of their art and in the matter of instruction'. A model school provided an example 'after which other schools may be created', but was mainly a school in which a candidate for teaching 'may practise his art and thus acquire the habits of which he listens to the theory'. As a Normal school was attended by candidate teachers only and the model school contained only children, the regimens of the two schools were totally different. Kay pointed out that his educational purposes, including the securing of efficient simultaneous instruction, required a model school of about 450 children distributed in a particular way. Both the number and the distribution are repeated in the minute, the meticulous Kay even allowing the 30 children, who he assumed in the letter would be 'casually absent', to appear in the minute as being 'probably absent from sickness or other causes'. In writing this minute Kay did not pull the Whig educational policy out of his pocket, as an overenthusiastic admirer has claimed. Nor was he a lonely pioneer uncovering educational vistas previously unglimpsed – he was collecting and codifying advanced contemporary practices. But the minute, which marked out the field on which the next decade's battles were to be fought, bears unmistakable signs of his imprint.[15]

In his 1843 letter to Russell, Kay spoke explicitly about the government's determination in 1839 'to assert the claims of the civil power to the control of the education of the country', and Blomfield certainly realized that the Committee of Council was a fundamental challenge to the Church's authority. Its provisions for religious instruction, and the extension of grants beyond the two societies, particularly to Roman Catholics, meant that the Church's doctrines and liturgy were no longer privileged. In strict logic the offering of the 1833 grant to the British and Foreign Society had undermined the Church's exclusive claims, but they could be rationalized as aid to another Protestant group and as an example of religious tolerance. The 1839 arrangements made such a rationalization impossible. Inspection was a dismaying assertion of the state's intrusive intentions, and the proposal to establish Normal and model schools declared its desire to shape teachers in its own way, the assurance that the chaplain would be a Churchman merely annoying the Dissenters without disguising the threat.[16]

In the press, parliamentary and pamphlet warfare which followed the announcement of the minute, the Church and the Tories mounted a spontaneously angry yet well-orchestrated campaign. In a secular age it is easy to underestimate the importance attached to the minute. Lord Ashley insisted that 'the control over and possession of the youthful mind of the country, and consequently the temporal and eternal destinies of countless millions' was at stake. The eternal destinies of millions have become unfashionably large stakes, at least in the Western world, but Ashley and many like him, inside the Church and out of it, saw themselves as participants in a momentous struggle. Peel put the matter concisely: 'if there is to be a national system of education, excluding the direct intervention of the National Church (at least only tolerating its intervention), there is an end of the Church, and probably an end of any religious feeling ultimately'. Such certainty was not universal. Many were as suspicious of Tractarian excesses as the High Church was of the latitudinarian views which it saw as eating away the fabric of belief. Yet, despite these differences, the Church's response was emphatic.[17]

The powerful ecclesiastical politicians, Howley and Blomfield, warned that the Committee's proposals reduced the Church to just another sect, though they were not as brutal as J.P. Plumtree, who desired never to place 'the blaspheming Jew, the idolatrous Romanist, the Unitarian denying his Christ, or the sensual Turk, on the same level as the humble and adoring believer of the Son of God'. Robert Wilberforce chose a military metaphor. 'Is the Church of England so completely a vanquished enemy', he asked, 'that it is to support the hostile garrisons by which its own faith is to be exterminated?' Howley argued that the distinction between general and special (denominational) religious instruction was logically impossible because 'the whole of Christianity consisted of peculiar truths'. Henry Phillpotts, the Bishop of Exeter, similarly insisted that there was 'hardly a dogma left unquestioned by one class of Christians or another'. Given that no formulation of Christian belief could be agreed upon by the denominations, the result of temporizing was as clear to Gladstone and Lords Stanley and Ashley as it was to Howley and Blomfield: it would lead to 'universal scepticism', to the belief that there was 'nothing certain', to a crippling indifferentism and latitudinarianism which would eventually dissolve religious belief.[18] The young gentlemen's capture of the National Society and the political standing of Howley and Blomfield probably deadened the voices more sympathetic towards general religious instruction. But if the Church appeared more unified than it was, the Committee of Council still had reason to fear it.

Other spectres could be set whirling through the political atmosphere to haunt the Committee. The Protestant Association cried 'No Popery', the Methodists protested against the use of 'the corrupt Romish translations of the Holy Scriptures', and *The Times* invoked the image of Jesuits 'swarming throughout this Protestant kingdom' because of the Committee's excesses. Blomfield found an additional bogy, the Central Society of Education, a loose association of radicals and liberals, established in 1836. Its membership included Brougham, Lansdowne, Russell, Spring Rice, Lady Byron and W.E. Hickson. Kay was not a member. Officially the Society had no policy but it acted as a clearing-house for radical educational thinking, in particular the Irish solution to the religious difficulties, the clear separation of religious from secular instruction. This 'secularist' solution drew Blomfield's anger and, whether from confusion or with the intention of linking the Committee with undesirable enemies, he frequently claimed that its plan agreed in substance and almost in words with the Society's 'exclusively secular' proposals.[19]

From attacks on the Committee's proposals it was a short step to attacks on the Committee itself. Lord Stanley launched a parliamentary cannonade typical of those who resented the Committee's power, the manner of its establishment, its independence from Parliament and its lack of bishops. Archbishop Howley insisted that the scheme made government 'the universal pedagogue, the sole trustee of all charitable funds for education, and the whipper in of all loiterers in the chase after useful knowledge'. It would appoint inspectors, choose teachers and textbooks and 'do everything but chastise the boys in person'. Peel's confidant, the ex-Whig Sir James Graham, identified the Committee of Council as the root of all evil and called for its removal; others implied that it was the plaything of malevolent and unseen powers, *The Times* hinting at unknown hands pulling Whig strings.[20]

Wilberforce, one of many who made the next step, attacked the Committee's secretary, speaking of 'the professional bias of the very respectable Poor Law Commissioner, whom the Board has selected as its secretary'. The poor, he added acidly, would not be attracted by 'the appointment of a poor-law Commissioner, Dr. Kay, (however individually able and estimable)'. Blomfield remarked that the members of the Committee of Council were busy men 'whose habits of life are not likely to have been such, as to qualify them for so delicate and difficult an office'. Would they not be

> acted upon, and moved as puppets, by a few artful and designing persons behind the scenes, who will pull the strings from time to time, and make the Privy Councillors gesticulate, and excite the mirth or the sorrow of the bystanders; and will themselves do all the mischief, without incurring any of the responsibility?

Their secretary might become 'the sole arbiter and director of popular education', and, Blomfield continued, 'what security have we, that he will not be a Socinian, or a Roman Catholic; nay, what security have we for his being a Christian?'[21]

His Bamford childhood had inoculated Kay against Roman Catholicism, but the suggestion of Socinianism was damaging. Socinians denied the divinity of Christ and rejected the doctrine of the Trinity; and Kay's links with the Manchester Unitarians were well known. He was not Unitarian, though as early as 1837 he had been forced to ask Thomas Chalmers to clear him from the charge, which he considered was a 'very gross outrage' and a foul calumny. In March 1840 a letter appeared in *The Times* asking if any of the paper's readers knew Kay's 'religious profession' and claiming that 'the *animus* of a board may be determined by the character of its secretary'. *The Times* coyly pleaded ignorance, and the Rev. Robert

Eden, vicar at Battersea, the parish in which Kay was then living, had
to reply that Kay and his family (this meant his mother and sister)
regularly attended the parish church, that his opinions were orthodox,
and that for many years Kay had attended the services of the
Established Church.[22]

Paz describes Kay's change as a conforming not a conversion,
whereas Smith attributes it to 'experience and reflection'. It is hard to
know why or when Kay conformed, as there is no trace of his changing
opinions in his writings. Though advancement was easier for a
member of the Church, Kay no longer had to conform to become an
assistant Poor Law commissioner or secretary to the Committee of
Council. The intense religious convictions of Robert and Hannah
Kay were to some extent displaced in their son's life by his social and
educational concerns. But they were never destroyed and Kay
remained devoutly, if in doctrinal terms tolerantly, religious – apart
from his anti-Catholicism and consistent suspicion of High Church
and Tractarian tendencies. As Kay's mother also conformed, a clue
to his attitude may lie with her. Before Kay had gone to Edinburgh
she wrote to him enthusiastically about the controversial and
theologically unorthodox Edward Irving, who was later deposed
from his ministry by the Church of Scotland. Hannah Kay noted that
he was 'exposed to much censure, from those who can only hear the
gospel in their own peculiar manner of having the truth stated',
whereas she thought that he had been 'raised up by Providence to
attract the attention and invite the attendance of such as perhaps
would never have heard such important truths from any other man'.
These sentiments anticipated the liberal Protestantism which she
and her son were to profess.[23]

Whatever the reason for Kay's conforming, his religious odyssey
placed him in an awkward position in the education debate. To
Dissenters he was one who had left their ranks, while members of the
Church saw the black clouds of Dissent looming over him. As
religious leaders pressed home their religious objections to the
Committee of Council, its secretary was particularly vulnerable.

While the clergy mounted their attack, Conservatives seized on the
13 April minute to belabour Melbourne's ailing ministry. After the
black farce of the Bedchamber crisis, when the Queen refused to have
Tories as her court ladies, Melbourne's government lasted two more
years, though in May 1839 its early demise looked likely. In these

circumstances the determination of Russell and Lansdowne to proceed with their educational plans was striking testimony to their commitment. 'We ought after having gone so far', Lansdowne wrote to Russell in March, 'to submit to be beat rather than to abandon our scheme without discussing it – we were so *decidedly* in the right, which is not always the case, that a discussion must lead to good hereafter if it does not produce it now.' It did not produce it at that time either. Nor did Kay's private negotiations with (among others) Blomfield, Frankland Lewis and Gladstone, who had read some of his writings on pauper education.[24]

On 25 May Kay wrote to the Whig journal, the *Morning Chronicle*, denying any link with the Central Society and complaining about 'the imputation of monstrous designs' to the authors of the Committee's plan. He insisted that the arrangements for religious instruction in the Normal school were not to be enforced in primary schools throughout the country, but allowed himself a revealing prophecy:

> that whatever barrier may be erected against the interference of the state, the accumulating weight and pressure of public opinion will, ere long, break it down, and that when that period shall arrive, the public funds cannot be applied to a plan of national education, from the benefits of which any number of children shall be excluded by religious tests.

He had expressed sentiments to Russell, but the *Morning Chronicle* letter had been written with the permission of the Committee of Council.[25]

This statement, made at the beginning of Kay's time with the Committee, identified the existence of barriers to the state's power, while asserting his confidence that it would ultimately prevail. But the years to come were to be full of battles in which Kay discovered that the state was much weaker than in some of the Continental countries which he and other educational reformers admired. Only part of Adam Smith's message had been heard, and the grip of laissez-faire economics and the industrial system it supported restricted the state's growth, even where, as in education, Adam Smith had favoured it. In such an atmosphere the determination of the Church, and especially of the young gentlemen, to preserve its traditional power over education was reinforced. His advocacy of the rights of the civil power never ceased, but again and again Kay was to find his way barred by the religious obstacle, and his office and his character attacked.[26]

On 28 May, the day after the *Chronicle* published Kay's letter, a meeting, organized at Willis's Rooms in London by the National Society and chaired by the Archbishop of Canterbury, condemned the Committee's proposals. Despite the antagonism the Committee pressed ahead with its plans and even explored sites for the dreaded Normal school. On 1 June, however, Russell postponed the Normal school proposal 'until greater concurrence of opinion is found to prevail'. Probably Melbourne was relieved as he thought that Normal schools would 'breed the most conceited set of blockheads ever known'. Kay's later claim that he had told the Committee that the proposal would fail was the hindsight of an old and sick man. In March 1839 his enthusiasm was high and he tried to persuade Lady Byron that Ealing Grove could, with suitable modifications, become a rural model school attached to the proposed Normal school. Russell's disappointment was long-lasting; in his memoirs he described the dropping of the Normal school as 'the throwing out of one of our children to the wolf'.[27]

The concession did not pacify his opponents. On 22 May, with the meeting in Willis's Rooms in mind, Peel had told Gladstone that 'the object of the meeting is political, in the highest and best sense in which the word, political, can be used'. His planning, however, was political in a more down-to-earth sense: part of the Tory campaign to unseat the Melbourne government. The Tories, Peel continued, had to be sure 'to induce the cooperation of such men as the Bishop of Salisbury . . . whose political leanings are in a tendency opposite to ours'. They were also to be

> cautious in availing ourselves of the legitimate aid of the party connections to which I have referred, that we do not give rise to the suspicion (however unjust) that we are not using Party to promote our views on Education, but making Education subservient to Party.[28]

In late May and early June the Tories and the Church planned a parliamentary campaign in which, if education was not subservient to party, it was certainly put to use by the party. Gladstone's diary has a number of entries of the kind: 'an interesting meeting of 8 or 9 at Sir R.P.s at 11 – on Edn & other great subjects', and Peel wrote of two or three meetings at the Duke of Wellington's attended by various lay peers, the Archbishop of Canterbury and the Bishops of London and Exeter. In accordance with the plan Lord Stanley, on 14 June, moved that the Queen revoke her Order establishing the Committee of Council and, in an intemperate speech, condemned Russell's proposals for religious instruction, though they were less radical than those which he had introduced into Ireland eight years earlier. Stanley's resolution was defeated by a mere five votes. The margin fell to two votes when the Tories moved in the committee of supply to reject the education estimates. In planning this move Peel conceded the difficulty of resolutions on a money vote, 'however cautiously they might be worded', because they could seem to be 'trenching on the privileges of the Commons'. Parliament voted solidly on party lines, but the calculated vehemence of the Tories' attack suggests that despite Peel's protestations the education debate, like other crucial debates of this period, was a battle in the party warfare which had the governing of Britain as its prize. In the Lords the Tories used their large majority to pass resolutions which included a request to the Queen that no steps should be taken to establish a plan for the education of the people unless they were first considered by the Lords. The Queen refused the request, but there must have been times during the debate when Kay congratulated himself on having retained his appointment with the Poor Law Commission.[29]

Kay struck back through the publication of *Recent Measures for the Promotion of Education in England,* a widely distributed pamphlet, which was unsigned but had the support of the Committee of Council. It was measured, laden with references to royal commissions, select committees and statistical investigations, redolent with Olympian certainty, and at times urgently polemical. Though conciliatory towards the Established Church, Kay protested against the 'industriously circulated misrepresentations' which the minute had encountered, and expressed his astonishment that 'the party calling themselves Conservative' was not leading the efforts to promote education among the working classes. He attempted to defuse the dispute over religious instruction by insisting that the Committee's plans were to apply only to the model school and not to all schools, but despite the failure of the Normal school project he discussed it in detail, claiming that it was the most important part of the Committee's plan.[30]

Kay's crucial assumption was that education for the working classes was limited in extent and poor in quality. He supported this assertion with evidence from bodies such as the Manchester Statistical Society and from select committees, beginning with Brougham's in 1816 and finishing with that of 1838 before which he had been a witness. His assertion has recently been contested, though

contemporaries, even critical Tory Churchmen such as the Archbishop of Canterbury and the Bishop of Exeter, supported it.
Whatever its accuracy, Kay believed it passionately, as (perhaps less
passionately) did the majority of his middle-class and aristocratic
contemporaries. It provided a spur for action.[31]

What made action urgent was Kay's fear of the decline in social
order. If the threat did not come from Luddism or machine-
breaking, there were the trades unions who tried by 'strikes, by hired
bands of ruffians, and by assassination, to sustain the rate of wages
above that determined by the natural laws of trade'. Kay was certain
that 'the anarchical spirit of the Chartist association will . . . become
every year more formidable'. 'We confess', he said,

> that we cannot contemplate with unconcern the vast physical force
> which is now moved by men so ignorant and so unprincipled as the
> Chartist leaders; and without expecting such internal convulsions as
> may deserve the name of *civil war*, we think it highly probable that
> persons and property will, in certain parts of the country, be so
> exposed to violence as materially to affect the prosperity of our
> manufactures and commerce, to shake the mutual confidence of
> mercantile men, and to diminish the stability of our political and social
> institutions.

About the same time as the publication of *Recent Measures*, the
government issued a proclamation against all who took part in
military drills with or without arms, authorized the formation of a
civil force to protect life and property and established a rural police to
control the outbreaks of disorder as the Chartists pressed their
demands. 'At this hour', Kay said with such actions in mind, 'military
force alone retains in subjection great masses of the operative
population, beneath whose outrages, if not thus restrained, the
wealth and institutions of society would fall.'[32]

Kay argued that 'the sole effectual means' of preventing anarchy
was to give the 'working people' an education which taught them that
their interests 'are inseparable from those of the other orders of
society'. As education was limited in extent and defective in content
the state was driven to take responsibility, just as it had already
'interfered' with the education of factory children, paupers and
juvenile offenders. With the experiences of East Anglia to support
those of Edinburgh and Manchester, Kay had grown impatient with
'the feuds of sects and the interests of bodies incompetent effectually
to deal with this national question', and in a striking conclusion to the
pamphlet he asserted that

if the whole of this kingdom were placed under an ecclesiastical interdict; if marriages could no longer be solemnised; if the dead were left unburied; and the Churches closed, terrible though the calamity would be, we find a parallel to it in that wide-spread and demoralising ignorance which paralyses all the healthful influences of society, if it does not convert its elements into engines of mutual destruction.

Kay supported state intervention in education because he was convinced that, without it, his imperilled society would collapse.[33]

He came to this position, from a cotton family background which supported the laissez-faire ethos, because he was captured by a vision of moral evil and by a fear of social disaster. But Kay's acceptance of state intervention was not accomplished in an intellectual vacuum – it *was* a pragmatic reaction to intolerable social evils; but it was more than that. Evil is partly in the eye of the beholder, and Kay had first to see evil and know it for what it was. His Dissenting childhood had helped teach him that, stocking his imagination with the sins of intemperance, sexual profligacy, improvidence and irreligion. In Edinburgh his medical education had taught him a more scientific observation and William Alison had shown him the social consequences of personal evil. Through his father, watching the power looms being destroyed at Bass Lane, Kay's family had had direct experience of these consequences. Then in Manchester and East Anglia he had had his own memorable confrontations, and in the face of public inaction, ignorance and malice, turned to municipal and central government action to find a remedy.[34]

The teachings of Jeremy Bentham and his followers may have helped him take that turn. He had been exposed to Benthamite ideas – from Chadwick, the Mills (to whom Nassau Senior had introduced him), and Senior himself: on 19 June 1839, at the height of the education controversy he had dined at the Seniors. Bentham's principle of utility made it possible for Kay to support free trade in commerce while arguing, without any sense of inconsistency, that to combat social and educational evils, state interference was more useful. Furthermore, as an assistant commissioner and as Secretary to the Committee of Council, Kay was in the position of a Benthamite expert bringing statistical knowledge and rationality to solve a social problem. But Kay's views went beyond Bentham, and back to Scotland. As well as learning to see evil there, he had found a solution: Chalmers had stressed the value of education; Stow had shown him how schools might be organized to produce moral and intelligent children, so that future generations could avoid the poverty, criminality and rebelliousness of their parents. Above all, Adam Smith had written of a society in which commerce unfettered by government was beneficial, in which common interests linked the classes, and in which government provision of education was justifiable and even necessary. It was no coincidence that in *Recent Measures*, when he wanted to find sustenance for his beliefs, Kay turned to Smith and quoted the famous passage from *The Wealth of Nations* in which Smith allows government to play a part in the provision of education for the 'labouring poor'.[35]

Recent Measures generated its own controversies, especially with Daniel Wilson, the Bishop of Calcutta, and Henry Phillpotts, the militant Tory Bishop of Exeter. Kay did not escape unscathed from these battles and later editions of *Recent Measures* contained some grudging apologies and minor changes. Phillpotts gained some concessions but, in the *Charge* which he gave to his clergy in October 1839, he showed his capacity for ecclesiastical street fighting by parading some misconceptions with self-righteous vigour. He described the pamphlet's concluding remarks as 'a foul and wicked calumny, which none but an anonymous libeller would dare to put forth'. Kay's reply was to print Phillpotts's comments side by side with the appropriate sections of *Recent Measures* and to write a new preface defending himself.[36]

The bitterness of the controversy and the passionate outbursts which flare amidst the official prose of *Recent Measures* contain a warning. At the Committee of Council Kay was an early example of an increasingly specialized and expert government bureaucrat. But he was not an early specimen of the impartial civil servant, who brought administrative continuity and impartiality while adjusting to the proclivities of changing governments. Never for a moment did Kay think of himself as impartial. He thought of himself as right, as fighting for a cause, as introducing policies to which he was deeply committed. He was constantly trying to persuade, to cajole, to correct, and his ultimate loyalty was to his cause, not to the governments he served, or even, finally, to his own personal advancement. Kay became a great civil servant, but his time at the Committee of Council began amid controversy, continued to be tumultuous, and never found him searching for bureaucratic obscurity. Like Phillpotts, he was a street-fighter; but on a different side.[37]

For six weeks in September and October 1839 Kay left *Recent Measures* to do its work and, accompanied by Tufnell, visited Paris and Germany, Switzerland and Holland. On 11 October 1839, a few days after returning to London, Kay wrote to Russell from his bachelor chambers in Albany in Piccadilly. He argued that a large grant for education (between £100,000 and £500,000 rather than the £30,000 of which Brougham had complained) would always be resisted and, as voluntary donations had failed, he proposed giving parishes and towns the power to levy an education tax. He had advocated the striking of an education rate in evidence before a select committee in March the previous year, but in the letter his plans were more elaborate – and closer to his 1836 suggestion that the powers of Boards of Guardians should be widened so that they evolved into rural municipalities. In his letter he wanted local taxation made subject to conditions, including 'the regulation of secular instruction according to the rules of the Ministry of public instruction, i.e. the Committee of Council'. If a grant for the establishment of Normal schools were made, the Committee could superintend them and 'issue rules for the regulation of the internal discipline and secular instruction of schools'. At the same time, inspection would be made more effective. Kay warned that his letter was 'imperfect probably both in principle and in detail', and he admitted that under the existing system it was impolitic and probably unconstitutional for the executive to try to regulate schools or use strong powers of inspection on issues other than the plan of the building – the grant was for the building of schools. However, his clear preference, which was to guide his future planning, was for a powerful ministry of public instruction (such as he had seen on the Continent) regulating locally managed schools supported by an education rate.[38]

The letter is consistent with a draft minute, which Kay produced before he and Tufnell left, in answer to a request for a policy document to assist the transfer of the administration of the annual grant from the Treasury to the Committee. His draft consistently endeavoured to widen the Committee's powers, despite the fact that in *Recent Measures* he had claimed that the functions of the Committee were similar to those of the Treasury. Spring Rice (now Lord Monteagle) objected to Kay's proposals as impractical, requiring an elaborate bureaucracy and likely to swallow up the whole grant. He was especially unimpressed with Kay's suggestion that the inspectors, whom the Committee was to appoint, could replace the societies in reporting on applications for grants. Monteagle viewed the inspectors' role as advisory, Kay wanted them to enforce the regulations, and to reduce the power of the two societies. The minute, published on 24 September, was a compromise between Kay's and Monteagle's views, and together with the letter, reveals his political immaturity. Having complained to Russell that the original scheme had caused the opposition 'to impute to the Government every monstrous design which their imagination could invent', he proposed a more radical plan which would have confirmed the suspicions of the Church and the Tories, and plunged the government into a battle for which it had no heart and which it could not expect to win. Russell took no action.[39]

In August 1840 Kay was to revisit Paris and, about the same time, Dublin. He used the public reports, dated 1 January 1841 and 15 December 1843, on his two trips to re-state the need for a Normal school and to publicize his ideas on the curriculum and methods of popular schooling. He and Tufnell had paid particular attention to Père Jean-Baptiste Girard of Fribourg; Emmanuel de Fellenberg whose establishment at Hofwyl, near Berne, was well known to Kay through Lady Byron; Johann Jakob Vehrli, who had taught at Hofwyl for 23 years but who was then conducting the Normal school at Kreuzlingen, and to the Mother School of the Brothers of the Christian Schools in Paris. Predictably Kay stressed the degraded state of pauper children, declaring that their teachers should not be hirelings whose main interest was the annual stipend, nor be drawn from those whose age, illness or lack of skill had driven from other occupations. 'The main object of a Normal School', he said, 'is the *formation of the character of the schoolmaster*' (Kay spoke exclusively of men). That schoolmaster was to be 'an agent of civilisation'; he also had to be prepared for a 'humble and subordinate position, and though master of his school, to his scholars he is to be a parent, and to his superiors an intelligent servant and minister'. The schoolmaster should share the qualities of 'the peasant-father' – 'an honest pride in the labour of his hands, in his strength, his manual skill, his robust health, and the manly vigour of his body and mind'. Kay wrote of Vehrli's simplicity, faith and insistence that a teacher should have 'a sense of the pleasures of a well-arranged family'. 'I am a peasant's son', Vehrli told his greatly impressed middle-class visitors. 'I wish to be no other than I am, the teacher of the sons of the peasantry.' Kay was charmed 'by the union of comparatively high intellectual attainments among the scholars with the utmost simplicity of life, and cheerfulness in the humblest menial labour'.[40]

When Kay returned to London in October 1839 he was more than ever convinced of the need for a Normal school. He and Tufnell, realizing that they could not hope for public money, unsuccessfully sought private sponsors; then they decided to support a Normal school at their own expense. Kay made the proposal to the Poor Law Commission at the same time as he wrote to Russell. 'If you approve, I will create it *at my own risk*', he told Shaw-Lefevre. 'All I ask is your approval.' Planning was swift for, on 18 October 1839, only ten days after his return from the Continent and a week after his letter to Russell, Kay sent Lady Byron details of his plans, including the fact that he had found a suitable house in Battersea. He also told her that 'unless I find a Vehrli, I see nothing for it, but my taking residence at Battersea'. He took up residence early in 1840 in the old manor house (called the Terrace House) which he leased from Shaw-Lefevre. Kay and Tufnell, hoping that eventually the financing of the institution would be taken up by 'abler hands', had established the Battersea Training School, a remarkable institution from the day of its origin. Neither the Poor Law Commission nor the Committee of Council gave it money but, at a time of great controversy, the Commission sanctioned its establishment and the Committee allowed its secretary to run the school as a private residential institution.[41]

Battersea in the early 1840s was a small village in a mainly market gardening area famous for its asparagus, though the arrival of the railway in 1838 was a harbinger of industrial change. The Terrace House, a somewhat neglected manor house, the remnant of a larger building, was to the north-east of the village, close to the Thames and next to St Mary's Church which had been mentioned in the *Domesday Book*. Not far from Battersea Bridge, then a wooden structure which was to inspire Whistler, was a marshy area once part of the common fields of the manor. In the 1840s it was the scene of sabbath desecration, prize-fighting, gypsy camps and fairs. Robert Eden, vicar of St Mary's, was a leader in the fight to persuade the government to make the area respectable by turning these notorious fields into Battersea Park.[42]

Kay's decision to go to Battersea was influenced by Eden's offer of his village school and his willingness to superintend religious instruction. Educated at Eton and Magdalene College, the 40-year-old Eden was chaplain to Queen Victoria, had been chaplain to King William, and eventually became Bishop of Bath and Wells and the third Baron Auckland. His religious views were moderate but inclining to the High Church. 'Under the shadow of Mr. Eden's wing', Kay remarked, '. . . nothing is to be feared from the Church' and, as he later informed Peel, the religious instruction was 'tolerant

162

Battersea College seen from the river

Church of Englandism'. This meant that a student who asked to attend divine service elsewhere than at the parish church would not be prevented, but would face the suggestion that he should not attend the Training School, lest 'a spirit of controversy arose'. Where national policy was concerned Kay defended the April minute, but at Battersea he had to accept the Church's power in order to retain the support of his influential patron.[43]

At the beginning of February 1840 the first boys, mostly orphans about 13 years of age, were moved from Norwood. They were to have three years' instruction in the Training School and to work as pupil teachers at the village school. By January 1841 there were 24 boys in this category, and acquaintances of Kay's, including the Bishop of Durham, the Earl of Chichester and Lady Byron, assisted with a grant of £20 per annum towards a child's expenses for clothing, board and education. A second group of nine men, about 20–30 years old, either came on the recommendation of friends or were being trained for schools under the responsibility of friends. Kay swiftly appointed masters (he sometimes called them tutors): William Horne, the teacher at Gressenhall who (in Kay's account) had indirectly assisted in the development of the pupil teacher system, was appointed when the school opened; Thomas Tate, later a well-known textbook writer; and Stow's protégé, Walter MacLeod, who moved from Norwood to take charge of the village school. He turned it into a type of experimental school and within a few years was being referred to as 'master of method', probably the first person in Britain to have that title.[44]

The regimen at Battersea shows Vehrli's influence. In the first months the students rose at half-past five and did household work until a quarter to seven, when they were marched to the five-acre garden. After an hour's work among its rubbish, withered grass and weeds, they marched to the toolhouse, left their implements, washed, and assembled for prayer in a specially prepared hall at eight o'clock. A passage of Scripture was read, a psalm chanted or a hymn sung, and prayers were said, often from a collection prepared by the Bishop of London. They breakfasted at half-past eight and studied from nine till twelve when they returned to the garden for an hour. Dinner was from one till two and, after another hour in the garden, the boys worked in their classes until five. Yet another hour in the garden followed. They had supper at six o'clock, and returned to class, working by dim candle-light from seven till nine when evening prayers were read. Then they went to bed. Occasionally Kay took them on long walks into the country to look at schools or to study a building of historical importance or some natural phenomena. On Sundays there were church services morning and evening, some study of the formularies, and the writing out from memory of a large extract from one of the sermons. These compositions were then read and discussed by the whole school.[45]

Experience and changing circumstances modified this timetable. When the garden had been brought into order, three of the four hours devoted to gardening were used for gymnastics, attendance at the village school, and lectures in the art of teaching. Similarly, when it became clear that the educational standard of the boys and the young men was low, Kay produced a plan to address its inadequacies through a preparatory education in the first year. Nevertheless, after the school had been going for four years, Kay was forced to argue that the course should be two years long and that no one under 18 years of age should be enrolled.[46]

To the rigorous timetable Kay added a complex system of weekly, quarterly and annual examinations. He also produced a uniform for the younger pupils – a plain dress of rifle green, which caused the students to be known as 'green birds', and a working dress of fustian cord. The older pupils had no dress restrictions but were watched for any peculiarities which threatened to tip into foppery. Kay thought that registers of moral merit encouraged rivalry and hypocrisy, but he organized time-books to check punctuality and kept records of household and outdoor work. Masters and students lived in the same house, rose at the same time, shared the same diet and ate in the same room. Apart from a matron who acted as cook, there were no servants, and all domestic duties were shared by the students. Cows, pigs, goats and poultry were bought and given into the charge of the older boys. By the time the masters went to bed they were probably as tired as the students for they accompanied them everywhere, worked in the garden with them and, in the autumn of 1840, assisted in the making of extensive alterations to the house. Kay summarized the Battersea philosophy when he remarked that the conceit of the pedagogue was 'not likely to arise among either students or masters, who cheerfully handle the trowel, the saw, or carry mortar in a hod to the top of the building'.[47]

Kay's fevered belief in his own ideas made it impossible for him to live at Battersea and not seek to control its activities. He worked in the garden, taught the art of teaching, attended prayers and divine service, led excursions to Norwood and Greenwich, visited the village school, devised examinations, and quietened the dormitories. A principal, he informed the Committee of Council, should be gentle and accessible, should devote his leisure to private interviews with the students, ensure that religion was not simply taught but was 'the element in which the students live', and be incessantly vigilant – for if he left 'the little republic, of which he is the head, to form its own manners, and to create its own standard of principle and action, the catastrophe of a deep ulcerous corruption, is not likely to be long delayed'. Kay said that he never assumed a tone of authority, preferring to correct a master's views by suggestion rather than argument. Thus without appearing to be directive, Kay was present in the school 'in each master's person by pre-occupying his mind rather than by exercising authority over his acts'. Of course, he was not as unobtrusive or as subtle as he claimed. 'I took the seat of the superior', he once said, sounding like the abbot in a monastery, 'and spoke in the name of the masters', occasionally asking them for their opinion but doing nothing which could impair their authority.[48]

Being in residence Kay's students and their teachers were removed from the distracting and mercenary lures of the outside world. The prayers, the sermons, the labour, the excursions, the meticulous timetable, the meals in common, the determination to ensure that 'the example of the master shall insensibly inform the habits of the scholar', the controlled leisure, the ubiquitous principal – everything was shaped towards the formation of character. The Training School was a total institution, though its model was not the asylum or gaol whose inmates are hidden away or punished. It had a clear moral and social purpose, the defence of a social order Kay perceived to be under threat, but, as was the case with pauper education, Kay's approach to the students was more generous and more complicated than a straightforward desire to protect society and his own class interests. John Hullah, the music teacher whom Kay brought to Battersea, wrote of visiting a Christian Brothers' school in Paris in August 1840:

> He [Kay] followed their teaching with close attention, and at the termination of one of the classes burst into a passion of tears, exclaiming, 'Would to God we had anything like these *men* (he would have said *papists* an hour before) in our schools!' A strange exclamation from a man very reticent on the subject of religious belief, and certainly, at the period of this visit to Paris, holding in horror everything bordering on Roman Catholicism.

This man, who had been so intent on exposing the duplicity of paupers, was driven by a passion which could turn the means of social stability, education, into an end with independent justification and demands.[49]

The passion and its ambiguities assailed Kay when he compared the Training School to a family in which his tutors occupied 'the parental seat'.[50] In pedagogic terms the analogy was generous because through it Kay asked for gentleness and affection in the handling of the students, though he had experienced enough of the tyrannies of middle-class family life to know that the analogy was ambiguous. A more arresting ambiguity arose from the fact that, at a time when the mother's role was being magnified, the family he invoked possessed no women as students or teachers – the cook, however, was a woman. Furthermore, the students had been removed from their natural families and placed in a residential institution so that values judged to be superior to those of their parents could be imparted. Yet, however obvious the contradictions in his thinking may now seem, they do not reduce the pedagogic significance of his comparison or, in the context of his time, its radical challenge to educational practice.

A paper Kay wrote at the Terrace House on 25 January 1841, which he called 'On the punishment of pauper children in work-houses', further reflected the ambiguity in Kay's thinking on the family. He commented on the ignorance of mothers in all classes, but especially the poor, and lamented the 'moral predispositions' of pauper parents; yet he urged teachers to fill their minds with 'sympathies for the children resembling the parental'. Despite these waverings his intentions were clear – the forbidding of corporal punishment in workhouse schools. Corporal punishment was a proof of the incompetence of the master – 'There is no tyranny so odious as that which Cowper denounced – the tyranny of full grown Dullness over defenceless dunces of its own creation', Kay wrote. Just as the abolition of torture had reformed judicial procedures, so the ending of corporal punishment would make teaching rational because teachers would be compelled to think about what they did. They would then realize that, though punishment might make the child obey the laws of the school, it was not likely to develop conscience, the awakening of which was the object of moral education. In any case, instant corporal punishment created an expectation that errors were followed by retribution, so that in life after school when no bolt fell after an offence was committed, evil people might be encouraged to act with impunity. They might forget what 'the Eye that never sleeps has in store for those who break His laws', the 'retributive providence' which ensured appropriate punishments for faults – the jealous lost their friends and the ambitious were objects of envy, while the honest were trusted and the meek were protected. 'I wish that this was true', a sceptical Poor Law Commissioner wrote in the margin.[51]

Any punishment required should be mild, given privately, and be free of any suspicion of bad temper. He suggested confinement in a warm room, lighted by a skylight, and perhaps combined with an employment which was appropriate to the offence. The children should feel that their conduct made them forfeit claims to respect, confidence and love, Kay believed, being untroubled by later generations' scruples about psychological punishment. He displayed revulsion when writing of workhouse schools in which the paupers 'seemed almost the football of a certain class – half-crazed by idleness and insobriety. I remember a Pauper Porter whose custom it was to kick every boy who came near him, or who passed through his Gate'. His great contemporary, Charles Dickens, condemned just these abuses, but others were not sympathetic. The Commissioner who doubted retributive providence took Isaiah as his inspiration when he commented:

> 'The renewal of the Golden Age.' The wolf also shall dwell with the lamb, and the leopard shall lie down with the kid, and the calf and the young lion and the fatling together, and a little child shall lead them. I fear we are not ripe for this at present.

He was right. Nothing was done. Ironically, Kay was not able to ensure the enforcement of these views at the village school in Battersea where caning re-emerged after its abolition had been proudly announced.[52]

The course of secular instruction and the teaching methods at Battersea also reflected a greater generosity and educational imagination than can be equated with a narrow pursuit of class interest. Aware that his acquaintances who were supporting students at Battersea wished to supply a teacher for the village school or a school on their estate, Kay had popular rather than merely pauper education in mind. He saw Battersea as producing schoolmasters who, having acquired the requisite skills, 'will diffuse them through-out the country'. The curriculum which he proposed, therefore, went beyond that offered in monitorial schools or the small private schools. Setting a model which was to be followed in teachers' colleges until the twentieth century, he divided the curriculum into two parts: first, because of the low level of their achievements, the students continued their general education; then they received their professional education by studying the art and practice of teaching. They were taught reading, and introduced both to the structure of the English language, through grammar, etymology, dictation and composition, and to the 'great minds' of English literature. They were even to get a sense of literary style. Then followed handwriting, arithmetic, the elements of algebra, mensuration and land surveying, book-keeping, some mechanics, geography, the outlines of the history of England, drawing (including drawing from models), and vocal music which Kay believed to have a powerful moral effect. Kay again drew on continental mentors to suggest how this curriculum should be taught: German work on phonics, Mülhauser for handwriting, Pestalozzi for arithmetic, Dupuis for drawing, and Wilhelm for music. Under the Committee of Council's patronage Wilhelm's methods were adapted for English use by John Hullah, whose fame spread from Battersea to many schools, including Eton and other Public Schools. This curriculum was swiftly embodied in manuals and teaching aids, in the development of which the Training School and MacLeod's village school played a crucial part. Materials were prepared to assist the teaching of phonics, writing, arithmetic, drawing and, most successful of all, Hullah's approach to the teaching of singing. Battersea had become the powerhouse from which a new orthodoxy was being generated and disseminated.[53]

Kay was fully aware that Battersea challenged not only school practices but also provincial and working-class cultures. Through phonics he attacked the provincial dialects which many students brought to Battersea. He noted that the middle and upper classes frequently used terms of Latin or Greek derivation which were not common in the vocabulary of the labouring classes: instruction in their meaning was therefore necessary. It was equally necessary to develop a sense of literary style in order to make complicated sentence constructions more accessible.[54] Kay realized the dilemma which plagues advocates of popular education: giving access to knowledge and skills which empower a social group may involve the destruction of parts of that group's culture. Like many of his middle-class contemporaries Kay did not hesitate in making his choice.

Kay devoted equal attention to the second half of his curriculum, the study of the methods of teaching. His ideas were similar to those in his reports on pauper education, though they were more formally stated and betrayed a greater, if idiosyncratic and eclectic, Pestalozzian influence. Kay borrowed the view that children should learn through their senses as an antidote to learning purely from books or by rote. 'What concerns the social state of man', he declared, 'may best be apprehended after lessons in the fields, the ruins, the mansions, and the streets within range of the school.' (Kay's practice, like Pestalozzi's, often departed from this view.) He also drew from Pestalozzi the theory of synthetic or constructive education ('I should prefer a simpler definition', the sceptical Commissioner had written when Kay used these expressions in his paper on punishment). The teacher broke learning down into small tasks which led logically from one to another, so that pupils always understood what they were learning and found the experience rational and rewarding. For example, under the phonic method children first learn the sounds, then the signs of the sounds (the printed letters), then the combination of the sounds into words and sentences. Provided that the teacher was adept at analysing tasks into their elements, all subjects could be taught this way, Kay, following Pestalozzi, believed. 'The easiest transition in acquirement', he said,

> is in the order of simplicity from the known to the unknown, and it is indispensable to skilful teaching that the matter of instruction should be arranged in a synthetic order, so that all the elements may have to each other the relation of a progressive series from the most simple to the complex.

Unfortunately manuals such as those being produced at Battersea became so minutely mechanical as to defeat the spirit of their compilers.[55]

Despite its shortcomings, this approach focused attention on the needs of the learner. Children were not so many pitchers to be filled with facts, as Dickens later had Gradgrind doing; they were 'rational creatures'. A child could be puzzled or made rebellious if a teacher loaded its memory 'not only with what it does not understand, but with what is revolting to its understanding'. Moreover, despite its epistemological naivety and its practical rigidity, the approach gave Kay a theoretical basis from which to continue his onslaught on authoritarian teaching. Nothing, he insisted dogmatically, was to be taught dogmatically. Constructive education was based on the assumption that the child was 'a being whose reasoning powers are immature, yet a rational creature, whose memory may be most successfully cultivated when employed in subordination to the reasoning faculty'. The child had to be brought, admittedly with caution, to the stage of being self-directed.[56] In this a child of the Enlightenment, Kay stressed that education was an affirmation that people and society could be changed. Of course, changed they had to be, if the social order which Kay valued was to survive, but he advocated a more generous curriculum and methodology than were necessary for the accomplishment of conservative purpose. He asked that the child should be treated humanely and as a rational being. He was not the first to insist that the working-class child should be considered in this way, but he was the first in Britain who held these views and simultaneously had the will and the opportunity to put them into practice on a national scale.

The claim, made by Kay, Tufnell and later historians, that Battersea laid down the lines upon which teacher education developed over the next 50 years, has been challenged. J.L. Alexander's analysis of the plans of the 'young gentlemen' shows that by May 1840, when Battersea had been going for three months, there were small diocesan training colleges in seven cathedral cities, and that plans for Queen's Hall, the central training college in London, predated Battersea. However, the college (eventually called St Mark's and built in neighbouring Chelsea) did not open until April 1841, triggered by shocked reaction to what Kay had done at Battersea. Commenting on the indifference towards the teaching of pedagogy in these colleges, Alexander notes that the Anglican training enterprise drew its inspiration from Newman and, rejecting any suspicions of utilitarianism, was antithetical to the idea of the trained elementary schoolmaster which motivated Kay.[57] Certainly he wished Battersea to be an affirmation of the teacher's significance in society. At a time when teaching the poor and the pauper was a despised occupation, Kay, for all the rules with which he hedged round his students, tried to give teachers a sense of worth. He did this because he wanted children taught rationally and with kindness and skill. In his own lifetime, and later, Kay's hopes were attacked and rejected; perhaps the affirmation of them, rather than the pedagogy which tried to embody them, was Battersea's greatest contribution to English education.

At the same time Battersea symbolized the ambiguities in Kay's thought. Throughout its life Kay consistently fought for the right of the civil order, the state, to enter the field of popular education, previously the preserve of the Church. When endeavouring to persuade his contemporaries about the need for government intervention he often invoked, and became preoccupied with, his fear of social disorder. When he wrote about how schools were to be run he was preoccupied with the more generous conceptions he had learned from Stow or Pestalozzi. Both preoccupations flowed into the government school system which eventually developed from his efforts and for more than a century government schools have grappled with these conflicting demands. Until the 1960s, liberal historians usually ignored the social pressure which led to the establishment of government schools and saw them as progressive and liberal institutions. Since the 1960s it has been common to see them as a middle-class, usually male-dominated, imposition on the working class. Where the liberals often romanticized flawed but vital institutions, some post-1960 historians too willingly sacrificed the intricacies of history before the god of tidy theory. They have been false to the historical experience of government-school teachers who have not seen themselves as the class oppressors of their students. Most ironically, having reduced government schooling to a subtle, or crude, middle-class plot, they were intellectually crippled when the time came to defend it against neo-conservative attacks on its legitimacy. James Kay's brave ambiguities contain a warning: government schools (and their predecessors which he helped to create) both control and empower their students. The balance at any one time is precarious.

During 1839 and 1840, Kay had another battle with the Church. Inspection was a common part of the programme of educational reformers. The ground had been prepared by continental example; the pervasive, though not precise, Benthamite influence; precedents such as factory inspectors or, more remotely, assistant Poor Law commissioners; and the acknowledged need for some form of accountability. The 13 April minute proposed the appointment of two inspectors of schools which had been granted public money, and Kay, who regarded inspection as second only in importance to the establishment of Normal schools, was gratified by (and probably drafted) a Committee of Council minute of 3 June 1839 which required inspection where new grants were given. The purpose was to secure 'a conformity to the regulations and discipline established in the several Schools, with such improvements as may from time to time be suggested by the Committee'. Though he knew that the issue of inspection was fraught with as many difficulties as the Normal school, Kay favoured the securing of conformity, only to be rebuked by Lord Monteagle, who thought that inspectors 'should merely inspect and report the facts. Opinion must do the rest; authority never will'. The June minute was immediately condemned, and the Committee made concessions – there would be no interference with religious instruction; inspectors would not exercise authority over the management of the schools, except to report the results of examinations; and one inspector would be appointed with the sole task of inspecting the National Society's schools. But the Committee would not allow the Society unchallenged power to report on its own arrangements or 'the right of excluding officers appointed by the State, to which they are to be indebted for a part of their resources'. Unwilling to accept any inspection that was not derived from or connected with the authorities of the Church, the Society was adamant that these resources, which it claimed amounted only to a third or a quarter of the building cost, gave the government no right to inspect 'and perhaps eventually to control, the entire discipline and economy of the school'.[58]

Increasing the pressure, the Church withdrew nearly all its applications for aid, or if grants had been offered, refused them. As relations grew more acrimonious and the two parties settled down to a bad-tempered waiting game, Russell and Lansdowne made a decisive step. In November 1839, through the Committee, they appointed two inspectors, the Rev. John Allen, chaplain to the Bishop of Chichester and a lecturer in mathematics at King's College, London, who was to inspect National schools, and Seymour Tremenheere, a barrister, a Whig and a member of the Central Society, who inspected other schools. Allen's was a clever appointment as he was known to be deeply religious, and it enraged Tories who did not know that he had consulted Blomfield on the issue. Blomfield advised him to accept the appointment, because 'if we are to have inspection it is better to have it in good hands'. From the Committee's viewpoint, this willingness to compromise was a helpful sign.[59]

Appointing inspectors was one thing; getting them to work in the way the Committee wanted was another. In the first months of 1840 the stand-off continued, though the Committee had some grounds for hope. The Church of Scotland accepted inspectors, and uneasiness grew in the National Society as Dissenters, who had not objected to the arrangements for inspection, applied for grants. Then in January 1840 Kay produced instructions in which inspectors were told not to interfere with the teaching or the management of the school, not to press suggestions which were unfavourably received, and to co-operate with the local school authorities (mostly clergymen). Early in June 1840 it became evident that moderate Church figures and even *The Times* had decided that compromise was necessary and that the National Society was too intransigent – 'foolish and petulant', the paper called it as the attack was mounted.[60]

A meeting took place late in June between Russell, Lansdowne, Howley, Blomfield and two other bishops. Kay informed his friend, the factory inspector Leonard Horner, that the meeting had gone well and that prospects for a compromise were good. However, Howley went down fighting. He produced proposals which, as Paz says, would have reduced the Committee to a paymaster – he particularly insisted that the appointment of inspectors should be made by the archbishops and accepted or rejected by the Committee. Meanwhile Lansdowne begged Russell to say nothing that would encourage the bishops 'to think we shall agree to the most objectionable point of their proposal, making the appointment of our inspectors originate with themselves'. By mid July agreement had been reached. The Committee would appoint inspectors of Anglican schools after consultation with the archbishops, who were at liberty to suggest names and could exercise a veto. The inspector's instructions on religion would be drawn up by the archbishops and were part of his general instructions, thus (at least symbolically) ensuring that the religious and the secular were not separated: the general instructions were to be sent to the arch-bishops before being published. The grants were to be distributed in proportion to the number of children being educated and the amount of money raised, an arrangement which favoured the Church as it was the wealthiest denomination and educated the most children. The National Society and the Committee of Council agreed to these proposals, which became known as the Concordat, on 15 July 1840. The Committee had made compromises and the Church had secured some protection. It had, however, made the most important con-cessions: there would be inspectors whose responsibility was to the Committee of Council, not the Church, and whose appointment was ultimately in the Committee's power.[61]

John Allen issued an early challenge to the Concordat when he refused to submit his reports through Kay or to address them to the Committee. Kay warned Lansdowne that the Committee's control of its inspectors was being tested and claimed that, as inspectors were appointed with no particular knowledge of education, they must 'either be the propagators of error, or they must be more or less responsible to the Secretary'. His threat to resign caused Allen to exclaim that 'few severer blows could be dealt to the cause of popular education in this country than the loss of your services'. But Allen refused to budge, asking Kay whether 'any clergyman will accept the office of inspector if he be bound to obey the injunctions of one who fills your situation?' The 'situation' had a double meaning: Kay's administrative position and his class status – Allen, who is said to be the model for Dobbin in *Vanity Fair*, had been educated at Westminster and Trinity College, Cambridge, and moved in social circles to which Kay could only aspire. 'I became inspector', he continued, 'being assured no such obedience was due from me.' Lansdowne, as became a grandee of superior kind, gave no ground: 'If Mr. Allen's report does not appear formally and distinctly addressed to the Lords of the Committee of Council', he told Kay, 'it must be sent back with a simple and dry direction (by my order if you will) so as to address it agreeably to the terms of the Minute.'[62]

'Plain and dry' was Lansdowne's suggestion, as Kay continued working on the instructions to inspectors. The final version, made in accordance with the Concordat, appeared in August 1840. Plain and dry it was not. Lansdowne wanted inspectors to report on whether public money had been duly applied, to record the effect of that application, including any improvements which might be applied elsewhere, and to give advice whenever it was sought. Instead Kay produced a letter which instructed inspectors to be circumspect advisors, and a list of questions which encouraged them to examine every aspect of schooling: the buildings, the classrooms and playgrounds, the moral and religious instruction, the means of teaching in secular subjects, the organization and discipline, the rewards and punishments, the methods of instruction, the arrangements for pupil teachers and monitors, the state of the attendance records and registers, the qualifications and attainments of the teachers, the school's method of government and its income and annual expenditure. The 174 obsessively detailed questions showed that, despite his remark to Russell that the regulation of schools apart from the buildings was impolitic and unconstitutional, Kay had just such regulation in mind. The obstacles to turning the Committee of Council into a ministry of public instruction were formidable, but so was Kay's determination.[63]

The inspectorate assisted Kay in another effort to bring his educational ideas before school promoters. As early as August 1839 he had presented the Committee with plans drawn up by the architect, Sampson Kempthorne, whom he was also recommending to Lady Byron for work at Ealing Grove, and on 20 February 1840 the Committee approved his 'Minute explanatory of the plans of schoolhouses'. Kay provided specimen forms for the contract, plans, specifications, estimates for building and even for the conveyancing. The use of such documents would save expense and, he claimed with more enthusiasm than accuracy, the Committee's plans would 'diffuse an acquaintance with the arrangements which have been sanctioned by extensive experience, as best adapted to different systems of instruction'. In recognition of the prevalence of the monitorial system in the schools of the two societies, the plans were designed for the mixed system of instruction, which combined a modified form of monitorial teaching with the simultaneous system. Even so they were probably better suited to simultaneous teaching, which Kay continued to argue was preferable. The lessons Kay had learned from David Stow could now be diffused more widely and the Committee's inspectors could report on their effectiveness.[64]

The educational empire which the state (for Kay, that was politicians in government and civil servants) was beginning to construct was a result of a schism in the ranks of those who ran Britain. The Church protested that the Committee of Council was a challenge by the civil power to its prerogatives and, though they proclaimed their good intentions, Russell, Lansdowne and Kay had determinedly issued that challenge. The Committee, born out of that determination, and political expediency, had its existence threatened, its policies condemned and its secretary attacked; but it survived to administer the parliamentary grant. Kay wanted to impose tighter conditions on the grant than his political masters would allow, and he had to watch as the Normal school was thrown to the wolves, and a high price paid for the Concordat. But the Church was forced to concede prime power in the appointment of inspectors to the government, and Lansdowne had ensured that they reported directly to the Committee of Council. Through inspection, letters, regulations, sets of instructions, architectural plans and manuals of method, Kay set out to influence the curriculum which schools were to offer, their methods of teaching and discipline, their sites and the shape of their classrooms (even to the detail of providing a lobby or a closet for hanging bonnets, cloaks or capes). Much work had to be done before popular schooling could be brought under government control, but through the Committee of Council, machinery had been created which the state could later use.

That machinery, Kay was already showing, could not be entirely controlled by the politicians who had set it up. Civil servants had their own ambitions, specialist knowledge, vested interests and ideals.

Despite the struggles Kay had reason for self-congratulation, though one dark cloud remained perpetually on the horizon. Melbourne's government continued in its seemingly endless state of disintegration and, when its end came, Kay knew that the Committee's fate (and his) would be decided by declared enemies of the civil power in education.

On 4 July 1836, while James Kay was in East Anglia dealing with recalcitrant paupers, the 18-year-old Janet Shuttleworth was in Hastings in Sussex writing in her journal about her family home, Gawthorpe Hall, at Padiham in Lancashire. The paintings of Canaletto, which she had just admired in the British Gallery, reminded her of those hanging in the dining room at Gawthorpe. Later that year her aunt, Elizabeth Shuttleworth, sent her a book, *The Spiritual Life*, and Janet remembered that, when she was a child and living at Gawthorpe, her aunt used to play the harp and sing to her. She also remembered her aunt singing at her christening (she was then four years old), or lying on the sofa in her room knitting stockings for the poor children of the neighbourhood.[65]

Despite the home-sweet-home sentimentality in Janet Shuttleworth's attitude to Gawthorpe, there can be no doubting her passion for the building and its accompanying estate, to which she was the sole heiress. The site of Gawthorpe had been acquired by Ughtred de Shuttleworth in 1388. The area then contained a few small hamlets dotted through heavily wooded country, and the Shuttleworths erected a fortified building. By the mid-sixteenth century they had accumulated wealth, principally through the efforts of Hugo Shuttleworth (*c.*1520–96) and his son Richard (1542–99). Marriage alliances, and perhaps land acquired as the monasteries were dissolved, contributed to their rise in importance. Richard, knighted by Queen Elizabeth in 1589 and a judge in Chester, made a considerable fortune at the Bar and invested heavily in land, including the Barbon estate which is still with the family. He planned the building of Gawthorpe Hall, but died in 1599 before it had begun. Gawthorpe was built by his brother Lawrence, between 1600 and 1605, in a striking setting below Pendle Hill on the banks of the Calder River. The speed of the building operation, which included the impressive

Great Barn which was simultaneously constructed, is evidence of strong commitment and organizational skills. On stylistic grounds Gawthorpe has been attributed to Robert Smythson, a major figure in English architecture, but it seems likely that Smythson provided a plan which may not have been fully followed. Whatever its provenance, Gawthorpe was an unusual building and testimony to the wealth of the Shuttleworths and the confidence with which they had assumed their place among the landed gentry of Lancashire.[66]

When Lawrence Shuttleworth died in 1608 Gawthorpe came into the possession of his nephew, Richard, perhaps the best known of the Shuttleworths, who at various times was High Sheriff for Lancashire and Member of Parliament for Preston. A colonel in the Parliamentary Army, he was in charge at the battle of Whalley when he decisively defeated the Royalists and brought Lancashire firmly into Cromwell's camp. After his death in 1699 the family moved from Gawthorpe, and for about 150 years the Shuttleworths were absentee landlords. It was Janet's father Robert who, about 1816, moved back to Gawthorpe and began renovations.[67]

Robert, a fascinating, intelligent, dark figure, was born in 1784, and became a barrister and Chairman of the Bench at Preston Sessions where he was called 'the People's Magistrate'. His legal and business interests kept him often in London but he followed the affairs of his estate closely, sending his estate manager, Paul Tickle, frequent letters from one of the Temple Inns of Court. Robert's views were expressed with terse vigour. He described one tenant as 'a most obstinate brute and I heartily wish his Rum and Milk would wash him into the next world', while of a debtor who had cheated him he remarked: 'I will either have my money or his carcase – all the attorneys in the land shall not protect him any longer.' He had other problems, about which he was equally frank. Instructing Tickle to find out who had cut the bell wires at Gawthorpe he suggested prosecution if the culprit was a particular woman but, he added, 'as for those little Bitches of maids they could not have wished to injure my Property, for I always paid them well for whatever they did for me'. In later years Janet did not seem to realize that one woman who importuned her family was her father's and not her grandfather's mistress.[68]

On 5 November 1816 Robert Shuttleworth married Janet Marjoribanks, the eldest daughter of Sir John Marjoribanks, the first Baronet of Lees and a member of a distinguished Scottish banking family. They made Gawthorpe their home and their only child, Janet, was born there on 9 November 1817. Robert Shuttleworth died, four months later, from what appears to be the result of injuries he sustained when he upset the coach he was driving, almost causing the death of his wife and daughter. He died a slow death. He was seriously ill and troubled with financial problems in December 1817. In January 1818 he decided to sell an estate he owned in Essex and, in the same month, writing from London, he told Tickle that he might not see Gawthorpe again. His suffering spilled out in criticism: 'you really . . . have acted so like a blockhead I have no patience to write about it'. On 13 January he felt that he was improving and that, if he could get 'this remaining disease' (he does not say what disease) cured, his strength would return fast. It did not, and he died at Gawthorpe on 6 March 1818. He might have been High Sheriff that year, the *Blackburn Mail* reported, but he had declined because of his health. As it was 'the great energies of his mind and body were very conducive to the peace, order and happiness of the country'. Janet Shuttleworth was left a widow with a four-month-old baby after only 16 months of marriage. She lived for a time at Gawthorpe but then moved away, though she visited it occasionally.[69]

On 8 April 1825 Sir John Marjoribanks gave Paul Tickle an account of a major change in Janet's life: she was to marry Frederick North, 'a Gentleman with a very good Property in Norfolk', who despite some encumbrances would bring 'a handsome income' to add to Janet's. He was two or three years younger but it was 'in every way an excellent marriage'. North came from a younger branch of the Earl of Guildford's family, which included a prime minister, Lord North, and there were 'greater improbabilities' than his succession to the title. More importantly, he was 'a very gentlemanlike young Man of the very best conduct', and it was impossible for Janet to have married a man who was 'more likely to do justice to my little grand-daughter's education'. North was less enthusiastic about Sir John Marjoribanks. A decent and honourable man who loved Janet Shuttleworth deeply, he was hurt by the Marjoribanks' attempts to secure a marriage settlement which gave excessive protection to Janet's fortune. They were 'tying my hands up famously', he confided to his diary. Sir John Marjoribanks, North believed, would never have accepted for his own son the 'very unusual settlements' proposed, though Janet was called upon to preserve the peace when some members of her family argued that the more reasonable settlement which North eventually gained was too much in his favour. Janet Shuttleworth and Frederick North were married on 16 June 1825.[70]

North's property at Rougham was less imposing than it had been because his grandfather, Fountain North, had destroyed the old house in which he felt he had been cruelly treated by his father. However, a farmhouse was converted into a comfortable home, though the Norths lived mostly in Hastings, for which Frederick became the Member in the Whig interest in 1832. He voted for the Reform Bill but bad health forced his resignation in 1837. In the meantime he pursued his business interests, looked after his Rougham estate, and kept an eye on Gawthorpe. The Norths had three children, two daughters – Marianne, usually called Pop, and Janet Catherine, usually known by her second name – and one son, Charles. Janet Shuttleworth's relationship with her half-sisters and -brother seems to have been unstressful, and they lived a comfortable life by the sea in Hastings, interspersed with visits to Rougham, Edinburgh, and occasionally Gawthorpe. North had accepted his wife's wish to keep up Gawthorpe Hall, despite the expense. It was to 'little Janet's' advantage – 'whom I really love, if, for her mother's sake, but absolutely for her own'. On visiting Gawthorpe a few weeks after his marriage North wrote:

> I cannot wholly understand the strange feeling which being at this place excites in me. There is something very painful in it (like many other painful feelings which excite at all events if they do not even irritate the mind) I cannot keep myself from indulging in it. I have felt them before once or twice. But there is a picture in the library (which I cannot doubt to be that of R[obert] Shuttleworth from its likeness to Janet [the child]) which disturbs my mind in the strangest manner. It is a weakness, and one that must be combatted. It is a harsh, rather powerful, and very intelligent countenance – but showing much ill temper – by no means of a liberal cast.

North exclaimed: 'Janet to have been under the control of such a character!' Yet this man had said on his deathbed, 'Marry again, soon; you will make any man happy, if woman can make him so.' Janet was of 'a nobler character', North concluded, 'and I will endeavour to render myself worthy of her'.[71]

When Janet returned to Gawthorpe in the summer of 1838, the year in which she turned 21, she too examined her father's portrait. She saw a different person from the one who had intrigued North:

> The very presence of my Father's picture does me good, I study it by the hour, trying to discover that I am like it, and endeavouring to read his character from that of his features, so that I may resemble him and be as loved and worthy of love as he by all accounts was.

James Kay-Shuttleworth (*The Graphic*)

Janet Shuttleworth, *c.* 1840 (courtesy of Lord Shuttleworth)

Her sense of family tradition, her deeply religious nature, and her sentimentality produced reflections as touchingly simple as those the portrait caused. Returned from church with Charles and Pop, she wrote that the Padiham church had for her acquired 'a more than ordinary degree of sacredness from the remains of my Father being interred there'. She was impressed to be 'worshipping the God of all in the same church, possibly on the same spot, where he has so often been similarly engaged'. She read and re-read his tombstone, studied his handwriting which she thought surprisingly similar to her own, calculated his age, wondered how different she would have been had he lived, and decided that 'it is doubtless best for me as it is – with GOD for my Father, why desire any earthly one?'[72] She did desire an earthly father, however, as her search to understand Robert Shuttleworth revealed. But, to some extent, parents are what children make them, and the Robert Shuttleworth she constructed was more like her heavenly father than the man who had married Janet Marjoribanks, pursued his debtors with anger, and paid his maids for whatever they did for him.

With her majority only a few months away Janet set herself, with help from 'Mr North', to master the affairs of her estate. She was determined to improve the land for herself and her heirs (even though she thought that she would have none), and not to be an absentee landlord who spent elsewhere money made on the estate. She conferred with her steward, her lawyer and neighbours, rode round the estate noting that her cottages needed much money spent on them, planned improvements at the Hall including the installation of an organ in its Long Gallery, struggled with accounts and business papers, calculated that the farm rents of £5,500 per annum would give her an annual income of £2,000, decided to buy a mill on the Calder partly because the weir constructed for its use caused flooding at the back of Gawthorpe, and met neighbours whose names were as familiar to her ancestors as they were to be for her successors – Dugdale, Townley Parker, Thursby, Scarlett, Diggle, Starkie. She took a particular interest in her colliery which, when in full operation, employed more than 200 hands. It was rented to Thursby and Scarlett for £800 per annum and a percentage of the coal taken out. She concluded that they took too little in order to keep up the price of coal, and determined to break their monopoly – it was 'bad for the country, bad for the poor, bad in every way'. She felt her youth and inexperience, and her gender – 'As a man I might do better, but as a woman I do not think I can'. Her laundry maid advised her to marry:

'be sure and get a good man, Miss, who'll be like to live here'. Others gave her similar advice, but she described as 'tiresome' the convention (which prevented her from coming immediately to Gawthorpe) that a young lady should not live alone. For all her uncertainty, Janet Shuttleworth planned to be a 'measter', as her tenants called her, to be reckoned with.[73]

Driven by a tortured conviction of *'noblesse oblige'*, she called on divine help. The responsibilities connected with 'the possession of property' extended, she decided, to caring for three old women who were receiving money in recognition of their claims to have been her grandfather's mistresses. 'Few things move my compassion more than a worn out aged sinner', she declared; and as 'these poor old creatures ministered to my grandfather's pleasures in their youth', she felt obliged to risk paying the wrong person rather than have the right one suffer. It was to her tenants and the working people of Padiham that she felt most obligation. The rural scenery and lifestyle which her father had known had been shattered by the cotton mills which had multiplied around (but not on) her estate, and she was upset by the physical and moral poverty she encountered. After a ride through Padiham she wrote: 'To see the multitudes, the shoals of unshod children, and the uncouth yet interesting parents, who live in my cottages is enough to make the most thoughtless land owner think seriously of the charge committed to one mortal.' It was wrong to do nothing and difficult to decide what to do. So she redoubled her determination to live on her estate, to encourage church attendance, to set up a lending library at Gawthorpe, and to improve educational opportunities. It might have been James Phillips Kay writing.[74]

Fatefully, she went to him for advice. On 3 October 1839 she wrote from Gawthorpe, telling Kay of her worries and her educational plans. She knew of his work and asked him, as others were doing at this time, to find a schoolmaster. He was to be sober, intelligent, healthy and a devout member of the Established Church – she would provide a seat for him in the Padiham church. The great evils of the neighbourhood were religious quarrelling and socialism – Chartists abounded and the Owenite and socialist spirit was 'highly dangerous to the religious and moral character of the poorer classes'. She referred to Kay's account of Wood's Sessional School (of special interest because of her Edinburgh family connections) which had 'not a little to do with my present application for though myself unknown I can hardly believe that the writer of that very interesting work is a stranger to me'.[75]

Just how that writer stopped being a stranger is not clear. No correspondence between them survives from 1840, though Janet probably had Kay's assistance when she added buildings to the school in the village of Habergham. She probably visited Battersea that year, and she later recorded that when she first knew him in London she contemplated the work he was doing, prayed for him and thought of him gravely, 'though not as connected with myself'. The next certain link was made through Caroline Davenport, wife of Edward Davies Davenport of Capesthorne in Congleton, Cheshire. She was Janet's cousin, the daughter of Robert Shuttleworth's sister, Caroline, and Richard Hurt; like Janet she was in pursuit of a teacher. In May and June 1841, in the Davenports' company (and that of bishops, 'smart ladies' and other members of society) Janet visited the Training School and the village school at Battersea, heard a class taught by Hullah sing in Cavendish Square, and inspected Norwood where Kay and Tufnell met them, rode back to London in their company and dined with them. Some intimacy had probably developed by this time as late in June, in a diary Kay kept for a short time, he reported receiving a note from 'my worthiest friend' which greatly dispirited him. 'God who knows our hearts', he wrote, 'will enable us to cherish each other without fear, suspicion or gloom!' This friend is given neither sex nor name, but a subsequent letter restored Kay to 'the most radiant sunshine'. Kay records a conversation with his family the previous evening in which they had all 'involuntarily' preferred the letter writer 'to every person they had ever seen, as the most adapted to satisfy my sympathies, and one to whom my experience might be most useful from my own capacity to understand my friend's most spiritual qualities'. At least, it seemed, this was not another Helen Kennedy. In June also, Janet wrote to Caroline Davenport, telling her of her plans for improving her tenants, plans about which her mother was lukewarm and at which Mr North scoffed. Janet also sent Caroline a description of a wedding she had attended in Bath. It was an awful ceremony, she said, 'and I felt how thankful I ought to be not to be tied to a mere fox hunter – as I once wished to be'. (Her half-sister, Marianne, remembered Janet as being 'quite innocent of anything but good works – schools, lending libraries, church-building were her delight', and she usually sat in one of the recesses of the Long Gallery at Gawthorpe 'working out her plans like Dorothea in *Middlemarch*'.)[76]

Later in that summer of 1841, at a party given by Caroline Davenport, Janet introduced Kay to her mother, who thought that he had 'a beautiful countenance' and enquired about him from his cousins, the Forts, when she returned to Gawthorpe. Kay's contact with the Davenports continued, and in September he visited Capesthorne where they talked about plans for the Davenports' son, Arthur. Matters came to a head in November when Kay again visited Capesthorne. Janet was present, as he knew she would be. So, at various times, were Tufnell, Lady Poore (née Agnes Marjoribanks, Janet's aunt), members of the Strutt and Greg families, the Bishops of Lichfield and Chester, some of the Stanleys from Alderley and Joseph and Ebenezer Kay who arrived from Cambridge where they were studying. In the setting of a gracious country home amid hunts for the last rose of summer on frosty mornings, discussions of farming, country walks, some party phrenologizing by Kay, singing from Lady Poore's daughters, billiards and 'squiddling' (idle chatter), the making of candle shades, the telling of ghost stories at which Kay excelled, paper puzzles, formal dinners and evening parties, Kay (on 23 November) proposed to Janet Shuttleworth and was accepted. Caroline Davenport was delighted with her success as a matchmaker and so, Caroline said, was Lady Poore. The news and the delight quickly spread. 'Is it true that Dr Kay is to marry Miss Shuttleworth?' the ex-Poor Law Commissioner, Thomas Frankland Lewis, writing from Rome, asked his son. 'If so (as I earnestly hope) pray wish him joy for me. She is a fortunate heiress to put herself and her worldly goods, into the hands of so good a man, and one so likely to make her happy.'[77]

The Shuttleworths and Norths were horrified. 'An absurd letter from young Janet', North growled into his diary on 19 November, four days before Janet accepted Kay-Shuttleworth's proposal, '. . . that a Dr Kay, a great Educationist, but a mere sub Commissioner of Poor Laws, is "seriously thinking of her, as she cannot mistake his manner" . . . in short that she is willing to be married, and to become Mrs Dr Kay'. It would not accord with the feelings of the Shuttleworths 'particularly as all we know about the man's family is that they were originally from Lancashire, relations of Mrs Fort, and probably Cotton Spinners'. He put it down to a passing whim of Janet's, though he noted that 'any penniless man' would be tempted by her Gawthorpe fortune. Janet North refused to approve her daughter's marriage to a person she had met only once, and then by her daughter's introduction and at the Davenports. When Janet Shuttleworth expressed her grief at this reaction North was confirmed in his belief that nothing would develop. Angry and deeply

Extract from Frederick North's diary, 19 November 1841, pouring scorn on Janet's concerned for his wife, North thought Janet 'a little fool'. Kay had told her of his 'extraction', he noted, 'which is not so "aristocratic" she is aware'. Somewhat impetuously, Janet North visited Battersea, met Mrs Kay – 'the Old Mother', North called her – and came to the same conclusion.[78]

North considered the Davenports' failure to consult Janet's mother 'perfectly infamous', something one read of in a novel but did not encounter in real life. Given the customs of the time, it did suggest independence and insensitivity. Mother and daughter were only 'removed by a post', a journey of twelve hours,

> and yet the daughter coolly allows herself to be given in Marriage (for it amounts to that) by an intriguing relation, whose own connubial sale (for I can call the Davenport marriage by no other name) should have taught her how little real good feeling, or judgement, influence men in that matter.

Caroline Davenport insisted that she and her husband had scrupulously avoided influencing events, that Kay was an affectionate son and brother, and that for someone with Janet's delicate health a physician would be a good husband. Her letter did no good. Janet North remained distracted with worry and Janet Shuttleworth hurt and disappointed. Frederick North consoled himself that 'young Janet was born a weak creature, and has never been, nor ever will be, otherwise'.[79] He underestimated her badly. For all her sentimentality and her sometimes supine willingness to place herself in God's care, Janet Shuttleworth's determination to marry showed that she could take her life into her own hands and defy convention.

'My wife', North recorded on 30 November, 'writes Kay an answer to his letters – enclosing a Shuttleworth Pedigree printed! it is rather an absurdity – but poor soul she is not herself on the subject.' She also asked Kay to take the Shuttleworth name on marriage, a suggestion North first interpreted as being a 'concession to the family pride of Janet's father – if it be permitted for feeling to remain to the Dead'. Janet North denied this interpretation, claiming, as Frederick put it, that her aim was 'to push the husband up in the world by thus giving him a sort of factitious Pedigree'. North thought that there was a good deal of vanity in it: 'she has for years puffed herself as the mother of this heiress, and she wants the heiress-ship kept up'. To everyone's surprise Kay agreed, even offering to suggest the idea himself to Janet Shuttleworth. She professed to be amused, said that she liked her mother's proposition, but expressed

concern that he should be known by any name 'but the one by which
the world now knows you as everything that is good and great'.
Nevertheless, she remarked that, though she would not have proposed the change, she greatly admired her own name and would
gladly see it united with his, either as a prefix or a suffix.[80]

A mollified but edgy Janet North was visited by Kay on
4 December. Janet Shuttleworth had instructed him on those he
would meet and even told him to shake hands with an old coachman
of whom she was fond. She gave her opinion that North thought ill of
everybody – 'it is his nature – mingled with much that is kind and
even generous'. Marianne, who was 11 at the time, remembered the
shock her half-sister's announcement had caused and how anxious
Kay had been at the visit. His composure would not have been helped
by a remark made by Catherine when Kay lifted her onto his knee in
an effort to hide his nervousness: noticing his baldness she asked why
his head came through his hair. North also thought that Kay seemed
nervous, though he admitted that he did not look his 36 years. He
noted that Kay had been to neither Public School nor college (North
had been to Harrow and Cambridge) but showed no signs of this
lack, 'beyond an occasional homission of his Hs'. To North's
astonishment Kay brought his 'things', as if he expected to be taken
in. They did not make him aware of his *faux pas* for, as North reflected,
'hospitality is a mere Arab virtue, so we made him a sleeping place in
Charlie's room'. Despite the social obstacles Kay came through the
meeting well. North decided that 'I really like Dr Kay very much'.
He thought him well informed, intelligent and a good conver-
sationalist – 'a purposelike, efficient and attractive man – and will
possibly make young Janet as happy as any husband could'. At the
time and in future years, North's opinion was to lurch between this
view of Kay and the view that he was a 'fortune hunter'. He also
decided during this first visit that Kay was not eager for 'the
Consummation of their Matrimonial Bliss' and would not marry
until after the winter was over. Given information that Kay's family
was respectable, North grimly quipped that 'none of them ever
hanged – but one certainly [was] now to be transported'. When all
else failed there was the virtue of resignation: 'Whether it be for good
or Evil – we must, at all events, make the best of it for Janet's sake.'[81]

Janet Shuttleworth and James had problems with other relatives.
The Marjoribanks were not pleased, nor was Janet's Aunt Elizabeth
who had heard that Kay's politics were radical. She was, Janet told
him, 'warm hearted and generous to a fault' but 'a most bitter

bigotted Tory' who had hoped that she would marry a Tory Lord. All would be well once she had met him. However, Elizabeth Shuttleworth was not easily changed. 'I can therefore only hope', she wrote to Janet on 30 November, 'that you have judged right for your own happiness by this rather peculiar connexion for a young lady in your position.' There were also problems with Kay's mother and sister, as the announcement of the impending marriage had come earlier than they expected. However, their letters pleased Janet, and she wrote affectionate and dutiful letters, saying that she would regard Hannah Kay as her own mother, in an effort to soothe their feelings. But the change of name, which challenged the Kays' family identity as seriously as the prospect of the marriage had struck at the Shuttleworths' family pride, caused great shock. On 5 December Robert Kay sent his brother a moving letter in which he said that, like his mother and sister, he was at first too disturbed by the news to be able to write. A letter from Kay, and the good reports he had received about Miss Shuttleworth, had reassured him. 'You are to us dear Brother the same whatever your name – so pray consult in this matter only what you consider right.' Robert enclosed letters to Janet which he and his wife, Rachel, had written. They felt themselves to be 'plain and somewhat blundering persons' and left Kay to make whatever use of the letters he wished. He passed them on to Janet who was pleased. 'You know me for a quiet, shy and nervous fellow', Robert finished his letter. 'Nevertheless I will go through what to me is fire and water to show my respect for one you love.'[82]

Despite Robert's support Kay was not at ease. In late January 1842 North was talking of the Shuttleworth connection being discouraged, and in February, with the wedding drawing very close, Kay was plainly depressed by his agreement to change his name. Neither his mother nor his sister was happy and Janet informed him that the Davenports were equally worried – 'Until they find your usefulness is not lessened and your position in the world is not altered it is only natural that they should continue to regret the change.' She protested that she could understand his mother and Hannah, especially, she added, optimistically overstating the frequency of an acknowledged practice, as they did not know 'how usual such changes are'. They would cease to grieve if they realized how strongly her mother and family felt about the change, and how much peace with them depended on it. Whatever his feelings, Kay adhered to his agreement and in later life showed no signs of regret or backsliding.[83]

Janet Shuttleworth had no doubts. 'I delight in your letters my own dearest James', she wrote on 18 December 1841. 'They come home to my heart with a force and freshness springing from the spirit in which they are written.' She saw Kay as a man set apart by God for great things, including 'the Christianization of the world by infusing a right spirit into the education of this and other nations'. She was willing to admit, however, that he was as liable to sin as any other man, though she could not express in words 'the value of such a husband'. Her task was to assist him, 'watch you lest success throw you off your guard – or difficulties too much depress you'. Much was expected from them both, she decided, and in particular they should spend their Sundays strengthening their faith in God and their affection for each other. When he had greater leisure – perhaps when he was staying at Gawthorpe – he should turn his great writing skill to convincing men of his real opinions on religion. She was probably worried about the accusations of Unitarianism – Caroline Davenport was and insisted that, whatever his background, he was now a sound Churchman. In the same letter Janet depicted her mother as estranged from the Marjoribanks, and receiving little support from the North family. She was worried by her mother's distress and agitation 'and the old fear of having done wrong crept over me'. But the feeling soon passed: 'Now I am only full of gratitude – and Hope – I am well – cheerful – happy – I love your Mother and Hannah more and more – and rejoice in the prospect of being one of a family which seems so united and full of affection for you'.[84]

By the end of December 1841, the die was cast, and the marriage date set for Easter the next year. Negotiations on the marriage settlement were well advanced, and Janet Shuttleworth believed that not only Padiham and Gawthorpe but the whole country and perhaps even the world would benefit from their union.

On 28 August 1841 the Melbourne government resigned and Kay added to his wooing of Janet Shuttleworth a less pleasant courtship. During the election he reflected how he, who was once so zealously involved in political activity, was now 'chiefly interested in questions of social reform which separate me from the exciting contests by which the country is now agitated'. With the election decided the survival of the Committee was at stake: it had no statutory basis and its membership and policies were at the mercy of the incoming government. Peel had led the Conservatives' parliamentary onslaught on the Committee, Sir James Graham, who had called for its abolition, followed Russell into the Home Office, and Baron Wharncliffe replaced Lansdowne as President of the Privy Council. Kay's links with the Whigs were public knowledge and *Recent Measures* had been a reminder of the differences between his views and those of leading Churchmen. His health was not good, and he was anxious and depressed. 'I ought not to be dispirited', he wrote on 6 July in his journal; but he was. Probably with the imminent departure of the Whigs in mind he added: 'I do not see a clear path for the accomplishment of any of my wishes, and consequently I work against the wind and stream.'[85]

Early in September Kay felt that his position was still in 'much obscurity', though others thought that he and Wharncliffe had got off to a good start. Despite the grounds for hope, however, Kay considered resigning if the Conservatives adopted undesirable policies. Never one to see himself as a detached civil servant, he wrote to Lansdowne, who expressed confidence that the Committee would continue and said that Peel wished 'to conciliate on this and some other points, on which he can do so without breaking with any of the interests on which he relies for support'. During these discussions Kay bravely argued that the Committee of Council represented the civil power in education and ought not to have clergy as members, and surprisingly Peel retained the Committee and continued to appoint lay members only. His decision, announced on 7 October 1841, was consistent with his ecclesiastical policy, but revealed the less than disinterested nature of the Tories' objections to Russell's original scheme. Having denounced the Committee and its secretary, they rejected the chance to remove both. Perhaps they decided that, as some mechanism had to be found to distribute the grant and, as they now controlled the Committee, Russell's scheme was good enough. The matters of principle, which had previously troubled them, vanished. And so, apparently, had opposition to the Com-mittee's secretary. 'I hope that Dr Kay, if he marry a Wife, will not cease to Education', declared Sir James Graham. 'The additional independence of his new position will only increase his influence and means of usefulness.'[86]

With the Committee's existence assured, Kay could work more confidently. One of his earliest acts was to continue the rescue of David Stow whose Normal Seminary had fallen into one of its customary financial crises. Very soon after Kay had been appointed to the Committee Stow had asked for assistance, and received it, on the condition that the right of inspection be granted. He successfully asked for more in February 1840, and he again requested aid in

March 1841. 'The present Liberal government', he wrote, 'with the Poor Law Commissioners and an *M D* of notoriety at their head or *foundation* rather have done more for real education alias Mental and Moral Training than has been done for two centuries past.' Kay sent John Gibson, who had been appointed as the Committee's inspector of Scottish schools, to report on the Seminary, pointedly instructing him that Stow and his colleagues had 'encountered peculiar Difficulties, because they have trod in a new Path, which their successors will find more free of obstruction'. On 31 December 1841 the Committee offered grants on conditions (eventually softened) which showed its wish to use its financial power as a means of control.[87]

As well as helping others, Kay's work for the Committee and at Battersea had a side benefit which assumed greater significance because of his courtship of Janet Shuttleworth. In 1841 it had become fashionable to visit Battersea, and Kay's journal and his letters contain many references to titled ladies and gentlemen who visited him or asked him to find teachers for them. Stow wanted infant teachers for Van Diemen's Land, but most requests came from landholders such as 'Miss Shuttleworth' who in July 1841 sent a teacher, his son and daughter to spend a fortnight living with Kay and visiting the best schools. 'You are here hatching your own eggs', Shaw-Lefevre said to him, when Kay said that he had no ambitions for the Poor Law commissionership which Shaw-Lefevre had vacated. 'You are in a situation which affords you opportunities of intercourse with the most distinguished men of your day.'[88]

Kay also met distinguished women. Among his best friends was Harriet Leveson-Gower, Duchess of Sutherland, grand-daughter of the fifth Duke of Devonshire, and one of the Whig ladies whom Queen Victoria's desire to retain caused the Bedchamber crisis. He conceded (to his journal) that she had a higher opinion of him than he merited, but declared that he was interested in her as a person, quite 'independently of all the splendour of rank and fortune' by which she was surrounded. The Duchess and her entourage visited Battersea and Kay dined at that fashionable and powerful centre of society, Stafford House. He met Dr Arnold of Rugby there, and was introduced to the King of Prussia. The King had 'conversed with me in the centre of a great circle of fashion and beauty for ten minutes', he told Janet, while wondering at his courage in expressing views on education different from those of His Majesty. 'Your opinion must have weighed with him', Janet assured him seriously, 'and I can well imagine that so given it would impress many besides.'[89] It was a whirling world in which he lived, working in Whitehall, visiting Norwood, presiding at Battersea, courting Janet Shuttleworth to the dismay of her family and the incomprehension of his, and mixing with nobility and royalty at Stafford House.

His family life was mingled with his public activities. His mother and sister lived at Battersea, making possible his dedication to his educational enterprises by helping to run the Training School. When his younger brothers were not at school or university they also lived at Battersea. Frederick North would have approved the path Kay had mapped out. Joseph, whom Kay judged to be persevering, ambitious and intelligent, and Ebenezer, who he thought had less self-control but was quicker, were being prepared for Cambridge. Tom was a problem, as he had been from birth. Physically feeble, he had been allowed to postpone 'the period of steady application' until he was stronger. There were fears that he might not be seized with the driving determination to make his way in the world which dominated the lives of his brothers, and might follow the example of John Phillips (Hannah's brother), who had written Kay a desperate and humiliating letter from a debtors' prison. For the moment, however, the brothers played a part in welcoming visitors to Battersea, accompanied them on walks to the village school, dined at Stafford House, and observed the professional and social world into which their eldest brother was drawing them.[90]

The entries in Kay's journal for 29 June 1841 give some sense of his way of life at this time. He rose at seven, attended prayers with the Battersea scholars, taught them elocution for an hour, read privately till a quarter to nine, then breakfasted while discussing with Joseph and Ebenezer a journey they were make to Wales with their tutor. After talking with Tate and Horne he rode to Whitehall, arriving about a quarter past ten. He was studying German in order to make the continental educationists more accessible and, when the German master failed to come, Kay attended to his correspondence while an artist made a medallion of his head (for his mother). He met a number of people including the Dean of Durham who brought him a list of German works on education which Kay immediately ordered from his bookseller; at noon he received a book on mesmerism in which he was interested. Having given instructions to a cabinet-maker who was making a device to help teach reading for a governess employed by an aristocratic friend, he consulted with a colleague who was preparing material on the phonic method. From two till three o'clock he paid some calls, then worked in his office until four.

At twenty past four he rode to Green Street to see Lady Byron, only to discover that she was out. He went on dispirited and walked his horse through Hyde Park, 'having no courage to speak to anyone'. He arrived home to dinner at a quarter past five (on other nights he might have gone to his club, the Athenaeum), met Eden to discuss problems at the Hospital School in Greenwich, and helped an assistant to prepare a manual on Mülhauser's methods of teaching writing. At ten o'clock he began to write private letters, at a quarter to eleven to read, and he retired to sleep at midnight. He had not given the devil much chance to find work for idle hands to do.[91]

The depression which gripped Kay when he was unable to see Lady Byron was not uncommon. In an unsurprised manner, as if they were part of ordinary living, Kay's journal refers to long gallops in the Park to shake off oppression or to get rid of a headache; to sleepless nights spent tossing in uncontrollable anxiety; to being disturbed by society engagements; to nervousness brought about by strain on his thoughts, and to sensations of extreme lassitude.[92] The dramatic collapse in Edinburgh and the distracted retreat from Manchester were violent eruptions of an anxiety and depression which constantly bubbled below the surface of Kay's life. As well as the Kay who presided over the Battersea experiment or fought to keep control of his inspectors in Whitehall or basked in the momentary attention of a circle of fashion and beauty at Stafford House, there was the lonely Kay who walked his horse through Hyde Park hoping that no one would want to speak to him.

Meanwhile in the first months of 1842 the preparations for marriage continued and Frederick North's moods fluctuated. Sometimes he pitied Kay, 'who with all his Vulgarity and want of "Race", has got a young wife of fortune beyond him, but of personal attractions most dangerously repulsive'. In fact a portrait painted in 1840 by the fashionable painter, Francis Grant, shows her to be an elegant woman, with a thoughtful, vulnerable, brooding face. At other times North decided that Kay had got what he wanted, 'station and fortune'; or concluded that the chances were 10,000 to 1 against Janet making a better match 'as regards her own happiness' than she had done. He tried to make the best of what could not be changed, but in the privacy of his diary he was resentful of Janet's uncaring attitude towards her mother. Typically he attributed a bilious attack she suffered in mid-February to 'overfeeding, and insufficient Air and

Exercise, which her little puny frame, and defective constitution cannot stand'. The doctor, he decided, 'undoubtedly is marrying a Patient and not a tempting Bride!' Before and after the wedding, Janet North remained 'intensely anxious as to how the marriage may turn out, for the bride's health and happiness'. Janet Shuttleworth was puzzled at her mother's behaviour, believing that, as she admired and respected Kay, she must be opposed to her marrying anyone at all. On all sides the blindness continued.[93]

Amidst this atmosphere James Kay and Janet Shuttleworth continued their courtship. Janet's letters occasionally show a sharp wit, as when she described two aristocratic Hastings acquaintances as '"good-hearted people" – that is they talk well – gamble – and do not pay their debts'. But mostly they are full of concern for Kay's work: through their marriage the rays of his good deeds would reflect on her and she would 'share in the blessings which attend your labours'. (Because of this attitude, a wedding present from Kay was oddly suitable – he gave her bound copies of all his writings from *Cynedrida* and the *North of England Medical and Surgical Journal* to *Recent Measures*. Morocco covers preserved what had drawn them together.) Janet continued to worry about his religious views, concluding that his silence proved the depth rather than the absence of faith – 'little as you speak of your love for Christ it is deeply grafted on your heart'. Kay seems to have been too ardent in other ways. Janet, with Caroline's agreement, decided that he ought not to be '*quite* so affectionate in manner' to her in front of people, especially at Hastings. But they did not want him to grow 'conventional'; that would 'destroy so much that is delightful in you – this never must be dearest James'. Kay wrote of his work or of social events at Battersea in which he thought she would be interested; 'I do not *content* myself now with *thinking* of you, my sweet love, nor with *praying* for you, I *write* to give you a little history of our happy evening'. In neither partner was there a sense of an overwhelming passion. Janet saw in the marriage the opportunity for good works and religious fulfil-ment, and probably an expression of her own independence. And while Kay was aware of Gawthorpe and what it stood for, he was not a simple fortune-seeker; as he told Janet of the happy evening there was an affection in his letter, though his expression of affection was always awkward. Janet was convinced that he loved her, and was confident that he would learn 'to *express* your affection for me more quietly – and yet retain your own delight-fully warm and affectionate nature'.[94]

North was determined that the negotiations for the marriage

settlement would be conducted with the utmost care. He stated his
aims bluntly in his diary: to tie up the property in trusteeship to
protect Janet's right of survivorship, to provide her with an annual
income independent of her husband of £1,000, and to require Kay to
pay the trustees £5,000 of his own money within two years. As Kay
had declared himself to have an income of £1,200 per annum (his
salary) and property worth £6,000 (most of which he had inherited
from his father) the £5,000 looked an impossible sum, but the income
from the estate was Kay's and, as North remarked, he could save
it from Gawthorpe rents. The settlement incorporated these arrangements and was signed at Hastings on 23 February 1842. The trustees
were Richard Shuttleworth, Janet's cousin, who could not attend the
wedding because of a hunting accident, Edward Marjoribanks, her
uncle, and Robert Kay.[95] Frederick North had protected the Shuttleworth property and, better than he realized, his errant step-daughter.
All was in readiness for the marriage, that turbulent nexus of
nineteenth-century familial, economic and personal power. And
religion. And hope and love.

Mr James Phillips Kay-Shuttleworth and Janet Shuttleworth were
married by Robert Eden in the parish church at Hastings according
to the rites of the Established Church on 24 March 1842. (With the
acquisition of 'Shuttleworth' Kay usually dropped the title of 'Dr'.)
Frederick North thought the bride as composed as a stone, the
bride's mother stirred up but showing nothing, and the bridegroom
very excited. Janet Kay-Shuttleworth wrote to her mother-in-law,
who was not at the wedding, that the marriage had gone 'most comfortably. We both and all behaved beautifully'. Robert Eden also
wrote to Hannah Kay, telling her that the church was crammed and
that Joseph had worn a magnificent waistcoat. Marianne North
remembered thinking that 'a medicine-chest was an uncomfortable
kind of thing to be stuck between bride and bride-groom in the
yellow chariot as they rolled away'.[96]

6 · The Committee of the Privy Council on Education, 1843–49

On Saturday, 23 September 1843 James and Janet Kay-Shuttleworth called at Burnley in an open carriage to bring Leonard Horner, friend and factory inspector, to Gawthorpe where he was to stay for a few days. Horner thought Gawthorpe 'a very perfect and entire Specimen of an old English mansion'; he particularly admired the Long Gallery with its family portraits, and the dining room with its oak music gallery. He also admired the Kay-Shuttleworths' educational work, whether it was building a school, organizing a village band, or encouraging a taste for gardening among their tenants. On Sunday after breakfast, which had been preceded by prayers, Kay-Shuttleworth and his three younger brothers taught Sunday school while Janet took Horner over the house, showing him hiding places made behind the panels during the Civil War and an old wooden board with names of her ancestors carved on it. In the evening there was a service and a sermon and John Hullah led them in playing and singing sacred music.[1] During this serious but pleasant weekend, Horner had the opportunity to lament with Kay-Shuttleworth the fate of educational clauses of the 1843 Factory Bill which Horner had helped to draft and which had been withdrawn after ferocious controversy.

The controversy, primarily with the Dissenters, had been inherited by the Conservatives and derived from the Concordat: the British Society, which favoured inspection, considered itself disadvantaged because it had no influence over the appointment or conduct of the inspectors of its schools. On 5 February 1841 the Committee of Council had considered a moderate memorial from the British Society which did not seek the privileges given to the Church through the Concordat, but asked for some concessions. The then James Kay had to explain to the Secretary of the British Society, Henry Dunn, why the Committee would go little way

Gawthorpe Hall, home of the heiress

towards meeting their requests, and to insist that their Lordships did not intend to appoint separate inspectors for schools which differed in worship, doctrine or discipline from the Church of England.[2]

Resentful, the British Society presented another memorial to Wharncliffe after the change of government, specifically asking for the same security with regard to inspection as the National Society had. Their Lordships gave little ground. Then in June 1842, the Society received a copy of a report by Tremenheere on 66 British schools in London which confirmed its worst fears. The Society described his savage attack on individual schools as 'unfair and extravagant' and the report itself as 'an elaborate attempt to show that the entire system of instruction pursued by the society is essentially defective'. Dunn called for its virtual suppression. His bitterness received powerful expression the following year when he wrote of

> *annihilating* inspection . . . Inspection, as the groundwork of reports intended to form and to foster, to mould and to guide public opinion in reference to education . . . Inspection, for purposes of rebuke, scorn, exposure. Inspection, to justify interference. Inspection, to furnish proof of a necessity for centralization, compulsion, despotic control. Inspection, undertaken for the sake of ruining the reputation, destroying the prosperity, and ultimately extinguishing, all schools founded and supported by voluntary contributions.[3]

Tremenheere was a friend and admirer of Kay-Shuttleworth, and was proud that all his work as an inspector had been devised to ensure that 'their ideas on Educational improvement could . . . be brought before the public'. Not long after submitting his report he met Kay-Shuttleworth on the steps of Nelson's monument and was told that the Council was considering suppressing it. Tremenheere insisted that that would be 'a cowardly act' and Kay-Shuttleworth, while agreeing with him, said that he would be forced 'to yield to the fears of the Lord President'. Wharncliffe, though conceding that Tremenheere had been tactless, did not suppress the report, and in November 1842 the *Eclectic Review*, the Dissenters' journal, published a powerful attack on the Committee, Kay-Shuttleworth and Tremenheere, but not Wharncliffe. Their resentment at the National Society's favoured position on inspection was explicit, Tremenheere was identified as an 'avowed foe', and it was, the article percipiently affirmed, 'utterly vain for Dr. Kay Shuttleworth to pretend that *his* ultimate design is anything short of a centralized national system of education'. Wharncliffe tried conciliation, and not until November 1843 did he give guarantees that the society would be consulted when an inspector for its schools was appointed and that no one would be recommended of whom the Society did not approve. Tremenheere, with whom the Society would in no circumstances work, had to be found other employment and Kay-Shuttleworth, whose support throughout the affair Tremenheere gratefully acknowledged, told him on 25 November 1843 that Graham had found an honourable solution, the inspectorship of mines and collieries and a rise of £100 per annum. He accepted the offer.[4]

The battle with the Dissenters was part of the context of the Factory Bill on which Horner and Kay-Shuttleworth co-operated. Gawthorpe provided another part. On the evening of 17 August 1842, Kay-Shuttleworth wrote to Lady Lovelace, Lady Byron's daughter, asking her and Lord Lovelace, her husband, to postpone a planned visit. He and Janet had rushed into Lancashire, 'hearing that the insurrectionary movement had extended to the valley of Todmorden and the Calder'. At Gawthorpe they were almost under siege: 'large bodies of men pass our gates daily – meetings are held on the hills, and in our immediate neighbourhood – and parties of men armed with sticks come (nominally to beg) to the house'. Defence and parleying with the 'beggars' had preoccupied them. Kay-Shuttleworth had sworn in the farmers and colliers, who were unemployed because they had been sent home from the mines, plugs having been taken from the estate's steamboilers to prevent them working. 'The sense of insecurity, and the imprisonment within doors would I think make Gawthorpe worse than a prison for you', he warned Lady Lovelace.[5]

In the desperate financial times of 1842, the Chartists had re-covered from the defeats of 1839 and were reasserting their demands, while the Anti-Corn Law League attacked the landed interests on the grounds that they increased the poverty and hunger of the working classes by keeping up the price of bread through protection. At the beginning of 1842 a royal commission had reported in horrific terms on the conditions which children faced in mines. Capitalizing on the moral outrage, Ashley secured the passage of the Mines Act (1842) which forbade the employment underground of women or girls, or of boys under the age of ten. The free traders, as anxious for the support of the working classes as were the Chartists, supported the Act. As Halévy has mentioned, it was easy to denounce the abuses of capitalism when they were perpetrated by Tories and protectionists rather than by the Lancashire millowners who provided the League with much of its drive. Matters came to a crisis in July. The price of wheat continued to rise and the Staffordshire coalowners decided to lower wages. With Chartists prominent, the miners organized a general strike which brought industry in the Potteries to a stand-still. The free-trade Lancashire manufacturers, though they had no love for the coalowners, gave notice of a reduction in wages hoping to force an insurrection which would frighten the government into seeing their viewpoint. They were successful. The strike spread to the cotton industry and the coal mines of Lancashire where, as Kay-Shuttleworth discovered, the 'plug plot' was developed to prevent the use of blackleg labour. However, the opportunistic alliance of free trade and Chartism did not hold, and when the League found that it could not control the disturbances it began to denounce them as the work of Chartist agitators. The government intervened, used the army to restore order, and the disturbances died down.[6] But to Kay-Shuttleworth, looking through the windows at Gawthorpe at the sticks in the hands of the 'beggars' outside, they were yet another warning of the precariousness of the social order.

Sir James Graham shared these fears and hoped that Kay-Shuttleworth would 'win back the poor deluded workmen from the error of their ways'. He immediately confronted Graham with his solution, popular education, but on 26 August 1842 Graham informed Peel that 'Every man has his nostrum. The Clerk of the Council for Education thinks that Moral Training and Normal schools will restore peace.' Though he did not despise education, Graham had decided that 'cheap Bread, plenty of Potatoes, low-priced American Bacon, a little more Dutch cheese and butter, will have a more pacifying effect than all the Mental Culture which any Government can supply'. Five days later a more conciliatory Graham told Kay-Shuttleworth that 'the education of the rising youth should be the peculiar care of the Government: its neglect is one of the principal causes of the Evil spirit, which now actuates large masses of the community'. But the danger was immediate and a scheme of national education too slow to meet it. Law and civil rights had to be upheld by power, and 'cannot with safety be left to the unaided protection of moral influences or even of religious restraint'.[7]

Despite this sturdy realism, Graham planned to include educational clauses in the Factory Bill which the political situation had made essential. On 12 January 1842, before matters had come to a crisis, the then James Kay told Janet Shuttleworth that Graham had called him back to his office after a meeting and they remained, Kay said, with naive, hushed honesty, 'for two hours alone', during which time Graham consulted him 'in the most flattering manner' on general education and the Factory Bill. In a desire to impress his future wife Kay may have overstated his importance, but he did take part in negotiations with Blomfield, Horner, and his fellow factory inspector R.J. Saunders. As the eventual proposal did not satisfy the Church, Graham did not proceed with it, and a cautious Peel told him in June that 'a more rapid advance in promoting good education will be made by the cautious and gradual extension of the power and the pecuniary means of the Committee of the Privy Council, than by the announcement at present of any plan by the Government'.[8] That the much maligned Committee should have become a key instrument of government policy again revealed the political opportunism of the Conservatives' reaction to the April 1839 minute and the creation of the Committee.

Probably influenced by the summer disturbances, Peel's govern-ment abandoned the policy of gradualism and decided on a set of educational clauses for a Factory Bill. Kay-Shuttleworth had worked to impress the government 'in terms of the *strongest* remonstrance' with the state of the northern manufacturing districts; and, despite his own reservations, Graham sent Peel two of the letters which Kay-Shuttleworth had written to him in August. Peel agreed with the views 'so well expressed by Dr. Kay', and by early September 1842 Graham was talking about the need to improve 'the means of education'. On 10 December, he asked Kay-Shuttleworth to weave a rope of sand: he was 'to keep open the door of friendly communication with the Bishop of London', frame clauses which met his views while not sacrificing 'tolerant principles' and, above all, prevent a rupture with the British and Foreign Society 'whose perverseness at this juncture may defeat the best chance for the diffusion of education which has presented itself in our time'. He was to work with Saunders who represented the Church's views and Horner who spoke for the Dissenters.[9]

Saunders had bargaining advantages. Both he and Horner were experienced factory inspectors, but Saunders had the Bishop of London behind him and, in Graham, a Home Secretary with a strong allegiance to the Church. On 27 December 1842, submitting a draft for Blomfield's approval, Graham referred favourably to Saunders's opinions and said that 'recent events', that is, the summer disturbances, had confirmed his own opinions on the education of factory children. He stressed that he did not want to bring to Cabinet any measure 'which I have not reason to believe is in Principle admissible by the highest Ecclesiastical Authorities'. Saunders, Kay-Shuttleworth and Horner were to produce clauses 'such as the Church might reasonably concede, and the Dissenters adopt, as a scheme of compulsory Scriptural education'. Graham had asked the impossible, as was made obvious in a letter of 30 December from Saunders to Kay-Shuttleworth, commenting on changes which Kay-Shuttleworth had suggested in various clauses. Having heaped praise on his work, Saunders remarked: 'The more, however, that I admire the talent and the zeal that can compass so much as you have done, the more do I lament the views and opinions you entertain on the religious part of the subject.' Saunders particularly objected to a draft regulation which allowed teachers not to be Church members. Saunders prevailed. The educational clauses to the Factory Bill made three hours' schooling per day compulsory, and to ensure the compulsion was meaningful, provided grants for the building of new schools which were to be supported from the poor rate. The schools were to be managed by a board of seven: the clergyman and two churchwardens, two members appointed by the magistrates and two millowners. The teacher, appointed by the board, had to belong to the Church and be approved by the bishop; church attendance was compulsory; and religious instruction was to be in accord with the Church's doctrines, though a conscience clause exempted children if their parents objected. Graham told Gladstone that the Bill gave the Church 'ample security, that every master in the new schools will be a Churchman: and that the teaching of the Holy Scriptures . . . will necessarily be in conformity with the Creed and understanding of the Master'. Ignoring the implications of this statement, he also said that it was 'a scheme of comprehension and concord'.[10]

In mid-December Kay-Shuttleworth wrote to Lansdowne, saying that the government wished to provide popular education which recognized 'the existing state of the law respecting Dissenters'. In his gracious reply Lansdowne referred to Kay-Shuttleworth as 'a personal and political friend', and promised his support, 'stopping short only of that which in this country it would be insane to attempt, a compulsory interference with the determination of parents in independent circumstances'. He lamented the unpredictability of political parties, 'especially where any popular prejudice is to be flattered, or vanity to be gratified', and he confirmed an invitation for the Kay-Shuttleworths to spend Christmas and New Year at Bowood. Immensely gratified as Kay-Shuttleworth was at such illustrious personal and political acceptance, he suffered for it. On 20 December, Wharncliffe told him that he would not have agreed with Graham, whose support Kay-Shuttleworth claimed, about the expediency of his writing to Lansdowne, though 'a casual conversation in the course of your visit to Bowood is a very different matter'. His former liaison with the Whigs was 'a notorious source of jealousy' so that there was much to fear if the correspondence became known. Two days later Graham wrote Kay-Shuttleworth a prickly letter seeking his agreement to a version of events which cleared him of impropriety and of any knowledge of the letter to Lansdowne, or of a visit that Kay-Shuttleworth had paid to Russell. Kay-Shuttleworth confirmed Graham's account, produced a laboured defence of his actions, and said that he was 'prepared to encounter any risk consistent with honour to secure for the Government a dispassionate consideration of any comprehensive measure for the improvement and extension of elementary education'. There the matter ended, another example of Kay-Shuttleworth's loyalty to his cause rather than the government he served.[11]

On 28 February 1843 Graham informally outlined his Bill to Parliament. The police and the soldiers had done their duty, he said, and 'the time is arrived when moral and religious instruction must go forth to reclaim the people from the errors of their ways'. The Bill paved the way for wider educational advances because, as Graham informed a supporter, 'If I succeed in large cities and the manufacturing districts, my plan is easily capable of extension.' As earnest of this hope the Bill contained a proposal for district schools – Kay-Shuttleworth had seized the opportunity to revive his much deferred idea. On 6 March, the day before formally introducing the Bill, Graham said, 'Mine is a measure of peace.' Peace was out of the question, and a stunned Graham began to realize that protests from outside Parliament posed the greatest threat to his plans. Fierce Dissent was on the march, stressing two among the multitude of objections it had to the Bill: the Church's control of the board of trustees and the requirement that teachers had to be members of the Church. With the Methodists reversing the support they had given the Church in 1839, Graham had no doubt of the seriousness of his position.[12]

In a brilliantly organized campaign Edward Baines Jnr exploited the grievances of Dissenters. He refuted 'the grievous charges made against the Manufacturing Districts' and stressed 'the voluntary zeal and liberty' of their inhabitants. In an open letter to Wharncliffe he denounced 'the mighty corruption which has been growing up within the last few years in the Church, and which is rapidly bringing back the Clergy of the Establishment to the doctrines, the rites, and the spirit of Popery'. The Bill, he insisted, placed schools paid from public money *'under the control and management of the Clergy of the Established Church,* and with such provisions as would make them *exclusively* Church schools'. The rising generation would be educated 'under the *exclusive and irresponsible control of the Clergy'*, not a surprising result of a Bill devised in part by Saunders, 'a very zealous and bigoted High Churchman'. As far as the *Eclectic Review* was concerned, the Bill aimed to produce 'a *preparatory ecclesiastical establishment,* a sort of Church of England Junior'. Dissenters varied in the number of objections they harboured, but all supported Henry Dunn's view that the Bill embodied a 'scheme of intolerant compulsion, adapted only to the military despotisms of the Church'. The pamphlets pumped out their message of opposition, large meetings condemned the Bill and, in a display of unity and discipline which was a rehearsal for the Corn Law agitation, petitions flooded into Parliament until it was awash with the Dissenters' anger. On 15 June, facing a divided Cabinet, Peel withdrew the Bill. It was a famous victory for Dissent.[13]

On 30 April 1843, the day before Graham returned his Bill, unsuccessfully revised, to Parliament, Kay-Shuttleworth again wrote to the Opposition. His letter to Russell (to which reference has been made a number of times in this book) explained his part in the measure, and reminded Russell that in 1839 he and Lansdowne had resisted the Church's claims for 'a purely ecclesiastical system of education' and had asserted the rights of the civil power. Kay-Shuttleworth claimed that he would have resigned from the Committee of Council had the Conservative government not continued to support that assertion, and that he had always fought to prevent the growth of any system which interfered with 'a comprehensive system of combined education'. (Kay-Shuttleworth used 'combined' to mean systems in which children of different religions attended the one school, with suitable arrangements made for religious instruction.) He attacked 'separate education', the system under which schools taught only the religion of those who controlled them, and so delivered schools into the hands of the clergyman. As the Church already 'absorbs nine-tenths of the parliamentary grant on a system tending to this result', the state would have to abandon any claims to regulating 'the religious constitution of the schools' and inspect only the secular instruction. The village school would be 'a *purely monastic institution*', quite the contrary to what Kay-Shuttleworth envisaged in a combined system 'in which the young might be brought up in charity with each other, rather than in hostile camps for future strife'.

More bluntly than he had ever done, Kay-Shuttleworth stated that the secular solution of 'Mr. Roebuck and the extreme radicals' was preferable to the separate system. (It is necessary to remember that in the 'secular' system the teacher taught the secular subjects, and religious instruction was offered by the appropriate ministers of religion.) However, Kay-Shuttleworth continued, secular schools 'will be denounced as infidel schools . . . and would be destroyed by a universal anathema'. Therefore, Russell had been right 'in attempting in the first place to establish common schools', that is, combined schools. Then, having written as 'the fearless and uncompromising advocate of a comprehensive system of combined education', a role he fulfilled in his unsuccessful arguments with Saunders, Kay-Shuttleworth came out in support of the Factory Bill. He told Russell that Peel and Graham 'clearly perceive the greatness of the principles for which they are contending' and would regard defeat 'as *fatal* to a system of National Education in this country'. He finished his letter by saying that this was also his opinion and that the defeat of the Bill might lead him 'for the present to abandon a hopeless struggle' or at least not to confine his energy to this battle alone.[14]

Russell struck at the contradiction in Kay-Shuttleworth's position. If education were to be civil and not ecclesiastical, 'there can be no ground for insisting that the schoolmaster should be a Churchman, and that the majority of the managing Board should be appointed in a way to secure a majority of Churchmen'. Russell invoked the 1828–29 Acts which opened civil offices to Catholics and Dissenters: 'yet here is a new civil office, with a salary paid by the public, restricted to Churchmen by a method as sure as the Sacramental test'. Russell then gave Kay-Shuttleworth a political lesson: 'with the encroaching spirit of the Oxford Catholics, as they call themselves, I cannot expect that a Bill to place education in the hands of the Church will be acquiesced in'. In a postscript Russell remarked that Kay-Shuttleworth's personal conduct 'is of course beyond all suspicion. You have been at all times anxious for a comprehensive scheme – I wish we had one.'[15]

Graham's belief that his proposals would be accepted by Dissenters has been described as being beyond comprehension and

Kay-Shuttleworth's support for the Bill is equally difficult to understand.[16] Perhaps the battles of 1839 and 1840 had led him to overemphasize the significance of the Church's support. He may also have been able to convince himself that the Bill's conscience clause would satisfy the Dissenters and enable the schools to be considered 'combined'. Moreover, the board of management, even if stacked by members of the Church, was an alternative to working through the parish. In that sense it was a civil institution and provided a precedent. Equally important precedents were established by the use of rates to support the running of the school and by some statutory powers which the Bill bestowed on the Committee of Council's inspectors. Finally, as Graham had said, the system provided a base from which a truly national education might grow. Driven by his belief in education and by the advances which the Bill embodied, probably convinced by the negotiations with Saunders that he could not get a better deal, and knowing that the schools would be supervised by the Committee of Council, he was blinded to the Bill's logical and political difficulties. He grasped at the straw that Graham offered and watched it break in his hand.

The Bill became the Factory Act of 1844, without the educational clauses. Ashley recognized the significance of the failure. The religious divisiveness was so great, and the victory of Dissent so telling, that 'united education' could 'never again be attempted'. First the Church and now Dissent forced Kay-Shuttleworth to retreat into the pragmatic gradualism which Peel had advocated before the preparation of the Bill. He also had the discomfort of knowing that a new and formidable foe had arisen. Baines had fed from his victory and, from his base among Kay-Shuttleworth's previous co-religionists, the Congregationalists, he mounted the case for strict voluntarism, the repudiation of all aid from the state. 'Who and what are these Congregationalists?' a startled Wharncliffe asked Kay-Shuttleworth in December 1843.[17]

> Mr David has since had a 'serious call'
> He never drinks ale, wine, or spirits at all,
> And they say he is going to Exeter Hall
> To make a grand speech
> And to preach and to teach. . . .[18]

Kay-Shuttleworth and his colleagues did their share of preaching and teaching in Exeter Hall, which had been built in the Strand as a nonsectarian hall for religious, scientific, and philanthropic meetings. Their endeavours were controversial and blurred the line between Kay-Shuttleworth's private and public responsibilities. In the autumn of 1840 the draft of a prospectus for Hullah's class, which began on 1 February 1841, caused Lansdowne to ask whether it was a private advertisement or a minute of the Committee of Council and, though a second draft gained his approval and his financial support, his question hung over the Exeter Hall classes during their entire existence. They were a private venture, but they drew on the work at Battersea, they were sanctioned by the Committee of Council, Kay-Shuttleworth was involved, and Wharncliffe associated himself with them. Hullah's classes, which aimed to teach schoolmasters and schoolmistresses how to teach singing, were a social and educational success – Queen Adelaide, the Duke of Wellington, Lansdowne and others attended and the classes gained publicity in the *Illustrated London News*. As Hullah's fame spread, he found himself teaching singing for its own sake, and his popularity became staggering: in July 1842 Wharncliffe informed the House of Lords that there were 50,000 people attending his classes or those of his pupils. Wharncliffe also mentioned that classes had been started in the teaching of drawing, writing and arithmetic to demonstrate the methods used at Battersea, and that these classes had undergone the same metamorphosis as had those in singing: 'mechanics, shopmen, and even those in a higher situation in life', had joined them simply to learn to read and write and draw.[19]

Fees paid by the students and subscriptions from Russell, Lansdowne, Clarendon, Morpeth and other friends of Kay-Shuttleworth's enabled the classes to start, but finance was always short. In October 1840, before the first class had been given, Lansdowne was asked if some of the parliamentary grant could be used to defray expenses, and he answered as Wharncliffe did, when during his term as Lord President he was asked the same question: he would like to assist but had no authority to divert money in this way. But in July 1842, Wharncliffe gave strong support to a petition from 1,600 teachers who had done the Exeter Hall course asking if the grant could be used for this purpose.[20]

Matters might have gone smoothly had Kay-Shuttleworth not given an extempore lecture entitled, 'The constructive method of teaching', at Exeter Hall in April 1842. Reproduced from shorthand notes and published in the *Saturday Magazine*, it was a typical explanation of his ideas and mixed a plea to treat the child as a rational creature with mechanical, Pestalozzi-derived explanations of phonics, as interpreted by the Committee of Council. Blomfield, who had subscribed to the music classes, attacked the Exeter Hall enterprise with the outlandish claim that a Normal school was being established without any religious instruction.[21] *The Times*, in a series of malicious and very funny misinterpretations, also moved into the attack. 'We have a class for this, and another for that', it said, echoing a complaint of Blomfield's, 'one for singing, and another for drawing, and, finally, one in which the art of "pædogogy, or the theory of teaching children the art of the alphabet *constructively*," (!) is most magnificently inculcated'. They had been told by 'Dr. K Shuttleworth' that

> every child, when he learned to say, for instance, the word, 'man', had to reconcile the fact that there were 26 letters in the English alphabet, and 86 sounds; and that these sounds were all represented by these letters. The child had to do all this 'by himself.' This was too bad; – it was too cruel.

'Upon the constructive method', *The Times* continued, 'children are to be no more vexed with being obliged to assume and do things, the reasons whereof they are ignorant . . . they are to be taught to boil kettles upon chymical synthesis, and to suck eggs by an analysis of the theory of *boring*'.[22]

Beneath the mockery, however, was an attack on what, according to *The Times*, Kay and the Committee stood for: centralization, uniformity and neutrality. Neutrality in particular annoyed the writers of the article who attacked a letter which (the then) James Kay had written in 1840 to the Manchester Mechanics' Institute urging that it keep its neutrality on religious matters. The Committee had given up its claim to keep schools of its own on the neutral principle, *The Times* argued, and was now trying to approach things differently. 'They teach first a singing class – then they establish "constructive" spelling – then writing; – and, it appears, arithmetic, and also drawing. No irreligious education! – not for the world.' And so the Committee would wriggle back to neutral education, without ever discussing it. *The Times* was uncompromisingly angry that 'schoolmasters and mistresses should be formed in this way, that education should be put in the hands of interlopers of this sort – random customers in spelling and writing – instead of persons who have had a thorough, sound, complete, and religious training'.[23]

The attack was successful. On 5 October 1842 Charles Greville wrote to his friend Henry Reeve that Wharncliffe and Kay-

Shuttleworth were extremely angry but that Kay-Shuttleworth had wisely decided to make no answer. Greville thought the attacks unjust and the misrepresentations gross, and he realized that some of the writers were opposed not just to Kay-Shuttleworth and the Committee but 'to every system . . . which is not under the control of the Church, and which does not inculcate its dogmatic theology'. Yet a week later Greville had reluctantly decided that Kay-Shuttleworth had to be muzzled and his philosophizing at Exeter Hall stopped, 'for it will not do to have the Council set up to be pelted with the ridicule and ribaldry of the Press. *The Times*, however, is really too bad'. With Kay-Shuttleworth taking some of the financial risk, the preaching and teaching at Exeter Hall were transferred to St Martin's Lane. A decrease in publicity deadened the controversy, but the scale of the operation grew smaller.[24]

While ill at ease with Exeter Hall, Greville was well disposed to the larger venture at Battersea. He visited it with illustrious company, including Russell, on 16 February 1842, and marvelled (as he had at Norwood) at the scholars' enthusiasm. Though James and Janet Kay-Shuttleworth had taken what Frederick North described as 'a small poky house in the remote district of Brompton', his mother and sister remained at Battersea contributing to the life of the Training School and making it easier for him to handle the pressure at the Council Office and at Gawthorpe estate. But despite their help, and the patronage of Prince Albert, the financial burden of Battersea was beginning to worry Kay-Shuttleworth and Tufnell. By August 1842, after £1,500 had been donated by friends such as Lord Morpeth (£500) and Lansdowne and Tremenheere, who each gave £100, they had spent £2,500, and that did not include the rent paid by the Kay family.[25]

In search of help Kay-Shuttleworth wrote to Peel, emboldened (or made desperate) because nothing had happened after the Committee of Council had delighted him by deciding in 1841 to include a sum in the estimates to defray some of Battersea's expenses. Nothing had happened, either, after he and Tufnell had given Wharncliffe a detailed account of their financial difficulties at the beginning of 1842, and asked for an annual grant of £1,000. Like many zealots Kay-Shuttleworth assumed his problems were important to everyone and did not hesitate to raise this relatively minor domestic issue with the Prime Minister. He stressed Battersea's conformity with the Established Church, claimed that it had been a model for other training institutions, mentioned its contribution to the development of new methods of teaching, and again asked for an annual grant of £1,000. He pointed out that he and Tufnell had waited two and a half years 'in expectation of aid from the public funds' and for a year since the Committee of Council minute 'inducing us to *depend* on receiving such aid'.[26]

It was not until November 1842 that the Committee of Council made a grant of £1,000, but in July 1843 Kay-Shuttleworth informed Peel that the grant would be exhausted by the autumn. He suggested that Battersea could either come into 'a still more intimate union' with the Committee of Council or work separately under a board elected by its subscribers. Economies had impaired the Training School's efficiency, he claimed, the masters were overworked (one had left England in the first stages of consumption), and it was necessary to raise staff salaries and appoint a principal who, unlike him, could live at Battersea. By the end of his letter he was telling Peel that Battersea had to be permanently connected with the government or he and Tufnell should be left 'to prepare for [its] immediate dissolution'. Action followed. The Committee granted £2,000 towards the expense of enlarging and improving the buildings on condition that a lease was taken on the premises and that satisfactory arrangements were made for the permanent support of the institution. But it was another one-off grant, not the annual grant for which Kay-Shuttleworth had been asking. Discussions with Wharncliffe followed, which included a suggestion that the trustees would take on the financial risks if proposals by Kay-Shuttleworth for payment by students, some of which were matched by government grants, were acceptable. The Committee ignored the proposals, increased the grant to £2,200, but kept it as a single grant. Kay-Shuttleworth was no better off. He estimated that Tufnell's and his expenses would rise to £1,500 per annum, and he drew the inescapable conclusion: 'We were unable to pledge our personal resources to this extent, and we could not claim the grant of £2,200 without providing for the permanent support of the establishment by arrangements satisfactory to their Lordships.'[27]

Throughout the negotiations Kay-Shuttleworth showed no squeamishness about the ambiguities of his position. He acted as he usually did in his Committee of Council dealings, not by observing a bureaucratic protocol but by doing what he considered was best for the cause. His requests for an annual grant showed that he wanted to bring Battersea under the Committee's wing, to turn it effectively into a government Normal school. However, the Tory-controlled Committee would hardly have wanted direct responsibility for a

Normal school, particularly as it involved a link with the controversial Kay-Shuttleworth. In the circumstances the support they gave was a remarkable tribute to Wharncliffe's commitment. For Kay-Shuttleworth, however, the choice had become simple: find another patron or close Battersea down. He flirted briefly with relying on private support but came to Russell's conclusion that individual effort would never be adequate. Lansdowne was equally unencouraging, and an unnamed friend believed that he would find it hard to attract students: only the 'extremest low party in the Church' would take teachers from Battersea, and the Dissenters would not take any. Kay-Shuttleworth would be left to supply friends such as Lord Radnor, Edward Stanley, the Whig Bishop of Norwich, and the Duke of Sutherland, 'excellent people in their way', but individuals whose exclusive support would weaken his standing as secretary to the Committee.[28]

With ruthlessly imaginative pragmatism, he offered Battersea to the Church, explaining to Russell and Lansdowne that the transfer was better than abandoning the institution. He told Blomfield on 5 October 1843 that the greatest contribution he could make to an appeal which the National Society had been running for the support of education in the manufacturing districts 'would be to confide the future management of these schools at Battersea' to a committee selected by the Society. His official position prevented him serving on such a committee but he suggested Blomfield, Howley, Lords Ashley and Chichester, John Sinclair, the secretary of the National Society, and 'my friend Tufnell' (whom, he admitted, he had not yet consulted about the plan but who later supported it). Kay-Shuttleworth hoped that this hierarchical but relatively liberal group would protect Battersea from the High Church element and preserve the structure of the schools, the jobs of the teachers, and Battersea's methods of teaching.[29]

Blomfield had his worries about St Mark's College and its intellectual and conservative principal, Derwent Coleridge, the poet's son, and Russell thought that Kay-Shuttleworth was acting wisely. Prince Albert was less pleased and asked to speak to Kay-Shuttleworth about the proposal, but the negotiations moved quickly. On 18 November Blomfield told Kay-Shuttleworth that he did not anticipate any difficulties, and armed with this assurance, Kay-Shuttleworth informed the Committee of Council that he had had discussions with Howley and Blomfield and that they were willing to take responsibility for Battersea. By early December the

National Society had formally agreed. Wharncliffe told Kay-Shuttleworth that Battersea 'placed both you and the Committee of Council in somewhat of a false position, and was a constant source of jealousy to both Church and Dissenters, from being looked upon as our model, to which we and you were determined to bring their schools'. Kay-Shuttleworth told William Thursby, his Gawthorpe acquaintance, that he had disenfranchised himself of 'that burthen' to enable him to attend to his private affairs, to look after his wife's property and to remove himself from any employment in the public service except with the Committee of Council.[30]

So, in a rather undignified search for financial support, Kay-Shuttleworth's Battersea endeavours ended. Blomfield spoke of Kay-Shuttleworth's and Tufnell's 'disinterested liberality', and in financial terms they were disinterested. However, in the educational politics of the time, Battersea was anything but disinterested. It embodied and helped to spread Kay-Shuttleworth's educational message. In a letter to Peel, he claimed that Battersea provided a model for other training institutions. It aimed at training the elementary schoolteacher, its regimen acted as a model for many colleges, it publicized the simultaneous method, and it placed great stress on pedagogy. To have to give Battersea to the National Society was a defeat and disappointment for Kay-Shuttleworth, but through it he had made an important contribution to the development of teacher training in England.[31]

While Kay-Shuttleworth was disentangling himself from his private ventures at Exeter Hall and Battersea he was heartened by new measures which the Committee of Council adopted. Though Wharncliffe rejected his proposals for support for students at training schools and annual maintenance grant for colleges, the Committee decided, in a minute of 22 November 1843, to give building grants to Normal schools, provided that they accepted inspection. They also offered grants for the improvement or building of schoolmasters' and schoolmistresses' houses, again on the proviso that the school was judged efficient by the inspector. Moreover, the Order of 3 June 1839, which had allowed the giving of larger grants to schools not connected with the two societies, especially in poor and populous places, was to be given effect. On the recommendation of an inspector, grants could be given for apparatus and furniture in new schools or for the conversion of Sunday schools to day schools, provided that one-third of the expense was met locally. It was hardly surprising, in the light of the responsibilities being given them, that the number of inspectors was to be increased to ensure that in 'the most populous and manufacturing districts' inspection took place at least twice a year.[32]

The minute was written after consultations, in which Kay-Shuttleworth took a considerable part, with both societies. There was clear agreement that the government grant system was based on an assumption of local effort, but Allen and Tremenheere, both supporters of this view, had argued that a complete reliance on private subscriptions was futile. The poverty of many of the schools they inspected contributed markedly to their unsatisfactory state, if only by ensuring that they failed to attract and keep good teachers. The new grants were a partial remedy for this state of affairs. The extension of the grant beyond the two societies had been made necessary because means had to be found to support the schools of the Free Church created in the Disruption of 1843 when Chalmers broke from the Church of Scotland. Similarly the need for more inspectors was appreciated by government and the National Society. Explaining a draft of the minute to Peel, Wharncliffe said that inspection was a joke and would remain so unless it was made 'periodically and frequently'.[33]

The continuity of Kay-Shuttleworth's policies was a striking feature of this minute. First, it *was* a minute and, as Johnson has pointed out, the Tories in Opposition condemned this method of bypassing Parliament, then used it when they came to government. There were also the arrangements made for inspection. Sinclair, on behalf of the National Society, wanted inspection based on dioceses, inspectors brought under the power of the bishops, and the publication of independent reports prevented. The 'Scheme for periodical inspection for England and Wales', which Kay-Shuttleworth put forward to Wharncliffe on 2 December 1843, required reports to be sent first to the Committee of Council, so the battle which concluded in the Concordat was fought and won again. As if to give a geographical expression to this victory, the inspectorial districts were drawn up without regard for diocesan boundaries: the civil power had asserted its independence and, within the limits of the Concordat, that of its inspectors. Kay-Shuttleworth resisted the suggestion that inspectors' salaries should be cut in order to help finance the increase in their number, arguing that inspectors should be University men of 'extensive acquirements and good manners' and that, as their jobs required 'peculiar knowledge, tact, and skill', the salaries offered should increase with length of service so that the inspectors were reassured about the value of their work. Early in 1844 Wharncliffe appointed five inspectors: four for Church schools, of which there were 479 in receipt of post-1839 grants, and a replacement for Tremenheere to inspect the 78 British schools.[34]

The provision of a grant for apparatus and furniture was the third example of the continuity of the secretary's policies. He had advocated this unsuccessfully in August 1839, before he and Tufnell visited the Continent;[35] but Kay-Shuttleworth under the Tories was able to resurrect what Kay had been unable to achieve with the Whigs. Making the apparatus grant dependent on the recommendations of the inspector was evidence of a fourth continuity: Kay-Shuttleworth's desire to limit the power of the two societies by increasing that of the inspectors. There was a fifth continuity: the grants for apparatus were a means of advancing simultaneous teaching and discouraging the monitorial system. Kay-Shuttleworth's approach might have been piecemeal but it was not haphazard – the extension of the civil power and the reduction of the influence of the Church consistently guided his actions. He suffered defeats, but he had a tenacious memory, a grasp of detail, an eye for the long haul and a hide thick enough to shrug off defeats and reintroduce policies when he thought there was a chance they might be accepted. He could even permit himself the grim satisfaction of watching the Tories take actions for which they had previously criticized the Whigs.

To continuity with the past Kay-Shuttleworth added planning for the future. Thus on 13 August 1844 he asked his inspectors to report on the incomes of schools in their districts. Similarly, as Richard Johnson has pointed out, he worked with W.G. Lumley, the Committee's legal adviser, on the trust deeds for schools receiving grants. The minute of 22 November 1843 had made the grant towards the building of Normal schools dependent on an appropriate deed of trust which had become important in Kay-Shuttleworth's strategy for increasing lay influence on schools. In the following years, particularly with the Revd William Kennedy, who succeeded Sinclair as secretary of the National Society, Kay-Shuttleworth and Lumley battled over the trust deeds submitted to the Committee by schools accepting grants. By the autumn of 1845 they had reached agreement with Kennedy and the National Society on a form of trust deed which ensured lay participation in boards of management while preserving the rights of the clergy. Both this agreement and the information on school incomes were to be of great use in future battles.[36]

Kay-Shuttleworth's attitude to inspection gave another example of his planning and of his characteristic way of working. When the National Society or the Dissenters criticized the Committee of Council as a step towards centralization and the building of a state machine hostile to their interests, they were identifying large social, economic and class pressures. But inspection was also a creature of the obsessive personality of James Kay-Shuttleworth. Unable to be in charge of anything without attempting to control it entirely, he sought to keep his inspectorate, whose appointment lay in the gift of the politicians, firmly in line. Despite his insistence that inspectors were merely advisers, the forms, plans, minutes and letters of instruction with which he bombarded them were aimed at equipping them to promulgate his and the Committee's ideas. He also helped to plan their itineraries and the weekly diaries which they were obliged to keep. As his assistant, Harry Chester, confided to him in July 1844:

> You know I have long shared your anxieties about the nonsupervision of the inspection – Every week, the establishment of a good system of regular, steadying, vivifying supervision will become more and more difficult of attainment - Young twigs soon grow into stiff boughs.

To prevent such a stiffening Kay-Shuttleworth devised a new form of diary in which the Council Office commented on suggestions made by the inspectors. Allen objected strenuously and the Committee supported him but, despite the setback, Kay-Shuttleworth did not slacken his efforts.[37]

In a voluminous personal correspondence, much of which is now lost, Kay-Shuttleworth counselled, cajoled and occasionally criticized the inspectors, sometimes forcing even the independent Allen on to the defensive. He once asked whether Kay-Shuttleworth had been writing him any more letters. 'I do not mean to say anything so uncivil or so untrue as that I should not have been delighted to have heard from you', but he had not, and was worried, if letters had gone astray, that his reputation as a man of business would suffer. When he was an assistant Poor Law commissioner, Kay-Shuttleworth told another inspector, contact with headquarters had given him 'a large implied moral sanction', while his detailed reports obtained him 'frequent if not constant signs of approval'. As a result he always believed that he had 'the entire moral and official support of the

central authority'. Kay-Shuttleworth did not want to yield power to
the men in the field, he wanted to capture it for the central authority.[38]

The scars of that struggle were deep, as another worry of Chester's
revealed. If he and Kay-Shuttleworth were 'effectually to supervise
the Inspectors our own positions must be improved and made
superior to theirs – Hitherto I must say I think we have all been
shoved into false positions; and have made our bricks without straw,
tools or thanks'. Chester's dissatisfaction may have been expressed
through illness for he was coming into the office at four o'clock to
attend to urgent business only. Kay-Shuttleworth, himself ill with
overwork, had retreated, in July 1844, to Gawthorpe and the Lake
District. Hearing of Chester's problems he offered to give up his
holiday and return to Whitehall, but Chester would have none of it:

> although as your junior officer, I have no official right to protect your
> interests, I certainly shall be guilty of insubordination in this
> particular – Your health absolutely requires relaxation shortly; and is
> not equal to a continuance of the harassing, fever exciting, depressing
> influences, which threaten to break you down – You *must have* an
> *easier* position, or you will break down – and this I am determined if
> possible to prevent.

He made the incidental complaint that he could not afford a carriage,
and decided that no one in Lord Wharncliffe's position could
imagine 'the depressing effect of going to London and back daily [he
lived in Highgate] when one has no conveyance but an omnibus', a
vehicle which he defined as '*a subtle poison consisting of noise, heat,
draughts, bustle and foul air*'.

At Gawthorpe Kay-Shuttleworth, free from London's noise, was
deeply depressed, and Janet was edgy with worry. During the Factory
Bill controversy she had told Joseph Kay that his brother's work was
comparable with the struggles for the abolition of the slave trade or
the emancipation of Roman Catholics. But in July 1844 she
reminded Kay-Shuttleworth that 'you could resign your Office
without hesitation on the score of money'. She did not want him
'sacrificed to mere routine and detail' when he was intended for '*some
great work*'. He was not to be a 'mere office slave', but by the time
there was a change in the Ministry, he would, in the prime of his life,
be 'driven out of the country by illness – the result of thankless and
almost useless toil'. A few days later, although distressed by 'the
exceeding nervousness and agitation which occasionally oppress

you', she had decided that 'God will guide us dearest Husband in our course', for 'to few has he given such duties and powers as to you'. She wished she could be at Gawthorpe but had decided to go to Tunbridge Wells to take the waters.[39]

Janet's remonstrance, as she called it, could hardly have found her husband more vulnerable. Her unrealistic romanticism, which magnified the significance of his work and blinded her to its difficulties, had first drawn her to him and helped to fulfil his need for respect. He believed that he was engaged on 'the greatest enterprise (rightly understood) of this time',[40] and to have this enterprise reduced to mere routine was profoundly depressing, especially as he knew that Janet's comments did lip the rim of truth. The unintended combination of her unimaginative, well-meant worrying and Chester's well-intentioned but tactless loyalty was devastating, particularly as there were still the Norths and the Shuttleworths to worry about. North was a gentleman adept at disguising his social superiority if he wanted to, but he seemed to want to less and less, and Kay-Shuttleworth would have had to be stolidly insensitive, which he was not, if he did not sense this attitude. Now with his wife and his closest professional associate telling him that his worth was not recognized and his work was dull and trivial, a principal bulwark of his self-respect was severely damaged.

From 1839 onwards attacks on that self-respect had ranged from the accusations of theological unorthodoxy to straightforward smearing, a common occurrence at a time of passionate feelings and loose libel laws. In 1841, for example, *Fraser's Magazine* had reported an anonymous Poor Law official, 'a very pet assistant-commissioner, a great industrial-education-monger', who wanted to build expensive schools to educate pauper children and who, when maddened by resistance of some guardians, had 'retired into an adjoining room, [and] swallowed a huge opium pill; for though he grudges the poor labourer his beer, and affects himself to disdain a cup of generous wine, the nasty *fee-losofer* is devoted to the Chinamen's vice'. In 1844 the *Quarterly Review* renewed the attack on the phonics books produced by the Committee of Council, casting doubt (as North had done) over Kay-Shuttleworth's pronunciation of 'the aspirate H' and concluding that 'no child, who shall be treated exclusively after Dr. Kay Shuttleworth's method, and limited to *his* reading lessons, will ever be able to read at all'. He wisely ignored these accusations as he had *The Times* articles, but with those articles and the *Eclectic Review*'s, and the campaigns against the 1839 minute and the Factory

Bill, he had been constantly under attack. In the summer of 1843 he had also rested at Gawthorpe and the Lake District, where he spent a short time with Janet, Joe and Hannah (his sister), but emotionally he remained desperately low.[41]

By 1844 Janet Kay-Shuttleworth was also showing signs of anxiety. She was sometimes torn between ambitions which strained the customary expectations for women and a conventional subservience to her husband. She was involved in proposals to have women deacons and to establish an institution for the education of governesses. When the parliamentarian, R.A. Slaney, came to discuss the governess question shortly after her marriage, he remarked that she was 'an amiable person and likely to use her large fortune to good purposes'. 'Had I been a man', she wrote to Joseph Kay in 1843, reflecting on those purposes, 'I should undoubtedly have chosen the Law as the profession most congenial to me'. She had been reading through some of her father's papers and responded to the intellectual challenges they set, though she puzzled over the morality of defending cases that were 'manifestly wrong'. She concluded the letter by remarking that her husband had gone out and, unless she delayed sending the letter, 'I cannot ask his approval of what I have said'.[42]

Frederick North's approval was harder to win. He noted that while professing to be economizing, the Kay-Shuttleworths employed five servants – yet 'the heiress of Gawthorpe' had no carriage. To the disappointment of an old servant, the Kay-Shuttleworth entourage would arrive at Hastings (assuming they had not cancelled because of a Committee of Council meeting or another inadequate reason) on the post – like 'paper parcels'. In May 1842 he remarked that Janet had expressed her delight at mixing with 'the great and wise of the country' and at seeing her husband 'universally looked up to by both classes'. He spilled his own views into his diary in November:

> My Janet is up to little, and seems perpetually suffering, but it is as much mind, as body – she never has, and I doubt if she ever will, get over the disappointment of her daughter's marriage. Kay, at the best, is but an adventurer, a successful one, and Respectable – but a man of no name, family, or position – he is cute enough, and looks well after the main chance – and seems disposed to make the most of his little wife . . .

With his cruelly attractive wit North described the younger Janet as 'a fragment from the glacier of Grundenwald' and was puzzled that his wife was so anxious to be with her daughter, when there seemed to be little affection between them. 'I suppose', he said in unimaginative bewilderment, 'it is caused, in some sort however, by her wish to know exactly how things between the Kays stand; in order to be of use to the young Married Lady.'[43]

The Kay-Shuttleworths' first child, Janet Elizabeth, was born on 6 May 1843, confounding North who had decided a few months after the marriage that there would be no children. The confinement and birth were uneventful, and though there were times when Janet seemed to be thriving, her health deteriorated after the birth, causing North to decide that 'poor thing, she is more adapted to be made a Nurse herself, than to Nurse a Baby'. In July 1844, again pregnant, she complained of the useless toil which was wearing her husband down, expressed the strange hope that hair might return to 'your poor bald head', and trusted in God's strength 'to make human weakness perfect'. She wished that she was a better helpmate – 'how earnestly I strive to conquer my weakness and ignorance'. Young Janet, North said about this time, was 'a perfect wreck and her husband quite tired, and in despair about her'. On 14 December with the baby due and in fear of her life, Janet wrote to Kay-Shuttleworth with some requests should she not survive childbirth. She wanted a few small gifts given to servants but her main concern was that he and the child (or children) should persevere in daily prayer. She listed the Biblical passages she wanted her daughter taught and asked him to deal truthfully and openly with her and to shield her by his integrity from those who confused truth and error. 'I can though not without many tears think calmly of leaving my child – I dare scarcely dwell on parting from my husband.' Four days later, on 18 December 1844, their son, Ughtred James, was born. 'The Gawthorpe turn out seems to be most uniformly successful', a mordant North wrote, 'and the little Misery (whom one hardly expected life for, herself), seems to be "enfante-ing" without encountering the average suffering attendant upon all Eve's daughters, in like circumstances.'[44]

The achievement of a male heir to Gawthorpe brought satisfaction, but it did not diminish Janet's problems of living with a driven depressed man. Nor could it control the cancer eating away at her husband's fragile personality. A man with no name and position, he had acquired both by marriage, only to find that Janet, whose ardour for the cause had drawn them together, now regarded what had to be done to further that cause as destructive. He was still as lonely as he had been when he tried to join the Manchester Infirmary or to marry Helen Kennedy.

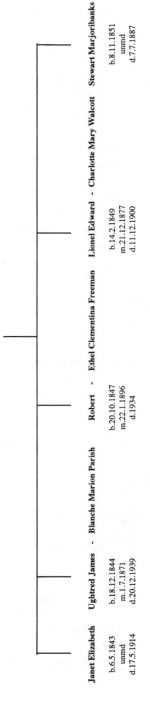

THE KAY - SHUTTLEWORTHS

James Kay m.24.2.1842 - Janet Shuttleworth

Janet Elizabeth	Ughtred James	-	Blanche Marion Parish	Robert	-	Ethel Clementina Freeman	Lionel Edward	-	Charlotte Mary Walcott	Stewart Marjoribanks
b.6.5.1843	b.18.12.1844			b.20.10.1847			b.14.2.1849			b.8.11.1851
unmd	m.1.7.1871			m.22.1.1896			m.21.12.1877			unmd
d.17.5.1914	d.20.12.1939			d.1934			d.11.12.1900			d.7.7.1887

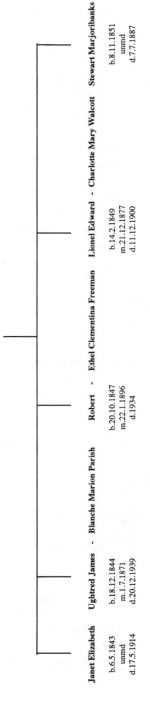

He found two outlets for his frustrations. The first was to consider entering Parliament. In May 1843 he told North that the 'confidential agent' for the Whigs had approached him about North's standing for Hastings again. North rejected the approach goodnaturedly, though in private he suspected that Kay-Shuttleworth wished to stand for Hastings himself. Kay-Shuttleworth made no move, but a parliamentary career was in the air for on 31 December North commented: 'We shall soon hear of you, as MP for Clitheroe – and occupying a new Cabinet Office, as Minister for Public Instruction'. Clitheroe was a family fiefdom, as North well knew, because the sitting Member, Kay-Shuttleworth's cousin, Richard Fort, was among the people North looked down upon – his father was 'Fort the Cotton-spinner of Read Hall – who was . . . born in a Gawthorpe cottage'. Kay-Shuttleworth made no attempt to challenge his cousin, but the allure of a parliamentary career had begun to tempt him.[45]

Then there was the estate. Shortly before their wedding, while he was subjecting the Norths to tales of his meeting with the King of Prussia, Janet North suggested that education and the King would distract him from Gawthorpe. Prompted by the suggestion, he asked his future wife to have her accountant, Charles Saunderson, audit the property, particularly the collieries. He planned to examine every detail, justifying his actions not as a check on Waddington, the estate manager, but as a means of acquainting himself with the business of his demesne. Saunderson was worried about the expenditure on the collieries and rather darkly told the then Janet Shuttleworth that, while he had no wish to be a prophet of evil, 'I never was – and perhaps I never shall be a Courtier'. He had no doubt, however, that 'by good and cautious management your fine Estate will yield what an humble individual as myself would call a princely fortune'.[46]

Shortly after the wedding, armed with Saunderson's audit, Kay-Shuttleworth descended upon the unfortunate Waddington, invited him to breakfast, and showed him that £15,000 had been expended on the colliery in the last three years at his discretion, without specific directions from anyone connected with the estate. Determined to implement Saunderson's recommendation that the colliery should be required to make a net cash profit each year, and not simply to record an increased value in stock and machinery, Kay-Shuttleworth informed Waddington that 'I was disposed to make myself Master of the whole affair, both in knowledge and in action', and that he would not be permitted 'the most trifling outlay either in improvement or on the colliery stock without my written authority'. This and much more, Kay-Shuttleworth reported, was 'communicated most kindly, and received by Waddington in a manner which impressed me favourably'.[47]

Kay-Shuttleworth had found a responsibility to which he applied himself with feverish dedication. 'There is *very very* much to be done here every way', he told Janet. 'I thought of my dear wife, and felt for the first time that I could make her a *worthy* return for her devoted love. Indeed my dearest I have never been so happy since we married as now when I find that I can be of great and lasting service to the Gawthorpe estate.' That service included a careful watch on the teachers' salaries. In December 1844 he praised one of the teachers, but 'for strong reasons connected solely with your own comfort and prosperity' he refused him a salary increase, offering instead a gift of £10 and the advice that 'as long as you continue to deserve my confidence, you may regard me as your protector and friend'. He renegotiated the complicated colliery leases – North admitted that he was glad not to have to deal with the mess into which the collieries had plunged, made Gawthorpe more habitable by preventing the smoking of its fires and blocking the draughts which swept through it, and he and Janet began to consider plans for major renovations. Kay-Shuttleworth was pleased with what he achieved, and North thought him to be 'not . . . quite honest or straightforward' and even 'unreasonable and grasping'.[48] For all his efforts he never acquired the combination of knowledge and detachment from the day-to-day management of the estate which came naturally to those accustomed to landed wealth. Just as he could not leave the details of school-buildings or curriculum to others, so, at Gawthorpe, he busied himself with every aspect of the estate and, no doubt to the anguish of Waddington, almost performed the task of estate manager himself. He was unpopular but extremely effective.

A letter written in November 1845 illustrates his approach. It instructed his agent that a new drainage programme was to begin in a small way so that its effectiveness could be checked. Kay-Shuttleworth reasoned that if it had been successfully and prudently done, he had a better chance of overcoming his tenants' reluctance to undertake similar programmes. He had studied Lord Derby's farms at Knowsley to ascertain how far apart the drains should be placed, and he knew how he wished his to be dug. If bad weather made draining impossible, he had prepared alternative work: the construction of a carriage road which had recently been laid out; quarrying, thinning the plantations, fencing to prepare for new plantations and, in the case of the horse and cart, the carrying of coal from a particular pit to Gawthorpe Hall, the colliery at Stockbridge, and the school. He required weekly reports on the employment of the men and monthly accounts of receipts and disbursements.[49] In every facet of the estate, the new master set out to render himself worthy of his wife's approval, and to ease the depression which weighed him down. The depression might have lifted briefly in January 1845 when the Royal Humane Society, wishing to encourage work on 'suspended animation', awarded him its Fothergillian Gold Medal in recognition of 'your eminent work on "Asphyxia"'. Kay-Shuttleworth had submitted his book some time before 1845 but at that stage a published book was not considered eligible for the award. When that policy was changed Kay-Shuttleworth and another doctor were awarded medals. His submission of his book, almost a decade after he had ceased medical practice, is an indication of how desperately he sought recognition of any kind.[50]

The minutes of 1846, a milestone in the history of English education, were announced in a minute of 25 August and embodied in regulations of 21 December. They enabled managers of schools to apprentice one or more of their most able students to the master or mistress of the school for a five-year term as a pupil-teacher. Students had to be 13 years of age, and inspectors examined them in a graduated syllabus (similar to Battersea's) of the subjects they would eventually teach, and in their teaching skills. At the end of the fifth year successful pupil-teachers were awarded a certificate. The Committee of Council paid pupil-teachers a small salary and provided the master or mistress with an annual loading for each pupil-teacher who successfully completed a year of apprenticeship. Each year, after a competitive examination organized by the inspector and the principal of a Normal school, the Committee of Council awarded exhibitions ('as many as they might think fit') to pupil-teachers who had obtained certificates. These 'Queen's scholars' received £20 or £25 per annum for three years to attend the Normal school, which was paid an annual sum for each Queen's scholar whom the inspector judged to have completed the year's work successfully. To perfect the circle of supply and demand, the Committee of Council gave schools which appointed an ex-Normal school trainee and which was declared efficient by an inspector, an annual grant towards the teacher's salary.[51]

Nothing explained the purpose of the minutes better than Kay-Shuttleworth's pamphlet, *The School, in its Relations to the State, the Church, and the Congregation* (1847). They were intended to 'raise the character and position of the schoolmaster; to provide for him a respectable competency', to produce better teachers by supporting more Normal schools, and to feed them with candidates of 'higher attainments and greater skill'. The school would become more popular among the poor by 'introducing their children to more honourable and profitable employments' and, through their increased efficiency, would 'create in the minds of the working class a juster estimate of the value of education for their children'.[52] There were major problems which the minutes did not solve, and did not even address – persuading children to attend school consistently, for example – but they were a major administrative achievement. They laid the basis for the training of teachers in Britain for the remainder of the century. Their course of study had a significant impact on the curriculum and methodology of elementary schools. They undermined the monitorial system by popularizing the pupil-teacher and beginning to ensure a supply of trained teachers. They reinforced the importance of local voluntary effort in the organization of popular education and supported its religious basis – in schools connected with the Church the clergyman (and in other schools, the managers) had to certify the moral character of the candidates for pupil-teacher, the parochial clergyman was to be present at the examination of pupil-teachers in the catechism and Scriptures, and the Normal schools, which had given such significant financial support, were all controlled by religious bodies. In the long run, however, the minutes' most important effect was to enhance the power of the inspectorate and increase the influence of the Committee of Council, the civil power in education.

They had other achievements which were not wholly unintended by-products. In *The School, in its Relations to the State, the Church and the Congregation*, Kay-Shuttleworth drew attention to the social mobility which the minutes encouraged – the scholars selected would mostly belong to the families of manual labourers, and would thus begin a career 'which would otherwise be rarely commenced'.[53] For women in particular, school-teaching increased social mobility and provided many recruits for suffragist and feminist causes. By funding the women's colleges started by the Church the state opened an avenue of liberation for young working-class or rural women, a narrow and twisting avenue, certainly, and one that led to a teaching service which discriminated against them, but one which opened prospects not visible from farm, factory or domestic service. At the same time, however, the minutes assumed the intellectual inferiority of women by allowing them to be exempted from examination in certain levels of subjects such as decimal arithmetic, mechanics, surveying, syntax, etymology and prosody, while containing the predictable expectation that they should increase their skills as seamstresses and in the teaching of sewing and knitting.

The minutes were another mark of the continuity of Kay-Shuttleworth's endeavours, particularly the increasing of the civil power in education – a power given an additional boost by the management clauses which were promulgated in 1847. They had a further continuity, Kay-Shuttleworth's work for pauper education. The 1844 Poor Law Amendment Act contained a provision enabling the establishment of the district schools of which he had for so long been an advocate. In 1846 he had persuaded the Committee of Council to accept a memorandum which gave £30,000 for the salaries of teachers in workhouse schools and which recommended the appointment of four or five inspectors to the Poor Law Commission who would act under the guidance of the Committee of Council. In the 1846 minutes provision was made for another recommendation of this memorandum, the establishment of a Normal school for teachers in workhouse schools. Money was put aside for this purpose and work begun to make a Normal school out of Kneller Hall, which had been built for the court painter in the early eighteenth century about a mile from Twickenham. Neither the district schools nor Kneller Hall proved successful, but they were testimony to Kay-Shuttleworth's pertinacity.[54]

Kay-Shuttleworth was the driving force behind the minutes but his own claims have helped to obscure their origin. In his *Autobiography* he describes the process by which he arrived at the minutes as being

> like that of a discovery in natural science. It was purely inductive. The inquiry how the organization and instruction of schools could be improved was like the interrogation of nature in search of an unknown law . . . If the method pursued were sound, if the observer were fairly intelligent, and if he had some power of generalization, the result might be relied upon with a confidence like that which attends the revelation of a natural law.[55]

However, the educational policies of the James Kay-Shuttleworth who wrote the minutes were not those of a detached intellectual or the incipient social scientist. They were a response to the 'old crones' in Edinburgh who begged Alison for money, to Manchester's Little Ireland, to the women screaming from windows in Bury St Edmunds, to the beggars armed with sticks outside the gates of Gawthorpe. They had been fashioned by the memory of the children's faces at Norwood, the example of David Stow in Glasgow and the teaching at the mother house of the Brothers of the Christian Schools in Paris. They were reactions to past experiences: the defeat of the Normal school proposal, the Concordat, Battersea, Exeter Hall, the 'young gentlemen', Edward Baines, and the Factory Bill. Far from being the result of cool rationality, the minutes of 1846 bore the marks of fear provoked by social disorder, of hope preserved despite bitter experience, of adaptation to political reality, and of a desire to gather power for the Committee of Council.

At other times Kay-Shuttleworth implied that he planned the 1846 minutes in 1839 but was prevented from implementing them because of the 'unabated jealousy' with which the Committee of Council was watched. He did not feel at liberty to disclose to anyone 'the plan of administration by the Committee of Council on Education, the vague outline of which I had conceived, but for the execution of which the time was not come'.[56] There were, indeed, clear continuities in Kay-Shuttleworth's policies, but the idea of a master plan devised in 1839 and pursued for seven tumultuous years is difficult to sustain. Kay-Shuttleworth claimed more than he needed to and his admirers conceded him more than was justified. In the controversies over the Normal school, the Concordat, Exeter Hall, the introduction of simultaneous instruction, and on other issues, he had fought hard, and frequently been forced into compromises which would have drastically altered any plan he made in 1839. Kay-Shuttleworth was a committed, obsessively determined, adaptable and pragmatic administrator, not the producer of secret, elegant plans or the discoverer of new natural laws. His administrative achievement in 1846 was to link the minutes' ingredients in a single scheme, to secure financial support from the government so that the required type of teacher could be produced, and by subsidizing the salary bill of schools who employed such teachers, to ensure that the new teachers were swiftly employed. His political achievement was to produce a package which avoided the fate of the 1839 Normal school proposal or the Factory Bill, while increasing the power of the Committee of Council, and of its maligned secretary. Battersea was the major catalyst for the minutes. Kay-Shuttleworth's 1843 letter to Wharncliffe, in which he sought an annual grant, produced an embryonic form of the minutes – it suggested retrospective government funding for certain Normal school students, certification through the inspectorate and exhibitions for selected students. In his 'Second report on the schools for the training of parochial schoolmasters at Battersea', dated 15 December 1843, Kay-Shuttleworth argued for the formation of a body of pupil-teachers in each of the great towns, the provision of fees and charges by the Committee of Council to cover their apprentice-ship, and the establishment of grants to support exhibitions at a Normal school. In November 1844 he submitted to the Committee of Council a scheme which had most of the ingredients of the 1846 minute, though the payments involved were less generous. And while he was maturing his own plans, Kay-Shuttleworth, as Johnson has shown, was gaining support from the inspectorate, partly through their criticism of the state of education in the country, and partly from direct suggestions as to policy. Frederick Cook and Henry Moseley were particularly influential. In January 1845 Cook provided detailed information on the working of the pupil-teacher system initiated by the London Diocesan Board and stressed the need to pay the teachers who instructed the apprentices, to provide certificates for pupil-teachers and to offer exhibitions which enabled chosen students to proceed to a training college. Moseley also argued strongly for exhibitions which could be linked to the pupil-teacher system.[57]

The momentous political battle surrounding the Corn Laws made it difficult for Kay-Shuttleworth to get parliamentary approval for his minutes. On 6 December 1845 Peel, lacking confidence in the support of his bitterly divided Cabinet for the repeal of the Corn Laws, had resigned and Lord John Russell was summoned by the Queen. Kay-Shuttleworth immediately informed Russell that he was able to 'restore into your hands the Education Department not only I trust uninjured, but, though not advanced by legislation, developed from being a mere limb of the Privy Council Office into a public department requiring reorganisation'. He had remained in his office, he said, to await Russell's return to power which brought the chance to complete the structure of a truly national system of education. But Russell could not form a ministry and Peel returned with a reconstituted Cabinet on 23 December, leaving Kay-Shuttleworth even worse off, as the supportive Wharncliffe had died four days earlier.[58]

Dejected but never long distracted from his plans, Kay-Shuttleworth wrote to Peel pointing out that the proposals he was nurturing had the support of the Bishop of London and the National Society. He also produced an important paper for Walter Francis Scott, the Duke of Buccleuch, who had succeeded Wharncliffe as President of the Privy Council. Entitled *The Present Condition of the Administration of the Parliamentary Grant* and hastily written in December 1845, it included most of the ingredients of the subsequent minute, and went further by advocating direct funding for elementary schools. Although written to brief Buccleuch, Kay-Shuttleworth had it printed and distributed to friends such as Lord Morpeth, and the Leveson-Gowers' daughter, Elizabeth Campbell, who had recently become Duchess of Argyll. The Duke of Sutherland remarked how 'very fortunate' it was that

> quietly and silently you have so far succeeded in raising an Office of Public Instruction; and perhaps when the *reality* has become established and familiar jealous sects may tolerate the name I hope some day to see a Minister of Public Instruction.[59]

Charles Blomfield was not so supportive when in March 1846 he discovered the existence of *The Present Condition* and was told that Kay-Shuttleworth had quoted him as being in favour of his plan. He complained of the indiscretion and Kay-Shuttleworth had no option but to confess to an angry Buccleuch, who pointed out that he would have to make the paper available to Blomfield and face a greater inconvenience – 'the cognizance by others, and we know not by whom, or by how many, of schemes confidentially submitted by you to the Committee of Council, upon which no decision or opinion has been pronounced'. Kay-Shuttleworth was reminded of 'the necessity as well as the propriety of abstaining altogether from communicating to friends however confidential papers of an official character'. His complete lack of repentance was illustrated when, in the midst of the dispute with Blomfield and Buccleuch, he wrote to his supporter, Lord Egerton, supplying him with arguments he might use to raise the subject of education in the House of Commons. Egerton did not oblige.[60] Throughout these difficulties Kay-Shuttleworth's health and spirits declined. The summer of 1846 found him morose and depressed, with the improvement, which followed a holiday he, Janet and Joseph Kay had taken in Bavaria the previous summer, proving to be temporary. Janet wrote to him from Sandgate, where she was taking a health cure, expressing the hope that he would recover health and energy, though she had resigned herself to seeing him grow weary, sleep badly night after night, and be 'silent – or nearly so'. She would abandon everything, even their children and Gawthorpe – 'and there was a time when I loved no living being in this world as I loved Gawthorpe' – if he would travel to some place where his work would not follow. She loved her children much but her husband 'infinitely more', and she was surer of him than she was of herself. Kay-Shuttleworth did no further travelling but thought again of a parliamentary career. Lady Elizabeth Campbell gave him sound advice: his work was wearing him down, and there would be less drudgery in Parliament, but there might well be 'the same deferred hope which sickens the heart'. Like Janet Kay-Shuttleworth, she suggested that he expect little from men and place his trust in God. Whomever he trusted in, Kay-Shuttleworth took no action, perhaps surprising Frederick North who had again decided, over-suspiciously, that he was intriguing for the Hastings seat.[61]

At the end of June 1846, with the Corn Laws repealed and his party split, Peel resigned. In Russell's ministry, the old aristocratic Whig families returned in force, and Kay-Shuttleworth watched Lansdowne return to the presidency of the Privy Council and Sir George Grey go to the Home Office. In July 1846, as the government settled into its deliberations, Walter Farquhar Hook, a High Churchman and Vicar of Leeds, published a pamphlet, *On the Means of Rendering More Efficient the Education of the People*, in which he argued that the educational wants of the country were so far from being met by the churches that the state should take over secular instruction, allow religious denominations to enter the schools twice a week and require scholars to attend a Sunday school or other place of worship. Originally sympathetic to the Oxford movement Hook had grown disillusioned, and partly out of this disillusionment, he made known the educational views which he had held since the late 1830s but, in the interests of Anglican unity, had not made public – he had merely whispered them to 'intimate and confidential friends as a kind of esoteric doctrine'. He had been in contact with Kay-Shuttleworth since April, and had shown him the manuscript, saying that if he thought that it would not benefit the cause, 'I have not the least objection to your committing it to the flames'. Kay-Shuttleworth knew a good thing when he saw one. He encouraged Hook to publish, and discussed points of difficulty, claiming that it was his job to provide information 'to all parties interested in promoting elementary education'. With Buccleuch's recent rebuke nagging at him, he told Hook that it 'may not always be prudent to avow that this had been done' and remarked how galling he found 'the official restraints which confine me within these limits'. For the moment, however, 'I must not be seen in this matter'.[62]

As Hook and Kay-Shuttleworth knew, Hook's views would create a furore. They did, and led to pamphlet and newspaper warfare every bit as personalized as the disputes of 1839 and 1843. Kay-Shuttleworth sent the pamphlet to Baines asking him what its effects were in the North and received the answer he must have expected – rejection; and an insistence that 'we should seek to attain an education as universal and of a higher moral quality and spirit than any stereotyped form that could be established by the State'. Through his *Letters to the Right Honourable John Russell on Education*, published in the autumn of 1846, Baines launched the voluntarist attack. Meanwhile Kay-Shuttleworth assured Hook that his writing had produced 'extreme consternation among the small *pedlars* who work the machinery of voluntary coteries against the national interests' and wrote to Russell of the coterie in the National Society who 'have abused their influence to retard national education'. Hook's 'knockdown blows', he rejoiced, 'have left them either stunned, or enraged with pain and shame'.[63]

While the debate raged outside Parliament, Lansdowne had no trouble within it. Though the minutes had been produced the previous year, he announced them to the Lords for the first time in February 1847, and listened as Howley and Blomfield agreed that they were 'exceedingly wise and prudent'. Even some Congregationalists led by Dr Robert Vaughan of Manchester ('a very able and distinguished minister', Kay-Shuttleworth called him) supported the minutes. The Catholics who, as Johnson has said, provided 'the classic case of the inadequacy of voluntary effort' but whose admittance would have provoked bitter protest, were kept at arms' length. Meanwhile Ashley concentrated on the Wesleyans who were initially hostile and had been left with the impression that aid to the Catholics was unlikely. Brandishing a Kay-Shuttleworth letter Ashley entered a meeting of Methodists in London which was about to pass unfavourable resolutions. He won them round, partly by arguing that, at least for the moment, aid would go only to schools which used the Authorized Version – that is, it would not go to Catholic schools. On 8 April, after a successful meeting with Methodists in Manchester he told Russell that his 'remaining Opponents are so many nine-pins, whom you may, and will, bowl down in your skittle-game of the H of Commons'. He added, 'Shuttleworth has done his *part admirably.*' The deal was formalized on 14 April and five days later the House had its chance to express opposition by refusing supply to the Committee of Council. During the debate John Bright attacked 'a very clever secretary, who, like other secretaries, was disposed to magnify the importance of his office'. A belated protest by the Catholic interest was checked, with Kay-Shuttleworth again providing Russell with useful advice, and supply was eventually granted. With the 1847 election looming, a concession was made to the Dissenters when a supplementary minute of 10 July removed the need for reports on the religious instruction of pupil teachers. The election, in which a fearful government faced hostile voluntarist opposition, passed without serious mortification, though there were some important losses. When a minute of 18 December gave aid to Catholic schools, Russell, Lansdowne, Grey and Kay-Shuttleworth could be satisfied that, even if deviously, they had accomplished their aim.[64]

By that time, however, Kay-Shuttleworth was embroiled in a controversy so bruising that it helped to end his time at the Committee of Council. The arrangements for the appointment, control and dismissal of teachers envisaged by the 1846 minutes were only as good as the Committee's arrangements for local management. Many schools were still controlled by the clergymen who might, the Committee feared, commit public funds to exclusive religious instruction. To prevent the reaping of a 'harvest of discord, confusion, or plunder' and to ensure 'the influence of the influential laity of the neighbourhood', Kay-Shuttleworth wanted a board of management for each school receiving aid. So did Kennedy at the National Society and in the spring of 1846, while the Conservatives were still in power, Kay-Shuttleworth's office sent four model clauses to the National Society and asked them to recommend them to school managers. After negotiations Howley and Blomfield, whom Kennedy described as 'omnipotent' in the National Society, were willing to accept the clauses, though Kennedy thought them imprecise and pressed for further negotiations. In September 1846 Kay-Shuttleworth, with the approval of Russell and the Chancellor, Sir Charles Wood, conducted secret negotiations with Blomfield and Howley. Kay-Shuttleworth was often to be accused of having deceived the Church but Kennedy's recollections in 1852 were quite clear – 'all you did (I doubt not) with the concurrence of the [by then] late Archbishop of Canterbury and the Bishop of London'. Howley had promised to support the clauses by November 1846 but, perhaps because of preoccupation with preparation of the 1846 minutes, they did not appear as a formal minute until June 1847.[65]

A school had to choose one of four clauses which were constructed to suit particular localities (populous districts of towns, rural parishes etc.). Under each clause the chair of a school committee was the clergyman or the licensed minister. Religious instruction was under his control, though in the case of a dispute in National Society schools an appeal could be made to the bishop. In all other respects, the minute of June 1847 insisted,

> the management, direction, control, and government of the said school and premises, and of the funds or endowments thereof, and the selection, appointment, and dismissal of the schoolmaster and schoolmistress, and their assistants, shall be vested in and exercised by a Committee.

The committees were to be composed differently depending on the type of school district, and could include unspecified numbers of lay people, local residents, landowners and subscribers.[66] Thus, although the clergy were prominent on the committees, the schools had been placed in the hands of respectable and wealthy lay people. Like the 1846 minutes, the management clauses marked the acceptance by the Committee of Council and Kay-Shuttleworth of a system of denominational schooling which relied heavily on voluntary effort and was controlled not by the parents of the children who used the schools, but by their social superiors. They were his last official shot in the battle, which had begun when the Committee was established, to assert the state's right in land which the religious bodies claimed was theirs. He had steadily gained ground, but at the cost of concessions which left a profound mark on English education.

To two groups, in particular, the management clauses guaranteed another disastrous expansion of the power of the state. While Baines continued his campaign against all state involvement, another formidable foe, George Anthony Denison, the Vicar of East Brent, defended the exclusive views of the High Church with harsh and intransigent vehemence. As all power and responsibility lay with the Church and its bishops and the local clergyman, the management clauses, the Committee of Council and its wily and untrustworthy secretary were anathema. Alexander has argued that the controversy over the management clauses made obvious, but did not create, divisions in the Church which were expressed in an internecine pamphlet warfare. Death, secession and changing views (Gladstone, now embarked on his fateful voyage towards liberalism, supported the 1846 minutes) had ended the cohesion and influence of the 'young gentlemen', but Denison stabbed his banner into the shifting sands and stood by it, a brave, consistent, and brutal fighter. 'I do not hesitate to declare *open war* . . . against the Committee of Council', he said in October 1849. He would work until 'this power, and this influence, is *fairly broken down and swept away*'.[67]

In the battle within the National Society and between the Society and the Committee of Council to modify the clauses, Denison prevented any swift agreement, and used the annual meetings of the Society to renew his attacks on the Committee and Kay-Shuttleworth. He found assistance from like-minded spirits such as Henry Wilberforce from East Fareleigh, who argued that in return for comparatively trifling aid the Committee of Council would 'dictate the whole system of control and management by which our future Church schools are to be regulated, and that for ever'. Kay-Shuttleworth had his defenders. They included the influential Richard Dawes whose parish school at King's Somborne had drawn the Committee's praise, and T.D. Acland, one of the original 'young gentlemen', who admitted that he once had 'serious fears of the influence of the Secretary' but now gave him 'every acknowledgement and praise'. Manning on the other hand exclaimed 'What a mess Kaye-Shuttleworth is making', but F.D. Maurice, a friend of Acland, exposed the divisions in the Church's ranks by describing Denison as 'a vulgar Church agitator, using the most sacred phrases for claptrap' and confusing the right of the clergy to have their own way with true Church principles. Maurice reported that he listened to speeches from clergymen at National Society meetings 'that it almost broke one's heart to hear' and saw 'demonstrations of a spirit which betokens schism and destruction'. The battle was to continue long after Kay-Shuttleworth had left the Committee. In the meantime Kneller Hall gave Kay-Shuttleworth's opponents another target. An article in the *English Review* in 1849 portrayed it as an 'infidel college' and the familiar arguments of 1839 were produced again, including a questioning of the need to have a Committee of Council 'with its secretary and inspectors'. Once more Kay-Shuttleworth was portrayed as the manipulative power behind the scenes who by 'unobtrusive' means exercised his 'remarkable talent' to get his own way.[68]

On one issue Kay-Shuttleworth got his own way quite unintentionally. In December 1846 he hastily produced a brief document for the Colonial Office on the education to be provided for the former slaves of the West Indies. The document, which had the (abbreviated) title 'Coloured Races of the British Colonies', was widely distributed and had a far greater impact on educational policy throughout the British colonies (not just the West Indies) than Kay-Shuttleworth ever imagined. His proposals were similar to those he was making for popular education in England, except that, predictably, he regarded the West Indians as being in greater need of 'civilizing' than the English or even the Irish working class.[69]

Insensitivity to national pride brought Kay-Shuttleworth and the Committee of Council into trouble much closer to home. They roused the anger of the Welsh by insulting their national pride and Dissenting tradition. The reports of the Council's inspectors had shown that the state of education in Wales, like that in many parts of England, was unsatisfactory, and on 10 March 1846 William Williams, Member of Parliament for Coventry, and a Welshman, asked in the House of Commons for a select committee to investigate Welsh education. Graham argued that there was no need for a select committee, and eventually it decided to appoint three special inspectors whose qualities were outlined in a memorandum prepared by Kay-Shuttleworth. They were to be 'familiar with the political and technical questions connected with elementary education' and, in order to reduce religious difficulties, should be lay members of the Church of England 'of liberal opinions and comprehensive views', that is, they were to be rather like him. The three selected were barristers – Ralph Robert Wheeler Lingen, J.C. Symons and R.V. Johnson. Only Symons could be said to have fulfilled Kay-Shuttleworth's criteria, as Lingen and Johnson were very superior young men whose acquaintance with elementary education was slight. However, all three shared Kay-Shuttleworth's inability to speak Welsh.[70]

The cumulative effect of their separately written reports, which came in about the middle of 1847, was devastating: they amounted to a frontal attack on Welsh culture, morality and identity. Symons was particularly offensive. He described the Welsh language, which he considered to have produced no literature to speak of, as 'a vast drawback to Wales'. Immorality prevailed 'rather from the want of a sense of moral obligation than from forgetfulness or violation of recognised duties'; the women were unchaste – night prayer-meetings contributed to this evil because of 'the intercourse which ensues in returning home'; and to complete the stereotypes, the Welsh were liars. 'I am confident that as regards mendacity', Symons decided with typical passionless arrogance, 'there is frequently no real consciousness that it is sinful, so habitual is disregard for truth whenever interest prompts falsehood'.[71]

The ensuing attack on the commissioners, the Committee of Council and Kay-Shuttleworth was led by Evan Jones, then editor of Cardiff's *Principality*. It was a spontaneous outburst of the anger of Welsh nationalists, Dissenters, and, as Baines was quick to realize, voluntarists against the English Church and state. Unable to speak Welsh, ignorant of Welsh culture, Establishment churchmen and representatives of the English state, the commissioners presented an easy target. So did Kay-Shuttleworth, and a *Principality* cartoon summed up the hostility – and the grounds for it. A man sitting in front of a table with a coal scuttle on his head, and his boots off so that his cloven hooves are revealed, speaks to three men wearing barristers' wigs:

> . . . you are to help their lordships (of the Com. of Council) to make out a case against voluntary religion, by collecting such evidence of its connection with immorality, disloyalty, and barbarism, as will disgust the public mind of England, thereby preparing it to sanction the (despotic) scheme in contemplation for driving the Welsh back to the true Church. The use of the Welsh LANGUAGE being known to be favourable to the propagation of earnest personal religion, both the LANGUAGE and the NATIONALITY of the Welsh, as well as their religion, are to be destroyed! Your *professional*, with your personal *art*, will enable you to select such witnesses, and cull such evidence, as may secure our object without exciting suspicion.

'Gathercoal Scuttleworth's final charge to the spies' is written beneath the picture, and 'the treachery of the Blue Books' became a contemporary Welsh commonplace.[72]

Smith endeavoured to absolve Kay-Shuttleworth of major responsibility, but J.D. Griffith has made that difficult. There is no evidence to support claims that Kay-Shuttleworth was involved in Williams's effort to get a select committee. Nor is there reason to believe that he chose the inspectors. Lansdowne was not likely to pass up the chance for patronage, and well-connected educational amateurs were not the sort of people Kay-Shuttleworth was likely to favour. The enquiry's terms of reference were drawn up and signed by Kay-Shuttleworth,

PICTURES FOR THE MILLION OF WALES.—No. 2.

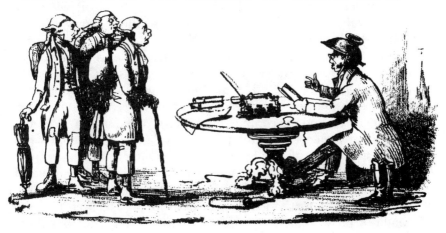

GATHERCOAL SCUTTLEWORTH'S FINAL CHARGE TO THE SPIES.

" The Whig Ministry are resolved to punish Wales for the danger-ous example it gives, to the rest of the Empire, by its universal dissent from our Church ! I now inform *you*, in confidence, that this is the real object of this espionage,—you are to help their lordships (of the Com. of Council) to make out a case against voluntary religion, by collecting such evidence of its connection with immorality, disloyalty, and barbarism, as will disgust the public mind of England, thereby preparing it to sanction the (despotic) scheme in contemplation for driving the Welsh back to the *true Church*. The use of the Welsh LANGUAGE being known to be favourable to the propagation of earnest personal religion, both the LANGUAGE′ and the NATIONALITY of the Welsh, as well as their religion, are to be destroyed ! Your *professional*, with your personal *art*, will enable you to select such witnesses, and cull such evidence, as may secure our object without exciting suspicion. My lords have authorized me to assure you that you shall be made *gentlemen (!)* on your return."

GATHERCOAL SCUTTLEWORTH YN GOLLWNG YMAITH YR YSPIWYR.

" Y mae y Whigiaid yn penderfynu cosbi y Cymry am eu *hymneill-duaeth*, yn yr hyn y rhoddant esiampl ddrygionus i'r deyrnas oll. Yr wyf fi am hyny yn dweyd wrthych chwi, *yn ddistaw*, mai gwir ddyben yr yspiaeth hon yw, *profi cysylltiad crefydd wirfoddol â barbariaeth, anfoesoldeb, a gwrthryfelgarwch, fel y ffieiddier y fath* grefydd gan y *Saison*, (anwybodus) *ac fel y delont yn foddlon* i gymeradwyo y moddion (gormesol) *a ddyfeisir, gan arglwyddi y* Cyngor, i yru y Cymry yn eu hol i'r "WIR EGLWYS." Ceir fod yr IAITH Gymreig yn wasanaethgar i daeniad crefydd bersonol ; rhaid i chwi gasglu y fath dystiolaethau i'w herbyn, ac yn erbyn holl arferion cenedlaethol y bobl, fel y gellir dystrywio y rhai hyn GYDA'R GREFYDD. Cewch gan yr OFFEIRIADAU (gwrthodedig gan y bobl) y fath dystiolaethau ag sydd eisiau. Er mwyn cuddio ein dybenion ewch at rai o'r Ymneillduwyr, ond yn benaf at rai a enwir i chwi fel rhai *lled hanerog*. Rhoddwyd i mi awdurdod i addaw y gwneir chwi yn *foneddigion (!)* ar eich dychweliad."

Cardiff: Printed by D. Evans, at the " Principality Office."

'Gathercoal Scuttleworth', as seen by *Principality*

but Smith sighted an earlier draft (since lost) on which alterations, later incorporated in the final version, were made in another hand. Smith claims that these alterations, and not Kay-Shuttleworth's original draft, contained the direction to look at the moral behaviour of the Welsh. Apart from the fact that, as Griffiths shows, the few examples which Smith gives of the changes to Kay-Shuttleworth's original version do not seem heavy handed, there is no reason to believe that the man who wrote *The Moral and Physical Condition of the Working Classes* would have blanched at investigating Welsh morality.[73]

There was, however, a difference between his reports on the Irish in Manchester and the commissioners' view of the Welsh. Whereas the commissioners relied heavily on the evidence of the clergy of the Established Church, Kay-Shuttleworth (or rather, Kay) had mixed with the Irish in their work places, homes and the cholera hospitals. Though his comments on their morality were condemnatory, they contained some realization of the social forces which created the condition the working class endured. Cut off by language from direct encounters and lacking Kay's passionate involvement, the commissioners went their superior way insulting a nation they had not attempted to understand. For all his faults, and his failure to realize the significance of language, Kay-Shuttleworth had been more sensitive than they were. But, whatever his responsibility, the Welsh commission involved him in yet another controversy which spawned tempestuous protests. As he worked at the Council Office or did the rounds of his estate, especially if he visited his collieries, Kay-Shuttleworth was weighed down with clamour and conflict. For all the achievements of 1846 and 1847, the burden grew heavier.

Unfortunately, external conflicts were accompanied by battles inside the Council Office and his family. In January 1848, Russell offered to place Kay-Shuttleworth's name before the Queen 'as one of the Civil Companions of the Order of the Bath'. 'I trust you will believe', Kay-Shuttleworth replied to Russell, 'that it is with a sense of the value of any sign of your approbation of my conduct as a public servant that I respectfully beg leave to decline the honor you propose to me'. When Lansdowne revealed that Prince Albert had suggested the honour, an embarrassed but unrepentant Kay-Shuttleworth wrote to the Prince's private secretary, G.E. Anson, pointing out that the honour was unexpected but that he had long ago decided that, if he ever received a distinction, he would accept nothing below the rank of a Privy Councillor – 'seeing for what purely political purposes all inferior honors have been employed'. To this less than ingratiating comment he added his thanks to the Prince: apart from 'the approbation of my own conscience' one of his highest ambitions was to deserve the favour of His Royal Highness and Her Majesty. From Windsor Castle, Anson replied that the Prince thought that, once Kay-Shuttleworth saw the list of those honoured, he would not think that an inferior order had been employed for political purposes. However, Anson revealed that he had the same ambition as Kay-Shuttleworth, but feared to appear ungracious by rejecting an award which the Queen had instituted to mark merit in her civil service. The reverberations were still being felt in May when Kay-Shuttleworth again found it necessary to stress that he had not known of Prince Albert's involvement when he declined the offer.[74]

He had given a more elaborate statement of his reasons to Charles Trevelyan, his equivalent at the Treasury, the day after he rejected Russell's offer. He claimed that he was not grieved to have received neither promotion nor honour from the government. 'I have a sufficient satisfaction in holding a position of considerable public influence and utility, and in the fact that whatever that position is, it has become in my hands.' When he took up this appointment, he had only a small fortune and 'my family had not held a position distinguished either by wealth, or public services'. Now he was married to the heiress of an ancient family which had a distinguished record of public service and he had an estate of 'upwards of ten thousand pounds'. He had given umbrage to his wife's family by following his sense of duty and 'resolving to remain in a subordinate executive office, and especially by recently refusing to enter Parliament'. He did not, therefore, consider himself at liberty 'to neglect their opinion so far as to accept an honor, which would in their eyes render my demerits only more conspicuous'.[75] There is no need to accept at face value his claim that he had chosen to remain in his inferior executive office, and the evidence suggests that rather than refusing to enter Parliament he had been denied the opportunity. But in view of Janet's reservations about his work, and the attitude of the Shuttleworths and the Norths, the rest of his explanation rings true. He had risen in the world but he was still trapped by his class origins.

The problem of earning respect from his family reinforced the pressing administrative reasons for a reorganization of the Council Office. In 1845 when writing *The Present Condition* for Buccleuch, he argued for 'the separation of the edn. dept. from the rest of the

Council Office, and the organization of a separate staff, upon the precedents which other departments of the service present'. In using the term 'education department' Kay-Shuttleworth was adopting a usage which had grown common (Greville himself used it), though strictly speaking there was no education department in 1845.[76] Yet as the importance of his work grew, as its tasks became more specialized, as the number of his staff increased, and as school managers, clergy, inspectors and teachers became accustomed to working with (or objecting to) his decisions, his office began to take on a separate identity, to be thought of as a department in its own right. For Kay-Shuttleworth and his staff, the office had attained a psychological, though not an official, independence. Their work was quite different from the ordinary routine of the Privy Council Office, and to express that difference, and to do the work properly, they needed a distinct organization. From 1847 onwards the struggle for independence became one of Kay-Shuttleworth's main preoccupations. Success would at one stroke guarantee a crucial administrative advance and, assuming that he was in charge of the new department, improve his status with Janet's family.

His financial arrangements were one expression of his struggle for independence. Official attention to them was surprisingly slow to develop. During the 1846 debate on supply William Ewart and Joseph Hume had pressed for a clearer picture of the Education Department's financial position, and Russell promised to meet the request. From 1839 until then, apart from tight-fisted treatment of requests for increases in the salaries of Kay-Shuttleworth's staff, the Treasury had been accommodating, even casual. In 1847, for the first time, Kay-Shuttleworth was required to itemize his expenditure in the annual estimate. His Department's money came from the annual parliamentary grant which had risen from £30,000 in 1839 to £40,000 in 1842, £75,000 in 1845 and £100,000 in 1846 and 1847. When questioned as to how he arrived at estimates of expenditure Kay-Shuttleworth was bravely honest: he assessed the likely contributions from the two societies, 'the circumstances of the times' and the probable resources of the societies. For new ventures, where there could be no guide from past contributions, Kay-Shuttleworth took into account the 'wants of society, as their expression is limited by the power to contribute the sums required as conditions of assistance', that is, as Johnson less politely but more lucidly suggests, he guessed. These estimates were approved by the Commons without close analysis and without the information which would have made analysis possible. The formidable Charles Trevelyan was aware of some of the difficulties and complained in 1842 of Kay-Shuttleworth's laconic replies to Treasury requests. His ideas of 'official regularity' were, he told Kay-Shuttleworth, 'set on edge by the summary and informal nature of your answers to our *References* – which answers seem to be intended rather as the basis of a letter to be prepared a clerk [*sic*] than to form the answer itself to our Reference'. But until 1847, such complaints were not translated into decisive action.[77]

By 1847 Kay-Shuttleworth had built up a surplus of £200,000, double the annual grant he received that year, and therefore a significant amount, even after allowing for large funds which were earmarked for applications which had been approved but not yet paid. Mason has put the matter simply: 'throughout Kay Shuttleworth's tenure of office the Education Department was awash with money'. But the halcyon days had ended. Sir Charles Wood was a member of the Committee of Council and, though he did not use that position to place direct pressure on Kay-Shuttleworth, he and Trevelyan began to probe the Education Department's financial ways. In February 1848 two select committees were established, one to examine miscellaneous expenditure, including that of the Education Department. The annual budget of £3,782,000 for this expenditure suggests that one explanation for Kay-Shuttleworth's success was that he spent a trifling amount of money. But the select committee was not to be trifled with and when Kay-Shuttleworth was examined on 16 June 1848 he was asked how his department had spent £125,788 the previous year when its vote was £100,000. Kay-Shuttleworth explained that there was no deficit – he had dipped into his surplus, which would have been unknown to Parliament when he was given his vote. The committee decided that the practice, which had been adopted by other departments, merited 'the close attention of the Treasury'. To make matters worse, Kay-Shuttleworth explained that, while he accepted that he should keep within the parliamentary grant, he did not feel bound to spend money in the precise way he had listed on the estimates.[78]

Kay-Shuttleworth had an uncomfortable time explaining his surplus, the manner in which he arrived at his estimate and the flexibility with which he interpreted it. He probably reinforced the opinions of John Parker, a Treasury official and a member of the select committee, who in April the previous year had told Wood that Kay-Shuttleworth was an electoral liability: by 'all the jargon and pedantry of his absurd minutes', he was turning the quiet lake of Sheffield into a stormy sea. Parker concluded that 'if we do not get rid of this Gentleman before the 3rd time of asking he will do the same thing for us'. Some defeated candidates sympathized with Parker's wish, and he struck another chord with his fellow bureaucrats when he complained that 'philosophers and wise men were becoming not merely guides but beacons'. What was the use of Senior, or George Lewis or Chadwick, he asked contemptuously, but 'to avoid whatever they recommend and more especially whatever they *do*'.[79]

The increased interest in Kay-Shuttleworth's entrepreneurial ways could not have come at a worse time. Greville described the Education Department, which he had watched take over more and more of his office space, as 'a very gigantic affair'. From the humble beginnings of 1839 its staff had grown to 35 by 1848: Kay-Shuttleworth and Chester, 15 inspectors, excluding Poor Law inspectors, 14 clerks, and the newly created positions of chief examiner, second examiner and statist. Technically the staff were responsible to Greville, as was Kay-Shuttleworth himself, but for all practical purposes it was Kay-Shuttleworth who controlled them. Yet, while Kay-Shuttleworth struggled, without a salary rise, to manage this rapidly expanding empire, Greville ran the whole Privy Council Office, excluding the Education Department, with four clerks – and an annual salary of £2,000.[80]

And, despite this increase, the Department was undermanned. Throughout the 1840s Kay-Shuttleworth battled with the Privy Council to enlarge his staff and to obtain better salaries, and although appointments eventually came, they were usually belated and did not relieve the demoralizing stress on his overworked and poorly paid staff. Clerks arrived at the Office, Greville reported with the casualness of a gentleman, about eleven in the morning, except for the Education Department's clerks who came at ten; the ordinary clerks left about four or five, but the Department's clerks often worked much later. The growing number of inspectors and grant applications, and the minutes of 1846, dramatically increased the amount and complexity of the work, especially as the final decisions, though based on inspectors' reports, were made by the Department. The intricate procedures constructed for the administration of the pupil-teacher system reflected Kay-Shuttleworth's obsessive personality, but his Department was finding its way through a political and religious minefield. Moreover, by requiring applicants to reflect on how their schools were conducted, the administrative process was educative, in the sense that it made school promoters more aware of the Department's policies.[81]

In January 1845, egged on by Kay-Shuttleworth, the Committee wrote to the Privy Council stressing the effect the strain was having on the health of its staff who had not even been accorded 'that recreation which is usually afforded to Clerks in Public Offices at certain periods of the year'. Kay-Shuttleworth returned to the point later in the year in *The Present Condition*, insisting that 'The existence of an official staff equal to the duties of the office is a question in which the existence of the office itself is involved.' He gained an increase in staff but by the end of the year another crisis was looming. As Johnson has pointed out, the difficulties he faced were repeated in other aspects of the Privy Council's work where new functions brought new and growing responsibilities and crippling work loads for the staff. The state was developing its newly acquired lands with insufficient resources and without a bureaucratic history on which to draw for lessons.[82]

Believing that he was making history, Kay-Shuttleworth grew increasingly frustrated by the stress, the ambiguity of the Department's position within the Council Office, and by the connected problem of his own status. In September 1846, his nervous exhaustion was so obvious that Lansdowne asked him to write a confidential letter 'explanatory of the circumstances causing this prostration'. Instead Kay-Shuttleworth waited until 3 May 1847 and wrote a non-confidential letter in which he pointed out the political sensitivity of his work, reminded Lansdowne that the Education Department 'absorbed the greater part of the staff of the Privy Council Office', and claimed that he had been put in a position resembling that of an under secretary of state. Yet, he continued, 'every gentleman employed in the Education Department is officially subordinate *not* to the Assistant Secretary of the Education Committee, but to the Clerk of the Council'. He was most apprehensive about attempts to execute the new minutes when 'official relations [were] so ill defined' and when the position of the officer directing them had 'neither dignity nor authority'. He could not hold this office with self-respect if 'I were not bound to your lordship and Lord John Russell by loyal and grateful feelings'; nevertheless, he continued, unless an alteration was made he would resign 'with the first change of administration'. Then, snatching at fragments, he asked for permission to employ a private clerk.[83]

Lansdowne sent the letter to Russell, attributing Kay-Shuttleworth's ill health 'to the state of the office'. With typical terse languidity he continued: 'he is intelligent, zealous, indefatigable, but write short, *he cannot*. Nevertheless, Lansdowne wanted action, partly for self-interested reasons:

> I will bend myself to anything you desire if the wheels can be made to turn – either add to the strength and reorganize the office according to the present demand upon it, upon my own responsibility, if you authorize it, or take and make the best of any new arrangement you and Wood will determine upon after seeing Shuttleworth, but I cannot sit down quietly and allow applications and questions to remain unanswered, till our new minutes come to disgrace, in which I shall be myself involved, from want of the means of working them.

Apart from giving Kay-Shuttleworth the private clerk, Russell did not know what to do, as Kay-Shuttleworth seemed to him to be 'in nearly the same position as Trevelyan at the Treasury – the man makes the office'. Moreover, Russell was being pressed by Kay-Shuttleworth for massive increases in the vote for education, and on 7 May 1847, only four days after the letter to Lansdowne, told Kay-Shuttleworth that 'in the present state of the Education question' he did not want the Committee to pledge itself to 'any expenditure which in the course of five years may require a greater annual vote than £150,000'. That was a substantial rise, but nowhere near the £250,000 or even £1,000,000 which Kay-Shuttleworth seems to have been pressing on Russell.[84]

Trapped by his dedication and the flexibility which was possible in a loosely structured civil service, Kay-Shuttleworth had made himself unique and indispensable – and brought himself great problems. He had made the office; yet to please the Shuttleworths the opposite would have been better: he needed the office to make him. Lansdowne and Russell, who understood and valued his achievement, even if they were sometimes troubled by him, were at a loss as to how to assist. Meanwhile the Treasury saw him and his department as the source of financial anomalies. Indispensable civil servants who are consumed by a cause, of ambiguous social standing and at the centre of political controversy have a way of becoming dispensable, as Edwin Chadwick found.

Russell must have passed Kay-Shuttleworth's requests for a dramatically increased vote to Charles Wood for, on 24 May, he told Russell that Kay-Shuttleworth's scheme 'will not do at all'. It would disturb the Privy Council without improving the Education Department. 'Far the best course', he decided, would be to give Kay-Shuttleworth extra assistance payable out of his vote of £100,000, think through the future of the establishment before the next estimate, 'and then vote it regularly as we ought to do'. It was in early April that Parker had suggested to Wood that it would be desirable to get rid of Kay-Shuttleworth, and his request a month later for a vote as high as £1,000,000 would have done nothing to cause him to change his mind.[85]

On 26 May 1847, three days after Wood's letter to Russell, Kay-Shuttleworth, writing from 38 Gloucester Square, where he and Janet had bought a house, made another attempt. Ironically he informed Lansdowne that the embarrassment of writing on a matter in which he was personally interested might have made his first letter 'imperfect from brevity and reserve'. Lansdowne had passed on Russell's remark about the man making the office and said that a means of removing the ambiguities of the Assistant Secretary's position 'did not present itself' either to his or Russell's mind. Kay-Shuttleworth set about driving home the need for action and went back to 1839 and Lansdowne's and Russell's determination to improve popular education and 'to vindicate the right of the government to interfere'. Amidst the uncertainties of that period they had three clear policies: education should have a religious basis, should not encroach on civil and religious liberty, and should be subject to civil authority only. These principles had been attacked and their defence 'has been in an unusual degree entrusted to the administrative action of the Education Department'. The Concordat showed how 'vigilant and careful administration' could prevent the perpetuation of 'the ignorantism of the schools, and an ecclesiastical supremacy over education'. Similarly the management clauses had defeated the clergy's instinct to exclude the laity from the management of parochial schools.

He attributed these results 'chiefly to administrative efforts, guiding the correspondence and personal communications of the Council Office, and giving an impulse, and a tone to the proceedings of the Inspectors of Schools'. In 1839 the Church had seen education as an ecclesiastical function, claimed control of inspectors and denounced aid to Dissenters and Roman Catholics; now its leaders accepted an inspection of civil origin, the management of the parochial school by a majority of laymen, the granting of a diploma to a schoolmaster directly from government, and the indirect prescription of the course of instruction in elementary and Normal schools through the regulations for pupil-teachers and Queen's scholars. Even the parochial schoolmaster was coming to regard the government rather than the Church as the source of his emolument, distinction and protection. It had been a mistake, Kay-Shuttleworth concluded, not to regard the Office from the beginning as 'a *peculiar Department* requiring a *peculiar fitness*'. He feared to 'utter one word which might savour of egotism' but he felt his responsibilities painfully and wanted appointments to his department which secured '*the most constant loyal and zealous support*' for the Council's principles. Above all, he believed that the internal administration of the Council Office should 'as early as possible be rendered in all respects independent of my person which the accident of ill health might any day withdraw'.[86]

A day after this dignified and desperate letter he wrote again to the Home Office, complaining that 'the inadequacy of the Staff of this Office' had prevented the execution of the resolutions of the Committee of Council, but nothing gained him the restructuring he desired. In July Wood's recommendation was acted upon and Kay-Shuttleworth was given extra staff. Treasury approved the provisional appointment of two examiners, a statistician and five clerks, but it had done so grudgingly and perhaps only in response to pressure from Lansdowne. And the ambiguities of Kay-Shuttleworth's position remained.[87]

Utterly dejected and grasping at straws, Kay-Shuttleworth turned again towards a political career. He contemplated a Scottish seat, and wrote to his sympathizer, the Duke of Argyll, whose reply, though penned with the best of intentions, was devastating. He wished he could help Kay-Shuttleworth because that would be to render a public service, but in Scotland local connections or a public name were needed to launch a parliamentary career. 'You', Argyll continued, 'have hitherto been working, as it were, *underground*, and the value of your services is more real than celebrated.' How deeply Kay-Shuttleworth felt that! And how ironic was the Duke's suggestion that he should use his government connections to find an English seat.[88]

While Kay-Shuttleworth struggled with Argyll's answer, a group of well-connected men arrived in the Education Department from Balliol College, Oxford, protégés of Benjamin Jowett. 'This is Balliol, I am Jowett', the verse went:

> All there is to know I know it;
> What I don't know isn't knowledge;
> I am Master of this College.

Jowett was not Master in the late 1840s but he had embarked on his campaign to place his best and brightest young men in positions of authority, where he could watch them grow in wealth and power while his prestige and power grew with them. Most of the positions grudgingly granted by the Treasury were filled by Jowett products: intelligent, upper-middle-class but not necessarily wealthy men, who shared his vicious snobbery and his conviction that the finely honed, but ultimately blinkered intellects which he had brilliantly cultivated really did possess the knowledge that was of most worth.[89]

First was Ralph Lingen, a Fellow of Balliol and an intimate friend of Jowett's, who in October 1846 had been attached to the Committee of Council for the Welsh Commission. Seven months later, to act as Lansdowne's private secretary, came Matthew Arnold, not the conscientious inspector that he was to become but affecting dandyism. Lingen had been his tutor at Balliol. A few months later, in July 1847, having finished his report for the Welsh Commission, Lingen was appointed as First Examiner. He had intended going to the Bar but, to Jowett's delight, was 'ensconced at the Privy Council Office' instead. In February 1848, after the Balliol circle had ensured that his ability and personal charm had time to work on Kay-Shuttleworth and the Whig ministers, Frederick Temple was appointed as Principal of Kneller Hall, but he worked with the Education Department while arrangements there were being finalized. Later, with Arnold's support, he was to become Headmaster of Rugby (as Arnold's father had been), and Archbishop of Canterbury. In November Jowett and Lingen secured the second examinership for Francis Sandford, Jowett making the revealing remark to Lingen that it would be difficult to find a better man at Balliol for the position. Finally, in this initial burst, Francis Palgrave, later the anthologist, came to be Vice Principal at Kneller Hall.[90] The religious views of the Oxford movement had caused Kay-Shuttleworth trouble enough; now another Oxford group, more worldly and liberal, was to have a damaging effect on him.

Johnson suggests that the link between the Education Department and Balliol College might have been made while Kay-Shuttleworth was seeking lay members of the examining board for teachers' certificates, or perhaps through Edward Stanley, the liberal Bishop of Norwich. However, there is no need to assume that Kay-Shuttleworth had much part in bringing the Balliol men to the Department. The appointments of Arnold and Lingen can be explained by patronage, and once they secured positions they worked with Jowett to appoint like spirits. Kay-Shuttleworth was sometimes consulted and a number of inspectors came from the statistical and educational circles in which he moved. But the examinerships were of greater prestige and Lansdowne, who was not noted for his reticence in making such appointments, may have acted without reference to Kay-Shuttleworth.[91]

However they came, the Balliol group were a major challenge to Kay-Shuttleworth. Greville adapted well enough to the new ways but he represented the senior civil servant of the past. He was reasonably well born, began his career at the Council Office at the age of ten with the job of Clerk Extraordinary, was aristocratic in lifestyle, a frequenter of country houses, well linked with the patrician politicians of the Whig and Tory parties, and preferred the days when 'ancient usage and practice' ruled. He represented a past that was fading, and Kay-Shuttleworth represented the fading present: he was the expert who brought knowledge and experience crucial to the plans of his political masters, a zealot whose allegiance was more to a cause than to a particular government. Unlike Greville, his work consumed him. The Balliol group represented the future, professional civil servants, cool, altogether more socially confident than Kay-Shuttleworth, more dedicated than they have been given credit for, and habitués of literary and artistic worlds which were closed to Kay-Shuttleworth. They were building the bridge between the universities and the higher ranks of the civil service which became an enduring feature of British public life.[92]

Their first impact was to increase tensions in the Department. When Lingen was appointed Examiner he became Chester's senior, thus, Jowett observed with polished malice, 'making the rest of his official life a bore'.[93] The relationship of the Balliol men, especially Lingen, to Kay-Shuttleworth was soured by their sense of superiority. As an administrator he won their admiration and his political achievements dwarfed anything they had achieved at that stage of their lives. In many ways he was better educated than they, as his Scottish degree was probably more rigorous and broader than anything Balliol offered. But Balliol's was the education of the powerful. It provided polish and the certainty that its possession marked out the educated man. Kay-Shuttleworth was making sure that Joseph and Ebenezer had the advantage of a similar education, but he could not undo his past.

The Balliol attitude to Kay-Shuttleworth – a mixture of condescension, contempt and a cool recognition that he might be useful – comes out in a letter from Jowett to Lingen in 1847. Jowett was contemplating the use of Parliament to secure university reform and, using the contemptuous term which Lingen employed, told Lingen of a visit by 'your master, "master Doctor Caius"', a reference to a sixteenth-century physician whose name could be rendered as 'Kay' and who had written an important study of epidemics. 'Shuttleworth's name', Jowett continued, 'is I think an omen of success in the scheme, at the same time he is as unfit as the two barbarians Hengist and Horsa to reform the University'. Much would depend on how he was advised by others, but though Jowett and his colleagues valued his usefulness, they were anxious 'not simply to be made a cat's paw of by Kay-Shuttleworth in a private speculation of his own'. Through these discussions, Lingen's contempt remained. Jowett reminded him that in mid-1848, 'you lay on the grass in our Garden attacking Shuttleworth in very vigorous English – six months afterwards you seemed to change your tone entirely – in the last letter [*c.*July 1849] you seemed to revert to your former view'. In his office as in his family, Kay-Shuttleworth was trapped by his social origins.[94]

About the time that Lingen was attacking him in Jowett's garden, Kay-Shuttleworth's health was close to collapse, and for parts of August and September 1848 he went on holidays in an effort to restore his strength. Temple pleaded with him to take '*absolute* rest for a few months', arguing that while his health was weak the government could always agree that 'the working head of the Education Department ought not to be in the anomalous position of an Assistant Secretary', and then put off action on the grounds that the man 'whose genius has hitherto originated all' was too ill to take the responsibility of a new structure. He suggested that Kay-Shuttleworth should jump at any provisional arrangement which left him as head of the Office while the negotiations continued, and tried to persuade him that, even if things went slightly wrong in his absence, nothing too disastrous was likely to happen. He also warned him not to risk losing Lingen who was dissatisfied with the conditions of his employment. By November, ill and despairing, Kay-Shuttleworth wrote to Lansdowne pointing out that one clerk had 'chronic congestion of the brain' (a stroke), and another a 'very sudden attack of congestion of the brain threatening paralysis'. Moreover, Lingen had left the office 'in a state of great nervous exhaustion'. On 9 December, while answering some questions from Peel, Kay-Shuttleworth collapsed in the Privy Council Office, fell to the floor and remained unconscious for about twenty minutes. He had had an epileptic fit.[95]

The 'falling sickness' had a terrifying history, even to the medically trained. Over the centuries its victims' frightening convulsions, their lapses of awareness, mood changes, hallucinations, and bizarre behaviour had associated epilepsy with madness or possession by the devil and made it shocking, shameful and utterly humiliating. It haunted those it struck, seemingly incurable, stirring the ghosts of ancestors from whom it had been inherited and placing the future generations at risk. The bedlam and the asylum were its natural habitats. For someone of Kay-Shuttleworth's temperament, it was an almost intolerable burden. Yet he took up that burden with a desperate but unflinching bravery and, while never publicly admitting to epilepsy (neuralgia, from which he suffered greatly, was often used as an explanation of his behaviour), he tried to live his life as if he had never been struck by the illness. The ghosts that haunted his mind never escaped in public.

There is insufficient information to determine the type of epilepsy he had. He was 44 when he collapsed in the Privy Council Office, rather late in life to have the first epileptic fit. However, eight years later, in circumstances which gave him every incentive to deny his illness, he wrote to an Eastbourne doctor saying that, for the first time in his life, he had suffered 'a sudden attack of convulsions with insensitivity' eight years earlier in the offices of the Privy Council. He identified the attacks as epileptic, said that there had been seven recurrences, and linked them with 'anything which disturbs seriously the emotions'. His earlier collapses at Edinburgh and Manchester and his illnesses while working at Whitehall may now appear in a different light, though the evidence is too thin to enable more than conjecture. What is clear is that on 9 December 1848 he fell into epileptic convulsions on the floor of the Privy Council Office.[96]

The next day he explained to Peel through an amanuensis that he had been prevented from completing the letter by a very sudden illness, and that he was confined to bed and forbidden exertion. Those who knew him showed that they understood how he would react. 'Pray do not let your zeal for the public hurry [you] into business before you are quite recovered', Russell wrote, while Trevelyan decided that his illness made the need for a thoroughly efficient second-in-charge even more obvious. Thomas Frankland Lewis came sorrowfully to another conclusion: he had better give up his office and try to recover his health for 'he never looked a strong man, and was always of a zealous anxious temperament'. Kay-Shuttleworth's efforts to come to grips with his illness and to protect the work he had done at the Committee of Council assumed tragic dimensions throughout the December of 1848 and the whole of 1849. On 20 December, less than two weeks after his collapse, he told Russell that he knew that he was aware of his part 'in the daily labours of the office in the preparation of parliamentary schemes, in the constant vigilance required for the direction of public administration, and in the violent party struggles which have occurred'. He had not set his own interests above those of the public, but after the serious warning he had received he was not at liberty to put his life, 'which is of some importance to my family', in unnecessary peril. Emphasizing that the duties of the assistant secretary 'would break down the stoutest constitution', he pressed for the appointment of a head of the department who would be an official member of the Committee of Council and a junior secretary of state. He did not claim the position, but said that he 'would not shrink from the labour and responsibility of such an office'. He also made an offer which must have wrenched his heart: 'I shall be quite as ready to retire in order to facilitate such arrangements as may be considered necessary for the public interests.'[97]

Russell consulted with Lansdowne who, on 29 December, gave an unerring estimate of 'poor Shuttleworth'. He would not be able to undertake the same amount of work as he had previously given himself, yet

> the loss of his services would be great to the publick, and from what I know of him, his relinquishment of all share in the business of the education department would be as fatal to him as his continuing charged with all the weight he has hitherto borne.

He suggested something close to what Kay-Shuttleworth wanted – a new organization in the office 'which they have long been led to expect' and which could not long be deferred, with Kay-Shuttleworth made a Clerk of the Privy Council and his 'superior duties . . . more exactly limited and defined'. Charles Greville, he assured Russell, had no objection to this. An alternative was to adopt a suggestion from Russell that he be offered a Privy Councillorship without salary. 'Shuttleworth', Lansdowne concluded, 'is not the only person (there have been two more examiners, both strong men) who have been overpowered by the mass of increasing details, which the progress and very success of the system has produced.'[98]

Only a few days after this letter, Kay-Shuttleworth, still seriously ill, returned to work and answered Peel's letter so satisfactorily that Peel expressed his pleasure at this 'proof of your amended health'. Kay-Shuttleworth set himself to tackle the most difficult issues facing the Education Department, including the management clauses, declaring that he would 'devote what strength I have left to the settlement of this question'. Friends, family and doctors were aghast, and despite his obsessive determination to return (which flared as soon as there was the slightest improvement in his health), Kay-Shuttleworth recognized that a complete break was necessary. On 23 February, Lansdowne informed Russell that 'repose, if he can but allow it to himself, is indispensable to him', but Kay-Shuttleworth could not allow it to himself until he had contacted Temple and Lingen about the appointment of a temporary assistant secretary. Temple refused on the grounds that he was a clergyman, and Lingen accepted, while reserving the right to change his mind if the position became permanent. Kay-Shuttleworth offered to resign if a suitable replacement could be found but could not bring himself to recommend anyone when Russell asked him for a name. Many years later Tufnell complained to Chadwick that Kay-Shuttleworth had supported Lingen rather than him when it came to choosing his successor. In fact Kay-Shuttleworth supported no one. His moods, his manoeuvres, and his decisions were constantly changing as he watched the department he had constructed at the cost of his health begin to slip from his grasp.[99]

As Kay-Shuttleworth was talking to Lingen and Temple, Lansdowne set about choosing a successor, informing Russell that he agreed with his view that the Office ought not to remain too long under 'a temporary arrangement'. Plainly assuming that Kay-Shuttleworth would not return, he said that 'Temple, if he would take it, would be preferable from all that I have seen of him, to any man that could be found as a permanent successor'. He thought Lingen clever and industrious, but in poor health and 'less conciliatory' in his personal communications. Lansdowne had to accept the less favoured person. In March 1849 Lansdowne sent Kay-Shuttleworth a draft minute explaining the leave of absence he had been granted. Kay-Shuttleworth returned it rewritten to emphasize that he wanted relief from 'the intolerable pressure of executive details' and that during his absence he wished 'to vacate the responsibilities and emoluments of the office of Assistant Secretary'. Lansdowne informed him that a reorganization of the Office was being considered, then Russell, revealing his hand for the first time, told Kay-Shuttleworth that the rank of Privy Councillor would be conferred upon him if he resigned.[100]

'I conceive', Kay-Shuttleworth replied, with a dignity which required a heroic effort from him,

> that your lordship is good enough to offer me these alternatives, viz.: 1. That, after a period of rest (during which I shall receive no salary), I shall be at liberty to resume the duties and position of Assistant Secretary, as hitherto defined; or 2. That, as a mark of approbation of my services, I may receive the rank of Privy Councillor upon my retirement.
>
> If I rightly understand the alternatives before me I cannot hesitate at once to prefer the distinction which you are so kind as to offer me, and to retire from my present office.[101]

Russell and Lansdowne had intimated that a reorganization was being considered, offered Kay-Shuttleworth the unreorganized *status quo*, which they knew he could not accept, and then provided an encouragement for him to refuse their offer. They had decided that Kay-Shuttleworth had to go.

Kay-Shuttleworth's proffered resignation was not officially accepted, perhaps because Lansdowne and Russell may have wanted to keep him as an alternative if Lingen proved inadequate or too ill. The Kay-Shuttleworths were going to the Pyrenees, North noted: 'he has entirely left the office – and is in high dudgeon with Ld Lansdowne, his late master, about something'. Not knowing the details, North guessed that there was a dispute over salary. Though, in line with Lansdowne's and Russell's offer, a humiliated Kay-Shuttleworth had, on 4 April 1849, relinquished his salary 'during the period that I may find it necessary to recruit my health abroad', his rejection struck at deeper strands of his personality than money could reach. He would have been even more devastated had he known that three weeks after he had relinquished his salary, Trevelyan informed the Committee of Council, as if the thought were new, that it had occurred to Their Lordships of the Treasury that as soon as it was convenient, though without increasing expenses, the Privy Council might consider separating that part of its Office which handled education from its other activities and placing it under 'the immediate superintendence of the Assistant Secretary'.[102]

The Kay-Shuttleworths left England at the beginning of May 1849 and returned at the end of August. Contacts with English colleagues were not completely cut – Kay-Shuttleworth discussed French politics with Nassau Senior in Paris in mid-May. However, the purpose of the trip was not accomplished; the rest did not restore Kay-Shuttleworth's health. Nevertheless, on his return he visited the Education Department and made clear his intention of resuming work. 'Shuttleworth is come back to England', noted Greville on 21 September, 'and is gone to Gawthorpe, meaning to resume his place here, greatly to the disgust of Chester and Co, and I believe of Lingen too, the latter however is absent, and I am afraid very ill.' He was very ill indeed. 'Poor Lingen I am sorry to say', Lansdowne had reported to Russell only five days earlier, 'is as ill as Shuttleworth tho' in a different way – the labour of the situation, thanks to the insatiable appetite of the clergy for funding or making difficulties is overwhelming.' For Kay-Shuttleworth, Lansdowne had a different story. Lingen and Temple were going well, he said, and were in tolerably smooth water on religious questions – despite the efforts of Denison and Manning. During his time on the continent Kay-Shuttleworth had kept in touch with educational developments in London, on one occasion sending a letter to his mother to pass on to Lingen – no one was to know of it, he said. But even if he had not been in touch he would soon have realized that Lansdowne's account was misleading.[103]

Shaw-Lefevre asked him on 8 December whether it was wise 'to form a fresh connection with the Committee of Privy Council'. Could he stay in it with a new government? Would he be able to delegate more responsibility? 'I doubt it much.' On 11 December Lansdowne with Russell's agreement indicated a desire to make permanent arrangements at the Education Department. Kay-Shuttleworth was not to be part of them. Her Majesty would be advised 'to express her sense of your great and zealous services by conferring upon you and your family the dignity of a baronetcy'. Arrangements would be made as soon as Lansdowne received Kay-Shuttleworth's answer. It came with an edge of bitterness. He expected soon to be fully recovered, had not withdrawn his resignation, and could have supervised his department if given authority; but in the position in which he had been placed, he could do so only by 'setting an example of self-devotion' which had destroyed his strength. He had opposed 'the most formidable social power in the country' and could not hope to conciliate either 'the extreme party which would reconcile the Church with Rome, or the party which would deprive the Church of her revenues, and separate her from the state'. With these feelings, and 'with great respect for your lordship, and many acknowledgements of the uniform courtesy and consideration which has marked your intercourse with me', Kay-Shuttleworth accepted the offer. There were still fears that he would refuse and, on 20 December, Shaw-Lefevre wrote with assurances 'of the propriety of your acceptance of an honourable distinction'. They were occasionally ill-bestowed, he admitted, but that was not the case in this instance. Moreover, it was 'very inexpedient to depreciate Titles of Honour' for they were marks of favour from the sovereign, and were incentives to exertion without introducing the 'sordid motive' of money rewards.[104]

Russell expressed his delight and his satisfaction and on 22 December the Queen granted 'the dignity of a Baronet of the United Kingdom and Great Britain unto James Phillips Kay-Shuttleworth, of Gawthorpe Hall, in the county palatine of Lancaster, Esq. and to the heirs male of his body lawfully begotten'. On Christmas Day Frederick North recorded that Janet had written from Gawthorpe to say that 'they are going to make Kay a Baronet, on retiring from his Place as Secretary to the Committee of Council on Education'. He decided that 'they could not well do less; for he has made the office; was, indeed, for some years, the Minister of Education. Cheaper reward too than a Pension, which I suppose, he was considered to have earned, but did not, in fact, want!' Janet had previously written that Lord Lansdowne had been 'ungrateful' and North, understandably but wrongly, decided that there must have been a time when the baronetcy was sought and refused.[105]

The new Sir James Kay-Shuttleworth could not bring himself to tell his mother of his resignation until 22 December. If he had retired without some mark of approval there might have been 'misunderstanding' or 'dishonour', he explained. The honour would not puff him up; in fact he felt humbled by 'my continued ill health and consequent retirement from a public career, and now by the necessity of this Badge of Honour, as a mark of the appreciation of my services'. But there was no mistaking the bitterness which seethed below his protestations of 'the uniform courtesy and consideration' with which Lansdowne had treated him: 'There is however a chance that justice will be done to our motives, if not now, possibly bye and bye if it please God to restore my health, and to justify my resolution to turn all his good gifts to good account.' On 8 January 1850 the final move was made. Lingen was appointed permanently as Assistant Secretary. The Education Department had not been reconstructed but Jowett had no doubt that Lingen's decision to accept the appointment was wise. He had been given the opportunity of 'doing good almost equal to a Prime Minister'; and it was 'most soothing and flattering after all your cares and anxieties'.[106]

Why Kay-Shuttleworth's cares and anxieties were so little soothed is not clear. He and the Whigs offered his health as the public and politically plausible explanation for his resignation. Yet it is not sufficient to explain the way in which he was treated. His resignation had been obtained before he left on the continental holiday which was supposed to restore him to full strength. It was obtained by making proposals which, both Russell and Lansdowne knew, were unacceptable and which ignored the stress at the Education Department and the ambiguities of Kay-Shuttleworth's position, both problems whose effect on his health had been acknowledged by Lansdowne. There were other reasons for ending Kay-Shuttleworth's time at the Committee of Council.

The internal differences in the Office and the public conflicts with Denison, Baines and the Welsh undoubtedly contributed to Kay-Shuttleworth's personal collapse, but they did not account for his resignation. The internal differences were not sufficiently well known or serious enough to warrant his going, and in the public controversies Kay-Shuttleworth was fighting to implement policies which Lansdowne and Russell supported. In any case, as they and the National Society knew only too well, trying to negotiate calmly with a person such as Denison was impossible. Furthermore, both at the time and afterwards, Lansdowne and Russell expressed admiration for Kay-Shuttleworth's endeavours. Perhaps they had decided that, while his motives were admirable, he was so politically controversial that he had outlived his usefulness. Whatever the reason, it was clear by early 1849 that he would go.

One of the reasons may well have been pressure from the Treasury which was worried by his unorthodox financial ways, opposed to his plans to reorganize the Department and desirous of ending his time at the Committee of Council. On 1 September 1849, just as Kay-Shuttleworth returned from the Continent, Wood wrote to Russell stressing the political necessity of the government's producing a surplus. To obtain that, 'the great desideratum . . . is to establish a more efficient control over the expenditure'. Permanent officers, in his opinion, had no proper notion of parliamentary responsibility and there ought therefore to be someone in charge who had to answer to the House of Commons. Wood was speaking of the

Ordnance Department but the situation he described was Kay-Shuttleworth's exactly. That same year Kay-Shuttleworth provided Wood with a paper saying that the Education Department's approximate surplus was £50,000 but in 1850 it had grown to £70,000 and Wood complained that the Committee of Council 'knew so little of their own affairs' that they would not believe that they had such a large balance. Kay-Shuttleworth had gone by then but the problem was one he had bequeathed his Office: accumulating balances of this kind was, in Wood's words, 'contrary to all principle'. He made it clear that if the probable expenditure of a department was £160,000, and he knew that there was a balance in hand of £70,000, he would make a grant of only £90,000, thus returning vigorously and precisely to the criticism which the 1848 Select Committee on Miscellaneous Expenditure had made of Kay-Shuttleworth's practice of not revealing his surplus funds.[107] Given their objections the Treasury chose a most effective way to get rid of him – it offered slow support so that the work pressure became intolerable, and simultaneously opposed his plans to reorganize the Department. But these Treasury attitudes could not have conquered without the concurrence of Russell and Lansdowne. They knew the significance and the cost of his contribution. Yet they were less than frank with him, understood but did not fight vigorously for the administrative reforms he wanted, and offered him a choice which was really an ultimatum.

The tragedy of Kay-Shuttleworth's downfall is not just a case of subtle and stubborn enemies and careless friends. He made his own contribution. His compulsive need to be involved with every part of the Education Department's work helped to cripple his health; his passionate belief in his cause set him apart, a lonely figure who bemused Wood, Parker and most of the Balliol group; and his relentless drive wore out supporters and angered enemies. To civil servants and politicians he was an awkward, prickly man who cared more for his cause than for the policies of the governments he served or for the customs of the Treasury. He lacked social position and the easy grace of the aristocratic and the upper-middle-class men among whom his working life was spent. He had married well, acquired a country house and an estate, become acquainted with the rich and powerful, and achieved much as a civil servant. Many in the educational world had some understanding of his contribution, and there were times when it seemed that he had gained acceptance; yet, at the age of 45, as he left Whitehall for the last time in his official capacity, he remained an outsider.

7 · Families, the family estate, novelists, and a novel, 1850–60

'You will smile', Hannah Kay said to her son in 1850, 'when I tell you I was asked yesterday, rather suddenly, how Sir James was – for a moment I thought only of Sir James Dark and wondered I was asked about him.'[1] But, she added, she had become accustomed to the changes in his life. In the first three or four years after Kay-Shuttleworth's resignation the tragic and tumultuous changes continued.

In 1850 Hannah Kay turned 70 and her daughter Hannah 44. They lived in London and worried about James's health. 'I wish I was with you to help your good Lady wife to nurse and take care of you', Hannah wrote to her son the day after his honour was announced. Sometimes they were entrusted with the Kay-Shuttleworth children at 38 Gloucester Square while their parents were attending to estate matters. Gawthorpe, like Battersea, could not have been developed as successfully without their assistance, and James Kay-Shuttleworth gratefully acknowledged it. Hannah (his sister) did not marry and devoted herself to the care of her mother and her nephews and nieces.[2]

Of the younger Kay brothers, Ebenezer and Joseph were making their way successfully. Both studied at Trinity College, Cambridge, Joseph completing his BA in 1845 and taking an MA in 1849 while Ebenezer, though a year younger, finished his BA in 1844 and took his MA in 1847. In 1845 Joseph had been appointed a travelling bachelor by the university and, under the influence of his eldest brother, spent much time in the next four years in Europe collecting material on the social and educational conditions of the working classes. In 1846, at the age of 25, he published a book, *The Education of the Poor in England and Europe*, and more important works appeared in 1850 and 1853. He was called to the Bar at the Inner Temple in 1848, where he joined Ebenezer, who after studying at Lincoln's Inn had been called to the Bar the previous year.[3]

The youngest brother, Tom, was causing anguish. He seems to have been employed for a time in the civil service, and after being sacked worked as a coach driver in Wales. On 11 December 1846, aged 21, he married Mary, the daughter of Judith and John Pritchard, landlord of the Goat Hotel in Beddgelert. When Mary died in 1848, a few days after giving birth to their daughter Louise, Tom went to London. Ebenezer expressed the hope that Janet's presence might restrain him – Tom wanted to behave well but his good intentions were like those of 'a steam engine off the rails'. And off the rails he went, for on 20 September 1849 he married Mary Pritchard's sister, Alice. Marriage to a deceased wife's sister was then illegal, and an angry Ebenezer told his sister: 'You must be aware that Tom's marriage is utterly void and that any children of Alice must be illegitimate. . . . Nothing can exaggerate my grief and disgust. I think the manner of doing it was so very wicked and heartless.' He asked Hannah to 'watch over dear mother with more than ordinary devotion if possible and comfort her under this trial'.[4]

Tom's life jerked uncertainly onwards, and by 1852 he and Alice had two daughters and a son. Kay-Shuttleworth managed to get him appointed to a minor position with the Committee of Council, but he resigned, amid hints of unsatisfactory performance, late in 1850. In October the following year he wrote to his mother and sister thanking them for letters and remarking on 'the quantity of ink used in the advice they contain' which, he said, was 'mighty satisfactory to your unworthy son and brother inasmuch as it showeth he hath not been forgotten'. He was unable to look after Louise, the daughter of his first marriage, who went to live with Judith Pritchard, in Beddgelert. Joseph and James urged Tom to work and to live economically. 'James has been very kind', Joseph said, and no harshness had been shown to Tom, 'except to refuse to do all he wishes.' Tom proved incorrigible and in October 1852 he and Alice went to Rickmansworth while his brothers tried to find him board and a job. He angered them by going to London and spending £5.6.4 in two days. Janet Kay-Shuttleworth was even angrier and concluded that 'Poor Tom's conduct is a terrible calamity to us all.' 'If he could now feel hunger and thirst', she told her husband, 'and learn what he may possibly be entailing on his poor children I would let him suffer them.' There had been family differences but Janet insisted – 'I cannot help saying this strongly' – let Tom feel the effects of his follies 'without any more of the gentle softening which so long as there was hope of his heart being touched by mercy was, perhaps, right'.[5]

James Kay-Shuttleworth's health continued to be a major concern. He and Janet were often apart in the early 1850s as he spent much time on the estate and she sought health cures, but they had two more children, Robert, born on 20 October 1847, and Lionel, born on 23 March 1849. The family concentrated on Kay-Shuttleworth's health and in his letters to Janet, their children, his sister and mother (and in letters they wrote to him) it is constantly canvassed: he is better, worse, has slept well or badly, is anxious or relaxed, his neuralgia has flared or has not appeared, he is fatigued or vigorous, but he is never better for long. Rather melodramatically he told Janet that he had 'a strong presentiment' that his time was short and his work nearly done.[6]

Soon after his resignation he gave an account of his illness to the mentor of his youth, W.P. Alison. He had been accustomed to work 12 hours a day and, during the last three years at the Committee of Council, had suffered from intolerance of sound, irritability when fatigued, and frequent pains in the back of the head in the evening. His sleep was occasionally interrupted by a shout or a snort or a scream. He also had slight neuralgic pains, his legs did not feel 'quite so strong as formerly' and he 'was frequently sensible of considerable stiffness in the lower extremities'. He described the collapse in the office and the subsequent problem: while he rested he felt well but once he attempted to work his pulse quickened and he felt 'a sense of fullness in the head'. Moreover, when he rode briskly over a reasonably long distance he suffered badly from neuralgia. He paused in his letter to describe the pain itself – 'sharp stings like the plunge of a stiletto' occurring every ten or twenty seconds along the femoral nerve either in the thigh, the knee, the tendons at the back of the knee or in the shin. Paroxysms of pain accompanied 'the excitement of conversation in a large party collected in a country house', or prolonged discussion on subjects that interested him. 'It is difficult for me', he said, 'after having spent a very active life to restrain myself from taking an undue interest in passing events – and to adopt the merely material course of existence which would probably be the most conducive to my health.'[7]

Like many a patient, Kay-Shuttleworth had not given his doctor the full information. Alison received another letter from Janet explaining that she had taken her husband's letter from dictation. She apologized for intruding on Alison – 'but a wife's anxieties must be pardoned – and I have observed several points respecting Sir James which he has not mentioned – and [of] some of which I believe he is not conscious'. His pulse was much more erratic than he admitted, he had told her that he feared softening of his brain, and at times he attributed his sufferings to a spinal injury. In April 1848, eight months before he collapsed in his office, she had been alarmed to notice that 'his jaws and head suddenly shook in a very strange manner' and he would have fallen from his chair had she not caught him. The shaking lasted two or three minutes but half an hour later he went to his office and refused to take advice. About two months earlier he had had a similar shaking which lasted for many minutes and had continued at intervals during the evening. He was so anxious that a friend who was present should not see it that, in what must have been a gruesomely pathetic farce, he covered his head with a handkerchief as if to avoid the light. He later admitted his alarm.

After noting that in the autumn of 1847 he had suffered from a bout of rheumatic fever and had not been able to take a rest from work, Janet, in a remarkably frank passage, revealed her own and her husband's desperation. For several years before his 1848 attack he had screamed in his sleep as often as nine or ten times a night,

> making 8 distinct kinds of noises, hysterical laughing, hysterical sobbing – ordinary laughing and talking, violent shrieks which can be heard at some distance and often awake the servants in the next room – or room above – shouting out words [such] as 'Murder' 'a [indecipherable]' – groaning, moaning gently as a sick child does in sleep, and a strange noise between a snort and a growl . . . I have heard him go over again long conversations apparently with yourself and other of his Edinburgh medical tutors and advisers – as though learning the elements of the profession – or consulting you as to his probable success – and this sometimes for an hour or two in an uninterrupted flow of words . . .

The incidence of these conversations had diminished since his collapse, though before it Janet had been frequently alarmed by his crying and sobbing, 'like an hysterical woman', as she put it. Lately he had often been depressed but had not cried in the same manner and was less easily irritated by trifles: 'Indeed his patience is wonderful, and surprises every one.' Finally Janet added that she did not believe that any suffering 'even that of labour' was more severe than he occasionally endured from a bad attack of neuralgia. Explaining that she did not wish her husband to be alarmed, Janet asked Alison to enclose any letter to her under cover to Miss

Poplawska 'as my Husband frequently opens my letters before they are brought to me' – a not uncommon practice at the time.[8]

The pain of neuralgia, the shame and fear of epilepsy, the screaming in the night, the humiliating sobbing, the throbbing of old but not departed anxieties – it was a harrowing and corrosive combination for James Kay-Shuttleworth, and scarcely less so for Janet. It would have been even more harrowing had they realized that, in his precisely observed and deliberate account of his neuralgic pains, Kay-Shuttleworth had sent Alison a textbook description of tabes dorsalis, a form of quaternary neurosyphilis. Sir John Walton, in *Brain's Diseases of the Nervous System*, describes the symptom of the 'lightning pains' of tabes dorsalis as 'stabbing in character', and as occurring in 'brief paroxysms in the lower limbs'. The attacks, which can be very severe, are usually localized, though the spot at which they occur may shift from place to place in the limb. The patient, Walton notes, 'feels as if a sharp object were being driven into the limb'. Lightning pains are of great diagnostic value and Kay-Shuttleworth's description raises the distinct possibility that he was suffering from neurosyphilis.[9]

Other indications support this diagnosis. Stiffness and loss of strength in the legs can accompany tabes dorsalis, while epileptic attacks are symptoms of general paralysis of the insane, another type of quaternary neurosyphilis, and the shaking of the jaw which Janet described is quite possibly Jacksonian epilepsy. Moreover, his son Ughtred mentions in his reminiscences that his father's health 'much improved in important respects' after he had recovered from Roman fever (almost certainly malaria) in 1869. In 1917 a considerable advance was made in the treatment of neurosyphilis by the introduction of malaria treatment. Kay-Shuttleworth had gone to Rome in search of better health and may have realized his hopes through a medical accident.[10]

Ughtred's comment is the more fascinating because so loyal a son would never have reported the cure had he realized its medical significance. The same explanation, lack of knowledge, can account for why Kay-Shuttleworth, a trained physician, gave so precise a description of the symptoms of neurosyphilis, when he would certainly not have wished to advertise to Alison or anyone else that he had been stricken by the disease. The first adequate account of tabes dorsalis was given by Moritz Romberg in 1846 and was not translated into English until 1853.[11] As Kay-Shuttleworth had ceased to practise professionally and was not mixing in medical circles, he had no reason to read textbooks on neurology and had no way of knowing of Romberg's findings.

Nor did Janet Kay-Shuttleworth: it is clear from her letter to Alison that she had no suspicion that her husband was suffering from syphilis. It was quite common for men with syphilis to recover from the first infection, to marry while free from the disease, to have a healthy family, and for the tertiary or quaternary syphilis to develop twenty or more years after the first infection. When this did develop it was not infective and for a time neither husband nor wife need have known the true nature of the disease. Perhaps this is what happened to the Kay-Shuttleworths. The rate at which tabes dorsalis develops is variable and in some cases considerable improvement can occur. If Kay-Shuttleworth had the infection, it was relatively mild and did not progress rapidly. Later in his life he may have begun to realize that the disease had claimed him but, if so, it did not humiliate him as it did many of its victims. He remained mentally alert until his death, and his death can be explained without syphilis being a cause.[12]

If Kay-Shuttleworth had neurosyphilis, he may have become infected when treating a syphilitic patient – he undoubtedly would have encountered some during the cholera epidemic, in his private practice, or at the dispensaries in Edinburgh and Manchester. If he were careless he might have been infected through a sore or open cut on his hand. That is, however, unlikely, especially as by character Kay-Shuttleworth was obsessively careful. Syphilis was commonly contracted through sexual intercourse – perhaps with someone such as the young woman who had given his cousin, James Kay, her address under the light of a lamp in Leith Walk in Edinburgh in 1826.

But though there is a strong case for believing that Kay-Shuttleworth had syphilis, it cannot be known for certain. Medical diagnoses of this historical kind have to be treated cautiously and, though the lightning pains are a striking symptom, other diagnoses can be advanced which, without detailed evidence to contradict them, can account for some of his symptoms. There is heavy irony in Kay-Shuttleworth's predicament. If a person so intent on improving the moral condition of the poor, and so aggressively condemnatory about the sexual habits of paupers, suffered from syphilis, he would provide a haunting parable of the human weakness of a moral reformer. He had become a victim of the disease seen as God's vengeance on sinners and, for those not powerful enough to keep the illness relatively private, as the epitome of social degradation.[13] If this were Kay-Shuttleworth's fate, it does not diminish his contributions to social and educational reform, nor lessen his personal tragedy. It ill behoves an age which penicillin has freed from fear of syphilis to judge his failings too self-righteously, especially as its reactions to the epidemic of AIDS, which raises many of the emotions stirred by syphilis in the nineteenth century, often perpetuate the same volatile mix of medicine and morality.

Alison's reply to Kay-Shuttleworth has not survived, though understandably he did not diagnose syphilis. He prescribed a diet and recommended an examination by a medical practitioner of experience and judgement. Kay-Shuttleworth went to his Manchester colleague, John Roberton, who attributed his symptoms to 'generally obscure constitutional sources', thus differing from Shuttleworth's self-diagnosis of irritation or chronic inflammation of the sheath of the spinal cord. He began to treat himself, passing on the details of his treatment to Alison, who was well aware that Roberton did not agree with the self-diagnosis.[14]

None of the treatments was successful and Kay-Shuttleworth sought relief in the baths at Wildbad in the kingdom of Württemberg in southern Germany. He went with Ebenezer at the end of August 1851, leaving Janet, who was expecting their fifth child in November, to stay at Broadstairs, the coastal resort in Kent, and then Windermere. At Cologne the travellers attended Mass in the cathedral and Kay-Shuttleworth, in ecumenical mood, desired to 'sympathise with all who worship the incarnate Saviour from the Quaker to the Catholic'. Baden was a different story: he could not stay because its famous gambling establishment 'overshadows everything with the Wing of Hell'. Once at Wildbad he took the waters and followed the regimen his doctors had suggested. He wrote regularly to Janet on the effect of the treatment on his neuralgia and fatigue, sent detailed instructions to ensure that *The Times* reached him, and asked about estate matters and (twice) the family plate, which he instructed Janet to keep with her when she went on a visit to the Davenports.[15]

With his faith in the treatment high, he spoke of going to watering places such as Eastbourne, Brighton and Hastings. Meanwhile, to the annoyance of Ebenezer, who was forced to return to England and be replaced by Joseph, he extended his stay. Insidiously, Kay-Shuttleworth's tragically destroyed health became part of another tragedy as he began to use illness as a means of exerting control. He told Janet that 'knowing of what value my health is to you, I have even for your sake a strong desire to perfect my cure' and hence would stay longer. He longed to be with her, of course, but for her sake would not hurry. 'Do you not feel dearest that the sweet pain of absence increases our love and will make us cling the closer to each other.' In his informative didactic letters to his children, the same note recurs. He told Ughtred, known as 'Ughty', who had caused Miss Poplawska some trouble, that no one could be more patient and skilful than Miss Poplawska, so if he failed to make progress the fault would be his. 'I am sure Ughty will show his love to me by being a good boy for when I am poorly nothing makes my pain come so surely as to hear that one of my little children has failed to be quite good.'[16]

His lack of self-awareness was illustrated when he wrote to Janet about the management of their children, warning against the exaggeration of slight faults and the habitual mild punishments which he blamed for his own lack of self-respect. This lack, he decided, 'seems to me to be peculiarly Ughty's danger. His condition is full of difficulty.' While his own fate was being mirrored in his son's, he decided that Ughtred was in the Marjoribanks mould. Prudence and circumspection made up for speed of reasoning, and what was lacking in brilliant courage was supplied by the sagacity which avoided danger. Ughtred had no part of 'my own too sensitive and suffering nature – neither its fatal power of introspection – its early growth of imagination and feeling – nor its later fruits of subtle thought'. Nor did he have Janet's 'gentleness, tenderness, ardour, unselfishness, and perfect good sense'. 'Now in Pussy' (as his daughter was called), he continued, 'I see much both of myself and you: and in Ughty I see much to love, and to train into a good and useful man.' He had made a declaration of what became a lifelong preoccupation based on flawed estimates of his own and his wife's characters.[17]

Towards the end of September, his health not restored (he had another epileptic attack shortly before he left Wildbad), he and Joseph began the return journey to London. In Heidelberg, which he thought at that season to be a cheerless and miserable place, he visited Dr Chelius, 'a very grave and impressive man', to whom he gave a minute description of the history of his illness. Dr Chelius concluded that he suffered from 'too great sensibility of the brain induced by too intense and prolonged mental labour', and that his condition was to be 'absolutely distinguished' from epilepsy. He was to take no medicine, rest completely, and in two months he would know whether the baths had done him any good. Chelius's opinion closely resembled those Kay-Shuttleworth had received from British

Changes at Gawthorpe: this view of the west front shows the openwork parapet and tall chimneys added in 1851

doctors, and 'perfectly without pain' he continued on his way to England, hoping against hope that he need not be haunted by the ghosts of epilepsy. Two weeks before the end of the two months decreed by Dr Chelius, that hope had gone. 'Wildbad did me harm', he told Janet North, 'but I shall get over that if I can keep quiet.' But for him keeping quiet was like writing short: he could not.[18]

As he struggled to regain health he executed his and Janet's scheme for the renovation of Gawthorpe Hall. Planning had begun in 1849 and the renovations, completed in 1852, were controlled by the fashionable and expensive architect, Charles Barry, who was working on the new Houses of Parliament. Barry considered that the exterior was 'a fine picture' but 'without a frame'; he therefore added an extra storey to the tower and crowned it with an openwork parapet on which the family names and mottoes were carved. A similar parapet appeared on the walls and tall chimneys which were placed at each corner. The result was a more dramatic skyline and, with some other changes, was designed 'to perfect and render more striking the original character of the building'. Barry also redesigned the entrance door putting up a four-centred arch with a window above. It carries the Kay and Kay-Shuttleworth arms. The Shuttleworth family motto, 'Prudentia et Iustitia', is inscribed on the inside of the lintel while on the outside appears the Kay motto, 'Kynd Kynn Knawne Kepe' (Kind friends know and keep). The origin of this motto is obscure but its convenient Ks help to explain its attractiveness.[19]

The many changes to the interior of Gawthorpe Hall made Kay-Shuttleworth's an insistent presence in the house: the Kay coat of arms was strategically placed and KS monograms appeared in a number of places, most spectacularly on the ceiling of the dining room. Gawthorpe Hall, he was determined, would always bear the marks of his existence. He carried out an extensive refurnishing programme, which used some designs by Augustus Pugin, and Barry designed formal gardens to set the restored building amid geometrical Elizabethan patterns.

In the early days of the work Janet Kay-Shuttleworth was closely involved, and she and her husband sometimes combined holidays at Windermere with their trips to Gawthorpe. They left the children in London with Miss Poplawska who features frequently in Janet's letters, which concentrate heavily on the next world. Kay-Shuttleworth was more intent on this world. He was happy that

'Mamma will have her old Hall restored', he told Ughtred, 'and that when his little boy is grown into a big man he will live there almost always and will take care that the tenants are justly dealt with – the poor are comfortably housed – [and] their children taught their duty to God and to man'. As time went by the responsibility for the renovations shifted heavily to him, partly because they fed his obsessive desire to control his environment, and partly because Janet's ill-health kept her in London or on holiday at Windermere or the seaside. Separation worried neither of them and in December 1851, two months after his return from Wildbad and only a month after the birth of their fifth child, Stewart Marjoribanks, Kay-Shuttleworth was back on the estate. 'Dearest wife', he wrote in a typically manipulative letter, 'Say whether you are pining for my return. I can come back any day.' He listed various tasks which he thought it prudent to complete, adding that he could finish them in a week, though 'they would greatly fret and worry me if I had to correspond about them from London'. Nevertheless, if Janet were unhappy, 'I should prefer to return home for a week' and to come back to Gawthorpe later.[20]

On one of the occasions when he feared he was close to death, he gave Janet a report on her estate. After the drainage programme was completed, they would be able to attract better tenants. The cost of the loan for the drainage was small, because the largest part of the interest was paid by the individual tenants. The improvements at Gawthorpe would cost about £5,000 and his savings, together with the repayment of some loans, including one from Robert Kay, would cover that cost and provide an additional £1,400 for the refurnishing. He was planning to keep at least £10,000 of ready money in a reserve fund, so that when the leases for the collieries ended they could work the collieries themselves, if they were not satisfied with the terms for letting them. Janet now had two beautiful houses, 38 Gloucester Square in London, and Gawthorpe, both luxuriously furnished, and an income so ample that he proposed to set aside £1,500–2,000 annually towards the fortunes of the younger children. This money might be used to assist with the working of the collieries but, since it would be unjust if Ughtred were given the £10,000 as well as benefiting from the improvements on the estate, any money that went towards the collieries from the fortunes of the younger children was to be seen as a loan.[21]

In March 1852, as the work at Gawthorpe was ending, Janet Kay-Shuttleworth acknowledged her husband's contribution: 'It has been especially your work and you know how *very very* grateful I am to you for all you have done at my old home – the Church, the schools, the House – and the care you are taking to improve the neighbourhood.' He should not think of his illness as a punishment for past sins, she consoled him, 'but rather as a merciful discipline to bring you nearer to GOD'. Frederick North for once came to the same conclusion as his step-daughter: Kay-Shuttleworth was 'a thorough Man of business – which his Neighbours will, I suspect, give him no credit for. He has his reward in a most flourishing state of the property.'[22]

Across the moors, about twelve miles as the crow flies from Gawthorpe, fame had come to Charlotte Brontë. In 1849 it became known that she was not just the only surviving child of the Rev. Patrick Brontë, the incumbent at Haworth, but Currer Bell, the author of *Jane Eyre*. In January 1850, as work progressed at Gawthorpe and as they exchanged letters with Alison, James and Janet Kay-Shuttleworth invited her to Gawthorpe, but her shyness and anxiety made such approaches unwelcome and she declined the invitation 'as neatly as I knew how'. Not to be put off, Kay-Shuttleworth wrote again, and having obtained an invitation, appeared at Haworth on Friday, 1 March. 'The baronet looks in vigorous health', Charlotte told her friend Ellen Nussey, 'he scarcely appears more than thirty-five, but he says he is forty-four [he was actually 45]; Lady Shuttleworth is rather handsome and still young. They were both quite unpretending.' They again urged Charlotte to visit them and to her alarm her father supported them, leaving her without an excuse. She agreed to go for three days, having refused the Kay-Shuttleworths' insistence that she return with them in their carriage immediately. 'Sir James is very courtly, fine-looking; I wish he may be as sincere as he is polished. He shows his white teeth with too frequent a smile; but I will not pre-judge him.' She wished the visit was well over.[23]

In mid-March she reluctantly took the train to Burnley where she was met by Kay-Shuttleworth and driven to Gawthorpe, a towering hall, 'grey, antique, castellated and stately'. Sir James, she decided, was 'a man of polished manners with clear intellect and highly cultivated mind'. He took her on quiet drives to old ruins and halls in the nearby hills and woods, and their dialogues by the fireside in his oak-panelled drawing room ('perhaps I should rather say monologues for I listened far more than I talked') did not oppress or exhaust her too greatly. On the whole she got on well with him. Janet

Kay-Shuttleworth she described as a little woman 'with a pretty, smooth, lively face' who made no pretensions to aristocratic airs, was frank, good-humoured and active, even if 'grace, dignity, fine feeling were not in the inventory of her qualities'. Her husband had these qualities, though 'frank he is not, but on the contrary – politic – he calls himself a man of the world and knows the world's ways . . . In him high mental cultivation is combined with an extended range of observation, and thoroughly practical views and habits.' If Kay-Shuttleworth had persuaded Charlotte Brontë to see him as he wanted to be seen, she was not deceived about his health: his nerves were acutely sensitive and the critical state of his health 'has exaggerated sensitiveness into irritability'. Janet's temperament seemed perfectly suited to nursing him and if her sensations 'were more delicate and acute she would not do half so well. They get on perfectly together'. It was hard for an anxious guest, seeing people of whom she knew virtually nothing, to understand them well, and Charlotte Brontë got a lot wrong.[24]

Yet when she was on more familiar territory Charlotte unerringly discerned a strong and strange personality:

> They have a young German lady as governess – a quiet, well-instructed, interesting girl whom I took to at once – and, in my heart, liked better than anything else in the house. She also instinctively took to me. She is very well treated for a governess – but wore the usual pale, despondent look of her class – She told me she was home-sick – and she looked so.

Rosa Poplawska, the German-Polish governess, had found a kindred spirit, and one who had herself been a governess.

Though the visit had gone better than she expected, Charlotte Brontë left Gawthorpe with a sword hanging over her head. The Kay-Shuttleworths had invited her to London for the season. She prized the 'extended range of observation' that this would bring her but, she informed William Williams, her publisher's reader, 'I tremble at the thought of the price I must necessarily pay in mental distress and physical wear and tear.' In a gracious letter to Janet Kay-Shuttleworth of 22 March 1850 she repeated her worries. 'I am angry with myself for not feeling more courage on the subject, but I am a great coward in some things. A life of seclusion may tend to develope [*sic*] the reflective faculties, but it stunts some useful practical points.' Kay-Shuttleworth kept pressing the invitation and, in response to her insistence that she would not be lionized, began to talk of 'small parties'. He had looked at her with a physician's eye and had seen at once, she told Ellen Nussey, that 'I could not stand much fatigue, nor bear the presence of many strangers.' But even the most skilful physician saw things from the outside – 'the heart knows its own bitterness and the frame its own poverty, and the mind its own struggles.'[25]

Kay-Shuttleworth's heart, frame and mind had received a battering in London and to have returned with Charlotte Brontë would have been something of a triumph. If the truth were known, he needed her more than she needed him. He might have opened some doors, though his links with the literary world were few. Matthew Arnold was not a powerful figure at that stage of his life, but Kay-Shuttleworth was acquainted with Dickens, perhaps through Edward Marjoribanks, Janet's uncle. During his time at the Committee of Council he and Dickens had discussed ragged schools and the Kay-Shuttleworths had met Dickens and his wife socially. Nevertheless, Dickens wittily parried a number of Kay-Shuttleworth's dinner invitations, remarking on one occasion that he was bidden to the marriage of a friend – 'one Dombey – and I am afraid if I stayed away, the Ceremony would scarcely come off; so much importance is attached to my presence. In fact, I give away the bride'.[26]

When her father's illness in early May forced Charlotte to cancel the London visit, she admitted to Ellen Nussey that she did not regret missing the ordeal – 'I would as lief have walked among red-hot plough shares' – but she did regret having to miss the opportunity to see and hear Dickens and Thackeray. Later in May came another delay, this time because Kay-Shuttleworth was seriously ill, two physicians attending him twice daily – 'company and conversation, even with his own relatives, are prohibited as too exciting'. A desperate Kay-Shuttleworth wrote two letters claiming that Charlotte had promised to wait until he was better; and, in a phrase which amused her, he asked her not to allow anyone else to introduce her 'into the Oceanic life of London'. She gave the promise for, as she told Ellen Nussey, 'I know something of him, and like part at least of what I do know.' How seriously she regarded his suffering was made clear by her hope that 'God will be pleased to spare his mind'. Lady Shuttleworth was much to be pitied, she remarked, adding: 'his nights, it seems, are most distressing'.[27]

Charlotte eventually went to London on 30 May and persuaded 'Sir James', who had recovered sufficiently to go London at the same time, that she had 'some little matters of business to transact' and would therefore stay with her publisher, George Smith. He lived with his mother at 76 Gloucester Terrace, a perilously short distance from the Kay-Shuttleworths in Gloucester Square, but he took charge of Charlotte, showed her the sights of London and arranged a reception at which she met major literary figures without being impressed by, or impressing, all of them. In her first three days in London, Kay-Shuttleworth called twice and Janet once. He was 'in a fearfully nervous state' and horrified Charlotte by talking of taking her to Hampton Court, Windsor and other places. 'God knows how I shall get on. I perfectly dread it', she said. It seems, however, that Smith protected her from these excursions.[28]

While Charlotte Brontë and James Kay-Shuttleworth circled each other, Janet Kay-Shuttleworth was writing to 'Mrs Gaskell', the wife of William Gaskell, minister of the Cross Street Unitarian Chapel in Manchester, and the author of the controversial *Mary Barton* (1848) and a contributor to Dickens' *Household Words*. None of Janet's letters has survived but her ideas interested Elizabeth Gaskell, even when they extended to suggesting that she write another novel which saw things from the viewpoint of millowners and thus counterbalanced *Mary Barton*. Janet had written a pamphlet on a group of deaconesses in Paris, and that and her interest in an establishment for invalid gentlewomen led to discussions of the role of women in the family and in social life. They may have met in Unitarian circles, and they saw each other at that fateful place for the Kay-Shuttleworths, Capesthorne, where Caroline Davenport, now a widow, continued to act as a brilliant hostess.[29]

In one of her letters Janet mentioned Charlotte Brontë's visit to Gawthorpe and, excitedly, Elizabeth Gaskell replied that she would 'like to hear a great deal more about her' because she was interested in her writings, and in what they revealed of 'her modes of thought, and, all unconsciously to herself, of the way in wh[ich] she has suffered'. On 19 August 1850 Janet invited Elizabeth Gaskell to meet Charlotte Brontë at Briery Close, a house which the Kay-Shuttleworths took when they holidayed at Windermere. She has left a famous description of 'a little lady in black silk gown':

> She is, (as she calls herself) *undeveloped*; thin and more than ½ a head shorter than I, soft brown hair not so dark as mine; eyes (very good and expressive looking straight & open at you) of the same colour, a reddish face; large mouth & many teeth gone; altogether *plain*; the forehead square, broad, and *rather* overhanging.

Charlotte Brontë (National Portrait Gallery)

Elizabeth Gaskell (National Portrait Gallery)

Janet Kay-Shuttleworth was ill which meant that 'Sir James' did much of the entertaining, one day driving his guests to Coniston to call on the Tennysons – the call was not made as it began to rain and they turned back.[30]

These drives made Charlotte Brontë's wayward spirit uneasy. She thought the Lake District scenery glorious but it was scenery '*as it can be seen from a carriage*'. She was only half at her ease and longed 'to slip out unseen, and to run away by myself amongst the hills and dales. Erratic and vagrant instincts tormented me', she added,

> and these I was obliged to control, or rather, suppress – for fear of growing in any degree enthusiastic, and thus drawing attention to – the 'lioness', the authoress – the she-artist. Sir James is a man of ability – even intellect – but not a man in whose presence one willingly unbends.

'Could I have wandered about amongst those hills *alone*', she said to Ellen Nussey, 'I could have drank in all their beauty.' Instead there was the carriage and company.[31]

Either on this visit or earlier Janet Kay-Shuttleworth made her contribution to the Brontë legend by giving Elizabeth Gaskell a description of life at Haworth. 'Such a life as Miss B's I never heard of before Lady K S described her home to me.' The village consisted of a few grey stone houses on the edge of a moor, and its bleak parsonage had not had a coat of paint or acquired a new piece of furniture since the death of Mrs Brontë 30 years ago. 'She had 6 children as fast as could be; & what with that, & the climate, & the strange half mad husband she had chosen she died at the end of 9 years.' While dying 'she used to lie crying in bed, and saying, "Oh God my poor children – oh God my poor children!" continually.' Mr Brontë vented his anger on things, not persons, and once during one of his wife's confinements he sawed up all the chairs in her bedroom, 'never answering her remonstrances or minding her tears'. The sitting room in the parsonage looked into the churchyard filled with graves, and Mr Brontë had not taken a meal with his children since his wife's death, unless he invited them to tea. 'All this Lady K S told me', she reported to a friend, going on to outline the rest of Charlotte's life with verve and amazed compassion. She reflected with less compassion and less insight on her host, judging him to be 'an eminently practical man . . . who had never indulged in the exercise of any talent which could not bring him a tangible and speedy return'.[32]

Charlotte Brontë's reaction was more complex. She told Ellen Nussey that she honoured Sir James's intellect, but could never have sympathy with his heart. He behaved to her with kindness and Mrs Gaskell believed that he had a strong friendship for her. But she felt that he was unforgiving, that 'the substratum of his character is as hard as flint' and that he had a 'natural antipathy' to authors as a class. 'Their virtues give him no pleasure – their faults are wormwood and gall in his soul.'

> Nine parts out of ten in him are utilitarian – the tenth is artistic. This tithe of his nature seems to me at war with all the rest – it is just enough to incline him relentlessly towards the artist class, and far too little to make him one of them. The consequent inability to *do* things which he *admires*, embitters him I think.[33]

Kay-Shuttleworth did not show Charlotte Brontë the poems he had written, nor did he tell her that he was planning a novel, but she had sensed a conflict which the more worldly Elizabeth Gaskell did not feel. Beneath the civilities at Briery Close, the guests pondered the character of their host and found it wanting, but in that August of 1850 a friendship was formed which issued in Elizabeth Gaskell's superb biography.

Rosa Poplawska was the highlight of Charlotte's next meeting with the Kay-Shuttleworths which took place in September at Gawthorpe. 'I saw the governess at Sir J.K.S.'s; she looked a little better and more cheerful – she was almost as pleased to see me as if we had been related – and when I bid her good bye, expressed an earnest hope that I would soon come again.' She noted with an expert eye that the children were fond of her and obedient, 'two great alleviations of the inevitable evil of her position'. Elizabeth Gaskell found other skills in the governess. In November 1850 she drew attention to a story of hers which was soon to be published in *Household Words* and told Miss Poplawska that she was most welcome to translate it 'if she thinks it worth while'.[34] Rosa Poplawska was to do much translating and to pass on the skill to her charge, the young Janet Kay-Shuttleworth.

Meetings between Charlotte Brontë and the Kay-Shuttleworths continued intermittently in the early 1850s. Late in December 1850, while Charlotte was staying at Ambleside with Harriet Martineau, they dined together and Kay-Shuttleworth called in his carriage a number of times to take her out. Charlotte told Ellen Nussey that he looked pale and wasted and she feared that he would not have long to live. She also met Matthew Arnold who was staying with his mother at their house, Fox How, a pleasant walk across the fields from Harriet Martineau's home. She thought him 'striking and prepossessing in appearance' but found his manner displeasing 'from its seeming foppery'. She discovered, as Kay-Shuttleworth assured her she would, that Arnold improved on acquaintance. However, her relationship with Kay-Shuttleworth did not improve and she deferred or declined his invitations if she could do so without being rude. She did 'begin to admit in my own mind that he is sincerely benignant to me'; and in June 1851 (when she dined with the Kay-Shuttleworths and Caroline Davenport, who she decided was 'a beautiful and – (I think) kind woman too'), she told her father that 'Sir James and Lady Shuttleworth have really been very kind, and most scrupulously attentive.' But her extreme shyness never diminished. In London in 1853, she summed up her feelings to Ellen Nussey: 'I really so much dread the sort of excited fuss into which he puts himself – that I only wish to see just as much of him as civility exacts.' But Kay-Shuttleworth continued his quest, ensuring, through his anxiety to know and to be seen to know Charlotte Brontë, that he saw less of her than he might otherwise have done.[35]

In the early sad years after his retirement, despite other pre-occupations, Kay-Shuttleworth found it impossible to resist the lure of public life. For a time Parliament beckoned again and he dallied with its temptations. He corresponded with constituencies at Hull, Bury and Macclesfield and in July 1851 was asked by the Working Men's Sanitary Committee of Macclesfield to become a candidate for the borough. Janet Kay-Shuttleworth told him that he was not well enough for public life which had always 'brought pain and nervousness'. If he were to introduce great subjects such as educational reform in Parliament 'and break down and be unable to work them yourself in the House', it would be 'a public misfortune' which would damage his cause and subject him to 'misconception and loss of future influence'. Moreover, if he became a parliamentarian he would 'put aside all private duties and interests and attend totally to Parliamentary duties'. She was not a selfish wife, Janet contended, and she had never grudged the loss of his society. But the private reasons of 'wife and children – home duties – tenants – schools etc are evident enough', and she reminded him of an illness and 'hysteric feelings' he had had at Wildbad.[36]

Kay-Shuttleworth's reply to the Macclesfield invitation made it extremely unlikely that anybody would wish to support him. If he were required to spend money in treating, bribes, in the employment of agents in private canvassing, 'or in any other way condemned by the votes of Committees of the House', he would not spend a shilling. Furthermore, he would consider Macclesfield only if five-sixths of the members of the registration committee supported him, and then he wanted a requisition from a very large proportion of the electors, particularly the influential ones. 'Before you take so much trouble you had better reflect whether a candidate whose health is less delicate and who has fewer scruples would not suit Macclesfield better.' In the light of such demands, which were driven partly by a fear of failure, Janet had little need to worry.[37]

Her argument that his standing would be diminished by a failed political career was given point by his role as an *éminence grise* in the education debates of the early 1850s. The Lancashire Public School Association, which had been formed in Manchester in 1847, advocated a policy of secular instruction given in schools financed from the local rates and controlled by local committees. Religious instruction was to be given at appointed times each week by religious teachers. It secured strong support from Liberal politicians, in particular Cobden, who told Kay-Shuttleworth 'that many more conscientious men of all parties will be driven to our remote refuge of despairing education-ists, the purely secular system'. In 1850 it re-named itself the National Public School Association and launched a national campaign. On 29 October Kay-Shuttleworth wrote a letter, the bulk of which was subsequently published in the *Manchester Guardian*, to R.M. Smiles, the secretary of the Association, expressing his sympathy with its work and his 'deep personal regret, that both in and out of the Church, the question of National Education should have been made the Battle Ground of great religious parties'. Nevertheless, he could not support a system of schools which was separate from the religious bodies of the country and in which religious influence did not pervade 'the whole discipline and instruction'. He kept in touch with the Association, hoping eventually to influence it.[38]

The Manchester and Salford Committee on Education, formed in 1850 to combat the Association, developed an Education Bill which favoured local control and local rates but retained religious instruction for all children, though in the hope of providing schools for all denominations. Kay-Shuttleworth joined its executive and wrote long and frequent letters to its chairman, especially when the

Committee decided that the Scriptures were to be read in all schools receiving rate aid. Fearing that this would alienate Roman Catholics and many others who 'would not tolerate any form of religious exclusion from civil privileges', he pointed out that he had fought for the promotion of education on a religious basis – 'The ship must be waterlogged and lurching into the whirlpool before I am tempted to abandon her' – but religious liberty was also crucial. He produced proposals to get round the Scripture reading problem, and for a time it looked as if the Committee and the National Public School Association might find common ground. They did not, and the Bill foundered. Though his main work was done behind the scenes, Kay-Shuttleworth was not afraid to complain if his views were given insufficient respect, once remarking to an influential member of the Manchester and Salford Committee, that 'to have permitted me to appear before your Committee to explain my views would have saved you a world of embarrassment in the approaching controversy'.[39]

Early in 1853 Kay-Shuttleworth made his first major statement since his retirement: *Public Education as affected by the Minutes of the Committee of the Privy Council from 1846 to 1852; with suggestions as to future policy*. A defence of the Committee's (and his) work, the book provoked predictable reactions – Kay-Shuttleworth's claims about Battersea were, an opponent said, 'a tissue of perversion' and 'enough to destroy the reputation for veracity of any public man'. In his opening chapters he discussed the monitorial system, inspection, pupil-teachers, the training colleges, the 1846 minutes, and the management clauses. He produced lengthy quotations, especially from Denison and Manning, to show the intransigence and extremism of 'a certain proportion of the clergy and of a much smaller body of laity, who had adopted exalted notions of the authority to teach, derived by an unbroken succession from the Apostles'. He took an obvious glee in the divisions within the Church, and he pointed with equal delight to differences in the voluntarist camp. He explicitly stated that he had intended to work towards the creation of a system of 'universally accessible and efficient elementary schools' and he described the achievements of the Committee, though considerable, as 'only preliminaries' to 'the universal diffusion' of elementary education. It might have seemed during Peel's government that the advance of the Education Department was confined to increases in the grants and in the number of inspectors and Normal schools; in fact, 'the principles of a great public policy were in operation, and were silently attracting to themselves, like centres of crystallization, a mass of precedent and authority, which was destined to become irresistible'.[40]

Public Education contained the important suggestion that local rates should be used to supplement the existing sources of educational income. It was an idea that he and many others had advanced before and was much discussed in the 1850s and 60s. For nearly 170 pages Kay-Shuttleworth took his reader through a maze of calculations and statistics designed to show the shortfall in educational finance if the existing sources only were used, and the contribution that rates might make. He provided an additional 80 pages of supporting appendices, and prefaced his discussion with a comment that he thought it best 'to retain the statistical reasoning in the form and place in which it will be most useful to those who do not shrink from the trouble of testing the analysis contained in these pages, and pursuing it to all its results'. Those who did not shrink from the trouble must have been few indeed. Charles Dickens was not among their company. 'I am so dreadfully jaded this morning', he wrote in April 1853, 'by the supernatural dreariness of Kaye [*sic*] Shuttleworth, that I feel as if I had just come out of the Great Desert of Sahara where my camel died a fortnight ago.'[41]

Once the statistical discussion begins, *Public Education* is supernaturally dreary; it is also quite mad. In his preface Kay-Shuttleworth described himself as 'worn with work, scathed by former controversies, and slowly restored to life after four years of suffering'. He was conscious that he was treading 'on the ashes and scoriæ of unexhausted fires, and that it may seem vain to desire to convert this crater into a garden'. But he drove himself through his world of statistics with an unwearied self-absorption that was as bizarre as it was stultifying and, having long ago lost most of his readers, arrived, triumphant, at his conclusions. *Public Education* is the work of a powerful mind that is partly out of its owner's control and, instead of creating gardens, builds forbidding statistical edifices, unaware that only a few similarly afflicted souls will wish to enter them. Three years after he finished *Public Education*, Kay-Shuttleworth, in a rare piece of self-deprecation, described himself as 'a Blue Book Cormorant'.[42] His indefatigable diving into official reports and statistics never produced a larger harvest than was displayed in this book.

Fortunately for many an authority figure, dreariness need not be an impediment to effectiveness and some of Kay-Shuttleworth's suggestions in *Public Education* were acted upon. In 1853 he persuaded the Committee of Council to issue a minute (a draft of which he wrote himself) which provided rural schools with a capitation grant. The minute embodied the new and potentially dangerous principle of a grant not dependent on local effort, that is, a subsidy. He was worried when it was extended to cover city schools, but when Gladstone and Lingen set about emasculating it he intervened to some effect. He acted as Russell's adviser on Bills on charitable trusts and Scottish education, and was effectively the author of Russell's unsuccessful but important Borough Bill of 1853, which under certain conditions proposed the subsidizing of schools aided by the Committee of Council from the rates. He also suggested that the Committee of Council might run more effectively and be more responsible to Parliament if, in addition to the Lord President in the House of Lords, a Vice-President were appointed from the House of Commons. His suggestion was taken up in 1856 when Lord Granville introduced the necessary legislation. These Bills, minutes and memoranda were openly argued for in *Public Education* and, as Richard Johnson was the first to notice, sections of the book sometimes appeared with little change in the memoranda or minutes and in some cases among the Gladstone papers.[43] Out of office Kay-Shuttleworth behaved no differently from the way he had operated while in office – he pressed his causes by whatever means, private or public, he judged the most effective.

On 21 October 1852 Kay-Shuttleworth wrote his daughter Janet, then nine years old, an affectionate, strange letter. Her little bedroom at Gawthorpe 'looks as though it expected you', fires were lighted in all the rooms on the ground floor and no chimney smoked, the schoolroom and Miss Poplawska's room were snug, and Mamma had a bell pull which could summon Janet to the boudoir or dining room. Everything was 'so warm and comfortable', and when Mamma was better 'we must all come and enjoy (if God will) our nearly restored home'. But, it seemed, God might not will it. 'We must try to be taught why it is that he would thus restrain us, and we shall perhaps find that he would mercifully keep us humble and obedient'. We needed to learn submission, though 'bye and bye we may all be a happy little family in our home at Gawthorpe.'[44] Kay-Shuttleworth was facing the collapse of his marriage.

About a year earlier, on 23 November 1851, the tenth anniversary of the day at Capesthorne on which Janet had accepted James's proposal, they had exchanged letters. Janet wrote from Gloucester Square. 'Many as have been my anxieties about you in these ten years and our cares of various kinds they have been the happiest of my entire life owing to your gentleness and constant kindness to me.' His reply, written on the same day, came, ironically, from Capesthorne, to which he was paying a weekend visit to break the rounds of his work at Gawthorpe. He had returned from church and was alone and could 'think over gratefully to God and affectionately to you, all that has happened since this day ten years'. Their wedded life had indeed been blessed with five children whose future was amply provided for, her health had improved and many of her hopes and wishes were fulfilled. 'How much have we to be thankful for? My own career has been wisely but mysteriously suspended, if not concluded. I resign myself gratefully and joyfully into the hands of God! Not my will but his be done. I have no desire for any future which he does not appoint.'[45]

In March 1852, as the work at Gawthorpe was nearing completion, Janet wrote of the ending of her own work in London – she had continued her interest in an institution for governesses, in women deacons, and in a home for invalid gentlewomen. Perhaps, she decided, he could learn the truth of 'that beautiful line of Milton's "They also serve who only stand and wait" with which I so often comfort myself now that I can do nothing more'. 'Surely, dearest husband', she continued, 'you and I need not wonder if we are also laid aside perhaps to prepare us for other duties – at all events to give us time for the land of GOD – Prayer and Meditation.' A graphic description of how she lived, which she gave to her sister-in-law, Hannah, in July 1852, showed that she was getting a lot of time for those pursuits. She had become the classic Victorian invalid, unable to leave her bed or sofa or to walk. She could not stand, though in the morning she sat up for three hours. The doctor had decided that she could go to Tunbridge Wells if a bed carriage were used. This involved Janet rolling from her bed onto the mattress from the carriage and being carried down to the carriage, lying in her usual flat posture. The carriage was driven to the rail, and a pair of horses met the train at Tunbridge Wells to take the carriage to her house. She was lifted out and carried to her bedroom where she rolled off the mattress and onto her new bed. She had 'less power than a child of a fortnight old'. In May 1853 Frederick North reported that Janet had not put foot to ground for nearly a year.[46]

From August 1852 until late October Janet stayed at Tunbridge Wells. For most of October, and probably for longer, she and her husband were apart. Their letters give details of their indispositions and of daily happenings. Janet was grateful to Miss Poplawska, who had given up her holidays to nurse her, and disturbed by a piano-playing lady next door. She expressed her relief that James, with his particular sensitivity to noise, did not have to hear her, or the children, and suggested that she move to Wales for a short time. Kay-Shuttleworth preferred a diplomatic letter, pointing out that she was 'confined to the sofa and very sensitive' and asking for the piano to be moved to another room. He also called upon 'my marital authority' to forbid a journey to Wales. Janet did not move, nor seem particularly disturbed by this assertion of authority, and two weeks later was enquiring how her 'Dearest Husband' had handled the Rent Day and all its fatigues. Rent Days were important social events on the estate and the Kay-Shuttleworths provided a dinner for their tenants to mark the occasion. 'Our health was proposed by the tenants', he reported, 'with three hearty cheers'.[47]

But successful Rent Days could not hide from Kay-Shuttleworth the realization that his wife was slipping away from him. It was in October 1852, while she was at Tunbridge Wells, that he wrote to their daughter Janet expressing the hope that 'bye and bye' they would be a happy family at Gawthorpe. A few days earlier he had told his wife that the alterations at Gawthorpe made him feel that it was 'our own home. We have expressed our own mind, feelings, and character upon it.' He hoped that she would 'love it for her husband's sake as well as for auld lang syne'. In an outburst of feeling, which he admitted was untypical, he said: 'Oh if I could find, Dearest Wife, some mode to express that love which should concentrate it all into one act of devotion how delighted should I be to enable you to realise its constancy and intensity.' Janet thought that the absence was doing him good. She wished that she could be with him to look after him when he suffered, or to read or write for him, 'but it pleases God to give me the trial of stillness and I trust I bear it with thankful cheerfulness'.[48]

The possessiveness and the insecurity expressed by the Ks in the engravings, plasterwork and mottoes at Gawthorpe, by the desire that he as well as 'auld lang syne' should be part of Janet's concept of Gawthorpe, and by the cry of love so agonizingly wrung from him, could hardly have been satisfied with this answer. Kay-Shuttleworth shared the expectations of a Victorian male that a wife should shelter within the private sphere of the family, leaving affairs of the world to her husband. Once, when she wished to advertise for a nursery governess, he told her not to write to *The Times*, even anonymously. He was 'jealous of my dear wife's appearing in print', he said. There was 'sanctity in reserve of female character which nothing but necessity should violate. The charm of that modesty is unspeakable to us who are sullied by contact with this world.'[49] But so private a life as she was living, so extreme a lack of contact with the world, was much more than he wished for. The trial of stillness was going too far.

The decisive year was 1853. On 30 January an uncharacteristically sharp Ebenezer reported that his brother was very busy and important, but was not getting on well with Janet. In these anxious times the Kay family confronted another sadness: on 23 April, after a long illness, their mother died at Briery Close. Hannah Kay was 72, and had been attended as closely at her death, as she had been in her life, by her daughter. Janet North, who knew something of mother–daughter relations, wrote a letter of condolence to Hannah, aptly remarking that she had lost 'the object of your life's devotion'.[50] There is no record of Kay-Shuttleworth's feelings at the ending of this intense and awkward relationship.

Shortly before she died Hannah Kay may have heard of the impending drama, but her death did not slow the disintegration of her son's marriage. In early April Janet had told Elizabeth Gaskell that she was going to Bad Homburg, a resort town just north of Frankfurt on the Höhe river. On 5 May 1853 North's diary recorded that his wife was 'fussing, even more than ordinarily, over Kay [the Shuttleworths and Norths, having bestowed a new name on James Kay, often neglected to use it] and young Janet – the latter wants to go to Homburg, *without* her husband, but with all the children – alleging health . . . Kay says this must not be, and has kicked out the doctors', saying that he would take her himself. All Janet's female friends had taken her part, North noted, 'delighted to have scenes, and Interest'. Janet North had been 'urged to assist in the Plot, which seems a strange interference between husband and wife, and against which I strongly protest'. The most powerful person in the land had been brought into it, an amazed North reported: 'someone has actually put Ld John Russell up to writing Kay, he must not be far from him, as he (Ld John) will want him in England, politically.'[51]

North was as well informed as the Shuttleworths were well connected – the following day, 6 May, Russell asked Kay-Shuttleworth not to go to the continent because he wanted his advice on two Bills. North concluded, rightly, that Kay-Shuttleworth was delighted with the compliment and, wrongly, that he would remain in England. By 13 May North and Pop (Marianne North) had gone to Dover, only to find that the Kay-Shuttleworth cavalcade had left for France. They found them in Calais – James and Janet, the five children, Rosa Poplawska, some nurses and a new maid. Kay-Shuttleworth was surprised that the Norths had arrived, but declared himself free from care 'so long as I am with Janet and the children'. The same day he set off with the children for Lille, in a second-class carriage, North characteristically noted. Janet, Miss Poplawska and the new maid were to follow, he added, so that 'My Lady' would not be troubled about lodgings.[52]

By 30 May the entourage was established at Homburg and the Norths, now back at Hastings, received a 'flourishing account' from Kay-Shuttleworth of Janet's condition. He had agreed to return home, and she was glad to be left alone. 'Such is young Ladies pleasing themselves in Matrimony', North reflected. 'It rarely follows, to my observation, that Marriages made without the perfect approbation of Parents, turn out altogether happy!' It was another month before Kay-Shuttleworth returned to England, without wife or children, and with the story that the separation was caused by the needs of Janet's health. It was not a difficult story to maintain for a short time, and close friends of Hannah Kay referred frequently to 'your dear Brother's prolonged separation from his Family' as if it were simply a trial which tore asunder 'affectionate hearts ennobled by every sympathy that exalts human nature'. As the months went by Kay-Shuttleworth and the Norths exchanged information on Janet's health, he secured for the delighted Pop the use of the opera box of Angela Burdett-Coutts, the philanthropist, with whom he had become friendly and, assisted by Hannah, who moved unquestioningly to her brother's aid, he entertained the Norths at Gawthorpe. In November 1853, North acknowledged that Kay-Shuttleworth had handled the affairs of the estate skilfully and that Gawthorpe had been much improved by Barry – 'yet after all the outlay, they cannot, wife or husband, live at Gawthorpe – health will not allow'. Kay-Shuttleworth was to spend much time there, though Janet, North correctly concluded, 'with all her original passion for the locality now seems to have no taste for it'. He decided that it was because she had sunk from an heiress 'into being merely the Baronet's Lady'.[53] In truth, Janet did not want to be the Baronet's lady either. She never saw Gawthorpe fully restored.

Russell and Lansdowne had allowed Kay-Shuttleworth to slide out of the career which gave him self-respect and a sense of worth; now Janet was rejecting him, even more destructively. The rejection had been emphasized in October, a few weeks before the Norths' visit to Gawthorpe. Early that month Kay-Shuttleworth had returned to Homburg to persuade Janet to return to England. On 12 October a German doctor, whose signature is indecipherable, wrote from Frankfurt, where Janet had been going for treatment, apologizing for being absent during Kay-Shuttleworth's visit, and assuring him that 'in every respect' Lady Kay-Shuttleworth was '*somewhat* better'. 'It seems that just during the week you were at Homburg, she was from some cause or other not so well as she has been before and as I have found her again now after my return.' The neat coincidence in time left Kay-Shuttleworth with few doubts about what 'some cause or other' was.[54]

The doctor provided the first explicit discussion of Janet Kay-Shuttleworth's condition. Her malady was not due to any organic disease or destruction of part of the spine, but to 'an excessive debility of the whole nervous system' and a corresponding excitability. It was of the utmost importance, therefore, that she have a 'most quiet life, just as she finds at her present place of residence'. The Homburg waters and some tonics she was taking agreed with her, and the doctor accepted Kay-Shuttleworth's opinion that 'the nutrition of her muscles can only be bettered by exercise, and that she will get the power of her limbs again in the same degree only, that she is able to exercise them'. Implicitly extending Janet's stay for a year, the doctor was optimistic that next summer she would be better able to profit from the baths; and he agreed to consult with 'my friend Professor Chelius of Heidelberg' if any unexpected change occurred.

About this time, and within a period of a year, a shattered Kay-Shuttleworth had four epileptic attacks, each a frightening reminder of the black precipice down which he might plummet. He fought on with great bravery, living as normal a life as his illness would permit and hiding his sufferings from the world as determinedly as he hid Janet's intentions. Then, as winter turned to the spring of 1854, he had an accident, of which both nature and cause are unknown. Charlotte Brontë mentioned the 'frightful accident', which imperilled his life and sight, to her friend, Margaret Wooler. 'I am glad to say', she reported in November, 'that, after much suffering, he is better – indeed quite recovered – with the exception of the lost eye which can never be restored'. He was forced to use a glass eye for the rest of his life, but that indignity was preferable to the complete loss of vision which at first seemed likely. Elizabeth Gaskell remarked, passing on her daughter's advice to George Smith, the publisher: 'Marianne begs you will watch his left eye, & provide him with Savoy biscuits.' Kay-Shuttleworth wrote of it himself on 6 May 1854, exactly a year after Russell had produced his devious request for advice. He told his daughter in Homburg that he had walked for four miles around Kensington Gardens and the Serpentine, reflecting on the beauty of nature and on how sight was taken for granted:

> if it were always night without a moon or stars, or if you were blind which would be the same thing, the light which is like one of God's brightest Angels might cover you with its brightest glory, and you could only know it by trying to think of what you now see.[55]

Failing sight and blindness are symptoms of neurosyphilis and the lack of details about the accident may arouse a suspicion that Kay-Shuttleworth realized the cause of his failing sight and contrived an accident to hide it. This is, however, unlikely. With neurosyphilis both eyes would probably have been affected and his sight would have continued to deteriorate. As only one eye was harmed, and as he read and wrote easily for the rest of his life, an accident is the more likely explanation.

By July 1854, with the marks of this trauma still raw, racked with fear of epilepsy and humiliated by his wife's continuing absence, Kay-Shuttleworth, accompanied by Hannah, had returned to Germany. Janet, while improving, was far from recovered, though occasionally Kay-Shuttleworth sent optimistic reports to friends. She had come to Homburg no later than 14 May 1854 and whether or not he visited her earlier Kay-Shuttleworth and Hannah were in Homburg in early September. They stayed in separate houses, Janet being with Sir Alexander Duff Gordon and his wife, Lucie, who was an old and close friend. On Friday 22 September Ebenezer and Joseph Kay were told by Edward Marjoribanks that Alexander Duff Gordon had informed him that their brother had been arrested by the police at Homburg for 'some acts of violence'. The affair is shrouded in mystery and, though there was clearly a severe crisis in the Kay-Shuttleworths' relationship, the acts of violence (whatever they were) do not seem to have directly involved Janet. On 17 October, by which time he had returned to Gloucester Square, she wrote him a letter which began 'My dearest James, Your letter received this afternoon is a real relief to me for I was becoming very anxious to know how you had borne your journey. I am truly thankful that my hopes as to the benefit you might derive from Marienbad [which he visited to take the waters on his way back to England] have not proved false.' In a mildly inconsequential way the letter gave details of her health, of a visit of Janet and Ughtred to the dentist in Frankfurt, and other family matters. It was signed 'GOD bless and preserve you, Your most affectionate, Janet KS'. It is not the letter of a person who, a few weeks before, had been the victim of an act of violence.[56]

Yet a crisis of some kind certainly developed for on the night of Sunday, 24 September, two days after Marjoribanks had given his message to the Kay brothers, Kay-Shuttleworth wrote to Thomas Greene, a Conservative politician and Westmorland landowner who had been a close friend of Janet's since her childhood:

> Circumstances have occurred here deeply involving the happiness of my dear wife and myself.
> She has always regarded you as a father.
> I trust you know with what feelings of affection and confidence I have always leaned towards your counsels.
> It is our mutual wish that with the least possible delay you would travel hither.
> To endure this at whatever inconvenience to yourself I am sure it will be sufficient to know that the presence of a friend who has the happiness of both of us at heart as well as the well being of our children is necessary.
> Owing to a most unfortunate complication of circumstances which I will in no respect venture to characterize our intercourse has been interrupted for a week, and a most erroneous impression has been received by some of our relations in England.
> This has occurred without the slightest abatement of any demonstration of affection on my part to my wife, and I cannot believe that her attachment to me is diminished.
> But the counsels and mediation of a wise temperate and kind friend are become indispensably necessary to both of us.

On 30 September Greene telegraphed his intention of coming.[57]

For a man with Kay-Shuttleworth's insecure pride this was a desperate letter, though precisely what to make of it, in the absence of detailed records, is difficult. The simplest explanation relies on the knowledge that Janet had again refused to return to England. Kay-Shuttleworth was brought closer to despair because on about 20

September he had travelled from Homburg to Heidelberg to consult Dr Chelius, who later put his opinion in writing: not only should Janet stay and keep the children with her but, for her own sake and his, her husband should not see her until winter was over. Distraught and desperate, Kay-Shuttleworth returned to Homburg, devastated by the recommendations of a doctor whom he had probably expected to be sympathetic. The 'unfortunate complication of circumstances', which was presumably the arrest and the events that led to it, took place at this time, probably on 22 September, the day on which the news reached Edward Marjoribanks. Kay-Shuttleworth was in a condition in which a violent action could easily be triggered, though what the act was, and how long he remained under arrest, are not known. No formal charges seem to have been laid. Perhaps he was locked out of Janet's apartment and caused a commotion in the street, or he might have had an epileptic fit and become involved in a clash with the police who could have mistaken his condition for drunkenness or madness. The 'erroneous impression' which relatives had received casts more confusion over an already shadowy set of occurrences.

To make matters more complicated the Kay brothers were receiving conflicting signals. When he first heard the news Marjoribanks had consulted with the family solicitor, as neither Ebenezer nor Joseph was in London, and had dispatched an agent to secure Kay-Shuttleworth's release. That seems to have been speedily done. On Sunday, 24 September, Ebenezer received a letter from Hannah containing nothing but good news and saying that James was at Heidelberg and would return the next day. If this letter were written about 20 September, as it probably was, it would have been perfectly truthful, because Hannah in Homburg would not yet have known about Dr Chelius's recommendations. Understandably, however, the letter made Joseph and Ebenezer doubly anxious as they already knew of their brother's arrest. They were made still more anxious when on Monday, 25 September, the day after Kay-Shuttleworth had written to Greene, a telegraph message arrived from him summoning both Joseph and Ebenezer to Homburg. Joseph left the following morning and would have arrived in Homburg well before Greene, though after the agent Marjoribanks had dispatched. The same morning, 26 September, Ebenezer received another letter from Hannah, dated 22 September, and still containing no news. Ebenezer exploded with impatience, hoping that Hannah would consider 'to how much unnecessary anxiety this

most absurd silence is putting us all'. Again the most likely
explanation is that, though she might have known Dr Chelius's
recommendations by that time, she either did not yet know of the
events that led to the arrest on 22 September, or they took place
before she had written.

In any case, on a Tuesday, probably 26 September, Dr Chelius
came to Homburg and had a long interview with Janet. Previously, at
Heidelberg, he had spoken with Lady Duff Gordon. On 1 October
his formal verdict, written from Heidelberg, appeared. Because of
pronounced erithismus spinalis, Lady Kay-Shuttleworth 'was
attacked during the course of the last year by paralysis of the lower
extremities (loss of sensation and of the power of motion)'. Careful
treatment had led to an improvement and she could now walk with
slight support. There had also been a favourable change in her
general health which suggested that a complete recovery might be
expected. To obtain that object Dr Chelius considered it 'absolutely
necessary':

> 1. that Lady K.S. should remain at Homburg next winter, that all
> mental agitation should be avoided & that all directions concerning
> the course of treatment hitherto pursued be carefully followed.
> 2. That Sir James Kay Shuttleworth should live at a distance from
> Lady K.S. during this time, a separation which will have the most
> beneficial effect upon Sir James's own state of health.
> 3. That the children should remain with Lady K.S. as their removal
> from her would be highly injurious.
>   If these measures are followed Lady Kay Shuttleworth's
> complete recovery may be confidently expected after a repetition of
> the use of the mineral waters of Homburg next Spring. On the other
> hand nothing is more certain than that if these measures are not
> followed Lady K.S. will suffer a relapse into her sad condition.[58]

Kay-Shuttleworth conveyed this devastating verdict to Janet
North by reporting that Dr Chelius had recommended that Janet
should remain in Homburg in the confident expectation that her
health would be permanently restored, and that the children should
stay with her – 'I told him it was my desire that she should be
surrounded by her children'. He explained that he regarded himself
not simply as her husband but as 'the representative of an anxious
family' and indicated arguments he had unavailingly put to Dr
Chelius: 'we should all feel relieved by his taking the responsibility of
so grave a decision with a full knowledge of the climate and of its
effects upon her in the preceding winter'. Of the requirement that he

should live at a distance, he said nothing. Nor did he mention the arrest. What he said of this to Ebenezer, Joseph, Hannah or Tom, who might have understood, Marjoribanks or Thomas Greene remains unknown, and reference to it never again occurs in the Kay-Shuttleworth papers.[59]

If many details of this European nightmare are blurred, its impact on Kay-Shuttleworth is not hard to estimate. He had been arrested for violent acts and Janet had decisively rejected him. To the traumas which had preceded his visit to Homburg, worse had been added. He had embarrassed himself and the Kays and, if the Shuttleworths wanted ammunition to attack him, he had supplied it in plenty. In the black world in which he lived only one faint light blinked – Janet might recover, as Dr Chelius had prophesied, and return to England and to him.

That hope was dashed in May 1855 when Janet, in a letter which has not survived, indicated that she wished to continue to live on the Continent and to keep the children with her. 'If my conscience could accept the plan which you propose', he wrote to her on 23 May, 'it would simply break my heart and leave you a lasting remorse.' He continued:

> There is an absolute necessity that whatever plan of life I submit to should be consistent with our mutual affection, and with the duties which we owe to each other and to the children. It should be such as to mitigate the anguish of our present most afflicting positions, and in some degree to enable us to bring up our children in the reverence and love of their parents.

He asked what further proof it was possible for him to give of his tenderness for her. 'Though my isolation, and my anxiety about you and the children have been in these two years the source of extreme suffering and critical illness, I have never uttered one reproach to you, nor one complaint to any human ear.' However, he had decided that he owed her 'the counsels of a faithful husband'. He could not take any step 'which implies my acquiescence in our continuing to live apart', for he and Janet would become the victims of 'evil tongues' and their children 'would receive this misfortune as their heritage', and suffer in their moral training and in their entrance on life from the example of their parents' separation.

'Return therefore to England, dear wife, on a different understanding', he continued. Her health might involve them living separately for another year, but he proposed a means by which, while still separated, he could have a part in the upbringing of their children. 'I have an absolute need of domestic sympathy. I could not survive, with the sense of duties to our children unperformed, in the dreary isolation in which I have spent the last two years.' Nor could he believe that his wife would want their children to be deprived of their father. 'First, as to the boys', he continued, striking a revealing note. The two oldest ought, as Janet agreed, to be prepared for a Public School and, except when they were with her, they should be with a tutor at Gawthorpe or elsewhere with him. In this way they would become acquainted with the tenants and neighbours, strengthen local attachments and prepare themselves for future duties on the estate. He had prepared a playground and boys' amusements, they would have ponies and he had brush gates to hang on the fences. They would visit Janet twice a year for six weeks each time.

For the two younger boys and for Janet, whom her mother wanted to stay with her, the reverse would apply – they would see their father twice a year for periods of six weeks and live with their mother the rest of the time. So the demands of the estate and the expectations of society for young boys and girls were reinforced in ways which neither parent, however much they differed, thought strange. 'I seek to reconcile my affection for you with this sense of duty to our children', Kay-Shuttleworth continued, praying that God would bring Janet 'to a full understanding of the feelings with which I write, and to spare us both the further misery in which a disagreement on this subject would involve us'.[60] In one of those contradictions with which his life was full he had achieved a self-detachment which, given his fragile personality and his anguished circumstances, was quite unexpected.

His realization of his rights, as the law then stood, is revealed in a letter which he wrote to Thomas Greene, the day before he wrote to Janet. He described the letter he had received from Janet as being 'most painful to me, from the absence of any consideration for me or for my happiness, in the proposals which she made'. He thought that she wished to deprive him of 'the society of all their children'. He hoped that Greene would think his reply (he provided a copy of the letter he intended to send Janet) consistent with 'the patient forbearance' he had shown through her illness, but feared that Janet thought that 'my affection will constrain me to sacrifice even my duty to our children to my love for her'. He was 'fully aware that my right to the custody and care of all my children is absolutely indisputable' and he was inflexibly determined not to give up any portion of that right.[61]

He won a Pyrrhic victory. Janet returned to England in July 1855, after Frederick North had offered her Rougham as a home. She was gratified but seems to have lived for some of the time at a friend's home in Wimpole Street. North thought she was 'without the least apparent feeling' and noted that she scolded the children perpetually. He painted a sad, jaundiced, picture of them: Puss was 'priggish and dwarfed', Ughtred, 'intelligent and amiable looking, but sadly cowed', Robin, unhealthy but 'clear and sharp, with much appearance of good humour', Lionel, 'a poor creature' who seemed mentally retarded, and Stewart 'by far the best of the lot'. Janet, he noted, 'never mentions Kay's name – to me and Pop, at any rate'. By October 1855 North acknowledged that the separation was complete.[62] For the next five or six years Janet lived in Eastbourne, while still spending substantial periods of time on the Continent. Her husband's proposals for the children were basically accepted, but if Sir James Kay-Shuttleworth came to his wife's house in Eastbourne, it was as a visitor.

What drove them apart? There are two family answers. The first remained the official explanation until (and indeed after) Janet's death, though it could have had little credence among the family and close friends: Janet was forced to live on the Continent for health reasons and James could not join her because of the demands of the estate which he managed faithfully for her and their children. The second answer is more convincing because it acknowledges the reality of the separation. In 1923 Ughtred gave the authoritative version:

> The distressing ailments of both my parents, coupled with my mother's promotion of a Prussian Pole, who was governess to my sister and myself, to be her inseparable companion, caused a lamentable estrangement from my father. This came in spite of their perfectly happy life together for more than ten years, and of the truth and faithfulness of the tie that bound them to each other. The separation of their lives, notwithstanding all the efforts that were made by my father, and by his and her best friends, was rendered permanent by the almost hypnotic influence that this woman gradually came to exercise. She seemed to me to cherish, besides a love of power, a hatred of my father and a determination to keep my mother at a distance from him.

The move to Germany, where Rosa Poplawska would feel at home, gave physical expression to the hatred and the love of power she was said to feel. The intense little governess, who attracted Charlotte Brontë and Elizabeth Gaskell, occupies a crucial place in the Kay-Shuttleworth family history.[63]

Ughtred was 79 when he offered this explanation, but it cannot be dismissed as the rationalization of an old man who was deeply loyal to his father's memory. Admittedly, making the governess the reason for the separation diminished blame which might otherwise be attached to his mother and/or father: an outsider was the cause, and family honour was in a sense preserved. But his assessment of Rosa Poplawska's influence was not a construction of his old age; it was also made when he was a child and young man, as his later letters to his father show. Furthermore, the same explanation was made by friends. The trusted Thomas Greene, writing to Kay-Shuttleworth in 1855, remarked: 'That poor Janet is labouring under some strange delusions stimulated by a designing woman I have no doubt at all, and I live in hopes that it may please God to open her eyes to the real state of things and dispel the mist of delusion which now blinds her.' Two years later, David Robertson, Janet's cousin, represented the view of at least one of the Marjoribanks, by informing Kay-Shuttleworth that time was widening the gap between him and his wife, 'as third parties' had come between them and exerted an influence which was 'fearful for ill, and never for good'. As telling, for its brevity, was Frederick North's comment when Janet returned from the continent in July 1855. Observing her he noticed another observer, Miss Poplawska, who watched Janet 'as a Cat a mouse'. He was relieved when Janet did not visit Rougham that year because he did not wish to meet the governess 'who must be largely responsible in respect of the now absolute separation between Kay and his wife'.[64]

There was undoubtedly a strong bond between Rosa Poplawska and Janet Kay-Shuttleworth, as Janet made abundantly clear when she was preparing for death. The twentieth-century mind moves easily, too easily, from an intense friendship between two women to a lesbian relationship. It would be wise to avoid such preconceptions: in Victorian England women commonly lived together without more than close friendship or convenience being assumed. Janet's religious faith was so deep-seated and puritanical that probably it would have been a barrier to lesbianism. Moreover, the agreement over the custody of the children ensured that a daughter remained with her, and having her daughter as a lifetime companion was an inconvenient arrangement if a lesbian relationship was contemplated.

There was much beyond the ties of friendship to bind Janet to Rosa Poplawska. Her decision to separate from Kay-Shuttleworth shocked her family as much as had her decision to marry him, especially as Janet North was very ill. Preoccupied with her daughter's marital affairs – Frederick described her as 'coughing and harping on the Kay-Shuttleworths' – she died on 17 January 1855. Five days later the grief-stricken North buried her, 'in cold snow, at the little Walton churchyard – All gone'. Janet did not attend the funeral and when she returned from Homburg in July North gave her her mother's diamonds. 'She made not a remark', he noted bitterly, 'except that they were all right.'[65] As far as he was concerned, her leaving Kay-Shuttleworth was simply the latest act in a life in which her preoccupation with her own affairs prevented consideration for her mother's wishes. The burden of such a judgement, which Janet could have been in little doubt about, was heavy. In any case her relations, and not only the male ones, held expectations for women of her class and religious convictions which made leaving a husband, whatever the cause, extremely unconventional and scandalous: it offended religion, good form and family honour. And not just family honour, but the very existence of the family itself. In mid-1853 when Janet first moved to Homburg the Kay-Shuttleworths' second youngest child, Lionel, was four years old and the youngest, Stewart, was less than two. To have taken the children from her husband when they were so young, even if she were driven by desperation or loathing, was an act of great bravery and independence. Janet Kay-Shuttleworth had exiled herself in a moral desert, and in her loneliness Rosa Poplawska's support offered solace and reassurance. Together they faced a world which repudiated and misunderstood them.

Yet, when this has been said, how could Janet, to whom her God and Gawthorpe were so important, have taken a decision which flew in the face of her religious beliefs and cut her off from her ancestral home? Epilepsy provides one reason. In June 1856, writing the letter (which has already been mentioned) to an unnamed doctor in Eastbourne, who was treating Janet and the children, Kay-Shuttleworth explicitly discusses his epilepsy, admitting to eight attacks and claiming that they were chiefly induced by 'anything which disturbs seriously the emotions'. The issue had arisen earlier, however. In April 1854 and again in April and May 1855 Lionel had had attacks of epilepsy. German physicians had told Janet that Kay-Shuttleworth's own attacks had an hereditary origin, and the children's nurse had been instructed to watch for them, and with some 'perversity' had 'confirmed Lady Shuttleworth's impressions'. And Lady Kay-Shuttleworth had passed those impressions on to her husband for in late 1854 and early 1855, desperate to influence his wife's views, he embarked on a private analysis of his family's past health. Mostly through an agent (probably his brother Robert who was now living near Rochdale) he probed the health and lifestyles of grandparents, his father, mother, uncles and aunts. Manufacturers and merchants, cotton spinners and weavers, former employees of the Kays, friends such as Thomas Jackson, family doctors, Rachel Kay (Robert's wife), relatives of Hannah Kay's family, and others, were interviewed. The conclusion of these interviews was that, whatever physical, mental or moral characteristics the Kays and the Phillipses had, they were not subject to fits or falling sickness. The only exception admitted was Hannah's unfortunate brother, who had once written to Kay-Shuttleworth from a debtor's prison. He had had fits, but as his character was so depraved by his 'sottish habits' they could be ignored, especially as his mind was never deranged.[66]

There was, however, the suggestion of a more important exception. A cousin of Kay-Shuttleworth's mother reported that she had heard that in the last months of what had been a very healthy life Hannah had suffered 'a slight convulsion such as occurs to aged people in the last stage of life'. The slight tremor this remark may have caused might have passed more swiftly if Hannah's death certificate had not stated unequivocally that the cause of her death was epilepsy. Kay-Shuttleworth, who must have known this diagnosis, ignored it and protested to Janet, as he later did to the Eastbourne doctor, that there was no hereditary tendency to epilepsy in his family.

Janet did not believe him. Whether or not she knew about his mother, she knew that he had epilepsy, and she shared the contemporary horror and some of the superstitions which surrounded it – she believed, for example, that the fits were likely to return on the same day in successive years. 'You may know what illusions', Kay-Shuttleworth wrote to the Eastbourne doctor, 'what false injurious and exaggerated apprehensions are in the mind of my dear wife', and, he added with Rosa Poplawska in mind, 'perhaps some of those about her'. Whatever her misapprehensions, Janet had no illusions about one matter – her husband suffered from epilepsy which could be passed on to their children. In early 1855, when Kay-Shuttleworth gave her the results of his family survey, she was 38 years old and could expect to have more children – the five previous children had been born in under ten years. Lionel's fits, the first of which had occurred when he was five (that is, in 1854), underlined the nightmare in which she was trapped: while she and her husband lived together she faced the prospect of bringing more tainted children into the world and passing on to future generations the insidious ghost that haunted hers. Did she have any sense that a more insidious and morally repugnant ghost had caused her husband's illness? Though the slightest suspicion of syphilis would explain the separation, the evidence suggests that neither Janet nor her husband had any.

Most likely the fear of epilepsy helped to drive Janet to the conclusion that separation was for her husband's good as well as her own. Lacking other means, she used the fear as a form of birth control, in which case Dr Chelius's instruction that Sir James Kay-Shuttleworth should live at a distance from Lady Shuttleworth had a physical as well as a psychological justification. For Janet separation could appear as a sacrifice ordained by God, a selfless act which ensured the purity of future generations; for her husband, it was devastating.

God, and the same physical necessity, could also be invoked for her severe invalidism. God's trials, like 'the trial of stillness' of 1852, could not always be understood but they had to be accepted as manifestations of his will. This trial made sexual intercourse impossible, especially when the invalidism was as extreme as Janet's. For her, as for many Victorian women, the sofa was a haven where she was protected from sexual demands, and being an invalid in Homburg made the protection more secure. Only one of their five children, Stewart, was conceived after the fateful day in December 1848 when Kay-Shuttleworth collapsed in the Council Office. He was born in November 1851. Some seven months later Janet's illnesses, which had often had her living apart from her husband as she sought cures, confined her to the sofa from which she could move only with the utmost difficulty.

Kay-Shuttleworth's personality made Janet's acceptance of God's will and the protection of future generations easier. Ill and depressed, haunted by his expulsion from public life yet unable to cope with its demands, the tortured being Janet described to Alison could not have been easy to live with. She had expected their marriage to be a partnership in which she assisted her husband to reform the villagers of Padiham and the country at large. Spurred by love of his wife, North saw Janet as cold and selfish – she parted with her children, he once remarked, 'as easily as if they were a couple of Rabbits'. He was overcritical, but even a little of the emotional coolness and self-centredness which he saw in Janet would have made her decision to separate easier. Her romantic views of human nature did not prepare her for the dreary complexities of administration, the bitterness of political debate, or the opposition of the Church. Still less did they prepare her for the effects of these conflicts on her husband whose shrieks at night awoke the servants, and for whom no achievement brought peace and all opposition engendered vexation of spirit. Kay-Shuttleworth's was not a personality which soothed and charmed, and while Janet could manage affection when they were apart, there were times, North reported, when she could not stand his company.[67]

Ironically the sceptical Frederick North helped to make the huge step of separation possible. Compared with the annual income of her estate, the £1,000 per annum guaranteed Janet by the marriage contract which he had negotiated was not large, and by the late 1850s Kay-Shuttleworth guaranteed her £2,500 per annum. Given the marriage customs of the time this was, and was recognized as, a generous settlement.[68] But that came later; the immediately available £1,000 made her independent life possible. It does not in any way diminish her courage or the anguish she suffered to say that money provided Janet Kay-Shuttleworth with a refuge which was denied to poorer women.

On 29 June 1854, as the Kay-Shuttleworths' marriage disintegrated, Charlotte Brontë married Arthur Bell Nicholls whose middle name had provided the Brontë sisters with their pseudonymous surname. He returned to the curacy at Haworth, which he had left when Charlotte refused an earlier proposal, and in November Kay-Shuttleworth offered him a better living, Habergham near Padiham. The parish church at Habergham, All Saints', was built in 1847 with the Kay-Shuttleworths providing the land and £1,300, and the Dugdales, the principal employers in the area, contributing £3,000. Kay-Shuttleworth seems to have considered that the living was in his hands, although strictly speaking it was in the gift of the Crown. The incumbent of All Saints', the radical, eccentric and financially irresponsible Edward Arundel Verity, warred incessantly with Kay-Shuttleworth and the Dugdales, and in November 1854 he was in embarrassing financial difficulties which Kay-Shuttleworth assumed (or hoped) would force him to leave the parish. Moreover, he was planning to sail to Patagonia as a missionary. The following year he left the parish, his pregnant wife and his debts to serve as a chaplain in the Crimea but he returned to dog Kay-Shuttleworth for decades.[69]

Kay Shuttleworth offered the curacy when he visited Haworth between 12 and 14 November 1854. Though seeing advantages in it, Nicholls declined because, as Charlotte said, 'during Papa's life, he is bound to Haworth'. Kay-Shuttleworth pressed the offer, again unsuccessfully, in January 1855 when the Nichollses paid a brief visit to Gawthorpe. More than the living was discussed on this visit, for Kay-Shuttleworth read them part of a novel he had begun, in which a young physician was a major figure. It must have been an eerie scene in Gawthorpe Hall as the would-be-novelist paraded his words before Charlotte Brontë who was pregnant and ill, more desperately than anyone in the room realized. While at Gawthorpe she aggravated a chill by taking a long walk in thin shoes over damp ground. Perpetually nauseous, she grew steadily weaker and died at Haworth on 31 March, probably of hyperemesis gravidarum, pernicious morning sickness in pregnancy. Elizabeth Gaskell wrote chillingly that, at the news of her death, the hearts of Haworth's villagers shivered within them as they thought of Charlotte's father and husband, who had fought over her while she was alive, 'sitting desolate and alone in the old grey house'.[70]

In July 1855, less than three months after his daughter's death, Patrick Brontë asked Elizabeth Gaskell to write a brief account of Charlotte's life and works. He hoped to forestall attempts by some less qualified writer to produce a biography and to correct articles and 'tracts' written about his daughter which he thought contained untruthful statements. A year later, having accepted the invitation, Elizabeth Gaskell confided to the faithful Ellen Nussey her doubts about getting access to material held at Haworth, including the manuscript of Charlotte's unpublished first novel, 'The Professor', some letters, and the beginning of the new story. She knew that, despite Patrick Brontë's protestations to the contrary, Nicholls had not been anxious to have a life written. She also suspected that he would be particularly uncooperative in releasing the material she most wanted. 'The Professor' was based on the time Charlotte had spent in Brussels where she had fallen in love with Constantin Heger, the husband of the owner of the school at which she had been a student and later a teacher. Her love was unrequited as his letters made clear, but getting access to these letters and the novel was an awkward problem. James Kay-Shuttleworth solved it.[71]

In February 1855, as Charlotte Brontë's death grew closer, Elizabeth Gaskell wrote to Janet about causes in which they were both interested, and she knew, soon after Janet's return to England in July

1855, that Janet was staying in London with friends. Her relationship with James Kay-Shuttleworth was less cordial. When she was invited to Gawthorpe in the same month, she told her daughter not to mention the invitation to anyone, and may not have accepted it. On 24 July 1856, however, she and Kay-Shuttleworth left Gawthorpe to pay a most important visit to Haworth. She had told him of her problem and he acted decisively. Both Mr Brontë and Mr Nicholls looked up to him, and he was 'not prevented by the fear of giving pain from asking in a peremptory manner for whatever he thinks desirable'. He was 'extremely kind in forwarding all my objects', she continued, 'and coolly took actual possession of many things while Mr Nicholls was saying he could not possibly part with them'. She came away with the manuscript of 'The Professor', the beginning of the new novel, 'Emma', and a collection of Charlotte's extraordinary juvenilia. Although her daughter reported that 'Mama has come back in very good spirits', she admitted that she did not feel easy in 'absolutely wresting things from him [Nicholls] by mere force of words'. However, she solved her moral dilemma easily: she continued to criticize the way in which Kay-Shuttleworth had obtained the material, then used it in her book. A self-righteous biographer needs to develop a slippery conscience.[72]

'The Professor' presented the ill-matched pair with a problem: what should they do with it? Kay-Shuttleworth was certain that it would add to Charlotte Brontë's fame and should be published, whatever the consequences. 'He over-rides all wishes, feelings, and delicacy', Elizabeth Gaskell told George Smith, the publisher. Though she thought the manuscript inferior to Charlotte's published work, she recognized that it was touched with her 'genius', would have an immense sale, and was interesting as an example of early promise which was afterwards realized. She also admitted that, as a reader of the life she hoped to write, she would feel her knowledge of Charlotte incomplete without access to 'The Professor'. But she dreaded its relation to Heger and his wife who were still alive. After reading the novel she found that it did not relate closely to the Hegers. On that ground, therefore, there could be no objection to publishing, but she insisted that Nicholls, not Kay-Shuttleworth, should decide whether or not to publish it.[73]

There was another difficulty. Kay-Shuttleworth praised the manuscript highly, but thought that there were 'certain coarse & objectionable phrases'. He offered to edit it and to 'expunge & make the necessary alterations'. Elizabeth Gaskell also thought that there was coarseness in the work and was willing to cut it out – 'For I would not, if I could help it, have another syllable that could be called coarse to be associated with her name.' However, she disagreed with Kay-Shuttleworth over the changes to be made and was 'sure from numerous passages in her private letters' that Charlotte would not have wished Sir James to edit her book. In the end Kay-Shuttleworth accepted that Nicholls should make the cuts, which he did – not severely enough, in Elizabeth Gaskell's opinion.[74]

So ended Kay-Shuttleworth's part in the Charlotte Brontë story. She had achieved the literary fame which, as young men in Edinburgh, he and John Addington Symonds had craved and towards which, with his public life curtailed, he turned again. Elizabeth Gaskell correctly judged that Charlotte Brontë would not have wanted him to edit her novel, yet both women were in his debt: without his imperious intervention, *The Professor* might not have featured in the Gaskell biography or the list of Brontë novels.

On 5 April 1860 Elizabeth Gaskell warned George Smith against 'Sir J.P.K. Shuttleworth' who, she said maliciously, had particular reasons for seeking Smith's company – 'he has generally a double set of motives for all his actions'. He had written a novel which he had partly read to Mrs Nicholls the last time she was at Gawthorpe and partly to her. It was his first literary endeavour since the poetry he had given to Janet to mark their wedding and a draft novel or story which has not survived but which he had shown to June Kennedy when he lived in Manchester. The warning came too late: Smith, Elder and Co. seem already to have accepted the novel for they published *Scarsdale* on 15 June. Vanity and a fear of criticism led to its anonymous publication. Kay-Shuttleworth even sought reviews anonymously: 'Tell me', he asked a contact at *Blackwood's Magazine*, 'whether any channels of literary criticism on a work of fiction written by a person in whom I am much interested, are open to you?'[75]

Elizabeth Gaskell gave the first recorded assessment of Kay-Shuttleworth's novel. He was a clever and painstaking man, she told Smith, and 'has really laboured hard to make this novel a good picture of country Lancashire society'. As the novel's subtitle suggests, Kay-Shuttleworth wanted to describe 'Life on the Lancashire and Yorkshire border, thirty years ago'. In this setting, which he knew intimately, he wrote of matters which had long been of concern to him: distressed and uninstructed weavers, manufacturers, civil unrest and riot, unions and secret societies, reforms in education and sanitation, the relationship of the aristocracy to the middle classes and, an increasing preoccupation, the relationship between the lord of the manor and his tenants. Even by the liberal standards of the Victorian three-volume novel, *Scarsdale*'s structure was loose and its plot diffuse. Kay-Shuttleworth had no compunction about stopping his narrative to hold stagey discussions on topics which he thought might improve his readers. One of *Scarsdale*'s heroes, Oliver Holte, who is an idealized version of James Kay (at the end of the book he goes to Manchester to work as a physician among the poor), travels widely in Europe, retracing the author's footsteps and discussing religion, politics and education with the real de Fellenberg and the imaginary Malvoisin, a character who owes something to de Tocqueville. Kay-Shuttleworth claims that these scenes will avoid the need for later digressions, but by the time the conversations are finished they have almost entirely dissolved the narrative interest.[76]

The characters in *Scarsdale* are stock types: criminals, agitators and poachers, weavers and farmers, benevolent landlords, a French aristocratic roué, a semi-Byronic aristocratic hero who is an irresponsible landlord made responsible by love, yet another dissipated aristocrat also redeemed by love, enlightened manufacturers, and a number of young women who are given different social stations but who are all lifeless and virtuous. The large cast never threatens to become interesting, as the author fussily drives them through his plot, managing their affairs and manipulating their fates, but not bringing them to life. Perhaps only once, in the character of Barnabas Collier, who is based on Kay-Shuttleworth's childhood friend, the crippled Sunday-school teacher, Thomas Jackson, does a reader feel that one of his characters might come to possess the author's mind. But the feeling does not survive for long, and other characters drawn from real-life models, for example Oliver Holte and Deloisir (who is based on the Mancunian autodidact, Roland Detrosier), are quite unconvincing.

Yet the novel is not without interest. Echoes of his rejection by Helen Kennedy (made louder because of Janet's rejection) sound throughout the novel. Oliver seems likely to marry well, having twice rescued one of the well-born heroines from danger and used his physician's skill to cure her illness. But he does not, and when he goes to Manchester to look after the poor, he goes alone. *Scarsdale* also reveals something of Kay-Shuttleworth's attitude to women. In a description of a young cottager there is, amidst the cliché, a hint of sexual feeling:

The glow of health in her round cheek; the swell of her full bosom, charged though it was with sighs; the perfect contour of her neck, down which fell two long, rich black tresses – an unusual and rather coquettish ornament in this district – showed, at least, that the recent grief, keen though its fang had been, had not poisoned her life.

But such mild outbreaks are rare. For the most part Kay-Shuttleworth's heroines are remote beings, morally superior to men, gentle, angelic, dignified, and without sexual feeling. A typical description of 'a beautiful woman, with calm and beaming eyes' stresses that her natural grace and beauty had been 'dignified by mental culture' and that her purity was 'not so much a sensitive shrinking from evil, as a sense of the ever-present help of God to the prayer of faith'. Such sentiments convey the same attitudes as those of the young man in his Edinburgh anatomy class shocked by the ribald jokes made over the naked body of a dead woman. Yet, over the intervening years, the sexual feelings to which he was not able to give expression in his novel had helped to drive his wife away from him, and may have led him to acquire syphilis.[77]

Scarsdale also has some value in giving an understanding of the region in which it was set. Kay-Shuttleworth was not an evocative writer and his many set-piece descriptions do not bring the region and its inhabitants to life. But he accurately described the district's topography, climate and scenery, and the customs, work and economic and social conditions of the 'borderers'. His acquaintance, William Rathbone Greg, who was critical of the novel, thought that Kay-Shuttleworth's delineation of 'the character and conversation of the natives' ('I mean', he speedily corrected himself, 'the lower classes of the district') was just, vivid and original. Greg also praised Kay-Shuttleworth's ear for the local dialect – he thought it had been captured perfectly, though there was too much of it and it slowed up the reading. Despite the opinion of Robert Lee Wolff, who in 1971 described *Scarsdale* as 'a remarkably subtle work of delicate social shadings', literary critics can safely pass it by, but linguists and regional historians will find value in its pages.[78]

The book did not cause a stir in literary circles or in the great quarterlies, but the *Norwich Post and Suffolk Herald* declared that it was 'one of the most remarkable novels of the century'. Most reviews were more guarded and judicious, and though they were fairly favourable, there was no rush to discover the identity of *Scarsdale*'s author. Thomas Hughes, who had published *Tom Brown's School Days* three years earlier, was sent a copy of *Scarsdale* and promised to keep the secret of its author's identity 'religiously'. Ebenezer Kay risked his elder brother's wrath by giving the brave advice that Kay-Shuttleworth should do the same thing: 'I should treat the publication as an amusement and should not acknowledge it.' Though Kay-Shuttleworth could pick among the reviews to find favourable comments, *Scarsdale*'s reception was disappointing.[79]

By 1860 Kay-Shuttleworth's life had fallen into a pattern which brought some predictability and a sense of purpose. Though no longer at the centre of the educational world, he remained important in it and kept in touch with what was happening. He corresponded with Russell, J.M. Lee, then Bishop of Manchester, Angela Burdett-Coutts and others on educational matters, and the hope that he might return to public life never fully left him. In 1857 Henry Moseley, whom he had appointed to the inspectorate and with whom he maintained a friendship, fed this hope with the comment that if his health recovered there was 'a great work reserved yet for you to do in Education'. Kay-Shuttleworth had expressed the same hope two years earlier when he told his children of his wish that God might enable him to resume 'the one great purpose of my life, viz to strive to make the condition of the workmen of England better and happier'. God did not co-operate and the next year Kay-Shuttleworth approached the Leveson-Gowers, asking the second Earl Granville, the son of Harriet Leveson-Gower who had introduced him to the grandeur of Stafford House, if there were any unpaid commissions he might perform for the public good. None emerged, nor did they emerge in 1859 when Kay-Shuttleworth again approached Granville and offered his services as an unpaid commissioner of charitable endowments.[80]

Family affairs were one preoccupation. Hannah now lived with him most of the time, bringing him the devotion she had previously given her mother. She ran his domestic affairs as a substitute wife, though day-to-day activities were controlled through servants, particularly James Lennard, a butler-valet, who had once worked at the Privy Council but who from the early 1850s was personally employed by Kay-Shuttleworth. Ebenezer and Joseph Kay were well established in their careers, and Robert's calico business continued, though it still had its difficult moments. In February 1858 he had enough money to contribute £50 (Kay-Shuttleworth contributed £100) towards helping the erring Tom and his unfortunate family, but he was still paying off loans advanced him by Hannah and Kay-Shuttleworth.[81]

Tom was the main problem. His irresponsibility and heavy drinking drove his brothers to a time-honoured solution – a spell in the colonies – in the hope that he would there find the discipline which had eluded him at home. With Kay-Shuttleworth's assistance Tom was dispatched to the south island of New Zealand (he arrived on 15 July 1859) where with a partner he established a timber business at Pigeon Bay, not far south of Christchurch. At least three of his children remained in England and were cared for by Joseph Kay and his wife May. Kay-Shuttleworth and Ebenezer continued their support when the business venture proved disastrous: Ebenezer paid some of Tom's debts, and in 1862 Kay-Shuttleworth is recorded as the owner of 202 acres in Pigeon Bay, land he probably had to repurchase after it had been forfeited by Thomas and his partner. Tom Kay named the cottage he built at Pigeon Bay 'Brookshaw', thus recalling the place from which his father had run his woollen manufacturing business. In anguish his thoughts had turned homewards, but the greater tragedy had befallen his wife Alice. With her family divided but still increasing (she had at least five more children in New Zealand), she struggled in a strange land against poverty and her husband's financial incompetence and drinking.[82]

Kay-Shuttleworth's prime preoccupation was with Janet and their children. Constantly attended by Rosa Poplawska, Janet remained an invalid, walking only short distances, and often being confined to bed for long periods. When she was in England Kay-Shuttleworth may have visited Eastbourne, perhaps at times such as Christmas, but he and Janet mostly communicated by letter. The children were educated by private tutors, though as the 1850s ended Kay-Shuttleworth and, to a lesser extent, Janet, began more deliberately to prepare their eldest son for public life and the administration of the family estate.

Ughtred was in his early teens. His sense of family history was deepened when his father took him to Rochdale where Robert Kay's business was then situated. Accompanied by his father and Joseph Kay, Ughtred inspected his uncle's calico works and slept at Rochdale 'where Papa was born'. They also visited Bamford and called at Thomas Jackson's cottage, met his wife and children, and saw him make a pair of shoes and play the violin. He was Papa's 'oldest living friend', Ughtred informed his mother. On another occasion they watched Joseph Kay examining witnesses at a court in Lancaster. Janet wrote to Ughtred about the part of the family estate at nearby Barbon, where in the past she had been warmly welcomed and called the Lady of the Manor. She asked him to love the warm-hearted country people as she did and to send her greetings to them. He attended audit dinners at Gawthorpe with his father, or studied plans of large enclosures which were to be planted with a great wood, of fields to be drained, streams to be dammed and ponds stocked with fish. He went to agricultural meetings and down a mine pit, he helped the gardeners to dig, rode a great deal, went fox-hunting on frosty mornings, and in the Long Gallery he romped, practised cricket and (perhaps because of these activities) watched plasterers at work. He played in a 'grand' cricket match in which the nine of Gawthorpe played an eleven from the schools at Habergham. 'The Coachman and I bowled and afterwards Lennard and I', Ughtred reported to his mother, having to admit a lack of success with the bat despite the Gawthorpe team's victory. On another occasion he and his father breakfasted at the Dugdales and as they rode home Ughtred heard someone say, 'Em's the Shuttleworths'.[83]

These experiences, through which he learned his role and the importance of his family in the locality, brought Ughtred some joy and excitement. But his happiness was always tempered by the brooding presence of Rosa Poplawska, a symbol for him of the separation of his father and mother. Mamma seemed better, though she had occasional pain in her side, he wrote to his father from Eastbourne in April 1860: 'Janet [his sister] is very affectionate and kind and Miss Poplawska keeps out of the way.' She did not always keep out of the way. Two years earlier, he reported that unfortunately his mother was speaking of going to Germany again. 'Miss Poplawska is talking to everybody about the pressing necessity of it, and I do not know what to say, I cannot think that going amongst all those Germans again can do her much good.' Whether it did or not, Janet went.[84]

In London his father kept Ughtred in touch with the Marjoribanks by dining with various members of the family including David Robertson and Frederick North. He took Ughtred to lectures on chemistry given by Michael Faraday and he bought him scientific equipment. They attended meetings of the newly formed Social Science Association in which Kay-Shuttleworth was taking a close interest, visited the South Kensington museum, the Crystal Palace, the Hanwell School for Pauper Boys, the British Museum, Madame Tussaud's, saw pantomimes in Rotten Row and accompanied by the younger Janet went to the Royal Academy.[85]

At Gawthorpe Ughtred had a practical example of political action when his father mediated in a strike of colliers in some of the local mills. Six men, 'all of them very young and no doubt not very wise', the fifteen-year-old Ughtred wrote to his mother in March 1860, had been dismissed because they had acted as delegates for a newly formed union. Their dismissal, added to grievances over conditions, had caused a strike. After various negotiations, culminating in a discussion with all the men in the dining room (watched by Ughtred from a hiding-place in the minstrels' gallery), Kay-Shuttleworth drew up a statement of grievances acceptable to the men, advised them to discontinue their union, and sent the statement to the owner of the pits involved. He agreed to readmit the delegates, to attend to the grievances and to ignore the union even though he too disapproved of its existence. The strike was called off, the men affirming, according to Ughtred, 'that if Papa will mediate for them there will never be any strikes'.[86]

Meanwhile Kay-Shuttleworth was establishing a base for Ughtred's political career. He invited to Gawthorpe writers such as Charlotte Brontë, Harriet Martineau and Elizabeth Gaskell, old friends from his Manchester days such as the Gregs and the banker William Langton, and politicians and members of the gentry, both local and more distant. When he was an old man, Ughtred could remember meeting in his youth people such as Bishop Lee of Manchester, Lord Shaftesbury, and Angela Burdett-Coutts. His memory was not playing him tricks, as his letters to his mother in the second half of the 1850s contain numerous references to the rich and powerful people who visited Gawthorpe. In a time-honoured manner James Kay-Shuttleworth used his country estate and its large house to provide a setting in which his eldest son could make the social contacts upon which a political career could be built. Where he had been weak, Ughtred would be strong.[87]

The pressure of his father's expectation on the young Ughtred was increased by the intensity of his mother's religious convictions. On the occasion of his twelfth birthday she wrote him a long and passionate letter. 'I must write to wish you a very happy birthday, and every blessing in this new year of your life which GOD in His infinite wisdom sees good for you.' She continued:

> My dear Boy, 12 years old is an age when the seriousness and importance of religion *may* be felt and understood. You are no longer a *little* boy – Many boys at this age earn not only their own bread but bread for others, many enter upon important duties . . . But there is a reason far more striking than any general one can be why 12 years old is a most important time in the religious life – And when Jesus was twelve years old they went up to Jerusalem after the custom of the Feast.

Janet wrote with fervour of what 'the Lord Jesus' had done in the Temple and concluded that he had gone to the Temple in order 'to show other children that 12 is the age for forsaking the ways of infancy and embracing the Christian cause – Jesus submitted to His parents – and so must every child long after twelve years of age'. (It would have been interesting to hear Frederick North's opinion of this statement.) She concluded her letter with a comment on her health: 'I cannot leave my room or couch, but there is provision for the sick in the ordinances of GOD's Grace, and the sick room is often the abode of the greatest peace and spiritual joy – even where sufferings abound'.[88]

Ughtred wrote a dutiful reply: 'I will strive to be truthful and also to be more thoughtful as I grow older. . . . And as I am growing older I will try to set my brothers and sister a better example of all goodness and kindness, as I pray every evening, than I have done yet. I see how important the age of twelve is.'[89] Ughtred was to fulfil many of his father's hopes and to live a life of honour and serious rectitude which might have satisfied his mother. But he was remote and slightly priggish, a man of diligence and industry rather than imagination or flair. It is easy to understand why; and it is hard not to feel a pang of compassion for a twelve-year-old who had come to realize how important the age of twelve was.

His schooling was of the greatest importance for both his parents who agreed that he should go to Harrow. 'Oh how glad I am', he wrote to his mother in June 1858, 'that it was settled that I was to go there.' He furnished her with a detailed account of the studies he was undertaking with a private tutor to prepare him for the school which he was to enter in January 1859 when he was 14 years old: Latin and Greek, mathematics, French and German (when he had the opportunity he spoke German with Janet who was a fluent German speaker). He realized that the standard he had reached in the classical studies would determine the form he was placed in at Harrow and he thought that it would be the upper fourth – if his place depended on mathematics he estimated that he would be in a higher form. It was his great desire, he said, to take a high place at the school and go to Cambridge to do mathematics. In the meantime he added to his studies English (he took daily writing lessons), the reading of Roman and English history, some political geography and chemistry.[90]

Ughtred's first two years at Harrow were disastrous. He had a series of crippling headaches and the surviving correspondence is full of requests to go home, confessions of failure, rushed trips by

Lennard to Harrow to bring him to Gloucester Square, and of letters between Kay-Shuttleworth, Janet, Charles Vaughan, Harrow's headmaster, and various doctors as they pondered what should be done. Ughtred was at least a solid student and probably much better; he was popular enough with the masters; and apart from one occasion he did not complain of being excessively bullied or badly treated by the boys. Yet he had a number of lengthy absences which greatly militated against his chances of success and began to wear away Vaughan's patience. After he had been a month at Harrow he wrote rather hopefully to his father that he was in the best house in the school, that there was little bad language and 'no bullying'. In fact there was 'only one *cad* (as they call them) in the house, a beast, and a cheat'. But by April he was ill and in May he gave his father a typical description of his condition:

> On Tuesday my head-ache came on again, it was very bad all day, & it was in vain that I tried to drive it away, by taking plenty of exercise, I was unable to finish my work that night, & next morning it was so bad that, though I persevered, & went up to school in the morning I got down very much, & in the afternoon was doing no work.
> The amount that one has to do in Smith's Form seems to be too much for me, as they seem to think, as I think, that it is that, and not anything else, which gives me these headaches, the hot weather has perhaps made it worse.[91]

Not surprisingly, he had failed to get his remove, that is, promotion to the next form, and the embarrassing absences continued. He wrote to his mother in September from Gawthorpe that he was 'certain that I shall do well if I am prudent and not impatient, because I have not got strength to do all that we could wish'. Perhaps she was consoled to know that he was, he considered, the fifth-best cricketer in the club.[92]

During these sad years Kay-Shuttleworth remarked to Edward Marjoribanks that he hoped that Ughtred would escape unscathed from school life. The Harrow of Ughtred's time was a hard place to escape unscathed from, and on one of Ughtred's contemporaries it left a very deep scar. John Addington Symonds, who came to Harrow in 1854 and was still there when Ughtred arrived, was the son of the John Addington Symonds whom Kay-Shuttleworth had known since their days of medical and literary pursuits in Edinburgh. As their sons' presence at Harrow shows, both fathers had outgrown the strict Nonconformity of their younger days, but their choice of school did

little to please their boys. Symonds Jnr often cried himself to sleep in
his first year at Harrow, he detested the physical ugliness of the
school and its setting, developed a bad stammer and was attacked
by a series of illnesses. He grew to be contemptuous of most of the
masters and was ambivalent about the headmaster, Charles Vaughan,
whom he thought hypocritical and whose scholarship the rather
priggish young intellectual judged to be thin.[93]

Symonds's memoirs reveal that the school's intellectual and
aesthetic deficiencies probably shattered him less than the boys' brutality and sexual immorality. A good-looking boy was commonly
addressed by a female name and regarded as accessible to all or as the
'bitch' of an older boy. The talk seemed to Symonds, as it would have
to Ughtred, incredibly obscene and, coming from the sort of families
they did, they were frightened by the brutality. Symonds was utterly
shocked when a friend, Alfred Pretor, told him that he was having
an affair with the headmaster and showed him passionate love-letters
from Vaughan to prove it. Understandably, when Vaughan once
began to stroke Symonds's thigh as they sat beside each other on the
sofa in the headmaster's study, Symonds (then 17 years old) was
greatly agitated. In the summer of 1859 Symonds blurted out what he
knew to the Corpus Professor of Latin at Oxford, where he had gone
after leaving Harrow. He was told that he should tell his father who
was unaware of what had been happening for, although Symonds had
kept a diary at Harrow which did record his feelings, his letters to his
family contained no hint of the state of affairs at the school. After
Vaughan had discussions with Dr Symonds and inspected a letter
from Pretor to Symonds Jnr, the headmaster agreed that he had no
alternative but to resign.[94]

In August 1859 Ughtred wrote to his father that Vaughan had
declared his intention to resign at the end of the quarter and that
people believed he had been offered a bishopric. His mother dismissed the rumour as one that had been afloat for many years, but
under unrelenting pressure from Dr Symonds Vaughan resigned. In
his circular to parents announcing his decision, in his last sermon in
the school chapel and at a farewell banquet in London, Vaughan
combined brave resilience, self-deception and hypocrisy to make his
going seem a triumph. He had been at Rugby under Arnold and had
striven to bring Harrow under the Arnoldian spiritual influence, and
he used these well-known facts in a typical explanation of his
resignation in a letter to Kay-Shuttleworth. Fifteen years was the
time Arnold had fixed and he had now served 15 at Harrow. 'I feel the

wisdom of his impression that a man may occupy such a post too long – even apart from questions of continued efficiency and prosperity – and have seen my way to carry out the principle in my own case.' It was better, he assured Kay-Shuttleworth, than 'seeking or waiting for the chance of any little preferment to remove me'. Vaughan was appointed vicar of Doncaster and when about four years later he was offered a preferment, the bishopric of Doncaster, he accepted it, only to be forced to resign when Dr Symonds again threatened to expose him.[95]

The incident was successfully hushed up and Ughtred probably never knew of it, but the corruption at Harrow which it symbolized, and the younger John Addington Symonds, played further parts in the lives of Ughtred and the Kay-Shuttleworths. Even as he was contributing to Vaughan's downfall Symonds had begun uneasily to realize that he shared Vaughan's love of the male sex but, deeply influenced by his father, he had determined to resist his inclinations. He later married Catherine North, Janet Kay-Shuttleworth's half-sister, and their marriage dissolved into misery as he lived an active homosexual life. Of Janet North's three girls, two made agonized marriages and, though Janet Kay-Shuttleworth and Catherine Symonds kept in contact with each other, neither was accurately aware of the other's misery. For Ughtred, Harrow's brutal harassments had a more immediate relevance and explain his headaches and his longing to return home. The coarse language and the brutality had a personal relevance when he was woken one morning in October 1859 by a group of boys who began to turn up his bed. He was rescued only when a sixth-form friend made them stop their persecution. 'School life is the natural life for a boy', Ughtred's mother told him but, though both she and her husband recognized that there were perils involved, neither realized how directly Harrow assaulted the religious and moral values they wished their son to hold.[96]

By the end of 1860 Ughtred had been two years at school and, despite frequent absences, battled for survival with the grim courage his father displayed. The 1850s had done little to resurrect Kay-Shuttleworth's public life, and they had seen the irretrievable collapse of his marriage and the humiliating arrest in Germany. He may not have had syphilis, and might not have realized it if he did, but the threat of epilepsy hung continually over him, and neuralgia often afflicted him. He had published one novel without exciting the literary world and he had begun work on another, he assiduously tended the estate, and he watched his family, and especially his eldest son, with intense care and hope. His unrewarded desire to return to public life, the final separation from Janet and his children, the death of his mother, and his own illness did not paralyse his endeavours. He turned 56 in 1860, in time to face challenges which called his life's work into question and which he faced with the same driven courage that had carried him through the 1850s.

8 · Challenges, the preparation of an heir, and depression, 1860–65

Sir John Pakington, the Conservative Member for Droitwich, who in the 1850s and 1860s was the parliamentary leader of the educational cause, watched as Acts on grammar schools, Public Schools and the universities gained parliamentary sanction while the ten Bills on English national education introduced between 1850 and 1860 (two by Pakington himself) failed. The religious disputes which had dogged Kay-Shuttleworth were not diminished and, though rising suspicions of administrative centralization supported the movement towards local rating, its introduction would add another level at which religious conflict could flare.[1] Moreover, there were causes other than religious conflict for the slowness of educational progress. Leadership was one. A changing membership whose commitment to education varied greatly made the Committee of Council an unwieldy mechanism. The addition of a Vice-President in the Commons did not provide a focused leadership as the relationship between the Lord President of the Council, the Vice-President, and the Committee itself was anything but clear. The inspectorate, which might have given a lead, was handicapped by its denominational loyalties, divided in its opinions, and unable to resist Lingen's determination to keep it so absorbed by the administration of the grants that it had no time to consider policy. And when it did express views at its annual meetings that worried Lingen, he had the meetings discontinued.[2]

Lingen's personality and beliefs differed in crucial matters from his predecessor's. Where Kay-Shuttleworth had come to accept that government should fund denominational schools (even if broader visions lingered in his mind), Lingen was 'secularist' by inclination. He had a sharper but less passionate intelligence than Kay-Shuttleworth, was equally hardworking, found compromise difficult and did not share Kay-Shuttleworth's willingness to work towards a goal in an opportunistic and administratively untidy way. Unlike Kay-Shuttleworth, whose unorthodox financial approach disturbed Trevelyan and Wood, Lingen wanted tight control over government expenditure. He saw himself as an administrator, not an educational leader, though his handling of the demanding administrative legacy created by the 1846 minutes indirectly helped to sustain Kay-Shuttleworth's reputation.

Most importantly, he did not share Kay-Shuttleworth's commitment to popular education. Where Kay-Shuttleworth pressed his views on government and Opposition alike, Lingen adopted the role of impartiality and administrative efficiency. As Johnson has pointed out, he consistently refused to act as an educational statesman and helped to create the image of the rational and detached civil servant. He remained snobbish, arrogant and sarcastic in dealing with inferiors, setting standards which later generations of civil servants with his background have maintained. His policy of detachment was politically as well as personally attractive because of the religious sensitivity surrounding education. He criticized the religious bodies who sought government money but did not want the House of Commons interfering in their activities; he thought that they preferred to leave relations between government and themselves in '*passionless hands, such as belong rather to bureaucracy than to Parliamentary Ministries*'.[3] Such cool rationalism was not for Kay-Shuttleworth, despite what he wrote about statistical societies. Moreover, his collapse warned Lingen that a personal obsession with work could lead to physical and professional destruction. Lingen learned the lesson well and finished his career in the civil service's highest post, Permanent Secretary to the Treasury; but in the 1850s his caution removed the insistent pressure for change to which Kay-Shuttleworth had subjected successive governments.

In these dispiriting days Pakington's parliamentary leadership was courageous but not productive until he revived an old idea. On 11 February 1858, in the dying days of the Palmerston government, he moved for a royal commission into the state of popular education in England, describing himself as 'a humble Member of this House, who has not even a party support to look to on this proposal'. His motion was successful but the government fell almost immediately leaving the Conservatives, led by the Earl of Derby, to put the commission into effect. Pakington, as the successful mover of the motion, might have expected the chairmanship of the commission, but Palmerston's government probably would not have given him the appointment. 'Whatever you do', wrote Earl Granville, Palmerston's President of the Committee of Council, to W.F. Cowper, the Committee's Vice-President, 'don't put Pakington on it [the commission] . . . it would be injurious to the cause and inconvenient to the government.' Pakington's fellow Conservatives were no kinder. Made suspicious by his criticism of the religious societies and his support for the establishment of education boards with the power to levy rates, they denied him even membership of the commission. He was given the post of First Lord of the Admiralty and placed at a safe distance from educational matters.[4]

Lingen wrote to Granville before the Liberal government fell, saying that he would be sorry to see any strong advocate of the present system put on the commission. Granville had suggested that Kay-Shuttleworth should be a member, but given this thinking there was no place for him, particularly as Lingen justified his recommendation on the grounds that advocates of the present system were 'deaf to everything but the cry for larger grants'. Once the Tories came into power Kay-Shuttleworth's appointment was out of the question. The fifth Earl of Newcastle, one of the largest landowners in England, was given the chairmanship and only one of the seven-member commission, Nassau Senior, favoured further extension of state intervention in education.[5]

Kay-Shuttleworth gave evidence to the commission on 26 and 30 January 1860. He took it on a lengthy tour of the controversies of his term of office, showing the development of the Committee's (and his) policies from the comprehensive system he and Russell had originally favoured to the denominationally based arrangements of 1846. Mindful of the compromises he had been forced to make as he strove to extend the state's power, he stressed the tentativeness of his approach and his willingness to accede to political realities, or as he put it, to his 'deeper appreciation of the exceeding strength of the religious principle of this country'. The Committee of Council had not sought to impose some supposedly perfect solution; it had been willing to learn from experience and to find the most acceptable ways to achieve its aim. He justified his actions by an appeal to social science:

> our present position is the result of experience – that exactly as in a scientific investigation you arrive at results, step by step, by an inductive process, and you do not know by how thin a film some great truth may be concealed from you; you are at any period of the induction obliged to confine your conclusions simply to the results of previous experience.

Nevertheless, 'in the present stage of the matter I know no system for which the country is prepared excepting the present'.[6]

On an issue of central concern to the commission, the rising cost of the parliamentary grant for education, Kay-Shuttleworth was initially vague and then ambitious, qualities which Treasury officials who remembered the late 1840s would have recognized. When asked to calculate what the government contribution might amount to in a few years, he argued that the growth of a national system was so slow that it would hardly keep pace with the population increase – which made it obvious (to him at any rate) that 'any such calculation would be of little value'. Later he conceded that the grant might rise from the existing £760,000 to nearly £1,200,000 in five years' time. Advocates of economy or parsimony would not have been pleased with the answer. Nor would he have inspired them with confidence that supplementation from the rates would solve the problem. He outlined his Manchester endeavours and remained in favour of rate support, but repeatedly stated that he was not sanguine about this approach. Municipalities would not accept extra financial responsibilities 'unless they had the entire regulation of the school', and transferring the control of schools from the religious to the civic authorities was politically impossible.[7]

He was pressed on issues which assumed great significance in the commission's discussions. The complex arrangements through which the Committee of Council distributed the grants, particularly after the 1846 minutes, caused great disquiet – in 1859, for example, £252,551 was paid on 20,000 separate money orders to individual pupil-teachers and teachers. Kay-Shuttleworth agreed that the office handled much detail but argued that it 'was subjected to extreme external jealousy' and procedures had been devised to make it 'impervious to external assault, to leave no joint of the harness open'. He agreed that the clerical work could now be diminished, but was reluctant to see the establishment of a single capitation grant which would cover what schools were presently given in a number of small and separate grants. Grants should continue to be determined by the inspector, he believed, but not paid to individual teachers. Instead a single grant could be paid to the local postmaster who would act as a banker and distribute the money according to a schedule drawn up in the office. In this way administration was simplified and some control over the criteria by which grants were distributed remained with the central authorities. He was strongly opposed to having a capitation grant distributed according to the results which students obtained at an examination, insisting that this would distract the inspector's attention from 'the general moral relations of the school and all the phenomena which meet the eye' and have him concentrate on 'two or three elements of education'. A general assessment of the school by an inspector, who took examination results into account but who looked more broadly at the way in which the school was conducted, would lead to conclusions which were more just.[8]

On 14 March 1861 the report of the Newcastle Commission was signed, and for a brief period it catapulted Kay-Shuttleworth back into the educational limelight. As the report itself admitted, the commissioners were divided. The majority welcomed the 1839 decision to grant public money to education and thought that the methods used to carry out the government's object had been successful. However, in a testimony to the dourness and longevity of the opposition Kay-Shuttleworth faced, the minority argued that 'in a country situated politically and socially as England is, Government has ordinarily speaking no educational duties, except towards those whom destitution, vagrancy or crime casts upon its hands.' The commissioners agreed that the existing system had given a powerful stimulus to school building, created a superior class of teacher and excellent models of teaching, stimulated voluntary contributions, and proved adaptable to 'the character of the people by leaving both the general management of the schools and their religious teaching free'. The commissioners also pointed to some problems:

> we have exposed great and growing defects in its tendency to indefinite expense, in its inability to assist the poorer districts, in the partial inadequacy of its teaching, and in the complicated business which encumbers the central office of the Committee of Council; and these defects have led us to believe that any attempt to extend it unaltered into a national system would fail.[9]

Influenced by some dubious statistics, the commissioners decided that access to education was diffused 'pretty generally and pretty equally' across the country and claimed that 'the great mass of the population recognizes its importance sufficiently to take advantage to some extent of the opportunities thus afforded to their children.' They concluded that the religious and moral influence of the public elementary schools had been great: 'A set of good schools civilizes a whole neighbourhood', the commissioners said. 'The most important function of the schools is that which they best perform.' They also praised the trained teachers which the 1846 minute was helping to produce. 'Intellectually and morally they are far superior to untrained teachers', the commissioners said, 'and there can be no doubt of their competence to teach elementary subjects thoroughly well to young children.'[10]

The schools and the teachers were doing their most important task well, but the commissioners were not satisfied. They argued that, although children left school at a early age and attended with little regularity, they were in school long enough 'to afford an opportunity of teaching them to read, write, and cypher'. Using an investigation of an assistant commissioner, J.P. Norris, they claimed that 'even in places where good schools exist . . . not more than one [student] in four reaches the first class' and 'not more than one in six learns to read with sufficient ease to retain, or care to use, the faculty in after life'. They considered that teachers neglected the more elementary subjects and the younger scholars to concentrate on the older pupils, and they decided that there was only one way to reform the schools: a searching examination of every child to determine whether he or she had learned 'the indispensable elements of knowledge'. 'There can be no sort of doubt', the report said, 'that if one teacher finds his income depends on the condition that his scholars do learn to read, whilst another is equally well paid whether they do or not, the first will teach more children to read than the second.' To simplify the administration, the commission recommended two grants: the government grant from taxation paid on the basis of attendance, and a grant from the rates given on the results of an examination in reading, writing and arithmetic, and administered by a county board of education.[11] Thus the commission ingeniously addressed four of its concerns: the improvement of instruction, the simplification of the grant system, the tapping of the county rates, and the decentralization of administration.

On 24 April 1861, about five weeks after the report had been signed, Kay-Shuttleworth wrote a public letter to Earl Granville, the President of the Privy Council in the Palmerston government, which had returned to receive the recommendations of the commission it had originally set up. The commission had erected an apparently firm buttress to sustain the existing system, the letter stated. It had rejected the arguments of the voluntarists, and approved the management of schools by religious bodies, the denominational inspectorate, and the training of teachers through apprenticeship and the Queen's scholarships. Nevertheless, some of the commission's suggestions were 'like a dry rot in the new timber'.

Kay-Shuttleworth knew only too well that the desire to curb educational expenditure had concerned previous Chancellors of the Exchequer and would trouble Gladstone, Palmerston's reforming Chancellor, for whom economizing was a political and personal imperative. He restated his view about the difficulties facing one possible source of finance, the rates, and, perhaps with the East Anglian Boards of Guardians in mind, asserted that civil and religious liberty could be in more danger from the ratepayers than from a government department which was subject to criticism by press and Parliament. He also reiterated his concerns about payment by results.[12]

The commission's desire to simplify administration led him to describe the Education Department as being in

> the condition of a juvenile hero outgrowing the suit of armour in which it was first encased. Its helmet, greaves, and gauntlets have become instruments of torture. In other words, the building is too small – departments have swarmed out of it into neighbouring streets – its staff is too slender – and the provisional character of its arrangements has been injuriously prolonged.

Despite its parlous condition, Kay-Shuttleworth saw his creation wearing a halo of bravery; but he had no illusions about the problems of its leaders. 'In their despair', he told Granville, 'the secretaries, worn out with the worry of an insufficient organisation, appeal to the Commission for relief', only to find that it had produced a plan which involved 'an increase of complication, risk, and expense'.[13]

The letter had little influence on Granville or on Robert Lowe, the Vice-President. Lowe, who turned 50 in 1861, had created a brilliant impression at Oxford, and during the 1840s had spent time in New South Wales, where he acquired a modest fortune and a reputation for having voted on both sides of every question. An albino, he was plagued all his life with a fear of blindness which matched his fear of democratic sentiments, and he displayed his formidable legal skills in his advocacy of a narrowly rationalistic liberalism – an 'illiberal liberal', one of his biographers has called him. But he was a man with a powerful mind whose intellectual consistency made him an effective speaker and writer, and a menacing controversialist. As he did not handicap himself by translating his intellectual principles rigidly into practice, his was a distinguished political career. On 11 July 1861, while the government was preparing its response to the Newcastle Commission, Lowe told Parliament that he wished to economize on the education grant 'and to make it go as far as possible'.[14]

His desire to economize had Ralph Lingen's support. Throughout the 1850s Lingen remained loyal to the 1846 minutes, though he had grave reservations about the system he was administering. An instinctive economizer who was dismayed by the idea of an ever-expanding Education Department, he fought to prevent the incautious extension of the grant system. The inspectors, because of their denominational allegiances and because they confronted the needs of the schools more dramatically than the central office did, seemed willing to change the grant into an outright subsidy rather than an assistance to voluntary effort. Lingen saw central direction as the only check on financial expansion, and he provided that direction by imposing his will and ways on the Education Department. Yet despite his unyielding and sometimes clandestine stringency, the Newcastle Commission confirmed that the parliamentary grant had grown steadily. Thus a Vice-President bent on economy was assured of Lingen's help. He was also assured of support from Granville who, at the height of the controversy which erupted over the government's response to the commission, admitted that its policies had resulted in an intentional pecuniary loss to the training colleges and schools.[15]

Gladstone's parliamentary record demonstrated his reluctance to grant money for educational purposes, and in November 1860 he had prepared committees to enquire into civil expenditure, including education. Plans for cuts were modified after discussions with some inspectors and the Duke of Newcastle, but even well-disposed politicians such as Russell agreed that the grant system had to be restrained. Once Newcastle's report appeared, the pressure for economizing increased and in his budget speech on 15 April 1861 Gladstone stated his conviction that excess in public expenditure was a great political and moral evil. Three years later, unrepentant at the furore his policy caused, he boasted to Palmerston of the 'great and salutary reform' they had secured in the administration of the education vote, and especially their checking of 'what was almost an inveterate tendency to rapid expansion'.[16]

When the Committee of Council met to decide their policy they chose the tactic which Kay-Shuttleworth had made a commonplace, the tabling of a minute in Parliament. In 1860 Lowe had organized a codification of Committee minutes – they had been published piecemeal since a codification in 1855. On 26 July 1861, the last day of the session, he tabled the government's response to the Newcastle

Commission in the form of a new code, the Revised Code. It had been drawn up by Lingen, who did not approve of all its provisions but who later explained that, in the light of the views of his superiors, 'I drew it just as, if I had remained at my old profession, I might have drawn a man's will or his marriage settlement.' Neither Lowe nor Lingen seems to have consulted anyone, certainly not the inspectorate whom Lowe had already announced he did not trust. The Revised Code was a striking example of the power acquired by the Education Department as personified in its Secretary and the Committee of Council's Vice-President. The timing of Lowe's tabling of the Code prevented discussion before Parliament rose, and suggested that he was anxious to circumvent political controversy. When the inevitable storm broke, Granville denied that the Committee of Council had tried to smuggle the minute through Parliament. But, at the very least, Lowe's tactic freed the government from the attention of the educational lobbyists while it framed the Code, and created a chance to study the Code's reception before Parliamentary discussion began.[17]

Like some subsequent commentators, Lowe defended the Code by appealing to the Newcastle Commission's finding that the teaching was defective. Actually the Revised Code ignored some of the Commission's most important recommendations: it did not introduce a capitation grant based solely on attendance and it avoided the suggestion of local rating. There were to be no grants for schools, other than the payment of a penny per scholar for every attendance over 100. One-third of this grant was to be forfeited if the scholar failed at an examination in reading set by the inspector, and failures in writing or arithmetic could see another one- or two-thirds vanish. Among the grants abolished by the Code were the capitation grant, the grants for books and apparatus, the augmentation grant given to teachers who successfully completed certificate examinations, the stipends for pupil-teachers, teachers' pensions, grants to evening and ragged schools, and some grants to training colleges. As compensation schools were offered an attendance grant for which many scholars would not qualify and which was subject to drastic reduction. This system of 'payment by results' was not entirely new – as the pupil-teacher and augmentation grants which Kay-Shuttleworth had introduced in 1846 demonstrated. But the earlier grants differed crucially from the Code. They were supplementary payments or rewards for success, whereas under the Code all pupils were to be examined and all a school's grant was made dependent on examination success. This 'uniform and universal principle', as A.J. Marcham points out, was 'Lowe's lodestar' which superseded all others.[18]

Moreover, the Revised Code was intended to satisfy the government's demand for economy. Delighted voluntarists such as Baines and Edward Miall, who was a member of the Newcastle Commission, hoped that the Code might be a step on the way to the abolition of state aid. For Robert Lowe the Code offered the simplification of administration that he, Lingen and the Newcastle Commission had sought – and the means to keep the famous promise he made on 13 February 1862. 'I cannot promise the House', he said,

> that this system will be an economical one, and I cannot promise that it will be an efficient one, but I can promise that it shall be one or the other. If it is not cheap it shall be efficient; if it is not efficient it shall be cheap.

It proved to be cheap: between 1861 and 1866 the grant fell 22 per cent while the average attendance rose 23 per cent.[19]

The Revised Code was greeted with howls of outrage from school managers, clergy, teachers and inspectors, and two months after announcing it, the government was forced to delay its implementation for six months. Still the protests continued, the vituperative pamphlets abounded, and angry meetings around the country sent deputations to Whitehall – 'Here they come', Lowe once said to Granville as the Committee's President prepared for another deputation, 'in number about five thousand!' Even by the nineteenth century's passionate and vindictive standards the debate was memorable. As it progressed old enemies found themselves in uneasy alliance: Kay-Shuttleworth, the Code's most politically important critic, found himself on the side of George Anthony Denison who saw the Code as an attempt to eliminate religious instruction from elementary schools.[20]

Kay-Shuttleworth's reaction is a convenient introduction to the controversy. On 4 November 1861, in a second letter to Earl Granville, he claimed that the Revised Code 'would destroy the existing system'. The claim was made from a position of strength because Kay-Shuttleworth's contemporaries acknowledged him as the founder of the system of English popular education. But it also exposed him to a damaging charge, that of wishing to defend his own creation. 'The most vigorous and uncompromising opponent that the new system has encountered, or is likely to meet, is the gifted author of the system which it attempts to supersede', wrote James Fraser, one of Newcastle's assistant commissioners and a defender of the Revised Code. In an effort to prevent his criticism being neutralized by such praise Kay-Shuttleworth claimed that his letter recorded the impressions of managers and teachers of schools.[21] He did have the support of teachers and managers, but personal concern gave force and passion to his letter. After his Manchester failures, Kay-Shuttleworth's life had gained meaning from his work as a civil servant. Now, at the very time when he faced rejection in his family life, these accomplishments were called into question. His campaign against the Revised Code was not vitiated by his emotional involvement, but opponents such as Fraser and Lowe struck a nerve which was more tender than they realized. In attacking the Revised Code Kay-Shuttleworth was defending his sense of worth.

His second letter to Granville argued that the Revised Code would result in an immediate reduction of £175,000. Kay-Shuttleworth denied that the instruction had been inadequate and that the Code would simplify administration. He insisted that, despite the formidable obstacles of inadequate attendance and (a familiar theme) of ignorant and demoralized parents who did not yet understand the value of education, the schools had been civilizing forces in the community. He contemptuously denounced Lowe's claim that the Code had introduced free trade into education as 'the arbitrary and indefensible application of a doctrine of political economy respecting supply and demand, bounties and protection . . . to a sphere of moral action in which it is totally inapplicable'. Statesmen who wished to civilize a nation had first to create the appetite for civilization: 'mental, moral and religious destitution have no appetite – they have no desire – they make no demand'. The teachers' task was not a 'trade': it was not done 'for pecuniary profit' but through 'a sense of moral and religious obligation, and a conviction that the wealth and strength of States, and domestic peace and prosperity, depend on the moral and intellectual elevation of the people'. Furthermore the conditions under which teachers worked and the intellectual and cultural background of their students varied so greatly that the proposed means of assessment were crude. In a deceptively simple statement, to which later generations of politicians and administrators have paid insufficient heed, Kay-Shuttleworth rejected Lowe's basic assumption: 'A capitation grant, based upon an examination of individual children', he said, 'does not pay for the work done in the school.'[22]

Correctly prophesying the Code's most destructive effect, its encouragement of unimaginative teaching and the grind after results, Kay-Shuttleworth saw the teacher as having 'to work like a horse in a gin-wheel, at the routine of teaching the elements, according to the mechanical standard of the Revised Code'. He attacked defenders of the Code who thought that teachers were 'too highly instructed – they are above their work' and who called for their education 'to be lowered to the level of their work'. He also commented bitterly on the Code's policy of having teachers bargain with managers for their salaries rather than being paid by the state: 'The teachers must, like corn and cotton, be subject to the law of supply and demand. They and the managers must make the best bargains they can.' The Code's attack on the system of training colleges, pupil-teachers and Queen's Scholars amazed him. When commenting on the first letter to Granville, Lowe had told Kay-Shuttleworth that Newcastle's report had destroyed 'the whole essence of the present pupil teacher system without as it seems being at all aware of the fact'. Now, well aware of the fact, Lowe had set out to do the same thing.[23]

Equally destructive of teachers' standing and self-respect was the reasoning Lowe used to defend payment by results. 'I believe', he said,

> that we must appeal to the passions of the human mind – that we must enlist hope and fear to work for us – that we must hold out a prospect of sufficient remuneration if the children are properly taught, and of loss if they are not, or we shall do nothing.

Not content with a policy based on the assumption that teachers would not work without incentives and punishment, Lowe asserted that the grant might become 'a grant to maintain the so-called vested interest of those engaged in education.' He did not want the system to pass out of the control of the Privy Council and Parliament 'into the hands of the persons working that educational system', for then 'no demand they choose to make on the public purse would any Ministry dare to refuse'. The vehemence of the teachers' response may have alienated some supporters, but the Code threatened to reduce their less than generous salaries, and Lowe offered them no choice except to be meek or rebellious.[24]

Kay-Shuttleworth saw teachers in a different light. He wrote of governmental (he meant his) efforts to create 'a new machinery of public education'. The teachers and the pupil-teachers were 'like the raw recruits of an army suddenly raised – brought into the field in successive battalions, on the verge of an immature manhood, and placed, as soon as drilled, in the front of difficulties and dangers'. They were 'the pioneers of civilisation'. Now they had been betrayed and elementary education brought close to ruin. Angrily he summarized his complaints. The Revised Code was

> an attempt to reduce the cost of the education of the poor, by conducting it by a machinery – half trained and at less charge; to entrust it to a lower class of ill-paid teachers, and generally to young monitors as assistants; to neglect the force of a higher moral and religious agency in the civilisation of the people, and to define national education as a drill in mechanical skill in reading, writing, and arithmetic. The State would pay less, and be content with a worse article.[25]

The pamphlet bore marks of hasty writing and of Kay-Shuttleworth's preoccupation with the minutiae of regulations, but the corroding obsessions of *Public Education* vanished, and he returned to the style and passion of *The Moral and Physical Condition*. The tone was not as consistent and the passion was sometimes lost amid the details of his argument, but the disappointments of the 30 years which had elapsed since the Manchester pamphlet had not dulled his conviction. The letter is a testament to his enduring belief in the civilizing power of education and contains his most explicit statement on the role of the state in educational and social welfare. Parliament and the executive government are 'created by the people for the promotion and conservation of national interests. This central power is embodied in the word State'. The state has a greater interest in the intelligence of the people than any other body, for on that intelligence depend the law, the police and the franchise, authority, the harmony of classes, the increase of wealth and national contentment, and the defence of the constitution against invasion or internal corruption and revolution. Education descends from the upper or governing classes to the lower who do not of themselves seek to be civilized but, like minors, are 'the care of the governing classes in some form' and have to be sought by the missionary or the teacher. They are rescued 'not by their own act, but by that of the State and the upper classes, to whom their progress has become a social and political necessity'. The State is best able to perceive 'this want of the commonwealth' because it best appreciates the dangers of ignorance, pauperism, crime and disorder. Kay-Shuttleworth described as fallacy the attempt 'to limit the power of the state to promote the intelligence and virtue of the people', especially if the claim were based on 'an abstract principle' such as the doctrine of free trade. The state's stake, he insisted, was greater than anyone else's, 'even than the Church established by law'.[26] He was asserting the rights of the civil power against its two strongest enemies, laissez-faire economics and the Church, and was revealing the mix of principle, passion, paternalism and idealism which underlay his vision of popular education.

Kay-Shuttleworth's reputation as 'the founder of English popular education', as Matthew Arnold had called him before the Revised Code was published, ensured that the letter would gain attention. Ten thousand copies disappeared very quickly: as Arnold said, it had sold 'like wildfire'. Kay-Shuttleworth distributed it widely and was encouraged by its reception from people such as Robert Eden and Pakington, who remarked that 'You, of all living men, have the best right to be the champion of the existing Privy Council system.' Gladstone promised to read the letter with care 'and I do not doubt with advantage'. Granville told Kay-Shuttleworth that he had read the pamphlet 'with the care which any opinion of yours deserves on subjects connected with education' but had not been convinced by it. Closer to home, Ughtred reported that his mother had not spoken directly about the letter, though she regarded the Revised Code as a breach of faith with the schoolmasters.[27]

On 30 November 1861, Lowe, on whom the defence of the Code primarily fell, used the semi-anonymity of the leader columns of *The Times* to publish a brilliant polemic which belittled Kay-Shuttleworth and mocked his views. (He differed from Lingen who deprecated Lowe's uncompromising attack on the old system: 'Sir James does not exaggerate the merit of his work, and his name will honourably live in connection with it.') Lowe opened with the standard ploy: 'Nobody is better entitled to a hearing on educational subjects', than Sir James Shuttleworth, who had to defend his own creations against 'the assaults of the Education Commissioners, and their virtual reversal by the Revised Code of the Privy Council'. His pamphlet, according to Lowe, was distressingly fragmentary and in parts unintelligible; moreover, he treated his arguments 'as a dog does a bone, taking them up, gnawing them, laying them down, and taking them up again, in an utterly inscrutable manner'. As for his writing style: 'Our standard of fair literary expression must be grievously "worsened," to use a favourite expression of Sir James, before we could bring it down to the standard of his pamphlet.' (The gibe hurt Kay-Shuttleworth who added a note to a reprint of his pamphlet giving Milton as an authority for the use of 'worsen'.) Of his educational achievements, Lowe remarked that 'the system of his own invention is perfect in conception, and only prevented from being perfect in execution by unavoidable causes.' In fact, far from being perfect, the schools 'have done everything . . . except the one thing which, as schools, they were especially bound to do, – taught reading, writing, and arithmetic'.[28]

Lowe's insistence that the schools had failed to teach the three Rs was conveniently impervious to argument. In 1862 J.P. Norris admitted that his calculations, which Lowe had used a number of times in Parliament to justify his claim that only a quarter of the students could read, were 'an unintentional mistake'. Lowe conceded that an error had been made, described the approach of the Rev. T.R. Birks, who had exposed the error, as being one of 'cabalistic ingenuity', and persisted in his argument, pouring scorn on those who spoke of the education of the people or of the nation. The Privy Council system, he said, was 'limited to the children of those who live by manual labour, and is, in fact, a species of out-door relief, administered by a central office'. The gap between this view and his father's hopes for popular education was clear to Ughtred Kay-Shuttleworth who noted Lowe's review of his father's pamphlet in his diary. His education for public life might have been sharpened when he saw the father he revered treated with such scant respect.[29]

Kay-Shuttleworth campaigned actively as the debate continued through the autumn and winter of 1861–62. He would come to no compromise with 'the rash, overbearing, and unskilful authors of this measure' which he regarded as 'an infantile blunder'. On 18 January 1862, apparently as an afterthought generated by an address to the Church of England Schoolmasters' Association, he wrote to the *Daily News* asking for a parliamentary enquiry to determine whether the Revised Code had been submitted 'with care' to the Committee of Council. He did not dispute that the Committee had approved the Code, but doubted whether it had been submitted for detailed consideration by the Committee and whether care had been taken to explain 'the subversive character of its arrangements'. His informant on the proceedings of the Committee was probably Russell, who was a member of Cabinet, and opposed the Code; on 4 January (three days after he and Kay-Shuttleworth had met at Pembroke Lodge), he said that the Code was depreciating all that had been done since 1839. He later attacked Granville, claiming that the Committee of Council had not been properly consulted about it.[30]

On 13 February 1862, at the beginning of the new parliamentary

Sir James Kay-Shuttleworth, *c.* 1860 (courtesy of Mrs Janet Young)

session, Granville defended the Revised Code in the Lords. As a counter to the view that he and Lowe had 'rushed out like Irishmen at a fair, to have a blow at something or somebody', he had been advised to stress that the government was providing a remedy for an admitted evil. It was also suggested that he should be gracious in expression 'even towards Shuttleworth'. Probably Granville would have acted in this way without advice, but he did express his 'great regard and affection for the Gentleman, whose friendship I have enjoyed for some years'. Nevertheless, he regretted that Kay-Shuttleworth's speeches and writings had departed 'from that judicial tone which his attainments, experience, and eminent service rendered to education fully entitled him to assume'. In the Commons Lowe opened the debate with a savage attack on his critics in a speech lasting three and a half hours. Kay-Shuttleworth sat with Ughtred in the parliamentary gallery and heard Lowe rehearse his usual arguments, attack the vested interest of teachers, and condemn the inspectorate. Ughtred reported the events to his mother, noting that he had seen 'a large number of distinguished people whom I had not ever seen before'. John Delane, the editor of *The Times*, told Granville that he greeted a victory 'inflicted on a class of persons whom policy compelled you and Lowe to treat with a respect they do not at all deserve'.[31]

However, despite his intransigence Lowe brought some concessions to offer Parliament, and may well have had to bring greater concessions if Granville and Gladstone had not supported him. The concessions did not bring peace, and on 11 March Ughtred Kay-Shuttleworth returned from the Zoological Gardens, where in the company of the appropriately named Mr W. Python he had been incubating some eggs of the Guinea rock snake, to find that the first copies of his father's latest book, *Four Periods of Public Education*, had arrived at Gloucester Square from Longmans. Kay-Shuttleworth's purpose was made clear by the dedication to Lansdowne and Russell, 'to whose sagacity, moderation, and firmness the country owes the establishment of the Committee of the Privy Council on Education and the adoption of the minutes of 1846'.

Four Periods of Public Education was a bulky apologia made up of earlier writings with minor editorial changes. The first of the four periods occurred before the Treasury grants of 1833 and was represented by 'The Moral and Physical Condition of the Working Classes' and the only substantial new piece in the book, a 'Sketch of the Progress of Manchester in thirty years, from 1832 to 1862', written to support the 1832 pamphlet and to illustrate the subsequent improvements in public health and education. From these dark days Kay-Shuttleworth advanced to the second period, illustrated through 'Recent Measures' and selections from his Poor Law reports, which concentrated on the apprenticeship of pupil-teachers and the two reports on Battersea. The third period was represented solely by the 'Explanation of the Minutes of 1846', and the dark ages of the fourth period by his two letters to Earl Granville. The book is a form of autobiographical testament to his public activities, assembled at a time when those activities were being undermined.[32]

Kay-Shuttleworth sent a copy of the book to Granville and in a reference to his two letters remarked that 'the rest of the book croaks like a Bird of Evil omen'. But he was clearly unrepentant as he referred to 'the years of resistance, vexation and struggle which could follow the confirmation of the Revised Code'. Lansdowne wrote an elegant and thoughtful letter which included the remark that 'it must be a great gratification to you to see the extension of a demand for knowledge of which you have contributed so much to lay the foundation'. The National Society's John Sinclair wrote in similar vein, and George Lewis said that the book had reminded him of things that had grown faint in his memory – 'I always consider you as having contributed more than any other person to the commencement of the sanitary movement'.[33] *Four Periods of Public Education* remains a convenient source of some of Kay-Shuttleworth's most important writings but its size and complexity ensured that it had little impact on the Revised Code debate.

That debate continued and on 28 March 1862 Lowe was forced to make further concessions. They did not still the agitation. Kay-Shuttleworth played a conspicuous part in drawing up another memorandum to Granville, in lobbying the sympathetic Russell, and in helping the British and National Societies to organize protests. But the war had been lost. Lowe railed at the concessions he had been forced to make, but he had won: payment by results was in place, and it stayed in place for another three decades.[34]

Matthew Arnold had intended to write an article attacking the Code from about October 1861 but delayed when he heard that Kay-Shuttleworth's pamphlet would soon appear, and it was not until March 1862 that 'The Twice-Revised Code' (by the second revision Arnold meant the changes announced by Lowe on 13 February) was published in *Fraser's Magazine*. Arnold thought that 'the pamphlet of a master of the subject – of the founder of our public elementary education, Sir James Shuttleworth' was admirable for experts but 'somewhat too copious' for the general reader; hence his own article. He pointed out that Kay-Shuttleworth had been taunted 'with not possessing the graces of style, the skill of the literary artist', but unlike those who taunted him he had a thorough mastery of the subject of popular education, and he had come to this knowledge in 'the only way by which this subject ever can be well known – he knows it because he loves it'.[35]

Arnold's witty, graceful and passionate article drew on Kay-Shuttleworth's letter and represented views which he did not consistently maintain in the future. But in 1862 he attacked the Code for its restricted view of the education to be offered to the poor:

> for every school-machinery which is thrown out of gear, for every glimmer of civilization which is quenched, for every poor scholar who is no longer humanized, owing to a reduction, on the plea that reading, writing, and arithmetic are all the State ought to pay for in our present State-expenditure for elementary schools, the State will be directly responsible.

The Code would not extend education, improve the education being offered in schools, or distribute the grant more effectively. It was a step towards abolishing state education. Arnold admitted that there might be folly in efforts to secure too ornamental an education, but identified the source of such efforts as 'something natural and respectable – the strong desire of the lower classes to raise themselves'. Even the faults of the teachers, he said, 'so visible, so pardonable and so little pardoned, proceed from this desire'. For all its faults, and Arnold was willing to admit them, 'there is something *vital* in the connexion established between the State and the lower classes by the old system'. It was because the Revised Code 'by destroying – under the specious pleas of simplifying, of giving greater liberty of action to managers – this vital connexion, takes the heart out of the old system, that it is so condemnable'.[36]

Arnold was aware that his anonymous article would easily be identified as his, and it was – Kay-Shuttleworth asked him for permission to reprint it and distribute it to Members of Parliament. Arnold did not have to worry – a dinner with the Lingens in June 1862 showed that relations between the Secretary and his ex-student were still cordial. Perhaps Balliol men understood each other.[37] But if Lingen and Arnold were closer in class, culture and social connections, Kay-Shuttleworth and Arnold were, at least at this time, closer in their educational thinking. Arnold's valuing of the state's role in education was integral to his vision of culture and was more elaborate and liberating than Kay-Shuttleworth's. But each saw that the Revised Code grew out of a view of public elementary education which restricted its educative power. Since the Revised Code controversy, those wishing to limit educational opportunity have often used Lowe's tactics. These essentially involve crippling the state's vision by imposing a rigid and restricted interpretation of its task through a centralized testing system. Lowe used the classic political justifications for this approach: a cry for economy, an insistence that schools should act as if they were part of the market economy, and an accusation that schools are inhabited by over-educated teachers and under-educated students. Whatever the limitations of their own views, Kay-Shuttleworth and Arnold saw this mean and unimaginative policy for what it was, and described it for their contemporaries and for later ages.

> It is totally exceptional. The state of things has no parallel in all history . . . There has been nothing like it in the history of the world for its suddenness, for the impossibility of dealing with it, or managing it in the way of an effective remedy.

Richard Cobden was speaking in Manchester on 3 November 1862 of the Lancashire cotton famine which was at its height from mid-1862 until the summer of 1863. Though its causes are still the subject of dispute, it probably began through overproduction rather than through a shortage of cotton. However, by the summer of 1862 the American Civil War had dried up the flow of cheap cotton from the southern states, and as the mills shut down, the smaller mill-owners, the cotton workers, and the shopkeepers and others who depended on them for custom were whirled out of work and into economic powerlessness. The scale of the disaster was too great for voluntary charity, and the Poor Law guardians were soon overwhelmed by the demand on the poor rate, though the impact of the famine varied greatly according to a place's dependence on the cotton trade. Lord Derby drew attention to the extent of the demand by pointing out that parish relief was running at £2,259 a week in September 1861, £9,674 the following September, and by November 1862 had risen to £17,681 per week. As the distress speedily deepened the call for financial assistance became pressing.[38]

Government action was delayed until the passage of the Union Relief Act of August 1862 which, in certain circumstances, allowed a distressed parish in a Lancashire, Cheshire or Derbyshire Poor Law Union to be assisted by rates in aid from other parishes in the Union. Before this Act had been passed, however, major efforts at relief had begun. On 25 April 1862, following a series of letters in *The Times* outlining the distress in the cotton districts, some London businessmen with interests in cotton manufacture met with the Lord Mayor of London to establish the Lancashire and Cheshire Operatives Relief Fund (known as the Mansion House Fund). Four days after the London meeting a group of Manchester men met that city's mayor in the Town Hall to consider forming a relief committee similar to those being formed in towns throughout the cotton district. Partly because they believed that the Manchester and Salford District Provident Society would handle the problem, no action was taken until 20 June 1862 when the Central Relief Committee was established in Manchester to collect subscriptions and distribute relief. On 19 July a group of Lancashire noblemen and Members of Parliament in London set up the Cotton Districts Relief Fund with Derby as chairman and Kay-Shuttleworth as secretary. The money was to be distributed through the Central Relief Fund in Manchester which was restructured – the General Committee, which established the fund, agreed to the appointment of a Central Executive Committee which distributed over £800,000 from 1862 to 1864. Derby was chairman of the Central Executive Committee and Kay-Shuttleworth its vice-chairman. By December 1862 the Central Relief Fund had replaced the Poor Law as the main support for relief in Lancashire, spending £46,000 per week by comparison with the guardians' £18,000. The Central Executive, though resented by some members of the original committee as a take-over by the London-based group, was the driving force.[39]

As well as being on the local relief committee in Burnley and the Board of Guardians at Padiham, Kay-Shuttleworth was an active member of the Executive Committee, sometimes working from six in the morning till nine at night. A chronicler of the cotton famine, John Watts, who observed his work at first hand, paid tribute to his 'intense activity of brain and persevering energy and administrative ability'. Kay-Shuttleworth was involved in the Executive's main work, the raising and the distribution of the funds, and he did a great deal of lesser bureaucratic work – changing the date of a committee meeting so that Derby could join a party at the York races or checking discrepancies in the returns from the local relief committees which received money from the Central Relief Fund. There were fewer discrepancies in Burnley's ('I presume, thanks to you', Derby wrote)

The Central Executive Committee (Cotton Famine): Kay-Shuttleworth is on the right, sitting back from the table

than in most others. Derby and Kay-Shuttleworth also discussed questions of policy including permanently enrolling or two or three regiments as a means of relief. Once again his pent-up energies were released in public service.[40]

They also issued in a familiar bureaucratic product, his *Manual of Suggestions for the Guidance of Local Relief Committees in the Cotton Districts* which appeared in 1863. Written on behalf of the Executive Committee, it attempted to bring consistency to the local relief funds' disposal of money given them by the Central Relief Fund. It included a scale according to which financial relief was to be allocated, and discussed who was eligible for relief, the kinds of relief to be given, the work to be done in return for relief and the respective duties of the Poor Law guardians and the local relief committees. Kay-Shuttleworth wanted relief money to assist those affected by the cotton famine, not to assist 'cases of purely chronic indigence' which remained the responsibility of the Poor Law guardians. When relief was given to victims of the famine, Kay-Shuttleworth tried to ensure that it was distributed in ways and on criteria which were close to those used by Poor Law officials. He wanted to bureaucratize charity. In his search for uniformity and his concern to avoid exploitation, there were many resemblances between Sir James Kay-Shuttleworth, a private citizen who was helping to administer philanthropic funds in a voluntary capacity, and James Phillips Kay, the assistant Poor Law commissioner who had swept through East Anglia a quarter of a century earlier.[41]

The cotton famine drew a less formal publication from Kay-Shuttleworth: *Words of Comfort and Counsel to Distressed Lancashire Workmen, Spoken on Sundays in 1862*, by 'A Country Squire – their Neighbour'.[42] The distressed Lancashire workmen and women who were forced to listen to these homilies found more counsel than comfort in them. Unimaginatively moralistic and paternalistic, they were part of the price the poor paid for charity.

Fortunately Kay-Shuttleworth did much more than offer verbal comfort and counsel. At a meeting of the Manchester Board of Guardians it was suggested that an educational test might be substituted for the labour test associated with the granting of poor relief. With the number of unemployed so large the test was difficult to enforce, and the cotton operatives bitterly resented traditional occupations such as stone-breaking and oakum-picking, which they associated with a pauperism quite different from the sudden unemployment into which the cotton famine had plunged them.

Schools for adults receiving relief had already been established by a few individuals and the Executive Committee, eagerly pushed by Kay-Shuttleworth, seized upon the idea. Fortuitously a fund, estimated at more than £15,000, arrived from New South Wales consigned to the care of Sir Daniel Cooper, a merchant and philanthropist who had returned to England after having greatly increased his fortune in the colony, and Edward Hamilton, a pastoralist and company director who had also returned to England after having done well in New South Wales. Cooper and Hamilton accepted Kay-Shuttleworth's proposal that the fund should be used for educational purposes and when the Central Executive were similarly persuaded schools were established, sometimes in old mills, offering sewing classes for women and some elementary instruction in reading, writing and arithmetic for both men and women. The Central Executive spent over £22,000 on educational matters between 1862 and 1864 and during the winter of 1862–63 there were 48,000 men and boys attending schools, while in March 1863 more than 41,000 women attended sewing classes. Practising what he preached, Kay-Shuttleworth had by August 1862 set up a sewing class in the farm-house at Gawthorpe.[43]

Kay-Shuttleworth reported to the colonists of New South Wales on the success of the venture and, according to R.A. Arnold, his 'rather unfortunate style of composition' and the colonials' 'ignorant impatience of long words' led to complaints that he was using the money to promote 'certain educational crochets'. Kay-Shuttleworth's link with denominational schooling, which seemed more obvious from the colonies than it was to adversaries such as Denison or Baines, caused much resentment in New South Wales and, fearing that the Australian contribution might be diminished, the Central Executive Committee persuaded the General Committee to repay from its general fund the money that had been taken from the New South Wales contribution. The schools continued to be supported from the general fund but Kay-Shuttleworth was left to ponder the strange ways of Australian settlers.[44]

As the winter of 1862–63 ended and the strain on the Poor Law and the relief organizations remained acute, the Executive Committee pressed for a new form of relief. They argued that many towns and municipalities would embark on extensive public works if the government provided long-term, low-interest loans, which would enable the provision of relief by the payment of a wage for useful work, such as the improvement of public roads, footpaths, places of public recreation and the sanitary condition of towns or villages. The Public Works (Manufacturing Districts) Bill of July 1863 enabled such proposals to be acted upon. Kay-Shuttleworth worked closely with Charles Pelham Villiers, President of the Poor Law Board, to frame the Act, and even took rooms in St James's Square so that he could be nearer the Athenaeum Club where some of the discussions took place. To the public work and approval, which he so greatly craved, Kay-Shuttleworth added private benefactions. Having encountered accusations of 'socialism' when he narrowly failed to persuade the Burnley relief committee to pay an hourly rate in its sewing schools, he took action of his own. In August 1862, using the estate's and not public money, he was paying 64 cotton operatives to work at Gawthorpe – the women sewed while the men made roads, quarried, drained and helped in other ways to put the grounds in order. They were paid wages at about the usual rate: working for four hours a day they earned 6/- a week. Kay-Shuttleworth also paid Padiham men to work on other parts of his estate in Westmorland, especially at Barbon.[45]

On occasions Kay-Shuttleworth faced disturbances similar to those he had encountered in East Anglia. In March 1863 the Executive Committee pressed the local relief committee at Stalybridge, which had been paying a higher scale of relief than usual, to reduce the relief (which was paid in cash) from 3s. 4d. to 3s. per head, and to pay the relief in 1s. tickets drawn upon shopkeepers, who could supply 7d. in goods and 5d. in cash. In this way, it was said, the waste of money through drunkenness and gambling would be reduced. Furthermore, either to ensure the performance of the day's work or to assist with the book-keeping, a day's pay was to be held back. On 20 March the operatives in the schools refused payment by ticket, local committee officials were jostled and the mill of an unpopular member of the committee had its windows smashed and some machinery damaged. Windows at the police station and at the relief committee office were also smashed and some clothes destined for relief were stolen. The Riot Act was read and police and Hussars sent from Manchester restored order and took about 70 prisoners.[46]

On Sunday, 22 March, *The Times* described 'peaceful and well-dressed crowds of holyday makers' looking at 'broken windows, and pavements strewn here and there with the fragments of stone, broken bottles, brick, and oyster-shells' that had been flung at the police. Further disturbances were put down by the police and fresh cavalry, though there were demonstrations and some violence in nearby towns. On 23 March, the Central Executive, chaired by Kay-Shuttleworth, lamented the disturbances and 'entirely approved' of the reduction of the relief and its distribution by ticket. 'Never in our history', thundered *The Times* on 24 March, 'from WAT TYLER'S time downwards, was there a mob more senseless, more ungrateful, or more stupidly ferocious than that which has just held possession of Stalybridge, and which threatens Ashton.' However, on the same day, discussions between the mayor of Stalybridge, the local relief committee and representatives of those on relief ended with a temporary acceptance of the committee's terms in the hope that future negotiations might secure some modification.[47]

While his father was in Manchester Ughtred was at Gawthorpe reporting on events in the locality. The Bacup valley would be first to rise, he said; Blackburn was likely to rise and Burnley might follow. Padiham was a peculiar case. Its relief was well managed and its committee unanimous, but the turbulent priest, Edward Verity, was creating 'immense mischief'. In 1862 in Padiham, Verity had formed the East Lancashire Central Operatives Relief Committee, which received over £200 from the Working Men's Central Committee in London. The supply dried up when it was revealed that Verity had been paid considerable expenses from the East Lancashire fund, but his influence remained strong and Ughtred reported his activities with trepidation.[48]

On 25 March, just as the protesters seemed to have been quietened, a group from Stalybridge, in which some clergymen were prominent, persuaded the Mansion House Fund in London to vote £500 to the Stalybridge relief committee, provided it returned to payments in cash. The local committee members were placed in an impossible position: if they accepted the £500 they admitted defeat; if they did not, their unpopularity would increase and they would be held responsible for the disturbances which would assuredly follow. They endeavoured to extricate themselves from their dilemma by resigning. The lamentations were loud. As relief, *The Times* decided, the £500 was ridiculous, but 'as a largess, flung out of a carriage window to a turbulent mob, or as a booty handed out to a highwayman, it is very handsome'. Ughtred thought that assisting those who rebelled against the local committee was a 'dreadful blunder'.[49]

With the secretary of the Executive Committee Kay-Shuttleworth went to Stalybridge the day after the Mansion House Fund's decision and persuaded the committee to rescind their resignation, saying that he would administer the relief by ticket himself if they did not. He then sat with the committee, without saying a word, while they negotiated vainly with a deputation from the protesters. In scenes reminiscent of Bury St Edmunds in 1836 he and the secretary were 'met with sundry unpleasant epithets and an occasional stone' – the secretary was hit on the shoulder by an old coffee pot – as they made their way to the railway station after the meeting. The next day Kay-Shuttleworth, who never lacked courage, returned to address the scholars from the schools. He expressed sympathy with their hardships, praised 'the unwearied attention of the ladies of the middle classes to the wants of the population', and stressed that the Executive Committee had to economize in order to make their funds last into the next winter. One of the most powerful arguments for the extension of the franchise, he said, had been 'the temperate, wise, manly, patient, and intelligent conduct of the Lancashire workpeople'. He also circulated a placard from the Central Executive, pointing out that, if the disturbances continued, there were many people elsewhere who would be grateful for all the Executive Committee could afford them. His uncompromising demeanour, the Executive's threat, and a rumour that the Mansion House Fund might have been stopped carried the day. After the meeting the relief committee's original proposal was accepted, the only change being that shopkeepers could give 6d. and not 5d. in cash when a ticket was presented to them. As was common throughout the distress in Lancashire, the cotton operatives did not tamely accept their plight and could be driven to violence, but in the end they could be persuaded to acquiesce in the existing social order.[50]

Kay-Shuttleworth worked for cotton relief causes until the distress was judged to be over. On 4 December 1865 the Executive Committee had its final meeting and 'Sir J. Kay-Shuttleworth' was among those singled out by the Earl of Derby for thanks. Even then he did not relinquish control. Under a scheme of his devising the money left in the Manchester fund when the distress abated was used to establish the Cotton Districts' Convalescent Fund, which built the Southport Convalescent Home and assisted the Devonshire Hospital in Buxton and the Children's Sanatorium at Southport.[51] The cotton famine took him back in the hurly-burly of political life, working with important politicians on a demanding task of civil service. He displayed the same willingness to experiment with administrative measures as he had shown in his halcyon days, the same driven idealism, and the same fear of public disorder.

During the cotton famine, Kay-Shuttleworth continued an

educational concern which had more success than the schools funded by the Australian colonists, though the famine helped to cause its demise. As early as 1854 he had started the Padiham Trade School to provide a more advanced instruction than the elementary schools, and to assist industrial training by teaching science and art. The enterprise was a failure, and Kay-Shuttleworth's attention turned to the evening schools sometimes attached to elementary schools and to mechanics' institutes. Kay-Shuttleworth proposed an East Lancashire Union of Institutions, which would cover about a dozen of these institutions within a ten-mile radius of Burnley. To improve the education offered in the schools, the Union, which was controlled by a central council made up of representatives of its member institutions and chaired by Kay-Shuttleworth, proposed to conduct examinations and to offer prizes. Successful candidates would obtain a certificate which, Kay-Shuttleworth vainly hoped, would lead employers to give them preference for jobs.[52]

The idea of a union of this kind was relatively new, but not original. However, the East Lancashire Union, which started in 1857, had two novel features: it offered a wider range of subjects for examination than was usual and it provided two certificated teachers, called 'organizing masters', who moved around the evening schools giving lectures and demonstration lessons and helping the local teachers to improve their skills. Candidate teachers were selected from the outstanding students, and they entered a similar relationship to the class and the organizing master as did a pupil-teacher. Eventually the local teachers who, like the candidate teachers, worked at other jobs during the day, were to come from the ranks of the candidate teachers. The echoes of Kay-Shuttleworth's days with the Poor Law Board and the Committee of Council are obvious, and he secured financial support from the Committee for the organizing masters and the candidate teachers.[53]

The Union started well. The main demand was for the elementary rather than the advanced subjects and, despite Kay-Shuttleworth's intentions, men heavily outnumbered women in the classes. However, the Union's evening schools did not share the mechanics' institutes' failure to attract the workers for whom they were designed – about 75 per cent of their students were cotton operatives. The number attending the examinations rose from 20 in 1857 to 175 by 1861, and the experiment with the organizing masters looked promising. In 1860 the Dean of Salisbury told Kay-Shuttleworth that the Union was 'the only successful attempt which has yet been made to supply the great educational want of the day – thoroughly efficient Evening Schools'. Kay-Shuttleworth had the more ambitious vision of providing the 'progressive education of the youth of the district from 13 to 30', and he argued that successful candidates should be able to be nominated for positions in the civil service 'irrespective of selection by means of parliamentary patronage'.[54]

The irrepressible Verity sneered that the Union's examinations were 'an attempt to dissect the minds of a few unfortunate working people . . . before the gratified gaze of a vain class'. The annual prize-giving lent his view some weight, as Kay-Shuttleworth endeavoured to attract the aristocracy, politicians and landowners to the ceremony. In 1859, having persuaded Brougham to preside, he lavishly entertained his 81-year-old celebrity at Gawthorpe. 'I wish to surround you in my own house with the scientific and thinking men of our country', he said, forgetful that the cause of Brougham's coming was the education of less eminent people. He later praised Brougham for making the first important efforts at educational legislation: 'That the people should be educated – was what your Lordship sought.' Preparing room for himself in the educational pantheon, he told Brougham that he (Brougham) was 'too much of a nobleman' to consider 'the *particular agency*' through which this aim would be achieved. Finding the means was what Kay-Shuttleworth wanted to be remembered for, and the East Lancashire Union was part of his search.[55]

His failure to persuade Gladstone to attend in 1865 came at a bad time. The Revised Code removed the Committee of Council's support and the local institutes, which had surrendered their jealously guarded autonomy to gain this support, found themselves with a financial burden – the Union's chief attraction, its organizing masters. By 1865 only four institutes were using them, whereas eight had used them in 1860. The cotton famine worsened matters. Though protesting that all was well and referring vaguely to income from subscriptions, Kay-Shuttleworth admitted to Ughtred that there were deficiencies in the Union's funds, but he expressed his determination to keep it afloat at his own expense until the cotton trade improved. But its fortunes did not improve. There were no prize-givings from 1867 to 1870 and, in 1872 when Kay-Shuttleworth withdrew his financial support, the Union ceased to exist. He claimed that the Union had pioneered the systematic teaching of science and, though that claim was too large, the Union did help to diffuse scientific knowledge in the district.[56] It was also a clear indication that Kay-Shuttleworth wished education beyond the elementary to be supported by government and made available to the children of his native county's working classes.

His work for the Lancashire Union passed unnoticed, but his time on the Executive Committee brought him official recognition. On 13 December 1863 Edward (later Viscount) Cardwell, who was Chancellor of the Duchy of Lancaster, invited Kay-Shuttleworth to be High Sheriff, the head of the administration of justice in the county. The position, now largely ceremonial, involved officiating at the opening of the assizes or the swearing in of juries, but it was busy, and the entertaining and travelling could make it expensive. The Lancashire gentry had sometimes to be pressed into accepting the office and Cardwell reminded Kay-Shuttleworth that, in 1861, when his name had been at the head of the rota which helped to decide who should be offered the post, he had declined on grounds of ill-health. Cardwell was 'glad to believe that this reason no longer disqualifies you' and mentioned that 'you have lately been distinguished by your services to the County on the Central Committee at Manchester'.[57]

Kay-Shuttleworth accepted the invitation, and during 1864 he flung himself into the work with characteristic compulsiveness. Hannah's support was crucial to his endeavours, as was the less conspicuous assistance of Lennard. He travelled much around the county and, as Ughtred remembered, entertained generously at Gawthorpe. Under-Sheriffs usually did much of the work of the High Sheriff but delegation was not in Kay-Shuttleworth's nature and his letters contain many references to the busy activity of his shrievalty. His motivation was familial: he was preparing the way, he told Ughtred, 'for my dear son on the circuit and in the County'.[58] For some of Lancashire's merchant, banking and textile families the obtaining of the High Sheriff's office meant a recognition of their new wealth and social standing. The Shuttleworths did not need such recognition, but the Kays did and, as he lavishly entertained the county's well-born and influential people, the erstwhile James Phillips Kay could reflect on the change in the class structure which made the position of High Sheriff available to him. The Kennedy family may even have noticed it.

Ughtred was constantly in his father's mind. His religious development proceeded satisfactorily and he was confirmed in 1861 at the age of 16, but his schooling continued to be a source of anxiety. He had returned to Harrow early in 1861 in another attempt to please his parents. He entered the house of the new headmaster, the 26-year-old H.M. Butler, who was destined to have a great impact on Harrow, though in these early days Ughtred found that he had made no improvement in the routine and customs of the house, and was strict and unpopular. Few of Ughtred's friends remained and he was placed in close proximity to 'a little lazy disagreeable fellow the Honourable Mr Ellis'. Ughtred stood out against his fellow students' principal amusement – betting on horses and in lotteries – was forced to fag for the head of the house, and acquired a new name, 'Spectre', because he was so pale and thin. Swearing was essential to popularity and as he did not swear he was, he told his father, 'one of the objects of torture'. He was 'spanked': 'I had to go into a room and lie full length on the top of a chest of drawers, and be hit by a long assembly of fellows, with twisted and doubled towels, my legs being tied together, and my arms held by a couple of big fellows.' He fell from the chest twice and could not break his fall because his legs were tied, but was let off with less than he expected when one of the boys called out that he was tender and might be hurt if he got too much. He had also to run the gauntlet of boys with twisted towels in their hands and was 'cobbed', which involved being given six cuts each from six boys with twisted towels, this time soaked in water. 'I bore the cobbing without a sound', he wrote, and got off more lightly.[59]

On 23 May, writing from the garden of Butler's house, Ughtred told his father that he had taken his advice on his health and 'all has been attended to that you wish but I am tormented with headache more even than yesterday and the day before'. Desperately he argued that 'we have given as fair a trial to me at Harrow as can be given without risk. Nobody can blame you with taking me away too soon.' Kay-Shuttleworth consulted Janet, who wrote from Vichy approving Ughtred's withdrawal; a doctor, who recommended it; and Butler, who decided that he would have set a good example had his health lasted. Ughtred left Harrow. 'You have told me more than once', Kay-Shuttleworth wrote to Frederick North to inform him of the decision, 'that your late wife's grand children would always be a subject of interest to you.' All of them were dutiful and affectionate but Ughtred was setting them an example in all respects: 'He never gave me one hour's pain in his life.' Harrow caused Ughtred much pain, but at the end of May 1861, aged 16, he became another old Harrovian who had to make his way in the world.[60]

His parents, who consulted each other by letter, were clear about the next step on that way: Ughtred should prepare himself for Cambridge. Though Shaw-Lefevre, from Poor Law days, warned that both a private tutor and a pupil were likely to be lazy and that there could be 'young lady associations – daughters, nieces, or cousins – with whom a young man of fortune is entangled', a tutor was hired and worked with Ughtred for the remainder of 1861 and for all of 1862. By early 1863 Ughtred was politely but stubbornly resisting his father. He did not want to go to Cambridge. 'I write this to beg of you', Ughtred said in a letter from Gawthorpe on 28 April 1863, 'that we may now speak to each other about these things openly, and that I may express to you my reasons for still urging you to accede to my earnest wishes on this subject.' If he went to Cambridge he would scarcely be able to be with his father and he could not, 'under the peculiar circumstances of our family, bear the separation'. He could obtain the numerous advantages of going to Cambridge in more congenial ways and had proved that he could work independently.

> My wish is this. Not to go to the University at all. To go to read law in London and to read here also so as to be able to be well prepared to be called to the bar at the end of 3 years. Then to go on the Northern Circuit with Uncle Joe, to try and really work there and prepare both for my many duties here, and for my public duties in Parliament &c.

His father had always consulted his wishes but he had been too young to ask 'so strongly about so important a thing before'. 'I assure you however', declared Ughtred, conscious that he had reached a watershed in his life and in his relationship with his father, 'that, after the trouble which Mamma's absence from you and all of us gives me continually, my greatest trouble is the prospect which has been hanging over me of my being obliged to go to Cambridge.'[61]

Ughtred was rarely so explicit about his mother and so determined to alter his father's planning. His bond with his father was close and, while determined, he was nervously concerned to avoid straining his father's affection. For Kay-Shuttleworth the struggle was equally momentous. He looked forward to Ughtred's having an illustrious public career so that he might vicariously experience the public recognition which he had grasped, tasted, but not been able to keep. And in a life starved of human affection his bond with Ughtred was his most intense personal relationship, closer even than that with his sister Hannah. When, a few years later, Ughtred fell from a horse near Marble Arch and suffered concussion which was at first thought more serious, Kay-Shuttleworth was distraught. 'It is curious', a friend observed, 'how wholly Ughtred has absorbed his affections.'[62]

Ughtred's rejection of Cambridge challenged his father's deepest hopes and feelings.

Kay-Shuttleworth insisted on the 'indispensable importance' of being in a large college like Trinity where Ughtred could compare himself with other men, and 'learn what will be required of you in competition with others in public life'. Without a college education a man lacked both 'the training which facilitates his intercourse with these men' and 'the moral and mental aptitudes which could enable him to succeed in his intercourse with them'. Clear-sighted about the social function of Oxford and Cambridge, and determined that his son should not have the handicaps he had faced, he enlisted friends and acquaintances such as Angela Burdett-Coutts, Nassau Senior and Charles Henry, or relatives such as Frederick North, in his campaign. At his club he pestered acquaintances with enquiries about his son's odd preference, and unaccountably impressed that 'two Oxford first class men' thought that a promising young man should be shaped in their image, he told Ughtred that they were strongly in favour of a university career.[63]

If his father insisted, Ughtred said, he would go to Cambridge, even though it meant a separation that was bad for both of them; but whatever happened, 'I wish and intend to become a useful man and not to live at home and do nothing'. By late July Ughtred's determination had been rewarded. He was to go to the University of London, which his Dissenting forefathers had started, and which offered a more modern curriculum than the two universities which had defined what 'university' meant. He studied science not law, having decided that he was beginning to understand what was meant by the 'Origin of the Species', and been captivated by Thomas Henry Huxley. It was a brave victory for Ughtred and as brave a capitulation by his father, who immediately began pressing friends such as the inspector, Joshua Fitch, for information he judged his son would require. Janet Kay-Shuttleworth, disappointed that Ughtred would miss the society of Cambridge's young men but fearing for his health, accepted the decision. By October 1864 Ughtred was ensconced at London. Huxley had given him 'exceedingly good natured and polite' advice, and he had settled into the chemistry course with 'three hideous young Japanese, a gentlemanlike intelligent-looking Parsee, an elderly grey-haired clergyman', and a man once a Roman Catholic priest and now an infidel. Despite this disconcerting company, Ughtred's scientific studies prospered, and he was eventually to write a successful textbook, *First Principles of Modern Chemistry*.[64]

Ughtred's informal education continued. Kay-Shuttleworth frequently discussed the estate with him, working carefully through routine matters of management and making him aware of new opportunities, such as ensuring that a branch of the main railway line came to the colliery on the estate. It was of '*paramount importance*', he told Ughtred. Without it, his efforts to build up 'the children's fortunes' would be put at risk, as would '*my efforts to keep up for you the position of the family in Lancashire*'. His personal morality was linked to the care of the estate: 'Never pass before you the example of any of the elder sons of any of our neighbours. They are bearers of *warning*.' He was not to play whist even for a small amount of money if out of his domestic circle, 'certainly never with anyone in a railway carriage'. He should not play cards or billiards in a public place or except among proven friends, for cards and gaming had ruined many an estate. He should eat lunch in his private lodgings, for in a public room he might be 'watched and entrapped by some of those sharks, always lurking about for young men'. The moral vision Kay-Shuttleworth offered his son was not purely prudential. 'Your life has, I trust in God', he wrote in 1864, 'a different destiny [from that of other elder sons]. You will I hope live a life of intellectual and religious growth.' He captured both the spiritual and prudential emphasis in instructions he gave Ughtred when he left him alone for the first time at Gawthorpe:

> *Have family prayers every morning and evening!*
> Act as if you were in my place.
> Take care of the office work.[65]

There were lighter aspects to Ughtred's training. He was to go on shooting trips, take outdoor exercise and play field sports and cricket. More refined pursuits had also to be followed: 'a few little bits of dancing are very necessary to complete my education in that branch', Ughtred informed his father in June 1864. And 'society' had to be conquered both in Lancashire and London. 'A new proof that my efforts to introduce you to the best society in Lancashire are successful occurred today', a delighted Kay-Shuttleworth told his son in November 1862, reporting an important invitation which had been received. In London Lady Caroline Hatherton (as the remarried Caroline Davenport was now called) and Angela Burdett-Coutts gave Ughtred entry to polite and powerful circles. Kay-Shuttleworth had stretched his range of political and social contacts in Manchester and London through his work for cotton relief which brought him closer to John Bright, Richard Cobden, and a politician who had strongly argued Lancashire's need, John Wilson Patten, whom in his youth Kay-Shuttleworth had attacked in the *Letter to the People of Lancashire*.[66] Thanks to his mother's family and to the education his father was giving him, Ughtred moved much more easily in these circles than his father had done.

Kay-Shuttleworth was particularly anxious that Ughtred should build bridges with his mother's family, both the Marjoribanks and the Norths. The link was assisted by Janet's half-sister, Catherine, with whom Ughtred became friendly, went riding and visited Harrow. When she married John Addington Symonds Jr, Ughtred attended the wedding in Bristol. He also grew closer to Frederick North, and disconcerted his father when he wrote to him on 18 April 1864 about North's disgust that the Conservative Opposition had made education a party question 'about which to chastise the Government and damage it throughout the country'. As these attacks had forced the resignation of Robert Lowe, Kay-Shuttleworth stiffly pointed out that he and North differed on many subjects because North was dominated by party considerations whereas he was more independent. He realized that Ughtred would form other associations, but 'it will be a consolation to me – in what remains of life – if we continue of one mind in most if not all things'. Ughtred produced a hasty answer in which, while putting North's views in the best possible light, he showed his disagreement with North and his opposition to Lowe. All that Ughtred said about the education question, the conduct of the government and the Opposition, and Mr North's views, a gratified Kay-Shuttleworth wrote to his son, 'gives me pleasure'.[67]

By 1865, Ughtred's education was proceeding so satisfactorily that Janet Kay-Shuttleworth warned him not to enter too swiftly into public life. Young men could be 'self-confident and presumptuous', Ughtred replied, and express opinions which hampered them later in life when they wanted to express 'maturer and often opposite convictions'. He did not plan to make public speeches on important matters for some years yet – he and Papa entirely agreed on this policy which they had often talked over. A man 'ought not to venture into public life till his preparation, which ought to be very careful and thorough, is complete' and until he was 'very well acquainted with the subject with which he will have to deal'.[68] Ughtred had just turned 20.

In the evening of 20 July 1864, his sixtieth birthday, Kay-Shuttleworth sat alone on his estate at Barbon and wrote Janet and

Ughtred a reflective and gloomy letter. 'It is a solemn time', he told his two oldest children, 'and I should be very insensible, if I did not *deeply* even *painfully* feel the import of this day of advanced life.' He was thankful to God that they had never caused him worry for if it had been otherwise 'I fear I could not have borne that further burthen'. He wanted to prepare them for the inevitable: what lay before him were 'declining strength – increasing infirmity – and a feebler capacity to help and protect you'. Ahead of Ughtred was the finishing of his science degree and the study of history, constitutional law, political economy and moral philosophy; Janet was to learn to speak and write English, French, Italian and German easily and eloquently. Both had to help him bring up their younger brothers. These considerations had weaned him from public life and given him domestic responsibilities which he had tried his best to discharge. Yet he was '*oppressed* with a sense of *duty unfulfilled*' and wished to die with a conscience full of charity and love. He asked to be forgiven where he had offended as 'before God I truly and sincerely forgive all offences against myself, and pray for God's mercy to my soul'.[69]

The melancholy tone of the letter is typical of Kay-Shuttleworth in the mid-1860s, though he had expressed some of its sentiments before. June and Helen Kennedy and Janet Kay-Shuttleworth had been the recipients of his self-engrossed expressions of love, and had experienced how he diminished the love that others might feel for him by making that love seem necessary to enable him to bear crushing burdens. Janet had also heard him accepting the ending of his public life and embracing the next temptation to resume it.

There were reasons for his depression. His neuralgia continued and he was frequently forced to walk with the aid of a stick – one illustration of the Manchester Executive Committee shows him sitting with his chair pushed back from the table and a walking stick at his side. His motor co-ordination had clearly declined: his handwriting, which in his youth and middle age was difficult to read but fluent, became waveringly spiky and very hard to decipher. He had frequently to use an amanuensis – most of the letters discussing Ughtred's last days at Harrow and the decision to allow him to leave are in Hannah's handwriting. Despite the loss of one eye his sight was good, and his intellectual power was undiminished. He continued to read widely – Ughtred reported to his mother in 1865 that he was reading a life of Caesar in French – and, though he complained that his low state of health and spirits made him 'unequal to prolonged and serious literary composition', he continued to work at his second

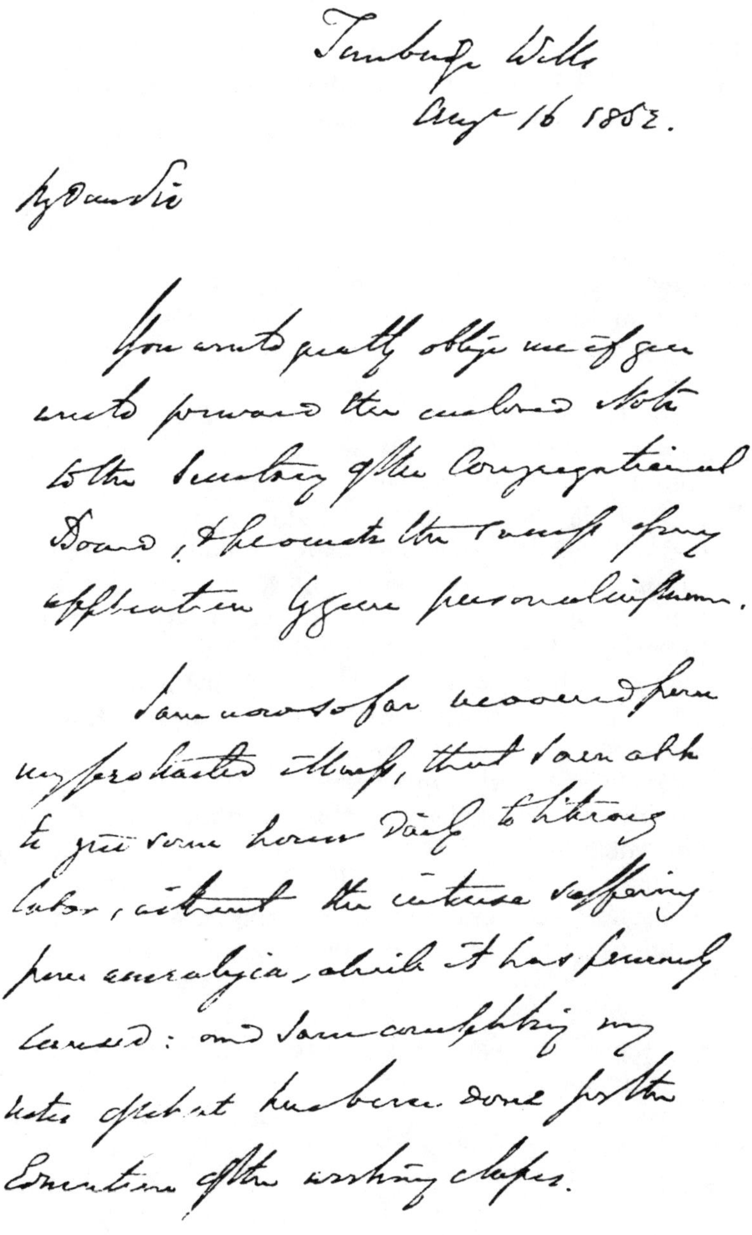

Tunbridge Wells
Aug 16 1852.

My dear Sir

You would greatly oblige me if you would forward the enclosed Note to the Secretary of the Congregational Board, & promote the success of my application by your personal influence.

I am now so far recovered from my protracted illness, that I am able to give some hours daily to literary labor, without the intense suffering from neuralgia, which it has formerly caused: and I am completing my notes of what has been done for the Education of the working classes.

'The intense suffering from neuralgia': a letter from Sir James in 1852

novel which he finished in 1869. He maintained a demanding
schedule during his work for cotton relief, the Revised Code debate
and his shrievalty. His was still a powerful personality and a
formidable mind, but the physical strain had left its mark.[70]

His depression was fuelled by his failure to accept the ending of his
public life, in the sense of holding a position such as he had held in the
civil service. Though he protested his slackening interest in politics
and his disenchantment with party, he was never content with the
domestic responsibilities and, for all its intensity, the surrogate life he
lived through Ughtred did not satisfy him. 'That which I can least
bear', he confided to his son in January 1864, 'is a stagnant life.' He
attacked the Whig aristocracy's power to protect traditional abuses:
'rotten boroughs, bribery and corruption of electors – undue
personal influence over voters – and an unequal distribution of
representation so as to favour the predominance of the Whigs'. On
the other hand, the Tories' incapacity, lack of foresight, and
selfishness made them incapable of defending 'the wholesome
traditions of the constitution'. He wanted a middle party composed
of 'philosophical reformers – and the most enlightened Whigs and
conservatives', but expected to be worn out or dead before such a
party proved possible. Yet, as the 1865 election loomed, he had long
conversations with friends such as William Langton over party and
personal manoeuvrings, and heard again the siren call of an old
dalliance which never lost its allure, Parliament.[71]

By 1865 Kay-Shuttleworth labelled the radical elements in the
Liberal party as 'revolutionary', and told Ughtred that if he were
young he would fight against manhood suffrage, the vote by ballot
and triennial parliaments. In late February, in preparation for a
general election, Kay-Shuttleworth was approached to stand as a
Liberal candidate for the seat of South Lancashire on the understanding that Gladstone, who had taken out insurance against his
uncertain hold on Oxford by nominating for South Lancashire, did
not stand. Kay-Shuttleworth and Gladstone were moving in opposite
political directions, and it was an ironic testament to their political
fluidity that their names should now be linked. For reasons which are
unclear, Kay-Shuttleworth declined the opportunity to stand. He
told Ughtred that he would not accept unless he were fully satisfied
about the extent and unanimity of Liberal support in every part of the
electorate and if expenses over £1,000 were guaranteed. Whether or
not his requirements were met is unknown, but he informed Derby
that he had numerous reasons for declining, including the feeling

that standing for Parliament immediately after their work on the Relief Committee exposed him to 'imputations as to the motives which had determined the extent of relief in particular districts' and though these imputations were unfounded he wished for the sake of the committee to avoid them. He and Ughtred supported his cousin, Richard Fort, who won Clitheroe when the Conservative candidate withdrew.[72]

He found some release from his depression on the estate. Road and bridge building and draining continued, the banks of the Calder were strengthened, walks were put in at Gawthorpe, fencing was extended and repaired, and the ground was prepared for croquet and plantations. Kay-Shuttleworth reported regularly to Janet on the finances of the estate. In a detailed statement (in Hannah's handwriting) which he sent with the audited accounts in 1863 he showed that the income was continuing to improve, but even on a prospering estate the distress had left its mark: the annual investment of about £2,000 which he made for the children (excluding Ughtred) had been absorbed, from October 1861 until April 1862, by the provision he had made for cotton relief. He guarded the estate with a single-minded determination never more clearly displayed than in the battles over railways and coal which landowners fought with intense bitterness. Thus in 1865 he wrote with cool triumph to Ughtred to say that, at his suggestion, the Lancashire and Yorkshire Railway Co. had adopted a line which was greatly to the advantage of Gawthorpe, adding perhaps £5,000 a year to the coal rental in five years' time. He had withdrawn from the directorship of a rival line because he thought it over-committed and likely to enable all the local coal fields to compete with the Shuttleworths in what he knew would be a very hard-fought battle. The Lancashire and Yorkshire offer had the additional advantage of assisting Richard Fort's ventures, thus enabling family co-operation, but giving no advantage to any rival company.[73]

From his personal income, not the estate's, he paid for the building in 1863 of a house and stables on Barbon, in Westmorland near Kirkby Lonsdale. The building and furnishing of Barbon Manor, he stressed to Ughtred and Janet in the letter he wrote to them on his sixtieth birthday, was 'the legacy of that sixtieth birthday' given to them and their brothers. The building of the 'shooting box' had been a plan of the Shuttleworth family and would end the need to preserve grouse at Gawthorpe 'to which both your parents have always been averse'. A hunting lodge to his sons, Barbon became for

Kay-Shuttleworth a place of escape, a sanatorium where he experienced some calmness and peace.[74]

But Barbon did not distract him from the larger estate and he did his best to maintain good relations with his tenants, the miners who worked for his colliery lessees and the local population. The Long Gallery at Gawthorpe was the setting for half-yearly Rent Dinners, and in the same setting and sometimes in the servants' hall he gave dinners to the miners. He was amused by their songs, even those which referred to poaching, and may have used the occasions to retune his ear to their dialect which he reproduced in his novels. This experiment had to be dropped because, as Ughtred later remarked, 'it was impossible to guard against some excess either of eating or drinking'. More successful was his decision in the 1860s to open Gawthorpe's grounds to the public for three or four hours on Sunday afternoons, especially in summer or autumn. He often walked among the visitors and Ughtred remembered that, if he passed a group whose hands 'remained in their pockets, and no hat or cap had been touched', he would sometimes bow formally to them and, to his satisfaction and amusement, attract some form of salutation. He had come a long way from the aggressive young man who, about 30 years earlier in his *Letter to the People of Lancashire*, had mocked lords who 'give us races in their parks, and lectures on the dignity of the aristocracy at our dinners'.[75]

For all the moments of importance on summer Sunday afternoons, Gawthorpe was a constant reminder of Kay-Shuttleworth's most painful rejection. The improvements he had made, his skill in managing the estate, and all the entwined Ks and Ss on its walls, could not hide the fact that Gawthorpe was Janet's family home and she did not live in it. His letters to her were sometimes headed 'My dear wife' and were often signed 'Your faithful husband'; and there is no reason to believe that he was not a faithful husband: certainly there is no evidence of any other attachment.[76] Yet the titles carried their own message: their relationship had become a sad masque in which they played out their roles as husband and wife, being united only by the roles. By the mid-1860s they had drifted further apart, not because of any new crisis but because a decade of separation made their separate lives seem normal.

Janet's health continued to be bad and a series of letters Ughtred wrote from Grand Parade, Eastbourne, in January 1862 were typical of the reports Kay-Shuttleworth received. Mamma was very pleased that he had come, though she had suffered much pain. A week later

Mamma's health had improved and she was able to see him a good deal more than usual; a few days later she could get up and even go into Janet's room, and might soon be able to come down to the dining-room for a short time each day. Then Miss Poplawska injured her ankle and went to bed, and 'as she sleeps in Mamma's bedroom I was unable to see Mamma yesterday morning'. In another few days, however, Mamma was feeling much better and planned to go to Brighton in a week's time. Just once, Ughtred glimpsed hope. 'I write you a scrap to tell you some excellent news', he excitedly informed his father in April 1861. Miss Poplawska was leaving Eastbourne for Germany 'either for good or for a very long time'. She was taking all her things with her and he would be surprised if she ever returned. His hopes rose higher the next day when he confirmed that in a few days Miss Poplawska was leaving for Prussia accompanied by her maid, and that Mamma's German butler was also returning to Germany. 'Thus she and all here leave Mamma (as I think never to return).' He intended to observe 'the anniversary of her departure as a feast!' But Rosa Poplawska either did not go or returned very quickly, and never again were Ughtred's or his father's spirits raised by the hope that she might leave.[77] Ughtred's youthful anguish indicates that his remarks in his reminiscences about Rosa Poplawska's hypnotic and baleful influence over his mother drew on deep memories. But memories they remained, and memories associated with a disappointment.

Young Janet, who turned 22 in 1865, had the same expectation of life as her mother: they would always be together. With her mother's health consistently precarious and Rosa Poplawska being a companion and not a maidservant, Janet was looked to for assistance. She wrote letters for her mother, attended to her when she was confined to her room or resting in a sitting-room unable to come downstairs, and travelled with her on the Continent or on her rare holidays at places such as Yarmouth or Brighton. She assisted with the education of her younger brothers when they were being taught by tutors and when they returned to Eastbourne on school holidays, her facility with languages being especially valued. Inevitably she was trapped amid the conflicting expectations of her father and mother. In 1862, for example, Ughtred indignantly told his father that his mother had decided that she needed a course of Vichy waters and baths and that she intended to take Janet with her. A trip the previous year had harmed Janet's health, Ughtred thought, and he argued that it was 'impossible under almost any circumstances to allow her to repeat that journey'. He also suggested that the time had come for the establishment of 'an understanding that you *must* see her for a certain time every year'.[78]

Janet went to Vichy. In 1864 she visited her father and wrote excitedly to Ughtred of seeing the Langtons, of the autumn tints at Gawthorpe, of her father reading aloud to her in the evenings, and of the 'jolly time you and I had together at Barbon. I shall never forget it'. The reality of her life immediately intruded, however; she was going abroad and it would be 'a good while' before they were together again. The following year Ughtred tried to arrange for Janet to come with him for a fortnight's visit to their father at Barbon. However, Janet was needed to look after her younger brothers, and her mother was ill. Unthinkingly betraying the depth of Janet's dilemma, Ughtred pointed out that he and his father were anxious that she should not leave 'if Mamma is not well' and if she 'could save Mamma fatigue or trouble' with the boys. Understandably Janet thought that there was no chance that she could come. For Kay-Shuttleworth the pain of the separation was marked. A trip to Scotland which they took together in 1863 gave him a rare opportunity for paternal pride: 'She is beautiful in her Pompadour dress', he told Ughtred, 'and evidently much admired.' On one of her visits he launched a campaign to have her meet English gentlefolk, perhaps as an antidote to the environment with which her mother and Miss Poplawska surrounded her. But he never lost the loneliness he expressed in a letter in October 1862. Asking her to visit him, he said: 'Remember how very much of your society I denied myself in order that you might be with your mother and have the benefit of the air. Remember how very deeply I feel my responsibilities towards my dear daughter.' They ought to be one in thought, feeling, opinion and affection, he concluded his letter, knowing that the circumstances had made that oneness unlikely.[79]

Kay-Shuttleworth's separation from his younger sons also continued, because they lived mostly with his wife or, as they became older, went to boarding school. By the mid-1860s the first stirrings of doubt about their futures began to quiver in his mind. Ughtred had reported that the 16-year-old Lionel, and Stewart, who was 14, were a little lazy and childish. Kay-Shuttleworth decided that Lionel did not thrive with petting, and wanted him treated with kindness as well as firmness, for harsh discipline made him 'sullen and obstinate'. There were echoes of older battles in this conclusion, which might have been reinforced by Ughtred's opinion that Lionel, when with his mother, was usually 'odd and rather noisy and rough'. He was a good worker, but there were ominous signs which Ughtred was well placed to recognize: in June 1864 Lionel was home from school with headaches. Kay-Shuttleworth planned to take him into the country daily – this was now very feasible, even from Gloucester Square, 'what with Underground & Above-ground railways &c.'. Stewart was a somewhat thoughtless child and he had 'fascinating winning ways' which made people spoil him; but, Ughtred confided to his father in July 1865, he was too fond of reading story-books and novels. Rather than forbidding such reading, Ughtred suggested that Stewart should be restricted to books from the school and dormitory libraries. Sagely Ughtred explained that 'his appetite for reading if kept in moderate bounds and encouraged in a wholesome way may be very useful to him'. No such appetite had shown itself in the rest of the children, Ughtred concluded with relief.[80]

Much more serious worries were developing with Robert, or Robin, as he was usually called. Like his two younger brothers, he attended Wellington College. Founded only in 1859, it had been chosen by Kay-Shuttleworth because of 'the preponderance of the middle class element which has before it the necessity of energetic action'. This character and 'the greater scope given to modern studies' had decided his choice of school for his younger sons: Harrow, for the eldest son for whom the estate, public life and Parliament beckoned, Wellington College for those who had to earn their living. Unfortunately Robin suffered severe headaches and the doctor was called in; by 18 April 1865 Robin had left Wellington (he was then 17) and was disconsolately considering his future. Ughtred asked his father if Robin's plans could be definitely settled as, even after allowing for exaggerations in the reports from Aunt Hannah, who was very sympathetic to Robin, there was no doubt that he was anxious and depressed. Kay-Shuttleworth arranged for Robin to work in the bank of his old friend, William Langton, but Robin could not bear the busy hours and routine of the bank and was suffering 'a very trying attack of some stomach derangement and sickness – with extreme faintness'. A merchant's office in Manchester was Robin's next place of employment, and in December 1865 Kay-Shuttleworth reported that Robin 'devotes himself to commerce and perseveres after trial'.[81]

Robin did not persevere for long, and a father for whom the work ethic was of consuming importance faced a son whom he could not understand. He was estranged from his wife and his meetings with his daughter came at intervals snatched from a programme he did not control. He guarded the interests of the Gawthorpe estate successfully and ruthlessly, but in the final analysis he was its manager, not its owner. The successes and excitement of his past were sealed off from him and could not be revisited. Public life on any continuing basis remained closed. Parliament had again beckoned but he had had to turn away. He was, in 1865, a 61-year-old man in ill health who lived in fear of epilepsy and perhaps of neurosyphilis. His depression was not hard to understand.

9 · The final years, 1865–77

The year 1870 marked the end of a major period in Kay-Shuttleworth's life. During this period he extended his activities in social and educational reform into new areas, watched his efforts for national education come to a culmination, and reached finality in his relationship with Janet, who went to live on the Continent, never to return to England.

The National Association for the Promotion of Social Science originated at a meeting in Brougham's home in Grafton Street on 29 July 1857. Kay-Shuttleworth may not have attended the meeting, though it drew inspiration from a conference in London on school attendance of which he had been one of the organizers. The Association, which met for the first time on 12 October 1857 in Birmingham, tried to advance causes he had espoused at the Manchester Statistical Society. Advancing knowledge, said G.W. Hastings, the Association's secretary, in words which James Kay might have used, showed 'an inseparable connexion between the various branches of physical science, and disclosed . . . a unity throughout creation, a vast expression of purpose based on a few simple laws'. Science offered the Association a methodology, a unifying principle, and a form of organization: the Association adopted 'the plan of assembling together occasionally' which had been popularized by the British Association for the Advancement of Science. It divided itself into five interest-groups, called 'departments': law-amendment, education, crime, public health, and social economy, and attracted reforming politicians of many hues, including Brougham, Gladstone, Granville, Shaftesbury, Russell, Pakington and Slaney. Through it Kay-Shuttleworth could also meet medical and civil service colleagues, such as Alison, Chadwick, Southwood Smith and Trevelyan.[1]

Brougham asserted that 'nothing of party, nothing of what is termed political, except in the good sense of the phrase' was to enter into the working of the Association. In fact the Association was intensely political in a reformist sense, though it did little to overcome the early self-criticism that no representatives of the working classes attended its meetings which were 'peculiarly concerned with their interests'. It brought together members of the aristocracy and the middle class, politicians and civil servants, intellectuals and practical reformers. Its influence began to fade in the 1880s, but for about a quarter of a century it promoted reforms in the fields designated by its departments, owing its success to careful negotiation, adroit lobbying, its influential membership, and the discussion generated through its annual conferences.[2]

Kay-Shuttleworth was virtually a permanent member of its council from 1857 until the early 1870s, and he was three times elected president of a department: of social economy in 1859, education in 1860, and economy and trade (the departments changed their names from time to time) in 1866. In his presidential address to the 1866 conference he shed a revealing light on his own views. The Association was founded, he said, 'on the idea that the growth of civilisation proceeds according to laws, the investigation of which is as much a matter of science as are the physical laws which govern the material world'. Both the physical and moral laws were the work of a supreme and harmonious intelligence and will, and were part of one design. All social and political changes resulted from 'the continuous operation of natural forces, which evolve phenomena in a regular succession. Nothing endures which is not in harmony with this law.' In general 'all sudden transitions in national polity' – for example, the changing of government from one class to another – 'unless brought about by the irresistible force of the growth of intelligence and virtue, partake of the character of revolutions, and of their weakness in the presence of surrounding conditions not in harmony with them'. Though the social laws were not yet fully understood, Kay-Shuttleworth was certain that, underlying all advances in national polity, there was 'the degree in which education has been extended, at any period, so as to prepare each class either to enjoy the benefits of freedom, or, which is much more difficult, to promote by active exertion, the growth of free institutions'. Never had this been better illustrated than by the behaviour of the operatives during the cotton famine. They accepted charity and conformed to 'an artificial social organisation of labour on public works, and attendance in day and sewing-schools' for years, while living on one-third of their income, and thus had proven their political intelligence and their 'patient martyr-like endurance for the sake of sacred principles.'[3]

To the faith in the unity of knowledge, in the possibility of a social science, and in the power of education which had characterized the young physician, Kay-Shuttleworth of the late 1860s and early 1870s had added a touch of Darwinism to justify his programme of cautious reform. Fittingly, he gave the address in Manchester. He and the Association were continuing the tradition of that city's statistical society by claiming a non-political, scientific status for social laws which they put to political ends.

On 18 June 1864 a deputation from the National Association for the Promotion of Social Science pressed upon the Prime Minister the need for a royal commission 'to enquire into the grammar schools and other endowed schools in the United Kingdom not yet reported upon and generally into the state of education of the middle classes'. The Newcastle Commission reported in 1861, and early in 1864 the Clarendon Commission had reported on the nine ancient Public Schools. The Schools Inquiry Commission, established in December 1864 under the chairmanship of Lord Taunton, brought the great school enquiries of the 1860s to a symmetrical conclusion, but it answered to more than a desire for tidiness. Middle-class education had been a concern throughout the century, and the National Association's education department had often discussed it, once led by Kay-Shuttleworth who had written about it in 1853 in *Public Education.*[4]

Allsobrook has sketched the scene which faced the Taunton Commission: 'A copse of seven or eight hundred endowed grammar schools was accompanied by a dense and ever-changing thicket of private schools, and a staid and limited plantation of more promising proprietary schools.' When the Taunton Commission reported at the end of 1867, it described a scene of chaos in overwhelming detail, 'the most complete sociological information pertaining to education ever assembled in this country', Brian Simon has said. Outdated statutes had been left unrevised or maladministered; a legion of incompetent teachers used bad teaching methods; a master was discovered who had taught no pupils for 30 years; trustees were often neglectful and sometimes corrupt; the passage of time, the folly of the law and the power of vested interests kept large endowments at places where there were few pupils, while elsewhere mere pittances were available to meet great need; there was a 'complete absence of all organization of schools in relation to one another'.[5]

The Commission recommended the creation of a central authority and the establishment of local authorities, subordinate to the central body but responsible for schemes of instruction, management and inspection. A three-tier system of schooling was to be organized. In the first grade, pupils destined for a liberal education would stay until they were 18 or 19 and learn Latin and Greek. In the second grade, pupils planning to enter the army, the civil service and the medical and legal professions (except for the highest branches) would stay until 16, would not be taught Greek, but would be offered two modern languages. In the third, where the leaving age was 14 and pupils were destined to be superior tradesmen or tenant farmers, they would learn the elements of Latin and a modern language. The report quoted Lord Harrowby, one of its witnesses, who made explicit the class basis of this arrangement: 'I should like to club the grammar schools with some relation to locality, and I should like to say, you shall be a good lower middle-class school; you shall be a middle middle-class school; and you shall be a higher middle-class school, that which is now called a grammar school.'[6]

On 8 May 1866 Kay-Shuttleworth gave evidence to the Commission, and in October he presented a paper on endowments to the annual conference of the National Association – 'a more weighty and suggestive paper than that of Sir James Kay Shuttleworth has never been offered for the consideration of this or of any other society', said Brougham, whose contribution to the reform of charitable endowments Kay-Shuttleworth had acknowledged. The paper drew on *Public Education* and gave a powerful expression of his views. 'No funds, in the just and wise application of which the public, and especially the poorer classes, are universally interested', he declared, 'were ever worse administered.' The Court of Chancery was basically judicial and could not originate proceedings; moreover, its interpretation of *cy près*, the principle of keeping as near as possible to the original donor's intentions, was rigid. As a result 'the most fantastic ideas of the morbid fancy of a recluse are as much respected as the wisest foundations of an enlightened and pious donor'. Like many writers he had his favourite example: a tobacconist who had left a field, the rent of which was to be held in trust 'to supply six poor women with snuff at *Bartholemy tide*'. The smaller bequests often consisted of rent charges which, through the lapse of time, were not collected and became absorbed into the estate. Its owners, especially if they were new, resisted payment if the charge were rediscovered, and the small charities could not afford legal action. Where the endowment was a house it often fell into disrepair, and there were many difficulties in the appointment of trustees. If endowments specifically for education could support a small school their conditions often made them unattractive to students; usually, however, they could not support a school, nor could they be transferred to aid other schools, nor used to provide a scholarship to a nearby school or an exhibition to a university.[7]

These endowments greatly troubled Kay-Shuttleworth because he accepted Brougham's calculations that, if combined, they might be worth 'half a million at least', and therefore be comparable with the parliamentary grant for education. His paper gave details of Bills he had prepared in 1841 and 1843 which were designed, among other things, to consolidate endowments so that they could be given to schools other than the one originally endowed, and to extend *cy près* so that endowments could be used to restore buildings, to enlarge the curriculum and to introduce modern improvements. These limited measures, he reported, 'encountered an insurmountable jealousy, though if they had passed into law, many trustees would have eagerly availed themselves of their provisions'.[8] In the bitter early years at the Committee of Council, his preparation of the Bills was evidence of political optimism; their retrieval 20 years later, at a more propitious time, was evidence of the tenacity with which he clung to his convictions.

The problem of endowments flushed out another cause he supported, the education of girls. The Taunton Commission recommended that girls' schools should be admitted to a 'direct and substantial' part in endowments where that was possible. Seven years earlier, in the midst of the Revised Code debate, Granville had asked Kay-Shuttleworth's opinion as to whether women should be admitted to London University. Kay-Shuttleworth condemned the existing method of educating women as 'objectionable' and argued that they should be 'trained in the subjects which we have considered requisite for the general education of young men'. He saw no real difficulty in having women sit for matriculation and university degrees, arguing that it need not infringe 'any feeling of decorum or delicacy', for the women could be examined separately and compete only with each other. The paternalism in these arrangements should not hide their contemporary liberality which, he warned Granville, would excite ridicule and obloquy. He returned to the issue in his Manchester address, arguing that endowments should be extended to assist the education of girls.[9]

Causes with which he had been concerned for much longer retained his attention. His paper lamented the fact that the Charity Commission was not 'empowered to exercise many of the administrative functions now so beneficially exerted by the Committee of Council on Education'. He wanted the Commission to have one or two commissioners added and become the executive of a committee of public charities 'under the Vice-President of the Committee of Council on Education, and in subordination to that committee'. His model was uncomplicated: the new Charity Commission should have the power to inspect buildings 'with a view to scholastic purposes' and, while 'it would not proceed authoritatively', should advise on the qualifications of masters, the curriculum and the methods of instruction. It should become, as the Committee of Council had under his supervision, 'a centre of administrative experience and skill'. 'It is marvellous', he said, restating his faith in the state's role,

> that a superstitious adherence to the bare letter of the English idea of self-government should have been preferred to an interference which would have rescued from fraud, mismanagement, waste, or pernicious application, a large part of a revenue exceeding a million and a half in annual value, and of which probably three-fourths of a million might be made the prolific seed of an efficient system of education for the middle classes and the poor.

England had refused to learn from the example of Europe in endeavouring to develop the intelligence of 'its entire peoples'. He knew only too well that 'few things had been more unpopular' than directing attention to the European example, but he persisted because 'the future of the nation requires the light and guidance of a generally-cultivated and refined mental power'.[10]

Education under the patronage of the state had now become necessary for the middle class. Indeed he had a wider vision: one Vice-President could represent the Education Department and the revamped Charity Commission in the House of Commons. 'I conceive that a Minister of Education already exists', he said, equating the Vice-President with a Minster and asserting that it was only a matter of time before he was admitted to the Cabinet. The sharing of a Vice-President could help to establish a relationship between the elementary schools, the grammar schools, and the universities. 'They might form a series of institutions, with means of transition from the lowest to the highest; thus establishing for the greatest capacities of all ranks an equality of privileges which, for political and social purposes, is of national importance.[11] Kay-Shuttleworth was one of the first to suggest that governments might develop a complete education system, which opened vistas of equal opportunity to the nation's students. Even if those vistas proved less rewarding than many hoped, to have seen them in the 1860s, and to have directed others towards them, was an act of imagination beyond the power of most of his contemporaries.

Kay-Shuttleworth put his ideas on middle-class education into practice at the local level. He was assisted by Joshua Fitch who, in October 1865, as an assistant commissioner of the Taunton Commission, visited Giggleswick School, an endowed school established in north Yorkshire during the reign of Henry VIII. Fitch remarked:

> if the inhabitants of this obscure little town understood their true interests they would soon admit that any scheme which was founded on an utter disregard of Giggleswick and Settle, but which promised to make the institution a flourishing and attractive school of the highest class, would in the end prove a far greater local blessing than one which allowed them to appropriate a revenue of £1200 to the elementary education of their own children.

Fitch had been well briefed by Kay-Shuttleworth, who was one of ten new governors appointed to the school by the Charity Commission the previous year. Only two months after he was appointed, Kay-Shuttleworth was in London negotiating with the Charity Commission and telling Ughtred that he would have more influence with the Commission than any other governor. He was determined to search for a 'more enlarged apprehension of modern educational requirements' than was being displayed by the old governors who were almost entirely local residents.[12]

The headmaster, J.R. Blakiston, who had sought this expansion since his appointment in 1858, was uncompromisingly committed to moulding the school along Arnoldian lines and was irked by restrictions placed on him by the old governors. Blakiston and the usher (senior master), who had both been appointed by the governors to freehold positions and could not be dismissed except for misconduct, disliked each other, as became very evident when Blakiston was summoned before the magistrates at Settle for inflicting corporal punishment too enthusiastically, and the usher was expected to be a hostile witness. To add to the school's internal problems, its boarding facilities were inadequate, yet the private board offered by residents of Giggleswick, who were anxious for the continuance of this longstanding practice, left much to be desired. Not surprisingly enrolments fell from 96 in the 1850s to 37 in 1865, and many of those enrolled, in Fitch's opinion, were doing work more suited to an elementary school, thus discouraging pupils interested in the higher form of education. It was 'a great scandal', he concluded, that there should be only 37 boys, of whom only four were boarders, in a school with a rich foundation, which was once a high-ranking school, which had new and handsome buildings capable of holding six times the present enrolment, and which could render great service to education in the North of England.[13]

By March 1866 Blakiston had accepted an appointment as an inspector of schools and the usher had resigned, but the opportunity for a change had been jeopardized because the governors were locked into a dispute with the inhabitants of Giggleswick. It arose from a new 'scheme', a constitution for the school, which had been agreed upon by the governors, both new and old, after discussions with the Charity Commissioners. A key factor in the scheme, which Kay-Shuttleworth supported, was the charging of a fee of £12 for each boy, irrespective of where he lived. Giggleswickians, used to having the endowment provide their children with free instruction, resisted the proposal. They based their arguments on custom rather than right, as it was clearly the founders' intention that the school should be open to children from all parts of England. Charles Savile Roundell, a barrister who joined the board of governors at the same time as Kay-Shuttleworth, described a meeting in the court house at Settle which was addressed by one of the governors. In the front sat 30 people of 'superior position', while the rest of the room was filled with small tradesmen and other respectable people, some of them in working clothes. Opposed to every word the governor said, they listened with 'such a disposition to show fair play, and such hard headedness and shrewd intelligence'. They gave the scheme no support and the governors were subsequently confronted with a demand for 50 and then 35 free places. At a governors' meeting on 21 October, the first to be chaired by Kay-Shuttleworth, the majority (18) favoured offering 30 free places to be drawn from an unlimited area, while a minority (six) led by Roundell were unwilling to compromise.[14]

Kay-Shuttleworth did not take a position at the meeting but forwarded its resolutions to the Charity Commissioners with a statement supporting the majority. Though in favour of a fee, he argued that in the short term the 'continuance of such an ancient usage' as free education was not a waste of school funds and should not at once be 'swept away'. By December 1865 the governors, worried by adverse court decisions elsewhere, had abandoned the idea of a fee and, pressed by Kay-Shuttleworth, tackled other problems. An 1867 scheme gave the headmaster control over the discipline of the boys and the power to appoint and dismiss assistant masters, but he could be dismissed by a two-thirds majority of the governors, without a reason being given. The governors also adopted a hostel system for boarders. The people of Giggleswick called the hostels the 'Governors' Folly', but under Kay-Shuttleworth's close supervision the buildings were completed in 1869. In the same year a new headmaster, George Style, whose appointment was monitored by Kay-Shuttleworth, began work, almost immediately becoming involved, as were the governors, in an unsuccessful attempt to merge Giggleswick with the school at nearby Sedbergh. By 1872, after delicate negotiations in which Kay-Shuttleworth played a leading part, Giggleswick secured approval for a new scheme which ensured that the school adopted the modern curriculum, including physics and chemistry, though Greek was not excluded. The scheme also provided for scholarships but required the payment of fees by boys who did not hold one. Giggleswick (and Burnley Grammar, where he was also Chairman of the Board of Governors) presented Kay-Shuttleworth with case-studies of the problems associated with endowments, but they benefited from the compulsive care he brought to any responsibility he assumed.[15]

On 19 March 1866 Ughtred Kay-Shuttleworth wrote to his father predicting the fall of the Liberal government. He was right: Russell resigned at the end of June and the Tories under Derby came in. Ughtred thought that if the Tories produced an appropriate Reform Bill it would succeed, 'and there would be at least *one* benefit obtained for the country from a Tory ministry – the settlement of the Reform question'. Derby's 1867 Reform Act, his 'leap in the dark', enfranchised only the better-off working-class men – to the relief of Janet Kay-Shuttleworth women did not gain the vote – but in 1868, at the first election to be held under its provisions, the Tories (now led by Disraeli) were swept from power to be replaced by Gladstone, who was bent on a programme of reform.[16]

For some people, and for Kay-Shuttleworth in some moods, especially those in which he attributed the moderation of the

Lancashire working classes to education, electoral reform followed from rather than caused educational reform. Though he continued to express such sentiments, Kay-Shuttleworth realized that the Reform Act presented him with a major opportunity, and in January 1868 he published his *Memorandum on Popular Education*. He made the obvious point about the necessity of educating the new electors, and grandiloquently declared that Parliament was the voice not only of the middle classes, 'but of the entire mass of the people, including the wealthiest and most privileged, but also – as never before – the humblest classes'. He gave a lecture on educational history (in which the 1846 minutes played a crucial part) and reached an uncompromising conclusion on the Revised Code:

> The Revised Code has constructed nothing; it has only pulled down. It has not simplified the administration. It did not pretend to accelerate the rate of building schools, or to improve their structure. It has not promoted the more rapid diffusion of annual grants and inspection to the apathetic parts of cities, or the founding of schools in small parishes and for the sparse population of rural districts. It has generally discouraged all instruction above the elements and failed in teaching them. It has disorganized and threatens to destroy the whole system of training teachers and providing an efficient machinery of instruction for schools. These ruins are its only monuments. It has not succeeded in being efficient, but it is not even cheap; for it wastes the public money without producing the results which were declared to be its main object.

He proposed an alternative system: the Committee of Council should provide one-third of the schools' income from the parliamentary grant and, through its minutes and inspectors, regulate the standard of education and the training of teachers; the committees of managers should raise another third from school pence and voluntary subscriptions; and the final third should come from a rate levied by newly established district education committees. Kay-Shuttleworth's reservations about the rates had not vanished, but the grant system's inability to provide the necessary money had driven him back to them.[17]

Kay-Shuttleworth distributed his pamphlet widely and among those who praised it was Matthew Arnold, who promised to use it in his own writings (a promise he kept). He informed his old chief: 'Lingen is really excellent, now at any rate, both in spirit and aim; what he needs is *more light*, and I quite long to give him this memorandum of yours to read.' Gladstone shared Kay-Shuttleworth's reluctance to support free education and told him that his suggestions on the Education Bill deserved 'the most careful consideration, as coming from you, and also in themselves'. W.E. Forster, who was to pilot the 1870 Education Bill through Parliament, said that Kay-Shuttleworth had done exactly what he wanted him to do, and expressed the hope that the Conservatives (still in power at the time he wrote) might bring in a Bill, because if there was 'the rag of a good principle' in it 'we can make it a good measure in Committee'. He also asked Kay-Shuttleworth what he thought of a speech by Lowe who was now advocating the use of rates. 'I wonder whether the parsons will see', Forster said in a postscript, 'that his [Lowe's] rate schools will utterly starve their denominational schools.' Lowe wrote to Kay-Shuttleworth to say that he was 'not at all bigotted' about his own proposals and that he was glad that they would be on the same side in the approaching campaign.[18]

The *Memorandum* contained a reference to another enemy. In Manchester on 11 October 1867 Edward Baines, in a speech to the Congregational Union, admitted that the voluntarist approach had failed, and he urged his fellow Congregationalists to accept government aid for their schools. Kay-Shuttleworth immediately invited Baines to Gawthorpe Hall, but Baines refused the invitation in a gracious letter. He acknowledged that 'as a practical man I am compelled to abandon the purely voluntary system, as untenable in competition with that which combines voluntary action and State aid.' However, he was afraid that if he came to Gawthorpe it might be suspected that he was 'under the fascination of your influence' – a suspicion which would reduce his chances of persuading his fellow Congregationalists to change their minds.[19]

The political reconciliation of Kay-Shuttleworth and Baines was symbolic. When the Liberals swept into power after the 1868 election the Nonconformists were, according to Edward Miall, 'the heart, and, he might say, the hands of the Liberal cause'. The ending of voluntarism released Nonconformists who favoured state aid from political restriction and they flung their impressive energy into the National Education League founded in 1869. From its headquarters in Birmingham the League led a powerful national campaign for compulsory, rate-aided, unsectarian education. Its definition of 'unsectarian' was ambiguous, and could mean 'the exclusion of the catechisms, creeds or tenets peculiar to any particular sect', or Bible reading without comment from the teacher, or secular education which completely excluded religious instruction. The rapprochement of Baines and Kay-Shuttleworth fed on this ambiguity: an ardent advocate of state intervention, Kay-Shuttleworth wanted a religious basis to education, and while Baines did not want aid confined to religious schools, he asked for Kay-Shuttleworth's support in 'the approaching conflict with a purely Secular and Rate-supported system of National Education'. The ex-voluntarist Baines gave his support to the National Education Union, an organization founded to combat the League, to have denominational religion taught in schools and to have rate support given to church schools.[20]

The struggle between the League and the Union kept education in the forefront of the political debate, despite the turmoil generated by Gladstone's reform programme. His appointment of W.E. Forster as Vice-President of the Committee of Council pleased Liberal Nonconformity. Forster was member for Bradford (his co-member was Miall) and a Quaker, though he had left the Society after his marriage to Matthew Arnold's sister. However, Nonconformist hopes were raised by his reputation as a Radical, rather than his exposure to the light which his brother-in-law was offering to the world, and to Lingen. Forster introduced his Education Bill on 17 February 1870 and, significantly amended, it received the Royal Assent on 9 August. The dramatic story of principle, passion and pragmatism which issued in the passage of the 1870 Education Act has been often told and need not be told again because, though it was of great personal significance to Kay-Shuttleworth, he watched the battle from the sidelines. He did, however, warn Forster that he would pay the price

> which every statesman has to pay in serving his country. You will have to do what I have done over and over again in this cause – you will have to disappoint some of your friends, in order that the education of the people may not be indefinitely postponed.

When, after the passage of the Act, a bitter Miall asserted that the government had betrayed the Nonconformists who had brought them to power, Forster might have judged Kay-Shuttleworth's words to be prophetic.[21]

Forster's Act gave the denominational schools, called 'voluntary schools' because of their reliance on charitable subscriptions, six months in which to supply the existing educational needs with the help of the government building grants. After the six months no new building grants would be made and, to adopt Forster's terminology, the gaps in the system would be filled by a school board, a body specifically designed to provide elementary education from the rates and elected by ratepayers on a generous franchise. The Lords rejected the proviso, which the Commons had passed after a bitter debate, that the elections should be by ballot. The proposal in Forster's original Bill was reversed and rate aid was denied to the voluntary schools who were compensated by an increased grant. However, clause 25 allowed school boards to pay the fees of needy children from all public elementary schools, thus diverting some rate money to the church schools and laying the foundation for future controversy. In the Board schools Cowper-Temple's famous amendment forbade the teaching of any denominational catechism or formulary. The voluntary schools continued to give denominational religious instruction but, to qualify for the government grant, they were required to allow children the right of withdrawal from religious instruction, which was to be given at the beginning or the end of a school meeting. Although the Act provided support for schools run by religious bodies, it adopted a secular stance over what was taught in those schools – government grants were to be given for secular subjects only. Education was not made free or compulsory, though Boards were given the power to introduce compulsion. Thus there was established the dual system through which Board and voluntary schools, with different forms of control, received grants from the Exchequer and charged fees. But the Board schools were assisted from rates, while the voluntary schools had the difficult task of raising sufficient revenue from subscriptions.[22]

Forster justified the Act on the grounds that the voluntary system had failed to supply the places needed if all children were to have access to an elementary education, that the education given was often defective, and that the private schools were in particularly bad condition. According to Forster, 'the result of the State leaving the initiative to volunteers, is, that where State help has been most wanted, State help has been least given, and that where it was desirable that State power should be most felt it was not felt at all'. In recent years Forster's statistics and those of other advocates of education have been queried, and the condition of the private schools, to many of which working-class parents were willing to entrust their children, has been defended. Given the nature of nineteenth-century statistics a strictly quantitative debate is unlikely to be conclusive, though William Stephens's authoritative study concludes that the private schools were little different in the 1860s from what they had been in the 1830s, that in many of them conditions were very poor, and that compulsion and the extension of public funding were essential for further progress. Overwhelmingly, contemporary opinion reported an education system which failed to reach many children and which gave many it did reach an ineffective schooling provided by poorly trained teachers in poor buildings. Inspectors and assistant commissioners, witnesses before royal commissions, the reports of commissions, newspaper editorials, the investigations of statistical societies, the multitude of pamphlets on education, the publications of the British and the National Societies, the charges of bishops, and the platforms of political parties – all speak of the failure of the existing arrangements. Nor was this agreement confined to the aristocratic and middle-class men who made up the Parliament. As Brian Simon has shown, radicals and the organized working class wanted elementary education to be extended to all children, though they wanted it to be secular.[23]

In any case, in disputes of this kind, reality can matter less than the manner in which it is perceived. And, as the parliamentary debate on the 1870 Act made absolutely clear, the argument was about how to extend public elementary education, who would control it, how it would be financed and what compromises would be made with the religious groups. It was not a debate about the need for education or whether the state should 'interfere' – for the most part, those issues were taken for granted. The long campaign of educational missionaries such as Kay-Shuttleworth had convinced the opinion-makers, who were influenced by the pressure created by the enlarged franchise and the view, reinforced by British industry's disastrous performance at the Paris Exhibition of 1867, that British commercial success required a literate and educated work-force. No one typified the change more than Gladstone. In May 1870, he sent Granville some educational papers with the comment that he was loath to trouble him with a quarter of an hour's reading; but he did, justifying 'this infliction' on the grounds that 'the subject of Education is so important and so arduous in regard to the "religious difficulty"'. Gladstone of 'the young gentlemen' would have found the expression 'religious difficulty' quite alien.[24]

The 1870 Act was in many ways an unsatisfactory compromise and stopped well short of providing a truly national system, even of elementary education. It filled gaps rather than building the coherent compulsory and free system that more radical visionaries desired. Yet it completed the foundation-building that Kay-Shuttleworth had begun at the Committee of Council. Through it, as Donald Jones has written, the role of the state was changed 'from the mere stimulation of the educational efforts of others to the assumption of direct responsibility for educating the nation's children. The basic foundation of a national system of universal, free, compulsory education had at last been laid.' In September 1870, a month after the Act had been passed, Kay-Shuttleworth spoke of 'the tact, sagacity, and the large and comprehensive legislative capacity of his friend Mr. Forster'. Despite its deficiencies, the Act carried further the work to which Kay-Shuttleworth had devoted most of his public career and upon which, as he grew older, he increasingly depended to give meaning and distinction to his life. That dependence was reinforced during the parliamentary debate when Forster remarked that Kay-Shuttleworth was 'a man to whom probably more than any other we owe national education in England'. Oxford, which had given him the mixed blessing of the men from Balliol, chose 1870 to recognize 'your great services in the cause of education'. At the instigation of Robert Gascoyne-Cecil (Lord Salisbury), it awarded him a DCL. Kay-Shuttleworth accepted the degree from the university which was closed to him in his youth, saying: 'My gratification in accepting this honour would be greater if I could feel that I had earned it by services at all proportionate to the reward.' He wrote with false modesty.[25]

On 15 March 1870, in an event so fitting that a novelist might hesitate to arrange it, Ughtred Kay-Shuttleworth, aged 25, made his maiden speech in the House of Commons on Forster's Education Bill. A.J. Beresford Hope, in congratulating Ughtred on his speech, referred to 'that eminent man, the father of the general educational movement in England, whose mantle, while he still lives, has so worthily fallen on his son'. Both the driven father and the dutiful son could feel satisfied with the compliment and the occasion.[26]

The father lost no time in writing to his daughter. 'Ughtred's speech', he told Janet, 'has been esteemed excellent, and has really excited much expectation of an honourable career.' He copied out a report from the *Illustrated London News* which said that 'a young man of fine form and pleasing though slightly precise aspect (!) rose . . . and thus Mr Kay Shuttleworth commenced his maiden speech'. The *News* continued:

> Doubtless he has an hereditary claim to be heard on the question of education and it is in no spirit of disparagement to him personally to

say that it might have been expected that he might not be under the influence of his own inspiration alone, but that he might be the medium for words of wisdom caught from the experience of another.

Ughtred spoke with gravity and clearness, the report continued, 'if perhaps there was some absence of the natural fulsomeness of youth'.[27]

Getting Ughtred into Parliament had not been without its difficulties. In February 1868, Ughtred held high hopes that he might win Clitheroe, as Richard Fort did not intend to stand and, perhaps with the family honour in mind, was offering his support to Ughtred. However, Fort died before the election and Clitheroe went to Charles Roundell, which may have added some tension to meetings of the Giggleswick Board of Governors. In late June Ughtred informed his mother that, somewhat unexpectedly, another chance had opened up. His father had been in London ensuring that the leaders of the Liberal Party and its Whip kept him informed of any favourable opportunity and, after it looked as though nothing would happen, both his and his father's name were suddenly mentioned as possible contenders for the seat of North-East Lancashire. (After the Reform Act North Lancashire had been divided into two seats, North Lancashire and North-East Lancashire.) Kay-Shuttleworth declined and urged Ughtred's claims to the chairman of the committee which was choosing the candidates, persuading him to suggest Ughtred's name to the committee '*on his own motion*'. The optimistic Ughtred thought that the objection on account of his youth (he was then 23) was untenable. He had not forgotten the letter he had written to his mother three years earlier about young men in public life who were self-confident and presumptuous. He would not, he assured her, be self-seeking as his entry to Parliament was 'more a great responsibility than an honour'. The tight political and family connection of Northern Liberals was illustrated by the fact that he was selected and stood with his cousin, William Fenton, whose father, John, had celebrated his election to the seat of Rochdale after the 1832 Reform Bill at a dinner addressed by the young James Phillips Kay.[28]

Ughtred was soon confronted with a dilemma from within his own party. Lord Hartington, later the eighth Duke of Devonshire, had represented the old North Lancashire division since 1857, sharing it with John Wilson Patten who had held the seat as a moderate Conservative since 1832. The reconstituted North Lancashire looked promising to the Conservatives who put up a second candidate, Frederick Stanley, the second son of Lord Derby. He and Wilson

Patten proved a powerful combination and by the end of July 1868 Hartington knew that he was in serious trouble. For a time a compromise was suggested by which the Conservatives would withdraw their candidates in the North-East division in return for an uncontested election in the North division. This assumed that Ughtred, the younger Liberal candidate in the North-East, would withdraw in favour of Hartington, having been promised first claim on the party for a vacancy after the general election. Hartington met Kay-Shuttleworth, who was managing his son's campaign, on a railway station, and put the proposal, making it clear that he did not himself support it. Kay-Shuttleworth needed no further encouragement and refused to withdraw Ughtred. To the delight of the Conservatives, who had in any case decided against a compromise and who considered him unpopular, Ughtred fought the election and was defeated. Kay-Shuttleworth explained to his wife that Ughtred's youth, in an election for so important a county division, had attracted envy and detraction, and he passed on the opinion of his old friend, Charles Henry, who attributed the defeat to the influence of the clergy on the smaller squires. Ughtred had been gentlemanly, his father explained, while at Padiham 'the women were crying, and the men silent'.[29]

Frederick North, who had been returned for Hastings after having lost the seat in 1865, was not silent. 'My dear Sir James', he wrote on 23 November,

> What Demon of Toryism, with its lurid wings, can be hovering over the Lancs Electorates!
> Ld Hartington – Ughtred – &, it may be, before you open this letter, Gladstone himself, to be rejected by Constituencies, that one felt assured, would be Liberal!

He considered that Ughtred had made himself a name and gained a popularity that would soon see him elected, but was sad that he and Ughtred would not sit together in Parliament, saying that 'it would have been a great pleasure to have lionized there my dear Janet's grandson'. One benefit which Ughtred did gain through the election was a closer acquaintance with Gladstone, and he received the important invitation to stay at Harwarden in October.[30]

Frederick North made possible Ughtred's election to Parliament by dying at a convenient time – on 29 October 1869. Shortly before his death William Scrivens, the Mayor of Hastings and a Liberal, wrote to Ughtred on North's behalf to tell him that North was dying and to ask him if he would be a candidate. Ughtred expressed his sorrow at the news, consulted his father, and accepted the offer, remarking that North would not want his opponents to steal a march and that there was to be no bribery or treating by his supporters. Her stepfather's death and her son's campaign produced conflicting emotions in Janet Kay-Shuttleworth. 'I will not touch on the many thoughts and recollections stirred by Mr. North's death', she wrote to her husband, as the circumstances of her childhood and marriage spun before her. She greatly preferred Ughtred to enter Parliament 'as the representative of our own county', but as this could not happen she wished him success.[31]

Ughtred swiftly prepared for the election, and secured the support of most of North's supporters, including his son-in-law, John Addington Symonds. The support was easier to obtain because of his friendship with Symonds and because North's son, Charles, who might have been the natural successor to his father, was not a serious candidate. As Janet Kay-Shuttleworth said: 'Charles seems to have no chance of applying the talents which he possesses . . . [it was] difficult to think of bringing him forward . . . when he has never taken a single step towards a public life.' With the advice of Symonds and Pop, who was desolated by her father's death, Ughtred chose an agent, and by 5 November he had his campaign organization in place. Of one of his competitors, Ughtred wrote that he was not a gentleman but a gin-distiller – his name was Vickers – who wanted notoriety and social position, and was not at all respected. By 11 November his canvassers were so encouraging that he was almost exultant. 'I am indefatigable', he told his father, recounting how every day he spent all day personally canvassing 'with successive good influential men'. On 17 November the brief campaign was over, and Ughtred had won. He expressed his gratitude for his father's training and influence, and for his 'generous readiness' to pay his election expenses. The Tories had called him 'Shuttlecock' and a 'Lancashire Lad' but he had overcome their taunts and he could now hear cries of 'Shuttleworth for ever'. For Kay-Shuttleworth the victory was especially sweet, as his grooming of Ughtred for public life had received so early a recompense. From the Continent Janet Kay-Shuttleworth wrote to tell her son that his victory would do his father good. She herself decided that God was good.[32]

In the late 1860s, before Ughtred's election brought a cause for celebrations, a despairing Janet often felt that God was almost alone in being good. She decided, probably in 1864, to live permanently at San Remo, bought land from a Dr Shuttleworth, a cousin, and entrusted to him the building of a villa and a chalet, each called Ponente. He mismanaged the affair so badly that, by early 1866, Janet was left with a larger villa than she desired and a debt of £5,000. In anguish and despair she turned for help to her husband, and the estate she had brought him. By 19 February 1866 Kay-Shuttleworth, more business-like than compassionate, accepted a plan which may have been suggested by Ughtred: the money would be lent to her free of interest from the savings set aside for the children on the security of the San Remo property. Though humiliated, she was grateful for the arrangement. 'I shall be much obliged', Janet wrote to Ughtred, 'to your thanking your Father on my behalf for having taken the matter so kindly into consideration.' Delays ensued, caused partly by a change in Janet's mind over some details of the arrangement, problems in determining the exact amount of money she owed to her creditors, unexpected difficulties and expense in transferring the land to her, and Kay-Shuttleworth's determination to ensure that the legal niceties were observed – perhaps he found this a way of resisting Janet's decision.[33]

In March 1866, as the lawyers argued, Janet told Ughtred that 'Sorrow and sadness draw me nearer to GOD, further from the world, further from the passing interests, the transient topics of this life ... the *only realities* concern the higher life.' However, San Remo's realities kept intruding, and on 12 June she was wondering 'what it must be like to have debts which did come of one's own fault', as she found difficulty in making 'even English people believe my real position'. A few days later her daughter informed Kay-Shuttleworth that unless the money was paid the contractor would take legal action, and that she and her three younger brothers preferred that the money should be lent unconditionally rather than having it kept for themselves. Their mother, Janet told him, was 'allowing herself scarcely anything beyond the barest necessities, (and denying herself much that any other invalid would consider necessary for her health), – in order that she may pay her debts'. Two weeks later, with the money still delayed, Ughtred received a letter from his sister in which she accused herself of having written on 'indifferent subjects' instead of confronting the matter directly, but 'we all especially I are too reserved and cold to one another, and have too much the habit of speaking and writing about things no one cares for, instead of expressing what our hearts are full of'. Perhaps value could be drawn from the trouble if it lead them to 'break through this ice' and draw closer to each other.[34]

The money came before a public legal hearing took place, but when Ughtred visited San Remo for Christmas 1866 he wrote to his father with a frankness which his sister might have found distressing. Little or nothing unpleasant had happened during his visit, he said, but his mother's concern for economy amounted almost to a delusion. They were well fed and comfortably housed but she stinted on servants so much that his sister's lot had become 'that of an attendant not to say a servant'. He thought it 'an absolute necessity on all accounts that there should be a good break in Janet's life'. In the next letter he withdrew some of his criticism, saying that his mother and Miss Poplawska managed the household, by which he meant that Miss Poplawska did, as the four servants were German or Italian (one of them a native of San Remo), and his mother spoke no Italian and not much French or German. But though Janet's life was not as hard as he had suggested, she did 'too much of mere servant's work' and 'held the third place here in position [and] in authority not to say also in Mother's thoughts'. Ughtred gloomily reported on Miss Poplawska that 'at no time when I have been with Mother has this woman's reign over her been so apparent and conspicuous'. She seemed to rule not by insinuation and suggestion but by direct influence and authority – 'Yet Mother (and Janet too if I mistake not) is quite unconscious of this.'[35]

So Janet Kay-Shuttleworth continued to live in her new home, receiving relatives and friends from England (John and Catherine Symonds were frequent visitors), reading the English papers when she had not cancelled them as an economy measure, and remaining isolated in the circle of English émigrés and tourists from the ordinary life of San Remo's inhabitants whom she thought cowardly and superstitious. The Villa Ponente was a daily reminder of the financial embarrassment she had suffered, and though she could lease most of its ground floor and the attic and so fulfil her promise to repay the loan, her resentment occasionally surfaced. It flared when Ughtred asked her about some fishing rights of which no one at Gawthorpe had knowledge. She also had none, but she wrote acidly that there might be many bits of property 'really belonging to me' which had lapsed because no one connected with her and her affairs had been told about them. She recalled that she once had 'a beautiful little rental book' which was written in her grandfather's hand and which had stood on her father's desk in the study at Gawthorpe.

Memories of her youth crowded into her mind and, setting aside her earlier gratitude for the restoration work which her husband had done, she remarked that 'the room, my own special sanctum, where I used to keep my books, and write, and rest, and settle accounts etc, was swept away by Sir Charles Barry, who could neither respect nor understand early and family associations'.[36]

Family associations brought more grief. Robin's career reached its nadir in November 1869 after incidents of an unknown kind. Janet was convinced that bad companions were to blame and thought that London and Manchester 'were equally full of danger for him' because of his associates. She invoked the remedy that had been applied to Tom Kay. 'The whole course of experience, history, and above all Scripture', she wrote to Ughtred on 6 November 1869, 'prove the value of being thrown into new scenes and circumstances'. Had not 'GOD Himself' called men 'to leave their country and their homes and begin life anew away from the idols and associations of youth'? Kay-Shuttleworth agreed with his wife's diagnosis, and had already drawn upon his cotton famine contacts to approach Sir Daniel Cooper, who was returning to New South Wales for a period of time. Cooper offered Robin a position in 'a respectable station' in Sydney. The sheep station turned out to be over 280 miles north-west of Sydney in Coonabarabran. Its heat and vast spaces contrasted dramatically with the rich, gentle landscape near Rougham where, with Charles North's co-operation, Kay-Shuttleworth thought his son might get a little practice in sheep-farming.[37]

Janet thought the opportunity provided by Cooper had been placed before them by God. Robin would have the guidance of an excellent old colonist and, when he returned in later years, his experiences and new companions would have strengthened his character: 'from a weak erring Boy, influenced by every undesirable companion he will have become a man, firm in those principles which he learnt in childhood, but which seemed to have failed him latterly'. Janet saw Robin for the last time in her life in March 1870 when he visited San Remo to say farewell. She accompanied him to Nice to see him on his way back to London and he sailed from there on 20 April. Ughtred and Stewart accompanied their father to the ship, and Ughtred informed his mother that his father had a long parting from Robin and was 'tired and nervous'. Janet was relieved by Robin's good prospects, but felt the pang of parting for those who remained in London and for Robin. Kay-Shuttleworth described Robin as 'grave, tender and thoughtful', understandable sentiments in a 22-year-old, who was being sent to the Antipodes by his parents to redeem his fortunes.[38]

The trouble with Robin came at a time when Kay-Shuttleworth was particularly vulnerable. In 1869 he holidayed in France and Italy and, though he came very close to San Remo, he did not visit his wife. Late in March he contracted the fever in Rome which has been mentioned in connection with the possibility of his having neurosyphilis and, as the doctors advised that he should travel in stages, his return to England was delayed. Late in May he wrote from Innsbruck to 'my dear little Janet' telling his daughter, in extremely shaky handwriting, that he had thought much about his family during his illness: 'It seemed to me that my task was not finished; and that as I had devoted myself to it with a single mind for many years, I might hope, with God's will, to be permitted to complete it.' For years, night and day, he continued, in an ungainly outburst, 'little mementos of affection' had reminded him of her – her slippers, which he sometimes wore, and a shawl which she had given to him.[39]

However, it was not Janet but Hannah who most concerned him at this time, because, while on his slow return to England, Kay-Shuttleworth learned that she was very ill. His first wish was to hurry home but, Ughtred told his mother, he thought it his duty not 'to follow his inclination to hasten home', but 'under God's blessing' to ensure that he was fully recovered. By 8 June 1869 the cavalcade had reached Wildbad and received the news that Hannah seemed to be sinking. Ughtred again insisted that his father should not hasten home, arguing that Robert (Kay) was in constant attendance on her. On 19 June, at Heidelberg, Kay-Shuttleworth learned that Hannah had died. 'Her devotion to Father it would be impossible to exceed', the younger Janet wrote to Ughtred the next day, 'but I am sure that you, old boy, can with equal unselfishness take even better care of him, because you have had more advantages to teach you to understand him and to be all that he wants.' Kay-Shuttleworth did not reach London until 25 June and a worried Ughtred reported that Hannah's death was a greater grief to his father 'and a greater loss than even I imagined'.[40]

One of Hannah's contributions was immediately emphasized as Kay-Shuttleworth experienced trouble in obtaining a housekeeper of the superior quality he required.[41] She had made possible her brother's public involvement, had helped with the rearing of his children, and had brought some uncomplicated affection to a life in which this was rare. In the long-gone days at Meadowcroft Hannah had waited for the return of 'dear Jemmy' from his studies at Edinburgh. He was now Sir James Kay-Shuttleworth, but Hannah, waiting in Gloucester Square at the end of her life for his return from the Continent, ill and without his wife, knew that some of those early hopes had not been fulfilled. Nor was her hope of seeing him again before she died. Her brother, with God's blessing, had resisted his inclination to hurry to her side.

Janet Kay-Shuttleworth died on 14 September 1872 at Bad Soden, a resort town a short distance east of Frankfurt, to which in her later years she often went to take the waters. Her invalidism was such that reports on her health took a similar tone, whether they contained good or bad news. On 31 December 1871 Janet reported to Ughtred that 'Mother' had been much better lately. She had dressed and gone to see the Christmas tree for a little while, and was now dressing every morning at 10 o'clock and staying up until 4 p.m. when she went to bed to avoid the cold. A few weeks earlier Ughtred had reported to his father that 'Mother' had been far from well, but was getting better. She moved about pretty actively but had not been downstairs for some time. Sickness and health merged to form a life dominated by invalidism: being well meant being less ill.[42]

If bulletins on her health were coloured with subtle shades of grey, those on her attitude to her husband were crisply black. As late as July 1871 Kay-Shuttleworth seem to entertain some hopes that Janet would return to England, and Ughtred was forced to dispel them in a letter whose laboured expression hints at his own suffering. He had formed 'a positive and clear opinion' after spending time with his mother in San Remo. 'I should be wrong if I did not refuse to encourage any idea in your mind of Mother's ever returning to England. I have no such hope.' He softened the blow by saying that travel could be injurious or perhaps fatal for his mother, and by assuring his father that he wished 'to add to these sad but deliberate lines' the warmest assurance of his love.[43]

Janet spent much time in her last years thinking of Gawthorpe. She was in part forced to do this: she had to sign leases, and she pondered over the impact that legislation on mines would have on her collieries. She approved of her husband's suggestion that land be set aside for a mission chapel, and on one occasion refused to sign any more building agreements or leases until he had set aside sites for three churches. She kept a photograph of the church at Padiham hanging above her couch between two views of Gawthorpe Hall, and her mind strayed back often to her youth – to November 1841 at Capesthorne, for example, when, though the estate was then 'wholly in my girlish hands', she had discussed plans for a public park at Padiham with her intended husband. She had written, she told Ughtred in February 1872, to his father to remind him of this plan which was 'so warm in my heart and mind in 1841'. She took this action though it had pleased God to remove her from active duties among 'my own people', as she once regarded the tenants and workers on her estate. Perhaps she had given too much of her heart to them and exaggerated the good she could have done. She was regretful that many worthy plans had 'long since blown to the winds', though she had come to fear that there 'may have been an element of *self* even in those which seemed the least selfish'. God perhaps had summoned her early 'from what might have been a snare under the garb of duty'. Nevertheless, she remarked pointedly, someone who was not born among these people could not be expected to care about them as much as she did.[44]

When Frederick North died, she brooded on her memories of him before he married her mother: he had seemed 'very handsome' and 'looked very young'. She was glad that North had given Ughtred the portrait which Grant had painted of her in her youth. She was not fully satisfied with it, she said, and neither was the painter; however, she conceded that 'a certain likeness was traceable in this picture' and she commissioned Ughtred to have two dozen photographs made from it. Christmas brought back other recollections. 'I now in old age', she wrote to Ughtred in January 1872 from San Remo, 'think of the Christmas Eves of the Norths at Hastings in my early youth', when people used to meet at Hastings Lodge to sing carols, and even her mother's Scottish habits did not prevent her from 'heartily enjoying the old English customs, and entering into the spirit of it'. She had received many congratulations, she added bitterly as the present recaptured her, 'on our supposed family gatherings here'.[45]

In that present, which was rapidly diminishing for her, there were joys, but also perils and sadnesses. The Villa Ponente brought stability and security. She still travelled to resorts such as Bad Soden, and she visited Wartburg where she went to Luther's cell and looked at his annotated Bible ('dear old Luther's room', she wrote to her children, '... Truly we stood on holy ground'). Friends such as Edward Lear came to see her; he drew water from her well and sent her a drawing of parrots by way of thanks. When Caroline Hatherton called, the days at Capesthorne could be mused over; and other events claimed her interest when she was visited by her half-sisters, Catherine Symonds and Marianne North, who after the death of her father embarked on a career of intrepid travelling and completed the many botanical drawings which she left to the Kew Gardens. Above all, for joy, there was the constant presence of her daughter and of Rosa Poplawska.[46]

For peril, there was the Franco-Prussian war; its outbreak led Kay-Shuttleworth to write to their daughter, urgently asking them to leave Bad Soden, where they had recently gone, for the safety of Switzerland. 'Your mother has the courage of a little lion', he said. 'She literally does not know what fear is.' They sheltered in San Remo until the declaration of peace, when she contented herself with the thought that Napoleon III would not live to see the Mediterranean become a French lake, 'thanks to GOD giving Victory to the armies of Germany'.[47]

For sadness there were her younger sons. Robin's progress was not promising and in December 1871 Kay-Shuttleworth told Ughtred that if he were younger he would go to Australia and settle him down. But it was Stewart, the youngest child, who was causing most concern. By April 1870, he was 18 years old, his parents had decided that he should leave Wellington College and take a tutor to prepare him for Oxford. Lady Hatherton expressed her worries about his habit of smoking and on 6 March his mother wrote from San Remo about more serious troubles. She began her letter, 'Dear Sir James', and remarked that as a child Stewart had never had much mental vigour. She had never considered any of their children to be 'what the world terms "clever"'; they were slow but sure in their development, so there was no need to be too discouraged about Stewart – except for his having fallen deeply into debt. She was aware 'how fearfully English tradesmen tempt the young who have rich relatives', but even as a boy he could never 'be impressed with the value of money'. As for his playing billiards, nothing could excuse it, and she would be thankful to know 'that he has abstained from public billiard rooms for a length of time – and given them up entirely'.[48]

'My dear wife', Kay-Shuttleworth wrote in a reply which dismissed Stewart's idea of going to Australia because he did not see in his son 'any of the qualities which would lead to success'. He was reluctant even to let him go unaccompanied to Paris on his way to visit her. By the end of 1871 the idea of going to Merton College had been abandoned on the advice of the tutor who thought that Stewart would be unlikely to pass the necessary examination. Furthermore,

Extract from a letter from Lady Kay-Shuttleworth to her husband Sir James, 6 March 1871, about the intended marriage of their eldest son there were 'several fast men in Merton', and Stewart might 'form associations which would lead him into extravagance if not vice'. On Christmas Day 1871 Kay-Shuttleworth confided to Ughtred that Stewart showed little sign of improvement, and was committing the unforgivable sin: he was shirking 'real work', and living 'an idle lounging life'. Bewildered, Kay-Shuttleworth decided that the Army was the solution and began to organize Stewart's enlistment.[49]

Meanwhile Ughtred was his consolation. His parliamentary career had started well and good reports continued to come in. He was dutiful and grateful. Billiard rooms did not attract him, and shooting and cricket continued to be his recreations. Most importantly, he married well, even if the news of his engagement to Blanche Marion, the youngest daughter of Sir Woodbine and Lady Parish, came as a complete surprise to Kay-Shuttleworth. He had just heard Ughtred's momentous decision, Kay-Shuttleworth wrote to his wife from the Athenaeum on 11 February 1871. He had no previous intimation of Ughtred's intentions and had seen Blanche only twice. A few weeks later, commenting on a letter from Janet to her son which enthusiastically accepted his choice, Kay-Shuttleworth said that, though Blanche was 'not of the highest style', her manner was radiant and 'full of light' and that there was no more beautiful woman in London at that time. Lady Parish was lovable and pleasing and he and Sir Woodbine were 'good and confidential friends already'. Janet's approval was uncomplicated: 'with so charming and lovely a young Wife as Blanche Parish, from all the accounts we receive of her, promises to be, he will have a happy home'. 'He has chosen for himself', Kay-Shuttleworth replied. 'The whole merit of the choice is his.' As a father, he maintained with some self-deception, he had hitherto left Ughtred 'to the promptings of his own pure nature and mature judgement'. He would continue to do so in the future.[50]

Ughtred and Blanche were married at St Leonard's-on-sea on 1 July 1871, and the next day Ughtred wrote from Tunbridge Wells telling Kay-Shuttleworth that 'your son and daughter are well'. He sent Blanche a copy of *Scarsdale*, knowing that she and Ughtred planned to holiday on the Continent for a month. They did not visit San Remo as Ughtred was anxious that Blanche should rest after the exhausting days and months through which she had just passed. Writing from Baslow six days after the wedding, he said, 'A more trying visit for my wife than one to my Mother, (whom she would see for the first time,) ... I could not imagine'. Janet did not seem disturbed by the decision, and in June she told Blanche, with hauntingly unconscious irony, that 'social and educational and sanitary reforms etc [are] just the topics in which a good "Housewife" can fully sympathize with her Husband, and even help him'. They met, very successfully, in November 1871 when Ughtred and Blanche stayed at the Villa Ponente. By March 1872 Janet was advising Blanche, who was now pregnant, that she should try to be calm – it was 'almost impossible for a woman to avoid great fatigues' after 'such severe shocks of mind and body'.[51]

A few months later Janet Kay-Shuttleworth prepared for death. On 15 August she chose the pages of an old Bible to write a message which she asked her daughter to copy for Ughtred. She wrote in pencil and so faintly that, Janet later reported to her brother, 'only I, who read it directly she had written it, could read it'. She knew that she was seriously ill and movingly captured the pain, self-deception, sadness and ambiguities of her life. She was at peace with God, she wrote, and forgave all who had injured her as she prepared to go to her only real home.

> I send my love to my Husband. He knows that I would thankfully have tended, nursed and served him so long as I lived, but for *his* sake more than for my own, and our children's, he *knows* I had to act as I have done. He does not know the pain it leaves me with. I trust we may meet in Heaven.

She commended Janet to her father's protection and that of her brothers. God would bless her,

> and He will bless and reward my faithful and unwearying friend Rosa Poplawska for her disinterested love and self-sacrifice for me and clear her from the calumnies of those who blame her without cause for being true to a suffering fellow Christian and following faithfully in the footsteps of her Lord. To whom I commend my soul and the souls of all I love.[52]

On 9 September, very near death, she again spoke of peace and took leave of all her dear ones, 'Husband, children, friends'. Ughtred was to let his father live 'if he wish it at Gawthorpe, dear old Gawthorpe, the home I gave him in my loving youth, by God's permission'. Again she commended Janet to the care of her brothers – 'She is a *most* precious child to me'. She asked for love for 'our Lancashire people' and returned, in the last written words which have survived from her, 'to that friend who has nursed me in all my illnesses and given up a good home and many advantages for my sake. When I am dead, may they be grateful and know the truth, and let us all meet in Heaven.'

Her last words asked God to be with 'my unborn grandchild'.[53] That grandchild, Angela (named in honour of Angela Burdett-Coutts), was born on 18 September 1872, four days after Janet's death.

Kay-Shuttleworth learned of his wife's death through Lionel, then 23 years old and pursuing medical studies at Cambridge, to whom Janet had written on 14 September, the day of the death, asking him to break the news to their father. The next day William Williams, his wife's solicitor, wrote to Kay-Shuttleworth, explaining that, by express word of Lady Kay-Shuttleworth, no warning telegram had been sent, as she was concerned by the effect travel might have on the delicate state of his health. He (Williams) had been sent a telegram in performance of a promise, but Lady Kay-Shuttleworth was dead when he arrived.[54]

So Janet Kay-Shuttleworth contrived to die in the company of her daughter and Rosa Poplawska, and without her husband or male children. She also ensured that she was buried in Germany – not in San Remo, and not with her ancestors in the graveyard of the church at Padiham whose photograph hung, between the two views of Gawthorpe Hall, above her couch in the Villa Ponente. Janet explained to 'my dearest father', from Bad Soden on 15 September, that her mother had expressed a wish both verbally and in writing 'to be buried at whatever place it pleased God to take her from'. Janet transcribed her mother's words:

> I wish to be buried in the Protestant burial ground of the place I die in. Should none exist, I then wish to be buried in whatever other cemetery may be near at hand, but I most expressly object to my remains being carried to any greater distance than may be absolutely necessary. Being simply a Christian, loving *all* Evangelical Churches, services by a Scotch, English, French, German or Italian Clergyman or Pastor will be equally appropriate at my funeral. I should be glad that a perfectly plain stone be placed by my heir in the Gawthorpe estates on the wall of Padiham Church, with the following words
> 'In memory of Janet, only child of the late Robert Shuttleworth of Gawthorpe Hall in the County of Lancaster Esqre. Wife of Sir James Phillips Kay Shuttleworth Bart. Born at Gawthorpe Hall Nov. 9 1817, died at Soden, September 14, 1872. O death, where is thy sting? O grave, where is thy victory? The sting of death is sin; and the strength of sin is the law. But thanks be to God, which giveth us the victory through our Lord Jesus Christ.
> Mors via ad Vitam'

She left directions for a tombstone to be put up in Soden and, there being no English church there, she was buried according to Lutheran rites on the morning of Monday, 16 September 1872, in the presence of her daughter, her friend and her solicitor.[55]

Having ensured that she died without her husband's knowledge, and been buried in his absence and that of her sons, Janet Kay-Shuttleworth left words of consolation, or words which could be turned into consolation, by those desperately in need of it. She had spoken of him very often, the young Janet told her father, 'always with the warmest love', and had told her many times to give her love to him,

> and tell you that her spirit would always be near you, – that during the last years her spirit *had* been always near you, nearer than ever before, that she felt that all clouds that had overshadowed your love for each other had been gradually clearing away, only too late for you to meet on earth, but she loves you now with that perfect love of which only glorified spirits are capable, and she looks forward to meeting you in Heaven, when it pleases God to take you.

Meanwhile he was not to grieve, but 'to go on working bravely, as you have done all these years carrying out her wishes – which are also yours, about the children she leaves you, the property etc'. Expressing her own views, his daughter told Kay-Shuttleworth that she thought it well for him that her mother 'would not let you watch her dying days, either here, or in anxiety alone at a distance, as would have been the case if Ughtred or Lionel had come'.[56]

Ughtred eagerly snatched consolation from Janet's letter which, he told his father on 19 September, had 'comforted me so much that I can write a little'. The previous day, when he had not yet seen Janet's letter, he wrote from the house which he and Blanche had bought at 35 Onslow Square to tell his father of 'the happy birth of our little daughter'. He added: 'I cannot write about our loss.' Janet's letter released the anguish of years and in his letter of 19 September he exclaimed that he was 'happier than I have ever been since a boy about my two dear parents. A great sorrow has been quite lifted off our spirits. Your great grief has been, in God's mercy, removed.' His mother had found peace and become once more 'her old natural self, and now she has rest and suffers no more'. Eventually, he said, 'we may join her who has gone first and . . . we may be *a Family in Heaven*'. In reply Kay-Shuttleworth said: 'emotion *grows* upon me so much as to the death of your dear mother and the revelation of her entire renewal of her old devoted love for her husband that I must *write little*'. Two decades of personal rejection had been posthumously removed.[57]

When David Robertson, Janet's cousin, received news of her death he wrote to Kay-Shuttleworth of the 'many happy days, years ago, she and I spent together'. They then had much in common and it had 'often vexed me when I thought of the little hope of our ever again meeting each other. Alas! now only too sadly verified'. His heart went out to his cousin's daughter – 'Poor little Janet's return will be very touching.' Janet's return to Gawthorpe had been delayed. As her mother had wished and Ughtred thought sensible, she had stayed with some women friends, so that she could 'give way to her grief and be tenderly comforted, and this will make her equal to the loving duty she sets before herself of being your comfort'.[58] First her mother's comfort, then her father's. Janet's life had been mapped out.

On 19 September Catherine Symonds wrote from Bristol, thanking Kay-Shuttleworth for his letter which included extracts from Janet's letter. She asked permission to show it to two or three people 'who have judged and judged harshly sometimes'. Janet's words 'would help so much to clear up misconstruction and teach charity and truth', she told Kay-Shuttleworth, judging that her half-sister 'must have been long thinking silently of all that was wrong and dark in life'. She continued: 'Miss Poplawska truly has a terrible account to render up one day, in putting distrust between you two. Such women are worse than murderers, I think.' It was not a conclusion that Janet would have liked. Nor, though she might have anticipated it, would she have appreciated the fact that after her death Rosa Poplawska, having fulfilled her last duty as her executor, passed out of the lives of the Kay-Shuttleworths. She had sisters in Berlin with whom she might have lived, and she may have kept an acquaintance with the younger Janet. But the quiet, well-instructed girl, who so interested Charlotte Brontë, no longer appears in the family's story, except in the guise in which Catherine Symonds saw her.[59]

A final ceremony remained. On Sunday, 22 September, the morning service at the Padiham parish church celebrated one of its benefactors. Janet had not yet arrived in England, Robin was in Australia, Stewart was preparing for army life elsewhere, and Ughtred did not attend, though he wrote to the vicar, giving the words his mother wished to have placed on the walls of the Padiham church. Only Lionel and her husband attended Janet Kay-Shuttleworth's memorial service. The sermon was preached by the assistant curate, William Chayter, in the unavoidable absence of the vicar. Kay-Shuttleworth wrote him a sermon, stressing the antiquity and the public contributions of the Shuttleworth family, as well as Janet's interest in the religious and social welfare of the people of Padiham. He drew attention to her concern for education, mentioning her financial and personal support at Habergham All Saints and the group of schools which had been completed at Padiham on Partridge Hill. 'She was in her character', Kay-Shuttleworth suggested the curate should say, 'a combination of high intelligence with benevolence – a mingling of the sweetest gentleness with rare courage and unflinching determination – an active spirit struggling with exceeding delicacy of constitution which was rare if not singular.'[60]

He defended the family honour and his precariously preserved pride by his explanation for her long absence. After the birth of five children, Kay-Shuttleworth suggested the curate should say, she was compelled to seek a warmer climate 'to prolong her life and to preserve her strength for the pursuit of all the benevolent objects to which she devoted herself'. Stewart's and Robin's unsatisfactory behaviour was given a similar gloss. Lady Kay-Shuttleworth 'cheerfully assented to the wish of her youngest son to enter the army, hoping that he would at least emulate the valour and self devotion of his puritan ancestors'. She likewise assented to the earnest wish of another son to emigrate to Australia to seek his fortune through a life of hardship and exertion as a sheep-farmer – 'for in her whole soul she abhorred effeminacy – a mere life of pleasure – or any shrinking from danger and hardship in the discharge of duty'. As so often happens, the life of the deceased was reconstructed at a memorial ceremony to serve and to solace the living.

On that Sunday morning in September, Janet Kay-Shuttleworth, whose body lay at Bad Soden, was remembered. The flag flew above the Padiham church at half-mast, muffled bells (one of which she had donated) tolled softly, the chancel was draped in black, the Kay-Shuttleworth coat of arms (on the tilted bannerets which had been used during her husband's term as High Sheriff) was placed in front of the pulpit, and a large congregation assembled, including many of her tenants who had been informed of her death by circular. The parish magazine reported that for many years Lady Kay-Shuttleworth had struggled against 'an extremely delicate constitution, and to her residence in the mild and salubrious clime of North Italy may be attributed the preservation of her life to the limit dictated by Divine Providence'. An 86-year-old man walked from and to Habergham to honour her memory. And in the course of his sermon, the Revd William Chayter used 'a good deal of matter furnished him by Sir James'.[61]

Janet Kay-Shuttleworth's will, made in 1868, was unambiguous. To her 'dear friend Rosa Poplawska', who was one of her executors, she left her Matthew Henry's Bible; to each of her sons, one of her large Bibles; and to Ughtred, a marble bust of her mother to be kept at Gawthorpe. To Janet she left the land at San Remo with its two houses, the Villa Ponente and the Chalet Ponente, all her money in funds or in banks, and her other possessions – furniture, books, jewels, trinkets, etc. – 'for her sole and separate use independently of any husband'. She gave her daughter the freedom of an independent income which Frederick North had secured for her.[62]

On Janet's death the estate passed immediately to Ughtred, the eldest son. Kay-Shuttleworth accepted the state of affairs. On 20 September, having told Ughtred that he could write little because of the emotion caused by the death of his wife and the revelation of her renewal of love, he wrote a detailed memorandum in which he started the process of transfer, which included having the estate's accounts audited and changing farms from his to Ughtred's name. He also stated that he wanted 'unimpaired fatherly care' over Ughtred's brothers and sister. *'They must owe all to me.* I wish you to abstain from helping them, or leading them to expect any aid from you in difficulties.'[63] With Gawthorpe and the income of the estate slipping from his grasp, he clung to paternal power.

The next day, wishing to be both sensitive and firm, Ughtred referred to his mother's 'last sacred messages of peace and love', which had given his father 'the only tribute for which you cared beyond that afforded by your own conscience'. His children, Ughtred continued, had 'wondered in and reverenced your life under your trial', and he hoped that in his new position, 'which might be a difficult one but for our love and unity', he would be able to relieve his father from care and labour. Two days later Kay-Shuttleworth pressed Ughtred to consult Ebenezer on legal questions, as he was 'a good disinterested adviser', and Langton on investment issues; but by then Ughtred had made up his mind about what he should do. A note written on 24 September sets out his understanding of the position: he was the heir to Gawthorpe estates, Gawthorpe Hall, and the house at Barbon; his mother's wishes were clear; his brothers were not provided for by any charge on the estate and would depend on what his father might leave them in his will; his father was not entitled to any income from the estate, but he (Ughtred) hoped to ensure his father's comfort and maintain his position as head of the family; he intended to appoint Messrs Farrer and Co., the estate's present lawyers, to be his London lawyers; he would honour his mother's wish that his father should continue to live at Gawthorpe as much as he wished; and he wanted Gawthorpe to be a place to which his sister and brothers could come.[64]

Three days later Ughtred explained that Blanche was still suffering discomfort and he could not leave her in London – it was presumably for this reason that he did not attend his mother's memorial service. However, he and Blanche had a proposal. First, he had only faint notions as to his father's income, but he believed that his property and savings would ensure that it was considerable, perhaps £3,000 per annum, and he guaranteed his father another £1,000 per annum from the estate. Ughtred recognized that the ample portions his father had saved for Janet and his brothers relieved him of the moral obligation of providing for them from the estate. Second, he had consulted Uncle Ebenezer, who agreed that there should be no 'noticeable disparity' in his father's mode of life and that of Blanche and himself. Ughtred, therefore, wished to provide his father with 'a pleasant house in the country' where Lionel and Stewart could have 'an entire change from their professional lives with sport and good society, and where you will be absolute master in every way'. He offered the house, grounds, stables and shooting at Barbon which would be 'absolutely *yours* during your life'. Barbon was the place to which he could move his establishment of servants from London (Kay-Shuttleworth had sold the Grosvenor Square house the previous year, and was using rented accommodation in Victoria Street) or at which he could leave his servants if he visited Gawthorpe. Third, he would have a 'congenial occupation' in developing the property at Barbon and its farm, plantation and schools. If he wished, Ughtred would annually set aside some money, and perhaps an additional capital amount, which his father could devote to permanent improvements, within certain limits, at Barbon. He should, of course, have a large portion of the family plate for his own use.[65]

On 29 September Kay-Shuttleworth wrote to Ughtred from Barbon to explain that he was 'quite unequal to thinking on the plan of life suggested to me in your affectionate letter'. His first duty was the transfer of the Shuttleworth estate, and when he thought beyond that it was of his other children; at the moment anything else agitated him. Then, in a sad and shakily written paragraph he told Ughtred:

> I must go on writing memoranda; – setting our agents to work to prepare the Estate accounts for audit; – and analyses for your guidance; – in short making everything ready for the close of my thirty years' stewardship.

He was like a runner 'who eagerly clutches the prize at the goal', a simile which reflected his feelings very poorly. He had made his peace with God and his conscience 'by the patient fidelity of love to your mother', by the nurturing of the children, and by 'the husbanding and development of their fortunes'. He needed time to think, to pray, and to let his feelings 'which are now in storm to subside'.[66]

He reported to Ughtred on 2 October that he had been 'quite unable to write or think for some days', and that he was 'inexpressibly weak and nervous', though he did remember to say that all unpaid income from the period before 14 September, the day on which his wife died, was due to him, not Ughtred. Not surprisingly, Ebenezer Kay, whose support for Ughtred did not waver, wrote to Ughtred on the same day, 2 October, to say that a letter he had received from his brother was extremely agitated. Janet, who had arrived at Barbon by this time, informed Ughtred that their father was not up to deciding, though he was considering the offer very carefully. She assured Ughtred that he was fulfilling his mother's wishes 'most amply' in what he was doing for their father and her brothers and herself.[67]

On 8 October an anxious Ughtred received his father's acceptance. 'You will not wonder', he wrote to his son, 'that with the breaking of the spring of all my life for thirty years, I have found myself incapable, for ten days, to answer your letter.' Until he received it, he had only brooded over his loss. Ughtred's letter came 'as an out-pouring of affectionate solicitude' which recognized his 'parental influence'. As he had ensured by his savings that the estate was free of charges for younger children, he was able to tell Ughtred that the estate could afford the annual sum required for him to live at Barbon and to maintain a house in London. He had purposely refrained from entering into details of 'my own or your income', he said with unconvincing sensitivity, because to do so would not become a father 'whose life has been the proof and pledge of his devotion to you'. However, he could sustain his position and live at Barbon, if £2,000 a year was put at his disposal from the estate. Janet told Ughtred that it had taken days of painful thinking before their father wrote his letter, and that he had been 'out of spirits last week'. Ughtred accepted the proposal with alacrity, thanking his father, 'as affectionately as I can for meeting me in the spirit in which I put forward my own crude ideas'. 'We have always been of one mind', Kay-Shuttleworth said to Ughtred the next day, 'we have always had implicit trust in each other: you have always been to me with dearest Janet the reward of patient suffering and effort.' Typically Kay-Shuttleworth mingled an expression of affection with an assertion of his rewarded suffering, but there was no equivocation about his acceptance of Ughtred's proposal. 'I adopt all that you propose for our future, without reservation or change.'[68]

There were many more formalities but, 24 days after Janet Kay-Shuttleworth died, her husband had accepted that he would have no further power over Gawthorpe and had agreed to live at Barbon Manor. Ughtred's offer was generous and graciously made, but Kay-Shuttleworth's delay in accepting it is not hard to understand. It brought him face to face with the reality of his situation. Though he was guaranteed a comfortable income, the estate which he had managed for 30 years was now taken from him. He was not lord of the manor. He could no longer walk in Gawthorpe's grounds on a Sunday afternoon greeting his tenants or the colliers he employed. Even Barbon Manor, which he had built and developed and in which he would live, was not his. The son whom he had trained to take his place, and whom he loved, and who loved him, had taken his place. He had been marginalized by a social system which used primogeniture to protect its wealth – a system he defended, though it had made him an outsider, as it had so many times before.

In the five years between his wife's death and his own, Kay-Shuttleworth remained active and his educational expertise continued to be recognized. He was called as an expert witness when a select committee was set up in 1872 to investigate whether the government ought to provide annuities for certificated teachers on retirement. As Ughtred was a member of this committee Kay-Shuttleworth had the satisfying opportunity of giving expert evidence before his son. As his long answers showed, he relished the chance to speak of his time at the Committee of Council. He denied that his 1846 minutes intended to found a general system of pensions for teachers, as the newly formed National Union of Elementary Teachers claimed, but he argued that teachers' stipends were too low and spoke in favour of a system of annuities for retired teachers. The committee's report did little to assist the teachers' cause, but Kay-Shuttleworth gave the National Union his support by speaking at their fifth annual conference in 1874.[69]

He also displayed a particular interest in Lord Sandon's 1876 Bill, which derived from the Conservatives' belief that the small voluntary schools, especially in the rural districts, were losing government grants because their students attended irregularly and were therefore more likely to do poorly at payment by result examinations. For these schools compulsory attendance offered the possibility of survival, as Sandon, who was a member of the National Society, realized – even before the Archbishop of Canterbury led a deputation to him asking for the extension of compulsory education. Donald Jones remarks that the Act was 'designed to preserve the supremacy of the Tories in the countryside'; Kay-Shuttleworth thought that it was going 'in the right direction, though feeble and confused'.[70]

In May 1876, in his last published writing, Kay-Shuttleworth reflected on the world of elementary education in which so much of his professional life had been spent. His article in the *Fortnightly Review* gives no indication of a decline in his interest in education or of a loss of ability to read the prevailing winds. He feared that, through the superior facilities which the rates enabled them to afford, the board schools might 'render certain the extinction of voluntary schools'. Paradoxically, the resultant increase in the charge on the rates might lead to the election of board members with 'a mission to restrain expenditure without much regard to the efficiency of schools'. He used the London School Board as an example of a growing resistance to the increase in school expenditure. He recognized that the Board had 'a gigantic task' and that it had acted with energy and courage, but he thought that its very zeal had led it into some over-sanguine schemes. So powerful a board should, he said, 'make its policy in harmony with national, as well as local arrangements'.[71]

His last years showed no slackening in his concern for high-quality teachers. Sometimes this was displayed in minor ways – by his willingness to write a preface for a book entitled *Work for Ladies in Elementary Schools* or his attendance at a conference on the work of the training colleges. He was more seriously involved with a scheme to train graduates to teach in schools higher than elementary. On 2 February 1875 Kay-Shuttleworth invited a group, which included headmasters, principals of training colleges, and inspectors, to a conference at his London home (he had now bought a house at 68 Cromwell Road). It decided to confer with the Charity Commission to see if educational endowments could be used for its purposes, held a conference with the Committee of Headmasters, and published *A Sketch for the Reasons for Establishing Training Colleges for Teachers of Schools Above the Elementary* (1875). This paper suggested that graduates should have a year's training at a university which might grant a diploma to those who were successful, that religious bodies might found halls of residence, and that women's colleges should be established for the training of assistant mistresses. However, the group's enthusiasm and inventiveness waned, in company with Kay-Shuttleworth's health, and it ceased activity.[72]

Kay-Shuttleworth maintained his links with Giggleswick. Under his chairmanship the enrolments expanded, and new classrooms, a lecture room, a chemical laboratory, a swimming bath and a sanatorium were built. A new house was provided for the headmaster and the hostel enlarged. As chairman of the board of governors he was a surrogate headmaster, concerned to leave his imprint on every aspect of the school's life. 'Sir James', a long-serving school employee said, 'practically *was* Giggleswick School at a very important and critical stage in its history'. He remained the chairman until his death, when his fellow governors noted that the present position of the school, compared with its position in 1864, was 'mainly due to the ability, experience, and constant care of their late Chairman, and is the best measure of his labours on its behalf'.[73]

The education of middle-class girls was another field in which his interest continued. After the meeting of the Social Science Association at Leeds in 1871 a provisional committee, in which Maria Grey and her unmarried sister Emily Shirreff were powerful figures, was established. From this developed the National Union for the Education of Girls of all Classes above the Elementary, the inaugural meeting of which was held in November 1871. It was almost obligatory to attach Kay-Shuttleworth's name to educational causes at this time and he appeared as one of the vice-presidents; he was also on the central working committee which the National Union established. This committee, following the model of the North London Collegiate School for Girls established by Frances Mary Buss, decided to establish a limited liability company to enable the establishment of public day schools for girls. Accordingly the Girls' Public Day School Company was launched at the Albert Hall in 1872. It aimed to offer girls an education similar to that given in the boys' Public Schools, though it was undenominational and professed to make no distinction on the grounds of class. Kay-Shuttleworth became one of its first shareholders.[74]

He gave time as well as money. He was active on the Council of the National Union and was once asked to be its chairman, but declined. He visited schools established by the Company, tried (typically) to persuade it to establish a system of inspection and examination, and on occasions acted as its counsellor. His caution might have slowed the Company's progress, except that his advice was not always taken.

Nevertheless, this advice, and his name, were of considerable value to a company which had embarked on the daring experiment of supplying girls with a public education.[75]

Another educational venture to which he gave much time was the Royal Commission on Scientific Instruction and the Advancement of Science. Established in 1870 and chaired by the seventh Duke of Devonshire, the commission reflected an increasing awareness that British industry was suffering by its tardy technological development and by its failure to appreciate the links between industry and science. In a series of important reports, the last of which appeared in 1875, the commission examined scientific instruction from the elementary school to the universities, in museums, the Science and Art Department, and other institutions. Kay-Shuttleworth's interest in science dated back to his unsuccessful experiments as a Sunday school teacher. He had supported scientific studies at Battersea, and had encouraged them while he was at the Committee of Council and after he had left there – he tried unsuccessfully in 1853 to produce a set of readers which included scientific material. He became a member of the commission, attended its many sittings with regularity, and chaired it on a number of occasions.[76] He did not provide intellectual leadership but he gave strong support to Huxley, who did; and he questioned witnesses and offered his suggestions with an intentness undiminished by age or illness.

Whether Kay-Shuttleworth worked on the Devonshire Commission or the Giggleswick Board of Governors, or tried to improve the training and conditions of elementary-school teachers, he was no longer a powerful administrator or a major player in educational politics. Yet, though his power base had gone, his reputation, his belief in the power of education, and the accumulated knowledge of a lifetime brought him influence. In 1832 he had written to Thomas Chalmers of his desire to advance education – 'this best cause' he had called it.[77] For all the vagaries of his life and all its disappointments, he was faithful to that cause.

The busy round of public activities upon which Kay-Shuttleworth engaged after the death of his wife did not distract him from family cares. Janet was his first disappointment. When she arrived in England after her mother's death, she stayed a few days with Ughtred and Blanche in London. Kay-Shuttleworth accepted this delay with an ominous resignation: because of it, each would be 'better disciplined to do our duty to each other'. Janet arrived at Barbon on 28 September 1872 to be met with the plans her father had 'for our humble quiet life together'.[78] She was at Barbon during the negotiations with Ughtred, but then made clear her intention of returning to San Remo. She lived in San Remo for the rest of her life, though she came to England from time to time and also invited her father to the Villa Ponente. According to the conventions of the time Kay-Shuttleworth had assumed, as Ughtred also had, that Janet would live at Barbon, and fill the place left vacant by his sister's death. Janet's relations with him were cordial, but she had no intention of serving him as she had her mother – and as Hannah Kay had served her mother and then him. She was a good linguist and used to living on the Continent, she had financial security, she had the Villa and the Chalet Ponente, and she had an opportunity for an independent life. She took it, calmly riding out her father's distress.

Ughtred took her part when Kay-Shuttleworth exclaimed in a pre-Christmas letter in 1874, 'I miss Janet terribly.' He had tried to devote himself to business to help him bear his solitary life, but: 'Unless I write, or read, or work, I think of Janet.' Ughtred replied that it was 'a great pity to fret', because Janet had lived so long for others and was in such poor health that it was good for her 'to spend a quiet winter with women friends in her sunny cottage'. Her staying in San Remo was inevitable, Ughtred decided, 'and it is not *her* doing or *yours* . . . Time will make all right, – unless we bother her to do what she feels she cannot yet.' Time did not make all right, and by 1876 Janet's health had deteriorated. Though she was 'as deceptively active and lively as ever', she had consumption, and needed to rest and avoid all risk of asthma.[79] Janet threw off the consumption and visited England and Barbon again, but she lived on the Continent until her death in 1914 at the age of 71. She did not marry, and was buried in Bad Soden with her mother.

Ughtred and Lionel caused their father little heartache. Ughtred had married sensibly, produced a grandchild, and was in the early and promising years of his political career. 'I have always cherished the wish that he [Ughtred] should attain high office', Kay-Shuttleworth wrote to his children, and even in the midst of the negotiations over succession to the estate, in a letter which Kay-Shuttleworth said was 'devoted to pure exact business', he could not contain his affection: 'But I love you my dearest Ughtred with unbounded love', he wrote. Ughtred returned that love, a little stiffly but sincerely, and though his parliamentary career did not reach the heights towards which he and his father aspired, it was honourable and useful. He held Hastings until 1880, contested Coventry unsuccessfully in 1881, and from 1888 to 1902 sat for what had almost become a family fiefdom, Clitheroe. In 1902 he was created Baron Shuttleworth and moved to the House of Lords. He worked on a number of royal commissions, was Parliamentary Under-Secretary for India in 1886, Secretary to the Admiralty from 1892 to 1895 and Lord-Lieutenant of Lancashire from 1908 to 1928. He died, aged 95, on 20 December 1939 as another war began, having lost both his sons in the First World War.[80]

Lionel was absorbed in his studies of anatomy, physiology and other subjects, Ughtred reported to his father; in fact he was 'a very satisfactory fellow'. He continued to be satisfactory, finishing his studies at Cambridge with an MA, becoming a Member of the Royal College of Surgeons, and following his mother to San Remo, where he became Vice-Consul. He remembered her and his brother in his children. Having married in December 1877, he called his first child Charles Ughtred, and the second, Janet. He died on 11 December 1900.[81]

Stewart was showing little sign of improving. His plan to enter the army was abandoned in 1873 or 1874 and for a while it seemed that he might go to Australia to work with the Learmonth family who, Kay-Shuttleworth remarked, were 'the most respectable and successful squatters in Australia'. The plan fell through, and by December 1874 Kay-Shuttleworth was so worried about Stewart that he did not want him to visit Ughtred in Onslow Square for Christmas – 'I do *not* want Stewart to come to London at present *even for a night*', he insisted. Another proposal to send Stewart to Australia also failed. It coincided with an unfavourable letter from Daniel Cooper about Robin, and Kay-Shuttleworth decided that he was 'averse' to Stewart's going. To his father's and Ughtred's satisfaction, Stewart developed an interest in estate management. By 1876 he had decided to emigrate to Ceylon [Sri Lanka] where, Ughtred was relieved to know, he would meet Aunt Pop, who had travelled to Colombo on one of her painting expeditions. Kay-Shuttleworth supported the idea, though he was sure that he would never see his youngest son again. He was right. Stewart successfully ran a plantation, helped by the money his father had put aside for him. He was in Ceylon when his father died. He was still in Ceylon when he died himself, unmarried and prematurely, in 1887.[82]

In Australia Robin was in trouble. Kay-Shuttleworth told Ughtred in June 1874, more than four years after Robin had left England, that he was afraid to guess why Robin had not been given higher duties.

Before he could be entrusted with capital he had to prove himself by managing a station, and there was no sign of that happening. Robin was still not managing a station in January 1875. He had been sent droving and the letters which Kay-Shuttleworth sent him twice a month were not getting to him regularly. A year later, Kay-Shuttleworth was so worried by Robin's lack of progress that he wrote to William Wilkins, once a trainee at Battersea and now the most important educational administrator in New South Wales, asking him to visit Robin for a week and report on him. Some sense of the unreality of this request must have struck Kay-Shuttleworth because he then suggested that Wilkins might send some competent man at his (Kay-Shuttleworth's) expense. If any reporting was done it made no difference to Robin who, Kay-Shuttleworth reported to Ughtred in March 1877, was 'on the spree'. Robin eventually went to Ceylon, probably because Stewart, feeling a kinship with a brother sharing exile, bequeathed him his tea plantation. His father never knew that the errant Robin, if Ughtred is excluded, became the wealthiest of his children. Like Lionel, Robin retraced some of his mother's footsteps: in 1896 he married Ethel Freeman from Eastbourne whose father, Alfred, had worked as a doctor in San Remo. He died in 1934.[83]

Kay-Shuttleworth's brothers, except for Ebenezer, who continued to live a successful and healthy life until his death in 1897, brought him sadness in his last years. Tom's behaviour during the 1870s brought the same grief and poverty to his wife and children as it had in earlier decades. Both Kay-Shuttleworth and Joseph Kay, though seriously ill, continued to assist Tom and his family financially (as Ughtred did after his father died), but emigration had not proved the remedy that Lady Kay-Shuttleworth had hoped for. Tom Kay died in 1878, as did Joseph who had been so generous to him. But where Joseph had provided adequately for his family, Tom left unpaid debts and the memory of the suffering he had caused.[84]

Joseph and Tom died the year after Kay-Shuttleworth did, but their brother Robert died before him. In late 1873 Robert's health had seriously declined and, on 3 January 1874, Kay-Shuttleworth wrote to Ughtred to tell him of Robert's death and of his intention to attend the funeral 'to bid my last adieux to the remains of my dear brother'. Two days later he reported that he had been to the funeral and that he 'had escaped all undue emotion'. Just as he had welcomed the delay in meeting Janet when she returned from the Continent after her mother's death, so now he measured out his feelings nicely – much more nicely than he could with Ughtred. He had been generous during Robert's life, however, for his brother died owing him £2,500.[85]

Two concerns which had recurred in Kay-Shuttleworth's career, though they preoccupied him less than education did, became important in the last years of his life: his desire to enter Parliament and his ambition for literary recognition.

Negotiations for the parliamentary seat of North-East Lancashire began when it was evident that Gladstone's Liberal government was facing certain defeat. On 24 March 1873, reading the writing on the wall, William Cavendish, seventh Duke of Devonshire, began discussions about Liberal candidates for North-East Lancashire, and Ebenezer Kay's name was mentioned. In June Devonshire wrote to Kay-Shuttleworth pointing out that the candidature of his eldest son was out of the question because he held a safe seat, and another son, Frederick Cavendish, was to take his chance in the West Riding. His youngest son, Edward, might stand, but was not altogether free as he had ties with East Sussex. Who, however, would stand with him if he did?[86]

In November, Devonshire told Kay-Shuttleworth that, while Edward would stand for East Sussex, he did not want that fact disclosed. Indeed, he wanted him to be invited to the Lancashire seat, and if North-East Lancashire were united in his favour Edward would become a candidate. By then Ughtred was being considered, but when his father warned him that the contest for the seat would be very close, Ughtred decided that the safer course was to fight the battle in Hastings. On 25 January 1874, as the election loomed, Kay-Shuttleworth informed Ughtred that Cavendish was certain to stand and that everything depended on the second candidate. He thought that Ughtred would win in Hastings, though he would have been gratified 'if you had found it to be your duty to become a candidate for NEL'. 'But we are in the hands of God', he decided. Ughtred knew what this meant: his father had decided to stand as the second candidate. His knowledge was confirmed when, on 28 January, he received a cable which said: 'I have just consented to become the second candidate for North East Lancashire availing myself of your aid.' Two days later Kay-Shuttleworth explained himself in more detail to Blanche Kay-Shuttleworth. He had been plunged unexpectedly into the contest and was not sanguine of success, but it had 'seemed indispensable' for him to go forward in order to confirm the connections of the family with the Liberal Party. Those connections were further tightened when Ebenezer, pressed by Kay-Shuttleworth, decided to stand for Clitheroe and, to complete the Kays' onslaught on Parliament, Joseph stood for Salford.[87]

Kay-Shuttleworth flung himself into the campaign with excited vigour, assisted by Lionel and Stewart and, when he could escape from Hastings, by Ughtred. Ughtred's presence helped to confirm the links of the family with the Liberal Party in Lancashire, and Kay-Shuttleworth stressed the part that motive played 'among my own reasons for encountering the fatigue and risk of this contest'. He was in his seventieth year and ill, but as in the past a contest revivified him. He was angry and embarrassed when his opponents claimed that he had served the interests of the Gawthorpe estate during the cotton famine by promising £1,000 for the fund then giving nothing. He had to produce a poster explaining that this was not true. Despite such checks to his electoral progress, he began to believe that he might be successful, and he basked in the approval of Devonshire and 'Lord Edward' who showed him 'an undue amount of deference'. Deference was not enough. The Conservative candidates polled 4,570 and 4,478 respectively, while Kay-Shuttleworth obtained 4,401 votes, about 100 more than Cavendish. He had come within 77 votes of entering Parliament. For a short time he considered contesting the validity of the election but decided not to press the case. Ughtred held Hastings but Ebenezer and Joseph were defeated. Both Kays and one Kay-Shuttleworth were numbered among the Liberal victims of Disraeli's victory over Gladstone.[88]

When Kay-Shuttleworth wrote to Janet after the election he was still elated with the combat. 'I am not in the slightest degree personally disappointed . . . I regret the result for the *Party*, but I expect no reproaches from them.' He had worked as hard as Lionel and Stewart and 'was decidedly the better for the excitement and labour'. On 13 February Gladstone wrote to thank him. 'I have had to lament the loss of your election in common with several others of special interest besides the indiscriminate slaughter of the mass.' Gladstone resigned the leadership of the House of Commons, and Kay-Shuttleworth was left to reflect on the cruelty of the fate which, after many false starts, saw him try for Parliament so late in his life, only to be part of a famous defeat.[89]

The defeat did nothing to diminish his fascination with politics and he constantly offered Ughtred his advice. His suspicion of the Radicals deepened further, and in a letter of January 1875 to Ughtred he dismissed Forster's claims to the Liberal leadership in Gladstone's wake. Forster's career began with 'the extreme working class radicals', Kay-Shuttleworth said; he was an ambitious man and one of Bright's lieutenants. In his management of the education question he 'seized an excellent opportunity, for an extreme radical, to make terms with the opposite party at the expense of his own friends. *And he succeeded.*' He rejoiced at Forster's success, 'but I do not admire the *mode* of his attaining it. Perhaps no other person could have done this *feat*; but it was a betrayal of the nonconformists who lifted him into the Cabinet, and they are not likely to pardon him.'[90] There was truth in the estimate, but he had forgotten his own comments on the friends he had lost as he pressed the cause of education.

Kay-Shuttleworth searched for recognition as a writer in the last years of his life as earnestly as he pursued his political ambitions. In 1873 Longmans, Green published his *Thoughts and Suggestions on Certain Social Problems contained chiefly in addresses to meetings of workmen in Lancashire*. Although it contained speeches given to meetings of workmen or at the East Lancashire Union, it also included addresses to the National Association for the Promotion of Social Sciences, semi-official documents, and pamphlets such as his 1868 memorandum. *Social Problems* included some interesting reflections on 'the treatment of idiots' and an address to a battalion of rifle volunteers, but Kay-Shuttleworth had expressed most of it before, except, perhaps, for his fervent imperial feelings. Were the Baltic and the Black Sea to become Russian lakes? Was Russia to dominate Suez and close the Red Sea? Why did England hold Aden, Malta, and Gibraltar, 'if not, in the name of civilisation, to secure a free pathway to the commerce of Christendom and Asia?' 'In short', he continued:

> are we . . . to abdicate the high trust committed to us, as the result of two thousand years of advancing civilisation and growing power, and to permit barbarism and disorder again to triumph, by the withdrawal of the protective influence of the Anglo-Saxon race?[91]

James Kay, returning to England with educational ideas garnered from the Continent, was more open-minded.

His second novel, *Ribblesdale*, was published in 1874. Unlike *Scarsdale* it was published under his name, though there is dispute about its authorship. A British Library duplicate, now in private hands, has a pencil note in volume 1 written by the art historian Katherine Esdaile, the wife of Arundell Esdaile, Secretary of the British Museum from 1926 to 1940. The note says: 'This book, though nominally by Sir James, was really written from his material by Andrew McDowall when he was his secretary in the late sixties. This my father [Andrew McDowall] told me about 1913.' Kay-Shuttleworth speaks specifically of dictating letters to a Mr McDowall in 1874, and though there is no conclusive proof that McDowall was his secretary in the late 1860s, he may well have been. They seem to have got on well as Kay-Shuttleworth's influence assisted McDowall to be appointed the first permanent secretary to the Girls' Public Day School Company, a position he held from 1874 till 1910.[92]

It is hard to know what to make of the claim. Katherine Esdaile's note is undated but, if she wrote it in 1913, it dates from 40 years after the event it describes – and probably it was written some years after 1913 as she appears to be working from her memory in choosing that date. Her recollection of what her father said may have been faulty; perhaps, after 40 or more years, he had blended the collecting of material for Kay-Shuttleworth with the writing up of material gathered by Kay-Shuttleworth, especially if he did a little of both tasks.

The book itself has obvious signs of Kay-Shuttleworth's style and preoccupations. It was set in the East Lancashire of 60 years past and its main concern, announced at the beginning of the novel, was a central theme of Kay-Shuttleworth's own life. 'The story', he wrote, 'is founded on the antipathies and rivalries of the ancient gentry with the families enriched by commerce.'[93] The most important of the book's plots embodied this theme. Rufus Noel, the son of Sir Hubert Noel of Mytton Hall, falls in love with Alice Hindle, the daughter of a rich woollen manufacturer. His rival for her love is Robert Hindle, Alice's cousin, and after various melodramatic events Alice chooses Rufus. Many of the character types from *Scarsdale* appear in the novel, including dissolute aristocrats, well-born, beautiful and highly moral women, as well as weavers, clergymen, squires, and sheep farmers. The novel's various plots are tighter than in *Scarsdale*, but rely on many devices from the Victorian novelist's repertoire which Kay-Shuttleworth had employed in *Scarsdale*. They include the improbable revelation of noble birth, apparitions and moments of gothic horror. The aristocrats are wooden types, as in *Scarsdale*, and speak the same elevated and stilted language. Characters from the lower classes again use the East Lancashire dialect, and are often portrayed as illiterate, superstitious and violent. Kay-Shuttleworth's involvement with education and his worries about disruption to the social order appear in the novel, though they are not as intrusive as they are in *Scarsdale*.

Apart from these similarities there are events which clearly draw on Kay-Shuttleworth's personal experience. The descriptions of life in the cattle fairs, in the weavers' cottages, and in the halls of the yeoman-squires and the Puritan manufacturers are said in the preface to be drawn from the author's experience and knowledge – and they certainly were within Kay-Shuttleworth's. Whalley Abbey, which is used as a setting at one stage of the novel, was very familiar to Kay-Shuttleworth. Rufus becomes interested in the lives of the poor when he visits a village stricken by typhus, Alice and her father develop schemes to improve the physical and moral welfare of the weavers and, during a famine, Hindle creates work for the unemployed. A clergyman, who is bribed to declare a marriage invalid and later goes to live in New South Wales, is named Everard Varley (Edward Verity?). As part of his effort to win Alice, Robert Hindle goes to New South Wales to a sheep station called Doonabarra, where he was more successful than Robin Kay was at Coonabarabran. And there is an unnecessarily long description of an election campaign run by Sir Hubert Noel which probably draws directly on experiences with Ughtred's campaigns for North East Lancashire and Hastings in 1868 and 1869. Andrew McDowall may have written some of *Ribblesdale*, but it would be unwise to rely too heavily on Katherine Esdaile's note. Kay-Shuttleworth's mark is on the novel, and the dubious honour of being the author of *Ribblesdale* seems likely to be his.

There is no doubt about the authorship of Kay-Shuttleworth's last novel, 'Cromwell in the North', though he endeavoured to hide his authorship by reverting to anonymous publication. His publisher, George Smith, was firm: books by anonymous authors had no chance of commercial success. Practised at rejecting authors, Smith found something to praise in the book, telling Kay-Shuttleworth in a letter of June 1875 that the amount of local colour in its description of northern scenes was unequalled since *Marmion*, 'but it is more an historical account of the period than a novel or story'. Its descriptions were too general, and it did not follow the fortunes of its characters 'with sufficient closeness to attract the readers of fiction'. It remains in nine notebooks in the Kay-Shuttleworth papers, unpublished and unfinished, a testament to Kay-Shuttleworth's literary determination and disappointment.[94]

It was written when Kay-Shuttleworth's health was failing and the act of writing was very difficult; a considerable amount of it was dictated to Janet. He probably began the manuscript in the early 1870s (he started the seventeenth of its 20 completed chapters in January 1875), and abandoned it in mid-1875 after Smith had rejected it. In his letter of rejection Smith gave the sales figures for *Scarsdale* and *Ribblesdale* – 750 and 473 copies respectively. He also sent a cheque for £27.17.6 to cover some unpaid royalties. The marks of his editing, in which he drew attention to authorial repetitions, survive on some leaves of the manuscript.[95]

'Cromwell in the North' is set in Lancashire and takes Cromwell's humiliating defeat of the Royalists at Preston as its central event. In this novel, aspects of regional life no longer concern Kay-Shuttleworth, and he produces an historical novel (among the experts he consulted was the Lancashire historian, William Abram).[96] The novel may be accurate enough historically, but it strains a reader's tolerance by its diffuseness, its lack of narrative power and by Kay-Shuttleworth's failure to bring his characters to life. As Heather Sharps suggests, Kay-Shuttleworth might have been attracted to the subject by its family connections – she points out that in 1648 Colonels Nicholas and Ughtred Shuttleworth commanded Round-head regiments. Moreover, though he did not attempt to depict the regional life of the period, as he had in his two previous novels, Kay-Shuttleworth set the novel in the Lancashire he knew so well. At one time he intended to call it 'Ravenstone' after a keep of significance in the novel but, for the first time in the title of a novel, he abandoned place for person and named it after Cromwell. Perhaps, as his life was drawing to a close, he found consolation in writing of a powerful man who imposed his will on the nation.[97]

Kay-Shuttleworth's literary endeavours did not receive the recognition which he and John Addington Symonds had coveted half a century earlier in Edinburgh. They did not deserve it. But his three novels, especially *Ribblesdale* and 'Cromwell in the North', which were written in the last decade of his life, were the products of an obsessive, brave and blinkered man, fighting illness, loneliness and disappointment at Gawthorpe, at Barbon Manor and at his home in the London street named after his hero. His fight was in vain. The books never rose above the ruck of the regional and historical novels of his time, and the educational, social and political messages he tried to convey through them had already been better expressed in his pamphlets and reports.

In 1876 and 1877 Kay-Shuttleworth's health steadily declined. He had a serious kidney failure and his neuralgia worsened. He continued his improvements at Barbon, but found the effort increasingly demanding; he and Ughtred exchanged many letters about political and educational matters; and he held occasional dinners at 68 Cromwell Road for illustrious intellectual company – in February 1876 the guests included Henry Irving, Matthew Arnold, W.H. Lecky, J.R. Green, Herbert Spencer and Francis Galton. But his failing health became manifest when, to the regret of Derby, he withdrew from the last of his cotton famine activities, membership of the board of governors of the Cotton District Convalescent Fund. The affairs of his children remained a major part of his interests, and Ughtred's political progress continued to satisfy him.[98]

In February 1876 he decided to visit the Riviera in search of relief from his suffering, and he talked of a family party at San Remo. He was still making plans in October, did not leave England until November and then, for reasons which are unknown, he settled at Cannes. Janet often came the short distance from San Remo to be with him, and they spent the Christmas of 1876 at Cannes. Ughtred, writing from Gawthorpe where the country was covered with a thin layer of snow and the night frost was sharp, described how he, Angela and their dog ran and cantered about the frozen roads or gathered round a nine-foot-high Christmas tree which had been brought from Barbon. He preferred this, he told his father and sister, to 'the radiant glory of the sunny Christmas at Thebes' where he, Blanche and Angela had been the previous year. In April 1877 Kay-Shuttleworth moved to San Remo, to stay for the first and only time in the house which his wife had built.[99] For Janet the Villa Ponente was full of memories of her mother, but they were memories which her father could not share.

By the time he arrived at San Remo Kay-Shuttleworth was too ill for concentrated work, but at Cannes he had bestowed some of his memories on Janet: he continued work on his last piece of writing, his autobiography. He had started in January 1874, when he wrote from Edinburgh of his intention of renewing his impressions of the Old Town in order that he could write a chapter of reminiscences of his college life. As the physical activity of writing had become increasingly difficult, he dictated parts to Janet; but his autobiography was not finished when he died, and it was not published until B.C. Bloomfield edited it in 1963. Strictly speaking, the manuscript, which lies in the Kay-Shuttleworth papers, has no title, but it has been referred to throughout this book as the *Autobiography* and Bloomfield's edition has been used.[100]

The first section of the book is entitled 'To review the sources of the chief impulses which have governed a life without egotism'. To the very end of his life, Kay-Shuttleworth's lack of self-awareness continued. Kay-Shuttleworth used 'egotism' to mean being self-preoccupied, or thinking too much about oneself, or being selfish, a usage which the *Oxford English Dictionary* records as being employed by F.W. Robertson whose sermons Kay-Shuttleworth greatly admired. So, Kay-Shuttleworth set himself the task of deciding what had been the chief impulses to govern his own unselfish life. He found them first in Edinburgh, they were reinforced in Manchester and East Anglia, and they received their most effective public expression during his time at the Committee of Council: they were the realization of the wants and sufferings of the poor, and the accompanying understanding 'how almost useless were the resources of my art [Medicine] to contend with the consequences of formidable social evils'. In Manchester, he recollected, the continuation of the political and social studies which he had embarked upon in Edinburgh, and the continuing opportunities he had for observing the poor, brought him to the conclusion that the physical condition of the poor could not be improved without 'an increase in their intelligence and virtue'. Other factors were important, hence his interest in public health and local government, but it was in education that he had placed his trust.

This explanation of the impulses that governed a life without egotism meant that his autobiography became the story of a public life, the story of his work for education. His story began when he was 20 years old, and was centred on his work as an assistant Poor Law commissioner and secretary to the Committee of Council. By the end of the first half of the autobiography, he had reached Norwood; in the second half, which he entitled 'An apology for fifteen years of administration and its consequences', he discussed the pupil-teacher system, Battersea, and the Revised Code. In several places he post-poned discussion of a particular matter to later chapters which time prevented him from writing, so that the unfinished autobiography gives an incomplete record of his career. What it does give is flawed by failures of memory and the determination of an old man, approaching death and jealous of his reputation, to defend his achievements by claiming credit which was not due to him. He maintains that he was the first to diagnose cholera in Manchester, that he suggested to Chadwick that he devote his time to improving public health, that he hit upon the pupil-teacher system before anyone else in England, and that he had worked, from the beginning of his days at the Committee of Council, towards the achievement of a coherent plan for the growth of education. None of these claims can withstand examination, but their assertion, and consequent rejection, have helped to distract the attention of posterity from achievements which can stand without any buttressing. By the end of the manuscript Kay-Shuttleworth had become engrossed in a discussion on the 'sinister influence' of the Revised Code on the education of teachers. The story of his life was lost as the apologia for his administrative years absorbed him. Kay-Shuttleworth had almost vanished from his own autobiography.

In a sense he was never in it. The autobiography passes in silence over his days at Bamford, at Leaf Square and Fenton's bank; John Clunie, William Henry, Thomas Jackson, Caroline Davenport, June and Helen Kennedy, Edward Verity, Charlotte Brontë and Frederick North are absent from it; so are his mother and father, his sister and brothers; so is Janet Shuttleworth; Wildbad, Bad Homburg, Heidelberg, Eastbourne and Bad Soden do not appear; nor do Gawthorpe Hall and Barbon Manor; he never becomes a parliamentary candidate or manages an estate; he does not edit a medical journal, run a Sunday school, become a member of the Established Church, or scheme to have railways pass his property; epilepsy and tabes dorsalis are not words he conjures with; he does not face blindness or force himself to write when he cannot properly control the movements of his hand; he does not pester members of the Athenaeum about the studies his son should undertake; he has written no poetry or novels; he is not born, he does not marry, he has no children. All these absences bestow a strange truth on his claim to have lived a life without egotism: as he describes himself, he has nothing that is separate from his public career, no identity except that which his work gives him.

James Kay-Shuttleworth was much more interesting and complex than the figure in the autobiography. His educational work was driven by his perception of an unstable society threatened by an ignorant population and by his desire to provide a richer intellectual and moral experience than England had previously given the children of the poor. His formidable advocacy of education, his commitment to asserting the power of the civil authority, his interminable wrestling with the Established Church and the Dissenters, his badgering of government and Opposition, his single-minded absorption in his work at Whitehall, his passionately composed minutes and regulations, his intriguing, and his adaptation to political reality – all this turbulent activity, which reduced him in his wife's eyes to a 'mere office slave', was driven not only by an intellectual vision, but by his search for personal certainty, for a sense of self-worth and self-respect. His public striving helped to assuage but could not dispel his private doubts; his efforts to protect the stability of society gained power and persistence because they vainly promised him some internal stability. Had he been a better and gentler man, had he fought less urgently for personal recognition, been a subtle and confident judge of his own interest, held a secure place in society, been the man without egotism whom his autobiography purported to describe, his effect on nineteenth-century social and intellectual history might have been less important.

On 5 May 1877 Ughtred asked Dr J.Weber, the London doctor who had treated his father for many years, to send an unnamed doctor (probably in Cannes) an account of Kay-Shuttleworth's health. Janet had sent a worried letter about her father's symptoms and Ughtred was concerned that the doctor should have the necessary information for treatment. Weber mentioned 'Sir James's reluctance to speak of his malady to any one, and especially to members of his family', but he did not need to hide a syphilitic condition from his children. Weber's account of Kay-Shuttleworth's health is concerned only with his acute uraemic poisoning and kidney failure.[101]

About two weeks later Janet telegraphed Ughtred with the news that their father's health had worsened, and Ughtred and Lionel, who by this time was house surgeon at St George's Hospital, rushed to San Remo. They decided that the onset of extremely hot weather and the need for special medical attention required their father's return to London. He made the journey safely, but on 26 May 1877, after a momentary struggle but no extended suffering, he died in the presence of Lionel and of his brother Ebenezer, who outlived him by 20 years. He was almost 73. As Janet had not returned to England, three of Kay-Shuttleworth's children were out of the country at his death. Ughtred wrote to each of them and arranged a private funeral. His father had left no instructions, and Ughtred had him buried at Brompton Cemetery, close to his Cromwell Road home. The *Burnley Gazette* said that he was 'generous to his tenantry' and a 'fine, fast friend of Padiham', and on the day of his burial the blinds of the Padiham Liberal Club were drawn, tradesmen put up their shutters, bells tolled, and the flags on the steeple of the Padiham Church flew at half-mast.[102] But the graveyard of that church, where he and his family had often worshipped and where many of his wife's ancestors were buried, had been denied him. Even in death he remained an outsider.

In Holy Trinity Church at Habergham-Eaves the Reverend E.C. Maclure, the vicar of Rochdale, preached a sermon on this Rochdale man. Kay-Shuttleworth, he said, had honour everywhere except in his own country where, through the prejudices of others and his own (unspecified) faults, 'our late neighbour found himself least appreciated where men thought they knew him most, and fought an uphill battle against local feeling and opinion'. But, Maclure continued, the pigeon-holes of the Council Office 'could alone unfold the almost Herculean labours which laid the groundwork for all his successors'. And, whatever the views of his neighbours, 'he hands down a compact and valuable estate, nursed by his personal care and replete with appliances for its development, in good order; its old family mansion at Gawthorpe restored; a residence erected in Westmorland; and he lays aside only with life his life's work'.[103]

His death was not much noticed by the papers, but in London tributes flooded in to Ughtred. Among them were some from old colleagues at the Council Office, from the inspector John Gordon, from Angela Burdett-Coutts and from acquaintances more closely associated with his professional activities – the Bishop of Manchester, the headmasters of Harrow and Giggleswick, Lord Sandon and Charles Trevelyan. Two in particular would have moved Kay-Shuttleworth. On the day of his death Ralph (now Lord) Lingen wrote to Ughtred with touching formality: 'I shall not address you by your title on so sad a day as this'. Your father, he said (putting aside the precious young Balliol man he had been), was 'one of my early and best friends'. He was 'one of the very ablest, most far-seeing, and public-spirited men I ever knew', and 'as an administrator I never knew his equal'. Kay-Shuttleworth's Manchester friend, William Langton, produced a sonnet which ended:

> His health and strength he spent to serve the State,
> The poor to raise, the young to educate,
> And sacred rights of conscience to protect.
> When wronged, his soul in patience to possess
> Proved him as large of heart as intellect.[104]

Ten years after Kay-Shuttleworth's death, a better poet chose prose to make a less heartfelt but more elegant and perceptive comment. Sir James Kay-Shuttleworth or 'Sir James Shuttleworth, as I shall . . . call him', wrote Matthew Arnold, was the founder of the

Department of Public Education, and 'a most remarkable man', who had 'never had full justice done to him'.

> He was not a man of high cultivation, and he was not a good writer. I am told that he might easily have become a powerful speaker, and I can well believe it; but he was not in Parliament, and his work was not to be done on the platform. As an administrator . . . he did not attract by person and manner; his temper was not smooth or genial, and he left on many persons the impression of a man managing and designing, if not an intriguer. But the faith in popular education which animated him was no intriguer's passion. It was heroic, it was a gift planted by nature, and truly and earnestly followed, cultivated, and obeyed. And he who had this clear vision of the road to be pursued, had a clear vision also of the means toward the end. By no other means than those adopted by him could a system of public education have been then introduced in this country. Moreover, in laying out popular education he showed in general an instinct wonderfully sound – he grasped the subject more thoroughly, made fewer mistakes, than any of his successors.

He was a religious man, Arnold continued, though distrusted by both Church and Dissent, and he thought the problem of supplying effectual religious instruction to be 'simpler than it is'. But he judiciously applied his knowledge of the secular programmes used in good schools on the Continent.

> I have already said that he did not attract, that he had faults; that both the clergy and the sects disliked and distrusted him. The general public was indifferent; it needed a statesman to see his value. Statesmen like Lord Lansdowne and Lord Russell appreciated him justly; they followed his suggestions, and founded by them the public education of the people of this country. When at last the system of that education comes to stand full and fairly formed, Shuttleworth will have a statue.[105]

Arnold's enthusiasm led him to excessive praise, just as his cultural predilections caused him to underestimate Kay-Shuttleworth's cultivation. He was also over-hopeful. Forces, some of which Kay-Shuttleworth had opposed in his lifetime, continued after his death to delay the full formation of a system of state education. Perhaps that is why the statue was never built.

Notes

1 · James Phillips Kay and family, pp. 1–20

1. John Lord (compiler), Pedigree of families who formed the congregation at the the Bury Presbyterian Chapel, Silver St, p.110 (manuscript held in Bury Central Library).

2. G.M. Ramsden, A record of the Kay family of Bury Lancashire in the 17th and 18th centuries (1978), pp.2, 3, 47 (typescript held in Local History Archives, Central Library, Manchester). A copy of the Kays' marriage certificate is in the Kay-Shuttleworth Papers (K-SP), John Rylands Library (Deansgate), Manchester. B.C. Bloomfield's A handlist of the papers in the deed box of Sir J.P. Kay Shuttleworth (1804-1877), College of St Mark and St John: Occasional Papers No.2, 1961, is the key to these papers. They have been numbered by the Library's staff; the marriage certificate is 338. Throughout this book the papers will be identified by this numbering – in this case, K-SP 338.

3. Schole's Manchester and Salford Directory 1794, p.163; Thomas Wild's statement, K-SP 455; Samuel Wilkinson's, K-SP 449; John Hall's, K-SP 451; Robert Porter's, K-SP 454, and summary statement, K-SP 465. These statements, and the others used in the following discussion, were gathered by James Phillips Kay – by then, Sir James Kay-Shuttleworth. The circumstances in which they were gathered are described on p.296.

4. Summary statement and statements by Wild, Nicholas Hoyle, John Parks, and Hall, K-SP 465, 455, 446, 460, 451. Bancks's Manchester and Salford Directory 1800, pp.99, 100; B. Nightingale, The Story of the Lancashire Congregational Union 1806–1906 (Manchester, 1906), p.27; Kay family book, Shuttleworth papers (SP), Estate Office, Cowan Bridge (EO,CB).

5. For details of the marriage – family tree, K-SP 336. For Robert Kay's attitudes to business, summary statement, K-SP 465. Deans' Manchester and Salford Directory 1808 and 1809, p.224; Pigot and Deans' Manchester and Salford Directory 1817, p.284; The Commercial Directory for 1818–19–20, pp.336, 339; J. Leigh's Directory of Bury and Rochdale 1818, p.68. For 1821, Pigot and Deans' New Directory for Manchester, Salford, etc. 1820–1, pp.92, 188, 298; for 1825, Pigot and Deans' Directory for Manchester, Salford, etc. 1824–5, p.417; for London and America, Hannah Kay to James Phillips Kay (JPK), 3 Nov. 1824, K-SP 18; for reduction of business activities, Hannah Kay to JPK, 6 and 30 May 1826, K-SP 42, 45.

6. Anthony Howe, The Cotton Masters 1830–1860 (Oxford, 1984), pp.24-5; for Rochdale, family tree, K-SP 336; for Ardwick, Deans' Manchester and Salford Directory 1808 and 1809, p.105; for Salford, Pigot and Deans' Manchester and

Salford Directory 1817, p.143, and Nightingale, *Lancashire Congregational Union*, p.150; for Leaf Square, *Pigot and Deans' New Directory of Manchester, Salford, etc. 1821–2*, p.92; for Meadowcroft, *Pigot and Deans' Directory for Manchester, Salford, etc. 1824–5*, p.417. The Kays were still at Meadowcroft in 1828 (Hannah Kay to JPK, 29 Dec. 1828, K-SP 59) but moved to Brookshaw sometime after that date.

7. Parks's and summary statements, K-SP 460, 465.
8. Wild's statement, K-SP 455. Lord's compilation includes the Kays; A.D. Gilbert, *Religion and Society in Industrial England* (London, 1976), pp.35–6; W.E. Harding, *The History of the Park Congregational Church, Ramsbottom* (Bury, 1931), pp.15–16; summary statement, and Hannah Kay to JPK, 23 Dec. 1824 – K-SP 465, 24.
9. Hall's, Porter's and summary statements, K-SP 451, 454, 465.
10. Nightingale, *Lancashire Congregational Union*, p.149; B.T. Barton, *History of the Borough of Bury and Neighbourhood, in the County of Lancaster* (Bury, [1874]), pp.158, 212–13, 217, 222–4; Owen Chadwick, *The Victorian Church* (London, 1966), pp.79–95; Erik Routley, *English Religious Dissent* (Cambridge, 1960), pp.112–18; H. Hale Bellot, *University College, London, 1826–1926* (London, 1929), pp.5–6.
11. Francis Room's, Mary Balleny's, summary statement, and Jackson's statement, K-SP 448, 463, 465, 462.
12. Harding, pp.15–21. 'Roby's Academy, Manchester 1803–1808', *Transactions of the Congregational Historical Society (TCHS)* Vol.13 (1937–1939), pp.41–2; and 'Dissenting chapels in and near Manchester, 1810', *TCHS*, Vol.6 (1913–1915), p.134. The Kays' second child, Hannah, was baptised at Roby's chapel – Church of Jesus Christ of Latter-Day Saints, *International Genealogical Index* (1981), p.41521. Nightingale, *Lancashire Congregational Union*, p.150. W.M. Arthur, *Bamford Chapel: Its Origins and History* (Heywood, 1901), pp.10–11 and Barton, p.280; Arthur draws heavily on the contemporary account in the Bamford Chapel, Church Book (minutes), held at Bamford Chapel, Norden Road, Rochdale. *Evangelical Magazine*, November 1801, p.454.
13. Arthur, pp.22–3 and Bamford Chapel, Church Book (Minutes); statements of Porter and Jackson, K-SP 454, 457; B. Nightingale, *Lancashire Nonconformity; or Sketches, Historical and Descriptive of the Congregational and Old Presbyterian Churches in the County* (Manchester, 1892), Vol.3, pp.254–62; Nightingale, *Lancashire Congregational Union*, p.150; *Evangelical Magazine*, December 1801, p.470.
14. Arthur, pp.14–15 and Bamford Chapel; Jackson's statements, K-SP 457, 462. 'Roby's Academy', pp.46–7; Gilbert, pp.53–7.
15. Room's, Balleny's, and summary statements, K-SP 448, 463, 465. Quotations from summary statement.
16. Hall's, Wild's and summary statements, K-SP 449, 451, 455 and 465. The quotation is from Hall's statement.
17. Hall's, Wild's, Parks's and summary statements, K-SP 451, 455, 460, 465 – the quotations are from Hall's statement; for Robert Kay's will, Prob.11/1845, Public Record Office (PRO), London.
18. Samuel Wilkinson's, Parks's and summary statements, K-SP 449, 460, 465; also Hall's and John Openshaw's statements, K-SP 451, 453.
19. Bamford Chapel, Church Book (Minutes); Jackson's and Porter's statements, K-SP 457, 454.
20. Wilkinson's, Hoyle's and Jackson's statements, K-SP 449, 446, 457.

21. The comments on James Kay's family life in this and the following paragraphs are based on letters written to him by his mother, and occasionally by his sister, when he was in his early twenties. They give the first available insight into the family and there is no reason to believe that the attitudes which they embody were different from those which pertained when he was younger. Hannah Kay to JPK, 11 December 1824, 30 and 6 May 1826 – K-SP 23, 45, 42. For Hannah before marriage: James Phillips to Hannah Phillips, Wednesday afternoon, no date, and Joseph Phillips to Hannah Phillips, 10 April 1800, SP, box F.

22. Hannah Kay to JPK: 3 November 1824, 14 April 1825, 16 February 1826, 3 April 1824, 30 December 1825, and 6 May 1826; and Hannah Kay (sister) to JPK, 5 November 1824 – K-SP 18, 32, 40, 10, 38, 42, 20.

23. Hannah Kay (sister) to JPK, 10 May 1826, K-SP 44. Hannah Kay to JPK, 30 December and 10 January 1825, 6 and 30 May 1826, 3 November 1824, and 7 November 1825 – K-SP 44, 38, 25, 42, 45, 18, 36. JPK-S to his children, 28 April 1858, K-SP 481.

24. Hannah Kay to JPK: 3 November and 23 December 1824, 7 November and 30 December 1825 – K-SP 18, 24, 36, 38.

25. *Dictionary of National Biography (DNB)*: James, Vol.10, pp.1138–40; Joseph, Vol.10, pp.1137–8; and Ebenezer, Supplement, Vol.22, p.928. Hannah Kay to JPK, 7 November 1825 and 16 February 1826, K-SP 36, 40.

26. Hannah Kay to JPK, 6 May 1826, K-SP 42.

27. James Phillips Kay-Shuttleworth (JPK-S) to Janet Kay-Shuttleworth (Janet K-S), 20 August 1851, K-SP 355.

28. John Clunie to JPK, 2 June 1822 and 9 February 1825, K-SP 5, 28. A prize Kay won at the school is dated June 1815, see Frank Smith, *The Life and Work of Sir James Kay-Shuttleworth* (London, 1923), p.2. He was still at Leaf Square on 1 June 1819 – poem by James Kay, SP, box F.

29. Quoted in 'Leaf Square Academy, Pendleton, 1811–1813', *TCHS*, Vol.13, 1937–1939, pp.113–15; H. McLachlan, *English Education under the Test Acts* (Manchester, 1913); Brian Simon, *The Two Nations and the Educational Structure* (London, 1974), pp.26–38, 56–62.

30. 'Leaf Square Academy', pp.107–13; the quotation is on p.108.

31. 'Leaf Square Academy', pp.113, 109, 117; Clunie to JPK, 29 March 1822, K-SP 4.

32. Smith, p.2; poem by James Kay, 1 June 1819, SP, box F.

33. For the Fentons at Bamford Hall: Porter's statement, K-SP 454; William Farrer and J. Brownhill (eds), *The Victoria History of the County of Lancaster*, Vol.5 (London, n.d.), p.138. Clunie to JPK, 10 January 1825, K-SP 25.

34. L.S. Pressnell, *Country Banking in the Industrial Revolution* (Oxford, 1956), note p.176; John Fenton to JPK, 12 March 1825, K-SP 31 and Hannah Kay to JPK, 10 January 1825, K-SP 25; Howe, pp.76-7.

35. Clunie to JPK, 9 February 1825, K-SP 28. A clear hint of the struggle appeared later – *Manchester Guardian*, 19 April 1828.

36. Notes by Dr W. Charles Henry, M.D., F.R.S., made in 1877 on the Edinburgh, Dublin and Manchester days of J.P. Kay, K-SP 1109; Clunie to JPK, 29 March 1822, K-SP 4; Editor, *Bolton Express*, to JPK, 5 December 1823, K-SP 9; Clunie to JPK, 29 March and 2 June 1822, K-SP 4 and 5.

37. E.B. Penny to JPK, 26 May 1821, K-SP 3; Arthur, p.15 and Bamford Chapel, Church Book (Minutes).

38. *Smith, p.4; Kay discussed Jackson in his *Words of Comfort and Counsel to Distressed Lancashire Workmen Spoken on Sundays in 1862* by A Country

Squire – Their Neighbour (London and Manchester, 1862), pp.11–12, and in
*Smith, pp.3–6. 'The first Manchester Sunday schools', *Bulletin of the John
Rylands Library Manchester*, Vol.33, No.2 (1951), pp.313–14; Jackson to JPK,
6 December 1824, K-SP 22.

39. *Smith, p.4.
40. *Smith, p.5; draft of an address [letter?] to Sunday school scholars at Bamford[?],
    K-SP 2; *Ecclesiastes*, chapter 8, verses 10–12.
41. A.L. Calman, *Life and Labours of John Ashworth* (Manchester and London,
    1877), pp.16–17; *Smith, p.6.
42. *Smith, p.8; Calman, p.15; Jackson to JPK, 6 December 1824, K-SP 22.
43. Clunie to JPK, 9 February 1825, K-SP 28; *Smith, p.8.

2 · The medical student, 1824–27, pp.21–45

1. A.J. Youngson, *The Making of Classical Edinburgh 1750–1840* (Edinburgh,
   1966), pp.2,v. This and the following paragraphs draw on Youngson.
2. Youngson, especially pp.40–2 (the quotation is from p.42) and 229–31;
   James Saunders, *Scottish Democracy 1815-1840* (Edinburgh, 1950), pp.82–3.
3. Anand C. Chitnis, *The Scottish Enlightenment and Early Victorian English Society*
   (London, 1976); Saunders, pp.85–9; and for the Evangelical movement, Stewart
   J. Brown, *Thomas Chalmers and the Godly Commonwealth in Scotland* (Oxford,
   1982), pp.211–13.
4. J.B. Morrell, 'The Edinburgh Town Council and its University, 1717–1766' in
   R.G.W. Anderson and A.D.C. Simpson, *The Early Years of the Edinburgh
   Medical School* (Edinburgh, 1976), pp.46–60, and 'The University of Edinburgh
   in the late eighteenth century: its scientific eminence and academic structure',
   Isis, No.62 (1971), pp.158–71; D.B. Horn, *A Short History of the University of
   Edinburgh* (Edinburgh, 1967), pp.52–71; Rex E. Wright-St Clair, *Doctors
   Munro: A Medical Saga* (London, 1964). For hostile comments, *Lancet*, 25
   November 1826, pp.254–7.
5. Horn, pp.58–71; Morrell, 'The University of Edinburgh', pp.169–70; A. Logan
   Turner, *The Story of a Great Hospital: The Royal Infirmary of Edinburgh 1729–1929*
   (Edinburgh, 1937); Alexander Grant, *The Story of the University of Edinburgh
   during its First Three Hundred Years* (London, 1884), Vol.1, pp.305–6.
6. Grant, Vol.2, pp.7–37; Horn, pp.108–9; Wright-St Clair, p.115; *The Life of
   Sir Robert Christison, Bart.*, edited by his sons (Edinburgh, 1885), Vol.1, p.68;
   Francis Darwin (ed.), *The Life and Letters of Charles Darwin* (London, 1887),
   Vol.1, p.36; David Hamilton, *The Healers: a History of Medicine in Scotland*
   (Edinburgh, 1981), pp.149–50; John A. Shepherd, *Simpson and Syme of Edinburgh* (Edinburgh and London, 1969), p.9.
7. J.L. Bardsley to Robert Kay, 24 August 1824, K-SP 14; William Johns to
   Christopher Anderson and William Nicol, both 26 October 1824, K-SP 16,
   17; James Williamson to JPK, 24 August 1824, K-SP 13. Hannah Kay to Miss
   White, 16 and 23 August and 15 September 1824, K-SP 11, 12, 15.
8. Henry Cockburn, *Memorials of His Time* (Edinburgh, 1971 edn), pp.20–2;
   Lancet, 23 June 1827, pp.362–5.
9. Records of medical students, session 1824–25, Special Collections, University
   of Edinburgh Library; Kay is student 248 and Henry 236; Notes by Dr W.
   Charles Henry. W.V. Farrar, Kathleen R. Farrar and E.L. Scott, 'The Henrys

of Manchester', *Ambix*, Vol.20, 1973, pp.183–208; Vol.21, 1974, pp.179–228; Vol.22, 1975, pp.186–204; Vol.23, 1976, pp.27–52; Vol.24, 1977, pp.1–26.

10. He joined on 7 January 1825: *General List of the Members of the Royal Medical Society of Edinburgh* (Edinburgh, 1906), p.43; Williamson to JPK, 24 August 1824, K-SP 13; James Gray, *History of the Royal Medical Society 1737–1937* (Edinburgh, 1952); Chitnis, pp.57–9; Hamilton, p.122; Notes by Dr W. Charles Henry; Francis Darwin (ed.), p.40; John Fenton (cousin) to JPK, 12 March 1825, K-SP 31; Hannah Kay (sister) to JPK, 10 March 1825, K-SP 30.

11. Notes by Dr W. Charles Henry.

12. *Reports of Proceedings at the Distribution of Prizes in St Mary's Hospital Medical School . . . with the address delivered by Sir James Kay-Shuttleworth BART* (London, 1857), pp.10–11, K-SP 1171.

13. Hannah Kay to JPK, 23 December 1824 and 8 February 1825, K-SP 24, 27. The first part of the 1825 letter was written by his brother Robert; his mother wrote her letter across Robert's.

14. Robert Kay to JPK, 3 March 1825, K-SP 29.

15. Hannah Kay (sister) to JPK, 10 March 1825, K-SP 30.

16. Hannah Kay to JPK, 3 November 1824, K-SP 18; Robert Kay (brother) to JPK, 8 February 1825, K-SP 27; Hannah Kay (sister) to JPK, 5 November 1824, K-SP 20; Hannah Kay to JPK, 14 April 1825, 3 November and 23 December 1824 and 8 February 1825, K-SP 32, 18, 24, 27.

17. For the factory, Hannah Kay to JPK, 10 January 1825, K-SP 25 and James Fenton to JPK, 12 March 1825, K-SP 31; Robert's progress, Hannah Kay (sister) to JPK, 10 March 1825, K-SP 30; for William Kay, Hannah Kay to JPK, 4 November 1824, K-SP 19 and William Kay (cousin) to JPK, 6 November 1824, K-SP 21; for ill-advised marriage, Hannah Kay to JPK, 23 December 1824, K-SP 24; family disputes and property settlement, Hannah Kay to JPK, 8 February 1825, K-SP 27; for deaths, Hannah Kay to JPK, 23 December 1824, K-SP 24 and Hannah Kay (sister) to JPK, 10 March 1825, K-SP 30.

18. Hannah Kay to JPK, 19 January 1825, K-SP 25; Jackson to Kay, 6 December 1824, K-SP 22; Johns to JPK, 4 February 1825, K-SP 26.

19. Hannah Kay (sister) to JPK, 10 May 1826, K-SP 44; letter written by physicians of the Manchester Infirmary, 7 September 1826, SP, box J. In his auto-biography, Kay said that he spent some of this period in Dublin – B.C. Bloomfield (ed.), *The Autobiography of Sir James Kay-Shuttleworth*, Education Libraries Bulletin, supplement 7, University of London Institute of Education (1964), p.3. (This document is what Smith calls 'the 1877 manuscript' in his *The Life and Work of Sir James Kay-Shuttleworth*. Throughout this book it will be referred to as *Autobiography*.) Kay's memory had failed him, but he did spend some of the 1826 summer recess in Dublin. Hannah Kay (sister) to JPK, 10 March 1825, K-SP 30; Hannah Kay to JPK, 14 April 1825, K-SP 32.

20. Kay (student no.253) signed the matriculation roll on 28 October 1825: Matriculation roll, Edinburgh University, held in Special Collections, Edin-burgh University Library. Details of his studies at Edinburgh are contained in records of medical students, session 1825–26, and a series of letters in SP, box J: letter written by physicians of the Manchester Infirmary, J.L. Bardsley, 1 September 1826; Edinburgh New Town Dispensary, undated; David Clark, 7 April 1828; Edward Turner, undated; John Aitkin, undated; W.P. Alison, 9 December 1827; Notes by Dr W. Charles Henry. For Dublin, W.C. Henry to JPK, 11 September 1826, K-SP 48.

21. Records of medical students, session 1826–27 – Kay is student 231; letters

from James Syme, 10 December 1827, Robert Graham, 11 July 1827, and James Buchanan, 7 December 1827 – SP, box J; *Autobiography*, pp.5–6.

22. *General List of the Members of the Royal Medical Society of Edinburgh*, p.117; Gray, p.319; *Life of Robert Christison*, p.130; Gray, pp.65–8, 135–6; Notes by Dr W. Charles Henry.

23. Hannah Kay to JPK, 30 December 1825, K-SP 38.

24. Hannah Kay to JPK, 7 November 1825, K-SP 36; James O. Kay to JPK, 13 February 1826, K-SP 39.

25. James O. Kay to JPK, 28 February and 8 May 1826, K-SP 41,43; *DNB*, Vol.1, pp.290–2; John D. Comrie, *History of Scottish Medicine* (London, 1932), Vol.2, pp.610–11, 108–11, Notes by Charles W. Henry, *Autobiography*, pp.4–6.

26. Notes by Dr W. Charles Henry; for Kay's paper, *Edinburgh Medical and Surgical Journal*, Vol.29, No.94 (1828), pp.37–66; W.P. Alison, 'Additional cases and observations illustrating the origin of tubercles', *Transactions of the Medico-Chirurgical Society*, Vol.3 (1829), pp.274–307 – comment on Kay, p.300; the review, *Edinburgh Medical and Surgical Journal*, Vol.30, No.96 (1828), pp.188–206 – reference to Kay, p.202.

27. *Edinburgh New Town Dispensary: Report and Treasurer's Accounts 1825*, University of Edinburgh pamphlets, EBF 9 (41445) 04/1; *Annual Report of the Edinburgh New Town Dispensary 1827* and *Statement Regarding the New Town Dispensary by the Medical Gentlemen conducting that Institution*, both held in University of Edinburgh pamphlets, SB 36204/2. Cockburn, p.283; Gray, pp.87–8; Olive Checkland, *Philanthropy in Victorian Scotland: Social Welfare and the Voluntary Principle* (Edinburgh, 1980), pp.200–4.

28. Based on *Autobiography*, pp.3–6.

29. *Autobiography*, p.6; draft of a letter from JPK to unknown, 1827, K-SP 49.

30. *Autobiography*, p.4; William Pulteney Alison, 'Observations on the epidemic fever now prevalent among the lower orders in Edinburgh', *Edinburgh Medical and Surgical Journal*, Vol.28, No.93 (1827), p.236 and *Annual Report of the Edinburgh New Town Dispensary*, p.10.

31. *Autobiography*, p.5; James O. Kay to JPK, 13 February and 8 May 1826 and Hannah Kay to JPK, 16 February (the quotation) and 30 May 1826 – K-SP 39, 43, 40, 45.

32. Adam Smith, *The Wealth of Nations* (1776), book 5, in Everyman edition, Vol.2, pp.264, 269; Andrew S. Skinner and Thomas Wilson (eds), *Essays on Adam Smith* (Oxford, 1975); R.H. Campbell and A.S. Skinner, *Adam Smith* (London, 1982); Chitnis, throughout.

33. A.C. Cheyne (ed.), *The Practical and the Pious: Essays on Thomas Chalmers (1780–1847)*, Edinburgh, 1985; and Brown – for Chalmers's visit, p.178; JPK to Thomas Chalmers, 26 May 1832, CHA 4.183.1, Chalmers collection, New College, Edinburgh.

34. Brown, pp.91–151; 'Introduction' and Mary T. Furgol, 'Chalmers and poor relief: an incidental sideline?' – both in Cheyne (ed.), pp.16–20, 115–29; John F. McCaffrey, 'Thomas Chalmers and social change', *Scottish Historian Review*, No.169 (1961), pp.32–60; quotations from Brown, p.138.

35. Olive Checkland, 'Chalmers and William Pulteney Alison: a conflict of views on Scottish social policy' in Cheyne (ed.), pp.130–40; Brown, pp.289–96. For the first to suggest the importance of Kay's Edinburgh experience, J.R.B. Johnson, 'The Education Department, 1839–1864: a study in social policy and the growth of government' (Ph.D. thesis, Cambridge, 1968), p.29.

36. *New Lapsus Linguae*, 17 January 1825, p.63, held in Special Collection,

University of Edinburgh Library; J.T.D. Hall, *The Tounis College: An Anthology of Edinburgh University Student Journals* (Edinburgh, 1985); *Smith, p.11; Notes by Dr W. Charles Henry; John Addington Symonds to JPK, 6 February, 8 May and 5 July 1828, K-SP 54,56,58. A memoir of Symonds is in John Addington Symonds, *Miscellanies* (Bristol, 1871), pp.ix–xxxi.

37. For the circumstances of the private publication, p.195. Preface to *Cynedrida*; Sharon Turner, *The History of the Anglo-Saxons* (London, 1828, first published 1807), Vol.1, pp.271–4; *Cynedrida*, p.31; Notes by Dr W. Charles Henry; Symonds to JPK, 5 July 1828, K-SP 58.

38. D.G. Paz, 'Sir James Kay-Shuttleworth: the man behind the myth', *History of Education*, Vol.14, No.3 (1985), p.186; *Cynedrida*, p.21.

39. *Cynedrida*, p.59; Symonds to JPK, 5 July 1828, K-SP 58.

40. J.P. Kay, 'On the cessation of the motility of the heart and muscles in the asphyxia of warm-blooded animals', Royal Medical Society Dissertations, Vol.88, pp.409–53 (held at Royal Medical Society, Edinburgh), quotation p.446. The original thesis in Latin, entitled *De Motu Muscutosum*, is in Thesis 1827, Special Collection, University of Edinburgh Library. Bichat's position is discussed in Notes by Dr W. Charles Henry, and Smith, pp.16–18. Evidence, oral and written, taken and received by the Commissioners . . . for visiting the Universities of Scotland, Vol.1, p.204, *BPP* 1837, Vol.35.

41. 'On the cessation of the motility of the heart', p.431.

42. For the date and examination procedures, *Lancet*, 3 May 1828, p.149 and Grant, Vol.1, pp.331–3. A copy of the thesis with the comments made by each professor is held by Lord Shuttleworth at Leck Hall. 'Edinburgh grinders and examiners', *Lancet*, 16 June 1827, pp.339–40; Williamson to JPK, 24 August 1824, K-SP 13; *Lancet*, 16 June 1827, p.340 and 3 May 1828, p.148; *List of Graduates in Medicine in the University of Edinburgh, from MDCCV to MDCCCLXVI* (Edinburgh, 1867), p.82.

43. Robert Kay to Hannah Kay, 10 May 1827, SP, box F.

44. The testimonials are in SP, box J.

45. M. Jeanne Peterson, *The Medical Profession in Mid-Victorian London* (Berkeley, 1978), pp.90–135; Henry to JPK, 23 September 1827 and 11 September 1826, K-SP 51,48.

46. Henry to JPK, 23 September 1827, K-SP 51; *Middlemarch* (Oxford, 1950), p.128.

3 · A Manchester doctor, 1828–35, pp.46–103

1. Alexis de Tocqueville, *Journeys to England and Ireland*, ed. J.P.Mayer (New Haven, 1958), pp.105-7.

2. Carlyle's comment on the noise is quoted in Steven Marcus, *Engels, Manchester, and the Working Class* (London, 1974), p.32; *Past and Present* (New York, n.d.), p.66.

3. De Tocqueville, pp.107–8.

4. Asa Briggs, *Victorian Cities* (London, 1963), p.85; Marcus, p.4; Duncan Bythell, *The Handloom Weavers: A Study of the English Cotton Industry during the Industrial Revolution* (Cambridge, 1969), pp.25–6; E.P. Thompson, *The Making of the English Working Class* (Harmondsworth, 1968), pp.207–13.

5. P. Gaskell, *The Manufacturing Population of England* (London, 1833), p.11; C.H. Lee, *A Cotton Enterprise 1795–1840: A History of M'Connel & Kennedy Fine*

Cotton Spinners (Manchester, 1972), pp.118–20; Gary Messinger, *Manchester in the Victorian Age: The Half-known City* (Manchester, 1985), p.27; Marcus, p.14; Briggs, p.89; Archibald Prentice, *Historical Sketches and Personal Recollections of Manchester* (London, 1970), pp.345, 351.

6. David Cannadine, *Lords and Landlords: The Aristocracy and the Towns 1774–1967* (Leicester, 1980), pp.46–7, 28.

7. Shena D. Simon, *A Century of City Government: Manchester 1838-1938* (London, 1938), pp.38–69; Arthur Redford, *The History of Local Government in Manchester* (London and New York, 1950), Vol.2, pp.3–9; V.A.C. Gattrel, 'The commercial middle class in Manchester c.1820–1857' (Ph.D. thesis, Cambridge University, 1971), and his 'Incorporation and the pursuit of Liberal hegemony in Manchester 1790–1839' in Derek Fraser (ed.), *Municipal Reform and the Industrial City* (Leicester, 1982), p.47; Raymond V. Holt, *The Unitarian Contribution to Social Progress in England* (London, 1938), pp.220–5; Howe, p.69.

8. *Lancet*, 23 February 1828, pp.754–7; Symonds to JPK, 8 May 1828, K-SP 56; Irvine Loudon, *Medical Care and the General Practitioner 1750-1850* (Oxford, 1986), p.321.

9. Peterson, pp.6–10, 16–23; Loudon, pp.88, 172, 227; S.W.F. Holloway, 'The Apothecaries' Act, 1815: a reinterpretation', *Medical History*, Vol.10 (1966), pp.107–29, 221–36.

10. Loudon, pp.208–23, 199–200, 133–8, 208–27; John V. Pickstone, *Medicine and Industrial Society: A History of Hospital Development in Manchester and its Region, 1752–1946* (Manchester, 1985), p.44; Katherine A. Webb, 'The development of the medical profession in Manchester, 1750–1860' (Ph.D. thesis, University of Manchester, 1988), pp. 267–8, 358. I have drawn heavily on these three works in this chapter. Michael Durey, 'Medical elites, the general practitioner, and patient power in Britain during the cholera epidemic of 1831–2' in Ian Inkster and Jack Morrell (eds), *Metropolis and Province: Science in British Culture, 1780–1850* (London, 1983), pp.258–9.

11. *MG*, 5 April 1828; Pickstone, *Medicine and Industrial Society*, pp.50–1; Brian Abel-Smith, *The Hospitals 1800–1948* (Cambridge, MA, 1964), pp.6–7; Roy Porter, *Disease, Medicine and Society in England 1550–1860* (London, 1987), p.38; B. Love and J. Barton, *Manchester As It Is* (Manchester, 1839), p.64; F.W. Jordan, *Life of Joseph Jordan, Surgeon* (Manchester, 1904), p.52.

12. *MG*, 19 April 1828; Notes by Dr W. Charles Henry; Hannah Kay to JPK, 2 April 1828, K-SP 55.

13. *MG*, 19 April 1828.

14. *Complete List of the Members and Officers of the Manchester Literary and Philosophical Society* (Manchester, 1896); Chris E. Makepeace, *Science and Technology in Manchester: Two Hundred Years of the Lit. and Phil.* (Manchester, 1984); Arnold Thackray, 'Natural knowledge in cultural context: The Manchester model', *American Historical Review*, No.3 (June, 1974), pp.672–709 and Joan Mottram, 'The life and work of John Roberton (1797–1876) of Manchester, obstetrician and social reformer' (M.Sc. thesis, University of Manchester, 1986), p.35; Joseph Aston, *A Picture of Manchester* (Manchester, [1826]), p.190; J.P. Kay, 'Observations and experiments concerning molecular irritation of the lungs, as one cause of tubercular consumption', *North of England Medical and Surgical Journal (NEMSJ)*, 1 February 1831, p.354.

15. Pickstone, *Medicine and Industrial Society*, pp.51–7; Irvine Loudon, 'The origins and growth of the dispensary movement in England', *Bulletin of the History of*

Medicine, Vol.55 (1981), pp.322–40; James Phillips Kay, *Defects in the Consti-tution of Dispensaries, with Suggestions for their Improvement* (London and Man-chester, 1834), pp.24–5.

16. Webb, pp.355–7; *Ancoats Hospital, 150th Anniversary 1828–1927*, Manchester, 1978, pp.4–5; Pickstone, *Medicine and Industrial Society*, pp.52–3, 83; F. Renaud, *A Short History of the Rise and Progress of the Manchester Royal Infirmary from the Year 1752 to 1877* (Manchester, 1898), pp.99–100; E.M. Brockbank, *The Foundation of Provincial Medical Education in England* (Manchester, 1936), p.60; *Reports of the Committee of the Ardwick and Ancoats Dispensary 1831, 1832, 1834*, all published in Manchester; *Lancet*, 11 July 1829, pp.465, 466.

17. Webb, p.356; Loudon, 'Origins and growth of the dispensary movement', p.336; J.P. Kay, 'Observations and experiments concerning molecular irrita-tion', pp.354, 358; Brockbank, pp.60, 100, 151; the *Reports of the Committee* contain details of its membership.

18. G. Heathcote to JPK, 11 June 1828, Symonds to JPK, 8 May 1828 and Hannah Kay to JPK, 29 December [1828] – K-SP 57, 56, 59. Symonds to JPK, 11 February 1833, K-SP 408 – Bloomfield dates this letter 1853, but D.G. Paz has noted that it should be 1833. V. Mary Crosse, *A Surgeon in the Early Nineteenth Century* (Edinburgh and London, 1968), p.150.

19. Symonds to JPK, 6 February 1830, K-SP 54. This letter is dated 'Saturday 6 February', a combination of day and date which occurs in 1830 but not in 1828 where Bloomfield tentatively places it; Webb, pp.512–16. R.V. Taylor, *The Biographia Leodiensis* (London, 1865), pp.415–16; S.T. Anning, *The General Infirmary at Leeds* (Edinburgh and London, Vol.2, 1966), pp.176–7. William H. McMenemey, *The Life and Times of Sir Charles Hastings* (Edinburgh and London, 1959), especially pp.57–64; W.R. Lefanu, *British Periodicals of Medicine: A Chronological List 1640–1899* (Oxford, 1984), p.11 and Symonds to JPK, 6 February 1830, K-SP 54. For the coalition and the conducting of the journal, W. Bandrew (?) to JPK, 15 December 1830, K-SP 61; Williamson to JPK, 22 February, 6 April and 26 May 1831, K-SP 62, 63, 65.

20. Introduction attached to *NEMSJ*, 1 August 1830; Pickstone, *Medicine and Industrial Society*, pp.78–80.

21. Lyon's articles were in *NEMSJ*, 1 August 1830 and 1 November 1830; Carbutt, 1 August 1830; Williamson, 1 February 1831; Symonds, 1 May 1831; Roberton, 1 August and 1 November 1830, 1 February 1831 – for Roberton, see Mottram; *NEMSJ*, 1 November 1830, p.264.

22. An anonymous article (1 August 1830, pp.105–26), reviewing Michael Thomas Sadler's *The Law of Population* (1830), has characteristic Kay touches but I have not found conclusive evidence that he wrote it. Kay's articles were: 'Two remarkable cases of disease in the circulating system', 1 February 1831, pp.278–85; 'Further experiments concerning suspended animation', 1 May 1831, pp.453–72 and, for the quotations, 'Physical condition of the poor', 1 November 1830, p.220; 'Observations and experiments concerning molecular irritation of the lungs', p.359. For byssinosis, Willis J. Elwood and A. Félicité Tuxford, *Some Manchester Doctors* (Manchester, 1984).

23. *Lancet*, 7 August 1830, pp.726–33; Williamson to JPK, 6 April 1831, K-SP 63; Symonds to JPK, 8 May 1831 and 11 February 1833, K-SP 64, 408.

24. Philip Whitwell Wilson (ed.), *The Greville Diary* (London, 1927), Vol.1, p.356. Symonds to JPK, 8 May 1831, K-SP 64; Asa Briggs, 'The background of the parliamentary reform movement in three English cities (1830–2)', *Cambridge Historical Journal*, Vol.10, No.3 (1952), pp.293–317; Thompson, p.889.

William Rathbone Greg to JPK, 24 December 1831, K-SP 67.
25. Kay, *Letter*, pp.10, 8, 16.
26. *Letter*, pp.14, 13, 7, 17, 23, 19, 23.
27. George Macaulay Trevelyan, *The Life of John Bright* (London, 1913), p.20.
28. Charles R. Dod, *Electoral Facts from 1832 to 1853 impartially stated*, edited by H.J. Hanham (London, 1972), pp.206, 173; W. Duncombe Pink and Alfred B. Bearan, *The Parliamentary Representation of Lancashire, (County and Borough), 1258–1885* (London, 1889), pp.269, 331; *MG*, 2 February 1833; H.J. Hanham, *Elections and Party Management* (London, 1959), pp.3–38; Howe, pp.101–5; C.P. Grenfell to JPK, 13 January 1833, K-SP 77.
29. Grenfell to JPK, 13 January 1833, K-SP 77; Charles William Molyneux to JPK [1834], and December [1834], 16 March 1834, 18 and 22 March 1833, 14 December 1834, K-SP 98, 99, 122, 83, 84, 154.
30. For the discussion of the Factory Act in this and the following paragraph, Elie Halévy, *The Triumph of Reform, 1830–1841* (London, 1961), pp.110–16 and Thompson, pp.371–84; Molyneux to JPK, 18 March and 18 April 1833, K-SP 83, 86.
31. Molyneux to JPK, 18 April 1833, K-SP 86.
32. Halévy, pp.173–7. Molyneux to Kay, undated but July 1834, and Tuesday evening, December 1834, K-SP 100, 99.
33. For Kay's intention to play a less active part in politics, E. Hopwood to JPK, 28 November 1834, K-S 150. Molyneux to Kay, Tuesday evening, December 1834, K-SP 99.
34. Grenfell to JPK, Wednesday morning [December 1834], K-SP 159; Molyneux to JPK, 14 December 1834, K-SP 154; Edmund Grundy to JPK, Sunday evening [December 1834], K-SP 151, Molyneux to JPK, 17 December 1834, K-SP 156 and Grenfell to JPK, 10 December 1834, K-SP 155.
35. R.J. Morris, *Cholera 1832* (New York, 1976); Michael Durey, *The Return of the Plague: British Society and the Cholera 1831–2* (Dublin, 1979); Margaret Pelling, *Cholera, Fever and English Medicine* (Oxford, 1978). Proceedings of the Board of Health Manchester (PBHM), Vol.1, 10 and 17 November 1831 (held at Local History Archives, Central Library, Manchester).
36. Durey, *The Return of the Plague*, especially pp.107–20; Morris, pp.170–92.
37. Roger Cooter, 'Anticontagionism and history's medical record' in Peter Wright and Andrew Treacher (eds), *The Problem of Medical Knowledge* (Edinburgh, 1982), pp.87–108. Cooter extends and modifies the interpretation offered by Margaret Pelling. For valuable comments on Kay's relationship to this discussion, John V. Pickstone, 'Ferriar's fever to Kay's cholera: disease and social structure in Cottonopolis', *History of Science*, Vol.22, 1984, pp.411–12.
38. Durey, *The Return of the Plague*, pp.103–5 and 'Medical elites', pp.258–9; the membership of the board is at the end of PBHM, Vol.2; 'Sketch of the progress of Manchester in thirty years from 1832 to 1862' in Kay-Shuttleworth, *Four Periods of Public Education*, p.88; *Autobiography*, pp.8–11; Report on Public Walks, 1833, p.357, *BPP* 1833.
39. PBHM, 1831: 11, 14, 17 November and 2, 14, 19, 21, 26, 28, 31 December 1832: 2, 4, 7, 14, 21, 28 January and 1, 15, 18, 22, 25, 29 February and 5, 7, 19 and 28 March 1832.
40. James Phillips Kay, *The Moral and Physical Condition of the Working Classes Employed in the Cotton Manufacture in Manchester*, (*MPC*) (London, first edition, 1832), pp.5–6, 14–15; 'Sketch of the progress of Manchester', p.88. The PBHM, 17 November 1831, record Kay's presence when the survey was first

mooted but do not indicate from whose initiative it originated. They also record the district medical officers on the back of a list of members of the local board at the end of Vol.2; Greg to JPK, 24 December 1831, K-SP 67.

41. G.M. Young, *Victorian England: Portrait of an Age* (London, 1961), p.26.
42. The first edition has no publication date but appeared in the first week of April 1832 – *MG*, 31 March 1832. The same issue of *MG* reports the Literary and Philosophical Society paper. The second edition was published on 24 November 1832 – *MG* of that date. 'Sketch of the progress of Manchester', p.88, contains Kay's inaccurate recollection of the time of publication.
43. *MPC*, pp.4, 5, 43.
44. *MPC*, pp.18, 24, 25, 23–4.
45. *MPC*, pp.21–3.
46. *MPC*, pp.19, 9, 41–2. Passages on pp.8–10, 19 and 26 are from his article, 'The physical condition of the poor'.
47. *MPC*, pp.29–46 – the quotations, pp.28, 29, 33, 38.
48. *MPC*, pp.45–6, 49.
49. *MPC*, pp.47, 49, 50, 7, 51–2.
50. *MPC*, pp.58, 60, 61.
51. *MPC*, pp.63, 69; Chadwick acknowledgement is quoted in Messinger, p.44.
52. *MPC*, pp.71–2.
53. Pickstone, 'Ferriar's fever to Kay's cholera', pp.408–12; *MPC*, p.6.
54. Messinger, p.43.
55. *MPC*, pp.6–7, 12, 19, 27–8, 20–1.
56. *MPC*, pp.8, 10, 11.
57. C.T. Thackrah, *The Effects of Arts, Trades and Professions on Health and Longevity* (Edinburgh, 1831); W.R. Greg, *An Inquiry into the State of the Manufacturing Population and the Causes and Cures Therein Existing* (Manchester, 1831); John Roberton, *General Remarks on the Health of English Manufacturers* (Manchester, 1831).
58. *MG*, 21 April 1832; the *Union Pilot* is quoted in Valdo Pons, 'Contemporary interpretations of Manchester in the 1830s and 1840s', *Stanford Journal of International Studies*, Vol.13 (Spring 1978), p.71; *Poor Man's Guardian*, 30 June 1832, p.448; Henry Gaulter, *The Origin and Progress of the Malignant Cholera in Manchester* (London, 1833), p.2; Friedrich Engels, *The Condition of the Working Class in England* (Oxford, 1958), pp.76, 58. Other comments occur on pp.73, 74, 75, 77, 103.
59. JPK to Chalmers, 4 June and 21 November 1832, CHA 4.183.2 and 4.183.4, Chalmers collection.
60. Durey, *The Return of the Plague*, Ch.7, especially pp.155–79.
61. Kay's activities are frequently mentioned in PBHM; *MG*, 4 August 1832; a series of letters written in July 1832, K-SP 69–73.
62. *Autobiography*, pp.9–10; Gaulter, pp.160–1, 37–9; PBHM, 18, 21 June 1832 and 22 August 1832; Mark Clifford, 'Medicine, politics and society: Manchester's 1832 cholera epidemic' (BA thesis, University of California at Berkeley, 1979), p.97.
63. Gaulter, p.137; PBHM, 9 July 1832; Morris, p.179.
64. Durey, *The Return of the Plague*, pp.179–80; Morris, pp.110–11; *Poor Man's Advocate*, 15 September 1832, p.3; PBHM, 3 and 4 September 1832.
65. Kay to Chalmers, 21 November 1832, CHA 4.183.4; Chalmers to JPK, 2, 26, 30 January and 14 December 1833, K-SP 75, 78, 79, 93. The second edition of Kay's pamphlet is that edited by W.H. Chaloner, 1970. It is referred to as

MPC2. For the quotations, *MPC2*, pp.8, 10, 11, 13.

66. The additional material includes the argument for street widening – it begins with a rewriting of the paragraph 'Unwilling to weary', *MPC2*, p.37 and concludes at the paragraph ending 'Lancashire', p.40. For the section on the pigs, 'One nuisance', p.41 to 'provided', p.42. For gaols and gin, the top of p.59 to 'spirits', p.60. For the assemblies of workers, 'The associations', p.107 to 'promoted', p.111. For the comments on education, p.95.

67. For religious instruction, *MPC2*, 'The fruit', p.65 to 'to them', p.67 and pp.114–15; for infant schools and domestic economy, *MPC2*, 'Before the age', p.70 to 'mothers', p.72.

68. For the poor law, *MPC2*, 'The poor-laws', p.45 to 'here', p.52; the quotations, pp.48, 49, 50.

69. *Autobiography*, p.11.

70. Kay to Chalmers, 21 November 1832, CHA 4.183.4; Report on Public Walks, 1833.

71. Mabel Tylecote, 'The Manchester Mechanics' Institution, 1824– 50' in D.S.L. Cardwell (ed.), *Artisan to Graduate* (Manchester, 1974), pp.55–86; Benjamin Heywood to Lord Brougham, 17 February 1825, Brougham papers, 30456, held at University College, London; *Report of the Proceedings of the General Meeting of the Subscribers and Friends of the Manchester Mechanics' Institution, 19 November 1832* (Manchester, 1832), and similar report for 14 January 1834, p.3; John Shuttleworth, *A Sketch of the Life of Rowland Detrosier* (Manchester, 1860); Simon, pp.217–20. Also for Detrosier, see below, p.302.

72. Leo H. Grindon, *Manchester Banks and Bankers: Historical, Biographical, and Anecdotal* (Manchester, 1878), pp.287–90; *MG*, 23 February, 23 March, 7 and 21 September 1833; *The First Annual Report of the Manchester and Salford District Provident Society, 1833* (Manchester, 1834), and *Third Annual Report, 1835*; Hugh Colley Irvine, *The Old D.P.S., A Short History of Charitable Work in Manchester and Salford, 1833–1933* (Manchester, 1933), especially pp.5, 8, 9.

73. Kay, *Defects in the Constitution of Dispensaries*, pp.6, 4, 23, 36; Pickstone, *Medicine and Industrial Society*, pp.81–3.

74. T.S. Ashton, *Economic and Social Investigations in Manchester, 1833–1933: A Centenary History of the Manchester Statistical Society* (London, 1934), pp.1–12. M.J. Cullen, *The Statistical Movement in Early Victorian Britain: The Foundations of Empirical Research* (New York, 1975), points out (pp.105–6) that Ashton draws on Thomas Read Wilkinson, 'On the origin and history of the Manchester Statistical Society', *Transactions of the Manchester Statistical Society 1875–76* (Manchester, 1976), which is based on information obtained from Langton. Chalmers to JPK, 14 December 1833, K-SP 93 – also C. Poulett Thomson to JPK, 6 November 1833, K-SP 91; *First Report of the Statistical Society, Manchester (FR,MSS)*, July 1834, Papers of the Manchester Statistical Society (PMSS), No.11, held at Local History Archives, Central Library, Manchester. Report of the committee appointed to revise the rules of the Manchester Statistical Society, 15 October 1834, PMSS, No.20.

75. David Elesh, 'The Manchester Statistical Society: a case study of a discontinuity in the history of empirical social research', part 1, *Journal of the History of the Behavioural Sciences*, No.8 (1972), pp.280–7; Ashton, pp.1–12; W.R. Greg, Brief memoir on the present state of criminal statistics, 16 October 1833, PMSS, No.2; *Prospectus of the Objects and Plan of Operation of the Statistical Society of London*, 23 April 1834, PMSS, No.8.

76. Untitled paper in Kay's handwriting, 1834, PMSS, No.5; *MPC*, p.5.

77. Cullen, pp.8–27; Victor L. Hilts, *Statist and Statistician* (New York, 1981), especially part 1; Harald Westergaard, *Contributions to the History of Statistics* (New York, 1969), p.136; Lucy Brown, *The Board of Trade and the Free-Trade Movement 1830–42* (Oxford, 1958), pp.76–93.

78. 'Analysis of the report of an agent employed by the Manchester Statistical Society in 1834 . . .', *Report of the Fourth Meeting of the British Association for the Advancement of Science; held at Edinburgh in 1834* (London, 1835), pp.690–1. This report is found with some slight changes in PMSS, Nos.17–19, 20.

79. *FR,MSS*; handwritten report, No.5, PMSS. For Heywood's survey, *FR,MSS* – the second study, Nos 38, 40, 43, 46, PMSS. Kay's paper, 'On the condition of the miners of Derbyshire', was reported in *FR,MSS* but no copy survives. 'On the means existing for the religious instruction of the working classes, in large towns, with suggestions concerning an enquiry into the subject' (1834) is another lost paper; it is reported in Nos 27, 28, PMSS; the dispensary pamphlet, No.7 in PMSS; the Mechanics' Institute lectures, No.4, PMSS. *Report of a Committee of the Manchester Statistical Society on the State of Education in the Borough of Manchester in 1834* (London and Manchester, 1835).

80. Paper No.5, PMSS.

81. *MPC*, p.47.

82. This analysis draws particularly on Philip Abrams, *The Origins of British Sociology: 1834–1914* (Chicago and London, 1968).

83. Kay, *Letter*, p.21; Heywood to Brougham, 30 October 1833, Brougham papers, 17565; No.6, PMSS.

84. G. Poulett Scrope, *Memoir of the Life of The Right Honourable Charles Lord Sydenham, G.C.B.* (London, 1844); Poulett Thomson to Kay, 15 March and 6 November 1833, K-SP 82, 91, and 22 and 30 January 1834, K-SP 105, 106. The November meeting is that reported by Kay in PMSS, No.5 and noted in *FR,MSS*.

85. *Westminster Review*, April 1833, pp.380–404; *Tait's Edinburgh Magazine*, No.11, 1833, p.675; *MG*, 5 May 1832; Gaskell, pp.94–5, 117, 136–7, 227, 250–1; George Condy, *An Argument for Placing Factory Children Within the Pale of the Law* (London, 1833), pp.55–8; Benjamin Heywood, *Addresses Delivered at the Manchester Mechanics Institution* (London, 1843), p.56; Leon Faucher, *Manchester in 1844: Its Present Condition and Future Prospects* (London and Manchester, 1844), pp.26–7, 57, 61–3. For contacts made at the Statistical Society, *FR,MSS*; the link with the Benthamites, *Autobiography*, p.14; Lord Kerry to JPK, 23 May and 10 August 1834, K-SP, 127, 133. For de Tocqueville at the Statistical Society, *SR,MSS*; de Tocqueville, pp.105, 106. For Cavour, G.B. Hindle, *Provision for the Relief of the Poor in Manchester 1754–1826* (Manchester, 1975), pp.51–2n.

86. J.T. Slugg, *Reminiscences of Manchester Fifty Years Ago* (Shannon, 1971; first published 1881), p.333; *Squib*, 2 March 1833, p.247 and 13 October 1832, p.84.

87. June Kennedy to JPK, 27 September 1833 and 16 February 1834, K-SP 88, 115; JPK to June Kennedy, c.15 and c.18 February 1834, K-SP 117, 118; Howe, pp.76–7. The Kay–Kennedy romance is reconstructed from the K-SP. Some of the letters are undated or inadequately dated, and the order of events cannot be determined with complete certainty. But the basic story is clear. I have gained from reading Graeme Davison's comments on this affair in his unpublished paper, '"A life without egotism": James Phillips Kay and the Manchester cotton lords, 1828–1835' (1981).

88. JPK to Helen Kennedy, 4 January 1834, K-SP 76. I have assumed that Kay

did not give this letter to Helen Kennedy because its first five and a half paragraphs are identical with a proposal written on 10 February (K-SP 111) which she did see. Even the distracted Kay is unlikely to have presented the same proposal twice! K-SP 111 wisely omits two and a half paragraphs from the earlier letter. There is a minor problem in the dating of the 4 January letter. Kay gave the year as 1833, falling into the common error of continuing the old year's date into the new. Bloomfield places it with the 1833 letters, but suggests 1834 (Bloomfield, p.5). The suggestion makes sense when the letter is placed in the context of the other correspondence.

89. Helen Kennedy's letters, K-SP 109 and 110, are not precisely dated. They were written from Ancoats on 'Saturday' and 'Sunday'. They make most sense, however, if placed at this part of the story. June Kennedy's letter of 4 February is K-SP 108.
90. JPK to Helen Kennedy, 10 February 1834, K-SP 111.
91. Helen Kennedy to JPK, undated, [February 1834], K-SP 107; June Kennedy to JPK, 15 February 1834, K-SP 113.
92. JPK to June Kennedy, 15 February 1834, K-SP 117.
93. June Kennedy to JPK, 16 February 1834, K-SP 115.
94. JPK to June Kennedy, c.18 February 1834, K-SP 118; June Kennedy to JPK, 19 February 1834, K-SP 119.
95. June Kennedy to JPK, 17 February, and 11 and 14 March 1834, K-SP 116, 120, 121.
96. Williamson to JPK, 19 March 1834, K-SP 123; R.S. McAll to JPK, 'Friday evening' [1834], K-SP 97; Webb, p.301, and letter to author, 4 March 1989.
97. Robert McAll to JPK, 26 April 1834, K-SP 124; Robert Kay to JPK, 28 November 1833, K-SP 92.
98. The bill is in K-SP 125; Jane Kennedy to JPK, 28 August and 8 September 1834, K-SP 136, 139; Mary Kennedy (another sister) to JPK, 19 September 1834, K-SP 137; Jane Kennedy to JPK, 15 September 1834, K-SP 140.
99. Jane Kennedy to JPK, 'Monday night', probably October 1834, K-SP 142.
100. Jane Kennedy to JPK, 'Monday night', probably October 1834, K-SP 142; JPK to Jane Kennedy, undated, but following K-SP 142, probably October 1834, K-SP 143; JPK to Helen Kennedy, undated, probably October 1834, K-SP 144.
101. JPK to Douglas, 12 November 1834, K-SP 146. This letter has no name for its addressee. Bloomfield suggests that it is William Langton, but it seems clear that it is Douglas. Other letters in this exchange are K-SP 141, 145, 147. JPK to Jane Kennedy, undated but probably October 1834, K-SP 143.
102. James Phillips Kay, *The Physiology, Pathology, and Treatment of Asphyxia* (London, 1834). Its reception may be gauged from comments from reviews published by Kay in *MG*, 23 May 1835. For Mackenzie's article, Smith, pp.17–18; *Lancet*, 24 May 1834, pp.315–16 and 7 June 1834, pp.387–9; W.H. Duncan to JPK, 27 August 1834, K-SP 135.
103. Medical papers of Dr Edmund Lyon, M/134/3/2/1–3, Local History Archives, Central Library, Manchester; Duncan to JPK, 27 August 1834, K-SP 135; Williamson to JPK, 'Thursday', September and 10 December 1834, K-SP 138, 152; Webb, pp.524–8.
104. Journal of Proceedings connected with the formation of a Medical Library, Reading Room, and Society, in Manchester, pp.1–28 (held in Medical Library, John Rylands Library, University of Manchester); E.M. Brockbank, *A Centenary History of the Manchester Medical Society* (Manchester, 1934), pp.4–8.

105. Manchester Royal Infirmary Weekly Board Minutes, Vol.21, meeting 4 May 1835 (held at Royal Manchester Infirmary). The arrangements for the election can be traced in the Weekly Board Minutes of 4, 11, 14, 18 and 25 May 1835. James Kay's donation is recorded at 25 May meeting. *MG*, 9, 23, 25 May 1835.

106. Proceedings of the General Quarterly Board [of the Manchester Royal Infirmary], 22 June 1826 to 3 June 1847, entry dated 28 May 1835 (held at Royal Manchester Infirmary). William Brockbank, *The Honorary Medical Staff of the Manchester Royal Infirmary, 1830–1948* (Manchester, 1965), p.8; *MG*, 30 May 1835; Symonds to JPK, 11 February 1832, K-SP 408; Notes by Dr W. Charles Henry; *MG*, 30 April 1835.

107. *Autobiography*, pp.16–19; K-SP 160, 161.

108. Earl of Sefton to JPK, 9 October 1833, K-SP 89; JPK to Brougham, 27 September 1833, Brougham papers, 46132. Letters to JPK from Hannah Kay (mother and sister), 6 August 1835, K-SP 162; Hannah Kay, 11 and 14 August 1835, K-SP 163, 164; Hannah Kay (sister), 10 November 1835, K-SP 166; Hannah Kay, 31 December 1835 and 11 February 1836, K-SP 168, 169.

109. De Tocqueville, p.107. De Tocqueville's journal entry was dated 2 July 1835. He met the Statistical Society the previous day, *SR,MSS*, PMSS No.51.

4 · Assistant Poor Law Commissioner, 1835–39, pp.104–141

1. *Autobiography*, p.25; Anthony Brundage, *The Making of the New Poor Law: The Politics of Inquiry, Enactment, and Implementation, 1832–1839* (New Brunswick, 1978), pp.82, 92–4, 98–100, 146–7.

2. For this and the following paragraphs, Brundage, pp.1–14, and John Knott, *Popular Opposition to the 1834 Poor Law* (London and Sydney, 1986), pp.13–38; J.D. Marshall, *The Old Poor Law, 1795–1834* (London, 1973), pp.9–11.

3. S.E. Finer, *The Life and Times of Sir Edwin Chadwick* (London, 1952), especially pp.69–95; Knott, pp.16–20, 43–4; Brundage, p.5.

4. Knott, pp.51–5.

5. Knott, pp.57–8; S.G. and E.D.A. Checkland (eds), *The Poor Law Report of 1834* (Harmondsworth, 1974), p.82.

6. Brundage, pp.75–80; Chadwick is quoted in Finer, p.69; Checkland (eds), p.337.

7. Rhodes Boyson, *The Ashworth Cotton Enterprise: The Rise and Fall of a Family Firm 1818–1880* (Oxford, 1970), p.189; Michael E. Rose, *The English Poor Law 1780–1930* (Newton Abbot, 1971), pp.107–9. In his *Autobiography* (pp.19–21) Kay claimed to have initiated the migration scheme. The available evidence does not support his claim. Report from James Phillips Kay, Esq., M.D. to the Poor Law Commissioners for England and Wales – On the migration of labourers from the southern rural counties of England to the cotton district of Lancashire (Migration of labourers), pp.183, 185, in First Annual Report of the Poor Law Commissioners for England and Wales (RPLC 1), *BPP* 1835, Vol.35.

8. Migration of labourers, pp.186, 188, 189.

9. JPK to Poor Law Commission (PLC), July 1835, MH 32/48, Poor Law Commission Papers (PLCP), Public Record Office (PRO), London.

10. Arthur Redford, *Labour Migration in England 1800–1850* (Manchester, 1964), especially pp.97–117.

11. *The Times*, 15 February 1836, p.6; John Fielden, *The Curse of the Factory System*

(London, 1969; first published 1836), pp.36, 66–7.

12. *British Parliamentary Debates (BPD)* 1841, cols 947, 941; G.R. Wythen Baxter, *The Book of the Bastiles; or the History of the Working of the New Poor-Law* (London, 1841), pp.356, 366; 'Of the salaries, expenses, and other charges for Commissioners . . .', p.127, *BPP* 1840, Vol.39. Kay was paid substantial amounts in travel expenses (for example, £660.6.4 in 1836 and £902.8.0 in 1837), but as he did much travelling they cannot fairly be added to his salary.

13. JPK to PLC, 4 August 1835, MH 32/48, PLCP.

14. Brundage, pp.86–8; *Autobiography*, p.26.

15. Anne Digby, *Pauper Palaces* (London, 1978), especially pp.3–7, 209–10, 217–18.

16. Digby, pp.1–3, 32–6, 52; JPK to PLC, 8 November 1835, MH 32/48, PLCP.

17. JPK to PLC, 3 October 1835 and 25 September 1836, MH 32/48, PLCP; JPK to PLC, 11 May 1836, MH 12/11837, PLCP; Aylsham Union to PLC, 21 September 1837, 12/8185, PLCP.

18. Report on the administration, under the Poor Law Amendment Act, in Suffolk and Norfolk, by James Phillips Kay, Esq., M.D., Assistant Poor Law Commissioner, RPLC 2, pp.146, 148, *BPP* 1836, Vol.29; JPK to PLC, 27 October 1835, MH 32/48, PLCP.

19. JPK to PLC, 7 December 1835, MH 32/48, PLCP.

20. Report on the administration, p.145; 'Letter from Dr. Kay to G.C. Lewis, Esq., on the cause of the efficacy of workhouses, and on the out-door relief of the impotent poor', in Remarks on the Third Report of the Irish Poor Inquiry Commissioners . . . by George Cornewall Lewis, pp.34, 35, *BPP* 1837, Vol.51.

21. Report on the administration, p.149; JPK to PLC, 7 December 1835, MH 32/48.

22. JPK to PLC, 7 December 1835, MH 32/48, 26 September 1836, MH 12/11991, and 5 November 1835, MH 12/11932, PLCP.

23. JPK to PLC, 7 December 1835, MH 32/48, and 26 September 1836, MH 12/11991, PLCP.

24. Fourteenth Report from Select Committee on the Poor Law Amendment Act, p.21, *BPP* 1837–38, Vol.18, part 1; JPK to PLC, 7 December 1835, MH 32/48, PLCP; Report on the administration, p.150.

25. JPK to Samuel Robinson, 25 June 1836, K-SP 176; JPK to Edwin Chadwick, 24 January 1836, Chadwick papers, 1130, University College, London.

26. Hannah Kay (mother and sister) to JPK, 6 August 1835, and Hannah Kay (sister) to JPK, 10 November 1835, K-SP 162, 166.

27. Robert Kay's will, PROB 11/1845, PRO; Hannah Kay (sister) to JPK, 10 November 1835 and Hannah Kay (mother and sister) to JPK, 6 August 1835, K-SP 166, 162; Robert Kay to JPK, 15 April 1836, K-SP 174.

28. JPK to Hannah Kay, 9 March 1836, K-SP 171; Robert Kay to JPK, 15 April and 12 November 1836, K-SP 174, 179; Robert Kay to JPK, undated, [1837], 13 July 1837 and 30 November 1838, K-SP 180, 182, 190.

29. JPK to Hannah Kay, 9 March 1836, K-SP 171.

30. Hannah Kay to JPK, 5 November 1835 and Hannah Kay (sister) to JPK, 10 November 1835, K-SP 165, 166; Hannah Kay to JPK, 11 February 1836, K-SP 169; Hannah Kay (mother and sister) to JPK, 6 August 1835 and Hannah Kay to JPK, 11 August 1835, K-SP 162, 163.

31. Hannah Kay to JPK, 11 and 14 August 1835, K-SP 163, 164; Hannah Kay (sister) to JPK, 10 November 1835, K-SP 166; Hannah Kay, 5 November 1835, K-SP 165.

32. JPK to Robinson, 25 June 1836, K-SP 176.

33. Hannah Kay to JPK, 17 July 1836, K-SP 177; Joseph Kay to JPK, 14 July 1838, K-SP 186.
34. Joseph Kay to JPK, 14 May and 1 June 1838, K-SP, 184, 185.
35. Hannah Kay (mother) to JPK, 7 July 1836, K-SP 177.
36. *Richard Oastler, King of Factory Children: Six Pamphlets, 1835–1861* (New York, 1972), pp.155, 62; Brundage, pp.145-80.
37. JPK to PLC, 23 February, 6 March and 18 October 1836, MH 32/48, PLCP; JPK to PLC, 17 March 1836, MH 12/8185, PLCP; Brundage, pp.120–2; Digby, pp.55–61; JPK to PLC, 11 September and 27 October 1835, 17 January and 6 March 1836, MH 32/48, PLCP; JPK to PLC, 23 July 1837, MH 32/49, PCLP; JPK to PLC, 10 October 1835, MH 32/48, PLCP.
38. JPK to PLC, 1 May, 13 October and 22 March 1836, MH 32/48, PLCP; JPK to PLC, 28 November 1838, MH 12/8502, PLCP; Digby, pp.123–9.
39. *Bury and Norwich Post*, 23 December 1835; a few details are taken from *Bury and Suffolk Herald* of the same date.
40. Thomas Grimsey and JPK to PLC, 17 December 1835, MH 12/11855; *Norwich Mercury*, 26 December 1835; *Bury and Suffolk Herald*, 23 December 1835; Knott, pp.72–4; Edsall, pp.34–7; JPK to PLC, 17, 20 and 21 December 1835, MH 12/11855, PLCP; T.W. Ellis to PLC, 22 December 1835, MH 12/11837, PLCP; JPK to PLC, 22 December 1835, MH 12/11932, PLCP; *Bury and Norwich Post*, 30 December 1835.
41. JPK to PLC, 23 December 1835, MH 12/11932, PLCP; JPK to PLC, 24 December 1835, MH 32/48, PLCP; JPK to PLC, 25 December 1835, MH 12/11932, PLCP.
42. JPK to PLC, 25 December 1835, MH 12/11932, PLCP; JPK to Chadwick, 24 January 1836, Chadwick papers, 1130; JPK to PLC, 24 and 26 December 1835, MH 32/48, PLCP.
43. JPK to PLC, 9 January 1836, MH 12/11855, PLCP; JPK to PLC, 27 December 1835, MH 32/48, PLCP.
44. JPK to PLC, 1 May 1836, MH 32/48, PLCP; JPK to PLC, 5, 14, 25 and 28 April 1836 and 22 February 1837, MH 12/8455; Heckingham Union to PLC, 20 July 1836, and Metropolitan Police to Chadwick, 18 April 1836 – both in MH 12/8455. *Ipswich Journal*, 23 April 1836; *Norwich Mercury*, 30 April 1836; Knott, pp.79–80.
45. JPK to PLC, 16 July 1836, MH 32/48, PLCP; *Bury and Norwich Post*, and *Bury and Suffolk Herald*, 20 July 1836; Brundage, pp.118–19.
46. JPK to PLC, 23 July 1836, MH 32/48, PLCP.
47. JPK to PLC, 10, 11 and 23 July 1837, MH 32/49, PLCP; *BPD* 1837, Vol.38, cols 1637, 1653, 1690–4, 1809–10, and 1837–38, Vol.42, 1014–15, 1037–8, 1050–1, 1170–3. Report from the Select Committee of the House of Lords appointed to examine into the several cases alluded to in certain papers respecting the operation of the Poor Law Amendment Act, pp.465–91, 519–23, *BPP* 1837–38, Vol.19, part 1.
48. JPK to PLC, 10 February 1838, MH 32/49, PLCP; JPK to PLC, 25 September 1836, MH 32/48, PLCP; JPK to Hannah Kay, 9 March 1836, K-SP 171.
49. Kay to PLC, 13 and 25 January, 2 February and 8 July 1836, MH 12/11855, PLCP; JPK to PLC, 7 February 1837, MH 32/49, PLCP.
50. JPK to PLC, 27 October 1835, MH 32/48; JPK to PLC, 15 November 1838, MH 32/50; JPK to PLC, 7 and 13 May, and 25 June 1836, MH 32/48, PLCP; JPK to PLC, 22 September 1836, MH 12/8429, PLCP. Brundage's book closely studies the significance of local government, and the limitations on the

power of the central authorities.

51. Brundage, pp.121–4; JPK to PLC, 25 September 1836, MH 12/8208, PLCP; JPK to PLC, 26 February 1836, MH 32/48, PLCP; Neil Arnot and James Phillips Kay, 'Report on the prevalence of certain physical causes of fever in the metropolis, which might be removed by sanitary measures', RPLC 4, pp.81–2, *BPP* 1837–38, Vol.28.

52. MH 1/15, 10 July 1838.

53. JPK to PLC, 3 September 1836, MH 12/8429, PLCP; JPK to Lewis, 7 January 1836, Chadwick papers, 1223; Report by James Phillips Kay, Esq., M.D., Assistant Poor Law Commissioner, relative to the distress prevalent among the Spitalfields Weavers, RPLC 3, *BPP* 1837, Vol.31 – also, JPK to PLC, 27 April 1837, MH 32/49, PLCP. Arnot and Kay, Report on the prevalence of certain physical causes of fever, RPLC 4, pp.67–83; Chadwick to Russell, 21 June 1838, Chadwick papers, 1733. J.P. Kay, Conduct of dissolute women in the workhouse, in Report of the Poor Law Commissioners . . . on the continuance of the Poor Law Commission, and on some further amendments of the laws relating to the relief of the poor, pp.178–81, *BPP* 1840, Vol.17. Report from Select Committee on education of the poorer classes in England and Wales, pp.1–42, *BPP* 1837–38, Vol.7. Fourteenth, Fifteenth, Sixteenth and Seventeenth Reports from Select Committee on the Poor Law Amendment Act, *BPP* 1837–38, Vol.18, parts 1 and 2.

54. Lord Kerry to JPK, 25 November [1835], K-SP 167.

55. J. Heath to PLC, 20 December 1838, MH 25/1, PLCP; JPK to PLC, 18 December 1837, MH 12/8429, PLCP; J.P. Kay, Report on the training of pauper children, Norwich 1838 (RTPC, 1838), p.140, RPLC 4, *BPP* 1837–38, Vol.28. Important studies are: Francis Duke, 'The education of pauper children: policy and administration, 1834–1855' (MA thesis, University of Manchester, 1968); and Alexander M. Ross, 'Kay-Shuttleworth and the Training of Teachers for Pauper Schools', *British Journal of Educational Studies*, Vol.15, No.3 (1967), pp.275–83.

56. Kay summarizes his views on apprenticeship in Report on the administration, pp.179–80; JPK to PLC, 23 July and 17 August 1937, MH 32/49, PLCP; JPK to Lady Noel Byron, 26 August 1837, folio 166–7, correspondence and papers of Anne Isabella Noel (1792–1860), Baroness Wentworth and Baroness Byron and her family 1669–1930 (the Lovelace Byron Deposit – hereafter LBD), the Bodleian Library, Oxford (New Library).

57. JPK to PLC, 19 and 29 August 1837, MH 32/49, PLCP. Kay's circular, which is undated except for '1837', is filed next to his letter of 29 August. R.J. Phillips, 'E.C. Tufnell, 1806–1886' (PhD thesis, Sheffield University, 1973).

58. E.C. Tufnell, 'Sir James Kay-Shuttleworth', *Journal of Education*, July 1877, pp.307–8; JPK to PLC, 7 September 1837, MH 32/49, PLCP.

59. JPK to PLC, 23 September 1837, MH 32/49, PLCP; MH 1/12, 20 September 1837, PLCP; Charles Mott to PLC, 27 December 1836, MH 32/56, PLCP; Tufnell to PLC, 29 September 1837, MH 32/69, PLCP; Mott to PLC, 9 November 1837, MH 32/56, PLCP.

60. MH 1/13, 2 October 1837, PLCP; Tufnell to PLC, 21 October 1837, MH 32/69, PLCP; JPK to PLC, 7 and 23 September 1837, MH 32/49, PLCP. For the context of Kay's normal school ideas, D.G. Paz, *The Politics of Working-class Education in Britain, 1830–50* (Manchester, 1980), esp. pp.14–16, 19–21, 36–41.

61. RTPC, 1838, pp.140-60; JPK to PLC, 29 December 1837, MH 32/49, PLCP.

The original report (in MH 32/49) is dated 'January 1838'. In the printed version 'January' is deleted. For Belgium and Holland, James Phillips Kay, Supplementary note to the first chapter, 'Training of Pauper Children', Report to the Secretary of State for the Home Department from the Poor Law Commissioners, pp.69–76, *House of Lords Sessional Papers*, 1841, Vol.33. W.A.C. Stewart and W.P. McCann, *The Educational Innovators 1750–1880* (London and New York, 1967), p.182.

62. RTPC, 1838, pp.140, 141, 144–6, 148, 149–150; Tufnell to PLC, 17 October 1837, MH 32/69, PLCP; W.E. Hickson to PLC, 13 August 1836, MH 10/7, PLCP. For Hickson, see Richard Aldrich and Peter Gordon, *Dictionary of British Educationists* (London, 1989), pp.112–13.

63. Henry P. Wood, *David Stow and the Glasgow Normal Seminary* (Jordanhill, 1987); William Fraser, *Memoir of the Life of David Stow; Founder of the Training System of Education* (London, 1858; first published 1836); Phillip McCann and Francis A. Young, *Samuel Wilderspin and the Infant Movement* (London, 1982), pp.20, 27, 107, 108–9, 123–4, 144–5, 185, 199; David Hamilton, *Towards a Theory of Schooling* (London and New York, 1989), especially pp.97–115; Select Committee on education of the poorer classes, p.39.

64. David Stow, *The Training System Adopted in the Model Schools of the Glasgow Educational Society; A Manual for Infant and Juvenile Schools, which includes a System of Moral Training Suitable for the Condition of Large Towns* (Glasgow, 1836). Kay used this edition. For the quotations, pp.20, 19, 16, 26, 17, 18.

65. Stow, pp.23, vii, 33, 123, 146.

66. Stow, pp.69, 172.

67. Hugh M. Pollard, *Pioneers of Popular Education* (London, 1956), pp.100–2; Stewart and McCann, pp.225–30; Hamilton, pp.78–85; Stow, p.97.

68. RTPC, 1838, pp.182–3.

69. For the plans, RTPC, 1838. For the architecture and apparatus, pp.155–7.

70. Select Committee on education of the poorer classes, pp.4, 7; JPK to PLC, 11 November 1837, MH 32/49, PLCP.

71. 'First steps as to pupil teachers', FPPE (1862) pp.287–8; *Autobiography*, pp.53–4; RPTC, 1838, pp.152–3; Victor Cousin, *On the State of Education in Holland, as regards Schools for the Working Classes and for the Poor* (London, 1838), pp.23–5.

72. Fourteenth Report from Select Committee on the Poor Law Amendment Act, pp.11, 3–4, *BPP* 1837–38, Vol.18, part 1; Report from Select Committee on Education of the Poorer Classes, p.20; JPK to PLC, 14 January 1839, 32/50, PLCP. For contemporary comments on Norwood and Aubin: B.P. Duppa, 'The education of pauper children in Union workhouses' in Central Society of Education, *Third Publication – Papers* (London, 1968), pp.286–8; James Phillips Kay, 'The Training of Pauper Children. Second report (1839)', RPLC 5, pp.91–9, *BPP* 1839, Vol.20 and 'An account of certain improvements in the training of pauper children, and on apprenticeship in the metropolitan Unions', in 'Training of Pauper Children' (1841), pp.127–200. JPK to PLC, 7 September 1837, MH 32/49, PLCP.

73. JPK to PLC, 10 December 1838, MH 32/50, PLCP; JPK to PLC, 26 and 19 February, 27 November, 11 January, 20 February and 14 January – all 1839, MH 32/50, PLCP; *Journal of the Statistical Society of London*, Vol.1 (June 1838), p.117. Kay's articles in this journal are listed in the bibliography.

74. JPK to PLC, 6 September 1838, MH 32/50, PLCP; JPK to Lord John Russell, 29 October 1838, Russell papers, PRO 30/22/3B, folios 350–3, PRO; PLC to

Home Office, 15 November 1839, MH 19/63, PLCP.

75. 'The training of pauper children. Second report (1839)', pp.94, 97.

76. 'The training of pauper children. Second report (1839)', p.97; JPK to PLC, Sunday, the last paper in MH 32/49, PLCP.

77. Tufnell to PLC, 15 August 1839, MH 32/70, PLCP; Tufnell to Chadwick, 27 November 1859, 5 September 1867, Chadwick papers, 1995; Report from Select Committee on Education of the Poorer Classes, p.11.

5 · The Committee of the Privy Council on Education, 1839–42, pp.142–196

1. Quoted in Hilaire Belloc, *The Cruise of the 'Nona'* (London, 1955), p.55.

2. James Murphy, *Church, State and Schools in Britain, 1800–1970* (London, 1971), pp.4–6.

3. Paz, *Politics of Working-class Education*, pp.11–14; Murphy, *Church, State and Schools*, p.17.

4. Paz, *Politics of Working-class Education*, pp.65–76; Melbourne to Russell, 27 November 1838 in Lloyd C. Sanders (ed.), *Lord Melbourne's Papers* (London, 1889), p.384.

5. Spencer Walpole, *The Life of Lord John Russell* (London, 1889), Vol.2, pp.468–9; Russell to Brougham, 3 October 1837, Brougham papers, 14425; Russell to Chadwick, 9 October 1836, Chadwick papers, 1733; R.E. Aldrich, 'Education and the political parties, 1830–1870' (M.Phil, University of London, 1970), p.208.

6. Norman Gash, *Reaction and Reconstruction in English Politics, 1832–1852* (Oxford, 1965), pp.60–2, 72–5.

7. John Morley, *The Life of William Gladstone* (London, 1904), Vol.1, pp.148, 179–80; M.R.D. Foot (ed.), *The Gladstone Diaries* (Oxford, 1968), Vol.2, pp.524, 539.

8. This account of the 'young gentlemen' draws on J.L. Alexander, 'Collegiate teacher training in England and Wales: a study in the historical determinants of educational provision and practice in the mid-nineteenth century' (PhD thesis, University of London, 1977), especially pp.59–63.

9. *Smith, pp.147–51; Paz, *Politics of Working-class Education*, pp.79–80; Alexander, 'Collegiate teacher training', pp.153–4; Spring Rice to Russell, 29 October 1838, Russell papers, PRO 30/22/3B, folios 346–9; Alfred Blomfield (ed.), *A Memoir of Charles James Blomfield, D.D., Bishop of London* (London, 1889), Vol.1, pp.311–12.

10. Papers on Education, BPP 1839, Vol.41; Paz, *Politics of Working-class Education*, pp.61–94; J.L. Alexander, 'Lord John Russell and the origins of the Committee of Council on Education', *Historical Journal*, Vol.20, No.2 (1977), pp.395–415; John Craig, *A History of Red Tape* (London, 1955), pp.149–50; A.S. Bishop, *The Rise of a Central Authority for English Education* (Cambridge, 1971), pp.19–21. BPD 1839, Vol.48, col.1839; D.G. Paz, 'The Composition of the Education Committee of the Privy Council, 1839–1856', *Journal of Educational Administration and History*, Vol.8 (1976), p.1.

11. Minutes of Proceedings of the Committee of the [Privy] Council on Education (MPCCE), Vol.1, 11 April 1839, ED 9/1, PRO; K-SP 199; 23 October 1840, Privy Council minute books, PC 4/19, held at PRO, Chancery Lane; John Earl Russell, *Recollections and Suggestions, 1813–1873* (London, 1875), p.376; *Auto-*

biography, pp.59–60; *Smith, p.61.
12. *Autobiography*, p.59; Paz, *Politics of Working-class Education*, p.90; Nancy Ball, *Her Majesty's Inspectorate, 1839–49* (Edinburgh and London, 1963), pp.43–4; Alexander, 'Collegiate teacher training', pp.166–7; Johnson, 'The Education Department', p.55. For the interview, *The Times*, 28 January 1839, p.4 – Johnson was the first to notice this interview.
13. MPCCE, Vol.1, 13 April 1839.
14. Thomas Adkins, *The History of St. John's College, Battersea* (London, 1906), pp.27–8; *Daily News*, 20 January 1862, p.5 – for the context of this statement see below, p.327. For discussions of the minute, Smith, pp.82–4; David Warwick, 'Sir James Kay-Shuttleworth (1804–1877); The genesis, development and influence of his ideas on education and teaching' (PhD thesis, Lancaster University, 1978), pp.214–16; Paz, *Politics of Working-class Education*, p.90; Alexander, 'Collegiate teacher training', pp.158–71; Johnson, 'The Education Department', pp.66–9.
15. JPK to Russell, 29 October 1838, Russell papers, PRO 30/22/3B, folios 350–3; Alexander, 'Collegiate teacher training', pp.167–8, 170. *Recent Measures* is reproduced in *FPPE* – for comments on the Normal school, pp.250–7; JPK to Lady Byron, 30 March 1839, LBD 76, folios 177–80; MPCCE, Vol.1, 13 April 1839; A.V. Judges, 'James Kay-Shuttleworth, a pioneer of national education' in A.V. Judges (ed.), *Pioneers of English Education* (London, 1952), p.118.
16. *Smith, p.148; Oliver J. Brose, *Church and Parliament: The Reshaping of the Church of England, 1828–1860* (Stanford and London, 1959), p.184; Alexander, 'Collegiate teacher training', pp.37–8; Johnson, 'The Education Department', pp.72–4.
17. *BPD* 1839, Vol.48, col.270; Peel's comment is quoted in Brose, p.184; James Murphy, *The Religious Problem in English Education* (Liverpool, 1959), pp.178–84.
18. *BPD* 1839, Vol.48, cols 593, 632, 1235 and Vol.47, 757; Robert Isaac Wilberforce, *A Letter to the Marquis of Lansdowne on the Establishment of a Board of National Education* (London, 1839), p.62; G.F.A. Best, 'The religious difficulties of national education in England, 1800–70', *Cambridge Historical Journal*, Vol.12, No.2 (1956), pp.155–73; *BPD* 1839, Vol.48, cols 1248, 1281, 279, 240–1, 1249 and Vol.47, cols 757–8.
19. Murphy, *Church, State and Schools*, p.2; H.F. Mathews, *Methodism and the Education of the People, 1791–1851* (London, 1949), pp.131–4; *The Times*, 25 May 1839, p.4. Richard Parkin, *The Central Society of Education, 1836–40* (Leeds, 1975); Richard Ely, *In Search of the Central Society of Education* (Leeds, 1982); Brose, pp.185,190; *BPD* 1839, Vol.48, col.1295.
20. *BPD* 1839, Vol.48, cols 229–59, 1304, 667–70, 655; *The Times*, 25 May 1839, p.4.
21. Wilberforce, *A Letter*, pp.48, 64; *BPD* 1839, Vol.48, cols 1305–6.
22. JPK to Chalmers, 13 December 1837, CHA 4.265.62, Chalmers collection; *The Times*, 20 and 21 March 1840, pp.5 and 7.
23. Paz, 'Sir James Kay-Shuttleworth', p.195; Smith, p.81; JPK-S to R.M. Smiles, 29 October 1850, M136/2/3/2976, Local History Archives, Central Library, Manchester; Hannah Kay to JPK, 3 April [1824], K-SP 10.
24. Lord David Cecil, *Melbourne* (New York, 1986), pp.358–65; Lansdowne to Russell, undated, but probably 1839, Russell papers, PRO 30/22/3C, folios 111–13 – the dating of this letter suggested by Alexander, 'Collegiate teacher training', p.169, n.72, seems correct. JPK to Russell, 24 May 1839, Russell papers, PRO 30/22/3B, folios 314–16; Foot (ed.), Vol.2, p.345.
25. *Morning Chronicle*, 27 May 1839, p.3.

26. The comparatively slow growth of the state in England is a major concern in Andy Green, *Education and State Formation: The Rise of Education Systems in England, France, and the USA* (London, 1990).

27. *The Times*, 29 May 1939, p.5; *Speech of the Bishop of London on National Education* (London, 1839); MPCCE, Vol.1, 1 June and 20 April 1839; Cecil, p.326; Adkins, pp.27–8; JPK to Lady Byron, 12 and 30 March 1839, LBD 76, folios 173–80; Russell, *Recollections and Suggestions*, p.374.

28. Peel to Gladstone, 22 May 1839, Gladstone papers, Add. mss, 44275, folios 25–9.

29. Fort (ed.), Vol.2, pp.602, 606, 607, 610; Peel's note of 17 July 1939 and Graham to Peel, 21 June 1839, both in Peel papers, Add. mss., 40427, folio 78 and 40318, folios 149–51; *BPD* 1839, Vol.47, cols.229–59; Donald H. Akenson, *The Irish Education Experiment* (London and Toronto, 1970), esp. pp.103–22; Paz, *Politics of Working-class Education*, p.86; *BPD* 1839, Vol.48, cols.1253–5 and Vol.49, col.128.

30. References to *Recent Measures* are to the version which was reprinted in *FPPE*. This version differs in some (for present purposes, unimportant) ways, which are discussed briefly below, from that originally published. *Recent Measures*, pp.189, 223, 250, 252–4, 258.

31. *Recent Measures*, pp.189–200; Phil Gardner, *The Lost Elementary Schools of Victorian England* (Beckenham, 1984); *BPD* 1839, Vol.48, cols.1239, 1277.

32. *Recent Measures*, pp.230 and 231; Halévy, *Triumph of Reform*, pp.220–1, 317–18; *Recent Measures*, p.228.

33. *Recent Measures*, pp.231, 233, 207–26, 205, 204, 233–4, 280–1.

34. This analysis owes an obvious debt to the debate begun by Oliver MacDonagh's 'The nineteenth-century revolution in government: a re-appraisal', *The Historical Journal*, Vol.1, No.1 (1958), pp.52–67. The debate is well summarized in Paz, *Politics of Working-class Education*, pp.7–10.

35. *Autobiography*, pp.14–15; S. Leon Levy, *Nassau W. Senior, 1790–1864* (Newton Abbot, 1970), p.103; *Recent Measures*, pp.200–1.

36. Josiah Bateman, *La Martinière. A reply to certain statements respecting the Bishop of Calcutta contained in a work entitled 'Recent Measures ...'* (London, 1839), p.93; *Recent Measures*, p.259. A grudging preface and an exchange of letters between Russell and Phillpotts is first printed in the tenth edition of *Recent Measures* – for Russell's comments, pp.xx–xxi (sixteenth edition). The eleventh edition of *Recent Measures* contains the new preface and, in an appendix, the comparison of passages from the *Charge* and *Recent Measures*. All this new material is reprinted in the sixteenth edition of *Recent Measures*, the edition I have used. I am grateful to Lord Shuttleworth for making it available. This edition was published by Ridgway in 1839, evidence of the interest created by the pamphlet which could not have been published earlier than mid-July 1839.

37. G. Kitson Clark discusses the type of civil servant Kay was in ' "Statesmen in disguise": reflexions on the history of the neutrality of the civil service', *The Historical Journal*, Vol.2, No.1 (1959), pp.30–9. See also Ian Hunter, *Culture and Government: The Emergence of Literary Education* (London, 1988), especially Ch.2.

38. JPK to Russell, 11 October 1839, K-SP 202; Select Committee on education of the poorer classes, pp.24–5, 31–2.

39. JPK to Lansdowne, 12 August 1839, Russell papers, PRO 30/22/3C folios 399–408; MPCCE, Vol.1, 24 September 1839; *Recent Measures*, p.238; Paz, *Politics of Working-class Education*, pp.104–5; JPK to Russell, 11 October 1839, K-SP 202.

40. The First Report (*FPPE*, pp.294–386) was published in 'Training of Pauper Children' (the House of Lords Sessional Paper, 1841), under the title, 'Dr Kay and Mr Tufnell on the Training School at Battersea'. A lengthy section of examination questions is omitted from *FPPE*. In *FPPE*, p.293 Kay points out that he was its sole author. The Second Report (*FPPE*, pp.387–431), called the 'Second Report on the schools for the training of parochial schoolmasters at Battersea', was published in MCCE 1842–43, 8vo edition, pp.251–81. For descriptions of the places visited, see First Report, pp.300–8; Second Report, pp.388–95; Pollard, pp.227–60 and Warwick, pp.172–201. First Report, pp.295–7; Second Report, pp.399, 396, 403; First Report, p.314.

41. First Report, pp.308–9; *Smith, p.93; JPK to Lady Byron, 18 October 1839, LBD 76, folios 181–2; Adkins, p.44. Warwick, pp.234–58; R.W. Rich, *The Training of Teachers in England and Wales during the Nineteenth Century* (Bath, 1933), pp.55–79; Alexander, 'Collegiate teacher training', pp.171–84; F.T. Smallwood, 'The story of Terrace House, Battersea (Old Battersea House)', *Surrey Archaeological Collections*, Vol.44 (1967), pp.110–12 – article drawn to my attention by Professor Peter Gordon. RPLC 7, p.24, *BPP* 1841, Vol.11.

42. Ben Weinreb and Christopher Hibbert (eds), *The London Encyclopaedia* (London, 1987), pp.43–5; Adkins, pp.34–44.

43. Eden, *DNB*, Vol.6, p.361; First Report, p.309; *Smith, p.94; JPK-S to Peel, 3 July 1843, Add. mss 40530, folios 387-8; 'Reports on Battersea Training School and Battersea Village School', pp.13–14, MCCE 1842–43, *BPP* 1843, Vol.40.

44. First Report, pp.310–11; E. Pleydell-Bouverie (Earl of Radnor) to JPK, 25 July 1838, K-SP 189; First Report, pp.311–12, 360; Adkins, pp.50, 59; Rich, p.78.

45. First Report, pp.314–15, 325, 319.

46. First Report, pp.362–3, 326–7; Second Report, pp.397, 399.

47. First Report, pp.330–2; Second Report, p.404; Adkins, p.62; First Report, pp.324–5, 312–13.

48. Second Report, pp.405–7; Adkins, pp.55, 61–3; *Smith, pp.110–11.

49. First Report, pp.358, 325; Second Report, pp.388–94; *Life of John Hullah, LL.D.* by his wife (London, 1886), p.26.

50. First Report, pp.323–4.

51. 'On the punishment of pauper children in workhouses', 25 January 1841, K-SP 223. B.C. Blomfield reproduced and edited the document – College of St Mark and St John: Occasional Papers No.1, 1961. The references (pp.12, 16, 15, 14, 13, 14, 17, 22, 21) are to the Occasional Paper.

52. 'On the punishment of pauper children', pp.21, 23, 18–19, 23, 10, 24; Adkins, p.60.

53. First Report, pp.309, 323, 333–56, 358; Second Report, pp.413–21.

54. First Report, pp.337–40.

55. First Report, pp.298, 302–3, 341–2; Pollard, pp.47–8, 54–5; First Report, pp.319–21; 'On the punishment of pauper children', p.11; Minute on constructive methods of teaching reading, writing, and vocal music, MCCE 1840–41, *BPP* 1841, Vol.20; Second Report, p.411.

56. 'The constructive method of teaching', p.43; First Report, p.355; Minute on constructive methods, p.20.

57. Tufnell, p.308; Adkins, pp.294–5; Rich, p.64; Report on St Mark's College, Chelsea, p.75, MCCE 1842–43, *BPP* 1843, Vol.40; Alexander, 'Collegiate teacher training', pp.63, 65–6, 72, 79–80, 83–4, 150–1.

58. This discussion is based mainly on Ball, *Her Majesty's Inspectorate*; see also, Paz, *The Politics of Working-class Education*, pp.98–103; John Hurt, *Education in Evolution: Church, State, Society and Popular Education 1800–1870* (London, 1971), pp.32–6; Johnson, 'The Education Department', pp.76–85. *Recent Measures*, p.245; MPCCE, Vol.1, 1 June 1839 – reproduced in *FPPE*, pp.182–3; JPK to Lansdowne,, 12 August 1839, Russell papers, PRO 30/22/3C, folios 399–408; John Sinclair (ed.), *Correspondence of the National Society with the Lords of the Treasury and with the Committee of Council on Education* (London, 1839), p.22; the National Society comment is quoted in Hurt, p.34.

59. Ball, pp.29–36; R.M. Grier, *John Allen: Vicar of Prees and Archdeacon of Salop* (London, 1889), p.84.

60. Ball, pp.36–9; 'Instructions for the Inspectors of schools', MPCCE, 4 January 1840.

61. Ball, pp.39–42; Leonard Horner to Katherine Horner, 14 July 1840, in Katherine M. Lyell (ed.), *Memoir of Leonard Horner* (London, 1890), p.17; Paz, *The Politics of Working-class Education*, pp.102–3; Lansdowne to Russell, [June 1840], Russell papers, PRO 30/22/3D, folios 161–2; Aldrich, pp.208–9.

62. *Smith, pp.99–100.

63. Lansdowne to JPK, 31 December 1839, quoted in *Smith, p.97n.; MPCCE, Vol.1, 4 January and 6 August 1840; Ball, pp.63–8.

64. MPCCE 1839, Vol.1, 15 August 1839 and 20 February 1840; Malcolm Seaborne, *The English School, its Architecture and Organization, 1370–1870* (London, 1971), pp.198–202.

65. Extracts from Janet Shuttleworth's journal (JSJ), 4 July and 9 December 1836, SP, box K. These extracts were copied after her death by her daughter, also named Janet. I have not found the original journal.

66. Roger Fulford, Notes on the history of the Shuttleworth family, unpublished manuscript in the possession of Lord Shuttleworth; Michael P.Conroy, *Backcloth to Gawthorpe* (Nelson, 1971); an anonymous paper (*c.* 1984) held at Gawthorpe Hall; National Trust, *Gawthorpe Hall, Lancashire*, n.p., 1984; National Trust, *Gawthorpe Hall* (Over Wallop, 1988). Mark Girouard, *Robert Smythson and the Architecture of the Elizabethan Era* (London, 1966), pp.90, 141, 154–5.

67. Fulford, Notes, pp.16–23a; National Trust, *Gawthorpe Hall, Lancashire*, pp.2–5 (this section of the pamphlet was written by Fulford).

68. Robert Shuttleworth's letters are in SP, box F. Those quoted: 3 January 1816, 12 December 1817 and 1 June 1815; Fulford, Notes, pp.61–2.

69. Ralph Richardson, *Coutts and Co., Bankers, Edinburgh and London* (London, 1901), pp.156–8; Mrs John Addington Symonds (ed.), *Recollections of a Happy Life, being the autobiography of Marianne North* (London, 1892), p.4. (Marianne North was Janet Shuttleworth's daughter by her second marriage.) Robert Shuttleworth's letters, 25 September 1816, 12 December 1817, January 1818 (without a precise date), 13, 21 January and 10, 11 February 1818, SP, box F; *Blackburn Mail*, 21 March 1818.

70. Marjoribanks's letter to Tickle of 8 April 1825, and other letters by him and his daughter, are with the Robert Shuttleworth correspondence, SP, box F. Frederick North diaries (FND), 30 April, 2, 5 and 16 May and 3 June 1825 – held at Rougham Hall, Norfolk, and used through the kindness of Mrs Pamela North; *DNB*, Vol.14, pp.613–14; John Stenton, *Who's Who of British Members of Parliament*, Vol.1, 1832–1885 (London, 1976), p.287.

71. FND, 25 May and 6 July 1825.

72. JSJ, 5, 12 and 9 August 1838.

73. JSJ, especially 1838 entries – 4 September, 10 August, 16 September, 7 and 12 August.
74. JSJ, March (no date), 15 May, 12 August 1838.
75. Janet Shuttleworth (JS) to JPK, 3 October 1839, SP, Ughtred's red box, EO, CB. This is the closest identification possible as a large collection of Shuttleworth papers, recently discovered is held at the Estate Office, Cowan Bridge, and is not catalogued; series of letters from Harriet Leveson-Gower to JPK in 1840, K-SP 204–9, 215–216a; the Sessional School material was probably that in RTPC, 1838.
76. Smith, pp.326–7; JS to JPK, 'Wednesday' [1841], SP, box P; extracts from Mrs Davenport's journals, 1841–3, 3, 4 May, 7, 10 June and Monday, September 1841, K-SP 221. The reference to the party is from an undated summary, p.21. The complete journals seem to have been lost. See Kay's 'Fragment of a journal (1841)', pp.5–6, K-SP 219 – the complete journal has also been lost. JS to Caroline Davenport, 24 and 30 June [1841], K-SP 227, 229; Symonds (ed.), p.6.
77. JS to JPK, 25 October 1841, SP, Ughtred's red box; extracts from Mrs Davenport's journals, beginning 16 November 1841, K-SP 221. Many of these entries are not precisely dated. They run until 26 May 1842. T.F. Lewis to G.C. Lewis, 23 December 1841, Harpton Court Collection (HCC), C/1721, National Library of Wales, Aberystwyth.
78. FND, 19, 22 November 1841.
79. FND, 24, 26, 27, 28 November 1841.
80. FND, 30 November and 2 December 1841; JS to JPK, 'Thursday' [1841], SP, box P.
81. JS to JPK, 'Thursday', [1841], SP, box P; FND, 4, 5, 6 December 1841; Symonds (ed.), p.11.
82. FND, 30 November 1841; JS to JPK, 'Thursday', [1841], SP, box P; extracts from Mrs Davenport's journals, 17 November 1841; Elizabeth Shuttleworth to JS, 30 November [1841], K-SP 235. A collection of letters in SP, box P: JPK to Hannah Kay, 28 November 1841; JS to Hannah Kay, 28 November 1841; JS to Hannah Kay, 4 December 1841. JS to JPK, 8 December [1841], K-SP 238; Robert Kay to JPK, 5 December [1841], K-SP 236.
83. FND, 23 January 1842; JS to JPK, 10 February 1842, K-SP 257; Joan Perkin, *Women and Marriage in Nineteenth-century England* (London, 1989), pp.51–2.
84. JS to JPK, 18 and 19 December [1841], SP, Ughtred's red box; extracts from Mrs Davenport's journal, not clearly dated, p.23.
85. Fragment of a journal (1841), pp. 13, 33.
86. Morpeth to JPK and JPK to Morpeth, 6 and 7 September 1841; K-SP 232, 233; T.F. Lewis to G.C. Lewis, 22 November 1841, Harpton Court collection, C/1718; Lansdowne to JPK, 16 December 1842 and 10 September [1841], K-SP 268, 234; *Smith, p.148; *The Times*, 7 October 1841, p.5; Graham to G.C. Lewis, 2 December 1841, Harpton Court collection, C/645; Johnson, 'The Education Department', pp.100–3.
87. Glasgow Educational Society to JPK, 22 August 1839 and JPK to Society, 21 September 1839, Minutes of the Committee of Council on Education (MCCE), 1841–42, pp.4–5, BSP 1842, Vol.33; Glasgow Educational Society to JPK, 5 February 1840, David Stow to JPK, 24 January 1840, K-SP 211, and MPCCE, 20 February 1840; Stow to JPK, 31 March 1841, K-SP 225 and JPK to John Gibson, 2 June 1841, MCCE 1841–42, p.11; Kay to Gibson, 31 December 1841, MCCE 1841–41, p.34; Wood, pp.39–42.

88. 'Fragment of a journal (1841)', throughout but especially pp.15, 44; Stow to JPK, 24 January, 3 and 17 February 1840, K-SP 211–13; E. Pleydell-Bouverie to JPK, 24 May 1841, K-SP 226; Sydney Smith to JPK, 28 June 1841, K-SP 228; Caroline Fox to JPK, 18 August 1841, K-SP 231; Russell to JPK, 30 December 1841, K-SP 242.

89. 'Fragment of a journal (1841)', pp.37–8; Leveson-Gower to JPK, 'Monday evening' and 30 March, both [1840], K-SP 204, 215; *DNB*, Vol.11, pp.1031–2; JPK to JS, 1 February 1842, K-SP 220; JS to JPK, 10 February 1842, K-SP 257.

90. 'Fragment of a journal (1841)', pp.4, 24–5; John Phillips to JPK, 11 November 1839, K-SP 203.

91. 'Fragment of a journal (1841)', pp.4–8.

92. 'Fragment of a journal (1841)', pp.10, 15, 11, 22, 24, 47.

93. FND, 9, 14, 12, 26 February 1842; JS to JPK, 10 February 1842, K-SP 257. The portrait is in the possession of Lord Shuttleworth.

94. JS to JPK, 10 and 14 February and 12 January 1842, K-SP 257, 258, 247; JPK to JS, 'Monday night', February 1842, K-SP 220.

95. FND, 6 and 24 February 1842 and 27 November 1841. Richard Shuttleworth to JS, 17 February 1842, K-SP 260. Drafts of the settlement are in K-SP 243, 244. The full settlement is held in SP, EO, CB.

96. FND, 24 February 1842; Warrant for change of name, 1 March 1842, held in 'Letters patent', Shuttleworth papers, Lancashire Record Office, Preston; Janet Kay-Shuttleworth (Janet K-S) to Hannah Kay, 24 February 1842; Robert Eden to Hannah Kay, 24 February 1842, SP, box P.

6 · The Committee of the Privy Council on Education, 1843–49, pp.197–257

1. Leonard Horner to his wife, 24 September 1843, in Lyell (ed.), pp.65–6.

2. Ball, pp.49–51; MCCE 1840–41, pp.16–17, *BPP* 1841, Vol.20; MPCCE Vol.1, 5 February 1841.

3. Ball, pp.51–4; MCCE 1842–43, pp.12–15, 18–26, and for the report, pp.22–62, *BPP* 1843, Vol.40; Henry Dunn, *The Bill or the Alternative* (London, 1843), p.12.

4. Ball, pp.54–8; Tremenheere Journal, pp.829–31, and Diary, 25 November 1843, Tremenheere papers, Penzance Library; E.L. and O.P. Edmonds, 'Hugh Seymour Tremenheere, pioneer inspector of schools', *British Journal of Educational Studies*, Vol.12, No.1 (1963), pp.65–76; *Eclectic Review*, November 1842, pp.481–502 – quotations, pp.486, 499.

5. JPK-S to Lady Lovelace, 17 August [1842], LBD 172, folios 80–1.

6. Elie Halévy, *Victorian Years* (London, 1961), pp.5–44.

7. *Smith, p.139; Graham to Peel, 26 August 1842, Peel papers, Add. mss 40447, folios 98–9; Graham to JPK-S, 30 August 1842, Graham papers, bundle 52B, Harvester Press microfilm, reel 7.

8. Paz, *Politics of Working-class Education*, pp.114–16; JPK to JS, 12 January 1842, K-SP 220; *Smith, p.141; Peel to Graham, 18 January 1842, Peel papers, Add. mss, 40446, folio 314.

9. JPK-S to Lansdowne and Graham to JPK-S, in *Smith, pp.143, 142; Graham to Peel, 26 August 1842, Add. mss, 40447, folio 99; Peel to Graham, 4 September 1842, Graham papers, bundle 53A (reel 8). Johnson, 'The Education Department', pp.117–41; Paz, *Politics of Working-class Education*, pp.114–25, Aldrich, pp.216–30.

10. Graham to Blomfield, 27 December 1842, Graham papers, bundle 56B (reel 8);

*Smith, pp.145, 142; Graham to Gladstone, 25 March 1843, Graham papers, bundle 59 (reel 9); Paz, *Politics of Working-class Education*, pp.115–16.

11. *Smith, pp.145, 143; Lansdowne to JPK-S, 16 December 1842, K-SP 268; Wharncliffe to JPK-S, 20 December 1842, K-SP 241. (Bloomfield's handlist tentatively dates this letter as 1841. It is clear from the context that it should be 1842.) Graham to JPK-S and JPK-S to Graham, both 22 December 1842, Graham papers, bundle 56B (reel 8).

12. *BPD* 1843, cols 78, 80–91; Graham to G.R. Gleig, 6 March 1843, Graham papers, bundle 59 (reel 9); Paz, *Politics of Working-class Education*, pp.118–19; Aldrich, pp.222–5.

13. Edward Baines, *The Social, Educational, and Religious State of the Manufacturing Districts* (London, 1843), pp.27, 11 and *Letter to the Right Hon. Lord Wharncliffe ... on Sir James Graham's Bill for establishing exclusive Church schools ...* (London, 1843), pp.70, 68, 69, 67 – included as an appendix to above; *Eclectic Review*, May 1843, p.593; Dunn, p.15; Paz, *Politics of Working-class Education*, pp.119–22.

14. *Smith, pp.147–50.

15. Russell to JPK-S, 2 May 1843, K-SP 271.

16. S. Maccoby, *English Radicalism* (London, 1935), pp.247–8.

17. Ashley to Peel, 17 June 1843, in C.S. Parker, *Sir Robert Peel* (London, 1899), Vol.2, p.561; *Smith, p.158.

18. From *Ingoldsby Legends* (1840), quoted in Weinreb and Hibbert (eds), p.270.

19. Smith, pp.128–31; Johnson, 'The Education Department', pp.110–13; Warwick, pp.252–8; Alexander, 'Collegiate teacher training', pp.188–90; *BPD* 1842, Vol.65, cols 7–13, 571; Wharncliffe to JPK-S, 3 April 1842, K-SP 266; *Life of John Hullah*, pp.29–31.

20. Smith, p.128; *BPD* 1842, Vol.65, cols 13–14, 18–19, 9.

21. Smith, pp.128–9; *BPD* 1842, Vol.65, cols 13–14, 18–19, 7–13, 570–1; J.P. Kay Shuttleworth, 'The constructive method of teaching', *Saturday Magazine*, No.647 (July 1842), pp.41–8.

22. *The Times*, 26 September 1843, p.4.

23. *The Times* 1842: 26, 23 and 28 September – each p.4; and 10 October, p.4. Kay's letter is reproduced in *British Critic*, No.59 (July 1841), pp.90–2.

24. Greville to Reeve, 5 and 12 October 1842, in A.H. Johnson (ed.), *The Letters of Charles Greville and Henry Reeve, 1836–1865* (London, 1924), pp.69–72; *Smith, pp.130–1.

25. *The Greville Memoirs* (London, 1885), Vol.2, p.86; G.E. Anson to JPK-S, 3 February 1842, K-SP 254; FND, 26 November 1842 and 17 January 1843; Tufnell to Chadwick, 28 May 1847, Chadwick papers, 1995; Smith, p.115n; Second Report, pp.425–6, 431; JPK-S to Peel, 8 August 1842, Peel papers, Add. mss 40513, folios 215–16.

26. MCCE 1841–42, p.40, *BPP* 1842, Vol.33; extracts from Mrs Davenport's journals, Wednesday [probably 23 June], 1841; *Smith, p.115; JPK-S to Peel, 8 August 1842, Peel papers, Add. mss 40513, folios 215–16.

27. Minute of 11 November 1842, in Copies of minutes, if any, of the Committee of Council on Education, passed subsequently to August 1840, p.1, *BPP* 1842–43, Vol.40; JPK-S to Peel, 3 July 1843, Add. mss 40430, folios 387–8; undated letter to Wharncliffe, Second Report – it survives only in this report as reproduced in *FPPE*, pp.423–6.

28. *Smith, pp.118–19.

29. *Smith, pp.119–22; Second Report, pp.427–30.

30. Blomfield to JPK-S, 23 and 25 October, 2 November 1843, C.J. Blomfield

papers, Letters Book (Diocesan), FP 372, Vol.38, Lambeth Palace Library; Blomfield to JPK-S, 18 November [1843], JPK-S 279; G.E. Anson to JPK-S, 15 November 1843, K-SP 280; JPK-S to Thursby, 8 December [1843], SP, Ughtred's red box.

31. Blomfield to JPK-S, 23 October 1843; Alexander, 'Collegiate teacher training', pp.59–202.

32. Minute, 22 November 1843, in Copies of all minutes, containing regulations as to the distribution of the Parliamentary grant for the promotion of education ... , pp.1–3, *BPP* 1844, Vol.38.

33. Wharncliffe to Peel, 12 and 19 October 1843, Peel papers, Add. mss, 40534, folios 132, 237–8; Ball, pp.80–4.

34. Johnson, 'The Education Department', p.146; John Sinclair, *Letter to a Member of Parliament on National Education* (London, 1842), pp.21–3; 'Scheme of periodical inspection for England and Wales', MCCE 1842–43, 8vo edition, pp.23–36 – quotation p.36; Ball, pp.85–90.

35. JPK to Lansdowne, 12 August 1839, Russell papers, PRO 32/22/3C, folios 399–408.

36. Circular letter, 13 August 1844, MCCE 1844, Vol.1, pp.121–5; Ball, pp.91–2, 94–6; 10 August 1840, Privy Council minute books, PC 4/19; Johnson, 'The Education Department', pp.151–2.

37. Chester to JPK-S, 22 July 1844, K-SP 286; Ball, pp.205, 75–6.

38. Grier, p.113; *Smith, p.156.

39. Janet K-S to Joseph Kay, 4 April [1843], SP, box J; Janet K-S to JPK-S, undated (but July) and 8 and 9 July 1844, SP, box 3, envelope 10.

40. *Smith, p.156.

41. *Fraser's Magazine*, Vol.23, April 1841, p.379; Janet K-S to Hannah Kay, 26 August [1844], SP, box J; FND, 21 August 1844.

42. May 1842, Journal of R.A. Slaney, held in the Morris-Eyton collection, Local Studies Library, Castle Gates Library, Shrewsbury; Janet K-S to Joseph Kay, 4 April [1843], SP, box J.

43. FND, 17 January 1843; 10 April 1842; 4 February 1844; 14 May and 26 November 1842; 4 March 1844; 17 June 1842.

44. FND, 17 June 1842; 4 March 1844; 22 June 1843; Janet K-S to JPK-S, 10 July and undated letter in July, 1844, SP, box 3, envelope 10; FND, 7 June and 18 December 1844.

45. FND, 14 May 1843; 28 and 29 March 1844; North to JPK-S, 31 December 1843, SP, Ughtred's red box; FND, 12 April 1842.

46. JPK to JS, 1 February 1842, K-SP 252; Saunderson to JS, 29 January 1842, K-SP 251.

47. JPK-S to Janet K-S, 27 March 1842, K-SP 265.

48. JPK-S to Janet K-S, 27 March 1842, K-SP 265; JPK-S to J.W. Gray, 26 December 1844, in envelope entitled 'Gawthorpe estate and schools', SP, Ughtred's red box; JPK-S to Peregrine Towneley, 8 December 1843, SP, Ughtred's red box; FND, 17 May 1843, 8 April 1844.

49. JPK-S to Calman, 28 November 1845, 'Gawthorpe estate and schools'.

50. Royal Humane Society, *Annual Report 1843*, pp.11–12; and Joseph Charlier to JPK-S, 15 January 1845, held at Royal Humane Society, Lancaster Gate, London.

51. MCCE 1846, *BPP* 1847, Vol.45. The minutes are reproduced in *FPPE*, pp.531–42.

52. J.P. Kay-Shuttleworth, *The School, in its Relations to the State, the Church, and*

the Congregation (London, 1847) – reproduced in *FPPE* as 'Explanation of the Minutes of 1846', pp.433–530. Page references are to *FPPE*.

53. *FPPE*, p.483.
54. Francis Duke, 'Pauper education' in Derek Fraser (ed.), *The New Poor Law in the Nineteenth Century* (London, 1976), pp.70–4; MCCE 1846, 8vo edition, Vol.1, pp.46–56 and pp.1–2; *FPPE*, pp.540–1; Ross, pp.275–83.
55. *Autobiography*, p.50.
56. *Autobiography*, pp.62, 64.
57. Second Report, pp.423–5, 396; Johnson, 'The Education Department', pp.186–90; Cook's report is dated January 1845 but appears in MCCE 1844, 8vo edition, Vol.1, pp.146–8, 183–6; Moseley's remarks are in MCCE 1845, 8vo edition, Vol.1, pp.344–5.
58. *Smith, pp.169–70; Johnson, pp.191–95.
59. *The Present Condition* is in K-SP 1168; Morpeth to JPK-S, 9 January [1846], K-SP 293; Elizabeth Campbell to JPK-S, 22 January 1846, K-SP 294; G.G. Leveson-Gower (Duke of Sutherland) to JPK-S, 24 January 1846, K-SP 295.
60. Blomfield to JPK-S, 20 March 1846, Blomfield papers, Letters Book (Diocesan), FP 372, Vol.58. (These letters are fading and are now very difficult to read.) Buccleuch to JPK-S, 23 March 1846, K-SP 296; *Smith, pp.170–1.
61. Janet K-S to Janet K-S (daughter), 9 August 1845, SP, Ughtred's red box; Janet K-S to JPK-S, 31 August 1846, SP, box 3, envelope 10; Elizabeth Campbell to JPK-S, 2 November 1846, K-SP 299; FND, 10 December 1845.
62. *FPPE*, pp.531–42; *The Times*, 22 and 26 August 1846, p.5. Alexander, pp.216–17; W.R. Stephens, *The Life and Letters of Walter Farquhar Hook* (London, 1878), p.447; *Smith, pp.174–7.
63. *Smith, pp.177–80.
64. This and the following paragraphs draw heavily on Johnson, 'The Education Department', pp.222–45; see also Smith, p.181; *BPD* 1847, Vol.89, cols 877, 882; *The School in its Relations to the State*, p.505; JPK-S to Russell, 31 March 1847, Russell papers, PRO 30/22/6B, folios 326–7. For Ashley's part and the negotiations, Mathews, pp.135–7; *BPD* 1847, Vol.91, cols 950–1, 983–4; Lansdowne to Russell, 7 April 1847, PRO 30/22/6C, folios 29–30; Ashley to Russell, 8 April 1847, PRO 30/22/6C, folios 35–7; JPK-S to Russell, 25 April 1847, PRO 30/22/6C, folios 176–7. For Bright's comment, *BPD*, 1847, Vol.91, col.1099; Supplementary minute of 10 July 1847, MCCE 1846, pp.18–19, *BPP* 1847, Vol.45.
65. Smith, pp.185–6; Johnson, pp.254–9; *The Times*, 24 June 1852, p.3; Wood to Russell, 'Wednesday', [September 1846], Russell papers, PRO 30/22/5E, folios 2168–9; MCCE 1846, 8vo edition, Vol.1, pp.25–33.
66. MCCE 1846, 8vo edition, Vol.1, pp.27–33 – quotation p.28; Peter Gordon, *The Victorian School Manager* (London, 1974), pp.1–2.
67. Alexander, 'Collegiate teacher training', pp.89–91, 214–16; Denison is quoted in Metropolitan Church Union, *History and Present State of the Education Question* (London, 1850), pp.91, 92.
68. Henry W. Wilberforce, *On the Danger of State Interference with the Trust Deeds of Church Schools* (London, 1847), p.18; Richard Dawes, *Observations on the Working of the Government Scheme of Education, and on School Inspection* (London, 1849), pp.7–8; *BPD* 1847, Vol.91, col.1288; Manning and Maurice are quoted in E.S. Purcell, *Life of Cardinal Manning* (London, 1896), pp.419, 431; 'Pauper education and Kneller Hall', *English Review*, September 1849, pp.109, 127.
69. 'Brief practical suggestions on the mode of organizing and conducting day-

schools of industry, model farm-schools, and normal schools for the coloured races of the British colonies', MCCE 1846, pp.30–8, *BPP* 1847, Vol.45. Bob Petersen's 'Black is the use of spades: agricultural education for the coloured races 1846' (Papers of the annual conference of the Australian and New Zealand History of Education Society, 1989) gives a telling analysis of this document.

70. *BPD* 1846, Vol.84, cols 845–60, 860–4; Smith, pp.203–6; J.D. Griffiths, 'Monmouthshire and the "Blue Books" of 1847', *History of Education*, Vol.19, No.3 (1990), pp.261–3, and his MA thesis of the same name, Institute of Education, University of London, 1985. (I am grateful to Dr Richard Aldrich for drawing this thesis to my attention.)

71. Reports of the commissioners of inquiry into the state of education in Wales, pp.iii-iv, 66, 56–7, 62, *BPP* 1847, Vol.27.

72. *Smith, pp.204-5; the cartoon and commentary are quoted from Griffiths's thesis, pp.15–16.

73. Smith, pp.201–5; Griffiths, 'Monmouthshire and the "Blue Books" of 1847', pp.15–37.

74. 1848: Russell to JPK-S, 11 January; JPK-S to Russell, 17 January; JPK-S to G.E. Anson, 20(?) January; Anson to JPK-S, 27 January; JPK-S to Anson, 28 May – K-SP 306–8, 310–11.

75. JPK-S to Trevelyan, 18 January 1848, K-SP 309.

76. *The Present Condition*, p.11; Report from the select committee on miscellaneous expenditure, p.236, *BPP* 1847–48, Vol.18.

77. Johnson, 'The Education Department', especially pp.279–87, 331–5 (this pioneering discussion has not been superseded); D.M. Mason, 'The expenditure of the Committee of Council on Education, 1839–52', *Journal of Educational Administration and History*, Vol.17, No.1 (1985), pp.28–40; *BPD* 1846, Vol.87, cols 1232, 1251, 1258; Estimate for public education, 26 March 1847, p.331, *BPP* 1847, Vol.35. For the annual grants, *BPP* 1845, Vol.80, col.917 and 1847, Vol.91, col.607; Report from the select committee on miscellaneous expenditure, p.474; Trevelyan's comment is quoted in Johnson, p.285.

78. Johnson, 'The Education Department', p.283; Mason, p.34; *BPD* 1848, Vol.96, cols 1055–63; Report from the select committee on miscellaneous expenditure, pp.468–9, 472–3, xxv.

79. Johnson, 'The Education Department', p.334; Report from the select committee on miscellaneous expenditure, pp.467–77; J. Parker to Wood, 4 April 1847, Hickleton papers, A4.52, EP Microform; Johnson, p.324.

80. Report from the select committee on miscellaneous expenditure, pp.468, 236, 234; Ball, pp.252–6, 197–8.

81. Johnson, pp.268–79; Ball, pp.196–201; Report from the select committee on miscellaneous expenditure, p.236. Johnson has a valuable analysis of the pressures created by the pupil-teacher system, pp.287–304.

82. 6 January 1845, Privy Council minute books, PC 4/19; *The Present Condition*, p.9; Johnson, pp.272–4.

83. JPK-S to Lansdowne, 26 May 1847, Lansdowne papers, Bowood; *Smith, pp.213–14.

84. Lansdowne to Russell, Wednesday afternoon, [4 May 1847], Russell papers, PRO 30/22/6D, folios 12–13; Russell to Lansdowne, 5 May 1847, Lansdowne papers; Russell to JPK-S, 7 May 1847, SP, Ughtred's green box.

85. Wood to Russell, 24 May 1847, Russell papers, PRO 30/22/6C, folios 330–1; *Smith, p.214.

86. JPK-S to Lansdowne, 26 May 1847, Lansdowne papers.

87. JPK-S to Home Office, 27 May 1847, HO 45/1926, PRO; Trevelyan to Committee of Council, July 1847 (no day given), Privy Council minute books, PC 4/19, p.365.
88. Argyll to JPK-S, 4 June [1847], K-SP 304.
89. Evelyn Abbot and Lewis Campbell, *The Life and Letters of Benjamin Jowett* (London, 1897). The verse is quoted in A.N. Wilson, *Hilaire Belloc* (Harmondsworth, 1986), p.46. The significance of the Balliol group was first noted in Johnson, 'The Education Department', pp.317–29. See also his 'Administrators in education before 1870; patronage, social position and role' in Gillian Sutherland (ed.), *Studies in the Growth of Nineteenth Century Government* (London, 1972), pp.110–38.
90. Johnson, 'The Education Department', pp.317–22; A.S. Bishop, 'Ralph Lingen, Secretary to the Education Department 1849–1870', *British Journal of Educational Studies*, Vol.16, No.2 (1968), pp.138–63.
91. Johnson, 'The Education Department', pp.317–19, and 'Administrators in education', pp.115–17; Ball, p.201.
92. Johnson, 'The Education Department', pp.323–6, and 'Administrators in education', pp.122–6.
93. Jowett to Lingen, *c.*22 March 1848, quoted in Johnson, 'The Education Department', p.326.
94. Jowett to Lingen, 'Sunday evening,' [1847], in Abbot and Campbell, Vol.1, p.188; Jowett to Lingen, 18 July 1849, quoted in Johnson, 'The Education Department', p.329.
95. Frederick Temple to JPK-S, 'Friday morning' [August 1848], K-SP 316; *Smith, pp.215–16.
96. JPK-S to an unnamed Eastbourne doctor, 30 June 1856, held by Lord Shuttleworth at Leck Hall. The circumstances in which he wrote this letter are discussed below, p.295.
97. *Smith, pp.216–18; Russell to JPK-S, 16 December 1848, K-SP 320; Trevelyan to JPK-S, 22 December 1848, K-SP 321; T.F. Lewis to G.C. Lewis, 13 December 1848, Harpton Court collection, C/1817.
98. Lansdowne to Russell, 29 December 1848, Russell papers, PRO 30/22/7D, folios 365–70.
99. *Smith, pp.218–19; Peel to JPK-S, 4 January 1849, K-SP 324; Lansdowne to Russell, 23 February [1849], Russell papers, PRO 30/22/7E, folios 370–1; Phillips, p.130.
100. Lansdowne to Russell, 23 February [1849]; *Smith, pp.219–20.
101. *Smith, p.220.
102. FND, 19 August 1849; 4 and 24 April 1849, Privy Council minute books, PC 4/19.
103. *Smith, pp.220–1; Nassau Senior Journal, A 1, 19 May 1849, Nassau Senior papers; Greville to Reeve, 21 September 1849, Greville papers, Add. mss 41185; Lansdowne to Russell, 16 September 1849, Russell papers, PRO 30/22/8A, folios 185–6; JPK-S to Hannah Kay, 19 August 1849, SP, box P.
104. *Smith, pp.222–3; Shaw-Lefevre to JPK-S, 20 December 1849, K-SP 331.
105. Russell to JPK-S, 25 December 1849, K-SP 335; *London Gazette*, 25 December 1849, in K-SP 332; FND, 25 December 1849.
106. JPK-S to Hannah Kay, 22 December 1849, K-SP 333; Jowett's comment is quoted in Johnson, 'The Education Department', p.341.
107. Wood to Russell, 1 September 1849 and 4 March 1850, Russell papers, PRO 30/22/8A, folios 124–9 and 30/22/8D, folios 46–9.

7 · Families, the family estate, novelists and a novel, 1850–60, pp.258–312

1. Hannah Kay to JPK-S, 2 January 1850, K-SP 340.
2. Janet K-S to Janet (daughter), 11 and 13 April 1849, K-SP 325,326; JPK-S to Janet (daughter), 16 April 1849, K-SP 327; Hannah Kay to JPK-S, 26 December 1849, K-SP 337.
3. *DNB*, Vol.10, pp.1137–8 and Vol.22, p.928.
4. Information on Tom Kay is drawn from 'Notes on the Kay family' by Professor Humphrey Kay of Pewsey, Wiltshire. I am grateful to him for making his research available. Joseph Kay to Ebenezer and Tom Kay, 1 September 1845 and Ebenezer Kay to Hannah Kay (sister), 18 July 1848 and 26 September [1849] – all in SP, box F.
5. Schedule of Education Department staff, 24 April 1849 and letters of 25 April 1848 and 1 January 1851, Privy Council minutes books, PC 4/19; Tom's letter is quoted in Humphrey Kay, 'Notes on the Kay family'; JPK-S to Janet K-S, 10 and 18 October 1852, K-SP 382,387; Janet K-S to JPK-S, 29 March 1852, K-SP 376.
6. JPK-S to Janet K-S, 18 February 1851, K-SP 345.
7. JPK-S to Alison, 12 January 1850, W.P. Alison collection, box 1, folder 3, held at Royal College of Physicians, Edinburgh. (I am grateful to Miss Sheonagh Martin, Edinburgh, for bringing this material to my attention.)
8. Janet K-S to Alison, 12 January 1850, Alison collection, box 1, folder 3.
9. John Walton, *Brain's Diseases of the Nervous System* (Oxford, 1985), p.269. My attention was first drawn to this diagnosis by Professor Humphrey Kay, a descendant of Tom Kay. Professor Kay was lately Consultant Haematologist to the Royal Marsden Hospital and Professor of Haematology in the Institute of Cancer Research, University of London. I benefited greatly from discussions with him and with Dr John Penman, lately Consultant Neurologist to the Royal Marsden Hospital, London. Professor Harold Attwood, of the Medical History Unit, University of Melbourne, and Dr Eric Cunningham Dax have also given advice for which I am most grateful. I am, of course, responsible for the conclusions drawn from the advice I have received.
10. Walton, pp.269, 267, 615, 268; Smith, p.345.
11. Walton, p.263; Webb Haymaker and Francis Schiller (eds), *The Founders of Neurology* (Springfield, 1970), p.508.
12. Walton, pp.268,271.
13. Richard Davenport-Hines, *Sex, Death and Punishment* (Glasgow, 1990), p.53.
14. JPK-S to Alison, 23 January and 17 March 1850, Alison collection, box 1, folder 3.
15. JPK-S to Janet K-S, 14, 20 and 29 August and 8 September 1851, K-SP 354, 355, 357, 358.
16. JPK-S to Janet K-S, 17 and 18 September, 29 August, 25 and 8 September, 20 August 1851, K-SP 359, 357, 361, 358, 356.
17. JPK-S to his children, 20 August 1851, and to Janet K-S, 17 and 18 September 1851, K-SP 355, 359.
18. JPK-S to Janet K-S, 23 September 1851, K-SP 360; JPK-S to Janet North, 8 November 1851, K-SP 363; JPK-S to Eastbourne doctor, 30 June 1856.
19. This and the following paragraph draw heavily on National Trust, *Gawthorpe Hall* (the quotations, p.43) and John Martin Robinson, 'Gawthorpe Hall, Lancashire – I and II', *Country Life*, 4 and 11 September 1975, pp.558–61, 630–3.

20. Janet K-S to Janet (daughter), 24 April, 3, 4 and 9 May 1850, SP, Ughtred's red box; JPK-S to Ughtred, undated, in envelope of letters from JPK-S to Ughtred, 1850–55, SP, Ughtred's red box; JPK-S to Janet K-S, 8 December 1851, K-SP 369.

21. JPK-S to Janet K-S, 18 February 1851, K-SP 345.

22. Janet K-S to JPK-S, 29 March 1852, K-SP 376; FND 2 November 1853.

23. Discussion of Charlotte Brontë is based on Margot Peters, *Unquiet Soul: A Biography of Charlotte Brontë* (New York, 1975); Charlotte Brontë (CB) to Ellen Nussey (EN), 25 and 28 January, 4 February, and 5 March 1850, in T.J. Wise and J.A. Symington, *The Brontës: Their Lives, Friendships and Correspondence* (Oxford, 1933), Vol.3, pp.69–71, 73.

24. This and the next paragraph are drawn from CB to William Williams, 16 March 1850 and CB to EN, 19 March 1850, in Wise and Symington, Vol.3, pp.82, 86–7.

25. CB to Williams, 16 March 1850, and CB to EN, 12 April 1850, in Wise and Symington, Vol.3, pp.82–3, 100; CB to Janet K-S, 22 March 1850 – this letter, which is not in Wise and Symington, is held at EO,CB.

26. Dickens to Forster, [? March 1839], in Madeline House and Graham Storey (eds), *The Letters of Charles Dickens*, Vol.1 (Oxford, 1965), p.527. This is the Pilgrim Edition. All following references are to it, though the changes in its editors are not noted. Dickens to Marjoribanks, 8 September 1843, Vol.3, p.557; Dickens to JPK-S, 28 March 1846, Vol.4, pp.526–7; Dickens to JPK-S, [Winter 1847–8], 5 October 1848 and 21 June 1847 – all in Vol.5, pp.220, 418, 96.

27. CB to EN, 11 May 1850, Wise and Symington, pp.108–9; Janet K-S to Janet (daughter), 9 May 1850, SP, Ughtred's red box; CB to EN, 21 May 1850 and CB to Mrs Smith, 25 May 1850, both in Wise and Symington, Vol.3, pp.110, 113.

28. CB to Janet K-S, 21 May 1850, reproduced in Madison C. Bates, 'Charlotte Brontë and the Kay-Shuttleworths, with a new Brontë letter', *Harvard Library Bulletin*, Vol.9, 1955, p.376; Peters, pp.287–94.

29. Elizabeth Gaskell (EG) to Janet K-S, 14 May and 16 July [1850], in J.A.V. Chapple and Arthur Pollard (eds), *The Letters of Mrs Gaskell* (Manchester, 1966), letters 72, 72a.

30. EG to Janet K-S, 14 May [1850] and EG to Catherine Winkworth, [25 August 1850], in Chapple and Pollard (eds), letters 72, 75.

31. CB to Margaret Wooler, 27 September 1850, and CB to EN, 26 August 1850, in Wise and Symington, Vol.3, pp.163–4, 148.

32. EG to Winkworth, [25 August 1850] and EG to Eliza Fox, [27] August 1850, in Chapple and Pollard (eds), letters 75, 79.

33. CB to EN, 26 August 1850, and CB to Williams, 5 September 1850, in Wise and Symington, Vol.3, pp.148, 155–6.

34. CB to EN, 2 September 1550, in Wise and Symington, Vol.3, p.152; EG to Janet K-S, 12 November [1850], in Chapple and Pollard (eds), letter 83.

35. CB to EN, 26 November and 18 and 21 December 1850; CB to Patrick Brontë, 21 December 1850; CB to James Taylor, 15 January 1851; CB to EG, [June 1851]; CB to EN, 19 and 24 June 1851; CB to Patrick Brontë, 26 June 1851 – all in Wise and Symington, Vol.3, pp.184, 189–90, 199, 248, 250–1, 252. CB to EN, 11 January 1853, in Wise and Symington, Vol.4, p.33.

36. *Smith, pp.239–40; Janet K-S to JPK-S, 27 January 1852, K-SP 347; Janet K-S to Janet (daughter), 21 August 1852, SP, Ughtred's red box.

37. *Smith, p.241.
38. Donald K. Jones, *The Making of the Education System 1851–81* (London, 1977), pp.16–20, and 'Lancashire, the American common school, and the religious problem in British education in the nineteenth century', *British Journal of Educational Studies*, Vol.15, No.3 (1967), pp.292–306; *Smith, pp.230–5; JPK-S to R.M. Smiles, 29 October 1850, M 136/2/3/2976, Local History Archives, Central Library, Manchester.
39. Jones, *Making of the Education System*, pp.21–2; *Smith, pp.232–9.
40. Andrew Reed, *Inspectors Inspected: A Review of the Operations of the Educational Committee of the Privy Council from 1846 to 1852* (London, 1853), p.9; *Public Education*, pp.7, 19, 54, 55, 6.
41. *Public Education*, p.113; Edgar Johnson (ed.), *Letters from Charles Dickens to Angela Burdett-Coutts, 1841–1865* (London, 1955), pp.223–4.
42. *Public Education*, pp.iv–v; JPK-S to John Potter, 2 October 1856, Autograph letters, Sir John Potter collection, No.68, held in Local History Archives, Central Library, Manchester.
43. *Smith, pp.245–6; Hurt, *Education in Evolution*, pp.82–3, 149–50; Johnson, 'The Education Department', pp.450–9; Jones, *Making of the Education System*, pp.23–4; Gladstone papers, Add. mss, 44571, folios 173–4 and 44573, folios 84–91.
44. JPK-S to Janet (daughter), 21 October 1852, SP, Ughtred's red box.
45. Janet K-S to JPK-S, 23 November 1851, and JPK-S to Janet K-S, 23 November 1851, K-SP 367, 366.
46. Janet K-S to JPK-S, 29 March, 1852, K-SP 376; Janet K-S to Hannah Kay, 31 July [1852], SP, box F; FND, 13 May 1853.
47. Janet K-S to JPK-S, 15 and 10 October 1852; JPK-S to Janet K-S, 13 October 1852; Janet K-S to JPK-S, 26 October 1852; JPK-S to Janet K-S, 26 October 1852 – K-SP 385, 383, 384, 395, 394.
48. JPK-S to Janet K-S, 13 October 1852, K-SP 384; Janet K-S to JPK-S, 15 October 1852, K-SP 385.
49. JPK-S to Janet K-S, 9 December 1852, held at Leck Hall.
50. Ebenezer Kay to Hannah Kay (sister), 30 January 1853, SP, box F.
51. EG to Janet K-S, 7 April [1853], in Chapple and Pollard (eds), letter 154; FND, 5 May 1853.
52. Russell to JPK-S, 6 May 1853, K-SP 415; JPK-S to Hannah Kay (sister), 14 May 1853, SP, box P; FND, 5, 13, 14 May 1853.
53. FND, 30 May and 28 June 1853; M.S. Jefferies to Hannah Kay, 26 December 1853, K-SP 432; FND, 2, 4 July and 1, 2 November 1853.
54. This and the following paragraph are drawn from the letter of the unknown doctor to JPK-S, 12 October 1853, held at Leck Hall.
55. JPK-S to Eastbourne doctor, 30 June 1856; CB to Margaret Wooler, 15 November 1854, in Wise and Symington, Vol.4, p.160; EG to Smith, [5 April 1860], in Chapple and Pollard (eds), letter 462; JPK-S to Janet (daughter), 6 May 1854, K-SP 436. Ughtred also refers to his injured eye in a letter written on 20 May 1854, SP, box P.
56. Angela Burdett-Coutts to JPK-S, 10 July [1854], K-SP 438; *Homburger Kur- and Bade-Liste (Cure and Waters Register)*, 14 May 1854, p.5 and 24 September 1854, p.541; letter to author from Der Magistrat der Stadt, Bad Homburg, 6 August 1991. I am grateful to Dr Margaret Pawsey, who conducted the research which led to this information. Ebenezer Kay to Hannah (sister), 26 September 1854; Janet K-S to JPK-S, 17 October 1854 – K-SP 441, 444.

57. JPK-S to Thomas Greene, 24 September 1854, K-SP 440.
58. JPK-S to Janet North, 'Saturday', [7 October] 1854, K-SP 439; Dr Chelius's opinion is K-SP 443. Following the convention of the time Kay-Shuttleworth in K-SP 439 addressed his mother-in-law as 'mother'. This has led Bloomfield to assume that the letter was sent to Hannah Kay, who was of course dead by this time. The assumption of the date of 7 October for the 'Saturday' (which is the only date given by Kay-Shuttleworth) is based on his comment in the letter that he was leaving for England in a few days and the last record of his presence in Homburg is 8 October – *Homburger Kur- und Bade-Liste*, 8 October 1854, p.577. The paucity of correspondence makes it impossible to be certain of the precise sequence of the events outlined here. What is absolutely clear, however, is Dr Chelius's verdict.
59. JPK-S to Janet North, 'Saturday', [7 October] 1854, K-SP 439.
60. JPK-S to Janet K-S, 23 May 1855, K-SP 467.
61. JPK-S to Thomas Greene, 22 May 1855, K-SP 466.
62. FND, 8, 19, 20 July and 10 October 1855.
63. Smith, pp.332–3.
64. Thomas Greene to JPK-S, 17 August 1855, and David Robertson to JPK-S, 22 April 1857 – held at Leck Hall; FND, 21 April and 10 October 1855.
65. FND, 30 November 1854; 21 July 1855.
66. JPK-S to an unnamed Eastbourne doctor, 30 June 1856; the details of the investigation, discussed in this and the following paragraph, crowd K-SP 1855.
67. FND, 24 July 1855, 10 February 1858.
68. Details of the settlement are given in a letter from Nassau Senior to his wife, 22 October 1859, Nassau Senior papers, E 336 (held at National Library of Wales, Aberystwyth); Greene to JPK-S, 17 August 1855 – held at Leck Hall.
69. Wise and Symington (eds), Vol.4, p.97; T.E.A. Verity, 'Edward Arundel Verity, Vicar of Habergham: An Anglican Parson of the Industrial Revolution', *Transactions of the Lancashire and Cheshire Antiquarian Society*, Vol.79 (1977), pp.73–94; Lilian Carr, *Point Me a Finger: The Story of All Saints' Church, Habergham, 1849–1974* (Habergham, [1974]), pp.1–15; Brian Hall, *Lowerhouse and the Dugdales: The Story of a Lancashire Mill Community* (Burnley, 1976), pp.14–16.
70. Elizabeth Gaskell, *The Life of Charlotte Brontë* (Harmondsworth, 1975), pp.522–4; Wise and Symington (eds), pp.160, 170–1; EG to George Smith, [5 April 1860], in Chapple and Pollard, letter 462. Kay-Shuttleworth reported to Ughtred on 13 April 1857 (in envelope of letters from JPK-S to Ughtred, 1850–55, SP, Ughtred's red box) that he was writing the second chapter of his book, which he was proposing to call 'Religio Medici'. It was eventually published in 1860 and called *Scarsdale*. Peters, pp.406–10.
71. Patrick Brontë to EG, 16 July 1855, and EG to Ellen Nussey, 24 July 1855 and 9 July 1856 – Wise and Symington (eds), Vol.4, pp.190–3, 201–3; Peters, pp.102–56.
72. EG to Janet K-S, [February, 1855]; EG to Marianne Gaskell, [27 July 1855]; EG to Janet K-S, 18 November [1861]; EG to Marianne Gaskell, [8 July 1855]; EG to George Smith, [25 July 1856]; Marianne Gaskell to Ellen Nussey, 25 July 1856 – all in Chapple and Pollard (eds), letters 231, 259, 494a, 251, 297, 297a.
73. EG to Smith, [1 August], 13 August, and 2 October 1856; EG to Emily Shaen, [7 and 8 September 1856] – in Chapple and Pollard (eds), letters 299, 301, 314, 308.

74. EG to Shaen, [7 and 8 September 1856] and EG to Smith, 2 October and 19 August [1856] — in Chapple and Pollard (eds), letters 308, 314, 303; M.M. Brammer, 'The manuscript of *The Professor*', *R.E.S.* New Series, Vol.11, No.42 (1960), pp.157–70.

75. EG to Smith, [5 April 1860], in Chapple and Pollard (eds), letter 462. The best study of Kay-Shuttleworth's novels is Heather Sharps, 'Sir James Kay-Shuttleworth, a regional and historical novelist' (B.Phil. thesis, University of Hull, 1973). See also her 'The educational and social content of Kay-Shuttleworth's novels', *Journal of Educational Administration*, Vol.13, No.2 (1981), pp.1–6 and 'Sir James P. Kay-Shuttleworth as a regional and historical novelist', *Notes and Queries*, Vol.27, No.1 (1980), pp.76–9. The earlier novel or story is discussed in a letter from 'J.K.' (presumably June Kennedy) to Kay while he was living in Mosley St in Manchester – K-SP 1158.

76. EG to Smith, [5 April 1860], in Chapple and Pollard (eds), letter 462; *Scarsdale; or, Life on the Lancashire and Yorkshire Border, Thirty Years Ago* (London, 1860), Vol.2, pp.38–76.

77. *Scarsdale*, Vol.2, p.158; Vol.3, p.223.

78. Greg to JPK-S, 9 July [1860], K-SP 524; Robert Lee Wolff, *Strange Stories and Other Explorations in Victorian Fiction* (Boston, 1971), p.15.

79. A collection of reviews and Ebenezer Kay's letter, dated 22 June [1860], are in K-SP 1173; Thomas Hughes to JPK-S, 1 August 1860, K-SP 527.

80. Russell to JPK-S, 22 March 1857; J.P. Lee to JPK-S, 10 March 1858; Angela Burdett-Coutts to JPK-S, 4 July 1857; Henry Moseley to JPK-S, 24 July 1857 and JPK-S to children, 28 April 1855 – all in K-SP, 471, 477, 473, 474, 481. Blomfield dates K-SP 481 as 1858 – the indistinct writing makes this easy to do. But internal evidence and the fact that it was written on a Saturday (28 April 1858 was a Wednesday) place it in 1855. G.G. Leveson-Gower to JPK-S, 1 May 1856 and 22 June 1859, K-SP 468, 492.

81. Robert Kay to JPK-S, 1 February 1858, K-SP 476.

82. This paragraph is based on Humphrey Kay's 'Notes on the Kay family'.

83. Ughtred Kay-Shuttleworth (UK-S) to Janet K-S, 2 September and 11 August 1855; Janet K-S to UK-S, 16 August 1855; UK-S to Janet K-S, 22 October 1856 – all from file of letters from Ughtred to his mother, 1855 onwards, SP, Ughtred's red box. JPK-S to UK-S, 16 July 1855, letters from JPK-S to UK-S, 1850-5, SP, Ughtred's red box. UK-S to Janet K-S, 5 September 1860, 21 September 1856, 1 and 15 February 1856, 7 August 1857, 18 October 1855, 18-20 October 1857 – all in letters from Ughtred to his mother, 1855 onwards. UK-S to JPK-S, 10 November 1959, K-SP 506.

84. UK-S to JPK-S, 11 April 1860 and 12 April 1858, K-SP 510, 478.

85. UK-S to Janet K-S, 9 June 1859, 19, 22 January 1858, 31 December 1860, 9 March 1858, 14 October 1858, 12 April 1859, 22 March 1858, 15 December 1856, 22 January 1857 – all in letters from Ughtred to his mother, 1855 onwards, SP, Ughtred's red box.

86. UK-S to Janet K-S, 24 March 1860, letters from Ughtred to his mother, 1855 onwards, SP, Ughtred's red box; Smith, p.341.

87. Smith, pp.333–4; UK-S to Janet K-S, 29 November 1856 and 25 March 1857, letters from Ughtred to his mother, 1855 onwards, SP, Ughtred's red box.

88. Janet K-S to UK-S, 16 December 1856, in a collection of letters from Janet to Ughtred, SP, Ughtred's green box. (Most of these letters are from his sister, but a few are from his mother.)

89. UK-S to Janet K-S, 18 December 1856, letters from Ughtred to his mother,

1855 onwards, SP, Ughtred's red box.
90. UK-S to Janet K-S, 7 June and 9 July 1858, letters from Ughtred to his mother, 1855 onwards, SP, Ughtred's red box.
91. For a typical sample of a large literature, see the collection of letters in K-SP 489. UK-S to JPK-S, 3 February and 5 April 1859, in a collection of letters from Ughtred to his father, SP, box P; UK-S to JPK-S, 26 May 1859, K-SP 491.
92. UK-S to Janet K-S, 8 May and 5 September 1859, letters from Ughtred to his mother, 1855 onwards, SP, Ughtred's red box.
93. JPK-S to Marjoribanks, 18 June 1859, SP, box P; Phyllis Grosskurth, *John Addington Symonds: A Biography* (London, 1964), pp.25–6, 28.
94. Grosskurth, pp.32–7.
95. UK-S to JPK-S, 2 August 1859, K-SP 494; Janet K-S to UK-S, 23 September 1859, K-SP 497; Charles Vaughan to JPK-S, 24 September 1859, K-SP 498; Grosskurth, p.37.
96. Grosskurth, p.35 – the North–Symonds marriage is a major theme of the book; UK-S to JPK-S, 6 October 1859, K-SP 502; Janet K-S to UK-S, 23 September 1859, K-SP 497.

8 · Challenges, the preparation of an heir, and depression, 1860–65, pp.313–356

1. Johnson, 'The Education Department', pp.347–59; Richard Aldrich, 'Sir John Pakington and national education' (PhD thesis, University of London, 1977), and his monograph of the same name (Leeds, 1979).
2. The discussion of Lingen in this and following paragraphs draws on Johnson, especially pp.416–42, 490–5 and A.S. Bishop, 'Ralph Lingen, Secretary to the Education Department, 1849–1870', *British Journal of Educational Studies*, Vol.16, No.2 (1968), pp.138–63.
3. Quoted in Johnson, 'The Education Department', p.423.
4. Richard Aldrich, 'Sir John Pakington and the Newcastle Commission', *History of Education Quarterly*, Vol.8, No.1 (1979), pp.22–5 – Pakington's quotation, p.24; Granville is quoted in Jones, *Making of the Education System*, p.40.
5. Jones, *Making of the Education System*, p.40; Donald Mason, 'Peelite opinion and the genesis of payment by results: the true story of the Newcastle Commission', *History of Education*, Vol.17, No.4 (1988), p.270.
6. Report of the Commissioners appointed to inquire into the state of popular education in England (the Newcastle Commission), Vol.6, pp.305–10, *BPP* 1861, Vol.21, part 6. For Kay-Shuttleworth's evidence, pp.299–325 and 368–90.
7. Hurt, *Education in Evolution*, p.186; Newcastle Commission, Vol.6, pp.309, 322, 310, 319.
8. Jones, *Making of the Education System*, pp.42–3; Newcastle Commission, Vol.6, pp.323–5, 371–2.
9. Newcastle Commission, Vol.1, pp.297–9, 542–3, *BPP* 1861, Vol.21. part 1.
10. Newcastle Commission, Vol.1, pp.293, 238, 273, 155.
11. Newcastle Commission, Vol.1, pp.154, 273, 157, 328ff.
12. *Letter to the Earl Granville, K.G., . . . on the Report of the Commissioners appointed to inquire into the State of Popular Education in England, 24 April 1861* (London, 1861), pp.555–8, 567, 568 – page references are to *FPPE*, in which the letter is reproduced.

13. *Letter to the Earl Granville*, pp.560, 561.
14. James Winter, *Robert Lowe* (Toronto, 1976); Ruth Knight, *Illiberal Liberal: Robert Lowe in New South Wales, 1842–1850* (Melbourne, 1966); BPD 1861, Vol.164, col.721.
15. Johnson, 'The Education Department', pp.467–82; Memorandum by the Lord President of the Council on the Revised Code, Russell papers, PRO 30/22/27,136.
16. D.W. Sylvester, *Robert Lowe and Education* (Cambridge, 1974), pp.44–6; Johnson, 'The Education Department', pp.482–4.
17. Winter, p.175; Connell, pp.203–4; Report of the Select Committee on Education, p.21, BPP 1865, Vol.6; BPD 1860, Vol.160, col.1293 and 1862, Vol.165, col.172; Johnson, 'The Education Department', pp.492–9.
18. Minutes of the Committee of the Privy Council on Education establishing a Revised Code of Regulations, BPP 1861, Vol.48, pp.365–84. This argument is based on A.J. Marcham's 'Recent interpretations of the Revised Code of Education, 1862' and 'The Revised Code of Education, 1862: Reinterpretations and Misinterpretations' in *History of Education*, Vol.8, No.2 (1979), pp.121–33 and Vol.10, No.2 (1981), pp.81–99. These articles offer a valuable introduction to differing views of the Code.
19. Miall is quoted in Marcham, 'The Revised Code', p.94n.; BPD 1862, Vol.165, col.229; for the expenditure savings, Sylvester, p.82.
20. *The Times*, 26 September 1861, p.6; Marcham, 'Recent interpretations', pp.125–6; A. Patchett Martin (ed.), *Life and Letters of the Right Honourable Robert Lowe, Viscount Sherbrooke* (London, 1893), Vol.2, p.219; for the continuing controversy over the Code, Marcham's two articles and Connell, pp.203–42, Sylvester, pp.80–115, Simon, pp.348–50, and Smith, pp.266–7.
21. *Letter to Earl Granville, K.G., on the Revised Code of Regulations contained in the Minute of the Committee of Council on Education dated July 29th, 1861* (London, 1861), p.576 (as with the first letter, the pagination is from FPPE); James Fraser, *The Revised Code of the Committee of Council on Education* (London 1861), p.30.
22. *Letter to Earl Granville, K.G.*, pp.609, 608, 611, 593.
23. *Letter to Earl Granville, K.G.*, pp.599–601, 615, 577, 578; Robert Lowe to JPK-S, 26 April 1861, K-SP 552.
24. BPD 1862, Vol.165, cols 206, 191.
25. *Letter to Earl Granville, K.G.*, pp.582, 583, 628.
26. *Letter to Earl Granville, K.G.*, pp.610–11.
27. Matthew Arnold, *The Popular Education of France* (1861), in R.H. Super (ed.), *Matthew Arnold: Democratic Education* (Ann Arbor, 1962), pp.114–15; Connell, p.211; Robert Eden to JPK-S, 3 December 1861, K-SP 584; *Smith, p.271; Gladstone to JPK-S, 5 November 1861 and Granville to JPK-S, 14 November 1861, K-SP 579, 578; UK-S to JPK-S, 26 November 1861, K-SP 582.
28. *The Times*, 30 November 1861, p.7; Lingen is quoted in Johnson, 'The Education Department', p.495; *Letter to Earl Granville, K.G.*, p.617n.
29. *The Times*, 30 November, p.7; for the Norris incident, 'Lies and statistics: a note on the Newcastle Commission', *History of Education*, Vol.9, No.3 (1980), pp.229–31; UK-S's diary at Harrow, 1861, in envelope A 11/06, in metal trunk, SP, EO,CB.
30. JPK-S to G.C. Lewis, 3 December 1862, Harpton Court collection, C/1638; *Daily News*, 20 January 1862, p.5; diary entry for 1 January 1862, from Miscellaneous correspondence, SP, box J; memorandum, 4 January 1862,

Russell papers, PRO/30/22/27, folios 130–2 and Russell to Granville, 26 March 1862, Granville papers, PRO 30/29/18/6, folios 93–4.

31. Edmond Fitzmaurice, *The Life of Granville George Leveson Gower, Second Earl Granville, K.G., 1815–1891* (London, 1905), Vol. 1, p.428; *BPD* 1862, Vol.165, cols 178, 191–242; UK-S to Janet K-S, 15 February 1862, letters from Ughtred to his mother, 1855 onwards, SP, Ughtred's red box; John Delane to Granville, 14 February 1862, Granville papers, PRO 30/29/19/16.

32. *BPD* 1862, Vol.165, cols 218–22; Winter, p.179; Eden to JPK-S, 3 December 1861, K-SP 584; entry for 11 March 1862, in Miscellaneous correspondence, 1862, SP, box J.

33. JPK-S to Granville, 12 March 1862, Granville papers, PRO 30/29/19/19; Lansdowne to JPK-S, 16 March 1862, Sinclair to JPK-S, 22 March 1862 and Lewis to JPK-S, 24 March 1862 – all in K-SP 594, 597, 598.

34. *BPD* 1862, Vol.166, cols 241, 831–2; for the approach to Granville (5 April 1862), K-SP 600, 601; Smith, p.275; Winter, pp.179–81.

35. *The Twice-Revised Code* is in Super (ed.), Vol.2, pp.212-43 – the quotations are from pp.212, 233; for Arnold's plans, pp.349–50.

36. Super (ed.), pp.228, 226, 234–5. D.M. Mason, 'Matthew Arnold and elementary education: a reconsideration', *History of Education*, Vol.12, No.3 (1983), has shown the inconsistency of Arnold's views, and the extent of Kay-Shuttleworth's influence on him.

37. Connell, p.223.

38. John Watts, *The Facts of the Cotton Famine* (London, 1866), pp.176, 121; P.J. Augar, 'The cotton famine, 1861–5: a study of the principal cotton towns during the American Civil War', (PhD thesis, Cambridge, 1979), pp.21–36; W.O. Henderson, *The Lancashire Cotton Famine, 1861–1865* (New York, 1969), pp.52–7, 68–74.

39. Henderson, pp.58, 78–80, 74–5; Watts, pp.156–60, 168–73; Norman Longmate, *The Hungry Mills* (London, 1978), pp.129–52.

40. JPK-S to Janet (daughter), 1 October 1862, K-SP 610; Watts, pp.172, 259; Derby to JPK-S, 10 August and 11 October 1862, K-SP 605, 611.

41. The *Manual of Suggestions* was reproduced in Kay-Shuttleworth's *Thoughts and Suggestions on Certain Social Problems* (London, 1873) – the quotation is from p.119. Longmate stresses the similarity with the Poor Law Board, pp.130, 152–3; Watts, pp.206–10.

42. The speeches were published in Manchester and London, probably in 1863. A copy is held in K-SP 1180.

43. Henderson, pp.87–90; Watts, pp.200–5; Longmate, pp.174–88; UK-S to Janet K-S, 8 August 1862, letters from Ughtred to his mother, 1855 onwards, SP, Ughtred's red box; for Cooper and Hamilton, *Australian Dictionary of Biography*, Vols 3, p.452 and 4, pp.329–30.

44. R. Arthur Arnold, *The History of the Cotton Famine* (Manchester, 1864), p.385; Watts, p.205.

45. Henderson, pp.59–67; Watts, pp.308–32; JPK-S to UK-S, 10 and 12 June 1863, K-SP 649, 651; Augar, pp.92–5; JPK-S to Janet (daughter), 15 August 1862, K-SP 606.

46. Arnold, pp.397–406; Watts, pp.263-6; Henderson, pp.111–12.

47. Henderson, pp.112–13; Watts, pp.266–72; *The Times*, 23 March 1863, p.12 and 24 March, pp.12, 9.

48. UK-S to JPK-S, 25 March 1863, K-SP 622; Henderson, p.73.

49. Watts, pp.274–6; Henderson, p.113; *The Times*, 26 March 1863, p.10; UK-S

to JPK-S, 26 March 1863, K-SP 624.

50. Watts, pp.277–81; *The Times*, 27 March 1863, p.5 and 28 March, p.14; the attitude of the cotton workers is a major theme of Augar's thesis.

51. Watts, pp.449–457; Longmate, pp.283–4.

52. James Kay-Shuttleworth, 'The industrial and social development of South East Lancashire', *Thoughts and Suggestions*, pp.60–2; U.J. Kay-Shuttleworth, 'On the East Lancashire Union of institutions having evening schools, in its bearing on the question of the education of the manual labour class', *Transactions of the National Association for the Promotion of Social Science, 1866* (London, 1867), pp.317–29. This and the following paragraphs draw heavily on John Dunleavy, 'The provision of education for working people in institutes in North East Lancashire, 1854–72' (PhD, University of Leeds, 1983).

53. U.J. Kay-Shuttleworth, pp.320–2.

54. Dunleavy, pp.43, 40, 20; U.J. Kay-Shuttleworth, p.325; H.P. Hamilton to JPK-S, 17 December 1860, K-SP 538; *Smith, p.252.

55. Dunleavy, p.33 (Verity quotation); JPK-S to Brougham, 30 October 1859 and 29 May 1961, Brougham papers, 24617, 32675; see also Kay-Shuttleworth's letters to Brougham, Nos 25240–3, 15077, 24616, 34625.

56. Gladstone to JPK-S, 28 November 1865; U.J. Kay-Shuttleworth, pp.325–7; Dunleavy, pp.188, 421, 386; J.P. Kay-Shuttleworth, 'The industrial and social development', p.61; JPK-S to UK-S, 8 October 1864, K-SP 702.

57. Edward Cardwell to JPK-S, 13 December 1863, K-SP 675; Howe, pp.254, 259–62.

58. Howe, pp.259–60. For typical comments on the shrievalty: JPK-S to UK-S, 12, 16, 20 January, 20, 22, 18, 28 March, 25 April, 22 November and JPK-S to Lionel and Stewart Kay-Shuttleworth, 16 January – all 1864. These letters are in K-SP 676, 680, 681, 684, 686, 683, 688, 693, 708, 679; Smith, p.341.

59. E.M. Goulburn to JPK-S, 31 January 1861, K-SP 544, 545; UK-S to Janet K-S, 18 March 1861, letters from Ughtred to his mother, 1855 onwards, SP, Ughtred's red box; UK-S to JPK-S, 1861: between 11 and 27 April, 25 March, 3, 6, 22 and 21 May, 30 April, 2 May – K-SP 553, 546, 557, 559, 567, 566, 555, 556.

60. UK-S to JPK-S, 23 May 1861 and JPK-S to Janet K-S, 27 May 1861, to H.M. Butler, 27 May and to North, 29 May – all in K-SP 571; D.M. Williams, 25 May 1861, K-SP 570; Butler to JPK-S, 30 May 1861, K-SP 573.

61. For the plan for Ughtred, see the correspondence in K-SP 571; Shaw-Lefevre's comment is quoted in Kay-Shuttleworth's letter to North in K-SP 571; UK-S to JPK-S, 28 April 1863, K-SP 629.

62. J.A. Symonds to Charlotte Green, 11 April 1867, SP, box P.

63. JPK-S to UK-S, 5, 6, 7 and 9 May 1863, and UK-S to JPK-S, 5 June 1863 – all K-SP 631, 633, 635, 644, 637.

64. UK-S to JPK-S, 5 May, 5 and 4 June, and 1 August 1863, 7 October 1864 – K-SP 632, 644, 643, 659, 700.

65. JPK-S to UK-S, 6 March 1863 and UK-S to JPK-S, 5 and 8 May and 1 and 8 June 1863 – K-SP, 618, 632, 636, 639, 646; JPK-S to UK-S, 22 November [1862], K-SP 613; JPK-S to UK-S, 21 July 1863, 20 and 22 March 1864, 4 October [1865] and 8 October [1863] – K-SP 652, 684, 686, 752, 666.

66. JPK-S to UK-S, 22 March [1864]; UK-S to JPK-S, 4 and 10 June 1863, 28 August 1862, 20 June 1864; JPK-S to UK-S, 22 November [1862]; UK-S to JPK-S, 17 June 1864; JPK-S to UK-S, 2 and 3 June 1863 – K-SP 686, 643, 650, 607, 696, 613, 695, 640, 641.

67. All letters 1864: JPK-S to UK-S, 16 January, UK-S to JPK-S, 18 and 25 April, 17 and 20 June, K-SP 680, 689, 694, 695, 696; UK-S to Janet K-S, 6 April, 22 August, 17 November, letters from Ughtred to his mother, 1855 onwards, SP, Ughtred's red box; UK-S to JPK-S, 17 October, 24 November, 18 April, JPK-S to UK-S, 19 April, UK-S to JPK-S, 20 April, JPK-S to UK-S, 21 April – K-SP 706, 709, 689, 690, 691, 692.
68. UK-S to Janet K-S, 4 February 1865, letters from Ughtred to his mother, 1855 onwards, SP, Ughtred's red box.
69. JPK-S to Ughtred and Janet K-S, 20 July 1864, K-SP 697.
70. JPK-S to UK-S, 10 January and 21 July 1863, 20 July [1864] – K-SP 615, 652, 697. The illustration is in Longmate, illustration 12; Hannah wrote the letters in K-SP 571; UK-S to Janet K-S, 21 March 1865, letters from Ughtred to his mother, 1855 onwards, SP, Ughtred's red box; JPK-S to UK-S, 10 January 1863, K-SP 615. The date for the finishing of his novel, *Ribblesdale*, is given in Janet K-S (sister) to UK-S, 2 November 1869, collection of letters from Janet (sister) to Ughtred, SP, Ughtred's green box. The novel was not published until 1874.
71. JPK-S to UK-S, 16 January and 21 April 1864, 21 February [1865], K-SP 680, 692, 720.
72. JPK-S to UK-S, 21 April 1864, and 1865: 21, 22, 28 February, 13, 15 April, and 17 June – K-SP 692, 720, 721, 722, 728, 730, 738; JPK-S to Hugh Mason, 24 June 1865 and to George Wilson, 30 June 1865, George Wilson papers, M20, Local History Archives, Central Library, Manchester; Philip Magnus, *Gladstone: A Biography* (London, 1954), pp.164, 170–2; UK-S to Janet K-S, 13 July 1865, letters from Ughtred to his mother, 1855 onwards, SP, Ughtred's red box; *Smith, pp.283, 335.
73. JPK-S to Janet K-S, 7 August 1863, K-SP 662; JPK-S to UK-S, 9 November [1865], K-SP 778.
74. JPK-S to UK-S, 7 and 9 May 1864 and JPK-S to Janet (daughter) and Ughtred, 20 July 1864 – K-SP 635, 637, 697; *Smith, pp.330–1; JPK-S to UK-S, 5 August [1865], K-SP 744.
75. Smith, pp.341–2.
76. For example, JPK-S to Janet K-S, 7 August 1863, K-SP 662.
77. UK-S to JPK-S, 7, 8, 9 and 10 April 1861, K-SP 548–51.
78. UK-S to JPK-S, 4 August 1865; JPK-S to UK-S, 2 and 6 August 1863; UK-S to JPK-S, 21 March 1862 – K-SP 743, 660, 661, 595.
79. UK-S to JPK-S, 31 July 1865; Janet K-S (sister) to UK-S, 8 October 1864; JPK-S to UK-S, 9 October [1863]; Janet K-S (sister) to UK-S, 9 October 1863; JPK-S to UK-S, 18 October [1865]; JPK-S to Janet K-S (daughter), 1 October 1862 – K-SP 741, 703, 667, 668, 765, 610.
80. JPK-S to UK-S, 6 and 7 August 1863; UK-S to JPK-S, 29 July, 5 August, 31 July 1865 – K-SP 661, 663, 740, 745, 741; UK-S to Janet K-S (sister), 27 June 1864, SP, Ughtred's red box.
81. JPK-S to Janet K-S (daughter) and UK-S, 20 July [1864], JPK-S to UK-S, 18 and 22 March 1864; UK-S to JPK-S, 18 April 1865 – K-SP 697, 683, 686, 733. UK-S to Janet K-S, 23 April 1865, letters from Ughtred to his mother, 1855 onwards, SP, Ughtred's red box; UK-S to JPK-S, 22 April and 17 June 1865, K-SP 735, 738; JPK-S to John Harland, 4 December 1865, msf 091 H15, Vol.2, No.75, Local History Archives, Central Library, Manchester.

9 · The final years, 1865–77, pp.357–410

1. *Transactions, 1857*, pp.xxi,xxvi, xv–xvi, 12. This discussion of the Association draws on David Ian Allsobrook, *Schools for the Shires: The Reform of Middle-class Education in Victorian England* (Manchester, 1986), esp. pp.16, 141–3; Richard Aldrich, 'Association of ideas: the National Association for the Promotion of Social Science', *History of Education Society Bulletin*, No.16 (1975), pp.16–21; Abrams, pp.44–9.
2. *Transactions, 1857*, pp.23, xxxii.
3. For his last appearance on the council, *Transactions, 1871*, p.xvii; these *Transactions* also list his chairmanship of departments. His 'Address on economy and trade', *Transactions, 1866*, pp.84, 86, 87, 96, 100 – this was republished in *Social Problems*, pp.1–39, as 'The laws of social progress'.
4. Allsobrook, pp.180, 4–5. This and the following paragraphs draw upon Allsobrook's work; *Public Education*, esp. Ch.4.
5. Allsobrook, pp.3–4; Simon, p.320; Schools Inquiry Commission, Report of the Commissioners, Vol.1, p.139, *BPP* 1867–68, Vol.28, part 1.
6. Schools Inquiry Commission, *Report*, Vol.1, pp.633–44, 577–9.
7. Schools Inquiry Commission, *Report*, Vol.5, pp.897–923, *BPP* 1867–68, Vol.28, part 4; James Kay-Shuttleworth, 'What central and local bodies are best qualified to take charge of and administer existing endowments for education . . .?', *Transactions, 1866*, pp.330–1, 332, 335–6, 333 – for Brougham's comment, p.406.
8. 'What central and local bodies', pp.336, 334–5; *Public Education*, pp.176–7, 180–2 (in footnotes).
9. Schools Inquiry Commission, *Report*, Vol.5, pp.897–923, *BPP* 1867–68, Vol.28, part 4; JPK-S to Granville, 9 May 1862, Granville papers, PRO 30/29/19/25; 'What central and local bodies', p.340.
10. 'What central and local bodies', pp.341, 340, 342, 346, 347.
11. Schools Inquiry Commission, *Report*, Vol.5, pp.908, 904.
12. Schools Inquiry Commission, *Report*, Vol.18, p.95, *BPP* 1867–68, Vol.28, part 15; Kay-Shuttleworth first attended a meeting of the governors on 7 September 1864, Giggleswick School, Minutes of governors' meeting, 7 September 1864 (held at Giggleswick School, Settle); JPK-S to UK-S, 22 November 1864, K-SP 613 – Bloomfield places this tentatively in 1862, but the content and the day it was written, Saturday, point to 1864 as the year; evidence of C.S. Roundell, Schools Inquiry Commission, *Report*, Vol.5, p.308, *BPP* 1867–68, Vol.28, part 4.
13. Edward Allen Bell, *A History of Giggleswick School from its Foundation, 1499 to 1902* (Leeds, 1912), pp.150–5, 159; Schools Inquiry Commission, *Report*, Vol.18, pp.93–4 and Vol.9, pp.112, 150, *BPP* 1867–68, Vol.28, part 8.
14. Bell, p.166; Schools Inquiry Commission, *Report*, Vol.5, pp.308–14, Vol.18, pp.94–5 and Vol.9, pp.150–1; Giggleswick School, Minutes of governors' meeting, 21 October 1865.
15. Schools Inquiry Commission, *Report*, Vol.5, pp.311–12 and Vol.9, p.151; Bell, pp.163–4; Smith, pp.307–8, 344; Sheila Fletcher, *Feminists and Bureaucrats: A Study in the Development of Girls' Education in the Nineteenth Century* (Cambridge, 1980), pp.47–8.
16. UK-S to JPK-S, 19 March 1866, K-SP 794; Janet K-S to UK-S, 19 May 1870, SP, box J.
17. 'A sketch of the history and results of popular education in England', *Thoughts and Suggestions*, p.153; Richard Aldrich, '"The growing intelligence and edu-

cation of the people"', *History of Education Society Bulletin*, No.22 (1978), pp.48–50; *Memorandum on Popular Education* (London, 1868), pp.66, 30, 67–8, 57, 56, 54.

18. All letters to JPK-S were written in 1868: Arnold, 17 and 26 January; Gladstone, 16 September; Forster, 27 January, Lowe, 28 January – K-SP 826, 828, 845, 830, 829. Lowe's speech was probably that reprinted as *Primary and Classical Education*, which was given in Edinburgh in November 1867. For Arnold's use of the *Memorandum*, see Mason, 'Matthew Arnold and elementary education: A reconsideration', pp.184–5.

19. *Memorandum*, pp.35–6; Edward Baines to JPK-S, 19 October 1967, Baines papers, 52/11, Leeds District Archives; Derek Fraser, 'Edward Baines' in Patricia Hollis (ed.), *Pressure From Without in Early Victorian England* (London, 1974), pp.201–2.

20. Murphy, *Church, State and Schools in Britain*, pp.62 (Miall quotation), 49–51; Jones, pp.57–61; Marjorie Cruickshank, *Church and State in English Education: 1870 to the present day* (London, 1863), pp.16–17; Baines to JPK-S, 19 October 1867.

21. Cruickshank, p.12; Jones, *Making of the Education System*, p.56; T. Wemyss Reid, *Life of the Rt Hon. W.E. Forster* (New York, 1970 ed.), Vol.1, p.495; Jones, p.66.

22. Jones, *Making of the Education System*, pp.64–7; Murphy, *Church, State and Schools in Britain*, pp.51–60.

23. *BPD* 1870, Vol.199, cols 442–3; for an example of recent analysis, see Carpenter; Stephens, pp.265–8; Simon, pp.363–4.

24. Jones, *Making of the Education System*, pp.51–5; Gladstone to Granville, 30 May 1870, in Agatha Ramm (ed.), *The Political Correspondence of Mr. Gladstone and Lord Granville, 1868–1876* (London, 1952), Vol.1, p.99.

25. Jones, *Making of the Education System*, p.67; Boards of Education for the Dioceses of Chester and Manchester, *Report of a Public Meeting . . . on Tuesday, September 27th, 1870* (Chester, 1870), p.27; *BPD* 1870, Vol.199, col.447; R.A.T. Gascoyne-Cecil, Lord Salisbury to JPK-S, 1 June 1870, K-SP 882; *Smith, p.293.

26. *BPD* 1870, Vol.199, cols 2016–21.

27. JPK-S to Janet (daughter), 23 March 1870, K-SP 876. The exclamation mark is Kay-Shuttleworth's.

28. UK-S to Janet K-S, 28 June and 6 March 1868, A 11/06, SP; Smith, p.336.

29. Hanham, pp.296–302; UK-S to Janet K-S, 10 and 17 July, 16 and 23 August, 22 November 1868, all in A 11/06, SP; JPK-S to Janet K-S, 29 November 1868, K-SP 846.

30. North to JPK-S, 23 November 1868, SP, Ughtred's red box; UK-S to Janet K-S, 20 September 1868 and UK-S to JPK-S, 1 October 1868, both in A 11/06, SP.

31. Hanham, p.293n; Scrivens to UK-S, 29 October 1869 and UK-S to Scrivens, 30 October 1869, both in A 11/06, SP; Janet K-S to JPK-S, 8 November 1869, K-SP 859; Janet K-S to UK-S, 18 November 1869, SP, Ughtred's green box.

32. 1869: Janet Kay-Shuttleworth to UK-S, 6 November 1869, SP, box J; UK-S to JPK-S, 3, 5, 7 and 11 November, K-SP 854, 855, 857, 861; UK-S to JPK-S, 17 November, A11/06, SP; Janet K-S (sister) to UK-S, 18 November and Janet K-S to UK-S, 18 November, both SP, Ughtred's green box.

33. Copy of a letter [by UK-S] n.d., and attached note by N[ina] H[ill] (Ughtred's daughter), 1939; F. Williams to JPK-S, 19 February 1866; draft of letter from JPK-S to Marjoribanks, 3 May 1866 (includes extract of letter from UK-S to Janet K-S, 19 February 1866); Janet K-S to UK-S, 27 February 1866; JPK-S to Williams (per Ebenezer Kay), 14 April 1866; Marjoribanks to JPK-S, 3 May 1866 – all K-SP, 783, 784, 797, 786, 795, 798.

34. Janet K-S to UK-S, 24 March 1866, SP, Ughtred's green box; Janet K-S to UK-S, 12 June 1866 and Janet K-S (daughter), 16 June 1866 – both K-SP, 799, 800; Janet K-S (sister) to UK-S, 2 July 1866, SP, A 11/06.
35. UK-S to JPK-S, 28 and 29 December 1866, K-SP 808, 809.
36. Janet K-S to UK-S, 17 April and 15 August 1866, and 9 December 1867, SP, Ughtred's green box.
37. Janet K-S to UK-S, 6 November 1869, SP, box J; JPK-S to UK-S, 3 November 1869, series of letters from JPK-S to UK-S, SP, Ughtred's green box.
38. Janet K-S to JPK-S, 8 November 1869, K-SP 859; Janet K-S (sister) to UK-S, 15 March 1870, collection of letters from Janet to Ughtred, SP, Ughtred's green box; UK-S to Janet K-S, 20 April 1870, series of letters from Ughtred to Janet K-S, envelope A 11/06, SP; Janet K-S to UK-S, 25 April 1870, box J, SP; JPK-S to Janet K-S (daughter), 17 July 1870, K-SP 881.
39. The fever is discussed in letters called 'My [i.e. Ughtred's] letters in 1869' in envelope in tin trunk, A 11/06, SP – the letter from UK-S to Janet K-S, 14 January 1869, makes it clear that Kay-Shuttleworth did not visit his wife. JPK-S to Janet K-S (daughter), May 1869 (day not given), K-SP 850.
40. UK-S to Janet K-S, 30 May, 8 and 20 June 1869, 'My letters in 1869'; Janet K-S (sister) to UK-S, 20 June 1869, SP, box P; UK-S to Janet K-S, 26 June 1869, 'My letters in 1869'.
41. UK-S to Janet K-S (daughter), 19 July 1869, 'My letters in 1869'.
42. Janet K-S (sister) to UK-S, 31 December 1871, in collection of letters from Janet to Ughtred, SP, Ughtred's green box; UK-S to JPK-S, 4 December 1871, K-SP 913.
43. UK-S to JPK-S, 7 July 1871, K-SP 907.
44. UK-S to JPK-S, 21 January 1871, K-SP 898; Janet K-S to UK-S, 23 June 1870, 20 November 1869, 7 February 1872 and 25 April 1870 – SP, box J.
45. Janet K-S to UK-S, 6 November 1869 and 6 January 1872 – SP, box J.
46. Janet K-S to her children, 3 September 1867, collection of letters from Janet Kay-Shuttleworth (sister) to UK-S, 3 September 1867, SP, Ughtred's green box; Edward Lear to Blanche Kay-Shuttleworth (Ughtred's wife), 15 December 1871, SP, box C.
47. JPK-S to Janet K-S (daughter), 17 July 1870, K-SP 884; Janet K-S to JPK-S, 6 March 1891, SP, box P.
48. JPK-S to UK-S, 25 December 1871, SP, box P; Janet K-S to UK-S, 25 April 1870, SP, box J; JPK-S to Janet K-S (daughter), 6 March 1871, K-SP 902; Janet K-S to JPK-S, 6 March 1871, SP, box P.
49. JPK-S to Janet K-S, 13 March 1871, SP, Ughtred's green box; JPK-S to UK-S, 25 December 1871, SP, Ughtred's green box; UK-S to JPK-S, 4 December 1871, K-SP 914.
50. UK-S to JPK-S, 13 December 1870 and 29 May 1872, K-SP, 895, 921; JPK-S to Janet K-S, 11 February and 6 March 1871, K-SP 901, 902; Janet K-S to JPK-S, 6 March 1871, SP, box P; JPK-S to Janet K-S, 13 March 1871, SP, Ughtred's green box.
51. 1871: JPK-S to Janet K-S, 1 July; UK-S to JPK-S, 2 July; Blanche Kay-Shuttleworth to JPK-S, 5 July; UK-S to JPK-S, 7 July – K-SP 904–7; Janet K-S to Blanche Kay-Shuttleworth, 6 June, SP, box C; Blanche Kay-Shuttleworth to JPK-S, 28 November; UK-S to JPK-S, 4 and 14 December – K-SP 912–14. Janet K-S to UK-S and Blanche Kay-Shuttleworth, 15 March 1872, SP, A 11/06.
52. Janet K-S (sister) to UK-S, 30 September 1872, SP, Ughtred's green box; her mother's words are held in SP, envelope 3, box 10.

53. SP, envelope 10, box 3.
54. Williams to JPK-S, 15 September 1872, SP, envelope 8, box 3.
55. Janet K-S (daughter) to JPK-S, 15 September 1872, K-SP 930.
56. Janet K-S (daughter) to JPK-S, 15 September 1872, K-SP 930.
57. UK-S to JPK-S, 19 and 18 September 1872, K-SP 933; JPK-S to UK-S, 20 September 1872, K-SP 934.
58. Robertson to JPK-S, 22 September 1872, SP, Ughtred's green box; UK-S to JPK-S, 19 September 1872, K-SP 933.
59. [Janet] Catherine Symonds to JPK-S, 19 September 1872, SP, box P. The Poplawska sisters are mentioned in Janet K-S to UK-S, 3 September 1867, in collection of letters from Janet K-S to UK-S, SP, Ughtred's green box.
60. G.T. Carey (a Gawthorpe employee) to UK-S, 23 September 1872; *St Leonard's Parish Magazine*, No.10, Vol.9 (1872) – both are in SP, Ughtred's green box. Kay-Shuttleworth's draft sermon is in K-SP 927.
61. *St Leonard's Parish Magazine*, and letter by Carey.
62. Her will is in SP, envelope 8, box 3.
63. For Kay-Shuttleworth's legal position, Perkin, *Women and Marriage in Nineteenth-Century England*, pp.65–6; UK-S to JPK-S, 19 September 1872 and JPK-S to UK-S, 20 September 1872 – K-SP 933, 934.
64. UK-S to JPK-S, 21 September 1872, and JPK-S to UK-S, 23 September 1872, K-SP 935, 937; note by Ughtred (it is not known to whom), 24 September 1872, SP, box P.
65. UK-S to JPK-S, 27 September 1872; JPK-S to Janet K-S (daughter), 7 May 1870; JPK-S to UK-S, 27 September 1872 – K-SP 944, 881, 943.
66. JPK-S to UK-S, 29 September 1872, K-SP 946.
67. JPK-S to UK-S, 2 October 1872, K-SP 948; Ebenezer Kay to UK-S, 2 October 1872, SP, box P; Janet K-S (sister) to UK-S, 30 September 1872, SP, Ughtred's green box.
68. JPK-S to UK-S, 8 and 10 October 1872; Janet K-S (sister) to UK-S, 8 October 1872; UK-S to JPK-S, 9 October 1872 – all in SP, Ughtred's green box.
69. Report from the select committee on elementary schools (certificated teachers), pp.56–64, 100–8, BPP 1872, Vol.9; National Union of Elementary Teachers, *Fifth Annual Conference, 1874. President's address and report of proceedings* (London, 1874) – K-SP 1198; Asher Tropp, *The School Teachers* (London, 1957), pp.123–4.
70. UK-S to JPK-S, 4, 10, 12, 16, 24, June and 6 August 1876, K-SP 1077, 1079–81, 1084, 1091; Jones, *Making of the Education System*, pp.74–9; *Smith, p.295; Gillian Sutherland, *Policy-Making in Elementary Education, 1870–1895* (Oxford, 1973), pp.125–45.
71. 'Some of the results of the Education Act and Code of 1870', *Fortnightly Review*, May 1876, p.695.
72. Louisa M. Hubbard, *Work for Ladies in Elementary Schools*, with an introduction by an old educator [Kay-Shuttleworth] (London, 1872); 'Memorandum in recapitulation of the Facts and suggestions discussed at the Conference on Training Colleges held on Thursday, March 21, 1872', in *Thoughts and Suggestions*, pp.295–305 – also K-SP 1192; Smith, pp.312–14; Rich, pp.259–60. The *Sketch* is K-SP 1202. 1875: Conference on establishing training colleges for teachers of schools above the elementary, minute book of meetings, 68 Cromwell Rd, February to June; H.J. Smith to JPK-S, 13 March; H.D. Harper to JPK-S, 7 and 11 May; C.H. Lake to JPK-S, 29 June 1875 – all K-SP, 1049, 1050, 1053, 1055, 1058.
73. *Smith, pp.309–10; Giggleswick School, Minutes of governors' meeting,

9 August 1877; Bell, pp.186–7.

74. Josephine Kamm, *Indicative Past: A Hundred Years of the Girls' Public Day School Trust* (London, 1971), pp.42–9; Margaret Bryant, *The Unexpected Revolution* (London, 1979), pp.102–3.

75. Kamm, pp.49, 56, 58, 60; *Smith, pp.311–12.

76. *Smith, pp.310–11; David Layton, *Science for the People: The Origins of the School Science Curriculum in England* (London, 1973), pp.33, 76–85, 106–11; J.W. Adamson, *English Education, 1789–1902* (Cambridge, 1930), pp.396–8, 420–2; Royal Commission on Scientific Instruction and the Advancement of Science, Vol.1, *BPP* 1872, Vol.25; Vol.2, *BPP* 1874, Vol.22, and Vol.3, *BPP* 1875, Vol.28.

77. JPK to Chalmers, 21 November 1832, Chalmers collection, CHA 4 183.4.

78. 1872: UK-S to JPK-S, 19 and 21 September; JPK-S to Janet K-S (daughter), 24 September; JPK-S to UK-S, 27 September – K-SP 933, 935, 939, 943.

79. JPK-S to UK-S, 14 December 1874, series of letters from JPK-S to UK-S, SP, Ughtred's green box; UK-S to JPK-S, 14 December 1871, K-SP 1044; UK-S to JPK-S, 31 March 1876, K-SP 1075.

80. JPK-S to his children, 20 July 1872, K-SP 923; JPK-S to UK-S, 20 September 1872, K-SP 934; Michael Stenton and Stephen Lees, *Who's Who of British Members of Parliament*, Vol.2, 1886–1918 (Hassocks, 1978), pp.196–7.

81. UK-S to JPK-S, 19 October 1872, K-SP 956; *Burke's Peerage*, 102nd edition, London, 1959, p.2061.

82. Blanche Kay-Shuttleworth to Janet K-S (sister-in-law), 10 August 1873, K-SP 978; JPK-S to UK-S, 10 August 1874, SP, box P; JPK-S to UK-S, 30 and 31 December 1873 and 3 January 1874, K-SP 998, 1000, 1004; JPK-S to UK-S, 14 December 1874, series of letters from JPK-S to UK-S, SP, Ughtred's green box; JPK-S to UK-S, 19 June 1874, K-SP 1030; JPK-S to Janet K-S (daughter), 18 April 1875; UK-S to JPK-S, 29 September and 17 December 1876; UK-S to JPK-S, 14 February 1877; JPK-S to UK-S, 3 January 1874, K-SP 1004.

83. JPK-S to UK-S, 19 June 1874, K-SP 1030; JPK-S to UK-S, 12 January 1875, series of letters from JPK-S to UK-S, SP, Ughtred's green box; JPK-S to UK-S, 6 February 1876, K-SP 1068; JPK-S to UK-S, 5 March 1877, SP, box P; *Burke's Peerage*, 102nd edition, p.2061; information on Robin supplied by Mrs Janet Young.

84. Humphrey Kay, Notes on the Kay family, especially the revealing letter he reproduces from Mary Kay (Joseph Kay's wife) to UK-S, 22 March 1878. There is a considerable amount of correspondence between the Pigeon Bay Kays and UK-S in SP, box F and in envelope 35.

85. JPK-S to UK-S, 31 December 1873 and 3, 4, 5 and 7 January 1874, K-SP 1000, 1004–7; JPK-S to UK-S, 27 August 1874, SP, box P.

86. JPK-S to UK-S, 24 March 1873, K-SP 963; William Cavendish (Duke of Devonshire) to JPK-S, 6 June 1973, K-SP 973.

87. JPK-S to UK-S, 10 and 15 November 1873, K-SP 987, 988; UK-S to JPK-S, 16 November 1873, K-SP 989; JPK-S to UK-S, 25 January 1874, K-SP 1010; Blanche Kay-Shuttleworth to JPK-S, 25 January 1874, K-SP 1011; cable from JPK-S to UK-S, 28 January 1874, K-SP 1199; JPK-S to Blanche Kay-Shuttleworth, 30 January 1874.

88. JPK-S to Blanche Kay-Shuttleworth, 26 January 1874, K-SP 1014; JPK-S to Janet K-S (daughter), 10 February 1874, K-SP 1017; election poster, 1 February 1874, K-SP 1197; Devonshire to JPK-S, 8 February 1874, K-SP 1016; JPK-S to Blanche Kay-Shuttleworth, 31 January 1874, K-SP 1015.

89. JPK-S to Janet K-S (daughter), 10 February 1874, K-SP 1017; Gladstone to JPK-S, 13 February 1874, K-SP 1019.
90. The letters of advice written in 1874-5 are too numerous to list. For Forster, JPK-S to UK-S, 29 January 1875, series of letters from JPK-S to UK-S, SP, Ughtred's green box.
91. *Thoughts and Suggestions*, pp.309–10.
92. The note in the British Library duplicate was drawn to my attention by Geoffrey Sharps of Scarborough, who owns the book. The note is reproduced in Howes Bookshop, *A Special Selection of Rare and Interesting Books*, catalogue 250, 1991, entry 299; for Katherine Esdaile, *DNB 1941–1950*, pp.239–40; for Arundell Esdaile, *Who Was Who, 1951–60*, p.352; for Andrew McDowall, Kramm, pp.68, 206; JPK-S to Janet K-S (daughter), 10 February 1874 and JPK-S to UK-S, 17 January 1874, K-SP 1017, 1020.
93. *Ribblesdale, or Lancashire Sixty Years Ago* (London, 1874), p.vii. As with *Scarsdale*, this discussion draws on the work of Heather Sharps.
94. 'Cromwell in the North. 1648. A Story', K-SP 1209; George Smith to JPK-S, 27 May and 2 June 1875, K-SP 1209. A valuable study of the manuscript has been done by Heather Sharps, 'Prolegomena to an edition of "Cromwell in the North". 1648. A Story' (MA, University of Leeds, 1977).
95. JPK-S to Janet K-S (daughter), 10 January 1875, K-SP 1046; Smith to JPK-S, 2 June 1875, K-SP 1057. Sharps has drawn attention to the editing – 'Prolegomena to an edition of "Cromwell in the North"', pp.85–85b.
96. W.A. Abram to JPK-S, 5 October 1874, K-SP 1036.
97. Sharps, 'Prolegomena to an edition of "Cromwell in the North"', pp.31–2; 'Ravenstone' is used as the title in JPK-S to Janet K-S (daughter), 10 January 1875, K-SP 1046.
98. Letter from Dr J. Weber to an unknown doctor, 5 May 1877, correspondence held at Leck Hall; page of a diary listing guests at dinner party, K-SP 1069; JPK-S to UK-S, 6 February 1876 and UK-S to JPK-S, 4, 10 and 12 June, 6 August 1876 – K-SP 1068, 1077, 1079, 1080, 1091; Derby to JPK-S, 9 June 1876, K-SP 1078; Robert Johnson to JPK-S, 19 July 1876, K-SP 1087.
99. JPK-S to UK-S, 22 and 24 February 1876, K-SP 1071; UK-S to JPK-S, 18 October, 24 December 1876, K-SP 1098,1108; JPK-S to Angela Kay-Shuttleworth (grand-daughter), 26 March 1877, K-SP 1119; JPK-S to William Cavendish (Duke of Devonshire), 21 April 1877, K-SP 1125.
100. JPK-S to UK-S, 3 January 1874, K-SP 1004. Bloomfield's preface to the *Autobiography* contains useful information about its production; the original is held in K-SP 1210.
101. J. Weber to unknown doctor, 5 May 1877, SP, Leck Hall.
102. Smith, pp.345-6; UK-S to Stewart Kay-Shuttleworth, 30 May 1877, SP, box P; *Burnley Gazette*, 2 June 1877, p.3.
103. *Burnley Gazette*, 2 June 1877, p.3.
104. All letters are to UK-S, and dated 1877: J. Goodall, 26 May; John Gordon, 29 May; Angela Burdett-Coutts, 27 May; J. Fraser, 28 May; H.M. Butler, 26 May; G. Style, 28 May; Lord Sandon, 12 June; Trevelyan, 1 June; Lingen, 26 May; Langton, [no date] June. All are in K-SP: 1130, 1139, 1134, 1137, 1131, 1135, 1144, 1142, 1133, 1141.
105. Matthew Arnold, 'Schools' in Thomas Humphry Ward, *The Reign of Queen Victoria* (London, 1887), Vol.2, pp.239–40.

Bibliography

Papers of Sir James Kay-Shuttleworth

These papers are found in two main collections. The first is in the John Rylands Library (Deansgate) Manchester. B.C. Bloomfield has prepared an invaluable guide to this collection: a handlist of the papers in the deed box of Sir J.P. Kay-Shuttleworth (1804–1877), College of St Mark and St John: Occasional Papers No.2, 1961. The staff of John Rylands Library have numbered the papers in the handlist, and I have used their numbering throughout this book. The abbreviation K-SP (Kay-Shuttleworth Papers) refers to this collection only.

The second collection is held in the Estate Office of the present Lord Shuttleworth at Cowan Bridge. I have called this collection the Shuttleworth Papers (SP) because, although it contains a great many papers of Sir James Kay-Shuttleworth, it is principally a collection of the papers of his son, Ughtred, the first Lord Shuttleworth. A part of the Shuttleworth papers has been sorted by Roger Fulford and placed in a series of envelopes and boxes which have been given alphabetical and numerical notation. But a very substantial group of papers has only recently been discovered. It has not been catalogued or indexed in any way. Where possible I have tried to make this material accessible by such unconventional referencing as 'Ughtred's red box'.

As well as the two main collections, there are three other sources of papers of Sir James Kay-Shuttleworth. A small set is held by the present Lord Shuttleworth at Leck Hall, Cowan Bridge. The Lancashire Record Office in Preston holds a valuable collection of Shuttleworth family papers, which contain a small number written by (or relevant to) Sir James. Finally, Frank Smith, in his *The Life and Work of Sir James Kay-Shuttleworth* (London, 1923), frequently quotes material written by or to Sir James which I have not been able to find in the other collections. I can only assume that these papers were made available to Smith when he was writing his book and have since been lost. When providing a reference for this material I have placed an asterisk before Smith's name. Thus '*Smith' refers to an original document which, so far as I am aware, is available only in his biography.

Writings of Sir James Kay-Shuttleworth (selected)

The most accessible collections of his writings are his own *Four Periods of Public Education* (1862), republished by the Harvester Press, London, 1973 with an introduction by Norman Morris, and (also with a valuable introduction) Trygve R. Tholfsen (ed.), *Sir James Kay-Shuttleworth on Popular Education*, New York, 1974.

Note: Books or articles written before his marriage are indicated by (JPK) at the end of the entry.

Address in *Report of Proceedings at the Distribution of Prizes in St. Mary's Hospital Medical School*, London, 1857, K-SP 1171
'Address on economy and science' (1866) in *Thoughts and Suggestions*
A Letter to the People of Lancashire, concerning the future of the commercial interest by the return of members for its new boroughs to the reformed Parliament, London, 1831 (JPK)
An account of certain improvements in the training of pauper children, and on apprenticeship in the metropolitan Unions, in 'Training of Pauper Children' (1841) (JPK)
'A sketch of the history and results of popular education in England' (1866) in *Thoughts and Suggestions*
Autobiography of Sir James Kay-Shuttleworth, The, Education Libraries Bulletin, supplement 7, University of London Institute of Education, 1964, edited by B.C. Bloomfield
Conduct of dissolute women in the workhouse, in Report of the Poor Law Commissioners . . . on the continuance of the Poor Law Commision . . ., BPP 1840, Vol.17 (JPK)
'Cromwell in the North. 1648. A Story', unpublished novel, K-SP 1209
Cynedrida, a masque; the river of the underworld; and other poems, privately printed, 1842
Defects in the Constitution of Dispensaries, with Suggestions for their Improvement, London and Manchester, 1834 (JPK)
De Motu Muscutosum (Thesis, 1827, Special Collections, University of Edinburgh Library). This is the original of 'On the cessation of the motility . . .'. (JPK)
Dr Kay and Mr Tufnell on the Training School at Battersea (1841) in 'Training of Pauper Children'; also reproduced as 'First Report' in *FPPE* (JPK)
'Earnings of agricultural labourers in Norfolk and Suffolk', *Journal of the Statistical Society of London*, Vol.1, July 1838, pp.179–83
First Report, see Dr Kay and Mr Tufnell
Four Periods of Public Education as reviewed in 1832–1839–1846–1862, London, 1862 (republished 1973)

'Further experiments concerning suspended animation', *NEMSJ*, 1 May 1831 (JPK)

'Increase of steam-power in Lancashire and its immediate vicinity', *Journal of the Statistical Society of London*, Vol.1, September 1838, pp.315–16

Introduction 'by an old educator' to Louisa M. Hubbard, *Work for Ladies in Elementary Schools*, London, 1872

Letter from Dr. Kay to G.C. Lewis, Esq., on the cause of the efficacy of workhouses, and on the outdoor relief of the impotent poor, in Remarks on the Third Report of the Irish Poor Law Commissioners . . ., *BPP* 1837, Vol.51 (JPK)

Letter to Earl Granville, K.G., . . . on the Report of the Commissioners appointed to inquire into the State of Popular Education in England, London, 1861

Letter to Earl Granville, K.G., on the Revised Code of Regulations contained in the Minute of the Committee of Council on Education dated July 29th, 1861, London 1861

Manual of Suggestions for the Guidance of Local Relief Committees in the Cotton Districts (1863), in *Thoughts and Suggestions*

Medical and Middle-Class Education. An address delivered at the Chatham-Street School of Medicine, Manchester, on Monday, January 21st, 1856, Manchester, 1856

Memorandum on Popular Education, London, 1868

'Notes illustrative of a previous paper on the training in schools of industry of children dependent from crime, orphanage, &c.', *Journal of the Statistical Society of London*, Vol.1, August 1838, pp.245–51.

'Observations and experiments concerning molecular irritation of the lungs, as one cause of tubercular consumption', *NEMSJ*, 1 February 1831 (JPK)

'On the cessation of the motility of the heart and muscles in the asphyxia of warm-blooded animals' (Royal Medical Society Dissertations, Vol.88) (JPK)

'On the establishment of country or district schools, for the training of the pauper children maintained in Union workhouses', *Journal of the Statistical Society of London*, Vol.1, May 1838, pp.14–27

'On the punishment of pauper children in workhouses', 25 January 1841, K-SP 223; edited by B.C. Bloomfield and published in College of St Mark and St John: Occasional Papers No.1, 1961 (JPK)

'Physical conditions of the poor', *NEMSJ*, 1 November 1830 (JPK)

'Physiological experiments and observations on the cessation of the contractibility of the heart and muscles in asphyxia of warm-blooded animals', *Edinburgh Medical and Surgical Journal*, Vol.29, No.94, 1828

Public Education as affected by the Minutes of the Committee of the Privy Council from 1846 to 1852; with suggestions as to future policy, London, 1853

Recent Measures for the Promotion of Education in England, London, 1839 (JPK)

Report by James Phillips Kay, Esq., M.D., Assistant Poor Law Commissioner, relative to the distress prevalent among the Spitalfields Weavers, RPLC3, *BPP* 1837, Vol.31 (JPK)

Report from James Phillips Kay, Esq., M.D. to the Poor Law Commissioners for England and Wales – On the migration of labourers from the southern rural counties of England to the cotton district of Lancashire, RPLC1, *BPP* 1835, Vol.35 (JPK)

Report on the administration, under the Poor Law Amendment Act, in Suffolk and Norfolk . . ., RPLC2, *BPP* 1836, Vol.29 (JPK)

Report on the prevalence of certain physical causes of fever in the metropolis, which might be removed by sanitary measures, RPLC4, *BPP* 1837–38, Vol.28 (JPK, with Neil Arnot)

Report on the training of pauper children, Norwich 1838, RPLC4, *BPP* 1837–38, Vol.28 (JPK)

Ribblesdale, or Lancashire Sixty Years Ago, London, 1874

Scarsdale; or Life on the Lancashire and Yorkshire Border, Thirty Years Ago, London, 1860

Second Report on the schools for the training of parochial schoolmasters at Battersea, MCCE 1842–43, 8vo edition; also reproduced in *FPPE*, pp.387–431

'Sketch of the progress of Manchester in thirty years from 1832 to 1862' in *FPPE*

'Some of the results of the Education Act and Code of 1870', *Fortnightly Review*, May 1876

'The constructive method of teaching', *Saturday Magazine*, No.647, July 1842

'The industrial and social development of South East Lancashire' (1864), in *Thoughts and Suggestions*

The Moral and Physical Condition of the Working Classes Employed in the Cotton Manufacture in Manchester, London, 1832, first and second editions (JPK)

The Physiology, Pathology, and Treatment of Asphyxia, London, 1834 (JPK)

The Present Condition of the Administration of the Parliamentary Grant, privately printed, 1845 (K-SP 1168)

The School, in its Relations to the State, the Church, and the Congregation, London, 1847

'The training of pauper children. Second Report (1839)', in RPLC 5, *BPP* 1939, Vol.20 (JPK)

Thoughts and Suggestions on Certain Social Problems, London, 1873

'Training of pauper children', Report to the Secretary of State for the Home Department from the Poor Law Commissioners, *House of Lords Sessional Papers*, 1841, Vol.33 (JPK)

'Two remarkable cases of disease in the circulating system', *NEMSJ*, 1 February 1831 (JPK)

Untitled paper, 1834, in PMSS (JPK)

'What central and local bodies are best qualified to take charge of and
administer existing endowments for education . . .?', *Transactions of the
National Association for the Promotion of Social Science, 1866*, London, 1867

*Words of Comfort and Counsel to Distressed Lancashire Workmen Spoken on
Sundays in 1862* by a County Squire – Their Neighbour, London and
Manchester, [1863]

Manuscripts and Private Papers

Alison collection (Royal College of Physicians, Edinburgh)

Anonymous paper, c.1984 (Gawthorpe Hall)

Autograph letters, Sir John Potter collection (Local History Archives,
Central Library, Manchester)

Baines papers (Leeds District Archives)

Bamford Chapel, Church Book (minutes) (Bamford Chapel, Norden Road,
Rochdale)

Blomfield papers (Lambeth Palace Library)

Brougham papers (University College, London)

Chadwick papers (University College, London)

Chalmers collection (New College, Edinburgh)

Correspondence and papers of Lady Noel Bryon and her family 1669–
1930, the Lovelace Byron Deposit (the Bodleian Library, Oxford – New
Library)

Frederick North diaries (Rougham Hall, Norfolk)

Fulford, Roger, Notes on the history of the Shuttleworth family (in
possession of Lord Shuttleworth)

George Wilson papers (Local History Archives, Central Library,
Manchester)

Giggleswick School, Minutes of governors' meetings (Giggleswick School,
Settle)

Gladstone papers (Add. mss, British Library)

Graham papers (Harvester microfilm)

Granville papers (PRO, London)

Harpton Court collection (National Library of Wales)

Hickleton papers (EP microform)

Journal of Proceedings connected with the formation of a Medical Library,
Reading Room, and Society, in Manchester (Medical Library, John
Rylands Library, University of Manchester)

Journal of R.A. Slaney, Morris-Eyton collection (Castle Gates Library,
Shrewsbury)

Lord, John (compiler), Pedigree of families who formed the congregation at
the Bury Presbyterian Chapel, Silver St (Bury Central Library)

Manchester Royal Infirmary Weekly Board Minutes (Royal Manchester
Infirmary)

Matriculation roll, Edinburgh University (Special collections, University of
    Edinburgh Library)
Medical papers of Dr Edmund Lyon (Local History Archives, Central
    Library, Manchester)
Nassau Senior papers (National Library of Wales)
'Notes on the Kay family' by Humphrey Kay of Pewsey, Wiltshire
Papers of the Manchester Satistical Society (Local History Archives, Central
    Library, Manchester)
Peel papers (Add. mss, British Library)
Proceedings of the Board of Health, Manchester (Local History Archives,
    Central Library, Manchester)
Proceedings of the General Quarterly Board (of the Manchester Royal
    Infirmary) (Manchester Royal Infirmary)
Records of medical students, sessions 1824–25, 1825–26, 1826–27 (Special
    collections, University of Edinburgh Library)
Robert Kay's will, PROB 11/1845
Royal Humane Society papers (Lancaster Gate, London)
Russell papers, PRO, London
Tremenheere papers (Penzance Library)

Official Publications

Annual reports of the Poor Law Commissioners for England and Wales,
    BPP 1835, Vol.35; 1836, Vol.29; 1837, Vol.31; 1837–38, Vol.28; 1839,
    Vol.20
British Parliamentary Debates
British Parliamentary Papers
Copies of all minutes, containing regulations as to the distribution of the
    Parliamentary grant for the promotion of education . . ., *BPP* 1844,
    Vol.38
Copies of minutes, if any, of the Committee of Council on Education, passed
    subsequently to August 1840, *BPP* 1842–43, Vol.40
Estimate for public education, 26 March 1847, *BPP* 1847, Vol.35
Evidence, oral and written, taken and received by the Commissioners . . . for
    visiting the Universities of Scotland, *BPP* 1837, Vol.35
Fourteenth, Fifteenth, Sixteenth and Seventeenth Reports from Select
    Committee on the Poor Law Amendment Act, *BPP* 1837–38, Vol.18,
    parts 1 and 2
Instructions for the Inspectors of schools, MPCCE, 4 January 1840
Minutes of the Committee of Council on Education (MCCE), published in
    BPP or as 8vo editions. (For the mysteries of these papers, see D.G. Paz,
    'A note on the quarto and octavo minutes of the Committee of Council'.)
Minute on constructive methods of teaching reading, writing, and vocal
    work, MCCE 1840–41, *BPP* 1840–41, Vol.20

Minutes of proceedings of the Committee of the [Privy] Council on Education (MPCCE), ED 9/1, (PRO, Kew)

Minutes of the Committee of the Privy Council on Education establishing a Revised Code of Regulations, *BPP* 1861, Vol.48

Of the salaries, expenses, and other charges for Commissioners . . ., *BPP* 1840, Vol.39

Papers on Education, *BPP* 1839, Vol.41

Poor Law Commission Papers (PRO, Kew)

Privy Council minute books, PC 4/19 (PRO, Chancery Lane)

Report from Select Committee on education of the poorer classes in England and Wales, *BPP* 1837–38, Vol.7

Report from the Select Committee of the House of Lords appointed to examine into the several cases alluded to in certain papers respecting the operation of the Poor Law Amendment Act, *BPP* 1837–38, Vol.19

Report from the Select Committee on elementary schools (certified teachers), *BPP* 1872, Vol.9

Report from the Select Committee on Miscellaneous Expenditure, *BPP* 1847–48, Vol.18

Report of the commissioners appointed to inquire into the state of popular education in England, *BPP* 1861, Vol.21, part 6

Report of the Select Committee on Education, *BPP* 1865, Vol.6

Report on Public Walks, 1833, *BPP* 1833

Report on St Mark's College, Chelsea, MCCE 1842–43, *BPP* 1843, Vol.40

Reports of the commissioners of inquiry into the state of education in Wales, *BPP* 1847, Vol.27

Reports on Battersea Training School and Battersea Village School, MCCE 1842–43, *BPP* 1843, Vol.40

Royal commission on scientific instruction and the advancement of science, *BPP* 1872, Vol.25; 1874, Vol.22; 1875, Vol.28

Scheme of periodical inspection for England and Wales, MCCE 1842–43, 8vo edition

Schools Inquiry Commission, Report of the Commissioners, *BPP* 1867–68, Vol.28

Supplementary minute of 10 July 1847, MCCE 1846, 8vo edition

Primary Sources, Books and Articles

Alison, William Pulteney, 'Observations on the epidemic fever now prevalent among the lower orders in Edinburgh', *Edinburgh Medical and Surgical Journal*, Vol.28, No.93, 1827

'Analysis of the report of an agent employed by the Manchester Statistical Society in 1834 . . .', *Report of the Fourth Meeting of the British Association for the Advancement of Science: held at Edinburgh in 1834*, London, 1835

Annual Report of the Edinburgh New Town Dispensary 1827 (University of

Edinburgh pamphlets, SB 36204/2)

Arnold, Matthew, 'Schools' in Thomas Humphry Ward, *The Reign of Queen Victoria*, London, 1887, Vol.2

Arnold, Matthew, *The Popular Education of France* (1861), in Super (ed.), pp.3–150

Arnold, Matthew, *The Twice-Revised Code* (1862) in Super (ed.), Vol.2, pp.212–43

Aston, Joseph, *A Picture of Manchester*, Manchester, [1826]

Baines, Edward, *Letter to the Right Hon. Lord Wharncliffe . . . on Sir James Graham's Bill for establishing exclusive Church schools . . .*, London 1843

Baines, Edward, *The Social, Educational, and Religious State of the Manufacturing Districts*, London, 1843

Banck's Manchester and Salford Directory 1800

Bateman, Josiah, *La Martinière. A reply to certain statements respecting the Bishop of Calcutta contained in a work entitled 'Recent Measures' . . .*, London, 1839

Baxter, G.R. Wythen, *The Book of the Bastilles; or the history of the working of the New Poor-Law*, London, 1841

Boards of Education for the Dioceses of Chester and Manchester, *Report of a Public Meeting . . . on Tuesday, September 27th, 1870*, Chester, 1870

Burke's Peerage, 102nd edition, London 1959

Carlyle, Thomas, *Past and Present*, New York, n.d.

Chapple J.A.V. and Pollard, Arthur (eds), *The Letters of Mrs Gaskell*, Manchester, 1966

Checkland, S.G. and E.D.A. (eds), *The Poor Law Reports of 1834*, Harmondsworth, 1974

Commercial Directory for 1818–19–20, The

Complete List of the Members and Officers of the Manchester Literary and Philosophical Society, Manchester, 1896

Condy, George, *An Argument for Placing Factory Children Within the Pale of the Law*, London, 1833

Cousin, Victor, *On the State of Education in Holland, as regards schools for the working classes and for the poor*, London, 1838

Dawes, Richard, *Observations on the Working of the Government Scheme of Education, and on School Inspection*, London, 1849

Deans' Manchester and Salford Directory, 1808 and 1809

de Tocqueville, Alexis, *Journeys to England and Ireland* (edited by J.P. Mayer), New Haven, 1958

Dunn, Henry, *The Bill or the Alternative*, London, 1843

Duppa, B.P., 'The education of pauper children in Union workhouses' in Central Society of Education, *Third Publication – Papers*, London, 1968

'Edinburgh grinders and examiners', *Lancet*, 16 June 1827

Edinburgh New Town Dispensary: Report and Treasurer's Accounts 1825 (University of Edinburgh pamphlets, EBF 9 (41445) 04/1)

Eliot, George, *Middlemarch*, Oxford, 1950

Engels, Friedrich, *The Condition of the Working Class in England*, Oxford, 1958

Faucher, Leon, *Manchester in 1844: Its Present Condition and Future Prospects*, London and Manchester, 1844

Foot, Michael (ed.), *The Gladstone Diaries*, Oxford, 1968

Fielden, John, *The Curse of the Factory System*, London, 1969

First Annual Report of the Manchester and Salford District Provident Society, 1833, The, Manchester, 1834

First Report of the Statistical Society, Manchester, July 1834, PMSS

Fraser, James, *The Revised Code of the Committee of Council on Education*, London, 1861

Fraser, William, *Memoir of the Life of David Stow: Founder of the Training System of Education*, London, 1858

Gaskell, Elizabeth, *The Life of Charlotte Brontë*, Harmondsworth, 1975

Gaskell, P., *The Manufacturing Population of England*, London, 1833

Gaulter, Henry, *The Origin and Progress of the Malignant Cholera in Manchester*, London, 1833

Greg, W.R., *An Inquiry into the State of the Manufacturing Population and the Causes and Cures Therein Existing*, Manchester, 1831

Greg W.R., Brief memoir on the present state of criminal statistics, 16 October 1833, PMSS

Greville Memoirs, The, London, 1885

Heywood, Benjamin, *Addresses Delivered at the Manchester Mechanics' Institution*, London, 1843

Hook, Walter Farquhar, *On the Means of Rendering More Efficient the Education of the People*, London, 1846

House, Madeline and Storey, Graham (eds), *The Letters of Charles Dickens*, Oxford, 1965

J. Leigh's Directory of Bury and Rochdale 1818

Johnson, A.H. (ed.), *The Letters of Charles Greville and Henry Reeve, 1836–1865*, London, 1924

Johnson, Edgar (ed.), *Letters from Charles Dickens to Angela Burdett-Coutts, 1841–1865*, London, 1955

Kay-Shuttleworth, U.J., *First Principles of Modern Chemistry*, London, 1868

Kay-Shuttleworth, U.J., 'On the East Lancashire Union of institutions having evening schools, in its bearing on the question of the education of the manual labouring class', in *Transactions, 1866*

Life of John Hullah LL.D., by his wife, London, 1886

List of Graduates in Medicine in the University of Edinburgh, from MDCCV to MDCCCLXVI, Edinburgh, 1867

Love, B. and Barton, J., *Manchester As It Is*, Manchester, 1839

Lowe, Robert, *Primary and Classical Education. An address delivered before the Philosophical Institution of Edinburgh*, Edinburgh, 1867

Metropolitan Church Union, *History and Present State of the Education Question*, London, 1850

National Union of Elementary Teachers, *Fifth Annual Conference, 1874. President's address and report of proceedings*, London, 1874

'Pauper education and Kneller Hall', *English Review*, September 1849

Pigot and Deans' Manchester and Salford Directory

Prentice, Archibald,*Historical Sketches and Personal Recollections of Manchester*, London, 1970

Prospectus of the Objects and Plans of the Statistical Society of London, 23 April 1834, in PMSS

Ramm, Agatha (ed.), *The Political Correspondence of Mr. Gladstone and Lord Granville 1868–1876*, London, 1952

Reed, Andrew, *Inspectors Inspected: A Review of the Operations of the Educational Committee of the Privy Council from 1846 to 1852*, London, 1853

Report of a Committee of the Manchester Statistical Society on the State of Education in the Borough of Manchester in 1834, London and Manchester, 1835

Report of the Proceedings of the General Meeting of the Subscribers and Friends of the Manchester Mechanics' Institution, 1832, 1834

Reports of the Committee of the Ardwick and Ancoats Dispensary 1831, 1832, 1834

Richard Oastler: King of Factory Children: Six Pamphlets, 1835–1861, New York 1972

Roberton, John, *General Remarks on the Health of English Manufacturers*, Manchester, 1831

Royal Humane Society, *Annual Reports, 1843 and 1845*, London

Russell, John, Earl, *Recollections and Suggestions, 1813–1873*, London, 1875

Sanders, Lloyd C. (ed.), *Lord Melbourne's Papers*, London, 1889

Schole's Manchester and Salford Directory, 1794

Second Report of the Statistical Society, Manchester, PMSS

Shuttleworth, John, *A Sketch of the Life of Roland Detrosier*, Manchester, 1860

Sinclair, John (ed.), *Correspondence of the National Society with the Lords of the Treasury and with the Committee of Council on Education*, London, 1839

Sinclair, John, *Letter to a Member of Parliament on National Education*, London, 1842

Slugg, J.T., *Reminiscences of Manchester Fifty Years Ago*, Shannon, 1971 (first published 1881)

Smith, Adam, *The Wealth of Nations*, 1776, Everyman edition

Statement Regarding the New Town Dispensary by the Medical Gentlemen conducting that Institution (University of Edinburgh pamphlets, SB 36204/2)

Speech of the Bishop of London on National Education, London, 1839

Stow, David, *The Training System Adopted in the Model Schools of the Glasgow Educational Society . . .*, Glasgow, 1836

Super, R.H. (ed.), *Matthew Arnold: Democratic Education*, Ann Arbor, 1962

Symonds, John Addington, *Miscellanies*, Bristol, 1971

Symonds, Mrs John Addington (ed.), *Recollections of a Happy Life, being the autobiography of Marianne North*, London, 1892

Taylor, R.V., *The Biographia Leodiensis*, London, 1865

Thackrah, C.T., *The Effects of Arts, Trades and Professions on Health and Longevity*, Edinburgh, 1831

Third Annual Report of the Manchester and Salford District Provident Society, Manchester, 1835

Transactions of the National Association for the Promotion of Social Science, 1857, 1866, 1871, London, 1858, 1867, 1872

Tufnell, E.C., 'Sir James Kay-Shuttleworth', *Journal of Education*, July 1877

Turner, Sharon, *The History of the Anglo-Saxons*, London, 1828

Watts, John, *The Facts of the Cotton Famine*, London, 1866

Wilberforce, Henry W., *On the Danger of State Interference with the Trust Deeds of Church Schools*, London, 1847

Wilberforce, Robert Isaac, *A Letter to the Marquis of Landsowne on the Establishment of a Board of National Education*, London, 1839

Wilkinson, Thomas Read, 'On the origin and history of the Manchester Statistical Society', *Transactions of the Manchester Statistical Society 1875–76*, Manchester, 1876

Wilson, Philip Whitwell (ed.), *The Greville Diary*, London, 1927

Wise, T.J. and Symington, J.A., *The Brontës: Their Lives, Friendships and Correspondence*, Oxford, 1933

Newspapers and Journals

Backburn Mail, 1818
British Critic, 1841
Burnley Gazette, 1877
Bury and Norwich Post, 1835, 1836
Bury and Suffolk Herald, 1835, 1836
Daily News, 1862
Edinburgh Medical and Surgical Journal, 1827, 1828
Eclectic Review, 1842, 1843
English Review, 1849
Evangelical Magazine, November 1801
Fortnightly Review, 1876
Fraser's Magazine, 1841
Homburger Kur- und Bade-Liste, 1854
Ipswich Journal, 1836
Journal of the Statistical Society of London, 1838
Lancet
Manchester Guardian
Morning Chronicle, 1839
New Lapsus Linguae (Special Collections, University of Edinburgh Library)

Norwich Mercury, 1835, 1836
Poor Man's Advocate, 1832
Poor Man's Guardian, 1832
Saturday Magazine, 1842
Squib, 1833
Tait's Edinburgh Magazine, 1833
The Times
Transactions of the Medico-Chirurgical Society, 1829
Westminster Review, 1833

Secondary Sources, Books, Articles, and Typescripts

Abbot, Evelyn and Campbell, Lewis, *The Life and Letters of Benjamin Jowett*, London, 1897
Abel-Smith, Brian, *The Hospitals 1800–1948*, Cambridge (Mass.), 1964
Abrams, Philip, *The Origins of British Sociology: 1834–1914*, Chicago and London, 1968
Adamson, John William, *English Education, 1789–1902*, Cambridge, 1930
Adkins, Thomas, *The History of St. John's College, Battersea*, London, 1906
Akenson, Donald, *The Irish Educational Experiment*, London and Toronto, 1970
Aldrich, Richard, 'Association of ideas: the National Association for the Promotion of Social Science', *History of Education Society Bulletin*, No.16, 1975
Aldrich, Richard, *Sir John Pakington and National Education*, Leeds, 1979
Aldrich, Richard, 'Sir John Pakington and the Newcastle Commission', *History of Education*, Vol.8, No.1, 1979
Aldrich, Richard, '"The growing intelligence and education of the people"', *History of Education Society Bulletin*, No.22, 1978
Aldrich, Richard, and Gordon, Peter, *Dictionary of British Educationists*, London, 1989
Alexander, J.L., 'Lord John Russell and the origins of the Committee of Council on Education', *Historical Journal*, Vol.20, No.2, 1977
Allsobrook, David Ian, *Schools for the Shires: The Reform of Middle-class Education in Victorian England*, Manchester, 1986
Ancoats Hospital, 150th Anniversary 1828–1977, Manchester, 1978
Anderson, R.G.W. and Simpson, A.D.C., *The Early Years of the Edinburgh Medical School*, Edinburgh, 1976
Anning, S.T., *The General Infirmary at Leeds*, Edinburgh and London, 1966
Arnold, R. Arthur, *The History of the Cotton Famine*, Manchester, 1864
Arthur, W.M., *Bamford Chapel: Its Origins and History*, Heywood, 1901
Ashton, T.S., *Economic and Social Investigations in Manchester, 1833–1933: A Centenary History of the Manchester Statistical Society*, London, 1934
Australian Dictionary of Biography, Vols.3, 4

Ball, Nancy, *Her Majesty's Inspectorate, 1839–49*, Edinburgh and London, 1963

Barton, B.T., *History of the Borough of Bury and Neighbourhood, in the County of Lancaster*, Bury, [1874]

Bates, Madison C., 'Charlotte Brontë and the Kay-Shuttleworths, with a new Brontë letter', *Harvard Library Bulletin*, Vol.9, 1955

Bell, Edward Allen, *A History of Giggleswick School from its Foundations, 1499–1902*, Leeds, 1912

Bellot, H. Hale, *University College, London, 1826–1926*, London, 1929

Best, G.F.A., 'The religious difficulties of national education in England, 1800–70', *Cambridge Historical Journal*, Vol.12, No.2, 1956

Bishop, A.S., 'Ralph Lingen, Secretary to the Education Department 1849–70', *British Journal of Educational Studies*, Vol.16, No.2, 1968

Bishop, A.S., *The Rise of a Central Authority in English Education*, Cambridge, 1971

Blomfield, Alfred (ed.), *A Memoir of Charles James Blomfield, D.D., Bishop of London*, London, 1889

Boyson, Rhodes, *The Ashworth Cotton Enterprise: The Rise and Fall of a Family Firm 1818–1880*, Oxford, 1970

Brammer, M.M., 'The manuscript of *The Professor*', *R.E.S.* New Series, Vol.11, No.42, 1960

Briggs, Asa, 'The background of the parliamentary reform movement in three English cities (1830–2)', *Cambridge Historical Journal*, Vol.10, No.3, 1952

Briggs, Asa, *Victorian Cities*, London, 1963

Brockbank, E.M., *A Centenary History of the Manchester Medical Society*, Manchester, 1934

Brockbank, E.M., *The Foundation of Provincial Medical Education in England*, Manchester, 1936

Brockbank, William, *The Honorary Medical Staff of the Manchester Royal Infirmary, 1830–1948*, Manchester, 1965

Brose, Oliver J., *Church and Parliament: The Reshaping of the Church of England, 1828–1860*, Stanford and London, 1959

Brown, Lucy, *The Board of Trade and the Free-Trade Movement*, Oxford, 1958

Brown, Stewart J., *Thomas Chalmers and the Godly Commonwealth in Scotland*, Oxford, 1982

Brundage, Anthony, *The Making of the New Poor Law: The Politics of Inquiry, Enactment, and Implementation, 1832–1839*, New Brunswick, 1978

Bryant, Margaret, *The Unexpected Revolution*, London, 1979

Bythell, Duncan, *The Handloom Weavers: A Study of the English Cotton Industry during the Industrial Revolution*, Cambridge, 1969

Calman, A.L., *Life and Labours of John Ashworth*, Manchester and London, 1877

Campbell, R.H. and Skinner, A.S., *Adam Smith*, London, 1982

Cannadine, David, *Lords and Landlords: The Aristocracy and the Towns 1774–1967*, Leicester, 1980

Cardwell, D.S.L. (ed.), *Artisan to Graduate*, Manchester, 1974

Carr, Lilian, *Point me a Finger: The Story of All Saints' Church, Habergham, 1849–1974*, Habergham, [1974]

Cecil, Lord David, *Melbourne*, New York, 1986

Chadwick, Owen, *The Victorian Church*, London, 1966

Checkland, Olive, 'Chalmers and William Pulteney Alison: a conflict of views on Scottish policy' in Cheyne (ed.)

Checkland, Olive, *Philanthropy in Victorian Scotland: Social Welfare and the Voluntary Principle*, Edinburgh, 1980

Cheyne, A.C. (ed.),*The Practical and the Pious: Essays on Thomas Chalmers (1780–1847)*, Edinburgh, 1985

Chitnis, Anand C., *The Scottish Enlightenment and Early Victorian English Society*, London, 1976

Church of Jesus Christ of Latter-Day Saints, *International Genealogical Index*, 1981

Clark, G. Kitson, '"Statesmen in disguise": reflexions on the history of the neutrality of the civil service', *Historical Journal*, Vol.2, No.1, 1959

Cockburn, Henry, *Memorials of His Time*, Edinburgh, 1971 edn

Comrie, John D., *History of Scottish Medicine*, London, 1932

Connell, W.F., *The Educational Thought and the Influence of Matthew Arnold*, London, 1950

Conroy, Michael P., *Backcloth to Gawthorpe*, Nelson, 1971

Cooter, Roger, 'Anticontagionism and history's medical record' in Wright and Treacher (eds)

Craig, John, *A History of Red Tape*, London, 1955

Crosse, V. Mary, *A Surgeon in the Early Nineteenth Century*, Edinburgh and London, 1968

Cruickshank, Marjorie, *Church and State in English Education: 1870 to the Present Day*, London, 1963

Cullen, M.J., *The Statistical Movement in Early Victorian Britain: The Foundations of Empirical Research*, New York, 1975

Davenport-Hines, *Sex, Death and Punishment*, Glasgow, 1990

Davison, Graeme, '"A life without egotism": James Phillips Kay and the Manchester cotton lords, 1828–1835' (unpublished paper)

Darwin, Francis (ed.), *The Life and Letters of Charles Darwin*, London, 1887

Dictionary of National Biography

Digby, Anne, *Pauper Palaces*, London, 1978

'Dissenting Chapels in and near Manchester, 1810', *Transactions of the Congregational Historical Society*, Vol.6, 1913–1915

Dod, Charles R., *Electoral Facts from 1832 to 1853 Impartially Stated* (edited by H.J. Hanham), London, 1972

Duke, Francis, 'Pauper education', in Fraser (ed.), *The New Poor Law*

Durey, Michael, 'Medical elites, the general practitioner, and patient power in Britain during the cholera epidemic of 1831–2', in Inkster and Morrell (eds)

Durey, Michael, *The Return of the Plague: British Society and the Cholera 1831–2*, Dublin, 1979

Edmonds, E.L. and O.P., 'Hugh Seymour Tremenheere, pioneer inspector of schools', *British Journal of Educational Studies*, Vol.12, No.1, 1963

Elesh, David, 'The Manchester Statistical Society: a case study of a discontinuity in the history of empirical social research', part 1, *Journal of the History of the Behavioural Sciences*, No.8, 1972

Elwood, Willis J. and Tuxford, A. Félicité, *Some Manchester Doctors*, Manchester, 1984

Ely, Richard, *In Search of the Central Society of Education*, Leeds, 1982

Farrar, W.V. and Kathleen R., and Scott, E.L., 'The Henrys of Manchester', *Ambix*, Vol.20, 1973; Vol.21, 1974; Vol.22, 1975; Vol.23, 1976; Vol.24, 1977

Farrer, William and Brownhill, J., *The Victoria History of the County of Lancaster*, London, n.d.

Finer, S.E., *The Life and Times of Sir Edwin Chadwick*, London, 1952

Fitzmaurice, Edmond, *The Life of Granville George Leveson Gower, Second Earl Granville, K.G., 1815–1891*, London, 1905

Fletcher, Sheila, *Feminists and Bureaucrats: A Study in the Development of Girls' Education in the Nineteenth Century*, Cambridge, 1980

Fraser, Derek, 'Edward Baines' in Patricia Hollis (ed.), *Pressure from Without in Early Victorian England*, London, 1974

Fraser, Derek (ed.), *Municipal Reform and the Industrial City*, Leicester, 1982

Fraser, Derek (ed.), *The New Poor Law in the Nineteenth Century*, London, 1976

Furgol, Mary T., 'Chalmers and poor relief: an incidental sideline' in Cheyne (ed.)

Gardner, Phil, *The Lost Elementary Schools of Victorian England*, Beckenham, 1984

Gash, Norman, *Reaction and Reconstruction in English Politics 1832–1852*, Oxford, 1965

Gattrel, V.A.C., 'Incorporation and the pursuit of Liberal hegemony in Manchester 1790–1839' in Fraser (ed.), *Municipal Reform*

General List of the Members of the Royal Medical Society of Edinburgh, Edinburgh, 1906

Gilbert, A.D., *Religion and Society in Industrial England*, London, 1976

Girouard, Mark, *Robert Smythson and the Architecture of the Elizabethan Era*, London, 1966

Gordon, Peter, *The Victorian School Manager*, London, 1974

Grant, Alexander, *The Story of the University of Edinburgh During its First Three Hundred Years*, London, 1884

Gray, James, *History of the Royal Medical Society 1737–1937*, Edinburgh, 1952

Green, Andy, *Education and State Formation: The Rise of Education Systems in*

England, France, and the USA, London, 1990

Grier, R.M., *John Allen: Vicar of Prees and Archdeacon of Salop*, London, 1889

Griffiths, J.D., 'Monmouthshire and the "Blue Books" of 1847', *History of Education*, Vol.19, No.3, 1990

Grindon, Leo H., *Manchester Banks and Bankers: Historical, Biographical, and Anecdotal*, Manchester, 1878

Grosskurth, Phyllis, *John Addington Symonds: A Biography*, London, 1964

Halévy, Elie, *The Triumph of Reform, 1830–1841*, London, 1961

Halévy, Elie, *Victorian Years*, London, 1961

Hall, Brian, *Lowerhouse and the Dugdales: The Story of a Lancashire Mill Community*, Burnley, 1976

Hall, J.T.D., *The Tounis College: An Anthology of Edinburgh University Student Journals*, Edinburgh, 1985

Hamilton, David, *The Healers: A History of Medicine in Scotland*, Edinburgh, 1881

Hamilton, David, *Towards a Theory of Schooling*, London and New York, 1989

Hanham, H.J., *Elections and Party Management*, London, 1959

Harding, W.E., *The History of the Park Congregational Church, Ramsbottom, Bury*, 1931

Haymaker, Webb and Schiller, Francis, *The Founders of Neurology*, Springfield, 1970

Henderson, W.O., *The Lancashire Cotton Famine, 1861–1865*, New York 1969

Hilts, Victor L., *Statist and Statistician*, New York, 1981

Hindle, G.B., *Provision for the Relief of the Poor in Manchester 1754–1826*, Manchester, 1975

Holloway, S.W.F., 'The Apothecaries' Act, 1815: a reinterpretation', *Medical History*, Vol.10, 1966

Holt, Raymond V., *The Unitarian Contribution to Social Progress in England*, London, 1938

Horn, D.B., *A Short History of the University of Edinburgh*, Edinburgh, 1967

Howe, Anthony, *The Cotton Masters, 1830–1860*, Oxford, 1984

Howe's Bookshop, *A Special Selection of Rare and Interesting Books*, 1991

Hunter, Ian, *Culture and Government: The Emergence of Literary Education*, London, 1988

Hurt, John, *Education in Evolution: Church, State, Society and Popular Education 1800–1870*, London, 1971

Inkster, Ian and Morrell, Jack (eds), *Metropolis and Province: Science in British Culture, 1780–1850*, London, 1983

Irvine, Hugh Colley, *The Old D.P.S., a Short History of Charitable Work in Manchester and Salford, 1833–1933*, Manchester, 1933

Johnson, Richard, 'Administrators in education before 1870; patronage, social position and role' in Sutherland (ed.)

Jones, Donald K., 'Lancashire, the American common school, and the religious problem in British education in the nineteenth century', *British Journal of Educational Studies*, Vol.15, No.3, 1967

Jones, Donald K., *The Making of the Education System 1851–81*, London, 1977

Jordan, F.W., *Life of Joseph Jordan, Surgeon*, Manchester, 1904

Judges, A.V., 'James Kay-Shuttleworth, a pioneer of national education' in A.V. Judges (ed.), *Pioneers of English Education*, London, 1952

Kamm, Josephine, *Indicative Past: A Hundred Years of the Girls' Public Day School Trust*, London, 1971

Knight, Ruth, *Illiberal Liberal: Robert Lowe in New South Wales, 1842–1850*, Melbourne, 1966

Knott, John, *Popular Opposition to the 1834 Poor Law*, London and Sydney, 1986

Layton, David, *Science for the People: The Origins of the School Science Curriculum in England*, London, 1973, pp.33, 76–85, 106–11

'Leaf Square Academy, Pendleton, 1811–1813', *Transactions of the Congregational Historical Society*, Vol.13, 1937–39

Lee, C.H., *A Cotton Enterprise 1795–1840: A History of M'Connell & Kennedy Fine Cotton Spinners*, Manchester, 1972

Lefanu, W.R., *British Periodicals of Medicine: A Chronological List 1640–1899*, Oxford, 1984

Levy, S. Leon, *Nassau W. Senior, 1790–1864*, Newton Abbot, 1970

Longmate, Norman, *The Hungry Mills*, London, 1979

Loudon, Irvine, *Medical Care and the General Practitioner 1750–1850*, Oxford, 1986

Loudon, Irvine, 'The origins and growth of the dispensary movement in England', *Bulletin of the History of Medicine*, Vol.55, 1981

Lyell, Katherine M. (ed.), *Memoir of Leonard Horner*, London, 1890

MacDonagh, Oliver, 'The nineteenth-century revolution in government: a re-appraisal', *Historical Journal*, Vol.1, No.1, 1958

Maccoby, S., *English Radicalism*, London, 1935

Magnus, Philip, *Gladstone: A Biography*, London, 1954

Makepeace, Chris E., *Science and Technology in Manchester: Two Hundred Years of the Lit. and Phil.*, Manchester, 1984

Marcham, A.J., 'Lies and statistics: a note on the Newcastle Commission', *History of Education*, Vol.9, No.3, 1980, pp.229–31

Marcham, A.J., 'Recent interpretations of the Revised Code of Education, 1862', *History of Education*, Vol.8, No.2, 1979

Marcham, A.J., 'The Revised Code of Education, 1862: reinterpretations and misinterpretations', *History of Education*, Vol.10, No.2, 1981

Martin, A. Patchett (ed.), *Life and Letters of the Right Honourable Robert Lowe, Viscount Sherbrooke*, London, 1893

Mason, D.M., 'Matthew Arnold and elementary education: a reconsideration', *History of Education*, Vol.12, No.3, 1983

Mason, D.M., 'The expenditure of the Committee of Council on Education, 1839–52', *Journal of Educational Administration and History*, Vol.17, No.1, 1985

Mason, Donald, 'Peelite opinion and the genesis of payment by results: the true story of the Newcastle Commission', *History of Education*, Vol.17, No.4, 1988

Mathews, H.F., *Methodism and the Education of the People, 1791–1851*, London, 1959

Marcus, Stephen, *Engels, Manchester, and the Working Class*, London, 1974

Marshall, J.D., *The Old Poor Law, 1795–1834*, London, 1973

McCaffrey, John F., 'Thomas Chalmers and social change', *Scottish Historical Review*, No.169, 1961

McCann, Phillip and Young, Francis A., *Samuel Wilderspin and the Infant Movement*, London, 1982

McLachlan, H., *English Education under the Test Acts*, Manchester, 1913

McMenemey, William H., *The Life and Times of Sir Charles Hastings*, Edinburgh and London, 1959

Messinger, Gary, *Manchester in the Victorian Age: The Half-known City*, Manchester, 1985

Morley, John, *The Life of William Gladstone*, London, 1904

Morrell, J.B., 'The Edinburgh Town Council and its university, 1717–1766', in Anderson and Simpson

Morrell, J.B., 'The University of Edinburgh in the late eighteenth century: its scientific eminence and academic structure', *Isis*, No.62, 1971

Morris, R.J., *Cholera*, New York, 1976

Murphy, James, *Church, State and Schools in Britain, 1800–1970*, London, 1971

Murphy, James, *The Religious Problem in English Education*, Liverpool, 1959

National Trust, *Gawthorpe Hall*, Over Wallop, 1988

National Trust, *Gawthorpe Hall, Lancashire*, n.p., 1984

Nightingale, B., *Lancashire Nonconformity; or Sketches, Historical and Descriptive of the Congregational and Presbyterian Churches in the County*, Manchester, 1892

Nightingale, B., *The Story of the Lancashire Congregational Union 1806–1906*, Manchester, 1906

Parker, C.S., *Sir Robert Peel*, London, 1899

Parkin, Richard, *The Central Society of Education, 1836–40*, Leeds, 1975

Paz, D.G., 'A note on the quarto and octavo minutes of the Committee of Council, 1839/40 – 1857/8', *History of Education Society Bulletin*, No.14, 1974, pp.54–8

Paz, D.G., 'Sir James Kay-Shuttleworth: the man behind the myth', *History of Education*, Vol.14, No.3, 1985

Paz, D.G., 'The composition of the Education Committee of the Privy

Council, 1839–1856', *Journal of Educational Administration and History*, Vol.8, 1976

Paz, D.G., *The Politics of Working-class Education in Britain, 1830–50*, Manchester, 1980

Pelling, Margaret, *Cholera, Fever, and British Medicine*, Oxford, 1978

Perkin, Joan, *Women and Marriage in Nineteenth-Century England*, London, 1989

Peters, Margot, *Unquiet Soul: A Biography of Charlotte Brontë*, New York, 1975

Petersen, Bob, 'Black is the use of spades: agricultural education for the coloured races 1846', Papers of the annual conference of the Australian and New Zealand History of Education Society, 1989

Peterson, M. Jeanne, *The Medical Profession in Mid-Victorian London*, Berkeley, 1978

Pickstone, John V., 'Ferriar's fever to Kay's Cholera: disease and social structure in Cottonopolis', *History of Science*, Vol.22, 1984

Pickstone, John V., *Medicine and Industrial Society: A History of Hospital Development in Manchester and its Region, 1752–1946*, Manchester, 1985

Pink, W. Duncombe and Bearan, Alfred B., *The Parliamentary Representation of Lancashire (County and Borough), 1258–1885*, London, 1889

Pollard, Hugh, *Pioneers of Popular Education*, London, 1956

Pons, Valdo, 'Contemporary interpretations of Manchester in the 1830's and 1840's, *Stanford Journal of International Studies*, Vol.13, 1978

Porter, Roy, *Disease, Medicine, and Society in England 1550–1860*, London, 1987

Pressnell, L.S., *Country Banking in the Industrial Revolution*, Oxford, 1956

Purcell, E.S., *Life of Cardinal Manning*, London, 1896

Ramsden, G.M., A record of the Kay family of Bury Lancashire in the 17th and 18th centuries, 1978, typescript (Local History Archives, Central Library, Manchester)

Redford, Arthur, *Labour Migration in England 1800–1850*, Manchester, 1864

Redford, Arthur, *The History of Local Government in Manchester*, London and New York, 1950

Reid, T. Wemyss, *Life of the Rt Hon. W.E. Forster*, New York, 1970

Renaud, F., *A Short History of the Rise and Progress of the Manchester Royal Infirmary from the Year 1752 to 1877*, Manchester, 1898

Report of Proceedings at the Distribution of Prizes in St. Mary's Hospital Medical School, London, 1857

Rich, R.W., *The Training of Teachers in England and Wales during the Nineteenth Century*, Bath, 1933

Richardson, Ralph, *Coutts and Co., Bankers, Edinburgh and London*, London, 1901

Robinson, John Martin, 'Gawthorpe Hall, Lancashire – I and II', *Country Life*, 4 and 11 September 1975

'Roby's Academy, Manchester, 1803–1808', *Transactions of the Congregational Historical Society*, Vol.13, 1937–39

Rose, Michael E., *The English Poor Law 1780–1930*, Newton Abbot, 1971

Ross, Alexander M., 'Kay-Shuttleworth and the training of teachers for pauper schools', *British Journal of Educational Studies*, Vol.15, No.3, 1967

Routley, Erik, *English Religious Dissent*, Cambridge, 1960

Saunders, James, *Scottish Democracy 1814–1840*, Edinburgh, 1950

Scrone, G. Poulett, *Memoir of the Life of the Right Honourable Charles Lord Sydenham, G.C.B.*, London, 1844

Seaborne, Malcolm, *The English School, its Architecture and Organization, 1370–1870*, London, 1971

Sharps, Heather, 'Sir James P. Kay-Shuttleworth as a regional and historical novelist', *Notes and Queries*, Vol.27, No.1, 1980

Sharps, Heather, 'The educational and social content of Kay-Shuttleworth's novels', *Journal of Educational Administration and History*, Vol.13, No.2, 1981

Shepherd John A., *Simpson and Syme of Edinburgh*, Edinburgh and London, 1969

Simon, Brian, *The Two Nations and the Educational Structure*, London, 1974

Simon, Shena D., *A Century of City Government: Manchester 1838–1938*, London, 1938

Skinner, Andrew S. and Wilson, Thomas (eds), *Essays on Adam Smith*, Oxford, 1975

Smallwood, F.T., 'The story of Terrace House, Battersea (Old Battersea House)', *Surrey Archaeological Collections*, Vol.44, 1967

Smith, Frank, *The Life and Work of Sir James Kay-Shuttleworth*, London, 1923 (see note under 'Papers of Sir James Kay-Shuttleworth' above)

Stenton, John, *Who's Who of British Members of Parliament*, London, 1976

Stenton, Michael and Lees, Stephen, *Who's Who of British Members of Parliament*, Vol.2, 1886–1918, Hassocks, 1978

Stephens, W.R. *The Life and Letters of Walter Farquhar Hook*, London, 1878

Stewart, W.A.C. and McCann, W.P., *The Educational Innovators 1750–1880*, London and New York, 1967

Sutherland, Gillian, *Policy-Making in Elementary Education, 1870–1895*, Oxford, 1973

Sutherland, Gillian (ed.), *Studies in the Growth of Nineteenth Century Government*, London, 1972

Sylvester, D.W., *Robert Lowe and Education*, Cambridge, 1974

Thackray, Arnold, 'Natural knowledge in cultural context: the Manchester model', *American Historical Review*, No.3, June 1974

'The first Manchester Sunday schools', *Bulletin of the John Rylands Library Manchester*, Vol.33, No.2, 1951

The Life of Sir Robert Christison, Bart., edited by his sons, Edinburgh, 1885

Thompson, E.P., *The Making of the English Working Class*, Harmondsworth, 1968

Trevelyan, George Macaulay, *The Life of John Bright*, London, 1913

Tropp, Asher, *The School Teachers*, London, 1957

Turner, A. Logan, *The Story of a Great Hospital: The Royal Infirmary of Edinburgh 1829–1929*, Edinburgh, 1937

Tylecote, Mabel, 'The Manchester Mechanics' Institution, 1824–50' in Cardwell (ed.)

Verity, T.E.A., 'Edward Arundel Verity, Vicar of Habergham: an Anglican parson of the Industrial Revolution', *Transactions of the Lancashire and Cheshire Antiquarian Society*, Vol.79, 1977

Walpole, Spencer, *The Life of Lord Russell*, London, 1889

Walton, John, *Brain's Diseases of the Nervous System*, Oxford, 1985

Weinreb, Ben and Hibbert, Christopher, *The London Encyclopaedia*, London, 1987

Westergaard, Harald, *Contributions to the History of Statistics*, New York, 1968

Wilson, A.N., *Hilaire Belloc*, Harmondsworth, 1986

Winter, James, *Robert Lowe*, Toronto, 1976

Wolff, Robert Lee, *Strange Stories and Other Explorations in Victorian Fiction*, Boston, 1971

Wood, Henry P., *David Stow and the Glasgow Normal Seminary*, Jordanhill, 1987

Wright, Peter and Treacher, Andrew (eds), *The Problem of Medical Knowledge*, Edinburgh, 1982

Wright-St Clair, Rex E., *Doctors Munro: A Medical Saga*, London, 1964

Young, G.M., *Victorian England: Portrait of an Age*, London, 1961

Youngson, A.J., *The Making of Classical Edinburgh 1750–1840*, Edinburgh, 1966

Theses

Aldrich, R.E., 'Education and the political parties, 1830–1870', M.Phil., London, 1970

Aldrich, Richard, 'Sir John Pakington and national education', Ph.D., London, 1977

Alexander, J.L., 'Collegiate teacher training in England and Wales: a study in the historical determinants of educational provision in the mid-nineteenth century', Ph.D., London, 1977

Augar, P.J., 'The cotton famine, 1861–5: a study of the principal cotton towns during the American Civil War', Ph.D., Cambridge, 1979

Clifford, Mark, 'Medicine, politics and society: Manchester's 1832 cholera epidemic', B.A., University of California, Berkeley

Duke, Francis, 'The education of pauper children: policy and administration, 1834–1855', M.A., Manchester, 1968

Dunleavy, John, 'The provision of education for working people in institutes in North East Lancashire, 1854–72', Ph.D., Leeds, 1983

Gattrel, V.A.C., 'The commercial middle class in Manchester c.1820–1857', Ph.D., Cambridge, 1971

Griffiths, J.D., 'Monmouthshire and the "Blue Books" of 1847', M.A., London, 1985

Johnson, J.R.B., 'The Education Department, 1839–1864: a study in social policy and the growth of government', Ph.D., Cambridge, 1968

Mottram, Joan, 'The life and work of John Roberton (1797–1876) of Manchester, obstetrician and social reformer', M.Sc., Manchester, 1986

Phillips, R.J., 'E.C. Tufnell, 1806–1866', Ph.D., Sheffield, 1973

Sharps, Heather, 'Prolegomena to an edition of "Cromwell in the North, 1648. A Story"', M.A., Leeds, 1977

Sharps, Heather, 'Sir James Kay-Shuttleworth, a regional and historical novelist', B.Phil., Hull, 1971

Warwick, David, 'Sir James Kay-Shuttleworth (1804–1877): the genesis, development and influence of his ideas on education and teaching', Ph.D., Lancaster, 1978

Webb, Katherine A., 'The development of the medical profession in Manchester, 1750–1860', Ph.D., Manchester, 1988

Index